Shakespearean Issues

Shakespearean Issues

Agency, Skepticism, and Other Puzzles

Richard Strier

UNIVERSITY OF PENNSYLVANIA PRESS

PHILADELPHIA

Copyright © 2023 University of Pennsylvania Press

All rights reserved. Except for brief quotations used for purposes of review or scholarly citation, none of this book may be reproduced in any form by any means without written permission from the publisher.

Published by
University of Pennsylvania Press
Philadelphia, Pennsylvania 19104-4112
www.upenn.edu/pennpress

Credits:
A portion of chapter 1 appears in *Shakespeare and Moral Agency*, ed. Michael D. Bristol (New York: Continuum, 2010). A version of chapter 2 appears in *Positive Emotions in Early Modern Literature and Culture*, ed. Cora Fox, Bradley J. Irish, and Cassie M. Miura (Manchester: Manchester University Press, 2021). A version of chapter 3 appears in *Shakespeare and Judgment*, ed. Kevin Curran (Edinburgh: University of Edinburgh Press, 2017). A version of chapter 4 appears in *Shakespeare and the Law: A Conversation Among Disciplines and Professions*, ed. Bradin Cormack, Martha Nussbaum, and Richard Strier (Chicago: University of Chicago Press, 2013). An early version of chapter 6 appears in *Writing and Political Engagement in Seventeenth-Century England*, ed. Derek Hirst and Richard Strier (Cambridge: Cambridge University Press, 1999). Chapters 10 and 11 contain some material that originally appeared as "Shakespeare and the Skeptics" in *Religion and Literature* 32 (2000). A version of chapter 12 appeared in *Religion and Literature* 47 (2016).

Printed in the United States of America on acid-free paper
10 9 8 7 6 5 4 3 2 1

A Cataloging-in-Publication record is available
from the Library of Congress
Hardcover ISBN 9781512823219
eBook ISBN 9781512823226

For Camille E. Bennett

        What you do
Still betters what is done.
         . . .
Each your doing,
So singular in each particular,
Crowns what you are doing in the present deeds,
That all your acts are queens.

CONTENTS

Introduction. The Leading Thought — 1

PART I. INDIVIDUALS

Chapter 1. Excuses, Bepissing, and Non-Being: Shakespearean Puzzles About Agency — 15

    Appendix. "Say it is my humour" — 43

Chapter 2. Happy Hamlet — 48

Chapter 3. Resisting Complicity: Ethical Judgment and *King Lear* — 66

PART II. SYSTEMS

Chapter 4. Shakespeare and Legal Systems: The Better the Worse (but Not Vice Versa) — 89

Chapter 5. *King Lear* and Human Needs — 112

Chapter 6. *The Tempest* (1): Power — 133

Chapter 7. *The Tempest* (2): Labor — 156

Chapter 8. *The Tempest* (3): Humanism — 171

PART III. BELIEFS

Chapter 9. Shakespeare and Skepticism (1): Religion   189

Chapter 10. Shakespeare and Skepticism (2): Epistemology   210

Chapter 11. Mind, Nature, Heterodoxy, and Iconoclasm in *The Winter's Tale*   228

Notes   251

Index   341

Acknowledgments   351

Shakespearean Issues

INTRODUCTION

The Leading Thought

As late as 10 years ago, I used to seek and find out grand lines and fine stanzas; but my delight has been far greater, since it has consisted more in tracing the leading Thought thro'out the whole.
—S. T. Coleridge

Estimating other people's intentions is one of the things that we do all the time.... Only in the criticism of imaginative literature, a thing delicately concerned with human intimacy, are we told that we must give up all idea of knowing his intention.
—William Empson

The essays that comprise this book all share a view on how to think about Shakespeare's plays and a commitment to doing literary criticism in a particular way. The essays vary in their foci—from dealing with passages (though not simply as "grand lines") to dealing with whole plays to dealing with multiple plays—but they are all committed to "close reading,"[1] and to reading, as we would now put it, "with the grain."[2] They are committed to making plausible hypotheses about authorial intention insofar as such intention can be inferred from material within the texts themselves (so that there is no distinction between "authorial intention" and "textual intention").[3] The interpretations will succeed if the reader finds that they make the texts more intelligible (which does not mean familiar or expected)—if, that is, they show that the details in question, whatever they may be, can be seen to serve a function within the work as a whole, and to cohere with other features of the work.[4] The essays employ the principle of charity—in the Davidsonian not the Augustinian sense: "If we want to understand others, we must count them right in most matters."[5] The idea is not that every detail in a work as long as a Shakespearean play is absolutely necessary to the success or intelligibility or force of the work—this might be true of a handful of lyric poems—but to show that the detail or details in question have some relation to thematic strands in the work ("tracing the leading Thought thro'out the whole").

This is where the matter arises of how the plays—as both texts and scripts—are to be thought about.[6] The guiding premise of my readings, and I am happy to call my procedures that,[7] is that the plays are constructed and designed with regard to intellectually compelling issues—"spirits are not finely touch'd / But to fine issues."[8] My picture is that when Shakespeare was reading widely and wildly to find material for plays—reading everything, high (classics and histories) and low (popular romances and plays)—what he was looking for was material that struck him as raising some issue he was interested in. Or rather, it could be put this way: as he was reading various things, looking for characters and plots, he found that some of those materials raised issues, and he pursued those issues as well as the characters and plots. Certainly, he wanted to entertain. But he wanted to explore issues in the process of doing so, and he took it that his audience wanted this as well. After all, he was competing with sermons—of enormous popularity—as well as with brothels and bear-baitings.[9]

The issues that I see the plays raising are philosophical and sociopolitical. It is these issues that provide the threads that I try to trace through the wholes. I do not mean to suggest that the plays are treatises in disguise or that the themes that I find are the only ones to be found. I do wish to claim that when we see the issues that are involved in various of the plays, many puzzling details can be seen to fall into place, and that these details can be seen as in turn illuminating and deepening the issues. Moreover, I will try to show not only that the plays explore issues but also that, at times, they take positions with regard to them. I do not hold the view that Shakespeare did not have "positions," or that, if he did, we cannot tell what they were. In some cases, the plays do produce aporias. But in other cases, in my view, they do not.[10]

Yet despite this philosophical orientation—or rather, along with or, better, within it—this is a book, unabashedly, of literary criticism. It does not apply philosophy to the plays but rather sees the philosophical issues as built into them, and, unlike some historicist work, it is not using the works that it treats to illuminate aspects of the culture in which they were produced (I will not say "the culture that produced them"). The essays do use philosophical concepts and materials from the culture to illuminate the plays—but only when fairly directly called for. That is the crucial matter. But what does it mean to say that a text "calls for" any particular critical or interpretive framework or response? Clearly this is a metaphor. The text in fact does not "do" anything. But it does have characteristics—features that I am willing to term facts—and these are what do the "calling." What I mean by a fact about a literary text is a feature of it that any competent reader would agree is present. The more of these that an interpretive framework can show to be meaningful and consistent with other such features, the more the framework proves its appropriateness—and, cannot we even say, its truth?[11]

This notion of doing, in the process of interpretation, what and whatever a text calls for eliminates many unnecessary dichotomies in literary theory and practice. It eliminates, for instance, the internal-external (formalist-historicist) dichotomy. If the text alludes to or mentions another text, a mythological story, a historical event or person, or an item in the world, that must be followed out—to the extent needed to elucidate the passage in question. What this extent is will be a matter of judgment and perhaps of audience. But the theoretical point is the same—some kind of "following out" is called for. The procedure I am recommending might be called promiscuous responsiveness. Such responsiveness has been claimed for "surface reading," but the orientation that I am adopting should also serve to dispel the dichotomy between "surface," literal, or "descriptive" reading, on the one hand, and "deep" reading, on the other.[12] I am happy to ally what I am recommending with what has been called "ordinary language criticism."[13]

What I mean by this is to advocate that we apply to texts the same attention to detail, and the same range and variety of responses that we, in the ordinary course of social life, apply to persons in general, and especially to ones we care about.[14] So the initial presumption is to take texts or persons in the most obvious sense (this is part of the "principle of charity" to which I have already referred). But with texts, as with persons, it sometimes seems that to get at the meaning of a stretch of language, the obvious reading seems insufficient or inappropriate. The language in question might seem out of context, unusual in mode, and so forth. At that point, I take it that a reading in more "depth" is called for. But in all such cases, one can supply reasons, within the principle of charity, why one made the move to go "beyond" or "beneath" the obvious or the surface. This is all quite ordinary and is a matter of judgment. In making such an interpretive move, one is not going "against the grain" of the utterance but rather is trying to capture what the utterance is actually meaning. In the case of a stretch of language within a literary text, one is trying to recognize what the author can plausibly be thought of as doing in providing language that provokes or invites the move to go beyond or beneath the obvious. This should also take care of the dichotomy between "suspicious" and nonsuspicious reading.[15] In my view, in literary criticism as in life, one needs a good reason, and one related to the particular instance, to be suspicious. Never being so would seem like a lapse, as would always being so (though these might not be ethically equivalent).[16]

But, as Dr. Johnson said, critical remarks are not easily understood without examples. So let me provide examples from the essays that follow of some of the different kinds of readings that methodologically "promiscuous" close reading can allow.

The opening essay, entitled "Excuses, Bepissing, and Non-Being," can be seen as going for "depth." It begins by considering two pleas for exculpation (one from *Hamlet* and one from *Othello*) in which it is difficult to tell whether the speaker of them is being ingenuous or disingenuous. I take it that Shakespeare, in these cases, meant to raise exactly that question (hence, "Excuses"— with a nod to J. L. Austin's great essay on the topic).[17] The middle section of the essay considers cases from *The Merchant of Venice*. It takes the puzzlement about Antonio's mental / emotional state with which the play opens to be announcing a theme. It then looks at instances where a character is given a circuitous or unexpected speech procedure—a lurch into narrative, for instance. Bassanio is considered, but Shylock becomes the focus as a character to whom Shakespeare gives a number of surprising turns, including a remarkable comparison of himself to a group who "Cannot contain their urine" (hence "Bepissing"). The final section of the essay considers a different set of cases in which a character is given a speech that is either unexpected or seems odd in relation to its immediate context. The cases are speeches by Iago. They all have to do with negative ontology (hence "Non-Being"). Here, with Iago, as in all the cases treated in this essay, I take myself to be following an "invitation," an invitation to go, in a directed way, beyond the realm of the usual—an authorial invitation, signaled in the text, to do so.

The Appendix to the first essay is a critique of an overly literal reading. This is one that assumes a particular "historicist" version of the literal. When King Lear asks (in the Folio version), "Is there any cause in nature that makes these hard hearts?" I had always thought that this was, as we say, a "rhetorical" question, and that the implied answer was no. But an influential school of recent critics takes it that the answer is yes, and would go on to explain the "cause in nature" through the framework of Galenic physiology. I still think that the answer is no, and that when Lear fantasizes about "anatomizing" (dissecting) Regan, he is speaking madly, not shrewdly. But now such a position has to be argued. The Appendix focuses on a speech of Shylock's that uses the key term of the Galenic framework, humor—meaning, of course, chemistry rather than comedy. I argue that the Galenic meaning is not at work in the passage, and that the speech is intended (certainly by Shakespeare and probably by Shylock) to be strange rather than familiar. The analysis tries to show that in this case, the literal (materialist) reading of the speech is a distraction from its real meaning and its real weirdness. The weirdness is the key. The attentiveness characteristic of ordinary life and of ordinary reading shows this speech to be extraordinary.

On the other hand, sometimes what is needed is respect for the "surface" and the literal. The second full-scale essay in the opening section is called "Happy Hamlet." Obviously, this title is meant to be provocative, but the hope is that, by the end of the essay, it will seem obvious, and not counterintuitive. The essay works by trying to take seriously—that is, literally—what the characters say about themselves and, especially, about each other. When Hamlet says to characters who have known him since childhood that he has lost all his mirth, this implies that he was and was known to be in that state. When Ophelia says that Hamlet had been "the glass of fashion," why not take her to be telling the truth? The essay argues that, even after his "transformation," Hamlet is still, as the play presents him, given both to mirth and to fashion. The essay takes seriously what Hamlet says about Laertes—"a very noble youth"—and Hamlet's sense of deep kinship with him. The essay's most controversial claim—perhaps even more so than disputing Hamlet's "melancholic" nature—is the attempt to see Rosencrantz and Guildenstern precisely as ordinary rather than as wicked. The essay relies on what we actually see them doing rather than on the devastating judgment on them that Hamlet comes to make. The point of all these "upward" revaluations—of Hamlet's emotional constitution, of the characters and moral standing of Laertes, Rosencrantz and Guildenstern (and Ophelia)—is to intensify the sense that I take the ordinary reader or viewer to have of the special affect of the play—that is, its sadness.

The concluding essay in Part I also attempts to recapture and to establish the literal and the ordinary. It deals with treatments of *King Lear* by two strong critics, Stanley Cavell and Harry Berger Jr. It critiques a symbolic reading of an important strand in the text by Cavell and, it critiques, in both commentators, negative moral judgments on characters who are (even less so than Rosencrantz and Guildenstern) not obviously wicked. The essay calls not only for literal reading but for normal moral judgments. Cavell is seen as surprising in his refusal to practice "ordinary language criticism" despite his designated and semiofficial patronage of it and his association with ordinary language philosophy.[18] He provides his own version of a well-established way of reading the play in which blindness is seen as symbolic. This allows him to use the language of blindness to make his negative moral judgments. Such judgments are regularly made by Harry Berger Jr., who is a systematically "suspicious" reader. His critical efforts are often devoted to establishing self-aggrandizing or vengeful motives where these are not obvious. The essential premise of my critique of both these critics is that the work in question does not provide good reasons to depart from literal reading and intuitive judgments, and, in fact, stresses the importance of literal, physical realities (the topic of the essay on the play in Part II of this book) as well as the beauty, in a world that contains true villainy, of benevolent motives and behavior.

So it should by now be clear that readings, on my view, can go wrong—in particular cases—either by being overly symbolic or by being overly literal. The general orientation of the essays in this book is toward literal reading, toward respecting "surface" meanings—unless that is, as I have suggested, the text *calls for* a different kind of reading. I have described how this works with regard to speeches or passages where strangeness of some marked kind invites a special sort of scrutiny. But this can happen with regard to more global features as well. Two of the essays in the book see the plays they treat as calling for a wholesale *rejection* of literal reading. The first of the essays on *The Tempest* argues that magic in the play is to be read allegorically or symbolically, and that to do so reveals and clarifies an important dimension of the play. Similarly, in the treatment of *A Midsummer Night's Dream*, the "juice" deposited in the eyes of the young males (and Titania) is not read as a literal love-potion. The play is seen to invite skepticism about nonnatural causes through the pretense of believing in them.

* * *

This book is organized in groupings that move from the more particular to the more general. As already indicated, the essays in Part I, "Individuals," are concerned with the presentation of and judgment on characters. Part II, "Systems," moves to Shakespeare's treatment of larger social, economic, and practical systems and questions. This is where the plays as treating "issues" comes to the fore.

The opening essay in Part II, argues, on the basis of key texts, that Shakespeare has a strangely negative attitude toward legal systems, and the more so the more that they are seen as systems (hence "The Better the Worse"). The essay begins with a consideration of the *Henry IV* plays, and it particularly focuses on the Lord Chief Justice, the figure who speaks for and embodies what one would think could only be seen as a virtue in a legal or ethical system: impartiality, not treating one's friends in a special way. The essay tries to show that (like some philosophers, then as now) the play is not so certain about the supreme status of this. The section, on *Measure for Measure*, sees that play as discounting the only model it presents for a working legal system. The play focuses on a fundamental function of any such system: proper punishment. The essay argues that this function disappears as an intelligible desideratum when the biblical perspective that is announced in the play's title takes over. The final section of the essay returns to *The Merchant of Venice*, which is seen as presenting an equivalent problem. We are introduced to an actual, historically recognizable polity (more so than the Vienna of *Measure*), a polity that has a developed legal system and a clear rationale for the aspect of the system that is in focus: the enforcement of contracts. The essay argues that in the course of this play, Shakespeare presents us with a situation where straightforward enforcement of a contract would produce a monstrous result, and where the argument for nonenforcement either undercuts the system itself or shows the system not to be committed to what it professes to be its defining value. So if the system works, it is a disaster; and if it does not work, it is a fraud.

The second essay in Part II returns to *King Lear*. It sees this play as concerned not with law but with justice, conceived in the largest possible human terms. As the title of the essay suggests, the play is seen as concerned with defining fundamental human needs, both physical and psychological. The essay argues that the play understands a certain level of physical "accommodation" to be necessary for any person to have a life commensurate with human dignity. Such a life is presented as a human right, and one that society should be organized to recognize. But the play is seen to understand human dignity in a nonphysical sense as well, a sense in which personal history is recognized. This means that the play insists on human difference as well as human sameness. This is a complex position—and the way that the term and idea of "superfluity" works in the play models this—but the essay tries to show that the play holds such a complex position, and coherently. This may sound as though the play is being approached as a treatise rather than a tragic drama, but, once again, as with the reading of *Hamlet*, the essay sees the affect of the play as essential to its arguments.

Part II concludes with a "suite" of three essays on *The Tempest*. The prominence of this play in the book—it is the only one to which three entire essays are dedicated—reflects the way in which the play is deeply involved with the kinds of social and political issues to which this part of the book is dedicated. The essays all revolve around the figure of Prospero, in relation to whom the "suspicious" approach is taken to be appropriate and authorially invited (in this context,

Harry Berger is approvingly cited). The essays move from the general to the particular, with Prospero at the center each time. The first ("Power") considers the play as a study of the possibilities for coercion in relation to persons, both European and non-European. The second ("Labor") considers work in the play in both its physical and its psychological sense. The third ("Humanism") takes up humanist self-construction and, especially, humanist pedagogy.

The essay on power considers the political and the colonial dimensions of the play. It distinguishes between "normal" (European) and "magical" (colonial) politics. In treating the latter, the essay draws the remarkable series of twentieth-century works that use the play to analyze actual colonial situations or colonial situations in general. It uses works that build out from Shakespeare as ways back to Shakespeare. This might seem adventitious, but I take it that there is a sense in which the play, in its semiallegorical suggestiveness, invites such extensions. The essay argues that *The Tempest* ultimately works to show the limits of coercive human power in both colonial and noncolonial situations. In neither case does it produce the desired results: happy slaves or transformed Europeans.

The essay on labor in the play follows, and follows from, the essay on power. It begins with the widely recognized borrowing from Montaigne's essay on cannibals that is used, almost intact, in Gonzalo's "Golden Age" fantasy. The essay argues—against many critics—that the passage is not undercut in the play. The idea of satisfaction without effort is seen as the key to Gonzalo's vision. The essay argues that effort is presented in the play as problematic ("vexed") at all levels. So Gonzalo's vision is reinforced as an ideal even in the face of what is seen as the directly competing one presented in Prospero's engagement masque, which is analyzed in some detail. But the essay has to confront the other, less well-known borrowing from Montaigne in the play, a borrowing from an essay ("On Cruelty") that seems to praise strenuous mental and emotional effort. My argument is that Montaigne is not actually praising such, and that in the play, as in Montaigne, high-class work and moral effort turn out to be further instances of the failure of power to produce contentment. "Idleness," on the other hand, as Montaigne shows (and not just in the primitivist context), can produce contentment. Here too, the affect of the play is seen as central to its content. The play is seen as longing, so to speak, to be free of itself.

Finally, "Humanism" takes up Prospero's behavior within his self-identified role as an expert in "the liberal arts" (on which being a *magus* depends). The essay assesses Prospero in the context of European humanism. His commitment to "secret studies" and withdrawal from public life are shown to be valued in one strand of the humanist tradition, but not in the one that was dominant in

England. He failed to rule in Milan. On the island he exercised, or attempted to exercise, the roles the previous essays examined—of moral reformer and of master. This essay examines his assumption of the related role of humanist "schoolmaster." It considers his practices and results with his two students, Miranda and Caliban. Miranda is shown to have learned eloquence and chastity, but to have been kept from developing anything like an adult consciousness. Prospero's educational role with regard to Caliban is shown to be more complex, and is judged against the most relevant humanist pedagogical theory, that of Erasmus. The relationship is shown to have begun on the Erasmian model but to have turned into a punitive one that is directly rejected by this model. Prospero is seen as just as responsible for Caliban's developed state of mind and character as for Miranda's.

Part III of this book, "Beliefs," moves from plays that are seen as raising social and political issues to plays that are seen as raising issues about belief. The first two essays in this section deal with the question of Shakespeare's relation to skepticism. This is an issue provoked by the plays but not, of course, named by them. The essays deal, in turn, with two different kinds of skepticism: religious (about the supernatural) and epistemological (about knowledge).

The first of these paired essays treats *The Comedy of Errors*, *A Midsummer Night's Dream*, and *King Lear*. *Errors* is shown to be a play that consistently mocks popular beliefs—in fairies, in exorcism (at least of a Catholic sort), and in witches. The play shows none of these to have any explanatory value or actual relevance. *A Midsummer Night's Dream* is, as I have already suggested, read in a similar way; the fairy framework is shown to have no explanatory necessity while perhaps serving a psychological function. Protestant or lay skepticism is seen as what is manifested in these plays. *King Lear* is seen as extending skepticism about the existence (or, at least, relevance) of the supernatural beyond any recognizable denominational position. The play is seen as continuing the mockery of exorcism and possession, and as going beyond this to question the very existence of divine presence in the world. But that is not the end of the discussion. The essay recognizes that there is religious language in the play, even Christian-sounding language, and holds that this cannot simply be ignored or discounted. The argument is that, as with the religious language in *Othello* discussed in the final section of the opening essay of this book, such language is to be taken seriously—but not literally. Respecting the "surface" in these cases does not entail literal reading. It entails understanding the function that this language has in a non- (or anti-) supernatural context.

The second of the paired essays on "belief" turns to philosophical skepticism in the plays, skepticism about the possibility of knowledge—of the world and of other minds. The essay argues that while Shakespeare is skeptical about such matters as fairies and exorcism, he is not an epistemological skeptic. Again, *The Comedy of Errors* is a key text. It is shown to present us with a central character whose dramatized experience seems to iterate the positions of both ancient and (uncannily) Cartesian skepticism. But, as the title of the play suggests, his epistemological situation is shown to be entirely a matter of errors, easily corrigible, and not a picture of human cognition in general. Knowledge turns out to be fully possible. The essay goes on to argue that something similar obtains with regard to skepticism about other minds. Plays that are often taken to manifest such skepticism, *Othello* and *Hamlet*, are shown, through attention to "surface" matters like plot and language, not to do so. The essay argues that Othello could and should have stuck with his demand for "the ocular proof," and that the evidence of the senses, when not artificially manipulated, is reliable. Misinterpretation is possible, but not inevitable. This is true of knowledge of other minds as well as of the world. Other minds can be hidden or ignored but are not inaccessible. The same is shown to be true in *Hamlet*. It can be difficult to find out the truth about the world and about other minds, but it is not the case that it cannot be done. There are cases of success with regard to knowledge of other minds dramatized in the play. Other minds are not a special problem. Access to them is no more (and no less) difficult than to one's own.

The final essay in the book provides something like an overall "reading" of *The Winter's Tale*. It sees the play as centrally involving the issue of the mind's relation to the world. The play, on this view, is concerned not with skepticism but with the fact that makes skepticism possible: that the mind and the world do not always align. The essay argues that the play presents such lack of alignment not as a general feature of the human condition but as a condition of madness. The world is seen as not only accessible to the healthy (normal) mind but as fundamentally benign. This is seen as leading to a kind of collapsing of the natural and the supernatural in the play, such that the natural becomes numinous. Two results that seem anomalous when brought together follow: an apparently softened attitude toward popular belief and a very strong resistance to idolatry. The former has to do with the status of wonder in the play. The latter, it is argued, flows from the assertion of benignity; the world ("Nature") is seen as reliable in a way that the mind is not, and special in a way that human invention cannot be. Faith, in the play, is seen as a restored belief in the benignity of the world, which reconnects the mind to "things," and keeps it from the disease of skepticism, which cannot get beyond "opinion." The language of the play is seen, on its "surface," as giving us all this.

The essays in this book speak to one another. George Herbert noted that in a book that works within a particular realm but is not completely linear, one point might unexpectedly connect to another, and both might connect "Unto a third, that ten leaves off doth lie." The ideal reader will perceive connections and, in Herbert's brilliant image, come up with "constellations of the storie." This book on Shakespeare will not (I am sorry to say) light you to "eternall blisse," but I do hope that its overall structure serves to deepen and enrich each of the individual essays.[19] Plays that are particularly interested in the kinds of issues in which the book is interested keep recurring, with different aspects of them in focus. *Hamlet* appears in three different essays, as does *King Lear*; *Othello* is treated in two, as are *The Merchant of Venice* and *The Comedy of Errors*. The three essays on *The Tempest* treat separate topics but are deeply interrelated. *A Midsummer Night's Dream* appears in a single essay but plays a crucial thematic role there. The *Henry IV* plays are brought into dialogue with *Measure for Measure* in what I hope is a productive way. *The Winter's Tale* is the culmination of the section on "belief," bringing together issues treated in the paired essays on skepticism. Certain words are multiply interrogated—"affection," for instance, and "humour." Certain critics keep recurring. This book is regularly in both Blakean (oppositional) and Aristotelian (affiliative) friendship with Stanley Cavell and Stephen Greenblatt. While the essays do not constitute a survey—in total, only eleven plays are treated—but they cover all the dramatic genres in which Shakespeare worked, and, taken together, they present a picture of some of the things that Shakespeare believed, some of the things that he did not believe, and some of the things that he wanted to believe. The book means to be surprising without being idiosyncratic, to make some new claims plausible (happy Hamlet, epistemological optimism) and to make some familiar topics (the complexity of motives, the deep social concerns, the awareness of colonialism and domination) resonate anew—all through what Nietzsche called "a goldsmith's art."[20]

PART I

Individuals

CHAPTER 1

Excuses, Bepissing, and Non-Being

Shakespearean Puzzles About Agency

My concern is about both Shakespeare's conception of moral agency and his conception of agency in general. I aim to indicate a peculiar feature in the latter. This seems to me more interesting than Shakespeare's conception of specifically moral agency, though I will begin with a puzzle about that. Insofar as moral agency involves the issue of moral responsibility—that is, the relevance to an action of (moral) praise and blame—there is a question that I wish to raise about Shakespeare's understanding of the issue. After that, I will turn to what I take to be the deeper and more intriguing puzzle, that about agency in general. But the first puzzle first.

Excuses

The question about moral agency is whether Shakespeare accepts the Aristotelian distinction between acting "in" ignorance and acting "due to" ignorance.[1] Acting "due to ignorance," for Aristotle, means acting in a way that one cannot be blamed for, acting in a situation where one simply did not know a morally relevant particular of one's situation (not knowing a morally relevant general truth is wicked [*NE* 1110b330–33]). For instance, though one knows that buying stolen property is wrong, one buys something in a situation in which one could not possibly have known (or reasonably be supposed to have known) that the object in question had been stolen. In this case, one is truly acting "due to ignorance." Such acts, for Aristotle, are pardonable, on the one hand, and do not properly generate regret, on the other. However, Aristotle holds that one is not acting "due to ignorance," even though one is acting "in ignorance," in a situation where one is responsible for the state that has put one into ignorance. The key examples are when a person is drunk or angry (*NE* 1110b16–1111a1–2). Aristotle holds that the actions performed in this state are not properly thought of as due to ignorance but rather due to drunkenness or wrath, and are therefore morally condemnable and generative of (moral) regret. The person did not have to get drunk ("had the power not to" get into such a state). That is perfectly straightforward. But Aristotle thinks that this also holds in the case of anger. If one says that one is simply the kind of person who is unable to control anger, Aristotle holds that one is responsible for letting oneself become that kind of person (1114a1–21). Here again, one is not acting "due to ignorance," but due to one's character—for which, Aristotle holds, one is also, in a deep sense, responsible (1114b20–1115a1–3).

I am not sure whether Shakespeare grasped this distinction or not. A test case would be a moment in *Hamlet*. After a great deal has happened, the prince asks, in very formal terms, that Laertes "pardon" him for a "wrong" he has done (5.2.204).[2] The reason Hamlet says he should be "pardoned" is that he is "punished with a sore distraction":

> What I have done
> That might your nature, honour, and exception
> Roughly awake, I here proclaim was madness.
> Was't Hamlet wronged Laertes? Never Hamlet.
> If Hamlet from himself be ta'en away
> And when he's not himself does wrong Laertes,
> Then Hamlet does it not; Hamlet denies it.
> Who does it then? His madness. If't be so,
> Hamlet is of the faction that is wrong'd—
> His madness is poor Hamlet's enemy.
> Let my disclaiming from a purpos'd evil
> Free me so far in your most generous thoughts
> That I have shot my arrow o'er the house
> And hurt my brother. (5.2.208–20)[3]

Hamlet presents his rash and excited action in killing Polonius, an action clearly done "in ignorance" (when he was too wrought up to be careful), as having been done merely due to ignorance (he did not know who was behind the arras). He does not take responsibility for allowing himself to get into the state in question (only dubiously called "madness"), and he does not allow for the obvious possibility that he could easily have found out who was behind the arras.[4] Presenting himself as already "punished" is a clever ploy, and in repeatedly referring to the whole episode as a "wrong" (rather than, for instance, a crime)—and not actually naming the "wrong"—he puts the episode into a primarily cognitive rather than a legal or ethical framework. The evasion of responsibility continues: he was "not himself" at the time; his "madness" was the agent, and therefore he is among the "wronged" parties. He speaks as if he accepts a very simple version of the voluntary, such that only chosen ("purpos'd") actions are to be thought of as such. Aristotle, on the other hand, makes it quite clear that the category of the voluntary must be much larger than the category of the chosen. The example Aristotle gives as an explanation of this distinction is immediately relevant to Hamlet: "an act done on the spur of the moment [is] a voluntary act, but [it is] not the result of choice" (1111b7–10).

I am genuinely unsure whether Shakespeare wants us to see Hamlet as being disingenuous and consciously sophistical here, or not. It does seem morally relevant that Hamlet did not intend to kill Polonius—he did it, to use one of J. L. Austin's very Aristotelian distinctions—by mistake though not by accident (he meant to stab *somebody*).[5] But the disclaimer seems too strong ("Hamlet does it not"). Surely Hamlet is enough of an Aristotelian to know the argument for one's responsibility for one's character, and also the argument that one's character is most fully revealed in "spur of the moment" actions (*NE* 1117a20).[6] Hamlet has given, after all, in his homily to his mother, something like an Aristotelian account of how, through habit, character is developed and can be potentially changed—"the monster Custom" can also be an "angel" and in its "wondrous potency" can almost "change the stamp of nature" (3.4.159–68).[7] Nonetheless, in the speech to Laertes, Hamlet seems sincere.

The ethical (as opposed to social) ideal to which he appeals is that of generosity. "Free me ... in your most generous thoughts," he says. This quality has been powerfully associated with Hamlet's own character by the shrewdest observer of character in the play. Claudius predicts that Hamlet will not examine the foils because Hamlet is "Most generous, and free from all contriving" (4.7.133), and this prediction turns out to be true. So we are certainly supposed to think that Hamlet knows about "generous thoughts." And, after all, he is condescending to explain himself—something that great aristocrats did not often feel obliged to do, even disingenuously, and, as the Folio emphasizes, he is doing so in public.[8] Perhaps the speech-act itself is more important than what it actually says. But that still avoids the question, since the whole issue is whether, or to what extent, he is being (or we are asked by Shakespeare to see him as being) disingenuous—in however grand a mode.

The puzzle is only deepened by Laertes's response, which seems, in some sense, to accept the apology.[9] Christopher Crosbie rightly speaks of the apology's "effectiveness."[10] I am genuinely not sure what Shakespeare means us to think of Hamlet's speech-act here. Perhaps we are to see it as part of a general perception on Shakespeare's part that persons often do not know whether they are being sincere or not, or can offer bad arguments to support good intentions (which we are to value above the arguments), or that disingenuousness is a complex business. Whatever we are to conclude about the moment in question, I think that it cannot be taken either as a straightforward, morally responsible account or as a straightforward piece of self-justifying and self-conscious sophistry.[11]

Let me adduce one other, parallel case, and then move on to what seems to me the greater Shakespearean puzzle. The other case where I am unsure how Shakespeare meant for us to evaluate a character's response to having acted badly responds directly to Aristotle's first example of an action done "in" but not "due to" ignorance—namely, an action done when drunk. When we first meet Cassio in *Othello*, he is presented as a model of high, almost exaggerated courtesy (2.1.96–99, 167–75). Yet in the next scene, when we see him (at Iago's prompting) getting drunk, Cassio behaves in a vile and murderously thuggish way.[12] Verbally, he "pulls rank" in a disgusting and obviously ungospel-like way in insisting that "The lieutenant is to be saved before the ancient" (2.3.106), and he is outrageously aggressive toward the gentleman (Montano) who attempts, in a reasonably polite way, to stop Cassio from brawling in the street: Cassio denies that he is drunk, and wounds the intervener, who is the governor of the island (2.3.147–52). When Othello arrives on the scene, Othello makes it clear what a deep breach of military protocol this whole episode is ("What, in a town of war . . . 'Tis monstrous" [2.3.209–13]). Meanwhile, Shakespeare has made it clear that Cassio was fully aware of his inability to hold his alcohol (he told Iago, "I have very poor and unhappy brains for drinking" [2.3.30–31]). Certainly Cassio could—and should—have resisted the pressure to drink. And he understands the full extent of what he has done. On sobering up, Cassio seems to accept moral responsibility and feels regret / remorse (for Aristotle, a crucial matter in determining the nature of the act and the agent [*NE* 1111a20 and 1150b31]). Cassio says, "I will rather sue to be despised, than to deceive so good a commander with so slight, so drunken, and so indiscreet an officer" (2.3.273–75). He goes on to say that he "frankly" despises himself (2.3.293).

The puzzle is that Cassio so readily decides (before Iago suggests it [see 3.1.33–34]) to appeal to Desdemona to help him get his position back—even though Cassio seems to recognize, in the lines just quoted, that it is not at all clear that he is worthy of getting it back. But Iago assures Cassio that Cassio is, in his self-castigation, "too severe a moraler" (2.3.294). The play seems to accept this, seems to accept that it is reasonable for Cassio to want his position back, and that it is acceptable for him to recruit Desdemona in his cause (though even she, despite her eagerness to help Cassio and to exercise her status with Othello, does have a moment in which she recognizes the problem—"they say the wars must make example" [3.3.65]). In Cassio's final appeal to Desdemona, Cassio recognizes the possibility that his offense may not be forgivable (3.4.116–23). But he seems to take this only partly seriously. The question remains as to whether Cassio was, in fact, "too severe a moraler" with regard to his behavior when drunk. Or is this another case where Shakespeare seems to let someone (an aristocrat) too lightly off the moral hook? Cassio is, after all, an admirable fellow—when, that is, he is not drunk or angry. So the question arises again: Does Shakespeare grasp Aristotle's point about such states? Or does Shakespeare take unacknowledged disingenuousness about regret to be normal?

Bepissing

Let me hasten now to what I take to be a deeper puzzle in Shakespeare's conception of moral agency—or rather, as I have already suggested, in his conception of agency in general. This puzzle may be related to the possibility raised above that Shakespeare thought that persons have an oblique and complex relationship even to their own sincere utterances. The issue that I am interested in is Shakespeare's sense of the thickness and sometimes opacity of motives. I want to make the general claim that this is true of Shakespeare, and that it is this view—that stated motives can be inadequate as explanations of a person's (character's) behavior—that leads to the perception that Shakespeare is a Freudian *avant la lettre*.

In this section, I will, for the moment, leave Hamlet behind, and focus on a play that explicitly thematizes the issue of the opacity of motives. This is the play that first enters the world as "a booke of *the Marchaunt of Venyce, or otherwise called the Iewe of Venyce*."[13] As the first part (and perhaps the second) of its possible titles suggests, in this play, motives should be straightforward; economics should rule. But right from its opening lines, the issue of the opacity of motives is presented, and the issue is dramatized at length with regard to the two possible title characters, the merchant and the Jew (though we will see that, as in *Hamlet* and *Othello*, a young aristocrat's speeches are also held up for scrutiny).

In the opening line of the play, Shakespeare's merchant asserts, to himself and his friends, "In sooth I know not why I am so sad." He claims to have no knowledge of the origins or nature of his mental / emotional state: "how I caught it, found it or came by it, / What stuff 'tis made of, whereof it is born, I am to learn" (3–5). The friends to whom the merchant (Antonio) is expressing his puzzlement are sure that they can explain Antonio's mental state. We learn from them that he is a maritime merchant-adventurer. The friends are impressed with the grandeur and scale of the merchant's operations, and profess to think, in the mode of comic hyperbole, that he must be experiencing anxiety at a commensurate level.[14] The poetry that Shakespeare gives them expresses both the grandeur and the vulnerability of Antonio's enterprises—their speeches culminate in the vision of a vessel returning from the East filled with luxury items that has its "gentle" side pierced by dangerous rocks, thereby seasoning and decorating the ocean with its cargo, scattering her spices on it and "enrobing" the roaring waters with silks (30–34).

Compelling as this vision is, Antonio rejects it. He insists that he is prudent enough not to have put all his wealth in one operation, and to have held back some of his capital (41–43). That seems like a good answer, so the friends try another tack. Love-melancholy was a well-known phenomenon: "Why then, you are in love." This is rejected immediately, with no explanation but a kind of childish revulsion. "Fie, fie" is all Antonio says about this psychological possibility (46). Unlike with the business-anxiety claim, no reason for the rejection of this hypothesis is given. It is simply rejected—viscerally, almost nonverbally. The friends have now run out of intelligible reasons for Antonio's melancholy, so they give up on the possibility of trying to provide such, opting, still in a comic mode, for the mystery of inborn temperaments. "Nature," Salanio says, "hath framed strange fellows in her time" (51). Some are prone to overmuch mirth—they "will evermore peep through their eyes"—or to uncontrollable mirth on occasions that would not seem to call for such: they "laugh like parrots at a bagpiper" (53). Other naturally strange fellows are the opposite, and are of "such vinegar aspect" that nothing, even a really good joke, can make them "show their teeth in way of smile." So the opening mystery is left unresolved, or ascribed, unhelpfully, to "Nature."

Three other characters now enter the scene and the first two depart, ceding their place to socially and perhaps emotionally "worthier friends" (61). Two of these three are simply accompanying the third, addressed as "Lord Bassanio," who has apparently been looking for Antonio. One of the two attendants attempts to take his leave with the other, but that one (Gratiano) takes up the theme explored by the first pair of friends. Antonio, Gratiano says, looks "not well." He too takes the cause of Antonio's condition to be psychological rather than physical, but Gratiano's approach is a moralized version of psychology. He suggests that Antonio has "too much respect upon the world" (74). Antonio asserts that he does not overvalue "the world," and that something like the "Nature" explanation is right. He adopts the world as stage metaphor in order to assert that the "part" that he "must" play in it is "a sad one" (78–79). Gratiano takes such playing to be a matter of choice rather than nature. He too believes in "strange fellows," and sees Antonio as being one of "a sort of men." But Gratiano takes the metaphor of "playing" to mean consciously taking on a part, and he accuses Antonio (again in a comic mode) of adopting the role of a highly sober man-of-few-words in order to gain a reputation "Of wisdom, gravity, profound conceit" (92). Antonio does not even respond to this speech, which is clearly a tour de force of comical satire rather than a serious hypothesis. Gratiano, having said his piece (for the time being), finally is willing to depart, and the actual plot of the play begins.

In this plot, the economic and the emotional are fundamentally intertwined. After "Lord Bassanio" and Antonio briefly comment on Gratiano's bravura performance, Antonio reminds Bassanio that he has revealed to Antonio a plan to court a "lady" whose identity Bassanio has not revealed (119). The reason for this reticence is now made clear. Money is going to be involved. Bassanio has been living beyond his means. He attempts candor about his situation, acknowledging, somewhat reluctantly, through a double negative, that Antonio is familiar with it ("'Tis not unknown to you"). He tries to present his financial condition and behavior in neutral, colorless terms—"How much I have disabled my estate"—but the sense of self-mutilation surfaces nonetheless. The next lines try to diminish the extent of the damage—"*something showing* a more swelling port / Than my faint means would grant continuance" (124–25). He has only exceeded by a bit; and again, he strives for neutral, almost technical language—"would grant continuance." But "swelling port" betrays him. It is minimized, but the phallic and social attraction of "swelling port" cannot be suppressed. The next lines are a model of almost conscious disingenuousness. This is another aristocrat who cannot quite face up to what he has done, and cannot quite inhabit the emotional space he is claiming. Bassanio purports not to be distressed by the lack of "continuance": "Nor do I now make moan to be abridged / From such a noble rate." "Make moan" suggests an awareness of the possible emotion that is being disclaimed, and "such a noble rate" makes it clear how much Bassanio admired, and continues to admire, the lifestyle to which he knows his means can no longer "grant continuance." But the speech has been avoiding the real problem. He has not simply run out of funds and "disabled" his own estate. His deeper problem is "the great debts" that he has accumulated, though even in acknowledging these he cannot bear to take very much responsibility or even to express very much remorse. Mitigation, as in "something showing," emerges again—"my time, *something* too prodigal" has left him "gaged" (130).

The key moment in the speech is the next one. It turns out that Antonio is Bassanio's major creditor. But the line that acknowledges this takes a crucial turn: "To you, Antonio, I owe the most" is perfectly straightforward, but it turns out that the "debt" is not only (as it obviously must be) "in money" but also "in love." It is this that leads Bassanio to think that he can now reveal the wooing plan through which he hopes "to get clear of all the debts I owe." Bassanio takes the emotional connection to have something like legal status; it gives him "a warranty" (132). We have already had a hint of the extent of the connection on Antonio's part in Antonio's eagerness to hear the details of the "secret pilgrimage" about which Bassanio has hinted to him. Antonio's eagerness continues, but at first with some care. He wants to know the plan, but he also wants to make sure that it is not a dishonorable one (there are, after all, dishonorable ways to secure "a lady"). Antonio expresses this carefully but nonetheless firmly; he will support the plan (yet undescribed)—"if it stand, as you yourself still do, / Within the eye of honour" (136–37). But then we suddenly move beyond the realm of prudence and even of friendship. If there is no question of dishonor, Antonio tells Bassanio, "My purse my person, my extremest means / Lie all unlocked to your occasions." Surely this is a case where the lines say more than the speaker intended. The purse being open is the intended meaning, as "unlocked" makes clear. The person being open is another matter—Shakespeare is indicating the arena in which the opacity of Antonio's mental state is located. The poetry is the means of revelation. There is little more that Shakespeare could have done to make the equation of purse and person more noticeable to the theatergoer or the reader; puns, alliteration, and anaphora are all deployed to make the phrase salient, and "extremest" is added to the mix.

Bassanio responds in an oddly indirect way. Instead of giving Antonio the requested information, he tells a story. The recourse to narrative always indicates that something complex is going on. The story evokes an aristocratic childhood practice (compare Hamlet's imagination of having shot an arrow "o'er the house")—finding a lost arrow by shooting another in the same direction—in order to guarantee that "what follows is pure innocence" (145), a phrase that undercuts itself by proclaiming itself. The analogy serves to minimize Bassanio's past prodigality (just youthful behavior) and to present the request that Bassanio is preparing to make as itself of no more consequence. The childhood context (as also perhaps in *Hamlet*) serves as a cover for adult embarrassment. There is no real conviction here in the reassuring quality of the analogy. The best Bassanio can promise is to return what Antonio will lend him—the second arrow, though exactly how the analogy is supposed to work in the case of money is unclear. The point, however, is not the promise but the appeal to protectiveness on Antonio's part. This is self-defense and rhetorical manipulation at work, disguised (to the speaker as well as the hearer?) as "innocence."

Antonio recognizes the presence of rhetoric, and he is hurt by it. He rebukes Bassanio for performing a rhetorical maneuver rather than directly relying on Antonio's assurance of love.[15] So Bassanio finally gets to the point, and Antonio and we finally hear the details about the "lady richly left" and Bassanio's plan for wooing her and the basis for his belief that he "should questionless be fortunate." At this point a further reason for Bassanio's hesitation, embarrassment, and circumlocutory rhetoric is revealed. Not only does Bassanio know that Antonio has provided him with more love as well as money than he has returned, it is now revealed that he has known all along that Antonio's claims to prudence were unjustified. Antonio does not actually have any cash. Suddenly, and for the first time in this interchange, Antonio uses the intimate form of address, saying, "Thou knowst that all my fortunes are at sea" (177). What Antonio told Salanio and Salarino was false. He has not held funds or property back ("Neither have I money nor commodity / To raise a present sum" [178–79]). He would not—perhaps psychologically could not—reveal this to his lesser acquaintances. There is an element of shame here on both sides. Antonio's imprudence is another area of his self-opacity (perhaps related in complex ways to the erotic one), and Bassanio must know, in some sense, that even at this point it is not the arrow but Antonio that he is "adventuring." Bassanio is inducing (seducing?) Antonio to enter into another world at least as dangerous as that of maritime commerce, the world of "credit" (180).[16]

The question now becomes "Where money is" (184). After an intervening scene that opens with a character (the rich lady with the classical name) playing at or with sadness while providing Gratiano-like satirical commentary on her suitors, we then read or see "Enter Bassanio with Shylock the Jew" (1.3.0).[17] Apparently "where money is" lands Bassanio there.[18] Why Antonio does not have

Christian friends who could be approached is never explained, though it might be understood in terms of a general scarcity of currency.[19] "Money," meaning a large amount of cash available for lending, seems, in this play, to mean "the Jew." Shakespeare's play featuring such a character (probably written circa 1595) is in continuous dialogue with Christopher Marlowe's earlier and highly popular *The Jew of Malta* (1589–90), where Marlowe's Jew is a merchant-adventurer like Antonio (though Barabas has an exuberant enjoyment of his commercial operations, his wealth, and his sybaritic lifestyle). By making the merchant and the Jew different characters, and making his Jew a moneylender, Shakespeare casts the figure in a much more traditional and culturally loaded role. He seems to be simplifying the figure. The world of Shylock seems exclusively economic. Everything is quite straightforward. Shylock names the specific sum that he is being asked to loan (not mentioned before) and the specific length of time for which it is needed. The only other fact about the deal that is mentioned is that "Antonio shall be bound" (1.3.6). This immediately raises the issue of suretyship, which was mentioned by Portia in a comical way, by this term, in the previous scene (1.2.77); the concept is now, in the contract scene, evoked by the more general term of being "bound" for someone else. "Antonio shall be bound" might well have been seen by the Elizabethans, and intended by the author, as another instance of Antonio's unadmitted imprudence. Standing surety—especially for friends—was notoriously dangerous and was strongly advised against in all prudential contexts.[20]

Bassanio, who lives in a hedonic world, thinks of the loan in such terms; "Will you pleasure me?" he asks Shylock (1.3.7). Shylock responds merely by reiterating the details of the loan. Shakespeare insists on the singleness of Shylock's focus by introducing into the dialogue a moment of explicit misunderstanding. When Shylock asserts that Antonio "is a good man," Bassanio assumes that Shylock is using the phrase in the normal way, as a moral evaluation. Shylock vehemently resists this reading: "Ho no, no, no, no," he corrects; and explains: "my meaning in saying he is a good man, is to have you understand me that he is sufficient" (12–16), meaning able to pay back the sum in question. Shylock gives voice in his own idiom to the anxiety we have already heard (and Antonio has discounted) about the vulnerability and uncertainty of maritime commerce, but Shylock decides that the man is "notwithstanding sufficient" (24), and he can take his "bond" to stand surety for Bassanio. Bassanio urges Shylock to take this on trust—"Be assured you may"—and there is, again, a moment of misunderstanding. Shylock insists that he needs direct evidence to be "assured," and insists on a meeting with Antonio. When Bassanio almost reflexively invites

Shylock to join them at a meal, Shylock makes it clear that, for him, social life has distinct spheres. Commercial life is one thing—"I will buy with you, sell with you, talk with you, walk with you, and so following"—but commensal life is something else ("I will not eat with you"), as is directly religious life ("nor pray with you") (30–34).

Just at this point, Antonio appears. Suddenly Shylock is given a soliloquy, the first such in the play and the first lines of verse that he is given.[21] It looks as if Shakespeare is going to present a truly stereotyped Jew. The soliloquy begins with Shylock occupying the position of the Pharisee who "thanked God that he is not as other men are ... even as this publican" in Luke 18:11.[22] He does not seem to know Antonio personally, but comments, "How like a fawning publican he looks." This is quite a complex reference, so it looks as if Shakespeare wants to clarify the situation by making the stereotype unmistakable—the next line could hardly be more straightforward: "I hate him for he is a Christian" (38). This is the Jew as filled not only with pride but with sectarian hatred. The next lines, however, shift the focus. The reason for Shylock's hatred is economic, not religious. "But more," he adds, "for that ... he lends out money gratis." We are given the specific economic result of this practice: it "brings down the rate of usance here with us in Venice" (40–41). The "hatred" between the merchant and the moneylender is fundamentally economic: "He hates our sacred nation, and he rails ... On me, my bargains, and my well-won thrift," which, Shylock says, Antonio calls "interest."

Shylock is totally caught up in this meditation. He fails to respond to Bassanio's introduction of Antonio, and Bassanio has to ask him, "Shylock, do you hear?" (49). Shylock responds by pretending to be attending to the deal at hand, but, as his soliloquy suggested, he is fixated on Antonio's interference with and critique of Shylock's business. After some perfunctory and perhaps disingenuous remarks to Bassanio about having insufficient funds on hand, Shylock finally welcomes Antonio in what seems like a courteous manner.[23] Antonio, without any return salutation, gets right to the point that Shylock was contemplating—Antonio's economic views and behavior. "I neither lend nor borrow / By taking nor by giving of excess" he states (57–58), though he allows that he will make an exception in this case.[24] For a moment, the topic is the deal at hand, but Shylock cannot retain his focus on it. He wants to return to the general topic. He speaks as if he is having trouble understanding Antonio's position. He presents Antonio's claim about "excess" as if it were a dream or a fantasy. "Methoughts you said," he begins, and paraphrases what Antonio has just claimed ("you neither lend nor borrow / Upon advantage" [65–66]).[25]

The Elizabethan theatrical or reading audience might have shared Shylock's puzzlement at this point. When Shylock was recounting Antonio's criticism of Shylock's business, Shylock said that Antonio calls Shylock's practice "interest" (1.3.47). But the audience would surely have been expecting another word here. They would have been expecting the word "usury," since interest on loans was legal in England as well as in Italy in the period ("usury" was then, as it is for us, a matter of degree).[26] Antonio, as Shylock correctly noted, equates the two terms. Not only will he not lend money at interest—certainly his prerogative—he will also, as he says, not borrow money at interest. It is not at all clear how he would be able to do this. It implies the existence of other lenders like himself, but the play gives no evidence of such, since he has to send Bassanio to Shylock. Antonio seems to exist completely outside the normal business world. Marc Shell rightly calls him an anti-interest "zealot."[27] It is part of the strangeness of his character; it goes along, somehow, with his apparent indifference to risk, or even courting of it. He need not have been the obsessed worrier that Salarino and Salanio conjured up in order to have some sort of appreciation of the dangers of his position, and to have taken some sort of protection against them. Rational assessment of risk—of the sort that we have seen Shylock doing—is not psychologically available to Antonio.[28] As we have already noted, his willingness to stand surety for his friend is another expression of this.

But Shylock wishes to explore the matter of "interest." After Antonio has affirmed the full extent of his position—never does he "use" interest—Shakespeare has the dialogue take a surprising turn. We begin to get some strangeness on Shylock's part (his hatred would not have been taken as such and, as we have seen, it partly has a rational basis). With no preface, he launches into a story. This is like Bassanio's narrative of the lost boyhood arrows. Psychological opacity might again be on display. And it is. Shylock begins to tell a familiar story from the Hebrew Bible. Just as he is beginning the story, Antonio interrupts to query its relevance to the topic of taking interest. Shylock insists on its relevance, even though "not . . . Directly" (71–72). The story is that of how Jacob grew rich by coming into possession of a large flock of sheep that would normally have been owned by his uncle Laban (Genesis 30:31–43).[29] There is no doubt about Shylock's overt point in telling the story: Jacob's successful wealth acquisition was due to his ingenuity, and ingenuity applied to acquisition (what Shylock calls "thrift") meets with divine approbation—as long as the means employed are not forbidden or criminal ("thrift is blessing, if men steal it not" [86]). But again, the character's intention is complicated by the poetry that Shakespeare gives him. Shakespeare wanted Shylock to narrate this particular story even though it was never—as far as anyone can determine—part of the usury debate.[30] Antonio's puzzlement is understandable. Shakespeare inserted the story into this context for Shylock, and wrote a particular kind of poetry for it. The striking feature of the passage is how Jacob's intervention into the copulation of the sheep is evoked; it is evoked in extraordinary biological detail. The sheep are "woolly breeders" who are caught "in the act," doing "the deed of kind"; the ewes are "rank" and "fulsome" (3.3.76–82). What these phrases do is to convey something like a hatred of sexuality and revulsion at normal reproduction.

Antonio disputes Shylock's reading of the story, seeing it instead as about grace rather than works, as "A thing not in his [Jacob's] power to bring to pass, / But sway'd and fashion'd by the hand of heaven" (87–88). It was, Antonio says, using a term that resonates in the economic context, a "venture," an act of faith, not something that could be routinely counted on.[31] But then Antonio asks the larger interpretive question—"Was this inserted to make interest good?"—and adds a powerful *reductio*: "Or is your gold and silver ewes and rams?" (90–91). The sense of bizarre sexuality implicit in Shylock's presentation of a scene of natural reproduction leads to this. Shylock says that he does indeed make his money "breed as fast" as do the sex-hungry sheep (91). But Antonio intends not a parallel but an opposition. He is tapping into one of the most long-standing and powerful critiques of usury, and indeed of all interest-taking. Running through the Western tradition from Aristotle on, the idea that money, something inanimate, "can breed," as Shylock says his money does, is seen as deeply, in Ezra Pound's words, "*contra naturam*."[32] We realize that, in telling his story as he did, Shylock was both consciously and unconsciously tapping into this—consciously in that he was certainly aware of the Aristotelian critique; unconsciously in that, in his presentation, "the deed of kind" is so mechanical as to be almost *contra naturam* in itself.

But after Shylock's insistence that Antonio "note" what he has said, and some moralizing by Antonio on how "The devil can cite scripture," the dialogue returns to the deal at hand. Shylock recurs to the matter of Antonio's behavior toward him, but now speaking out rather than meditating. It now seems that there was an interpersonal relationship between them.[33] The speech begins as a recapitulation of the soliloquy, but now in second-person rather than third-person terms. Instead of "he rails ... On me, my bargains, and ... my thrift," Shylock says, "you have rated me / About my moneys and my usances" (102–3). The focus remains on economic practices. But then Antonio's behavior is presented as more personal and more vicious—"You call me misbeliever, cut-throat dog," the latter perhaps invoking the famous blood-libel.[34] Antonio's behavior is now presented as having a physical dimension. Shylock mentions—three times—that Antonio regularly spit on him, and, twice, that Antonio kicked him, spurned him "as you spurn a stranger cur."[35] But Shylock's focus is on the "dog" charge—the idea that Antonio does not see Shylock as operating in the human community. The "stranger cur" is the key image. Ignoring the "stranger" issue, Shylock asks, "Hath a dog money?" (117). His point is that economic life is part of the human world, and should be recognized as such, and that he is operating within the rules of the economic-human world, the world that recognizes property rights. His appeal to "use of that which is mine own" relies on a deep legal pun on "use."[36]

It looks as if Shylock has, rhetorically and situationally, forced Antonio into offering some kind of apology or at least mitigation. But this is not what happens. Surprisingly, even shockingly, Antonio is not only completely unrepentant but vows to continue the behavior in question—in its verbal form ("I am like to call thee so [dog] again") and even in its grossest physical form ("To spit on thee again, to spurn thee too"). I think that we are to recognize this embrace of the most vulgar forms of physical violence as part of Antonio's pathology in relation to business, his desire to separate himself as far as possible from the economic world in which, in his status as a merchant, he is necessarily involved.[37] His deepest fear would be for someone to ask the question "Which is the merchant here, and which the Jew?"[38] After his affirmation of past and future violence, Antonio returns to the matter at hand. Since he cannot see the economic realm as existing and having validity in itself, he puts the transaction at hand into the terms in which he prefers to think, interpersonal ones. In a sense, it could be said that he now accepts Shylock's view of borrowing and lending as part of the human social world. But now the "stranger" part of "stranger cur" comes into operation. Antonio refers back to the Aristotelian critique of usury, but now folds it into a different framework. He tells Shylock:

> If thou wilt lend this money, lend it not
> As to thy friends, for when did friendship take
> A breed for barren metal of his friend?
> But lend it rather to thine enemy,
> Who if he break, thou may'st with better face
> Exact the penalty. (127–32)

This introduces a whole new conceptual and historical tradition, that of Deuteronomy—though, perhaps significantly, Antonio does not name his source.

As Benjamin Nelson's book on usury makes clear, many of the historically and conceptually important questions about usury have to do not with the properties of money or the question of rates but with the issue of what constitutes a community—of "brothers and others" as W. H. Auden, following Nelson, puts it. Antonio's contrast between how one lends to friends versus enemies harkens back to a key passage in Deuteronomy, which says, in the King James translation, "Thou shalt not lend upon usury to thy brother . . . but to a stranger thou mayest lend upon usury" (23:19–20).[39] Nelson points out that "stranger" here (*nokri*) meant persons as distinct as possible from the brotherhood of the clan or community, the *mishpaha*. Saint Ambrose continued the thought in explaining that "a stranger" meant an enemy, someone to whom one could legitimately do harm.[40]

Antonio is urging Shylock, the Jew, to stay within the Deuteronomic framework, the framework that, in its purest and least practical form, prevented Christians from lending at interest, since for the Christian, as the parable of the Good Samaritan makes clear, no one is supposed to be a stranger, but all persons are supposed to be neighbors or brothers. Antonio completely accepts the Deuteronomic framework, as his treatment of Shylock as "stranger" suggests. His world is one of friends and enemies, where entirely different rules apply to the two categories. He assumes, naturally, that the Jew would fully enter into this world as well. Shylock does enter into it—but in a completely surprising way. For Shylock to accept Antonio as a "stranger" or enemy would be utterly rational, given their history and Antonio's gleeful embrace of it. But Shylock seizes on the other side of the prohibition, taking it as defining friendship rather than as regulating behavior within preestablished grounds, and taking Antonio to share this view.[41] Noting that Antonio is the one who is manifesting ill-will—"look you, how you storm" instructs the actor playing Antonio how to say the "when did friendship take" lines—Shylock surprisingly tells Antonio, "I would be friends with you and have your love." What this means is that he will make the loan "and take no doit / Of usance for my moneys" (136–37a).

This is a delicious moment. Shylock is acting in the "Christian" way. He is offering, in this scene of moneylending, entirely to give up his professional and culturally determined identity.[42] Antonio is shocked. He must make some sort of recoiling gesture, since Shylock says, "And you'll not hear me" (137b), and states, using a key word, "This is kind I offer"—a meaning of the term very different from that of "the deed of kind," though the connection to biology is not irrelevant. Antonio is completely silent in response to this. Bassanio steps in and states, "This were kindness" (139). Why Shylock makes this turnabout is completely unclear. Perhaps he wants to assume the high moral ground and prove that he is capable of such behavior, which Antonio clearly thinks him incapable of. But the sudden shift is never explained.

Shylock then complicates the situation. Showing, once again, how closely he has listened to Antonio, Shylock picks up the mention of "the penalty"—a notion first introduced into the scene by Antonio (at 132). Amanda Bailey has shown that a penalty clause could not actually apply to a loan with interest.[43] So for there to be a penalty, the loan would have to be a "friendly" one. The whole legal situation has changed. The contract is now a "single bond" between Shylock and Antonio (Bassanio is no longer a principal, so to speak); Antonio is the recipient of the loan, no longer a surety for it.[44] The "penalty" or forfeit for nonpayment of the interest-free loan within the time specified is the famous pound of flesh. Shakespeare has Shylock introduce this feature in a way that intensifies the opacity of his motives. Shylock presents this new contract—which has nothing at all to do with usury now—as a "merry sport" (141), perhaps playing on or within the "friendship" framework. Now Antonio finds his voice. He can, once again, see Shylock as malicious, and he agrees "to seal to such a bond." He can now mock the idea that Shylock is showing "kindness" (149). Bassanio is horrified at the proposal, and, to his (nonmonetary) credit, urges Antonio not to take it. But Antonio reassures him, in terms that are almost certainly hyperbolic, that his forfeiting is extremely unlikely.[45] Shylock accepts this, and insists on the purity of his motives, meaning that there is no economic aspect to this "merry bond"—"what should I gain / By the exaction of the forfeiture," since "a pound of man's flesh" (as opposed to a pound of sheep's or cow's or goat's flesh) has no market value (159–63). He insists on this version of the contract; he will not make the loan on any other terms ("If he will take it, so, if not adieu" [165]).

Whatever Shylock is doing—whether he is making a point about his capacity to enact "kindness" and to be, as Antonio mockingly says, a "gentle Jew" (173), or whether he secretly believes that he will be able to exact the penalty and enact hatred—he is no longer acting in the world of rational, economic motives. It is as if, in another conversational turnabout, he has adopted Antonio's reading of the story of Jacob and the sheep, and has entered into a "venture," a thing "not in his power to bring to pass." Probably we are to understand that Shylock is himself unsure of what he is enacting, and of what it is that he wishes. Perhaps, in some sense, he really does want Antonio's love. Perhaps the "bond" does stand for some sort of imagined bodily closeness. The language of it is oddly erotic: "your fair flesh"; "What part of your body pleaseth me" (146–47).

In any case, profit-making, and usury with it, have entirely disappeared as an issue, and we are in a much more mysterious world.

As the play continues, it looks as if Shylock's motives get clarified—to himself and to us. By act 3, he has been outraged by his daughter's elopement with one of the "foppish" Christians (see 2.5.35), taking with her some of Shylock's cash and treasure. One of Antonio's friends points out that this will lead Shylock to enforce the penalty on Antonio should the situation allow it, even though Antonio himself (as far as we know) was not involved in the elopement: "Let good Antonio look he keep his day / Or he shall pay for this" (2.25–26). Shylock has become a figure of hatred. When confronted by Antonio's friends about the economic irrationality of enforcement of the penalty, should Antonio forfeit, Shylock has an answer. The pound of flesh has always stood in for the non-economic. "What's that good for?" Salarino asks. "It will feed my revenge," says Shylock. This is all quite straightforward, and even makes economic sense: "He hath disgrac'd me, and hind'red me half a million, laugh'd at my losses, mock'd at my gains, scorned my nation, thwarted my bargains, cooled my friends, heated mine enemies"—and all because "I am a Jew," and therefore unredeemably other (3.1.49–53a).

Shylock, however, presents himself as mirroring Christian behavior—that is, actual Christian behavior. He sounds exactly like Marlowe's Barabas, who sees a model for his actions in Christian violence, greed, and hypocrisy.[46] Shylock notes that "if a Jew wrong a Christian, what is his [the Christian's] humility? Revenge!" He is acting, Shylock says, "by Christian example": "The villainy you teach me I will execute, and it shall go hard but I will better the instruction" (3.1.61–66). But Shakespeare is not Marlowe, however much Shakespeare may have learned from his prematurely deceased contemporary. Between the lines that I have quoted about the propriety of and rationale for revenge come the lines about human biological and psychological community that have made this speech famous: "Hath not a Jew eyes?" etc. (53b–59a). Shylock wants the focus to be revenge, but Shakespeare gives him lines that constitute a plea for human solidarity—"kindness" in the deepest sense—that transcends religious and other difference.[47] "Hath not a Jew eyes?" cannot be taken from its context. But it also cannot be kept within it. As in the establishment of the "merry bond"—where Shylock might, in some sense, be sincere in wanting the love of a man he knows he hates—Shylock's desire for community might well be deeper than mere commonality in villainy. He may be wrong in thinking that all he wants is revenge.[48]

The last moment in *The Merchant of Venice* that I will discuss is, like the opening of the play, a section that not only enacts but actually thematizes the matter of the opacity of motives. At the beginning of the trial scene, Shylock is given the opportunity to disclaim publicly his "strange apparent cruelty" in seeking to extract the penalty from Antonio. The Duke gives him the opportunity to treat the pound of flesh provision as if it were truly a "sport" ("thou but leadest this fashion of thy malice / To the last hour of act" [4.1.18–19]), and enjoins him to act in a "gentle" manner. This should be the moment when Shylock lists all the good reasons he has for hating Antonio. He should repeat, in public, the points he made to himself in the contract scene ("He hates our sacred nation"), and the points he there made to Antonio ("You call me misbeliever... spit upon my Jewish gaberdine"). This is his chance to make his hatred for Antonio and desire for Antonio's death perfectly and publicly legible. He has the Duke and many Venetian aristocrats hanging on his words (the stage directions in both the Quartos and in the Folio specify that "the Magnificoes" enter along with the Duke and Antonio's party). Shylock will never have a grander and more public occasion in which to air his personal grievances against Antonio. The assembled company wants to know why he is committed to enforcing the penalty rather than receiving his principal back (he has not, as far we have yet seen, been offered it, but the idea might be that he could, as often actually happened, offer Antonio an extension, in which period Antonio might have raised the principal).[49] Shylock could also, if he wished, give his "economic" reason ("were he out of Venice I can make what merchandise I will" [3.1.117–19]). Instead, however, of commanding the stage with any of his many previously articulated reasons for exacting the penalty, Shylock says:

> You'll ask me why I rather choose to have
> A weight of carrion flesh, than to receive
> Three thousand ducats. I'll not answer that! (4.1.40–42)

He refuses to answer the "why" question just at the point when it seems his answer would be most apropos. "I'll not answer." He acknowledged from the beginning that "a pound of man's flesh" has no direct economic value (1.3.161–63), but he has since made it clear that he does have an answer to the "What's that good for" question: "if it will feed nothing else, it will feed my revenge" (3.1.47–49). Shakespeare could have put that great speech here, at the trial scene, where it would seem to be much more functional than it was in a private conversation with two minor Venetian hangers-on. But instead of expressing or explaining his feelings, Shylock shifts the ground entirely: "say it is my humour. Is it answered?" (42).[50] He knows perfectly well that this would not normally be considered an "answer" to the "why" question. He goes on, however, to give an account of human behavior that does, in a sense, serve as a response, if not an answer, to the question. Human behavior need not be obviously rational. He provides a series of cases here that function the way stories (the lost and found arrows; the copulating sheep) did earlier in the play—as an alternative to the discursive mode. The first case is put in the first person:

> What if my house be troubled with a rat,
> And I be pleas'd to give ten thousand ducats
> To have it baned? What, are you answer'd yet? (4.1.43–45)

Shylock here seems to speak for absolute freedom of choice (within the realm of legality) with regard to personal expenditures. It is a familiar economic world.[51] It is a world of wishes and preferences and choices, if not a world of rational bases for such. Yet after this example of what would seem a strange piece of behavior that is consciously chosen, Shylock then gives some pictures of human behavior that have increasingly little to do with choice, that move to the truly, as Aristotle would say, nonvoluntary (not the involuntary, which includes things chosen under duress [*NE* 1110b]). After presenting himself as the cheerfully prodigal rat-baner, Shylock shifts into a mode of general observation of the human condition; we are back to contemplating, as in scene 1, "sort[s] of men":

> Some men there are love not a gaping pig!
> Some men are mad when they behold a cat!
> And others, when the bagpipe sings i' th' nose,
> Cannot contain their urine. (4.1.46–49a)

The first line here might be seen to mediate between the world of preference and the world of nonrationality. "Love not" is rather mild, and may or may not be in the world of choice, but the "gaping pig" suggests an element of visceral horror. The examples move from the understandable (one need not be a Jew or Muslim to find something slightly disturbing about the pig "gaping," either from its mouth or its cut neck) to the puzzling ("Some men are mad when they behold a cat") to the truly visceral and Pavlovian ("when the bagpipe sings … Cannot contain their urine").[52]

These cases just seem to come to Shylock; he seems to be a kind of connoisseur of such things, zany things, which might be comical in another context. The picture is of persons helplessly under the "sway" of compulsions, of persons doing things over which they have absolutely no control. It is as if Shylock had heard Salanio's speech about "strange fellows." But that speech at least had an intelligible context. The Duke and the aristocrats are certainly to be represented as puzzled as to why Shylock is citing these cases. "Now for your answer," Shylock says. He makes it clear that he is presenting these cases as analogous to his own state of mind in the present: "As there is no firm reason to be rend'red" in these cases, "So can I give no reason," he insists, before adding that he also "will not." However, between the "As" and the "So," instead of merely referring in a general way to the examples he has cited, he reiterates them in order, and does so in a way that, in each case, intensifies it. In the first, the men who "love not" a gaping pig now "cannot abide" it; in the second, the strangeness of the response is emphasized in relation to the object of it, which is now "a harmless necessary cat." But it is the third, and already strangest, case that receives the most major embellishment. Instead of simply "a bagpipe," it is now "a woolen bagpipe," and the social and phenomenological situation of the person who "cannot contain [his] urine" is fully evoked. He "of force / Must yield to such inevitable shame, / As to offend himself being offended" (55b–57).

Shakespeare seems to have associated the bagpipe, with its oddly biological sound ("i' th' nose") and appearance, evoking male genitalia ("a woolen bagpipe"), with the production of compulsive behavior.[53] Salanio's speech had already cited people who are somehow compelled to "laugh like parrots at a bagpiper" (1.1.53). Shylock seems to be presenting himself, and all of us, as such strange fellows. When, at the end of this speech, Shylock turns from those opaque instances to a familiar named passion, he wants to give the passion a quality of viscerality—"a *lodg'd* hate"; and when he recharacterizes the "hate" as "a certain loathing" (59), the phrase, in its odd, almost fussy detachment and vagueness, has just the quality of unwilled aversion that the examples support. Bassanio is right in saying, "This is no answer." The Duke is dead silent.

But what is Shakespeare doing in giving Shylock this speech? Shylock begins, as we have seen, with the case of the rat-baning. Probably he intends the other examples to be parallel to it. But we have seen that they are not, and we have noted that the recapitulation of the cases adds the element of shame and self-violation to the picture.[54] I do not think that Shylock intends this any more than he intended the element of sexual disgust in the account of Jacob's trick; or the demand for love and possibly bodily closeness in the merry bond; or the element of positive brotherhood though the body in "Hath not a Jew eyes?" There is something in Shylock that is deeply ashamed at whatever it is he sees (or does not see) himself as doing in the courtroom or council-chamber.[55] Perhaps what is at work—here, and in all the moments just mentioned—is Shylock's ambivalence about "kindness," about human embodiment: is it positive (as in "fed with the same food") or negative, as in his disgust with reproductive sexuality? His refusal to answer the "Why are you doing this?" question might be, as he says, a matter of inability as well as refusal ("I can give no reason, nor I will not"). We are way past economic rationality here, and even, apparently, past the "rationality" of justified hatred.

We might think that Freudian psychology could answer the "why" question in individual cases, but these "answers" are certainly opaque at the time to the agent. Shylock might "be Shakespeare" in the sense that, in the final speech we have examined, Shakespeare gives his Jew a speech that expresses, more powerfully perhaps than any other in the corpus, Shakespeare's sense of the lack of access that persons often have to the actual springs of their own behavior. Shylock seems himself to be in the grip of some kind of compulsion to assert the power of compulsion, to deny the relevance of "reasons," even if this means offending—demeaning, shaming, verbally bepissing—himself as well as others. This is not a case of attempting to deny responsibility by appealing to irrational forces ("Hamlet does it not"), but, weirdly, of accepting responsibility because of irrational internal forces—that is who, or what, I am. It is not even the Aristotelian point about being responsible for one's own character. There is a strong sense in this passage that reason and choice never entered into the picture at all—not at an early or a later stage in some process (compare *NE* 1114a19-21). The only term that Aristotle has for such behavior is "brutishness" (which, interestingly, he associates with childhood trauma [*NE* 1148b23-30]).

Non-Being

The Merchant of Venice points to something general in Shakespeare's conception of the human agent. Even when there is a straightforward motive for a character's behavior—ambition, for instance, in *Macbeth* (or even *Richard III*)—it can be shown that those characters are not fully aware of what they actually want. Let me conclude this set of reflections by adverting to the most famous case of "motivelessness" in Shakespeare.[56] Again, my topic is Shakespeare's conception of character and agency. The question can now be said to be, If conscious intentions do not count as real—that is, fully explanatory—motives for Shakespeare, what kind of thing would? What does a "real" motive look like for him? The case of Iago helps with this, and adds something to the case of Shylock.

The first sixty-four lines of *Othello* consist basically of speeches by Iago, and they are speeches about his motives. In the first of these speeches we hear of his resentment at not getting the job of Othello's lieutenant, a job that Iago is fully convinced that he deserved. "I know my price," he says; "I am worth no worse a place" (1.1.10). This is framed not as vainglory but as proper pride. Maybe there is a critique here of classical ethics, of the idea of "proper pride," or maybe the critique here is of the stance or tone that this conception generates in Iago, the tone of mockery and resentment (not a stance that Aristotle recommended for the person with "proper pride").[57] We might learn more from Iago's second long speech, a discourse on proper service as Iago sees it, on how manly, non-"obsequious" followers maintain the "forms and visages of duty" while truly only serving ("attending on") themselves (45–50).[58] This, for Iago, is to have, as he says, "some soul" (53)—meaning, as Machiavelli would say, "spirit," *animo* (not *anima*).[59] Shakespeare would seem to be giving us a picture of a perfect hypocrite, skilled and self-aware. The speech ends with a contempt for "outward action" based not, like Hamlet's, on its inability fully ("truly") to express the inward, but on the opposite, on its contemptible ability to do so, to "demonstrate / The native act and figure of my heart" (60–61). The point is not that the inner cannot be expressed but that, for the properly self-regarding, it should not be. Everything is set up for the speech to end with the culminating and, in this context, properly proud assertion "I am not what I seem."

But that is not what Shakespeare gives us. Instead we get the very strange assertion "I am not what I am." Either this is a slip of the pen on Shakespeare's part—though both the 1622 Quarto and the first Folio have the same line—or a slip of the tongue on Iago's.[60] If, as is much more probable, it is the latter, what is Shakespeare doing in this line? It is, as virtually every commentator has noted, the first, and one of the most spectacular, of the biblical echoes in the play. Shakespeare has Iago culminate his elaborate self-presentation with a negative version of one of the most famous and mysterious moments in the Hebrew Bible, the moment in Exodus (3:14) when, in response to the request that Moses makes of God to be able to answer the query Moses knows he will get regarding in whose name he is claiming to act, God either does or does not—depending on one's interpretation—give His name, saying (in all the Protestant English Bibles of the century), "I am that I am" (in Douay-Rheims, "I am who I am"). This is an echo that Shakespeare surely expected many people in his audience to catch. But what does it mean? The figure who makes this riddling utterance in Exodus is asserting—in all the Christian translations of the Bible (though perhaps not in the Hebrew Bible itself)—some sort of absolute ontological priority, however one understands this.⁶¹ Iago cannot be purposely echoing this in the negative, but nor can he be seen as merely, as E. A. J. Honigmann says in his note on the line, being "profane." Shakespeare gives Iago this slip, this allusion, in order to alert the audience (many of whom would have been biblically literate) that although they seem to be seeing and hearing a character with a solid if rather sinister sense of himself, Iago might rather in some deeper sense be, and recognize himself as being, a figure who does not have a self. There is no "I am" just at the point where one seemed to be powerfully unfolding.

So let us pursue further the question of what the biblical / theological reference does here. It does not mean to interpret the Bible. Rather, it uses the Bible to interpret the character that Shakespeare is creating. The play as a whole can be seen as in dialogue with the founding story for the Judeo-Christian conception of history. *Othello* is Shakespeare's *Paradise Lost*. This has many implications, but the one that I want to pursue here concerns the matter of motivation—of devilish motivation. Milton's explanation for Satan's revolt is Satan's "sense of injur'd merit"—precisely the motive that Shakespeare initially gives to Iago. Milton thought this motive truly explanatory. An injury to "pride" (proper or not) seemed very deep to Milton; it is the narrator's as well as Satan's own account of Satan's motivation.⁶² But Milton can be seen as more committed to classical ethics and to a classical (especially Greek) ethical psychology than Shakespeare was.⁶³ Shakespeare, the more "secular" poet, seems to have needed a deeper and more mysterious explanation for the diabolical. The idea of sheer negativity seems to be what drew him. What the perverted biblical echo at the end of Iago's speech helps us to see is that the conception that Shakespeare had of Iago's "motives," such as they are, is that they are not ordinary, recognizable, easily statable ones like the "sense of injur'd merit" (or the sexual revenge avowed by Iago at 1.3.386), or a combination of sexual revenge and sexual desire (avowed by Iago at 2.1.289–95). What Shakespeare seems to be suggesting is that it is the mere existence of goodness that drives Iago to a fury. In a Neoplatonized biblical context—suggested by the prominence of the Exodus echo—one might say that it is the fact of anything at all existing that drives Iago to a fury. That is the kind of thing that Shakespeare seems to have thought of as a motive. "Corruption can consume the good only by consuming the being," writes Augustine.⁶⁴ It took Shakespeare's genius to make something as abstract and metaphysical as Augustine's conception of evil as a deprivation of being into a plausible character in a more or less "realistic" drama.

The point can be elaborated further. When Iago finally sees his general plan take—thanks to Cassio's drunkenness—a specific shape involving Desdemona's future advocacy for Cassio, Iago summarizes the result he hopes for, with regard to Desdemona, Othello, and Cassio, thus: "So will I turn her virtue into pitch / And out of her own goodness make the net / That shall enmesh them all" (2.3.355–57). Again, *Paradise Lost* comes to our aid. Toward the end of the final book, after the archangel Michael explains to Adam that Satan will ultimately be defeated, Adam, "Replete with joy and wonder," bursts out: "O goodness infinite, goodness immense! / That all this good of evil shall produce, / And evil turn to good" (*PL* 12.471–72). This is the theme of *felix culpa*—the "fortunate fall"—that, as A. O. Lovejoy demonstrated long ago, was widely echoed from the late classical to the medieval period in vernacular and literary texts as well as Latin and liturgical ones.[65] Shakespeare again expects many in his audience to recognize that the Satanic plan is exactly the reversed mirror image of this: "out of good still to find means of evil" (*Paradise Lost* 1.165). In the Christian scheme, the happy cosmic outcome of the Fall is a testimony to the benevolence of God; the Fall was necessary to the full revelation of this in Christ. In Shakespeare's (in)version, the relation of the result to the original situation is more intimate. Iago knows that there is something inherent in goodness that he can use against it. He has the Neoplatonic sense of goodness as inherently active and overflowing.[66] Again, it is not a matter of will, but of being.[67] Desdemona simply is the kind of person who will be overflowing with charity. It is both a decision and, as Roderigo says, a "condition" (2.1.247). "She's framed as fruitful / As the free elements" (2.3.336–37)—compare Salanio on how "nature hath framed" fellows.[68] Desdemona's goodness of being includes a happy excess of both goodness and being—as in the positive moral dimension of her moist palm (4.1.36–38). So again, the principle of negativity is clarified by reference to its theological opposite. What goodness cannot be is envious or grudging—a Platonic principle that is fundamental to Plotinian ontology.[69]

There are moments in the play when Shakespeare explicitly presents Iago in something like these terms. In the scene in which Iago and Desdemona banter about the nature of women, and Desdemona, grand lady that she is, sets Iago the task of praising her, Iago gives a reason for not wanting to play the game, a reason that, again, seems to say rather more than he intends. He says, in attempting to refuse the playful challenge, "O gentle lady, do not put me to't, / For I am nothing if not critical" (2.1.118–19). The context is playful, and Iago does pride himself on his "tough-mindedness" (which in this case, *pace* Eliot, is cynical), but Shakespeare clearly wants us to think about what it would mean to be "nothing if not critical."[70] To take the claim literally, it would mean that without an object to demean or destroy, such a person would be nothing, would not exist. Again, as in the ontological argument, existence is a good, and has a positive dimension.[71]

In this framework, Iago's passion to destroy Othello must be seen to derive from Othello's grand complacency, his capacity for love and for joy, for being fully in the world—for being fully. "O my fair warrior" is a truly wonderful moment (in all senses [2.1.180]). When Cassio expresses his hope to be reconciled to Othello, Shakespeare gives Cassio a formulation that is strikingly Pauline and Neoplatonic. Cassio says that he hopes "that I may again / Exist, and be a member of his [Othello's] love" (3.4.133). Othello's love is like Paul's invisible church—a mystical body to which it is the highest privilege to belong, and with which and only within which one "exists."[72] So the *culpa* from *felix* principle must be seen at work in relation to Othello too. Iago states that "The Moor" is "of a constant loving, noble nature" and will probably "prove to Desdemona / A most dear husband" (2.1.287–89). So he must be destroyed.

Yet the clearest account of Iago's actual motivation comes in relation not to Othello or Desdemona but to Cassio. At the beginning of the fifth act, we watch Iago going over the reasons why both Roderigo and Cassio must, one way or another, be killed. His motive for wanting Roderigo out of the way is very ordinary ("He calls me to a restitution large / Of gold and jewels that I bobbed from him" [5.1.15–16]). From the beginning of the play we are given a straightforward motive for Iago hating Cassio—Cassio beat him out for the lieutenancy. But the next "motive" we are given seems a bit strange. Iago claims to think that every significant male above him in (at least) social rank has slept with his wife. He first states that "it is thought abroad" that Othello has done so; Iago does not seem actually to believe this, but seems to adopt it as something that will stand in for a motive (1.3.386–89). In his next soliloquy, he still does not assert belief in the charge but claims that he finds the mere suspicion of it intolerable (2.1.294–95). Iago revels in presenting Othello as "the lusty Moor"; practically the first reference Iago makes to the marriage is to envision, in gross and racist terms, sexual intercourse of an animalistic kind between the couple (the "old black ram" is "tupping" the "white ewe" [1.1.87–88]—this is oddly and significantly reminiscent of Shylock's account of Laban's sheep).[73] But it is Cassio whose erotic potential seems truly to fascinate Iago.

Where Iago seems to imagine Othello's sexuality as gross, Cassio's seems to intrigue him. His first thought is merely general—Cassio is handsome ("a proper man"). But then he notes to himself that Cassio has "a person and a smooth dispose" that is "framed"—again this word for what comes from nature—to attract women (and make them false [2.1.396–97]). "Smooth" here hovers nicely between the physical and the behavioral. In the next scene, we see Iago watching Cassio's "smoothness" in action. Cassio pays elaborate courtly attention to Desdemona—which drives Iago into a frenzy of imagined physical degradation (wishing that Cassio's fingers, which he is kissing toward Desdemona, were "clyster-pipes").[74] Roderigo makes the mistake of thinking Cassio's behavior with Desdemona "but courtesy"; Iago sternly reminds him, in his best homiletic mode, that "when these mutualities so marshal the way, hard at hand comes the master and main exercise" (2.1.259–60).[75] In the soliloquy that ends that scene, Iago claims to "fear Cassio with my night-cap too" (306). Iago imagines sexual magnetism through the imagination of his wife's vulnerability to it—a point of view that he wishes to transfer to Othello. Iago's *narratio* of "laying with" Cassio and being passionately kissed and cuddled by him is an obvious homosexual fantasy, but what I want to highlight is the elegant speech that Iago imagines for Cassio's address to Desdemona. "Cassio," like a Jonsonian lover, echoes Catullus: "Sweet Desdemona, / Let us be wary, let us hide our loves" (3.3.421–22).[76]

So when it comes to finding a reason for the murder of Cassio, it looks as if erotic jealousy should suffice (the loss of the job ceases to be an issue once Iago replaces Cassio as Othello's lieutenant [3.3.481]). But the formulation that Shakespeare gives to Iago is completely unexpected. "Smoothness" and "courtesy" might have led the way to it, but one would never have expected that Iago would give as his reason for killing Cassio (or having Roderigo do it) this statement of his relation to Cassio:

> He hath a daily beauty in his life
> That makes me ugly. (5.1.19–20a)

"A daily beauty in his life"—one could hardly imagine a more magnificent tribute to someone who prides himself on "manners" and courtesy. That Iago has made Cassio ugly (in his drunkenness) no longer seems to count for anything; nor does the refusal or inability of Cassio to accept the seriousness of this behavior that we have examined; nor does the supposed adultery with Emilia, which seems to be long forgotten. In Iago's mind, Cassio is not the flawed human being that the play reveals to us (and that Iago has helped to reveal), but an idealized figure—Cassio at his most "smooth." It is the image of this that is intolerable, the ease and happiness in his being, social and ontological, that we saw in Cassio's "flirtation" with Desdemona. We are back to the "clyster-pipes," but now with self-consciousness of the ugliness of the thought.

One of the things that is interesting about the "daily beauty . . . makes me" formulation is that it is put objectively rather than subjectively. Cassio's normal way of being does not make Iago feel ugly; rather, it makes him ugly. It provokes, necessarily provokes, in Iago "clyster-pipe"-type thoughts—ugly, envious, destructive ones. An aesthetic framework turns out to have enormous power and relevance. This is part of the deep Neoplatonism that we have been tracing in the play. For that tradition, beauty, goodness, and fullness of being run together. For evil as negativity to prevail, they must all be destroyed. "Corruption can consume the good only by consuming the being." For evil to prevail, non-being must prevail; the nothing that can only be critical must prevail. Being is the enemy. One of the things that makes the lines about Cassio so extraordinary is that at this moment, Iago seems to understand all this. He has found a "motive." The aesthetic framework clarifies and intensifies the self-hatred (or hatred of the non-self). If the contrast were directly with goodness, the opposite quality produced in the agent who does not have it could be a source of pride, a position that Iago, like Milton's Satan, sincerely thinks that he can inhabit ("Evil be thou my good" [*PL* 4.110]; "these fellows have some soul," etc.). One can—at least professedly—revel in one's wickedness. But no one revels in being ugly as such—just as no one revels in not existing.[77]

But Shakespeare did not want to leave the matter there. I am not sure that it was because Iago could not dwell in such self (or non-self) knowledge.[78] That may be right—or perhaps Shakespeare thought he had to provide something more intelligible for those in the audience who would not "get" the metaphysical point. In any case, he has Iago add, as a clear afterthought, what seems like a prudential motive. "And besides," says Iago, "the Moor / May unfold me to him—there I stand in much peril" (5.1.20b–21). This seems to make sense until one tries to understand it. What is it that Othello could say to Cassio that would endanger Iago? Othello could question Cassio about his conversation with Bianca supposedly about Desdemona (4.1.131–58) and about the handkerchief. Cassio would tell the truth and deny the accusations. But what leads Iago to think that Othello would believe the denials? Othello does not, after all, believe the very strongly phrased denials of his charges that Desdemona provides. He has demonstrated his "changed" state in public as well as in private (4.1.268b). So Iago's apparently more plausible motive does not, in fact, withstand scrutiny. But perhaps Iago himself had the ordinary sense of what a "motive" is, and took his point about Cassio's effect on himself as merely an observation.

But Iago does come close to something like self-knowledge—which he ends his role in the action by refusing to divulge. "What you know, you know," he tauntingly asserts (5.2.300). The authorities know, through various means (Emilia's heroic outspokenness, Cassio's recollections, letters found in Roderigo's pockets [!]), the facts of what Iago has done. What Othello wants to know is why. He asks the authorities to "demand" this of Iago. This leads into the final fantasy of the play, stated three times, emphatically in the final lines: that torture will open Iago's lips (5.2.302, 331–33, 367). Shakespeare got the focus on torture from the Cinthio story on which the play is based; there, "the Moor" is tortured, which he endures "with great steadfastness" (and is later "slain by Disdemona's relatives"); and eventually, with regard to a later and unrelated act of villainous slander, the Iago figure ("the Ensign") is "tortured so fiercely that his inner organs were ruptured," and he dies miserably.[79] Shakespeare uses the torture issue to point to the mystery. It is clear that whether or not torment will "ope" the lips of Iago, the tormenters will not and cannot get what they want. What sort of answer could they expect to the "why" question. They would not be able to hear the kind of motive that Iago actually has, and he could not truthfully give them the kind of thing they want to hear—something normal and intelligible. Iago's taunt will stay in place.

My argument is that through Iago, as through Shylock, Shakespeare is working to complicate our thinking about agency and motives. In the case of Iago, Shakespeare, on my view, had to draw on theology to find a conception sufficiently mysterious.[80] The fact that Shakespeare was almost explicitly using such a conception in creating Iago is perhaps what allowed him to give Iago—as opposed to Shylock—something like, as I have tried to show, actual self-knowledge. Shylock simply knew that, despite everything, he could not actually explain (or even, perhaps, fully face) the psychological content of his own actions. Hamlet thought he stood in a special relation to his own actions and motives, a relation different from that which he had to those of others. But the play leads us to doubt both of these assumptions.[81]

APPENDIX

"Say it is my humour"

The aim of this appendix is to meditate further on the weirdness of Shylock's non-"gentle" nonanswer to the Duke's opening appeal to him. This speech, beginning "Say it is my humour" and ending with the "woolen bagpipe" (4.1.42–57), is certainly one of the weirdest—perhaps *the* weirdest—speech in the whole Shakespearean corpus. I take that to be a reason to pay special attention to it. I will address an influential proposal for how we should think about this speech (and other ones) in Elizabethan literature. The historico-critical proposal at issue rests on the status of the Galenic psychophysiological theory of the four humors in the Elizabethan world-picture, and on a particular way of reading passages that purportedly rely on this theory.[1]

The speech would seem to invite this reading. Gail Kern Paster, perhaps the major "humoralist" critic, has accepted the invitation. She is, as far as I know, the only critic to have analyzed the speech at length, and it is her reading that I will consider in detail. Curiously, the only other commentator I know of who has dealt really seriously with the speech is Richard Posner in his law and literature textbook. I will consider his view as well.

Paster calls the speech "brilliant" (three times).[2] We can return the compliment to her; her reading is so. But I think that, nonetheless, it is misleading. As one would expect from one of the leaders of what I have called "the new humoralism," it is the word "humour" that sets Paster's reading in motion. She sees the scene as "humoral" from the beginning, stating that when the Duke describes Shylock to Antonio as "a stony adversary, an inhuman[e] wretch" (4.1.2), this language is "implicitly humoral" (204). This means that we are to take "stony" as literally as possible—just as, later in the scene, we are to take mercy in Portia's great speech "as a liquid" (208). This kind of literalism and materialism is crucial to the humoralist critical framework, and seems to me one of the ways in which it is misleading.³

It is not at all clear that the Duke, in speaking of Shylock as "stony," is making a claim about Shylock's physical constitution any more than the Duke is doing so when he speaks of the "brassy bosoms" and "hearts of flint" of supposedly barbaric non-Europeans (4.1.30). Paster is certain that the answer to King Lear's question—"Is there any cause in nature that makes these hard hearts?"—is yes (208). But is it not more plausible to think that Lear, in his desperation and madness, is looking for a simple solution ("Let them anatomize Regan") for something that is actually a mystery (compare Kent's puzzlement at how "one same mate and make" could produce "such different issues")?⁴ To return to Portia's speech, the "gentle rain from heaven" is an analogue for the ethical or spiritual truth that it is constitutive of mercy or grace that they are *given*, and cannot be compelled or earned. The source may be a passage from Luther.⁵ Physiology is irrelevant.

Paster sees Shylock as building on and making brilliant use of "the duke's own discourse of the natural body." Paster elides the Duke's asserted expectation of "a gentle answer" from the Jew (33). That is a complex formulation, one that is both flaunting and trying to reject its irony, but the Duke's expectation / exhortation has its existence within the realm of religion and ethics. What is at issue here is not a picture of the body and its (supposed) chemistry but a normative conception of the natural. The Duke is appealing to something that he takes to be—or hopes to be—fundamental in human nature, an impulse toward "commiseration" with human suffering that does not require either training or a social network (it is present, he claims, even in "Turks and Tartars, never train'd / To offices of tender courtesy"). This issue is "humaneness," an ethical quality. Paster sees this. But she insists, nonetheless, that the speech is a "discourse of the body," one to which Shylock responds by employing his own counter-discourse of "the natural body" and the "natural status of his bodily 'humour' and its capacity for antipathy" (204).

But is it clear that chemistry enters into this conversation at all? The question arises even with regard to Paster's key term. Shylock does indeed cite his "humour." But the example he gives of it has nothing to do with bodies. The illustration of his "humour" that he gives is the passage about paying a fortune to have a rat baned (4.1.42–45). "Humour" here seems to mean something like "whim," and giving into it is entirely a matter of will—if "I *be pleas'd to give* ten thousand ducats" (4.1.44; emphasis mine). Shylock can be seen to be developing his mention of the city's (presumably economic) "freedom" (4.1.38). "Humour" in the singular might not be in the same realm as "humours" in the plural. Paster elides the lines about baning the rat. Her citation of the passage (204) goes right from "say it is my humour" (line 42) to "some men there are love not a gaping pig" (line 46). Not surprisingly, the lines that Paster elides are precisely the ones on which Richard Posner is helpful. Posner quotes the rat-baning lines in order to see Shylock as making a point that, according to Posner, will become "a commonplace of liberal theory—the subjectivity of value."[6] Shylock is explaining, for Posner, "that value is determined by willingness to pay, which is a function of the preferences and resources of each individual." We are in a world of preferences and resources.[7]

But then Shylock goes on to give the lines about the pig, the cat, and the bagpipe. On these lines, Posner has nothing to say. He elides the bagpipe. Paster, on the other hand, now has much to say. She sees the phobic cases as indicating "the involuntary power of the humors over the subjectified body" (205). But it is important to note that Shylock does not recur to "humor" or "humors" here. Instead, he introduces a new term. He speaks of "affection," which, he states, is the controller ("Master" or perhaps "Mistress"—there is a textual problem here) "of passion," which it [affection] directs in a positive or negative way ("sways it to the mood / Of what it likes or loathes" [4.1.50–52]).[8] This is extremely difficult, and no one, to my knowledge, has come up with a satisfactory account of what "affection" means here. But surely that is what a truly adequate reading of the passage would require. Paster does not even take note of the term. A number of thinkers from Aquinas on have distinguished between affections and passions, but Shylock does not seem to be using the distinction in the normal way (where "affection" is higher and more intellectual than "passion," and involves judgment).[9] The word seems to produce obscurity in Shakespeare, as in the famously difficult speech in which Leontes meditates on the word in *The Winter's Tale* ("Affection!—thy intention stabs the centre," etc. [1.2.138–46]). But in *Macbeth* the term is used to describe something like the overall constitution of the psyche when Malcolm claims to have an "ill compos'd affection" in which there is bottomless "voluptuousnesse" and "staunchless avarice" (4.3.77). This seems to be close to the usage in Shylock's speech.

So, the one example in the speech that does involve the word "humour" is the one that presents a piece of behavior that is *not* involuntary (or, as Aristotle would say, nonvoluntary). Paster is right about the other cases (the pig, the cat, the bagpipe); they do not involve choice. Paster sees Shylock's citing of these as a strategy; Shylock aims to produce an unanswerable argument on the basis of "an agreed upon instance of what comes before cultural inscription" (205). But this, I think, captures neither the intended nor the unintended meaning of the lines. Most of all, it ignores their deep weirdness. Aside from the key question of why Shylock *would want to* portray his antipathy to Antonio as involuntary, and to say that he "can give no reason" for it when we know full well that he can give many, any full reading of the speech would have to deal with the bizarreness of the instances. It may or may not be bizarre to "love not" a gaping pig (though probably the Elizabethans would have thought that it was so), but the person who cannot abide a "harmless necessary cat" is clearly bizarre and comical, and the poor urinator is even more so. These are instances of pathology, not of naturalness. In seeing the speech as pointing to a fundamental human substratum—"an agreed upon instance of what comes before cultural inscription"—Paster ignores the obvious zaniness of the examples.

Moreover, Paster's account ignores another major fact: Shylock has already given a speech about the fundamental psychobiological identity of humans, of "what comes before cultural inscription." In "Hath not a Jew eyes?" Shylock has given the speech that Paster thinks Shylock's initial trial-scene speech is. In the earlier speech, Shylock also distinguished between passions and affections ("hands, organs, dimensions, senses, affections, passions" [3.1.53–54]), but the examples he there provided are universal, and not at all pathological: "Fed with the same food, hurt with the same weapons, subject to the same diseases," bleeding if pricked, laughing if tickled. These do indeed come before cultural inscription. They are responses that are truly natural and not at all eccentric or, as Shylock says about the men who cannot abide a cat, "mad."

Paster's analysis of the "humour" speech, though she deals with much more of it, is similar to Posner's in a fundamental way: they both see Shylock as *making a point* in the speech, as putting forth some sort of rational argument (hence Paster's thrice-repeated "brilliant"). But this occludes the element of shame in the speech, an element that, as we have seen, Shylock insists upon in his recapitulation of the instances of irrational behavior that he has listed—"such inevitable shame, / As to offend himself being offended" (4.1.56–57). To her credit, Paster does take this on. Shame is something in which she is highly interested.[10] I have to say, though, that I find her treatment of it in this immediate context very difficult to follow. Here, she sees "the shame of the humoral body offended by the environment (here Venice) containing things that it cannot help but find disgusting (pig, cat, bagpipe, Antonio) and the reciprocal shame of that environment offended by the social consequences of its disgust" (206). I take it that the referent of 'it' and "its" in this sentence is "the humoral body." I find it hard to see the reciprocity here, and how Venice is shamed by Shylock's response to

Antonio. Paster argues that the Venetians would be ashamed that someone could find Antonio repulsive. But it seems more likely that they would see this as horrifying and (if they are as dense as Gratiano is) unintelligible. I do not see how or why they would feel shame. The shame seems to accrue entirely to the afflicted persons, the stand-ins for Shylock himself.

There are other details with which I would quarrel in Paster's treatment of this passage and in other readings like it (for instance, her reading of Bassanio's lines about "the current" of Shylock's cruelty as "humorally based" and involving blood and gall [207]—neither of which is mentioned), but let me hurry to some sort of conclusion. Obviously, I have to face up to the hard question. If Shylock is not making a rational argument (about the irrational) in this speech, then what is he doing, how are we to read the speech? I think that we need first of all, as I have emphasized, to recognize its weirdness, not to see it as somehow rational (either modern, with Posner, or "brilliant," with Paster, or even biblical, with Kenneth Gross).[11] I think that the speech is something of a non sequitur, that it has the status of something like a piece of Shakespearean metacommentary. As I have argued above, I think that Shakespeare wants to remind us—at a moment in which the issue does not seem at all to arise—of the opacity of motives, of how an agent, even a very self-conscious and intelligent one, can be unaware of the complexity of his motives.

From a less "meta" point of view, I think that we are to see the speech as one in which Shylock's unconscious is surprisingly erupting, in which he is (without fully intending to do so) acknowledging that he feels some shame and some sense of irrationality in his insistence on the pound of flesh, some sense that he is disgracing rather than dignifying himself. After all, he could have surprised the Christian community, taught them a real lesson, by (as the Duke suggests) forgiving Antonio a moiety of the principal—just as he surprised Antonio in the loan scene by (contrary to all of Antonio's assumptions) taking "no doit / Of usance" for the loan. Or he could just have taken the money and run. He is seriously offered two (4.1.83 and 206) or even three (4.1.223) times the original amount (I am not sure how seriously we are to take Bassanio's willingness to pay the principal "ten times over" [207], though Shylock could have said "sold" at that point). But Shylock knows that he is committed to something stranger here, just as he must (in some sense) have known—as Shakespeare surely did—that there was something odd in a vision of human biological community and vulnerability leading to a justification of revenge.

CHAPTER 2

Happy Hamlet

Hamlet is "the melancholy Dane," and his play is one of the world's great tragedies. But there is a way in which emphasis on the supposed truth of the first of these assertions can be seen to diminish some of the force of the undoubted truth of the second. *Hamlet* is certainly not the most painful of the "great" or "mature" Shakespearean tragedies—*Othello* and *King Lear* compete for that honor—but *Hamlet* can be seen as the saddest of them. Part of this sadness springs from the fact that, unlike Lear, Othello, or Macbeth, Hamlet did nothing at all to initiate the tragic situation in which he finds himself. But what intensifies this sadness, I will argue, is the sense the play gives us that there was an alternative life for Hamlet. King Lear may have had a few years of contentment ("rest") with Cordelia after his abdication and (initial) apportionment of the kingdom, but this was to be, at best, a muted crawling toward death.[1] Othello may, as Iago thinks, have had a happy marriage if Iago had not intervened, even though modern criticism has raised doubts about this.[2] It is hard to imagine the Macbeths living happily, even with children. I will argue that, by contrast, Hamlet was not melancholic by nature (or humoral unbalance); that he was happy in the period before the events that form the plot began; and that there was every reason to suppose that such happiness would continue, since we see the components of it. I will even try to show that some of what Yeats called the "gaiety" of Hamlet continues after the "perfect storm" that defines the plot of the play: the death (as it turns out, murder) of King Hamlet and the accession to King Hamlet's place, political and nuptial, of the late king's brother, Hamlet's uncle.[3]

"As you were when we were at Wittenberg"

To see the play in this way requires that we take Hamlet himself as capable of participating in *and enjoying* key aspects of both the contemplative and the active life.[4] It means basically agreeing with Ophelia that Hamlet, before his "transformation," truly possessed and happily manifested the "courtier's, soldier's, [and] scholar's" best qualities.[5] This is controversial enough in the world of criticism today—a large book on the play recently espoused exactly the opposite view[6]—but my view also entails seeing the people that Hamlet was involved with, especially those in his own generation, in a basically positive light as well, so that his implied past interactions with them (along with some of his present ones) seem positive, and the destruction of all of them profoundly sad. "Golden lads and girls"—or something like that—is what we must see lost.[7] This is even more controversial. Almost no one these days has a good word for Laertes or even for Ophelia (except when she's mad), let alone for Rosencrantz and Guildenstern. But I will see what can be said positively for all of these components of Hamlet's pre-crisis world, all of whom should, under normal circumstances, have continued in the ways they were then. My focus will be on what Julia Lupton calls the play's "horizontal strands" rather than its "awful longitudinals."[8]

Yet for reasons that are nowhere given, Lupton also speaks of the "grim Elsinore childhoods" of Hamlet and Ophelia.[9] Yet Elsinore in the late Elizabethan period was anything but grim. Shakespeare was, as far as we know, the first teller of the Hamlet story to shift its locale to Elsinore in particular, and he is insistent on the location (Elsinore is mentioned four times in the text).[10] What this means is that the locale of the story was the castle of Kronborg, which, from its reconstruction in the 1570s on, was one of the grandest, newest, and most heavily armed of Renaissance palaces—all of which, according to Gunnar Sjögren, was "well known" to the Elizabethans.[11] So Hamlet, and perhaps Ophelia, grew up in a grand and very contemporary structure. We are told little about Hamlet's early life, but we do know that he idealized his father—as, it seems, both a model human and a model male ("'A was a man . . . I shall not see his like again" [1.2.186–87])—and he had a devoted mother (in the present, we are told that she "lives almost by his looks" [4.7.12], and there is no reason to think that this was not the case in the past). The one early memory strand of Hamlet's that is reconstructed is riotously joyous. His father's court jester "bore [Hamlet] on his back a thousand times," and Hamlet loved him (having kissed his lips "I know not how oft"), and, even as a child, appreciated the jester's performances—his gibes, gambols, songs—and was part of a festive community in this appreciation; the jester's "flashes of merriment" were wont "to set the table on a roar" (5.1.179–85).

The other thing that we know about Hamlet's early life is that he had two friends who were "of so young days brought up with him," and were close to him not only in age but in spirit and activity ("neighbour'd to his youth and haviour" [2.2.11–12]). In naming these characters, Shakespeare is, again, being absolutely historically correct and contemporary. At the coronation of Christian IV in 1596, there were no fewer than nine Guildensterns and seven Rosencrantzes among the attendant Danish aristocrats—so the ethnicity and class status of Hamlet's friends are assured.[12] And we know that Hamlet was genuinely fond of them. It is his uncle who mentions the affinities in youth and "haviour," and his mother reports to the two young aristocrats that Hamlet enjoys telling stories about their shared youthful exploits—"he hath much talk'd of you," and she believes that there are not two men living "To whom he more adheres" (2.2.19–21).[13] Hamlet's mother and uncle appeal to the "gentry" of the two youths, and expect them, given their past relationship to Hamlet, to "draw him on to pleasures" (2.2.22, 15).[14] I realize that this reading requires that we take the words of Claudius and Gertrude here at face value, but I cannot see any reason not to do so. Their plan depends on what they say being true.

Their confidence seems justified. When Rosencrantz and Guildenstern find Hamlet, they address him quite formally as a social superior. Rosencrantz says, "God save you, sir"; Guildenstern addresses him both more intimately and more formally as "My most dear lord." In what we now recognize as a typical gesture of (using Lupton's terms again) establishing horizontal rather than vertical social relations, Hamlet changes the register and addresses them as "My excellent good friends" (2.2.221–23). Michael Neill has called attention to the complexity and problematic nature of such a gesture, as has Christopher Warley, but it seems to be something that Hamlet quite spontaneously does, and is quite committed to doing.[15] He does the same when he first meets Horatio, who addresses Hamlet even more formally than Guildenstern does, with "Hail to your lordship," and whose "your poor servant," Hamlet changes to "my good friend" (1.2.159–63). Hamlet insists, at the end of the encounter with "the thing" on the battlements, that precedence be ignored—the "Nay" in "Nay, let's go together" only makes sense as a gesture of this sort. Hamlet seems genuinely to enjoy setting friendship above hierarchy. This can, again, be seen as a hierarchical prerogative, but even so it is significant that Hamlet chooses to exercise the prerogative in this way, and so regularly.

When Hamlet asks his "excellent good friends" Rosencrantz and Guildenstern how they are doing, he playfully urges them to extend their metaphor about their location on Fortune's body, and himself turns the metaphor in a bawdy direction, which the friends are happy to adopt (2.2.225–36). It's all quite lighthearted. Hamlet makes it clear that (as we already know) the two have not, recently, been living in Denmark. In the Folio text, he turns bitter, puzzling the two by calling Denmark a prison; he banters with them about the subjectivity of feelings and about the (supposed) insubstantiality of ambition; and invites them, in a gesture that is now familiar, to "go together" with him ("shall we to th' court?").[16] They insist on his taking precedence ("We'll wait upon you"), and he tells them that he will not "sort them" with "the rest of his servants" because he is "most dreadfully attended."[17] I do not think that this implies that Hamlet thinks of them as truly among his servants (as Warley does). At this point in both Q2 and the Folio, Hamlet turns to them and asks, with obvious sincerity, announcing that he is momentarily giving up being witty, "but in the beaten way of friendship, what make you at Elsinore?" (2.2.270).

It is tempting to see this as a turning-point moment. At the equivalent moment in relation to Horatio, Horatio makes the joke about "a truant disposition," and then answers directly ("I came to see your father's funeral" [1.2.176]). Rosencrantz, on the other hand, tells what we know to be a bold-faced lie ("To visit you, my lord, no other occasion" [2.2.271]). Hamlet does not believe this, but he seems willing to give them a chance to admit what he guesses, correctly, to be the true situation ("Were you not sent for?" [2.2.274]). I think that he really wants them to "deal justly" with him. He pressures them by reference to their history, and presents this very positively in three different modes: "by the rights of our fellowship, by the consonancy of our youth, by the obligation of our ever-preserved love" (2.2.284–86). Hamlet is laying it on here, but, again, I think that he really wants them to come through. With some hesitancy, and after another appeal to love ("if you love me," says Hamlet [2.2.290]), they finally do fess up. Hamlet then gives them his set humanist and anti-humanist speech about "the paragon of animals" who is also "the quintessence of dust" (2.2.303–8). He is playing with them—pretending, for instance, that he does not know why he has "lost all [his] mirth—but it does not yet seem to be cruel play. He does not dismiss them, and he is extremely interested to hear their report about the actors who are coming to the castle. When the actors are about to appear, Hamlet professes to be worried lest Rosencrantz and Guildenstern be offended that he will greet the players more warmly than he did them (2.2.367–71).

I do not see why he should even raise this issue of what he beautifully calls "th' appurtenance of welcome" if he were not actually concerned about it. It seems like a moment of exquisite social tact. He then trusts his childhood friends with the knowledge, phrased obliquely but still unmistakably, that he is not really mad ("but mad north-north-west"). It is no part of any strategy to tell them this. His final words to them in the scene are "My good friends, I'll leave you till night. You are welcome to Elsinore" (2.2.540–41). This may be read as ironic, but need not be.

There is no doubt that in Hamlet's next significant encounter with the two, after "The Mousetrap," Hamlet treats them harshly and with contempt, using the recorder to show his sense of them as merely instruments of the king's, and directly calling them liars (3.2.341–50). He has come—perhaps through the experience of seeing Ophelia as a willing pawn; perhaps through his newfound assurance that Claudius is his father's murderer (and the assumption of Gertrude's connivance)—to see his friends now only in relation to the King and Queen, from the latter of whom they are bearing a message.[18] Now being frank about being "sent for," Guildenstern says, "The Queen your mother . . . hath sent me to you" (3.2.303–4). When, at this point, Rosencrantz and Guildenstern attempt to mobilize the language of friendship, Hamlet fiercely resists. Guildenstern says that it is love that leads him to press Hamlet about the cause of his "distemper," and appeals to the idea that love and duty can, at times, lead to "unmannerly" boldness (3.2.339–40). There is no doubt that, as a general maxim, this is true (think of Kent in the first scene of *Lear*).[19] Hamlet pretends not to understand (3.2.341).

Yet there might be real feeling and real pathos in Rosencrantz's reaction to Hamlet's newly caustic treatment of them: "My lord, you once did love me" (3.2.326). This has something of the ring of Sir Andrew's "I was adored once" in *Twelfth Night*, and it echoes Ophelia's "I was the more deceived" when Hamlet tells her, "I loved you not" (3.1.119–20).[20] After all, what do Rosencrantz and Guildenstern think that they are doing? Like everyone else, they do not know that Claudius is a murderer. They have been sent for by a concerned stepfather, who is also their monarch, together with a concerned mother, to try to help the two get some insight into why their son and son-in-law has indeed apparently lost all the mirth (and the good manners) that had previously characterized him. The young aristocrats have no reason to think that there is any other motive for their being sent for. But what of their eagerness to be used by the reigning monarchs, giving up themselves "in the full bent" (2.2.30) to be used by them? It is easy for us to see this as sleazy or worse, as Hamlet comes to do. We tend to see them, in an analogy that is almost impossible for us not to use, as "good Germans."[21]

But would Shakespeare and most of his audience have seen them in a parallel way? The two have a very high view of kingship and its importance to the body politic, but virtually all Elizabethans would have agreed that on the monarch's "weal depends and rests / The lives of many" (3.3.14–15). When Hamlet tells the two that he will simply give them the insight that they have been sent to acquire, so that their secrecy "to the King and Queen moult no feather" (2.2.294–95), he may actually be respecting their situation. Frank Whigham reminds us that satiric depiction (and our own assumed high-mindedness) "can blind us to the probability that most young Elizabethan hopefuls" were more like Rosencrantz and Guildenstern than they were like Sidney or Castiglione.[22] Rosencrantz and Guildenstern certainly do not offer any resistance to the king and queen's requests (which they rightly see as equivalent to commands [2.2.27–29]), but it is important to remember that they have not been asked to do anything obviously improper or immoral.[23] They are about to be sent to accompany a depressed friend on a trip. As far as the play lets us see, they are neither fools like Osric nor willing executioners like Goneril's Oswald. They are loyal servants to their monarchs, but it is not clear that they have knowingly betrayed their friendship to Hamlet. Horatio, in his low-key way, is shocked at Hamlet sending them to their death—"So Guildenstern and Rosencrantz go to't" (5.2.56). Hamlet responds (in the Folio) with an unproven allegation ("they did make love to this employment") and in both texts refuses, on appallingly hierarchical grounds, to feel any guilt about their deaths. He sees them, despite their courtly origins, as persons of "baser nature" who should not have ventured into a conflict of "mighty opposites" (5.2.60–62)—which seems to mean the mightiness of those who are or would be kings.[24] There is no reason to think that Rosencrantz and Guildenstern would have known the contents of the "grand commission" (5.2.18) that they were delivering.[25] They should have been nearer to Hamlet's conscience (see 5.2.58).

Let me now turn to the other members of Hamlet's generation with whom he has long-standing relationships, beginning with Ophelia. Since the death of Hamlet Sr., young Hamlet seems to have intensified his wooing of Ophelia ("he hath very oft of late / Given private time to" her [2.2.91–92]), but there seems to be no doubt that he was courting her before. He apparently was in the habit of writing her letters (including at least one with a confessedly poor attempt at poetry [2.2.115–20]), and of following up the letters with words "of so sweet breath compos'd / As made the things more rich" (3.1.98–99). Despite the (completely understandable) concerns of Ophelia's father and brother, she and Hamlet seem to have comported themselves admirably—"he hath importun'd me with love / In honorable fashion" (1.3.110–11).[26] But can we think that the cessation of this relationship is really a major loss? There has been a good deal of focus recently on the cultural significance of Ophelia's madness, but this is clearly a matter of "after."[27] I am interested in "before." With regard to that, she can be thought of as another moral weakling willing to be manipulated by an authority figure. Again, I think that this is an anachronistic perspective. Just as I believe most Elizabethans would have applauded the care for Ophelia's honor shown by her father and her brother, I think that they would have understood, if not applauded, daughterly obedience to a father.[28]

But there is more to be said. Female compliance is often (by us) judged harshly. Yet Ophelia, like Desdemona, is a person of wit and spirit. Ophelia is skeptical about Laertes's initial characterization of Hamlet's behavior as "trifling" (1.3.5). Her "No more but so?" (1.3.9) can be seen as manifesting disbelief rather than belief. After the longer speech in which Laertes concedes that Hamlet might be sincere but introduces class, political, and other considerations, Ophelia answers her brother with surprising shrewdness and humor.[29] Assuring Laertes that she will indeed remember what he has told her, she turns the tables on him and says, "But, good my brother, / Do not as some ungracious pastors do / Show me the steep and thorny way to heaven / Whiles like a puff'd and reckless libertine / Himself the primrose path of dalliance treads" (1.3.45–48). This is intellectually and morally sharp, and very wittily phrased ("a puff'd and reckless libertine").[30] Later, she gives an extraordinarily vivid narrative of Hamlet's intrusion into her closet in a state of surprising dishabille and inarticulateness (2.1.77–100)—a narrative that is powerful enough to change Polonius's estimation of the relationship (2.1.102–6, 110–13)—and she stands up to Hamlet's barking at her about female dishonesty with lovely ingenuousness and directness (3.1.109–20).

She reacts more in sorrow than in anger to Hamlet's unintelligible advice for her to go to a nunnery (in Protestant Denmark), and to his general misogyny.[31] She focuses on what has apparently happened to him rather than on her own hurt feelings. But what is most striking about Ophelia's reaction—aside from its selflessness—is that she shares Hamlet's Renaissance humanism. She cannot have heard him musing on what is "nobler in the mind" regarding suffering and indignity, but her first line after his noisy exit is "O, what *a noble mind* is here o'erthrown" (3.1.153; emphasis mine). She comments on his new disregard for fashion (is he dishabille again?), but keeps her focus on "that noble and most sovereign reason" (3.1.159)—again falling in line with the many assertions of the crucial, ethically significant, and distinctively human status of reason that we have already heard (from Horatio at 1.4.28) and especially from Hamlet himself (at 1.2.150, 1.4.28, and 2.2.304). In the equivalent speech in Q1, Ofelia speaks of Hamlet's intellect as "the jewel that adorned his feature most."[32] Finally, let me add that Ophelia, like Desdemona, is no prude. Like any intelligent aristocratic lady of the period, she is accustomed to off-color jokes. When Hamlet makes a crude joke to her about "country matters," she does not manifest shock or displeasure, merely noting, "You are merry, my lord" (3.2.120).

Ophelia's brother receives, if anything, even worse treatment in most critical accounts. Laertes's role in the play is to be a "foil" for Hamlet. One might say that this is explicit in the text. Hamlet calls Laertes this—but only with punning regard to their fencing skills, their skills with literal foils (5.2.250–53). The normal critical conception of Laertes as a "foil" for Hamlet is with regard to the supposed contrast between them as revengers. Hamlet is thought to be the scrupulous avenger; Laertes the unscrupulous and savage one. The supposed contrast has three bases: Laertes's arousing of a popular rebellion and bursting into Claudius's palace at the head of one (4.5.110ff.); his lack of hesitation in embracing revenge; and, supposedly in most pointed contrast with Hamlet, his willingness, with regard to the murderer of his father, "To cut his throat i'th' church" (4.7.125).[33] To take the question of lack of hesitation first, it must be recognized that Laertes's situation, from an epistemological point of view, is entirely different from Hamlet's. Laertes is given, in short order, a perfectly clear picture of his father's death. There is no doubt, in his mind or anyone else's, how it happened. Hamlet, on the other hand, is given an account of his father's death by a "thing" that is certainly, in the modern sense, a "questionable shape" (1.4.43); doubts about the status of this thing (regularly referred to as "it"), and therefore about the status of its claims, are inevitable, especially given the play's Protestant context, with Hamlet having been a student at Wittenberg.[34] That the thing encourages the belief that it comes from purgatory would, from a Protestant point of view, simply confirm its demonic status, since belief in purgatory is itself "a wicked device of the devil."[35] The thing's reference to the importance of Catholic last rites ("Unhousel'd ... unanel'd") would be similarly viewed. What exactly Hamlet believes the thing to be in the immediate aftermath of his confrontation with it is unclear. His mention of Saint Patrick (1.5.142), supposedly the keeper of Purgatory, may be a joke (*pace* Greenblatt).[36] In any case, when Hamlet calms down, he is very (and very properly) worried that "The spirit that I have seen / May be a devil" (2.2.594–95).

With regard to the popular rebellion, the major thing to note is how little is made of it. The fact that the rebellion seems to happen easily may suggest that there is some general discontent with Claudius's reign, but this is not developed.[37] The rebels, insofar as they are represented at all, seem focused on Laertes becoming king—in which Laertes manifests no interest whatever. All he cares about is being, as he says, "reveng'd / Most thoroughly" for the death of his father (4.5.135–36). He leads the rebellion against Claudius only because he thinks Claudius responsible for this. Hamlet, on the other hand, is the designated successor to the throne (1.2.109), and does not need to stir up whatever popular discontent exists to get at Claudius. But the major supposed difference remains: Laertes's willingness with regard to his father's murderer "To cut his throat i'th' church." The obvious contrast here is with Hamlet's unwillingness to do this when he has exactly that opportunity. As Margreta de Grazia has shown, there is a long tradition, from the eighteenth century on, of refusing to take at face value Hamlet's explicit reason for not cutting Claudius's throat when he might do it "pat, now a is a-praying" (3.3.73). Hamlet, in this line of thinking, cannot seriously have wanted to send Claudius's soul to hell; he cannot have had such a "diabolic" idea.[38] Only a crude soul like Laertes could have wanted this. Supposedly, Hamlet cannot stand the idea of killing an unarmed man who is kneeling in prayer—perhaps cannot stand the idea of revenge at all—and so he finds a fierce-sounding excuse for not seizing the moment. In order to disguise "a delicate disposition," he pretends to desire "a savage enormity."[39]

But Hamlet has made it clear all along that he does indeed want to see the souls of his enemies in hell. One of the worst things that he can think of—almost as bad, he says, as his mother's marriage to his uncle so soon after his father's death—is to meet his "dearest foe in heaven" (1.2.182). For some reason, this line has gotten remarkably little attention. De Grazia does not mention it. Hamlet is appalled at the idea of one of his enemies going to heaven. He wants his enemies to go to hell. He tells Claudius, in a (sort of) joke, to go there (4.3.34–35). Although part of what is presented as "most horrible" about the murder of Hamlet Sr. is not only what happened to his body but that he was not given any opportunity to prepare spiritually for his death (1.5.76–79), Hamlet has no compunction about specifying that exactly the same thing happen to Rosencrantz and Guildenstern. The letter that Hamlet wrote to the English king to substitute for the one that Claudius composed insists that the bearers be put "to sudden death," which is explicitly specified to mean "no shriving-time allow'd" (5.2.46–47). So, Laertes's stance with regard to this issue is no more crude or unconstrained than Hamlet's is.[40] Hamlet is in fact more cold-blooded about wanting his enemies to go to hell than is Laertes, who never specifies this. If there is a moral difference here, the balance is in Laertes's favor.

I have already suggested that Laertes's concern for his sister's honor can be seen as admirable. I have yet to find any commentary on the language that Shakespeare gives to Laertes when Laertes shifts from considering Hamlet's special status as (essentially) crown prince to considerations of the fragility of virginity and honor. After making the general observation that "Virtue itself scapes not calumnious strokes," Laertes says:

> The canker galls the infants of the spring
> Too oft before their buttons be disclos'd,
> And in the morn and liquid dew of youth
> Contagious blastments are most imminent. (1.3.38–42)

This is the language of some of Shakespeare's most lyrical sonnets (for instance, sonnets 5, 12, 15, 54, 65, et alia). The speaker of these lines can hardly be seen as a coarse sensibility. We do not know whether, in France, Laertes is putting into practice the "precepts" about behavior in the social world that Polonius bestowed on him or whether Laertes is indulging in the "wanton, wild, and usual slips" that Polonius later enumerates (2.1.25–26).[41] But we do know that Polonius, by his own account, is overly suspicious (2.2.113–15), and in any case the audience would almost certainly agree with Polonius that "gaming" etcetera are merely "slight sullies" on the reputation of a young aristocrat.

It is as an aristocrat that Laertes is presented. He is consistently concerned with the behavior-regulating principles that Hamlet calls "honour and dignity" (2.2.526).[42] In the course of the play, Laertes has to deal with the destruction of what we know of as his entire nuclear family (his mother seems to be long deceased; she is never mentioned or even referred to). Laertes's love for his intimate family is demonstrated—he is not being ironic in appreciating "A double blessing" from his father (1.3.53)—and with regard to both father and sister, his concern for how they are treated postmortem would have been seen as entirely and admirably class-appropriate. He is, and would have been recognized as being, entirely right in protesting his father's "obscure funeral," with "no trophy, sword, nor hatchment o'er his bones, / No noble rite, nor formal ostentation" (4.6.210–12).[43] He is admirable in desiring further ceremony for his sister—even if "her death was doubtful" in the sense of being a possible suicide (5.1.220).[44] Roland M. Frye is certain that the officiating figure is wrong in denying her a musical "requiem": "A great deal of music would have been expected, even if the funeral had been that of a commoner, and much more of course for the burial of a prominent court lady."[45] Frye even claims that Laertes was doing something proper and familiar in taking the improperly exposed shrouded body into his arms.[46] On this view, Hamlet, who is now willing to acknowledge his love for Ophelia, simply wants to get in on the pious and loving act.

Hamlet sees Laertes not as a contrast to himself but, on the contrary, as a kind of double. He says this explicitly with regard to their situations; they have both lost their fathers unexpectedly, and Hamlet can easily, by reflection, project himself into Laertes: "By the image of my cause I see / The portraiture of his" (5.2.76–77). But there is more to the doubling of these characters than this. Hamlet consistently views, and treats, Laertes as "a very noble youth" (5.1.217). Just as we should take seriously Ophelia's sense of Hamlet before the crisis as a model Renaissance aristocrat (courtier, soldier, scholar), we should recognize the substance behind Osric's rhetoric about Laertes as "an absolute gentleman," the "card or calendar of gentry" (5.2.107–10). It is worth recalling that Polonius's last instruction to Reynaldo about what Reynaldo should do in France with regard to Laertes is "let him ply his music" (2.1.73).[47] It is also worth saying that with regard to matters of "formal ostentation," Hamlet—despite his apparent disdain for externals (to which we will return)—is just as concerned with "honour and dignity" as Laertes is. In Hamlet's first soliloquy, where he expresses his revulsion at his mother's remarriage, Hamlet takes note of Claudius's comparative lack of physical attractiveness and martial prowess, and closes with a reference to incest, but the main focus of Hamlet's disgust is the speed of the marriage: "But two months . . . ere these shoes were old . . . a beast . . . would have mourned longer . . . O most wicked speed" (1.2.138–57). The issue here is not just personal revulsion but shame and impropriety. Frye makes clear how utterly shocking this speed would have been to an Elizabethan audience, who would have expected a period of public mourning for an aristocratic or royal death of a least many months.[48] Here too, Hamlet's case is the portraiture of that of Laertes.

Unless we see Hamlet and Laertes as figures who were both, under normal circumstances, model Renaissance aristocrats, and who should have been, under normal circumstances, friends and perhaps happy brothers (-in-law), much of the poignance of the final movement of the play is lost. This movement starts by giving us a glimpse of what the normal relation between these two aristocratic youths should have been. One of the small mysteries in the play is why it includes the elaborate account of the "bewitching" horsemanship of the Norman,

Lamord (4.7.80–89). Horsemanship was one of the great aristocratic skills—recall the opening of Sidney's *Apology for Poetry*—and the point of the Lamord passage is to bring us into that world.[49] But the feature of that world that is the focus of the discussion here, and the reason for Claudius bringing up Lamord, is not horsemanship but fencing, another prized gentlemanly pursuit (despite Polonius listing it as one of the "wild" activities in which Laertes may be engaged [2.1.25]).[50] Lamord brought to the Danish court (not clear under which king), a "report" of Laertes's extraordinary skill for "art and exercise" in his defense, especially with that very fashionable weapon, the rapier.[51] Laertes was extolled for many virtues (Q 4.7.72), but this one galvanized Hamlet into aristocratic emulation.[52] In an odd phrase (especially from Claudius), this praise did "envenom" Hamlet with envy of Laertes (4.7.102; and see also Q 72–74).[53] Laertes, though he is determined to revenge his father's death on Hamlet, and wishes to be "the organ" of Hamlet's death (4.7.69), can see nothing at all unusual or significant in this aristocratic rivalry—"What out of this, my lord?" (4.7.105). He sees it as utterly normal and unsurprising. It exists in the world of happy aristocratic exercise and friendly competition. As Claudius says, Hamlet is eager "to play with" Laertes (5.2.195). This is what their world should be.[54]

Laertes does not put two and two together—until Claudius spells it out for him—because, as I have suggested, the fencing match seems so normal and so innocuous to him. Hamlet, until he is forced by word and by circumstance to see it otherwise, also sees the fencing match in this way. He imagines, somehow, that he and Laertes are still in the world they should have been in, the world in which their duel, with the betting on it, would be a "brother's wager." Hamlet has been looking forward to it, and in fact has been "in continual practice," ever since Laertes's departure for Paris (5.2.206–7). Despite the foreboding that Hamlet feels, which on a combination of religious and philosophical grounds he decides to ignore, it does seem to be his pleasure "to play with Laertes" (5.2.195). The power of this vision of friendly and courtly aristocratic emulation gives rise to the pre-duel moment when Hamlet agrees to takes Laertes's hand and to issue the formal apology to him that begins, "Give me your pardon, sir. I have done you wrong" (5.2.222). He asks Laertes to pardon the wrong—killing Laertes's father—on the basis of a class or status solidarity that he takes to have an ethical dimension: "Pardon't *as you are a gentleman*" (emphasis mine).[55]

What this seems to mean here is that Laertes understands the importance of intention in determining the nature and culpability of an action. Hamlet knows that Laertes understands the legal importance of this, since a claim to nonintentionality had to lie behind Laertes's demand for more extended funeral rites for Ophelia.⁵⁶ After Hamlet's claim that he was "not himself" when he killed Polonius, Hamlet returns to a direct plea: "Let my disclaiming from a purpos'd evil / Free me so far in your most generous thoughts / That I have shot my arrow o'er the house / And hurt my brother" (5.2.236–40). He returns to the matter of intention, and again to the matter of what it means for Laertes to be, as Hamlet sees it, in the deepest sense, "a gentleman."⁵⁷ It means to have "generous thoughts"—which seems to mean, among other things, being the sort of person who is capable of forgiving a wrong done to him by someone who is genuinely penitent for it and also professes continuing goodwill (of the sort "a brother" would have).⁵⁸

Laertes responds to this speech in an extraordinary way. Instead of rejecting its arguments as specious, or its contrition as unconvincing—both of which would be points well taken—Laertes professes to accept its goodwill. He claims, from a generally human point of view, to be satisfied by Hamlet's speech, saying, "I am satisfied by nature," but he insists that in terms of public "honor," he cannot forgive Hamlet until he has been assured by "some elder masters of known honour" that he (Laertes) will not be thought to have done something dishonorable in doing so (5.2.246). Meanwhile, he concludes, "I do receive your offer'd love like love / And will not wrong it" (5.2.247–48). What is extraordinary about this is that Hamlet has nowhere used the word "love." But Laertes sees, in what is certainly intended as a "most generous" thought, that love is what lies behind Hamlet's words.

The question naturally arises as to whether Laertes is simply being hypocritical here. He is, after all, about to select carefully the "unbated and envenom'd" rapier (after having mistakenly chosen another [5.2.261]). Yet it is hard to feel Laertes's words as simple hypocrisy, just as it is hard to take Hamlet's apology as merely disingenuous.⁵⁹ Laertes seems to respond not just to the words of Hamlet's speech but to the emotion and the bond that Laertes sees as implied in them. Laertes is, in the sense required, "a gentleman." Further proof that Hamlet's words have genuinely moved Laertes comes in Laertes's comment (to himself) after he has reassured Claudius that in the third "pass" he will wound Hamlet, that it is "almost against [his] conscience" to do so (5.2.300). Only Hamlet's words could have caused this shift from Laertes's prior commitment to lack of conscience with regard to his revenge. (Whether Laertes's failure to wound Hamlet in the first two passes reflects some ambivalence is completely undecidable; Hamlet may simply be the better fencer). The two noble youths end up exchanging forgiveness (5.2.334–36). In Q1, Leartes adds love.⁶⁰ They both die in what really should have been—had life in Elsinore proceeded as it should have—a "brother's wager."

Mirth in Funeral

The first part of this essay attempted to demonstrate that Hamlet led a happy life, among attractive people, before his world was thrown "out of joint." His experience was filled with "meditation or the thoughts of love" (1.5.30), and his consciousness was filled with "saws of books" and such images as "youth and observation copied there" (1.5.100–01)—books and life; what Bradley called "his joy in thought and observation."[61] This section attempts to demonstrate the continuities between Hamlet's life before and after, that he retains many of his qualities, characteristics, and even pleasures. To describe him simply as "melancholy" captures very little of what we actually see of him.

Ophelia saw Hamlet as a sharp dresser—"The glass of fashion" (3.1.155). One might think that this was something that he gave up, but that is less clear than it might be. His first extended speech (1.2.76–86) is usually read as a rejection of externals, of all "trappings" in favor of a deep interiority that (supposedly) cannot be adequately manifested. But that is not exactly what the speech is saying—or rather, it is not all that the speech is saying. The word in the speech that seems to me rarely to be given its proper weight is "alone"—"'Tis not alone my inky cloak, good mother."[62] The claim is not that the garment does not "denote" the state of mind of the wearer, but that it does not fully do so. The point is not that it does not contribute to such "denoting"—rather the claim is that it does do so.[63] The fact that any piece of "haviour" can be played—which is undeniable—does not mean that it cannot also be sincere. One can "know not" seeming and still employ such. That one can feel that even sincere "haviour" does not fully express one's interior state is merely another fact. Furthermore, it is important to give full weight to something that is unmistakable on stage: what Hamlet is wearing. He is, under the circumstances—a grand court scene where, presumably, everyone is quite colorfully dressed—making a point, a point about appropriate "haviour" and costume. He is wearing black. If he actually thought such matters were trivial or worse, he would not be displaying the "customary" suit. There is, moreover, one other thing to say about this, and here, again, I am indebted to the work of Roland Frye. Frye calls attention to the actual garment that Hamlet is wearing. An "inky cloak" was a spectacular piece of mourning clothing, covering the wearer from head to foot (it included a hood).[64] It was often expensive; in Q1, Hamlet refers to his "sable suit," a notoriously expensive material that Hamlet later refers to as such (in bantering with Ophelia before "The Mousetrap," he jokes that he will get "a suit of sables" to signify his mourning [3.2.127]).[65]

Finally, it should be said, that, in the Renaissance as now, black was the most fashionable color. As Frye says, Hamlet's garb "would associate him with such young Renaissance nobles and princes as so often appear painted by Moroni, Titian, Bronzino, Veronese, and others."[66] In *The Book of the Courtier*, Federico of Montefeltro, one of the most authoritative speakers, expresses the opinion that "black is more pleasing in clothing than any other color," and points to the practice of the Spanish, who are, as another speaker has already stated, "the masters in Courtiership."[67] Hamlet is, *avant la lettre*, exactly following Polonius's advice with regard to clothing—"rich, not gaudy" (though Polonius sees the aristocrats of France rather than Spain as especially "select and generous" in this [1.3.70–74]). Hamlet can be seen, in other moments, as maintaining his participation or leadership in fashion. His shocking dishabille in Ophelia's closet certainly reflects his unhappy inner state and felt need, after the encounter with "the thing," to banish "fond records" from his consciousness (1.5.99). But it also, as he must know, corresponds almost perfectly to the standard dress of the melancholy lover. Rosalind, in *As You Like It*, gives the formula "your hose should be ungartered, your bonnet unbanded, your sleeve unbuttoned, your shoe untied, and everything about you demonstrating a careless desolation."[68] Hamlet follows this almost to the letter (though he has no hat).[69] Another instance is Hamlet's famous dialogue with the skull in the graveyard scene. This seems to have been an innovation on the stage, but Frye points out that the young aristocrat with a skull was a well-established motif in the visual arts from 1519 on.[70] The gorgeous Franz Hals painting of a *Young Man with a Skull*, though of a later generation (1641), strikingly illustrates the fashionableness of the motif.[71]

None of this is meant to cast doubt on Hamlet's sincerity at any of these moments. The point is just to suggest that Hamlet's concern with attire and "haviour" can be seen to continue after his much-noted "transformation." In the present of the play, he both is and is consciously enacting being the melancholy prince—as elegant mourner, lover, and intellectual (black was also the color of the academic gown).[72] Another continuity from before to after is more explicit in the play and more central to it. Rosencrantz and Guildenstern are, as we have noted, instructed to draw Hamlet on "to pleasures" (2.2.15), and their major success at this, in relation to which "there did seem in him a kind of joy" (3.1.18), is to tap into his love of theater. They knew about this from long experience, including the way Hamlet was "when we were at Wittenberg."[73] This continuity is explicit in the play. The company that has traveled to Elsinore happen to be "even those" that Hamlet was "wont to take such delight in, the tragedians of the city" (2.2.326–27).[74] He is extremely interested in their situation, asking, "How chances it they travel?" (2.2.328); in Q2, he gets a detailed account of their rivalry with the children's theater, and is utterly fascinated by it (2.2.335–58), even (and very oddly) linking the "strangeness" of the theatrical success of "the boys" with the success of Claudius as king, and with the general problem of understanding the irrational (2.2.359–64).

Shakespeare cleverly links Hamlet's love of theater to his humanistic attitudes and knowledge of the classics.[75] Rosencrantz and Guildenstern immediately see the *contemptus mundi* that Hamlet is pretending as antithetical to the enjoyment of theater ("If you delight not in man, what Lenten entertainment the players shall receive" [2.2.314–15]). But with regard to the theater, Hamlet is a kind of aristocratic purist. His taste is not for the kinds of plays that succeeded in the public theater but rather for highly rhetorical adaptations of classical material, the kind of thing that was "Caviare to the general" (2.2.432–33).[76] He enjoys describing in detail, with regard both to plot-construction and diction, the kind of plays that he likes, and, in an astonishing moment, decides to show off his love of such plays by reciting, from memory, with only a tiny false start, eighteen lines of a play about the fall of Troy, one that he, presumably, heard a number of years ago (before the face of the boy actor in the company was "valanced" [2.2.419]). I am sure that we are meant to think that Polonius was right in evaluating this performance as "well-spoken, with good accent and good discretion" (2.2.462–63). Hamlet's plan for testing the veracity (and, as he thinks, nature) of "the thing" is one that only a died-in-the-wool humanist and theater-lover could seriously propose. After indulging in some hyperbolic self-reproach—which itself might be seen as a sort of perverse rhetorical and psychological pleasure—Hamlet recalls something that he claims to have "heard" about the theater and the special power of theatrical art: "That guilty creatures sitting at a play / Have, by the very cunning of the scene, / Been struck so to the soul that presently / They have proclaim'd their malefactions" (2.2.584–89). Wherever we are to imagine that Hamlet "heard" this fantasy about the power of theater (perhaps in Wittenberg), it is easy to locate where Shakespeare got it. In praising "high and excellent tragedy," Sidney's *Apology for Poetry* makes reference to a story in Plutarch of "the abominable tyrant Alexander Pheraeus, from whose eyes a tragedy well made and represented, drew abundance of tears, who without all pity had murdered infinite numbers, and some of his own blood."[77] Sidney takes the story with a grain of salt, but Hamlet seems actually to believe it.[78] He is delighted with the plan, and is in high spirits from the preparation of the performance (lecturing the players on acting), through the performance itself (commenting from the sidelines), and, especially, after its apparent success.[79]

It may be something of an overstatement to see "theatre and diplomacy" as the "respective areas of expertise" of Hamlet and Claudius, but András Kiséry's formulation has something to it.[80] The larger point is that Hamlet enjoys using his education and enjoys exercising his intellectual powers ("About, my brains," he says when coming up with the Mousetrap idea [2.2.584]).[81] Soon after his excitement at the play, another moment of enjoyment is Hamlet's decision to see the relation between Claudius and himself as a contest in (military) ingenuity. Hamlet is utterly delighted at this conception of their situation: "'tis the sport to have the engineer / Hoist with his own petard ... O, 'tis most sweet" (3.4.208–11). This is as enthusiastic as Hamlet gets about almost anything. But he has been enjoying exercising his intellect all along. And his intellect primarily manifests itself in verbal capacity. He loves to talk. He is a wit and consistently manifests a rather mordant sense of humor. As Bernard McElroy (following Bradley) says, "Hamlet's sense of humor is ubiquitous"; it "never deserts him even at the nadir of his fortunes."[82] He loves many different literary and rhetorical modes: satire (re old men [citing a "satirical rogue" at 2.2.196], re lawyers [5.1.196–210], and re courtiers [5.2.183–91]); lectures (on natural and acquired vices [in Q2, 23–38], on acting technique [3.2.1–35]); homilies (these mainly to women—to Ophelia [3.1.121–51] and to his mother in the closet scene); and, of course, meditation (the reflective soliloquies). Hamlet insists—and demonstrates—that he can even rant "as well as" anyone (5.1.270–78). Like his creator, he cannot resist a pun. His first words are a snide one (on "kind") and his last words a profound one (on "rest," sending us back to the central soliloquy). The sadness of the play is encapsulated in that final sentence of his, since the last thing that we want to hear from Hamlet, that wonderful talker, is silence.

Finally, a few words about the play's final words. They strike the note of lost potentiality that, I have argued, is meant to be a large component of the play's final affect: Fortinbras opines that Hamlet was likely "had he been put on / To have prov'd most royal" (5.2.402–3). Many critics, however, take this to be ironic, or worse. They are said by Fortinbras—Fortinbras! And Hamlet as a soldier! Lupton calls Fortinbras a "thug," and she speaks for the majority of critics.[83]

The odd thing about this is that, like the usual critical treatment of Laertes, it completely ignores what Hamlet says about the character. Hamlet describes Fortinbras (in Q2) as "a delicate and tender prince" (4.5.48)—a remarkable phrase, one that describes another beautiful and educated young man. Fortinbras's "unimproved mettle" and "sharked up" band of "lawless resolutes" are in the context of characterizing an enemy (invaders from the north), and even there the enterprise is recognized as having "some stomach to it" (1.1.99–103).[84] The evaluation that Hamlet later gives of Fortinbras's substitute military endeavor is admiring, not deflating. He recognizes that everything changes "when honour's at the stake" (4.5.56 [from Q2]). Unless one thinks that Hamlet having the scholar's tongue disqualifies him from employing and appreciating the soldier's sword, one has to accept that Hamlet fully endorses this central aristocratic value.[85]

He has done so since the beginning of the play. He was concerned not only with national honor—regarding the "custom / More honour'd in the breach" (1.4.15–16)—but also with the honor of his friends. Horatio's joke about having a "truant disposition" elicited from Hamlet a surprisingly fierce (and not obviously jocular) response: "I would not hear your enemy say so" (1.2.170). He has within him, as he warns Laertes later, "something dangerous" that those who provoke him should fear (5.1.255–56). As his horror at the idea of meeting his "dearest foe in heaven" indicates, Hamlet lives in a world of friends, enemies, and honor. As he lies dying, Hamlet is concerned not only with the succession but with the status of his "name." He does not wish to leave "a wounded name" behind (5.2.349–50). Young Fortinbras knows about young Hamlet. I think that we are meant to take Fortinbras seriously when he says that Hamlet, had he been put on, would have proved "most royal"—bringing together his father's military prowess and his uncle's diplomatic skills and intelligence. "Had he been put on"—the sense of a wonderful lost future is real. But Hamlet would have appreciated being given grand (and appropriate) obsequies. There is no irony here.

CHAPTER 3

Resisting Complicity

Ethical Judgment and *King Lear*

Something odd has happened in recent criticism of *King Lear*. Two of the strongest and most influential critics of our time, Stanley Cavell and Harry Berger Jr., have devoted a great deal of effort to showing that, when the play is looked at closely, there is virtually no difference between the characters normally characterized as "good" (Berger almost always uses scare quotes for this word) or at least (if I may coin an intuitively obvious ethical category) mixed, and those who are wicked (or "wicked").[1] This critical practice has produced, as I will try to show, some quite bizarre claims along with a number of less spectacular dubious or false ones. The interesting question—aside from understanding the mechanisms that produce these readings (which will constitute the bulk of this essay)—is why these readings, if they are as flawed as I have suggested, have had the power and influence that they have had. Subsequent critics often state that "Cavell has established" this or that, or "Berger has established" this or that.[2] I wish I could give a really good account of the success of these readings and of the ways of reading these essays represent. What follows will serve as a preliminary attempt.

With regard to Cavell, part of the success derives from his special standing in the world of literary criticism. Cavell brings with him the authority that comes from his constantly signaled membership in a more intellectually elite group within the academy than literature professors: he is a professional philosopher. But other philosophers have written on Shakespeare without having made a dent or even a ripple in our field.[3] The reason why Cavell has been so singularly influential may have to do with the fact that his philosophical work with literary texts is done more or less within the protocols of our field.[4] So he speaks as an insider and an outsider simultaneously—a very powerful position. His conception of philosophy does not generally involve technical work (though he has done this in some of his "straight" philosophical writing),[5] but rather revolves around terms that are resonant in the worlds of ethics, psychology, and religion: recognition and acknowledgment. These are the terms that, for Cavell, represent an antidote to or overcoming of the ongoing philosophical and human problem of skepticism, though not an "answer" to it, since Cavell thinks a direct answer impossible and self-entangling.[6] His *agon* with skepticism does not involve us in the issues of certainty or truth but rather in the needs and fears that Cavell sees as underlying the raising of these issues, so we are put in the (for us) more comfortable world of existentialized psychology rather than in the (for us) foreign world of sustained epistemological inquiry.[7] So Stanley Cavell speaks to us in a language that is almost our language in a voice that is not exactly our normal voice. He speaks, to use the biblical phrase, as one with authority.[8]

Harry Berger does so too—but in his case because of his standing as an established and prolific critic.[9] Both write with extraordinary fluency. Their prose often has a rhetorical and argumentative flow that makes criticism of single assertions difficult. Moreover, Berger is a stylist (Cavell is a powerful writer, but not a distinguished prose stylist in any normal sense). Both of them are extremely intelligent, obviously so—which has to be part of their power. But certainly not all of it. I have tried to suggest where some of Cavell's special standing in our field comes from. Berger's derives not only from his extraordinary and wide-ranging productivity but also from his conscious appropriation of some of the Cavellian *mana*, and also, more substantively, from our attraction to something like "tough-mindedness."[10] We are suspicious of categories like goodness, and more comfortable with low (self-interested) than high (altruistic) motives. So the motives of the "good" (or not obviously wicked) are to be interrogated, where the motives of the wicked are taken to be obvious.[11] Some generalized, more or less Freudian psychology easily comes into play here (though Berger allies himself with Lacan's critical revision of Freud).[12] What also enters the picture—more so for Berger than for Cavell (though it is present in Cavell)—is the pleasure of moralizing omniscience, of knowing better than the characters what drives them, what their true motives are. These are always dark.[13] This is a highly satisfying and implicitly self-congratulatory position, as "tough-mindedness" is in general. So its appeal is reasonably clear.

But let me now turn to specifics. I will spend more time on Cavell's essay on *Lear* than on Berger's essays on the play—though the critique of these seems to me of equal theoretical importance—not only because of the length and density of Cavell's essay but because of the quite extraordinary status that Cavell's essay has in current studies of the play. It is always referred to positively, even reverentially (examples are too numerous to cite). Sarah Beckwith is certainly right in speaking of the essay as "profoundly influential."[14]

Asserting the Symbolic

The *Lear* essay begins—to my mind very promisingly—with a meditation on the odd split in the history of literary, especially Shakespearean, scholarship between "character criticism" and, though Cavell does not call it this, "close reading."[15] He (again to my mind, rightly) sees this split as odd and means to demur from it. He seems to oppose in particular a kind of criticism that purports to trace, as he somewhat mockingly puts it, "something called the symbolic structure or the pattern of something or other in the piece" (40). Instead he proposes a kind of reading that attends to the specificity—a repeated word here—of the particular words that particular characters say, a way of reading that sees words as meaning deeply "not because they mean many things [taken to be the New Critical approach] but because they mean one thing completely." This is analogized to the task of "ordinary language philosophy," which, according to Cavell, consists in the task of "placing those words with which philosophers have always begun in alignment with human beings in particular circumstances who can be imagined to be having those experiences and saying and meaning those words" (42). So it looks as if the task will be to try to come to terms with the exact things that characters mean in saying what they say.[16] The "depth" of the meaning will not lie "under" but within the "surface" of them.[17] It looks as if the literal will not have to be transcended in favor of some sort of hidden "symbolic structure."

The main body of the essay then turns, quite logically, to an essay by Paul Alpers that argues for and tries to exemplify what would seem to be exactly the sort of reading that Cavell seems to advocate.[18] Alpers's essay is a prolonged and eloquent critique of what he calls the "sight-pattern" reading of the play put forth by many critics—Robert B. Heilman being the most notable.[19] This is indeed a reading in terms of "symbolic structures" or a "pattern of something or other." In particular, it is a pattern in which both sight and blindness are treated symbolically and morally, so that sight is equated with some sort of "insight," and blindness with some sort of materiality or obtuseness, so that literal sight can involve "blindness," and blindness can involve "sight." This culminates in the moment when Gloucester's (literal) blinding finally allows him to "see" (that is, have "insight"). Alpers, on the other hand, wants the blinding to be taken literally—as an act of supreme human cruelty (140), without any metaphysical dimension. He treats the "recognition scene" between Lear and Cordelia in the same literal, nonmetaphysical way. One would think that Cavell would applaud all this, and would go on to try to be even more consistently literal and nonmoralizing than Alpers manages to be.[20] But Cavell (despite an irenic footnote [46 n. 3]) positions his essay not as an extension but as a corrective of Alpers. That is where the trouble begins.[21]

Cavell lodges two charges against Alpers's reading of the blinding of Gloucester. The first is ethical, the second methodological. The ethical charge is in the supposedly mediating mode of the footnote. Cavell says that if the readings proposed by Heilman and company are "hysterical," Alpers's reading of the blinding is "overcasual" (46). So Cavell will avoid both extremes. But I find it difficult to understand how a reading that focuses on supreme cruelty, and takes note of the fact that eyes not only are of special importance to human beings but also are "exceptionally delicate and vulnerable" (141), is to be reckoned "casual." (I take "*over*casual" to be merely rhetorical here.) What is missing, Cavell asserts, is "a *meaning*" (emphasis his). But why does the action itself not count as having a *meaning*; why must it signify something else? Cavell thinks that the answer to this lies in the methodological charge against Alpers—Alpers does not "follow the words." When one does this, Cavell claims, the special *meaning* of the blinding emerges, the symbolic meaning of it.

Before revealing the special meaning that following the words of the blinding scene will provide, however, Cavell mentions that "of course" words already used by Lear, Goneril, and Gloucester himself "implicate all of them spiritually in Cornwall's deed" (47). I have to confess that I simply do not understand what this is supposed to mean, what this "spiritual" implication is. The claim is that these characters have all "implanted" in the play "the idea of punishment by plucking out eyes," and this is what "implicates" them. But let us (following the example of J. L. Austin and Wittgenstein) look at the actual instances—or rather "follow the words," but do so in their actual contexts. Cavell provides no quotations or citations here, but it is easy to find the passages that he has in mind. Lear has said, "Old fond eyes, / Beweep this cause again I'll pluck ye out / And cast you with the waters that you loose / To temper clay" (1.4: Q 289–91; F 271–74a).[22] This has nothing to do with actual blindness. Lear is expressing shame that he has allowed Goneril's actions toward him to make him weep. As Alpers points out, eyes function as many things other than organs of sight in the play (135, 141).[23] Here eyes produce tears and have shown affection ("old fond eyes"). Lear is trying to get rid of his emotional vulnerability to Goneril ("this cause"), not his vision. Gloucester has indeed also mentioned eyes being plucked out, and in the very scene of his blinding. But he has not imagined this in terms of "punishment." He imagines it, as Alpers suggests, as the most extreme form of cruelty. He tells Regan, "I would not see thy cruel nails / Pluck out his [Lear's] poor old eyes," and he barely imagines this as a human possibility—his next line is to imagine Regan's "fierce sister / In his anointed flesh [to] rash boarish fangs" (3.7.53–55). The context is one of preventing such cruelty. But, for Cavell, the mere mention of the phenomenon of blinding, even as virtually unimaginable, apparently qualifies as an invitation or incitation.

But this leaves Goneril. She too, according to Cavell, is implicated "spiritually" in the blinding of Gloucester. This part of the claim makes it clear how determinedly Cavell is avoiding the literal. Goneril is not "spiritually implicated" in the blinding. She is literally implicated in it. It is her idea. When Cornwall, Regan, and Goneril were contemplating how to punish Gloucester, Regan's idea was to "Hang him instantly" (3.7.4). Goneril is the one who suggests, "Pluck out his eyes" (3.7.5). Committed as I am to the literal, I do not want to say that Goneril's relation to "Cornwall's deed" is the same as that of Cornwall himself or of Regan. After all, Goneril is exiting when she makes this (lovely) suggestion, and she leaves before Gloucester is brought in. But it seems likely that once Cornwall has decided that he cannot follow Regan's advice ("We may not pass upon his life" [23]), Cornwall recalls Goneril's alternate suggestion. It is hard to think that Goneril would not have participated fully had she been present, but even apart from this, Goneril's relation to "Cornwall's deed" is rather different than that of Lear or of "Gloucester himself." And Goneril exits with Edmund. If anyone who was not present for the act is implicated in the blinding, it is he. It is he, after all, who "informed against [Gloucester]" to Cornwall and company "And quit the house on purpose that there [F: their] punishment / Might have the freer course" (4.2: Q 91–92; F 60–61). Cavell does not mention him.

Cavell has to keep the idea of implication "spiritual." To do so allows him to shift the register from the literal and physical to the psychological: "The physical cruelty symbolizes (or instances) the psychic cruelty which pervades the play" (47). The *meaning* of the blinding is psychological. The question becomes what the action means psychologically to its perpetrator, Cornwall. It must be related to "Cornwall's needs," which must be psychological. So Cavell has maneuvered himself to home ground. He can deploy his central philosophical concern with issues of recognition and acknowledgment. It is no accident that the

Lear essay, in its original context in *Must We Mean What We Say?*, immediately followed the essay "Knowing and Acknowledging." Cornwall cannot bear to be seen, which means being recognized, by Gloucester. This is the motivation that Alpers has missed, the *meaning*. What Cornwall is doing is preventing Gloucester "from seeing *him*" (Cornwall; again, Cavell's emphasis). Cavell thinks that if we "follow the words," this becomes clear.

So let us, again, try to follow the words. Cavell is right that when Cornwall stomps on each of Gloucester's eyes, Cornwall states that something in particular will not be seen. But is this something Cornwall himself? In the first case, Cornwall's response is to Gloucester saying, "I shall see the winged vengeance overtake such children" (3.7.64); in the second case, the response is to the heroically intervening servant saying to Gloucester about Cornwall, "you have one eye left / To see some mischief on him" (79–80). To the first claim, Cornwall responds, "See 't shalt thou never" (64); to the second, after starting to say, "If thou see vengeance" (69), and being interrupted by his servant, Cornwall continues, "Lest it see more prevent it" (80). So, if we "follow the words," the psychological factor that leads Cornwall to blind Gloucester is not the idea that *he* (Cornwall) cannot, in his shame, bear to be seen by Gloucester in doing what he is doing. What Cornwall is concerned about is the idea that Gloucester will witness or possibly be the agent of some sort of providential punishment of Cornwall. The "seeing" that is being foreclosed is in the imagined future, not the present. And it is not clear that this motive is best seen as psychological rather than pragmatic. Cornwall imagines that the blind Gloucester will not in any way be a threat to him. This was, as Regan points out later, a miscalculation ("where he arrives he moves / All hearts against us" [Q 4.5 and F 4.4: 9–11]), but the blinding was, in any case, done out of calculation as well as out of anger and religious (or superstitious) fear.

It is important for Cavell that Cornwall be, at some deep level, feeling shame, since shame is the emotion that Cavell has a philosophical account of, and his belief that it is central to *King Lear* accounts, as I have already partly suggested, for why his analysis of the play stands as the culmination of his first book. Cavell takes it as an axiom that cruelty "cannot bear to be seen," and he speaks, portentously, of "evil's ancient love of darkness" (47). One knows what he means by this—light and darkness are given moral and symbolic values in many religious and metaphysical schemes—and a certain kind of wicked person does indeed crave darkness in order not to see as well as not to be seen (Lady Macbeth's invocation of "thick night" is a very clear instance [*Macbeth*, 1.5.49]). But Cornwall is not a wicked person of this sort. Like the other major villains of the play, Goneril and Regan, Cornwall does not feel any shame (Edmund seems to have a momentary bout of it as he is dying). The villains in the play are notably self-righteous, and they feel entitled.

In blinding Gloucester, Cornwall thinks that he is properly—and with some restraint—punishing a traitor (blinding was especially associated with treason).[24] The "vile jelly" is the eye of a traitor—a loathsome being (compare Edgar calling Edmund "a most toad-spotted traitor" [5.3: Q 133; F 130]). Throughout the blinding scene, Gloucester is "the traitor."[25] And there is good reason for the charge. As Edmund concludes from the letter that Gloucester has secretly received and shown to him (3.3) and that Edmund has passed on to Cornwall (3.5), Gloucester is in collusion with an invading army. He is "an intelligent party to the advantages of France" (3.5.9–10). When Regan and Cornwall insist that Gloucester reveal to them where he has "sent the lunatic King," and then ask him why he has sent the king where he has (to Dover), they are not trying to extract information from Gloucester. They are trying to get him to confess his treason. They already know where Gloucester has sent the king, and why. Before Gloucester is brought onto the scene, Oswald has already told Cornwall and company that Gloucester has sent the king "towards Dover" where Gloucester "boasts" that Lear will find "well-armed friends" (3.7.18–19). When Oswald encounters Gloucester at Dover, Oswald is astonished to find the "bold peasant" that Edgar is pretending to be take up his cudgel in defense of "a published traitor" (Q 4.6.221; F 4.5.226).

Cavell finds the whole issue of Dover in the play a great mystery and puzzle. But this shows that, in pursuit of his themes, he is not truly attending to the words, let alone the plot. He wonders "why Regan assumes that he [the blinded Gloucester] is going to Dover" (53). But Gloucester has known since he received the incriminating letter that "a power" sympathetic to Lear's injuries has gathered (3.3.12), and he has instructed Kent and company to take Lear to Dover (3.6: Q 84; F 47). Why everyone is focused on Dover is not a great mystery. Where else would a French invasion begin? Cavell states that "it is now commonly appreciated" that when the blinding scene began Gloucester had "no plans for going to Dover" (52). Whether or not this is true about the state of the criticism, the question is what "we must incline to the King" in 3.3 means. It comes right after the mention of the invasion. I simply cannot understand how Cavell can speculate that Regan's "Wherefore to Dover?" taunt "may have put that destination in Gloucester's mind" (53). It was, unequivocally and explicitly, already there. Cavell is correct that in the scene immediately following the blinding, Gloucester tells the Old Man who offers to aid him that he (Gloucester) has "no way" (4.1: 16, 18), meaning no destination. But to "follow the words" here should, again, surely mean to get the point—not what "the words" mean in themselves but in context. Gloucester is trying to protect the Old Man who has been a tenant of his family for generations. Aiding a traitor was dangerous. Gloucester rightly notes that supplying comforts to Gloucester "may hurt" the devoted tenant (4.2: Q 10–14; F 13–17). Yet when the vagrant beggar, who has no fixed residence, appears, Gloucester immediately indicates that he aims to go to Dover. It is true that, as Cavell says (53), Gloucester only reveals his intention to commit suicide there at this point. But that simply provides yet another reason for going there (a suitable cliff).

But we must return to the *meaning* of the blinding. It relates not only to Cornwall's deep psychological needs but also, and perhaps even more so, to "necessities of Gloucester's character" (47). This is the moment when the symbolic and the moralizing readings come together. The blinding "takes on symbolic value" (47) and the blindness-as-insight pattern comes into play through what Cavell sees as Gloucester's "immediate and complete acquiescence in his fate." Gloucester accepts his blinding as somehow appropriate, as "retribution." It leads him to "an insight into his life as a whole." But is any of this true? Gloucester's immediate response to his blinding is not to acquiescence but to call for vengeance; he wants his son to be outraged, to "enkindle all the sparks of nature / To quit this horrid act" (3.7: Q 84–85; F 83–84). When Regan gleefully points out that in calling on Edmund to do this, Gloucester is calling "on him that hates thee," and who made the "overture" of Gloucester's treasons to Cornwall and herself (adding, with typical self-righteousness, that Edmund is "too good" to pity a traitor), Gloucester has his "insight." His realization is about Edgar (he has nothing to realize about Edmund, since he has been given the information about him). In response to the truth that is thrust upon him about Edmund, he exclaims, "O my follies! Then Edgar was abused." This seems to indicate that he realizes that, like himself, Edgar was a victim of Edmund ("abused" suggests this). "Follies" is plural—he realizes that he made two mistakes at once: believing Edmund and punishing Edgar. In the next line, he asks the "Kind gods" to forgive him. I take it that this is what Cavell would point to as the textual warrant for stating that Gloucester finds his treatment by Cornwall somehow appropriate. If the phrase does imply this—which is doubtful, since it seems to be merely a general epithet—the bad behavior for which Gloucester certainly feels he needs forgiveness and *may* feel that he deserved punishment is entirely in relation to Edgar. "I stumbled when I saw" (4.1: Q 17; F 19) is about Edgar.

But that is too straightforward for Cavell. The blinding must be shown to manifest a perfect poetic justice; it must have "the horrible aptness of retribution" (47). Gloucester's "insight" must be "into his life as a whole," not merely into one disastrous episode. So Cavell insists that Gloucester has gotten his life and his feelings wrong. He has attached his shame to the wrong thing (48). It is his treatment not of Edgar but of Edmund that he should truly be ashamed about. This is where he has truly done something wrong, and something for which, Cavell will show, his blinding his appropriate. So Cavell shifts, as the text does not, from Gloucester's relation to Edgar to Gloucester's relation to Edmund. This allows Cavell to deploy, once again, his key ethical term. Gloucester's great moral failure, which can be seen to define his character and "his life as a whole," is his failure to acknowledge his bastard son, Edmund. The key shift, again, is from the physical to the psychological. But before examining the claim about acknowledgment, it might be worthwhile to (again) attend to the literal. What Gloucester did to Edgar is not merely to have disinherited him. His plan was to make use of Cornwall's authority to send Edgar's "picture ... far and near" to enable anyone who sees Edgar to capture him and present him for execution, and to proclaim further that anyone who harbors Edgar will be punished by death (2.1.59–62). Gloucester will also make it impossible for Edgar to flee the country since he will bar all ports (79). Edgar testifies that this plan has been carried out ("No port is free, no place / That guard and most unusual vigilance / Does not attend my taking" [2.3.3–5]).[26]

So Edgar is condemned to being hunted to death in as close to a systematic national search as early modern resources would allow. But let us return to the issue that, from Cavell's point of view, we (and Gloucester) are really meant to take seriously—that of acknowledgment. Almost the first thing that Gloucester says in the play is that he has regularly acknowledged Edmund: "I have so often blushed to acknowledge him that now I am brazed to it (1.1.9–10). Cavell does take note of Gloucester's use of the word, but insists that Gloucester has not done the acknowledgment in the proper interpersonal way (48). The (past) blushing is a problem. It connotes shame, which Cavell uncontroversially takes to include the desire to hide (not the act but the self) and also—this is his special interest—the refusal to let oneself be recognized by another, which he takes to be the precondition for recognizing another (49).[27] Of Gloucester's relation to Edmund, Cavell writes: "He [Gloucester] does not acknowledge *him* [again, Cavell's emphasis], as a son or a person" (48). This is the great failure. But what exactly does it mean in context? Gloucester does acknowledge Edmund as a son (which he did not have to do). He has also paid for Edmund's education ("his breeding... has been at my charge" [8]), which he did not have to do. Both of these actions by Gloucester give Edmund a certain status. Alan Macfarlane notes of bastardy in the period that "though its ascription might be libelous, [it] was not greatly disapproved of, *as long as the child was maintained*" (emphasis mine).[28] Heavy weather has been made—by Cavell (49) and many others—of the fact that Edmund "has been out nine years, and away he shall again" (1.1.31). But in the Tudor-Stuart period aristocratic children were often "out" for a considerable period of time for breeding.[29]

Cavell says that Gloucester does not acknowledge Edmund's "feelings of illegitimacy and being cast out" (48). But does Gloucester encourage such feelings? And what is the evidence that Edmund feels "cast out"? Gloucester states that even though he has another son, one who is both elder and legitimate, that son (Edgar) is "no dearer in [his] account" than Edmund is (1.1.19). Berger takes this to mean that Gloucester likes them both equally little, yet Berger knows that that is not the intended (or contextual) meaning.[30] Edmund never expresses any feeling of being "cast out," and states that he is quite certain that he is as dear to his father as Edgar is. In a line that critics rarely quote, Edmund asserts quite confidently that "Our father's love is to the bastard Edmund / As to the legitimate" (1.2.17–18). Edmund is apparently perfectly well acknowledged as a son and as a person. What he is not acknowledged as is as a primary heir. This is a matter of law, not of interpersonal feelings, and is treated by Edmund as such. He resents his legal, not his personal situation, and what he resents in his legal situation is as much his birth order as his birth status. As a second son, Edmund would not be Gloucester's heir even if he were legitimate.[31] The introductory scene between Gloucester, Kent, and Edmund ends with Gloucester working to incorporate Edmund into the courtly world (as both Kent and Edmund recognize and beautifully enact).

But Cavell is unrelenting. Like almost all other critics, he deplores Gloucester's ribald and casual description of Edmund's begetting. I will not go to the wall for this, but I think it possible to see even these remarks as an attempt on Gloucester's part at acknowledgment, at doing something like acknowledging Edmund's mother: she, unlike him, was not committing adultery (their relationship was "ere she had a husband"); she was beautiful ("yet was his mother fair"), and the sex seems to have been enjoyable, perhaps all the way around ("there was good sport at his making"). In any case, Cavell sees Gloucester as full of shame here, and once he can establish that, the whole failure-to-recognize-and-be-recognized dialectic can come into play. Gloucester is not willing to "see" Edmund, and therefore to be seen by him. This produces a truly astonishing sentence. Cavell and Heilman converge. Cavell's tone is not as delighted as Heilman's ("The vile jelly, the material seeing, had but caught reflections from the surfaces of life.... His physical and material loss is his spiritual gain"),[32] but the moralism and sense of satisfaction are equally strong (as is the prominence of "spiritual"). Cavell's claim is even more startling (we are accustomed, after all, to the pat kind of supposedly Christian, supposedly Platonic paradoxes that Heilman postulates). Cavell states, unequivocally, that "Gloucester suffers the same punishment he inflicts" (49).

But that is quite insane. Whatever wrong Gloucester (supposedly) did Edmund, it surely is not "the same" as having one's eyes gouged out. Cavell's explanation of this claim smacks of bad faith. Cavell writes: "In his respectability, he [Gloucester] avoided eyes; when respectability falls away and the disreputable come into power, his eyes are avoided" (49). One hardly knows what to say about such a sentence. "Respectability" is a very odd axis on which to place the events in question, and insofar as one wants to use this terminology, "respectability fall[ing] away" has nothing to do with Gloucester's recent behavior, which has been heroic in aiding his "old master" ("Though [F "If"] I die for it, as no less is threatened me, the King my old master must be relieved" [3.3.16–17]). There is something truly odd in speaking of the outright villains of the play—all of whom, including Edmund (in prospect), are highly "reputable"—as "the disreputable." But most of all, the weirdness and moral insanity culminate in speaking of Gloucester's eyes being "avoided." This is either a bad pun or an intolerable euphemism (or both). His eyes are not "avoided." They are smashed by the heel of a boot.

What is lost in the shift from physical to psychic cruelty is both the physical reality of the blinding of Gloucester and the special horror at the perpetrators thereof, since, according to Cavell, practically everyone in the play blinds Gloucester. Again, Cavell is unrelenting. Lear's mad harping on Gloucester's blindness in the scene between the two old men at Dover is Lear "picking at Gloucester's eyes" (51). It is "active cruelty ... deliberate cruelty" (50–51). Cavell will not see it as Lear trying, in a mad way, to come to terms with what has happened to Gloucester—which he first discovers here. When Lear says to Gloucester, "If thou wilt weep my fortunes, take my eyes" (Q 4.6.164; F 4.5.169), he is not, as Cavell says, offering Gloucester "a crazy consolation." Lear is offering Gloucester sympathy. He is sorrowing for Gloucester. One might well want to say that he is *acknowledging* Gloucester's situation. Lear is saying (meaning) that Gloucester's situation is such that Gloucester can save his weeping for himself; what Lear is expressing is the thought that Gloucester's situation is at least as bad as Lear's own. It is a moment of lucidity, not of madness. The next line is "I know thee well enough; thy name is Gloucester." Cavell sees Lear as asserting the uniqueness of his own suffering, saying, "Your eyes wouldn't have done you any good anyway in this case; you would need to see what I have seen to weep my fortunes" (51–52). But at this moment, Lear is not focused on himself. He is actually focusing on another, on Gloucester. But for Cavell, we are back to the notion of being "spiritually" implicated, and the word, in this same odd usage, recurs here. Lear's "picking" at Gloucester's eyes "spiritually relates Lear to Cornwall's and Regan's act in first blinding Gloucester" (52). Again, to use a word that was supposed to indicate Cavell's own commitment, the *specificity* of Cornwall's and Regan's "act"—again spoken of in the most general way (recall "Cornwall's deed")—is lost. Cornwall and Regan are not the ones who "first" blind Gloucester. They are the ones who do so.

But the character who is most powerfully tarred by the brush of Cavell's version of the sight-pattern is Edgar. Condemning Edgar for not revealing himself to Gloucester until Edgar is armed is something of a cottage industry in Shakespeare studies.[33] Cavell contributes mightily to it (as does Berger, as we shall see). Cavell sees Edgar as, like almost everyone else in the play, "avoiding recognition," which is then immediately—and, again, I would say, bizarrely—equated with "mutilating cruelty" (54). The moment in question is indeed a puzzling one, and something like "avoiding recognition" may be involved. But again Cavell's reading of the passage is oddly tone-deaf. As in Cavell's reading of "If you would weep my fortunes, take my eyes" and his understanding of what Cornwall does not wish Gloucester to see, Cavell's analysis is oddly (for someone powerfully affected by J. L. Austin) unconcerned with identifying the actual speech-act being performed.[34]

The passage in question is when Gloucester exclaims:

> Ah dear son Edgar,
> The food of thy abused father's wrath,
> Might I but live to see thee in my touch,
> I'd say I had eyes again. (4.1.19–22)

I think that it is possible that this moment could and perhaps should be staged with Edgar-as-Tom hiding off to one side, so that he can see Gloucester and the Old Man and comment on the sight, but cannot hear their words. In support of this staging, I note that if "Tom" were in plain sight, the Old Man would not say "How now, who's there?" right after Gloucester's speech (23). The Old Man seems just then to be noticing the presence of another person whom he cannot see.[35] Cavell (like most critics) is certain that Edgar hears the speech, so that Edgar "deprives Gloucester of his eyes again" (55). This links him, "as Lear was and will be linked, to Cornwall and the sphere of open evil"; it shows Edgar's "capacity for cruelty," which is "the *same* cruelty as that of the evil characters" (55; Cavell's emphasis). But whatever it is that Edgar is doing or not doing here—even assuming that he does hear the relevant words—it is certainly not "the *same* cruelty" as that inflicted by Cornwall on Gloucester ("deprives Gloucester of his eyes" is, like "his eyes are avoided," a formulation that obscures obvious difference, and functions, with regard to the diegetic reality, as another unbearable euphemism).

But there is more to be said. Again, I am not convinced that Cavell is following the words. He treats the "Might I but live" lines as if Gloucester were saying that being able to embrace Edgar would cure his blindness. But Gloucester is not saying this. He is saying that if he could embrace Edgar, he would *say* that he had eyes again. Gloucester is imagining a counterfactual hyperbolic exclamation that he would make in the imagined situation. By not revealing himself, Edgar is depriving Gloucester of the experience of "seeing" Edgar "in [his] touch," and of the chance to make the imagined joyously hyperbolical rhetorical assertion. If we are going to "follow the words," we must take the whole utterance, including "I'd say," into account.

But this is still to avoid the matter of avoidance. Whether or not Edgar hears Gloucester's exclamation, the fact is that he does not reveal himself to his father in 4.1. This is what he is constantly critically rebuked for (and, in the Folio, rebukes himself for—"Never, O fault" is a Folio-only moment; the Quarto has "O father" [5.3: Q 186; F 184]. But the play itself makes it clear that it is not easy for a father who has radically abused a child to deal with what he (the father) has done. Gloucester knows that he has wrongly disinherited and proscribed Edgar. But he does not know that Edgar was "Tom," who "made [Gloucester] think a man a worm," though Gloucester did have some intuition of a connection between "Tom" and Edgar (4.1.32–33). Lear we are told later is (in the Quarto) avoiding Cordelia out of, as Kent wittily puts it, "A sovereign shame" or, a few lines later, "a burning shame" (Q 4.3.42, 46). It does not seem "cruel" to want to spare one's parent from this, if possible.[36] Edgar's revelation of his identity as Poor Tom to his father at a moment when Edgar is armed (5.3: Q 187; F 185) can be seen as protective of his father, not—as Cavell takes it—of himself. Refusing to let oneself be recognized can be a matter of protecting another rather than oneself from shame. The moment should also be recognized as Edgar's last chance to reveal himself, since he did not know whether he was going to survive the single combat with Edmund. But, for Cavell, such accounts are insufficiently psychological—or rather, they are not psychological in the right way.

Space does not permit me to deal with Cavell's reading of the "love-test" in the first scene, since I want to move on to Harry Berger's critiques of Edgar and company, but suffice it to say that two of Cavell's major claims about this moment do not seem persuasive to me: first, that Lear is avoiding love in this exercise rather than clumsily seeking it; and second, that what Lear actually wants is flattery, the pretense of love. Cavell creates a witty paradox in saying that in speaking the truth to Lear, Cordelia would not be giving him what he wants but would be providing "*dissembled flattery*" (65; Cavell's emphasis) rather than the real (false) thing. Since one cannot pretend to feel something that one does feel, and since Cordelia does love Lear, she cannot pretend to do so (62).[37] This seems too clever by half, as the British would say, and too peremptorily dismissive of less tricky, more "ordinary" accounts of both Cordelia's behavior and Lear's desires.[38]

From Symbolism to Cynicism

One of the striking features of both Cavell's and Berger's interpretive work is that they are aware of objections to their procedures. Cavell notes of his reading of the opening of *Lear* that "it may be felt that I have forced this scene too far in order to fit it to my reading" (66); elsewhere in *Disowning Knowledge*, he speaks of (and defends) the "over-excitement" (158) of one of his readings (this is in relation to his treatment of *Coriolanus*, which is again oriented against a reading that would insist on the literal—in that case Brecht's [146]).

Berger acknowledges two objections to his critical procedures: cynicism and anachronism. The first is the deeper and more important. C. L. Barber (in conversation?) is said to have launched the charge of cynicism, and stated that Berger's readings lack "the minimal level of sympathy for and generosity toward the fictional objects of his criticism" that is necessary for anything like an adequate response to "the human claims" that characters make on the critic (50).[39] Berger's answer to this is that in his demonstrations of the "complicity" ("spiritual implication" Cavell would say) of the not obviously wicked with the very obviously wicked, Berger, the "structural" ironist, is only assigning "responsibility," not guilt (52). Berger insists that he is not using "the language of praise or blame" in arguing for such complicity (68). He is not adopting "the unpleasant perspective of the ethical judge" (52). But this—like his even more outrageous claim that his readings of the motives of characters "have nothing to do with the unconscious" (53)—is disingenuous. Complicity is certainly a term of ethical judgment, as its presence in legal contexts confirms. What all this shows is that Berger feels the strength of the charge of cynicism.[40] With regard to the charge of anachronism, he believes this charge to be "less securely grounded" than that of cynicism (52). I am not sure. The early moderns certainly did not hold that there was no such thing as goodness, but only "goodness." Even Machiavelli did not think this (his doubt was not about the existence of goodness but about its usefulness in the political world); neither did Luther or Calvin insofar as they held that regeneration had an ethical as well as a soteriological dimension. We will examine later a particular case where the two charges against Berger's practice come together.

With regard to negatively judging characters who are not obviously wicked, Berger's position with regard to Cavell is that of Regan's to Goneril's first speech: it is right as far as it goes but "comes too short" (F 1.1.71). Again, Edgar is the focus. Antagonism between Edgar and Gloucester is taken as a given based on Edgar's status as Gloucester's heir (55). So Edmund (as not having this status) can be finessed, and Edgar's "complicity" begins earlier than Cavell thinks it does. As Poor Tom, Edgar is filled with rage (61). Here as elsewhere, the key to Berger's reading is his commitment to what he calls, only semi-ironically, "the value of the victim's role" (42), where this "value" is seen in its implied (and, by the agent, enjoyed) accusatory power and licensed desire for retaliation. On this view, all suffering can be turned into a version (or enactment) of aggression. Unsurprisingly, the "sight-pattern" again emerges. When Edgar states that one of the supposed fiends who supposedly torment Tom "gives the web and the pin, squinies the eye" (Q 3.4.104), Edgar must be referring to the father who (long before 3.7) has "obscured vision"; and when, during the "mock-trial" (Q 3.6.20–21), Edgar babbles "Look where he stands and glares! Want'st thou eyes at trial madam?" Edgar is referring to blindness and "conducting his own trial, probably of his father" (62).[41] What this means is that Edgar had long "entertained the idea that blindness would be a just symbol, if not a just punishment" for—and here Berger's reliance on Cavell surfaces—"Gloucester's inability truly to see him" (63). What shocks Edgar after the blinding is not, for Berger, Edgar's sight of his father "poorly led" (F and Qa) or "parti-eyed" (Qb) but "the shock of [his own] complicity" in the situation: "presumably what he cannot bear about his father's maimed appearance is his having entertained this idea" (of maiming and blinding him [63]).[42] These readings are not only forced and dramatically unlikely, but it seems fair to say that they do manifest less than a "minimal level of sympathy for and generosity toward the fictional objects of his criticism."

We must take note of how "presumably" is used here. It represents a deeply characteristic move in Berger's criticism. The word makes sense when it refers to something implied by the text but not explicitly stated or shown, something noncontroversial (Lear, for instance *presumably* went to Cornwall's residence before appearing at Gloucester's). But that is not how Berger uses it. He uses it, as above, to assign motives. As I have suggested, he always knows better than the characters do what their true motives are, and he is happy, as in this case, to assign their true motives to them. He has no commitment to capturing what the characters ostensibly mean or what is plausible in a dramatic context. With regard to his commentary on the speech that opens *Henry IV, Part 1* Berger states that "it may have been apparent that when I was describing Henry's motives in the preceding section, I was sloppy and evasive in my treatment of their intentional or cognitive status" (244). But as the casualness of "it may have been apparent" makes clear, Berger is not actually worried about such a procedure. His "Lacanian" conception of "text" demands this, since it always involves attending to "the textual matrix" rather than its mere verbal surface—which he thinks is all that performance can capture.[43] What is under the "surface" must always be darker.[44]

Even when Berger attempts acknowledgment of virtuous intent, he cannot allow it to stand. Of the mock-miracle that Edgar produces for his father, Berger asserts handsomely that "there is no doubt in my mind that Edgar's 'Why I do trifle thus with his despair / Is done to cure it' is to be taken at face value" (63). But the next sentence begins, "It is nevertheless the case that this is an act of symbolic parricide." The next paragraph, treating Edgar's revelation of the identity of "Tom" to Gloucester, begins with the words "The execution of Gloucester." In this discussion, Berger usefully cites a sentence (64) from the source of the Gloucester strand in *Lear* (Sidney's *Arcadia*) in which a blinded and penitent father notes that his good son has been a poor "historian" in not blaming his father.[45] Berger writes—and here it is again—"Edgar was presumably a better historian" (64), meaning that he did punitively blame his father for his sufferings. But, again, what other than a premise about psychology justifies this "presumably" is never made clear. In a parallel moment involving interpersonal history, Cordelia insists on being, in the relevant sense, a poor historian in asserting that she has "no cause" for punitive anger toward her father. Naturally, this moment annoys Berger. He has his own reading of it—in terms of "complicity." Cordelia is complicit in helping Lear "refuse to acknowledge the wrong he did her" (xii). This is not only remarkably ungenerous but bizarre, given that Lear has just said, "If you have poison for me, I will drink it" (Q 4.7.69; F 4.6.66).

As this suggests, Cordelia does not escape Berger's search for darker purposes. With regard to Lear's original plan in the opening scene, we are told that "the thought of Lear's setting his rest on her kind nursery (a heavy phrase! a heavy rest) must surely be oppressive to her, though she is not likely to admit it to herself" (42). Again, a feeling is attributed to a character by sheer postulation—here by way of "must surely" rather than "presumably." The critic knows much better than the character what she is (must be) feeling. Why this "must surely" be so is never explained, and the heavy parenthetical interjections of "heavy" are sheer rhetorical manipulation. All of this rests on a psychological theory that sees resentment as the most fundamental human response.[46] Berger offers a similar reading of Cordelia's "For thee, oppressed King, I am cast down," where an expression of other-directed sadness and empathy is read as resentment (46). "For" is read as "By." Berger knows that this is not what Cordelia means to say, but as always, this does not matter. The text, apart from context, could conceivably be read this way, and therefore this reading must be admitted. All verbal possibilities are actual, especially if they, as Berger says, incur "a worse meaning" (46).

No good deed goes uncriticized. Here Berger diverges from Cavell. Cavell is not afflicted with generalized cynicism. He is basically sympathetic to Cordelia in the first scene, in however strained a fashion, and he speaks lyrically of the "gratitude and relief" properly evoked by the words and behavior of France in the scene. Cavell not only defends such feelings but asserts that he sees "the validity of such feelings as touchstones of the accuracy of a reading of the play" (65). This is a surprisingly strong claim. Berger will have none of it. The king of France is overly self-satisfied, and "diminishes [Cordelia] by dwelling on his largesse" (43). The King is chided for "indulging nice antitheses" ("Most choice forsaken, most loved, despised" [1.1: Q 240; F 250]), and these are somehow "at her [Cordelia's] expense." Berger makes a fine historical-legal point in stating that France is "invoking the law of salvage" in "I take up what's cast away," but this is somehow held against the King, as if he meant only the negative sides of the "nice antitheses."[47] That France is doing something unimaginably grand is irrelevant. Moreover, the "nice antitheses" can be read differently. Shakespeare seems to be showing the character trying to find words to conceptualize the situation and his feelings—"'Tis strange . . . My love should kindle" [1.1: Q 243–

44; F 253–54]). Denigrating Cordelia hardly seems the point. However, Berger is certain (and here we get the words again)—"*surely* France's condescension *must* rankle [Cordelia]" (44; emphasis mine). This is the point where anachronism and cynicism coincide. "Condescension" is indeed a relevant notion, but a bit of historical work can easily recover the very positive sense that the term (and concept) normally had in the period (a society in which hierarchy was accepted as normal appreciated moments when it was ignored).[48] Further, Cordelia is blamed—I see no other word for it here—for committing (as she says) her father to her sisters (Q 1.1.261; F 1.1.271)—as if at this point she had a choice in the matter. But that is mere plot. Her words committing her father to the "professed bosoms" of her sisters are seen as intending his punishment by the sisters rather than as urging them to live up to their "large speeches." But again, "whatever she consciously intends" does not matter (44).

Berger is committed to reading the play only in personal and psychological terms. Here Cavell and Berger come together. Berger's successive chapters are "*King Lear*: The Family Romance" and (as subtitle) "The Gloucester Family Romance." Cavell's ideological commitments are less obvious and more original (his particular battle with skepticism), but he too shares the private, interpersonal focus. This leads these critics to ignore such plot matters as war, resistance, and treason, and either to occlude or to downgrade one of the most striking and distinctive thematic strands of the play: its concern for the material conditions of human life.[49] Cavell simply does not mention such matters; they do not vector into his focus. Berger is aware of the sociological aspect of the play but finds it ludicrous and / or irrelevant. After quoting the extraordinary speech (prayer in the Folio) about "Poor naked wretches" (3.4: Q 23–32; F 28–36) that Lear makes just before he actually encounters what looks to be one of such, Berger states that "on the face of it," this speech might seem to be "converting wretchedness to fellow feeling" (38). But we know all about "on the face of it." Lear is—and here we get another "presumably"—imagining himself regaining power (as if, after Lear says, "I have ta'en / Too little care of this," he were continuing to address himself when he exhorts "Pomp" to "take physic"). Lear is making, Berger says with a kind of sneer, "what sounds like a suggestion for better housing and other economic reforms" (38). But that is only what the speech "sounds like."

The main point for Berger is that "these reflections are conspicuously irrelevant" to Lear's experience and to the play as a whole (38). The only real function they can have is psychological. When this speech is brought into alignment with Lear's initial speech banishing Cordelia, "the conspicuous irrelevance of Lear's prayer comes to seem more like conspicuous evasion." So we can criticize Lear for this speech too. In it he is merely evading his responsibility for his mistreatment of Cordelia and revision of his initial plan. Yet before the end of the first act, Lear has already condemned himself for bad judgment (1.4: Q 257–59; F 240–42) and said of Cordelia "I did her wrong" (1.5: Q 23; F 21). Berger skips over almost everything in the first two acts of the play after the opening scenes: the refusal of housing and "accommodation" to Lear by Goneril and Regan and company; the specific "shape" and social position that Edgar adopts. The "prayer" for the poor is the only piece of this aspect of the play that Berger considers, and his final comment on this speech is that it is "facile" and "misdirected" (39). Lear cannot actually be expressing concern for the poor; he cannot actually be building on his own wretched situation to expand his sphere of sympathy and concern. We must not be distracted by what the speech "sounds like."

I hope that it has now become clear that something has gone very wrong in these critical accounts. Obviously they are right about some things: there is language of blindness in the play as well as the enactment of it; the timing of Edgar's revelation to his father is something to be thought about, as is the dynamic that leads Cordelia to so outrage Lear in the opening scene. Stanley Cavell and Harry Berger are intelligent people, as are the critics who have followed them. So was Robert Heilman. But there is something in the world of literary criticism that allows the odd results that we have examined to emerge—and not only to emerge but to be taken as definitive or at least highly persuasive. It looks as if what is needed in literary criticism is something like ordinary awareness and common sense. In the actual world, the difference between, on the one hand, avoidance or delayed revelation, and on the other, physical mutilation, is obvious and hardly needs to be argued for. Motives—whether an action is done out of love or hatred—matter. Conscious intentions matter. The "face value" of an utterance is generally not to be discarded; a special argument is needed for doing so. Kenneth Gross, in an essay on Berger that is generally admiring, nonetheless finds himself asserting that there have to be times when such utterances as "Take this gift" or "I honor you" are not "inevitably subject to suspicion."[50] Moreover, the nature of actions matters—sending one's father to be tortured is different from creating a fiction to preserve his psychic equilibrium. Imperfection is normally distinguished from wickedness; moral growth is normally applauded rather than dismissed.[51] And, in the actual world, "better housing and other economic reforms" really do matter.

What is odd is having to say these things. Dr. Johnson rejoiced when he was able, as he said, "to concur with the common reader."[52] As literary critics, and as readers of literary criticism, we need to maintain our common sense, and not (to use one of Wittgenstein's favorite formulations) allow ourselves to be "bewitched" by "shrewd" or "deep" remarks or schemes that cannot survive the light of common day. Literary criticism as well as philosophy sometimes needs to be brought "home."[53] It seems strange to have to say this of an "ordinary language" philosopher, but, as I have already suggested, I think that Stanley Cavell—in at least some of his literary criticism, especially the essays on *Lear* and on *Coriolanus*—does not in fact do "ordinary language criticism," and that such criticism, together with "ordinary" ethical sense, is what is needed to bring literary criticism into alignment with how literary works actually mean and function in the world of "ordinary" human life.[54] This is not to say that there is nothing beneath the "surface" of literary works, but only that the surface must be taken fully into account before anything else is concluded, and that we must proceed to the depths only when the surface invites or requires that we do so.[55]

PART II

Systems

CHAPTER 4

Shakespeare and Legal Systems

The Better the Worse (but Not Vice Versa)

One of the great advantages that literary texts have over others is that literary texts—unlike, for instance, legal ones—do not have to resolve the problems that they raise; they just have to raise them in interesting and provocative ways. This may be true of some philosophical texts as well, though even these sorts of philosophical texts tend to suggest some sort of resolution or accommodation of the difficulties they note. Literary texts do not even have to do that. With this in mind, the problem that I want to raise and ponder in the following essay is this: while there is no doubt that Shakespeare was able to imagine a great range of things, one of the things that he seemed consistently unable to imagine was a reasonably attractive and well-functioning legal system. What I will try to show, in fairly brief compass, is that in every instance in which Shakespeare seems to imagine such and to give it the recognizable features of such, he also immediately raises issues that complicate, undermine, or call into question the possibility and even desirability of such a thing.

Impartiality

I will focus primarily on the second part of *Henry IV*, a play that has figured relatively little in the recent spate of work on Shakespeare and the law.[1] This play seems to be committed to highlighting and endorsing one central feature of a properly functioning legal system: impartiality, the law applying equally to everyone within its jurisdiction. This would seem to be an unquestionable good. The figure who embodies this in the play is, appropriately, the Lord Chief Justice of England, who had, on an occasion referred to but not dramatized by Shakespeare, ordered Prince Hal, the heir apparent of the kingdom, to confinement for showing gross disrespect for the Chief Justice and his position (striking him, in the earlier play on this material).[2] It is significant that Shakespeare chose not to stage this scene. I do not think this was because Shakespeare did not want to show his Prince Hal behaving in that way but rather because Shakespeare did not want to present his Lord Chief Justice demeaned, visibly, in that way. What he did want is to have the Lord Chief Justice explain at length the rationale for his behavior, and to do so just at the moment of Hal's elevation to the kingship. When Shakespeare has Hal, about to be formally crowned King Henry V, recall the "indignities" the Justice laid upon him, Shakespeare has the Justice reply thus:

> I then did use the person of your father;
> The image of his power lay then in me;
> And in th' administration of his law,
> Whiles I was busy for the commonwealth,
> Your highness pleased to forget my place,
> The majesty and power of law and justice,
> The image of the King whom I presented,
> And struck me in my very seat of judgment;
> Whereon as an offender to your father,
> I gave bold way to my authority
> And did commit you.[3] (5.2.73–83)

There are two major features, not entirely compatible, in this eloquent and detailed account. The first of these, and probably the dominant one, is the Chief Justice's stress on "personation."[4] He uses the term in exactly the Hobbesian sense of a "person" being an entity entitled to act publicly as an agent either of himself or of someone or something else.[5] The stress on this in the passage is very strong—"the person of your father; / The image of his power ... The image of the King." An "image" here is thought of not as a simulacrum but as an agent, a representative, someone in whom the power of someone or something else is made present ("The image of the King whom I presented"), a "presenter" rather than (or as well as) a representation.[6] This conception of legal entitlement culminates in a reference to "authority" (which will be Hobbes's key term), and to a merging of the representative and the represented: "struck me ... as ... your father." The other conception of legal "authority" in the passage is the less absolutist, more procedural one that Lorna Hutson is interested in.[7] The mention of "th' administration of his law" mediates between the two conceptions, where the impersonality of "th' administration" and potentially of "law" is qualified by the personal pronoun, "his law." The next line, however, moves fully into the alternate conception: "I was busy for the commonwealth." Suddenly the King has disappeared, and the Chief Justice acts in the name and authority of an abstract political body, the normal English translation of *res publica*.[8] The young prince is an exalted individual, "Your highness," who acted willfully ("pleased to forget"), while the Justice's authority is abstract and structural, coming from, as he says, his "place." In the next line the legal system becomes its own king: "The majesty... of law and justice." To add to this mix, the final reference to the Justice's "place" gives it a kind of biblical sacrality in the mention of "my very seat of judgment."[9]

The one thing that we can say about the conceptions of "authority" in this passage is that they are both impersonal. When the speech finally arrives at an "I-Thou" relation—"I did... commit you"—and seems to involve some personal passion ("I gave bold way"), it turns out that that the actual agent of punishment is "authority," and there is—and this is the key claim—nothing directly personal in it ("an offender to your father"). In all of this personation, there are no people. The new king is being asked to give the matter "cold considerance" and to speak in his "state" (98–99). He does so, and commends the Chief Justice's "bold, just, and impartial spirit" (along, it should be noted, with commending his own willingness to condescend to be judged in this way). So impartiality of this sort would seem to be an unquestioned and unquestionable virtue. If legal reform were truly at the heart of this play, the Lord Chief Justice would be its hero.[10]

Yet, in the play, the interchange between the new king and the Lord Chief Justice is embedded in another context. Surrounding the scene in which the above speech occurs are scenes at the home of a much lesser man of law, a country justice, Master Robert Shallow (the Lord Chief Justice is not given a name; he exists entirely as a position). These scenes evoke in detail the life of a nonaristocratic country estate (like that of Petruchio in *The Taming of the Shrew*). In the first of them (5.1) we see Justice Shallow arranging a supper for his visitor, Sir John Falstaff. Falstaff is amused at how concerned Shallow is with the details of his estate, and how close Shallow is to his servants ("Their spirits," says Falstaff quite grandly, and in highly Latinate and semilegal terms, are "married in conjunction, with the participation of society" [5.1.65–67])—a kind of "participation" very different from that by which the Lord Chief Justice participates in the power of the king. The head of the servants seems to be one Davy. In the midst of the "business" of arranging for the supper, Davy interjects a legal matter. Just as we are on an ordinary country estate here, we are made privy here (entirely in prose) to an ordinary legal dispute, one that does not involve princes and Lord Chief Justices.[11]

Suddenly and startlingly, we are in the world of specific (and perhaps actual) ordinary people.[12] Davy says to Justice Shallow: "I beseech you, sir, to countenance William Visor of Woncot against Clement Perkes a' th' Hill." Justice Shallow replies that he is familiar with the legal record of the defendant in this case—"There is many complaints, Davy, against that Visor"—and assures Davy that "that Visor is an arrant knave, on my knowledge." Davy's reply is worth quoting in full:

> I grant your worship that he is a knave, sir; but yet God forbid, sir, but a knave should have some countenance at his friend's request. An honest man, sir, is able to speak for himself, when a knave is not. I have served your worship truly, sir, this eight years; and if I cannot once or twice in a quarter bear out a knave against an honest man, I have but very little credit with your worship. The knave is mine honest friend, sir, therefore I beseech your worship let, him be countenanced.
> (5.1.40–48)

Now, obviously this is funny, and meant to be so. But it raises some issues that the play is very interested in, and that Shakespeare is very interested in. There are two major issues here: the first is the relation between justice and friendship (or other personal relations—here, service); the second, the whole matter of dealing with transgressions (since the fact of Visor's "knavery" is stipulated).

The first of these is an issue with which the entire span of the *Henry IV* plays has been concerned. Aristotle noted, in his immensely influential treatment of friendship in the *Nicomachean Ethics*, that "when people are friends, they have no need of justice."[13] What Aristotle means by this is not at all clear. He may mean, as Christine Korsgaard argues, that friendship is the model for justice, and includes it; or he may mean, as Bernard Williams would argue, that there is a deep difference between the kinds of relationships that the terms denote.[14] Shakespeare's view seems to me closer to Williams's. One might be tempted—as a modern, and not at all following Aristotle—to say that friendship operates in the "private" realm, and justice in the "public" one.[15] But Shakespeare has set up the *Henry IV* plays in a way that keeps the two realms in constant juxtaposition, and threatens (or promises) to allow them to mingle.

Things that seem, from the point of view of the public realm, to be obvious values, are put under pressure by this juxtaposition. E. M. Forster famously (or infamously) wrote, "If I had to choose between betraying my country and betraying my friend, I hope I should have the guts to betray my country."[16] Forster was being consciously provocative here, but he did have a point about the importance in our lives of "love and loyalty" to individual persons. He thought Dante agreed with him.[17]

The figure who primarily exercises the pressure on impersonality in the *Henry IV* plays is not Davy but the character who describes himself (I am certain with complete accuracy) as having been "born about three of the clock in the afternoon, with a white head, and something a round belly" (*2H4*, 1.2.186–88). The Falstaff of the plays is completely Shakespeare's creation. That Prince Hal frequented the taverns of London is an inevitable part of the story; that he did so with the primary companion that Shakespeare gives him is not (in fact, as all Shakespeare scholars know, Shakespeare had to apologize for the historical name that he had initially used to insert this figure into the fictional-historical context, and had to change the figure's name from "Oldcastle" to "Falstaff").[18]

The very beginning of the *Henry IV* sequence sets in motion the pressure on public and abstract values. The opening line of the first play, spoken by the eponymous character, ends on the word "care," which here means something like "anxiety" or "worried concern." The public world, the world of politics (and of law) is a world of care and of constant strife. The second scene of the play introduces us to an alternate world. On the one hand, it is a world of lawlessness; Falstaff fantasizes that when Hal is king, there will be no gallows standing in England (this could merely signify a lack of capital punishment—many thinkers and juries thought that there were too many crimes that were supposed to be capital[19]—but Falstaff clearly means it to signify no punishments whatever for crime). Yet on the other hand, the world for which Falstaff stands seems to be a world of abundance, of enjoyment, of leisure, of companionship, and of freedom from "care." Peace, in the King's opening lines, pants and is "shortwinded"—like Falstaff. The Prince has to goad Falstaff into performing an actual robbery. Falstaff's "vocation," as he wonderfully and outrageously claims, is highway robbery, but his life seems mainly to consist of sharing drink and, most of all, talk—talk of all kinds (insults, jokes, etc.)—with his longtime companions.[20] What he seems to offer, most of all, is a realm of happy and shared play. When, at the end of this hitherto all-prose scene, Hal steps out from it and gives a serious, blank-verse soliloquy explaining that he is not really engaged in the world in which he seems to manifest "the participation of society," and that his apparent engagement with this world is in fact a calculated strategy for making an impression on the political world, we cannot but feel a kind of shudder. "Cold consideration" and lack of concern for one's relationships with particular persons are already under pressure. "I know you all," Hal says chillingly.

I want to pause for a moment on this assertion and ask what exactly it means. What exactly is the knowledge that is in question here? It is impartial—one might say, judicial—knowledge, knowledge of all the faults, limits, and crimes of this group. It is the kind of knowledge that would be appropriate to a Stoic sage—"Unmoved, cold, and to temptation slow."[21] Hal here manifests exactly the characteristics that Erasmus's Dame Folly claims make Stoics incapable of true friendship and true social participation. She thinks that friendship involves precisely not noticing faults, and she claims that in the unlikely event that "it should happen that some of these severe wisemen should become friendly with each other, their friendship is hardly stable or long-lasting, because they are so sour and sharp-sighted that they detect their friends' faults with an eagle eye."[22] Hal is not like the (Stoic) wise man who disrupts a party "by his gloomy countenance,"[23] but Hal does share the wise man's attitudes and "cold eye." Even when Hal is apparently participating in the social world, he keeps reminding Falstaff of the gallows (*1H4*, 1.2.38ff.). On the other hand, while Hal is, in his way, participating in Falstaff's world, he takes it upon himself to act as if he shared Davy's view that "a knave should have some countenance at his friend's request." In part 1, Hal lies to the sheriff, the watch, and the Lord Chief Justice himself, who have come to Eastcheap in pursuit of Falstaff and company for the robbery at Gadshill. "The man, I do assure you, is not here," says Hal, directly lying (2.4.505); and in one of his final speeches in part 1, Hal assures Falstaff that he will lie for him again: "If a lie may do thee grace, / I'll gild it with the happiest terms I have" (5.4.156–57).[24]

A great deal depends on what is contrasted with the world of politics and law, the world of "cold considerance." In part 1 of *Henry IV*, two worlds contrast with the legal-political one—not just the world of Falstaff but also that of Hotspur. It is easy to think of Hotspur and Falstaff as opposites, and, in relation to courage or martial heroism, they surely are so. It is therefore easy to generate a tidy "Aristotelian" scheme with Hotspur at the extreme of martial foolhardiness, Falstaff at the extreme of cowardice, and Hal as the "golden mean" between them.[25] That is certainly plausible. But the more interesting, and, I believe, deeper reading of the plays sees Falstaff and Hotspur as equally divorced from the world of "cool reason" and of "policy."[26] Hotspur is consistently associated with the world of "imagination." In the first scene in which we see him, "Imagination of some high exploit / Drives him beyond the bounds of patience"; "He apprehends a world of figures... / But not the form of what he should attend" (*1H4*, 1.3.197–98, 207); in the battle in which he dies, he is seen as having "with great imagination / Proper to madmen, led his powers to death" (*2H4*, 1.3.31–32). Like Falstaff, who asserts, very memorably, that "the lion will not touch the true prince" (*1H4*, 2.2.267), Hotspur's imagination is filled with themes from romance (his uncle, Worcester, brings him into the plot against Henry by presenting it as equivalent to walking, Lancelot-like, over "a current roaring loud / On the unsteadfast footing of a spear" (*1H4*, 1.3.191–92).[27] Hotspur and Falstaff are both "lunatics," brilliantly projecting lunar mythology ("To pluck bright honor from the pale-faced moon"; "let us be Diana's foresters... minions of the moon") (*1H4*: 1.3.200; 1.2.25–26). They are both drunks. Hotspur is the first inebriate that we meet—"drunk with choler?" Northumberland asks him (*1H4*, 1.3.127). And Hotspur and Falstaff share both a deep contempt for the "frosty-spirited" (see Hotspur at *1H4*, 2.3.2 and Falstaff on "the cold blood [Hal] did naturally inherit from his father" at *2H4*, 4.3.116). They share an equally deep contempt for respectable citizens and their wives, who do not know how to swear "a good mouth-filling oath" (see Hotspur on his wife's "in good sooth" at *1H4*, 3.1.240–50 and Falstaff on "yea-forsooth" knaves at *2H4*, 1.2.36).

The key fact about the second part of *Henry IV* is the one that is made momentarily ambiguous at the opening: that Hotspur is dead. There is no heroic dimension to war or to negotiation (Hotspur haggles for fun and honor; see *1H4*, 3.1.130–35).[28] Whereas the great martial triumph in part 1 was a hand-to-hand combat between two impressive warriors, the military triumph in part 2 is a triumph of treachery—although understood as being legally and politically mitigated by being treachery to the treasonous (a practice that the Elizabethans had perhaps come to countenance in their dealings with the Irish).[29] Moreover, the prince in question—not Hal, but his brother, John—insists, probably correctly, that from a technical and legalistic point of view, he does not break his word with the rebels when he has them arrested and proscribed after a parley and a negotiated peace. He promised, "Upon [his] soul," that he would redress the "griefs" that the rebels had listed in their "articles," and he said, "If this [that is, redress of the listed complaints] may please you, / Discharge your powers" (*2H4*, 4.2.60–61). He fully intends, he says, to keep his word and to redress the griefs. The rebel lords had not specified that they would not be arrested and executed, so John is not, technically, breaking his word with them at all.[30]

Shakespeare keeps the basic contrast of the whole *Henry IV* sequence in our minds by having Falstaff, in the scene following this one, give a long soliloquy on the cold-bloodedness and antifestive nature of Prince John ("he drinks no wine" [*2H4*, 4.3.87]). But the theme is present even in the "victory" scene itself. Prince John offers the rebels not only his "princely word" but also a promise of friendship and conviviality: "Let's," he says, "drink together friendly and embrace" (4.2.63). Both he and his right-hand man (Westmoreland) actually drink to the leaders with whom they have just made a treaty. Drinking "together friendly" is, needless to say, Falstaff's world in the play. He is right that Prince John has, in fact, nothing to do with it. But perhaps this is too benign a view of what Falstaff stands for. The Lord Chief Justice sees Falstaff as standing for legal impunity—"power to do wrong," as he says (*2H4*, 2.1.128). The dying King Henry IV presents a tremendous vision of lawlessness as terrifying, a vision in which conviviality merges into serious criminality. He sees Hal as going to allow ruffians not only to "swear, drink, dance / [and] Revel the night" but also to "rob, murder, and commit / The oldest sins the newest kind of ways." Lest this latter sound oddly attractive, Shakespeare gives the dying king an image of almost biblical force to represent lawlessness: "the wild dog / Shall flesh his tooth on every innocent" (*2H4*, 4.5.124–32).[31]

Yet what we actually see contrasted with the world of politics and law in the play is not a world of spectacular and violent injustice but merely the world of conviviality. In his first interchange with the Lord Chief Justice, Falstaff explains that he has used the law concerning his status in the military to evade the law's claim on him ("I was then advised by my learned council in the laws of this land-service" [*2H4*, 1.2.133–34]),[32] but the realm of law truly enters Falstaff's world when Mistress Quickly sends for officers to arrest him on a suit of debt (and perhaps of breach of promise—with regard to his supposedly having promised to make her "my lady thy wife" [*2H4*, 2.1.90]). When Falstaff physically resists the officers, the Lord Chief Justice appears again, insisting on decorum and asking Sir John, "Doth this become your place, your time, your business?" (*2H4*, 2.1.64). But public decorum is not involved in the resolution of this suit. The resolution comes, when, after a bit of unstaged private conversation, Falstaff says to Mistress Quickly (Ursula?), "Go, wash thy face" (she has been crying), "and draw [that is, withdraw] the action [that is, the suit]." "Come," he says, "thou must not be in this humour with me." Then he asks her, "dost not know me?" (*2H4*, 2.1.149–50). That settles the matter.

We return to the key word. This is a very different kind of "knowledge" of another person than that with which Hal "knows" all his companions. Hal's is detached and "moral" knowledge, connected to judgment and to (what Folly would call) relentlessly accurate assessment; the "knowledge" to which Falstaff appeals is intimate and forgiving, accepting of an entire person as such, and connected to (a part of) love.[33] Falstaff's borrowing and Mistress Quickly's lending (and perhaps his occasional hint that she will become his "lady") are part of a long-standing and well-understood relationship between these particular persons, a relationship that has gone on for years on this basis, and that includes mutual indulgence. Later on in the second act of part 2, when Falstaff and Doll Tearsheet are exchanging insults, Mistress Quickly notes that "this is the old fashion" between Falstaff and Doll, and insists that they must "bear with another's confirmities" (2.4.57)—a wonderful malapropism that combines infirmities with settled states of character, and that exactly replicates Dame Folly's claim that friendship involves an ability "to wink at one another's faults."[34]

Hal enters part 2 in between the two tavern scenes. As in part 1, he enters speaking prose (though to Poins, rather than to Falstaff), and as in part 1, he engages Poins in playing a trick on Falstaff. But, also as in part 1, he reminds his companion, in what passes as a humorous mode, of the reality of the social situation they are in, saying to Poins, "What a disgrace is it to me to remember thy name, or to know thy face tomorrow" (*2H4*, 2.2.14–15). He addresses Poins as "one it pleases me for fault of a better to call my friend," and tells Poins that he (Hal) has harmed his reputation by "keeping such vile company as thou art" (2.2.40, 47). Poins registers no offense at this, either because he is afraid to (which is unlikely), or he is used to being addressed in such a way (which is likely), or (and) because he takes Hal to be "joking" (highly likely). But these are hardly loving jokes. In part 2, Falstaff pretends to make a move parallel to his appeal to the lion's "instinct" in part 1. To escape the trap that Hal has set for him here, Falstaff claims that in equating Hal with Poins as another dim-witted athlete (*2H4*, 2.4.241–52) in explaining Hal's "love" for Poins, he (Falstaff) was protecting Hal's reputation by dispraising him "before the wicked" (2.4.316). Instead of Doll and Mistress Quickly being, as Hal urges them to be, offended by being referred to as "the wicked," the scene ends with both of them bidding tearful farewells to Falstaff, and with Quickly reflecting on how long she has known Falstaff: "Well, fare thee well. I have known thee these twenty-nine years, come peascod-time" (2.4.379–80).[35]

I mentioned earlier that Shakespeare places the great interchange between the new king and the Lord Chief Justice between two scenes featuring Justice Robert Shallow. The first is the scene of preparation for supper that we have examined, with Shallow and Davy; the scene that follows the young king's dedication of himself to the Lord Chief Justice is one of full-scale conviviality. Though

I am sure that Colin Burrow is right that the Elizabethans would have recognized Shallow and Silence as corrupt justices of the peace, the scene is more one of holiday than of license.[36] It is filled with mottoes of good fellowship, all variations on a theme: "There's a merry heart, good Master Silence," says Falstaff; "the heart's all," says Davy (consistent with himself); "a merry heart lives long-a," sings the surprisingly lively Silence. Justice Shallow commends to Bardolph Davy's loyalty: "The knave will stick by thee, I can assure you that." When Bardolph responds, "And I'll stick by him, sir," Shallow replies, interestingly and surprisingly, "Why, there spoke a king" (5.3.63–67). Moments later, Pistol arrives with the great news; Saturnalia has come to the realm—"golden times." "I speak," says Pistol, "of Africa and golden joys" (5.3.97). The scene ends on a note that does seem to move the mode from festivity to license. Falstaff says, "Let us take any man's horses—the laws of England are at my commandment" (131–33). We know from the previous scene, in which the new king took the Lord Chief Justice as his new surrogate "father" (5.2.140), that this is not at all true. But we cannot help but wonder, if we have not seen or read the play before, how the young king is going to adjudicate between friendship and impartiality in this crucial case. Before the confrontation to which the whole play—perhaps the whole two-part sequence—has been building,[37] Shakespeare interpolates a little scene (*2H4*, 5.4) in which Mistress Quickly and Doll Tearsheet are arrested by a beadle, and there is suddenly, and without any preparation, talk of them being involved in a murder.[38] Yet it is still hard to root for "whipping-cheer."

The great moment arrives when Falstaff gets the king's ear and addresses him thus: "My King! My Jove! I speak to thee, my heart!" Shakespeare has carefully prepared for this line. Falstaff has been equated with Saturn (*2H4*, 2.4.261), and Hal with his son, Jove (*2H4*, 2.2.166–67). Jove notoriously dispossesses (and castrates) Saturn, and ushers in, ultimately, an age of law and lead rather than one of gold, freedom, and Saturnalia. But the key word is "heart." This is the word that captures much of what the alternative to law has been, and it is the word that suffused the party at Shallow's. The new king, however, has, as he has told the Lord Chief Justice, buried his "affections" (5.2.124). He addresses Falstaff with "cold considerance," saying:

> I know thee not, old man. Fall to thy prayers.
> How ill white hairs becomes a fool and jester!
> I have long dreamt of such a kind of man,
> So surfeit-swelled, so old, and so profane;
> But, being awak'd, I do despise my dream. (5.5.47–51)

Hal has moved from the coldness of "I know you all" to the coldness of "I know thee not," where the positive and the negative assertions mean the same. Here the new king recognizes and specifically rejects the kind of knowledge on which Falstaff relies. We recall "Dost thou not know me?" Hal, now Henry, treats Falstaff truly impartially, relegating to unreality the personal relation between them. Falstaff is now simply a nameless and indecorous "old man." The acknowledgment that Henry does offer—Falstaff as part of a dream—renounces the whole realm of alternatives to what Sidney called the "brazen" world of ordinary history and politics (we recall that our very first description of Falstaff, by Hal, was to see Falstaff as an inhabitant of a dreamlike Land of Cockayne in which historical time was replaced by material and festive abundance: "hours were cups of sack, and minutes capons" [*1H4*, 1.2.7–8]).[39] Falstaff has already noted that "if to be old and merry" and fat—"surfeit-swelled"—"be a sin," then "Pharaoh's lean kine" are to be loved (*1H4*, 2.4.465–67). But a different biblical reference is evoked in Henry's speech of nonrecognition. The new king is echoing one of the most chilling passages in the Gospels. Jesus is explaining why few will be saved, that many who desire to be so will not be able to pass through the "straite gate." He tells the parable of the harsh and resolute housekeeper: "When the good man of the house is risen up, and hath shut to the dore, and ye beginne to stand without . . . saying, Lord, Lord open to us; and he shall answer, and say unto you, *I knowe you not*. . . . Then shal ye beginne to say, We have eaten and drunke in thy presence. . . . But he shal say, I tel you, *I know you not*" (Luke 13:24–27; emphasis mine). This is hardly a moment of charity.

So where does this leave the theoretical question, the question of impartiality? Of course Hal / Henry could not put the laws of England at Falstaff's commandment. But Shakespeare has worked hard to make us feel that the triumph of impartial justice is hardly to be celebrated. It is indeed hard to love "Pharaoh's lean kine." And it is hard not to feel that Davy, for all his outrageousness and simplicity, had a point.

Punishment

Having dwelt on the second part of *Henry IV*, and on the issue of impartiality, I will turn, more briefly, to other plays in which Shakespeare shows himself equally unhappy with other fundamental features of law. We have considered only one of Davy's points, that about friendship. We have not considered his remark that "An honest man, sir, is able to speak for himself, when a knave is not."

This raises the issue of punishment. Here again, Davy is right: the issue is only of interest in relation to the guilty (it is obvious that the innocent should not be punished). The play of Shakespeare's that considers this issue most sustainedly and directly is *Measure for Measure*. There it looks as if an overly lax legal system, one in which punishment has been neglected, merely needs to be supplanted by one that will attend to the matter properly. In this view, the character of Escalus in the play is the model for such a judicial position, one that (again) occupies a "golden mean," a sensible middle between overlaxity and overseverity.[40] There are a number of problems with this view. The first is that Escalus, despite the opening lines of the play extolling his qualifications, turns out to be a rather minor character, and his one clear judicial achievement— sending Mistress Overdone to prison—hardly seems like a great triumph (though he may also, as David Bevington and Virginia Lee Strain claim, try to straighten out the constabulary in Elbow's ward).[41] Escalus is set up, in the final act of the play, as a complete dupe, and appears, quite surprisingly, as an eager voice for harsh interrogation and torture (5.1.309ff.).[42] But the major problem with taking Escalus as a model is deeper than these matters. The issue on which the play is focused is not that of the behavior of a good judge. The focus of the play, as its title suggests, is on a more fundamental problem: whether judgment—in the sense of assigning punishment for offenses against the law—is in itself a desirable thing. If the answer to this question is negative, then it is hard to see how there can be a legal system. I will try to demonstrate that the play leaves us in precisely that perplexity.

Shakespeare attains a number of aims by making the locus of his examination of the viability of legal systems the regulation of sexuality (he derives this issue from his source material, but that simply shifts the question to why he chose this material).[43] Within this realm, Shakespeare's focus is not laws against rape or molestation but laws against prostitution and "fornication." Of these, the first is something that, as the play clearly recognizes, could be legalized. When Escalus asks the male bawd in the play, Pompey, whether his "trade" is "lawful," Pompey answers, "If the law would allow it, sir" (2.1.223–24), and Pompey continues in the play as the voice for awareness of the possibility of legalizing various practices. He points to the way in which interest-taking ("usury") has sometimes been illegal and sometimes—in the Elizabethan-Jacobean present (within limits)—not so;[44] he sees usury and prostitution as equivalent, and notes that "of two usuries, the merriest was put down, and the worser allowed by order of law" (3.2.6–8).[45]

Pompey also raises the question of whether the existence of prostitution responds to a fundamental need in human nature and society—"Does your worship mean to geld and splay all the youth of the city" (2.1.228).[46] The cogency of many of Pompey's retorts lends point to Constable Elbow's malapropisms— his confusing of benefactors with malefactors, for instance—since Shakespeare wants there to be a real question on the issue of "Which is the wiser here, Justice or Iniquity?" (3.1.174). Moreover, Pompey's final identity in the play—his punishment in being assigned to be the executioner's assistant—makes it seem as if he had been performing an equally useful service to the commonwealth in his previous role, since he is told, by an authoritative character (the virtuous Provost) that he and the executioner (pointedly named Abhorson) "weigh equally" (4.2.28). As Pompey says, with his normal sense of the way in which "legality" can be arbitrary, "I have been an unlawful bawd... but now I consent to be a lawful hangman" (4.2.15–16). This equation seems to raise the status of the bawd and lower that of the executioner, who is, after all, a necessary part of any legal-punitive system that includes capital punishment.

The issue of the basis for prostitution in human nature and society carries on, certainly, into the issue of "fornication." The sexual crime here is again one that makes the matter of criminalization dubious. The Elizabethans may have thought that "sodomy" (whatever that is) was abominable, and adultery legally punishable, but the matter of consensual noncommercial (hetero-) sexual relations between unmarried persons was obviously in a different category.[47] The issue is especially cloudy in a case like the one presented in the play, where the couple is (at least) engaged—and, by some definitions, legally married.[48] For the appointed deputy to prosecute the (male) offender in such a case to the letter of the law—the newly revived (though never quoted) statute apparently prescribed death for fornication—obviously raises a number of questions: first of all, does the statute itself make sense applied to either member of the "offending" couple; and second, is the statute, if it does make sense, being properly applied in the case at hand? The first issue is raised in the play—by Pompey, as we have seen, and also by the rakish know-it-all and man about town, Lucio. But, oddly, the second issue never is. When Escalus attempts to convince Angelo not to prosecute the "fornicator," Claudio, to the full extent of the law, Escalus does not offer any legal argument in Claudio's favor. He appeals first to a general sense of proportion ("Let us be keen, and rather cut a little, / Then fall, and bruise to death" [2.1.5–6]), and second, to the fact that the condemned "had a most noble father" (2.1.6–7).[49] Escalus does not attempt any version of the kind of statutory interpretation that Constance Jordan has illuminated.[50] He does not raise the question of whether Claudio's actions actually constitute "fornication," even though Claudio himself has claimed that he and Juliet were actually (legally) married: "Upon a true contract / I got possession of Julietta's bed ... She is fast my wife" (1.2.134–36).

Escalus's major argument for clemency to Claudio is, rather, something like an appeal to human nature, and specifically to the possibility that with regard to sexuality—a presumed universal—Angelo might have "err'd" in the same way Claudio did: "Had time coher'd with place, or place with wishing" (2.1.10–13). This is the issue on which the play focuses: Should the moral status of the judge affect the judgment that he (or she) should render? Does it matter that Angelo can be imagined to have committed the crime in question, or even—to put the question more strongly, as the play comes to—that he has in fact done so? Angelo himself sees the issues involved very clearly and answers extremely cogently. First of all, he notes that there is a crucial difference between intention or imagination and action—"'Tis one thing to be tempted, Escalus, / Another thing to fall" (2.1.17–18). Second, and even more important, the whole issue is irrelevant: "The jury passing on the prisoner's life / May in the sworn twelve have a thief or two, / Guiltier than him they try" (19–21). But so what? Why is this a problem? The law proceeds with regard to the particular case before it—"What's open made to justice, / That justice seizes."[51] To put the point most sharply, Angelo asks, "What knows the laws / That thieves do pass on thieves?" (22–23). This is a completely coherent position. A legal system is precisely that, a system, and if the system is functioning properly, then it is functioning properly. That is what matters. This is a view that allows for the administration of justice, or, if that seems too grand a way of putting it, at least for the working of—as I have said, and Angelo suggests—a legal *system*.[52]

This is the view that the play contests. The most riveting scene in the play (2.2) is that in which Isabella, the novice-nun sister of the condemned "fornicator" attempts to persuade the deputy, Angelo, to have mercy on Claudio. Isabella's primary argument is the appeal to human nature with regard to sexuality that Angelo is presumed to share: "You would have slipp'd like him" (2.2 65). She then adds a theological dimension to this appeal—we are all sinners in the eyes of God: "How would you be / If He, which is the top of judgement, should / But judge you as you are?" (75–77). Remarkably, Angelo is able to withstand this. He sticks to his formalist position—his own moral status is irrelevant: "It is the law, not I, condemn your brother" (80); and his own feelings are irrelevant (we are back to the issue of impartiality): "Were he my kinsman, brother, or my son, / It should be thus with him" (81–82). Angelo has some further arguments—some dubious claims about deterrence and irredentism—but he is basically sticking to his major, formalist point.

What is interesting about this scene, and about the rest of the play, is that Angelo is brought to renounce this perfectly coherent view. Isabella presents a searing and unforgettable picture of human pleasure in abusing authority (2.2.112–24), but her central argument is the one that has been on the table since Escalus first raised it (and Pompey, in his own way, echoed it), the argument from shared human (sexual) nature: "Go to your bosom, / Knock there, and ask your heart what it doth know / That's like my brother's fault. If it confess / A natural guiltiness, such as is his, / Let it not sound a thought upon your tongue / Against my brother's life" (137–42). When Angelo does find himself responding sexually to Isabella, manifesting "a natural guiltiness" in doing this, he completely forgets and contradicts his earlier recognition of how a formally constituted legal system operates. From "What knows the laws / That thieves do pass on thieves?" he has gone entirely over to exactly the opposite view: "Thieves for their robbery have authority / When judges steal themselves" (176–77).

Oddly, for the rest of the play his revised view is taken to be axiomatic.[53] The most shocking moment in the plot—even more shocking than the onset of lust in Angelo—is when Angelo fails to acknowledge the "*tu quoque*" and insists on the execution of Claudio despite their newly revealed kinship in sexuality. Yet Angelo never returns to legal formalism ("It is the law not I, condemn"); rather, Shakespeare supplies him with a self-interested motive (Claudio might take revenge on him for his "bargain" with Isabella [4.1.26–30]). The formalist view is entirely forgotten—and with it the distinction between being tempted and falling, between a thought or feeling and an overt action (Angelo adopts the alternative view before he has acted upon or even attempted to act upon his newfound impulse). The play comes to reject a legal framework that holds that "Thought is free"—or, as the Roman maxim puts it in Justinian's code, *Cogitationem poenam nemo patitur*.[54]

The great attack on "Thought is free" is the Sermon on the Mount. G. Wilson Knight was right about its centrality to *Measure for Measure* (though not, as we will see, in his triumphalism about this).[55] Jesus's relation to the moral teaching of the Old Testament, as embodied in the Decalogue, is not to abrogate this teaching but to "fulfill" it, which seems to mean to make it more demanding: "Ye have heard that it was sayd unto them of the olde time, Thou shalt not kil.... But I say unto you, whosoever is angrie with his brother unadvisedly, shal be culpable.... Ye have heard that it was sayd unto them of olde time, Thou shalt not commit adulterie. But I say unto you, that whosoever loketh on a woman to lust after her, hath committed adulterie" (Matthew 5:21–22, 27–28). The point of recognizing one's own sinfulness in this way—"A natural guiltiness"—is to learn the most important moral lesson of all: "Judge not" (Matthew 7:1). The great moral feeling is love, and the great moral action, forgiveness. This means love and forgiveness of everyone, since it is hardly an achievement to love one's friends (5:46), and—to return to Davy—the innocent do not need to be forgiven. But then, in God's eyes, as Isabella has noted, no one is innocent—"all the souls that were, were forfeit once" (2.2.73)—and so we all need and must give such blanket forgiveness.[56]

This view does not seem to leave a place for any sort of legal system—or rather, the only one conceivable would postulate a judge (like Christ at the Last Judgment) who does not have to be forgiven for anything. The Duke in *Measure for Measure* imagines such a creature. "He who the word of heaven will bear / Must be as holy as severe"; such a judge will not punish anyone for any behavior toward which he can discern an impulse in himself: "More nor less to others paying / Than by self-offences weighing" (3.2.254–59). The Duke may, to give him more credit than he probably deserves, originally have thought of Angelo as being such a creature, but the Duke does not put himself forth in this theocratic and perfectionist guise. Lucio attributes the Duke's "lenity to lechery" to the Duke having "some feeling of the sport" (3.2.94, 115–16), but this is simply a cynical version of the appeal to universal fallen nature, of which, in this play, sexuality in general is the sign ("a natural guiltiness"). Some version of Lucio's claim is simply true; no human being can, with regard to bodily needs and impulses, live up to the standard that Angelo apparently professed. The Duke appointed Angelo as one who "scarce confesses / That his blood flows, or that his appetite / Is more to bread than stone" (1.3.51–53). These are exactly the terms in which Lucio mocked Angelo: "a man whose blood is very snow broth" (1.4.58). So, as the play demonstrates through the case of Angelo, there is no human being who is "holy" enough to justify being "severe." The Duke in disguise as a friar—thereby perhaps affirming some theocratic impulse—manipulates the plot to make sure that no major injustice or wrong is done: Claudio is not executed and Isabella not violated.[57] But the Duke, even unhooded, does not attend to *legal* justice.

The key character for showing this is Barnardine, another purely Shakespearean invention (like Falstaff).[58] If the legal system were working at all, and able to provide punishments as well as pardons, it would differentiate clearly between the legal situations of Claudio and Barnardine. Claudio's legal guilt—as a "fornicator"—is, as we have seen, questionable at best, and the "crime" at issue questionable (and questioned). But Barnardine is a murderer—a major crime in any imaginable legal system. The Provost, a model of integrity in the play, sharply distinguishes between the two prisoners condemned to execution: "Th' one has my pity; not a jot the other, / Being a murderer" (4.2.59–60). Moreover, the play works to eliminate any legal argument (other than opposition to the death penalty itself) that would work to mitigate or prorogue Barnardine's execution: his stay in prison has not led him to be in any way reformed or penitent; there is no shadow of doubt about his guilt, which has recently become "apparent" and is "not denied by himself" (4.2.135–45). If there were ever a model candidate for execution—or for the severest penalty that the law allows—it would seem to be Barnardine. In Shakespeare's source, the equivalent figure is executed.[59] A legal system that does not treat Barnardine differently from Claudio can hardly be said to be functioning.[60]

But this is exactly what happens in the play. Both Claudio and Barnardine are spared from execution and freed from prison. The reason for sparing Barnardine has nothing to do with law as such. The Duke claims that to execute Barnardine "in the mind he is / Were damnable" (4.3.67–68). This is a theological position, not a legal one; where these came together in the legal tradition, what was "damnable" was to send someone to execution about whose guilt there was "reasonable doubt."[61] But the theological tradition was much more scrupulous. This is the Duke's view. What matters is not to be as sure as possible about what Barnardine has done but his state of mind (here equivalent to soul). To follow the law, and execute Barnardine for what he has unquestionably done, would violate a higher law, which forbids knowingly sending someone to (likely) damnation. The horror of this runs deep in the period. Othello would not kill Desdemona's soul by (as he thinks) executing her before she confesses her sins (5.2.31–54); Hamlet shows the depth of his hatred for Claudius, and (we can now gather) his own willingness to "dare damnation" by wishing to kill Claudius's soul.[62] To execute an impenitent murderer would, on this view, be worse than (or at least equivalent to) the murderer's own crime. Impenitence makes the criminal free from the death penalty—at least until he or she is properly "prepared" to die (Barnardine, according to the Duke-Friar is "A creature unprepar'd, unmeet for death" [4.3.66]). Impenitent Elizabethan and Jacobean criminals condemned to execution sometimes had their executions delayed so they could "prepare."[63] The assumption (often triumphantly recorded in pamphlets) is that they used such a remission to do so. But, in the cases recorded in the pamphlets, and in Desdemona's "case," the execution did occur.[64] Concern for the soul of the criminal delayed but did not cancel earthly justice.

In *Measure for Measure*, it does. At the end of the play, when the Duke has returned to put right (after a certain amount of testing) the situations that his withdrawal has created, it looks as if some semblance of actual legal thinking, however minimal, might be restored: what matters is what actually happened. "He knew me as a wife," says Mariana, regardless of what Angelo thought he was doing (5.1.229). Isabella, thinking, as she must, that her brother is dead, accepts his fate as at least legally intelligible: "My brother had but justice / In that he did the thing for which he died" (446–67). He did the thing. She, who had been the great spokesperson for the legal relevance of what's in "your bosom" (2.1.137), becomes the spokesperson for the view that it is only acts that are legally relevant. Of Angelo's defloration plan with regard to her, she argues that since—for whatever reason—"His act did not o'ertake his bad intent" (5.1.449), he has not committed any crime.[65] She provides an alternate formulation of "Thought is free"—"Thoughts are no subjects" (451)—and points out that intentions are "but merely thoughts" (452).

So, it looks as if the pendulum has now swung strongly in the opposite direction from the conflation of intention and action that defines the position of the Sermon on the Mount. Only acts are to be punished. But it turns out that these are not punished either. It turns out not to matter that Claudio, revealed to be alive, "did the thing." This may seem a reasonable outcome—except Barnardine is also pardoned. He also did the thing, and in his case also, this apparently does not matter. The commutation of his sentence is not temporary, and he is not to continue in prison. Barnardine is given an absolute pardon. His crime—a murder—is dismissed as a mere "earthly fault" (481), though he manifests no sign of apprehending anything "further than this world" (479). What matters, it seems, is that maybe, however unlikely the prospect, he may in "times to come" do so (483). He is remitted to the "hand" of the friar, not the Provost. The whole idea of punishment is mocked (as it was when the Duke as a "traitor" was threatened with being racked "joint by joint" [309–10]). Lucio claims that having to marry a woman he has gotten pregnant on a promise of marriage (3.2.193–94) is "pressing to death, / Whipping, and hanging" (5.1.520–21). Like the rack, these are the most dire of early modern punishments—made into a joke.

To conclude, as Knight does, that the ending of the play shows the Duke's original leniency "to have been right" is to ignore completely the topic that the play set out to confront: the issue of enforcement for lawbreaking.[66] As August Wilhelm Schlegel noted, it is hard to see how the Duke's original purpose "has in any wise been accomplished."[67] If anything, the situation in Vienna as the play concludes is worse than it was at the beginning. The surprise ending that

Robert Falls devised for his production was shocking and certainly nontextual but it was not, thematically, a non sequitur.[68] Not only is Barnardine free but Pompey is employed by the state. Even with regard to brothels, it is not clear that the situation has significantly improved—if their abolition is held to constitute an improvement.[69] But all that does not matter. We are made to feel "the sublime strangeness" of the Sermon on the Mount.[70] But what if it is not the case that "the world is going to end before your next mortgage payment is due"?[71] In the ongoing world, we are left with an *aporia* where a legal system should be. The title phrase turns out not to define law—"Measure still for measure" (5.1.409)—but to cancel it out. Judge not.[72]

Legality

Finally, let me turn to the play in which Shakespeare can be seen to give his fullest treatment of a legal system at work. In *The Merchant of Venice* Shakespeare does seem to want to give a sense of a system. It is a system that is seen primarily in terms of protecting commercial interests in a multiethnic and multinational situation. The "justice of the state" of Venice is presented as needing to be impartial because "the trade and profit of the city / Consisteth of all nations" (3.3.28–31).[73] Property rights are to be protected. The economic argument that Shylock puts forth in the great trial scene is not a defense of usury—that, long ago in the play (by the end of act 1, scene 3), ceased to be an issue.[74] In his characterizing "the justice of the state," Shylock does not pick up on his defense of licit ingenuity—if that is what it is—in the Jacob-Laban story but on a much less striking and marked moment in his earlier defense of himself to Antonio. He says in the earlier scene that Antonio's verbal and physical abuse of him is "all for use of that which is mine own" (1.3.108). Property, private property, Shylock says, is what is at issue—"that which is mine own." The sovereignty of ownership is ratified in the play by no less a character than Portia. In explaining that Bassanio has come, in an emotional sense, to "possess" her, Portia regrets that a procedure (here, the casket choice) must ratify this "ownership," and laments that "these naughty times / Put bars between the owners and their rights" (3.2.18–19). Ownership should be absolute. What she sees as "naughty" is exactly what Shylock says that Antonio is doing in contesting the contract.

But perhaps there are proper and recognized limits to property rights, and, in particular, to ownership. What Shylock points out is that in the Venetian society in which he lives, there seem to be few such limits. Shylock refuses to accept the idea that, in pursuing his property rights, he could possibly be doing something wrong. He makes a speech that has attracted remarkably little interest from our economic critics, new or old. He says something, very forcefully, that seems to be a non sequitur, but is not. Speaking to the assembled Venetian aristocrats, he says:

> You have among you many a purchas'd slave,
> Which, like your asses, and your dogs and mules,
> You use in abject and in slavish parts
> Because you bought them. (90–93a)

"You bought them" is clearly presented by Shylock as something recognized as an unanswerable argument. He pursues the point, noting that the owners in question will not endure interference—even of an ethical and "Christian" sort. Of the slaves, he asks the slave-owners:

> Shall I say to you,
> Let them be free, marry them to your heirs?
> Why sweat they under burdens? Let their beds
> Be made as soft as yours, and let their palates
> Be season'd with such viands? (93b–97)

Again, Shylock notes, unquestionably correctly, what the answer to such humane and egalitarian proposals would be: "you will answer / 'The slaves are ours.'" This picture of Venetian society turns out, historically, to be true (as is, no doubt, the justification he imagines being offered for it).[75] The question becomes how Shylock thinks this is relevant to his situation vis-à-vis Antonio. He says that the pound of flesh is "dearly bought"—which is true (3,000 ducats is presented as a large amount of money)—but what he is really saying is not just that he has bought the pound of flesh but that he has bought Antonio, and that in a society in which persons can be property, this is perfectly intelligible.[76] No answer is ever given to this argument. The critic who has thought hardest about this matter, Amanda Bailey, argues that Shylock is mistaken in thinking that he has an absolute right over his forfeit (the pound of flesh), but the play does not make the distinctions that Bailey claims that English law would have made.[77] She may be right that Shylock does not recognize (or chooses not to recognize) the complexity of "the animated gage," but what Bailey fails to note is that Shylock's argument about slavery and the ownership of persons is never disputed in the play. In fact, the speech is never responded to in any way. Immediately following it, the need for an outside judge is suddenly proclaimed by the Duke (103–6).[78] The proceedings have to wait for the legal expert, and in the rest of the trial scene, the legal trumps the economic.

The first thing to be said about the contract that is at the center of the legal case in the play is that no one in the play ever asserts that Shylock's contract with Antonio is unenforceable on the face of it.[79] Certainly a judge contemporary with us would assert this, and probably a Venetian judge contemporary with Shakespeare would have.[80] But no one in the play does. On the contrary, the validity of the contract is repeatedly affirmed.[81] At the very beginning of the trial scene, Antonio states of his situation vis-à-vis Shylock that "no lawful means can carry me / Out of his envy's reach" (4.1.9–10). When "Balthazar" enters, and after "his" credentials are verified and he is apprised "Which is the merchant here, and which the Jew," Balthazar's first words to Shylock are "Of a strange nature is the suit you follow, / Yet in such rule, that the Venetian law / Cannot impugn you as you do proceed" (4.1.173–75). What Shylock wants is enforcement of a contract that no one takes to be invalid. The Duke initially called on Shylock to show "gentleness and love" (24)—not legal terms. Later the Duke plies Shylock with an extralegal argument, an argument about transcendent, otherworldly justice—"How shalt thou hope for mercy, rend'ring none?" (87). Portia / Balthasar, of course, develops this further. Predictably, given the symbolic role of Judaism in the play, Shylock is unmoved.[82] He may have a different conception of the relation between justice and salvation ("What judgement shall I dread, doing no wrong" [88]), but what Shylock is arguing for is not cosmic justice but legal enforcement. He is relying on the legal system. He believes in it.[83]

Though it may seem odd to say this, it seems to me that if the legal system of Venice were shown to be working correctly—with respect to its own principles—and if Shylock continued, for whatever reason, not to take money in lieu of the specified forfeit, he should have been allowed his pound of flesh. What this means is that a system that allows for property in persons can produce monstrous results that are perfectly legal.[84]

But, as we all know, Shakespeare does not allow the system to work in this way. The "no jot of blood" proviso brings the proceedings to a halt. This can be read in a number of ways—all of them unattractive. The first reading would be that this proviso is an obvious dodge, an extreme and absurd legalism, since if the initial contract were valid, the conditions necessary for its fulfillment would have to be acceptable as well. The second reading, suggested by Charles Fried, sees this proviso as consistent with the extreme formalism and literalism of the Venetian legal system as we are given it in the play. Fried argues that Shylock, given his own view of the law, must be viewed as "seeing the force" of this argument.[85] This hardly makes the system an attractive one, despite Fried's modified defense of it. We watch Shakespeare's most famous spokesperson for mercy succeeding in outlegalizing the spokesperson for law. Unless we wish to stand with the ironically named Gratiano, we can hardly cheer for this. That Gratiano occupies this position can be seen as Shakespeare's way of trying to ensure that we (the audience) will not.

But there is more to be said. Even if one takes the view that the "no jot of blood" proviso is not absurd, Portia emerges as disingenuous in her earlier assertions of the validity of Shylock's contract, since the "act" to which she suddenly appeals would have invalidated the contract in the first place. And let us pause for a moment over this "act" (which, apparently, no one has ever heard of until this moment). The "act" seems to have to do not with the shedding of blood in general but specifically with "Christian blood": "If thou dost shed / One drop of Christian blood, thy lands and goods / Are (by the laws of Venice) confiscate / Unto the state of Venice" (4.1.304–7). Shylock is astonished ("Is that the law?" he asks), and he is assured that Portia / Balthazar can produce the text (which she never does). One might have thought that the blood in question in this case just happened to be Christian, since it was Antonio's. But that cannot be right.[86] The (unproduced) law must state that it applies only to aliens, since otherwise every assault on any Christian in Venice that produced bloodshed of any kind would fall under it.

This becomes obvious when Portia activates her further proviso, the "other hold" (also unknown to all present) that the laws of Venice have on Shylock. Whether or not her claim that this other law applies in this case is valid, this law—now quoted—explicitly distinguishes between "aliens" and citizens, and is specifically aimed only at aliens ("If it be proved against an alien . . ." [4.1.345]). Despite the fact that "the trade and profit of the city / Consisteth of all nations," it turns out that the Venetian system, as it is presented in the play, is no more committed to impartiality than it is to honoring valid contracts.[87] Shylock, who seems to be a well-established resident of Venice, enjoying at least the status of a *habitator*, is suddenly simply and somewhat unaccountably an "alien."[88] So it turns out that "Christian blood" is quite crucial. After the second legal trick is played on Shylock, Portia succeeds, through putting pressure on the Duke, to allow the court to feel that it has behaved in an especially merciful way in exempting Shylock from some of the provisions of this lovely (and extremely vague—"by direct or indirect attempts") anti-alien statute. To borrow a term from Harry Berger, we might call this process "mercifixion."[89] To show "the difference of our spirit" between Shylock and the Duke, Shylock is spared execution (364–65). But he is radically diminished in his estate and rights, if not impoverished (a fate that Shylock sees as equivalent to death [370–73])[90]—and, oh yes, he is forced to change his religious identity and become a Christian.[91] So the picture of a legal system that we are given is that it either acts truly impartially and allows monstrosities as legal, or acts partially—to protect a ruling elite.[92]

So what are we to conclude from all this? Shakespeare certainly did not want to "kill all the lawyers"[93]—he made copious use of them in his own life—but he did seem to find that whenever he thought hard about legal principles or legal systems, he found himself profoundly uncomfortable.

CHAPTER 5

King Lear and Human Needs

Dramatic tragedies involve the representation of one or more humans suffering. This is true whatever theory of tragedy one holds. Often the focus is on mental or emotional suffering, on what Macbeth calls "the torture of the mind" (3.2.22). The suffering depicted can have a somatic dimension, as in Macbeth's sleeplessness or Othello's epileptic fit, but the physical is not normally the focus. Even in *Oedipus Tyrannos*, with its self-blinded hero, the focus is on "the torture of the mind." *Philoctetes*, with its evocation of loathsome physical suffering and social isolation, is a striking exception. Tragedies regularly depict material losses—loss of kin is an obvious one, along with loss of homeland and position—but normally what is lost is something grand and something peculiar to the individual in focus. The fall of an individual from a high estate is the succinct and cogent medieval formula.[1] Before the twentieth century, tragedies rarely focused on what might be called routine suffering—or, to put it more sharply, the sustained and everyday physical or social suffering of ordinary people. They rarely treated, for instance, being cold or hungry or, in one's own society, being homeless as a life-long or group condition. Poverty as a social condition, in other words, is not generally a topic for tragedy any more than unredeemed physical suffering is.[2] *King Lear* is unusual not only in its onstage depiction of physical disfigurement but also in its concern with the social condition of poverty—or rather, with its concern for poverty as a social condition.[3] The nature of this concern, its depth, and the recourse that the play imagines for it are matters of critical controversy that I will address.

Penury in Contempt of Man

Right from the beginning, the *King Lear*'s social imaginary includes basic social and physical deprivation. When Lear first bursts out at Cordelia, the speech is a magnificent piece of oratory, invoking, with cosmological pagan grandeur, "the sacred radiance of the sun, / The mysteries of Hecat and the night [Q: might]," "the operation of the orbs"—all to witness what it means to make a formerly loved person into a "stranger" (1.1: Q 98–106; F 108–14).[4] This is a very strong formulation. A "stranger," on this account, is someone to whom it is not clear that one owes any duties at all, someone to whom one has no obvious bond.[5] Cordelia has just affirmed her "bond" to Lear, and explicated it to him.[6] The bond exists, she says, because "You have begot me, bred me, loved me," and she therefore owes him a series of reciprocal duties (86–88; 95–97).[7] Lear responds to this point by point. He "disclaims" each of these bond-creating connections. Taking the social and emotional ones first, he sums up in a single phrase what Cordelia meant by his having "bred" (i.e., educated) and loved her.[8] He disclaims all "paternal care" (103; 111). He then moves to the biological connection (her "begot me") when he disclaims "Propinquity and property of blood" (104; 112). He says that he will henceforth hold her forever "as a stranger to my heart and me." This leads Lear to the thought of "stranger" human groups. His mind turns to the *ethnos* that, for the ancient world from Herodotus on, marked the limits of recognizable human life, the Scythians.[9] Then Lear goes even further, and thinks about cannibals—a category that identified the most extreme ethnic and ethical other.[10] Lear says that both of these, a "barbarous Scythian" and any male figure who eats his children ("he that makes his generation messes"), will be more welcome to him than his now former daughter (106–10; 114–18).[11] This is clearly a moment of psychological opacity like Shylock's image of the self-bepisser, where unacknowledged shame is powerfully present beneath the image (Lear is in effect the one who is devouring his offspring).[12] But putting aside the psychological density here, what is salient in this speech is the particular form that Lear imagines his deprivation of his daughter taking. He says that the most alien social being will be "as well neighbored, pitied, and relieved" by him as his "sometime daughter" will be (110; 118).

This is a remarkably detailed and informative way in which to imagine abandonment. It implies that persons need to be "neighbored, pitied, and relieved"—that aid from other persons, from a community of some sort, is a fundamental necessity, and that to be in a condition to need such things is more or less normal.[13] The first word of the triad contains the others. For "neighbor" to be used as a verb in a way that is not geographical or spatial is extremely unusual; the *OED* gives only one instance from the period (while oddly mistaking the *Lear* instance for a spatial usage).[14] Shakespeare wants us to think of "neighboring" as an activity, as something that one does—or, in this case, that one refuses to do.[15] Here, for this moment, the play leads us to think about what it would mean not to be "neighbored," to live in a world where no one felt any sense of social connection to one. The rest of the line gives the content of social connection. It involves a recognition of the other, a feeling for the suffering of the other, and action taken on the basis of that feeling (the suffering of a "neighbor" is pitied, which leads to its being relieved). The lawyer's great question to Jesus, "Who is then my neighbour?" (Luke 10:29), points to the crucial status of the term.[16]

As it turns out, Cordelia, though disinherited, does not have to experience anything like what Lear imagines here. The fairy-tale aspect of the story emerges when the King of France, to his own amazement—and wildly against all plausibility—decides to marry Cordelia without any dowry and indeed "dowered" with her father's curse. Invoking something like the law of salvage, France decides to "take up" what has been "cast away" (242; 252).[17] The figure who does experience what Lear in his curse imagined is the rejected virtuous child in the subplot that Shakespeare added to the Lear story. This addition was entirely Shakespeare's invention (just as the addition of the Polonius family story to the Hamlet story almost certainly was).[18] Without the addition of the Gloucester family story to Shakespeare's *Lear*, poverty and something approaching recognizable social death would have entered the story only in the special case of the dethroned and abandoned king. The devotion of the mistreated virtuous (and legitimate) son to the father who has been blinded by the usurping (and bastard) wicked son is taken, as is well known, from a minor episode in Sidney's *Arcadia*, an episode that Shakespeare recognized as parallel to the Lear story: a father entirely and disastrously mistakes the moral character of his children, and yet is still loved by the rejected virtuous one. In Sidney, the life of the virtuous son is spared by the servants the father ordered to kill him, and the son is let go "to learne to live poorely." He becomes "a private souldier."[19] Nothing of the virtuous son's life in this state is narrated except that he did well in this role. The decision to have the mistreated virtuous son take on the disguise that he assumes in Shakespeare's play was entirely Shakespeare's invention. This disguise extends the range of social imagination in the play to include a figure as far from civilization as the Scythian and yet as familiar as the nearest town, village, or country road: the vagrant beggar.

To live as such was "to live poorely" indeed. The sturdy vagrant beggar was the nightmare of the Elizabethan state and the object of parochial and national legislation; "the sixteenth century," as R. H. Tawney put it, "lives in terror of the tramp."[20] Social history has shown that there was not a fully rational basis for this terror, but the terror itself is an established fact.[21] In the play, Edgar clearly needs to protect himself; he has been "proclaimed" (2.3.1) and aid to him declared a felony. An obvious plot device would have been to have had Edgar escape to France, where the other virtuous rejected child is queen, yet, as Nahum Tate correctly noted, in Shakespeare's play, Edgar and Cordelia have no contact whatever (they "never changed word with each other").[22] Through Gloucester's efforts "no port is free" to Edgar; this means Edgar's "exile" will have to be internal.[23] So Shakespeare has him decide to take on the role of "Tom o' Bedlam." It has been said that it is "no wonder" that Edgar "who has become nothing by being denied" finds "Poor Tom such an appropriate disguise."[24] But there is a wonder here. Edgar did not have to go to such a length. All disguises work in Shakespeare. Kent becomes "Caius" simply by changing his manner of speech, shaving his beard, and, presumably, changing his clothing (1.4.1–4); Edgar's later disguise as "a most poor man" with a northern accent seems to work perfectly well (Q 4.6.210; F 4.5.215ff.). Shakespeare wanted the particular figure of "Tom o' Bedlam" in the play. As Simon Palfrey notes, the question is, "Why *this* disguise?" (emphasis his).[25]

Edgar states with great precision what he must do to "assume" the physical dimension of the role. He has to ruin and degrade his physical appearance: "My face I'll grime with filth, / Blanket my loins, elf all my hair with knots" (2.3.9–10). The physical degradation will force him to "with presented nakedness outface / The winds and persecutions of the sky" (2.3.12–13). This is the first mention in the play of "nakedness" and the first hint that the physical universe might be hostile to the unprotected human. But Edgar wants to go further. He will take on the appearance not only of a filthy tramp but of one who is also mad, a "Bedlam." So he will become grotesque and self-mutilating. Here too his instructions to himself are startlingly precise. The "Bedlam beggars" on whom he will model himself "Strike in their numbed and mortified bare arms / Pins, wooden pricks, nails, sprigs of rosemary" (15–16). But he understands further that the point of the physical condition is social. These figures go about among people in circumstances slightly less immiserated than their own, people who have, that is, some sort of fixed abode, however flimsy—"low farms, / Poor pelting villages, sheepcotes, and mills"—and the Bedlams, with the "horrible object" of their physical appearance, and "roaring voices ... Sometimes with lunatic bans, sometime with prayers / Enforce their charity" (2.3.16–20) in this "geography" of poverty.[26] These beggars are figures who are barely "neighbored"—they are "relieved" as often out of fear of their wild curses ("lunatic bans") as out of pity. They must use extreme measures to "enforce" charity.

Yet in the soliloquy that we have been examining, Edgar has not yet actually taken on the persona of "Tom." He is contemplating what it will mean to do so. He has just "bethought" himself of the idea (2.3.6). The interesting question is why Shakespeare wanted to include this soliloquy, and to do so here. This little scene—if it is a scene—is not necessary to the plot and, in fact, interrupts the narrative line of Lear's story.[27] Edgar could, after all, soliloquize about his disguise when he appears in the storm in act 3. But Shakespeare wanted the detailed verbal evocation of "Tom's" appearance and behavior; he wanted his theater audience to imagine "Tom" in great detail, to picture him in their minds, before they actually saw him on stage. And Shakespeare wanted something more. He wanted Edgar to make a conceptual point about the figure. In taking on this guise, Edgar says that he will be adopting "the basest and most poorest shape / That ever penury in contempt of man / Brought near to beast" (2.3.7–9).[28] This suggests that extreme poverty can make what is recognizable as human life almost impossible—or, to put the point positively, that certain minimal material conditions must be met before a life that can be recognized as human is possible. "Contempt of man" here means "disdain for the status of the human." The agent of this contempt is not "the cosmos," but a specified human social situation—"penury."[29] The question of the material conditions for what counts as a human life has been introduced into the play—right in the middle of the dramatization of the immediate aftermath of Lear's revised division plan.[30]

What we realize is that the Lear plot comes to focus on exactly the issue that Edgar has raised. "Contempt of man," it turns out, can work on various levels, and these turn out to be interconnected. If we consider the Lear plot in itself, apart from the Gloucester plot, we recognize that, after the opening scene, the first two acts of the play are devoted to a systematic attack, by his elder daughters, on Lear's social identity. The attack moves along two fronts.[31] They both have to do with Lear's followers. The first concerns Lear's retinue, his hundred knights; the second, the treatment of a single servant not part of that group (Kent as "Caius"). Thomas G. Olsen has made it clear that one of Shakespeare's innovations in his treatment of the Lear story is the prominence of the issue of Lear's retinue.[32] The attack on the retinue is sustained and systematic. Lear proposed a "monthly course" of alternating residences (1.1: 122; 130), and began, naturally, with his eldest born. The first speeches that we hear / see Goneril address to Lear, after her consummate performance in the love-test, are attacks on his followers. Her rhetorical genius is again on display. Her tone is of outraged reasonableness; she manifests her righteous indignation not in exclamations but in icily controlled syntax, with a special mastery of the relative pronoun "which" (196, 198; 183, 185). Her picture of the bad behavior of the retinue is unforgettable; her court has been made to seem "more like a tavern or a brothel / Than a great [F: graced] palace" (1.4: 233–34; 214–15).

A great deal depends on whether we, as critics, readers, or audience, accept Goneril's claims here. It has become a kind of convention in stage and film productions to do so.[33] Goneril, along with Regan and Cornwall, presents herself as the voice of prudence in the play.[34] If she is right, there is a prudential basis for the reduction of Lear's retinue. Redress is a matter of "necessity" (1.4: 200; 186). But we recall that Milton called necessity "the Tyrant's plea" (*Paradise Lost* 4.393). Is it clear that we need to accept Goneril's representation either of the situation or of her motives? The more disordered that we take Lear's followers to be, the less gratuitous the actions of Goneril and company are. So the fact of the matter and the issue of prudence become crucial. I will argue that the more we accept the prudential account of the attack on the retinue, the less we understand its actual role in the play.

So let us examine the evidence for Goneril's view—other than the rhetorical brilliance of its formulation. The first thing to say about this view, once we have fully heard it, is that Lear immediately and strongly denies it. He does not deny being imperious; after all, his first words when he appears on stage at Goneril's are "Let me not stay a jot for dinner" (1.4.7), and the Folio states that his arrival is announced with horns and that he comes with "Attendants."[35] But nothing further is specified. Lear insists that his followers are "men of choice and rarest parts" (1.4: 250; 233). But this merely gives us competing assertions. What is interesting, and has not been given sufficient weight in criticism and productions, is that Lear's view is supported by the only member of his retinue who actually speaks in the play. When Goneril's "Gentleman" (or, in the Folio, Oswald) executes Goneril's command to be systematically and provocatively rude to Lear (1.3.11–12), a member of the retinue (designated "Servant" in Q; "Knight" in F) speaks out.[36] The Servant / Knight asserts that "his duty cannot be silent" when he sees his master wronged ([1.4: 58–9; 60–61]. This parallels Kent's "Think'st thou that duty shall have dread to speak" in scene 1 [1.1: 137; 145]), but this character does not have Kent's social status and relation to Lear, so he cannot, as Kent could, be "unmannerly" (see 1.1: 135–36, 143–44]). Instead, the Servant / Knight speaks in a very careful and mannerly way, beginning, "I beseech your highness pardon me, if I be mistaken," and conveying a deep regard for decorum. "To my judgment," he says, "your majesty is not entertained with that ceremonious affection as you were wont" (1.4.51–53). "Ceremonious affection" is a lovely and rich phrase; it suggests an ideally unified social world, a world in which—as Lear intended the opening scene to be—ceremony and affection are not at odds.[37] The phrase opens a vista into a nontragic social world, a social world that Cordelia, for the brief moment when she is in charge of Lear, tries to create.[38] The figure who uses the phrase can hardly be seen as "disordered," with manners that could "infect" a court (Goneril at 1.4: 229–31; 211–13).

On the other hand, let us examine a moment of "confirmation." Regan has been informed, in a letter, of Goneril's view of Lear's retinue.[39] When Regan hears from Gloucester of Edgar's (supposed) wicked behavior, she creates an entirely fictitious scenario, hypothesizing that Edgar must have been "companion with the riotous knights / That tends [F: tended] upon my father" (2.1.93–94). Gloucester naturally says that he knows nothing of this, but Edmund, seeing an opportunity, steps in to confirm the connection (96), and Regan ties it all up quite neatly: the riotous knights "have put [Edgar] on the old man's death / To have the spoil [F: th' expense] and waste of his revenues" (98–99). Edgar's entirely imaginary behavior confirms Goneril's report. Moreover, there is a further problem with the prudential critique of Lear's retinue. The rationale for it (a little like Iago's motives) keeps changing. The initial rationale is the one we have noted, the retinue's supposed rowdiness. But later in the scene (in a Folio addition), Lear's retinue has become, for Goneril, a semi-military threat (F 1.4.295–96); and when Regan picks up the critique, she appeals to an administrative difficulty (2.4: 210–12; 229–30). There is little doubt that the goal is for the sisters to whittle down, systematically, the size of the retinue. But is it so clear that the number is the issue? I would suggest that the number is only important because it is the number that Lear specified ("to be followed / With such a number" [2.4: 222–23; 241–42]).[40] The point is not decorum, defense, or efficiency. The point is to deprive Lear of what he thinks he needs to be himself, of what he needs to maintain his identity.[41]

The parallel strand in the Lear story reveals the same purpose. But where the attack on the retinue was planned and coordinated, the punishment of Kent / Caius arises spontaneously. It is part of the tragic and ironic structure of the play that the only staged "evidence" for Goneril's account is the behavior of Kent (as Caius)—in particular, Kent's / Caius's behavior toward Oswald, Goneril's steward. Kent and Oswald are set up as opposites from the very first moment that Kent reappears; Kent claims that there is an "antipathy" between them.[42] Kent's first action in his new guise is to trip Oswald when Oswald is defying Lear (1.4.75–81). When we next see Kent / Caius encountering Oswald,

Kent insults him at length and physically assaults him. This seems to be clear confirmation of Goneril's account; Cornwall states: "This is a fellow of the selfsame colour / As our sister speaks of [in her letter]" (2.2.129–30). Cornwall calls for the stocks. But Caius has come to Gloucester's residence (where this scene is taking place) on the King's business. The King's messenger, however crude-seeming, is "personating" him.[43] To treat Caius in the way that Cornwall intends is to show disrespect to Lear. Caius explains: "You shall do small respect [F: respects], show too bold a malice / Against the grace and person of my master / Stocking his messenger" (123–25). Gloucester recognizes this, and it elicits his first gesture of protest against Cornwall (who is, after all, his "master," his "arch and patron" [2.1.57–58]). In urging Cornwall not to stock Caius, Gloucester explains why this punishment is a particular act of disrespect. "Your purposed low correction," says Gloucester, "Is such as basest and contemnèd'st wretches / For pilferings and most common trespasses / Are punished with."[44]

Cornwall certainly knows this. "'Twill be ill taken," says Gloucester (F 147; Q 150: took), and so it is. When we next see Lear, after he has cursed Goneril and been deprived by her of half his followers [1.4: 282; 264]), he has resolved to take up with his other nonexiled daughter. He is sure that he will find Regan "kind and comfortable" (1.4: 293; 276)—where the second of these terms, as much as the first, has an emotional sense—we would say "comforting."[45] But we know that Regan and Cornwall have been informed by both Goneril and Lear of the strife between them; both Goneril and Lear have sent messengers with letters (Oswald in Goneril's case, Kent / Caius in Lear's).[46] Immediately upon reading Goneril's letter, Regan and Cornwall left their residence in the middle of the night to turn up, unannounced, at Gloucester's (see 2.1.78, 118–20). It is clear that this was done to make sure that Lear's messenger would find them "from home" (2.4.1). When Lear next appears, he has followed the couple to Gloucester's. The transit—presumably to Cornwall's and then to Gloucester's—is unstaged, and the lack of hospitality is barely mentioned ("'Tis strange" [2.4.1]). Shakespeare clearly wanted the first experience we see or read Lear having after his angry departure from Goneril's at the end of act 1 to be the sight of Caius in the stocks.[47] The whole effort of act 2, scene 2 has been to get him there.[48] Lear is so shocked at the sight that he has difficulty taking it in; he has to be convinced that it was actually done on the express orders of his "son and daughter" (2.4.12). His comment on the situation seems hyperbolic: "'Tis worse than murder / To do upon respect such violent outrage" (15–16; 17–18). But he recognizes that disrespect, as Kent stated when the stocks were first brought out, and as Gloucester underlined, is exactly the point. Ostensibly, the stocking of Caius is punishment for his aggression toward Oswald, but the primary purpose of this punishment is semiotic—it is a message for Lear. The message is, indeed, disrespect, contempt. Cornwall and Regan do not care who Lear, socially, is or has been, and they are signaling this. Such behavior can be seen as "worse than murder" in that murder need not imply contempt.[49] Lear's identity, his history, do not matter—or rather, they matter only as a target.[50]

Long after Kent / Caius is finally freed (at 2.4: 107, 121), Lear still has trouble processing the fact that his servant had been stocked (152; 171). Even when initially confronted with Goneril and Regan together, he is still obsessed with the issue.[51] When Cornwall, with full self-righteousness, assumes responsibility, Lear can still barely believe it. As Goneril and Regan begin to work in concert, the issue of the retinue returns. The numbers game continues. After Goneril's "what need you five-and-twenty, ten, or five?" Regan moves in with "What need one?" (231, 233; 250, 252). With this devastating but completely expectable question, the key term for the (mal-) treatment of Lear has shifted from "respect" to "need"—though, as we shall see, the link between the terms is deep and important. Lear responds to the proposed elimination of his retinue with an exclamation that, suddenly, is phrased generally rather than in terms of his own situation: "O reason not the need" (234; 253). He continues with a line that shows—for the first time since his opening curse on Cordelia—a wide social awareness. Instead of defending his own "need" for his retinue, he reiterates the point that Edgar has already made about the material basis of a life that can be called human. Lear knows nothing of that speech and of Edgar's decision to take on the persona of "Tom." Completely on his own, and quite surprisingly—if one does not remember the line about being "neighbored"—Lear makes the assertion that "our basest beggars / Are in the poorest thing superfluous" (234–35; 253–54).

It seems that beggars and the poor are on everybody's mind; the Fool had already (in the Folio) sung about "Fathers who wear rags" (F 2.4.41); Gloucester is aware of "basest and contemnèd'st wretches." "Our basest beggars"—everyone knows about them. But one might ask how they can be "in the poorest thing superfluous." Lear explains this in his next line and a half: "Allow not nature more than nature needs, / Man's life is cheap as beasts'" (2.4: 234–35; 254–55). Being "superfluous" here means possessing anything that is not strictly necessary for biological existence. Lear is making, as Edgar did somewhat less explicitly, what we would call the Aristotelian (or Arendtian or Agambenian) distinction between *zoē* and *bios*.[52] Hannah Arendt speaks of "the chief characteristic" of the "specifically human life" as that "it is full of events which ultimately can be told as a story, establish a biography ... *bios* as distinguished from mere *zoē*."⁵³ "Mere *zoē*" is what Lear earlier called "base life" (2.4: 185; 204). What the human needs—to have a biography—is more than what the biological needs. Margreta de Grazia mocks Lear for pleading "for the retention of his unnecessary retainers as if such holdings were a human right," but when this plea is read correctly, that is exactly what it is.⁵⁴

To deny or forget the distinction between *zoē* and *bios* is either cruelty or madness. In acts 1 and 2, we see the denial as cruelty. In the storm scenes of act 3, we see it as madness. Lear has felt himself on the edge of madness ever since Goneril unleashed her denunciation of him, his fool, and his retinue, and he simultaneously recognized the mistake he had made regarding Cordelia. Act 1 ends with Lear praying not to go mad (1.5.40). In act 2, he is again afraid that Goneril will make him so (2.4: 188; 207). In his act 3 dialogues with the storm—encouraging its apocalyptic rage (3.2.1–9), accusing it of complicity with "two pernicious daughters" (3.2.21–23), calling on it to punish those who have committed secret crimes (3.2.52–58)—Lear is right on the edge. But, in the continuation of the storm scenes, when Edgar appears on stage as Poor Tom, Lear goes over. Generalization gives way to projection; he asks "Tom," "Did'st [Q: Hast] thou give [Q: given] all to thy [Q: thy two] daughters?" (3.4: 42; 47). In his madness, Lear ignores the lengthy autobiography that Edgar produces for "Tom" (3.4: 75–81; 79–85) and focuses on Tom's pathetic physical condition—seeing the human only in terms of *zoē*: "Thou," says Lear to Tom, "art the thing itself" (3.4: 95; 98–99). He then explains what "the thing itself" is: "Unaccommodated man is no more but such a poor, bare forked animal as thou art" (95–96; 99–100). Accommodation stands here for what the "superfluous" stood for in the earlier speech. Through an act of mad identification and empathy, Lear attempts to descend to the level of "the thing itself" by tearing off his clothes, which he characterizes, from the "animal" point of view, as "lendings."⁵⁵

Humans do not possess their clothes or other made things in the same way that they possess their biological properties. Or perhaps the non-mad point is that, to be human, they do. Even *zoē*, for humans, involves more than biology. To be something more than a forked animal one might need to be an animal with a fork—or other such "lendings," accommodations, or "superfluities." Such matters are not "patently appliqué" to the human—or rather, it is madness to see them as such.⁵⁶ With regard to the distinction between humans and animals in the play, it should be said that the point about the human need for accommodation—or, rather, the need for accommodation in order to be human—has nothing to do with the superiority of other animals to biologically human ones. With the possible (and trivially ludic) exception of the snail, the other creatures are presented as no more capable of dealing with "the enmity of the air" and "Necessity's sharp pinch" than humans are (2.4: 179–81; 198–200); even the strongest and fiercest of them share vulnerability to the elements—"the cub-drawn bear . . . the lion and the belly-pinched wolf" all need shelter (Q 3.1.12–14).[57] As Andreas Höfele points out, "at its most devastating"—i.e., in *King Lear*—Shakespeare "flattens" the human-animal divide.[58] It may be that humans have the same responsibility to other creatures as they have to other humans ("Mine injurious [F: enemy's] dog / Though he had bit me, should have stood that night / Against my fire" [4.7.34–6; 4.6.30–31]). Only humans, it seems, can produce, in the fullest sense, "accommodation."[59]

Showing the Heavens More Just

So, if the play is clear about lack of "accommodation" as a threat to a recognizably human life, does it suggest any way of guaranteeing access to such a life? Again, perhaps surprisingly, it does. Lear's elder daughters deny him not only what is necessary for a *bios*, but even what is necessary for *zoē*. Lear had earlier mocked the idea that his daughters might fail to "vouchsafe" him "raiment, bed, and food" (2.4: 125–26; 144–45), but that is exactly what, in their moralistic and pedagogical mode (Lear "must needs taste his folly" [2.4: 261; 280]), they do. Lear, as we saw, had expected to find Regan "comfortable"—never thinking that he would ever need comfort of the sort that Gloucester later provides ("I will piece out the comfort [of the lodging] with what addition I have" [3.6.2]). The play shows that the line between inflicting social and inflicting material deprivation is easily traversed. When Kent finds Lear in the storm, with no retainer but the Fool, Kent offers to lead them to a nearby "hovel" that will provide something like what the sisters and Cornwall have refused. It will provide "some friendship" against the storm (3.2.61–62)—the social term has become material.

Kent provides a more traditional term for "accommodation"; he says that, after he installs Lear and the Fool in the hovel, he will go back to Gloucester's house and try to "force / Their scanted courtesy" (3.2.67). This recalls "Tom" imagined as trying to "enforce . . . charity"; Kent too will, he imagines, have to resort to extraordinary means to enforce courtesy. The two terms are treated as virtually equivalent. What Gloucester refers to as "charity" to Lear, Edmund refers to as "this courtesy forbid thee" [3.3.14, 19]). But "courtesy," like "ceremonious affection," describes an ideal of social life. The semantic and conceptual range of "courtesy" here covers the whole realm from protection to respect. But the play is now focusing on the physical. When Gloucester says that the king "must be relieved," he is using the term in exactly the way that Lear did in speaking of the need to be "neighbor'd, pitied, and relieved."[60] We speak of "relief workers." Kent's intervention leads Lear to attend to his literal situation. Lear sees that the Fool is cold, and acknowledges that he himself is so too. This gives Lear another insight into the issue of "need." He recognizes that physical suffering can make the bottom of the scale of values visible. He appreciates the possibility of the hovel. "The art of our necessities," he says, "is strange, / That [And] can make vile things precious" (3.2.70–71). "Our necessities"—Lear is here explicitly speaking in the name of humanity, but the "necessities" here are biological, though the articulate recognition of them is human. The hovel remains such, but, under the circumstances, is recognized as (strangely) "precious." As John Gillies points out, the fundamental distinction between being inside and outside (a physical structure) is highlighted in the play; "inside" is "a comfort zone"—however meager ("Some friendship . . . 'gainst the tempest").[61]

Yet when Kent brings Lear and the Fool to the hovel, Lear refuses to enter. He first gives a personal reason for this behavior, though one that does involve a general claim. The general claim is for the paramount nature of mental suffering. Mental anguish provides an anesthetic against physical pain. "The tempest in my mind," says Lear, "Doth from my senses take all feeling else" (3.4.12–13). But physical pain, when it is felt, can in its turn provide an anesthetic against the more detrimental pain: "This tempest will not give me leave to ponder / Things that would hurt me more" (22–23; 24–25). But *King Lear* is not a work that will downplay physical suffering. Lear's next speech is very different. It returns to the literal situation and to the issue of "our necessities." But now the object of concern is not the generically human. As in "O reason not," Lear moves from thinking about "need" to thinking about the situation of "the basest." Yet, despite that earlier speech, and Lear's longstanding awareness of the human need to be "neighbored," one still might not have thought Lear capable of the utterance that Shakespeare now gives him. "Reason not the need" was conceptual, though agonizingly personal for Lear. Here he conjures up, in his own mind, the physical situation of those who share what he is experiencing, but who do so more intensely and have done so routinely—not, as he has, for the first time in extreme old age.

The speech addresses a particular social group that its opening three-word phrase identifies. Its first word ("poor") is an adjective that is indeterminate between the objective and the affective and its third ("wretches") a collective noun that (in the period) could express both love and contempt; in between is the word that does the substantive work. The focus is bodily vulnerability:

> Poor naked wretches, wheresoe'er you are,
> That bide the pelting of the pitiless night [F: storm],
> How shall your houseless heads and unfed sides,
> Your looped and windowed raggedness, defend you
> From seasons such as these? (3.4: 24–28; 28–32)

The imagery is of enduring ("biding") torture—the stressed plosive b's and p's seem to imitate the strokes of a whip. The "wretches" are imagined in terms of particularized bodily deprivations, starting from "houseless heads" and moving downward to "unfed sides." Their overall appearance is then evoked, with terms that are affective through the surprising concreteness with which they are imagined: "looped and windowed raggedness." We are approaching the level of detail in which Edgar first imagined the Bedlam beggars, but now entirely in the mode of pathos without any hint of the bizarre (no bare arms stuck with nails or sprigs of rosemary).[62] Palfrey rightly speaks of "the speech's cherishing almost maternal touch."[63]

But there is more to this speech than empathy. Lear surprisingly rounds on himself, recognizing that the issue of poverty had not, when he was in power, been a pressing one for him—"O I have ta'en / Too little care of this," he says. But what would it mean to take sufficient "care of this"? What would lead the powerful to do so? As Michael Ignatieff notes, "Need" as such "is powerless to enforce its right"; it has power in itself "only if the powerful understand themselves to be obliged by it."[64] Lear's answer to this conundrum is to project from his own newly direct experience. But it is not clear that this projection is madness; he is not projecting details of his *bios*. He understands the structure of what has happened to him. He recognizes that the kind of awareness he is manifesting has been produced by the kind of experience he is having. Strong medicine was needed. The Folio is justified in calling this speech a prayer (3.4.27) in that it is asking for something to happen, something that is not in the power of the speaker to bring about. But instead of the addressee being, as in Lear's earlier storm speeches, the winds, or "the great gods," the addressee is now a second social group—all those with wealth and status. They are adjured to undergo harsh, cathartic treatment. "Take physic, pomp," says Lear. He is indeed imagining the equivalent of "a violent bodily process" here, a purge or emetic.[65]

Lear then explains what the purge or emetic is to be: radical bodily exposure. "Expose thyself to feel what wretches feel," the rich are told (3.4: 30; 34). As in "pitied, and relieved," feeling is seen as producing action, but here it is physical feeling that produces the psychological feeling that produces the action. Through such a process the wealthy and grand will be enabled to "shake the superflux to them [wretches] / And show the heavens more just" (31–32; 35–36). Undoubtedly this is a call for some kind of redistribution of wealth. Certainly, in the violence and extremity of its language, it goes beyond what Stephen Greenblatt calls a "modest" vision of a "trickle down" to the poor?[66] This is where the line imagining the result of this shaking of the superflux becomes important. The question becomes what it means to "show the heavens more just." Walter Cohen is on the right track in seeing the line as "a secular, materialist inversion of religion" in which "social justice guarantees metaphysical justice, rather than the other way around."[67] But even this formulation might not take the full measure of "show the heavens." The ascription of this greater justice to the heavens is presented as a fiction. There is only human, not "metaphysical" justice. Human action is needed to produce this sort of justice, some reasonable distribution of goods—and *the appearance* that it comes from "the heavens."[68] This would make the "miracle" that Lear is imagining exactly parallel to that which Edgar produces for his father.[69]

It is worth noting that Lear comes to the vision of social reform on his own, through his own experience. It is only after this speech that he encounters a poor naked wretch in the person of Edgar as Tom. It is then, as we have seen, that Lear shifts fully into madness, and enacts the idea that the proper response to wretchedness is to adopt the condition of the wretched rather than to alleviate it. But the idea of social justice—of economic justice—has been released into the play. It might seem a stretch to see the play as intended to produce the sort of catharsis that Lear imagines here—rather than the sort that Aristotle imagined—but the play is clearly meant to be strong medicine for the audience. This might explain the extraordinary amount of stage time given to the persona that Edgar adopts. He almost completely usurps the role of a voice apart from normal speech that was previously held by the professional fool. The Fool announces Tom as "a spirit" (meaning a demon?), and then virtually disappears from the dialogue (before actually disappearing).[70] "Tom" occupies and dominates the literal center of the play.

It is hard for us to imagine the impact that seeing and hearing this figure on stage probably made on the Jacobean audience. They were not used to seeing such figures dramatized in the way that Shakespeare does here. The stage-beggar was normally, like the beggars in the "rogue literature," a confidence man.[71] In fact, the first mention of "Tom o' Bedlam" in *King Lear* is in the context of a major con. In setting up his plot against Edgar, Edmund says (in the Folio), "my cue is villainous melancholy, with a sigh like Tom o' Bedlam" (1.2.125–26).[72] Shakespeare followed the con model later in his career, in a comic mode, with the figure of Autolycus in *The Winter's Tale*. I have already mentioned that the able-bodied ("sturdy") vagabond-beggar was both the nightmare of Elizabethan society and a familiar reality. The phenomenological world of such a figure was not normally evoked on the stage. William C. Carroll speaks of "the signal lack of suffering on the part of the non-Shakespearean exemplars."[73] And it is suffering, above all, that Shakespeare gives us in the figure of "Tom." We are given a full account of "what wretches feel."[74] That this is presented to us through the imagination of a former high aristocrat does not lessen the vividness of the picture, though it might make the evocation more remarkable.

Lear claimed that mental suffering is worse than physical, and "Tom's" evoked experience is of madness as well as of physical deprivation. The great majority of Elizabethan and Jacobean madmen thought they were bewitched or possessed.[75] "Tom" says that he was pursued by "the foul fiend," who tried to get him to commit suicide ("laid knives under his pillow and halters in his pew" [3.4: 46–47; 51–52]). He experiences both physical and mental anguish. The fiend Flibbertigibbbet "hurts the poor creature of earth" (3.4: 101, 105; 106, 109). We get into the particulars of "Tom's" experience, even learning what he is imagined to eat—"the swimming frog, the toad, the tadpole, the wall-newt and the water [newt]" (115–16; 119–20). Those items "Tom" presumably sought out on his own (Richard Halpern memorably calls him "a gourmet of the abject").[76] But when "Tom" felt possessed ("when the foul fiend rages") his diet was even more disgusting. He "eats cowdung for sallets, swallows the old rat and the ditch-dog, drinks the green mantle of the standing pool" (117–19; 121–23). The experience of being the object of the Elizabethan Poor Laws is specifically evoked; Tom is "whipped from tithing to tithing," since no community feels obliged to take him in, and, as one of the "basest and contemnèd'st wretches" to whom Gloucester alluded in protesting the stocking of Kent (Q 2.2.134). Tom is "stock-punished" (120).[77] And always we are reminded that "Tom's a-cold" and (supposedly) quite mad. He enters fully into Lear's madness—whether or not this includes the mock-trial.[78] Linda Woodbridge is certainly right that "Shakespeare did not have to go this far to dramatize the wretchedness of poverty."[79]

Luckily, we are not entirely in the position of having to guess at what sort of impression the figure of "Tom" made on the early Jacobean audience. We have one of those rare and precious bits of information about how something in one of Shakespeare's plays appeared to his actual audience. The title page of the only version of *King Lear* published during Shakespeare's lifetime, the Quarto of 1608, gives the author's name and status, "M. William Shak-speare," prominently in large and bold type at the top of the page; a little further down, it states, in somewhat smaller but still large type, the title or subject matter of the play ("His True Chronicle Historie of the life and death of King LEAR and his three daughters").[80] But then, just above the middle of the page, in type of the same size and arrangement as that of the title, and centered as the rest is, it adds, in italics for the first line, "*With the unfortunate life of* Edgar, *sonne* / and heire to the Earle of Gloster, and his / sullen and assumed humor of / TOM of Bedlam." "TOM of Bedlam," on a line by itself, stands at almost the exact center of the page. It is clear that this figure is mentioned because of the memory of his presence on stage, since the next lines go on to assert, in bold italic but smaller type, that the printed text is "*As it was played before the Kings Majestie at Whitehall upon S. Stephans night in Christmas Hollidayes*," followed, in smaller roman type, "By his Majesties servants playing usually at the Gloabe on the Bancke-side."[81]

The prominence of "TOM" on the title page must have reflected the prominence that the publisher took the presence of the figure on the stage to have had for the theater audience: "You've seen it (or heard about it in performance), now read it." "Tom" must have been a topic of conversation, and a draw. The only striking language on the title page is in relation to this figure. That the persona of Tom was "assumed" is straightforward (though elegantly put); that it is a "humor" is worth noting, since the word seems to mean something like "behavior"; but that the "assumed" behavior is described as "sullen" is interesting, and fascinatingly opaque. It seems to suggest ill-tempered and perhaps, as the *OED* suggests, "baleful, malignant."[82] In Shakespearean usage, the word goes with "froward" and "peevish" and "disobedient" (all applied to difficult women).[83] The word suggests that the audience did not see the figure as comical but rather as troubling. Of the various types of pretended beggars in the rogue literature, one is said to be "*sullen* both in looke and speech," and to use this to enforce charity—"compelling the servants [of a household] through feare to give them what they demaund."[84] In the storm scenes, Gloucester and Kent do not share Lear's empathy for "Tom."[85] Gloucester wanted to leave him in the "hovel" [3.4: 158; 162]; Kent was only humoring Lear in arguing that Tom be allowed to come along to the new shelter (with "fire and food") that Gloucester provided; basically, as Edgar later says, Kent "Shunned my [i.e., Tom's] abhorr'd society" [Q 5.3.204]). It is possible that the Jacobean audience found watching and hearing such a figure on stage to be an experience almost as unnerving and harrowing as the blinding of Gloucester or the death of Cordelia. It might have felt like taking "physic." And memorable.

In case we have missed the social and political point, Shakespeare makes it again in the double plot. After the audience has been forced to witness something else from which it is normally and specifically shielded (Gloucester's blinding), Shakespeare has the mutilated Gloucester perform another act of personal charity. Gloucester has been enacting charity (or courtesy) since Lear was sent out into the storm. But there the object of his care was a special and personal case—"The King my old master" (3.3.16–17). But in the scene after the blinding, when Gloucester enlists "Tom" to lead him to Dover, Gloucester's charity is to someone he knows only as a "madman and beggar too" (4.1.29; 31), though for some reason, this figure made Edgar come into his mind (32–33; 34–35). Gloucester tells this suffering (apparent) stranger, "take this purse ... that I am wretched / Makes thee the happier" (4.1: 63–64; 60–61). As in Lear's speech to "poor naked wretches," there is no concern about the "worthiness" of the recipient—in fact, the able-bodied "Tom," who claims to have been regularly whipped, would have been recognized as the opposite of "worthy."[86] To Gloucester, "Tom" is simply someone whom Gloucester takes to have experienced extreme abjection, to have been whipped by the cosmos into subjection—"thou whom the heavens' plagues / Have humbled to all strokes." But in commenting on what might be called the social geometry of the action ("I ... wretched ... thee happier"), Gloucester is led to reflect further, and to generalize—just as Lear does after realizing that he had himself taken "too little care" about the problem of the poor. Gloucester recognizes himself as part of a group of people, a whole social class, that has failed to show sufficient care.

Lear's "prayer" is really more of a fantasy, and its relation to "the heavens" is critical if not oppositional. Gloucester's speech, on the other hand, is truly a prayer. He sees the action that he has just performed as in conformity with what "the heavens" command of persons in the social state that he had inhabited. Switching from informal address to "Tom" ("thou") into formal address ("you"), Gloucester prays that "the heavens" transform the inner lives of persons such as he had been.[87] Again, "feeling" is the key:

> Let the superfluous and lust-dieted man
> That slaves [Q: stands] your ordinance, that will not see
> Because he does not feel, feel your power quickly.[88] (4.1: 65–67; 62–64)

Unlike Lear in "Expose thyself," Gloucester does not specify exactly what the rich and spoiled are to "feel," but it has to be something like a pang of conscience or fear of moral retribution. Where Lear sees the transformative feeling as empathy based on physical suffering (or the imagination of it), Gloucester seems to conceptualize the transformative feeling psychologically, as guilt or dread—as in Lear's earlier call for divine "summoners" (3.2.59). But in both cases the result is to be some sort of widespread social reform. Again, superfluity is the name of the condition that needs to be massively corrected. With regard to this, Gloucester is more specific. Where Lear's call for the shaking of the "superflux" to the poor moved into the general ethical realm ("more just"), Gloucester's call relies equally on the idea of justice, but puts it in distinctively economic terms. The idea is that "distribution should undo excess." Moreover, Shakespeare has him state what the result of such "distribution" would be—"That each man have enough" (67–68; 65–66).[89]

Distribution strikes us as a remarkably modern and technical and perhaps even radical term.[90] But Judy Kronenfeld has shown that it was the normal term in the period both for private, individual almsgiving and for nationally or locally legislated charity (that is, the poor rate).[91] It could have radical implications, though it did not have to.[92] Again, as with Lear's speech, the question is whether the social process being envisioned is "modest" or large-scale. "Distribution" leaves the matter open, but again the key, as in Lear's speech, is the final line. The vision—even the concept—of each person having "enough" is extraordinary. *Pace* Samuel Fleischacker, who claims that until the early nineteenth century no one saw "the basic structure of resource allocation across their societies as a matter of justice, let alone regarded justice as requiring a distribution of resources that meets everyone's needs," the idea in the lines, backed up, as we have seen, by much else in the play, is that there is some level of material possessions to which every human must be seen to be entitled.[93] And this, as a matter of justice.[94]

One of the things that makes the idea remarkable, especially in an early modern text, is that what it envisions was probably not possible in early modern Europe—at least under existing social conditions. It is not clear that the societies were producing enough food, and so forth, for each person to have "enough."[95] The reach of "distribution" in the existing world might have been limited in this way. Actual social security might not have been possible. But the imagination of it was.[96] Here we can turn to one of the greatest pieces of social thinking in the period, a work that Shakespeare could easily have known.[97] More's *Utopia* presents widespread labor (with no exemptions for women, clerics, or aristocrats), together with communism, as the answer, as a system that truly allows for each person to have enough.[98] It is not clear that Shakespeare's play imagines any institutional means for producing this result. But it certainly articulates this result, the idea of each person having, from a material point of view, "enough," and the play sees this ideal as rational, proper, and devoutly (or undevoutly) to be wished.[99]

Epilogue: The Superfluity Problem

There seems to be a paradox at the heart of Shakespeare's play. On the one hand, the play attacks "superfluity" and sees it as something to be undone. On the other hand, the play defends the importance of the "superfluous." Unless the play is hopelessly incoherent in its social vision, the term cannot be used in the same way in both cases.[100] In the great pleas by Lear and Gloucester for the undoing of superfluity, the term must mean something like "wealth and material possessions in excess of what anyone can be said to need"; in the second case, in Lear's great plea for respecting the superfluous, the term means, as we have seen, something like what is needed for a life that can be said to be that of a human rather than that of a "poor, bare, forked animal." Even the "basest beggars" are on the human side of that line. Lear's point is the importance of that line. If Lear were saying that the very poor have more than they need in general—where superfluity means excess—then de Grazia would be right that Lear's claim is an example of "illogic."[101] But that is not what Lear is saying. He is making a more limited and more fundamental point. He is saying that the "superfluous" defines the human. The beggar's rags and Lear's retinue both fall on the same side of the line. This is what de Grazia fails to understand. But the beggar, as Edgar says, is just over that line ("near to beast"). Redistribution moves the poor further above that line. But the question becomes how much further. Is the idea for everyone to end up in the same place, so that having "enough" means that everyone has the same amount? This would be a leveling account. But the play also seems to care about what Kent calls "differences" (1.4.83). This seems to push in a hierarchical direction. James H. Kavanagh thinks that the play is, in fact, incoherent on this matter, and that it is part of the ideological work of the play to disguise this.[102] But are there ways of resolving the apparent contradiction?

One way of doing so would be to deny the leveling impulse completely, and to see the play—despite "token acts of redistribution"—as committed to keeping the social and economic status quo in place.[103] This is de Grazia's position.

She cites Ignatieff's distinction between what a person needs and what a person is due, and claims that the latter pertains only to the rich and privileged.[104] This ignores Ignatieff's further assertion that "these two criteria [for judging social justice], though conceptually distinct, can never in fact be separated in any fully human concept of obligation."[105] Another way of resolving the contradiction would be to accept that the play has an important economic vision but to see this as significantly modified by its concern for hierarchy. This is Kronenfeld's view: the "enough" that each person can be imagined rightfully to have is conceived, in the play, as "relative to his rank."[106] So the play does have a certain economic daring but it remains, socially, just where de Grazia thinks that it does.

This would be a plausible reading if the play did not also contain scathing attacks on mere hierarchical status, on "robes and furred gowns"—as both luxury items and as symbols of official positions (4.6.158; 4.5.158). To assert that "a dog's obeyed in office" hardly shows a respect for hierarchy or "office" as such (4.6.151; 4.5.151). Kronenfeld acknowledges (unhappily) that at moments like these, the play indeed "feels 'radical.'"[107] Here I think we can rely on Henry James's maxim that "in the arts, feeling is always meaning."[108] The play simply cannot be read or theatrically experienced as a paean to rank and hierarchy. The social hierarchy that the play implicitly respects would be coordinated with personal qualities. It might be taken to include, for instance, the possession of a functioning social conscience. It would see such a conscience as taking into account what a person has been when considering who he or she is. Identity is not a matter of place or (*contra* de Grazia) property, but it is, partly, a matter of personal history.[109]

That a person's history is—or becomes—part of a person's identity is a view that allows for something like an optimistic social premise to emerge from this unquestionably bleak play. The ending of the play should not lead us to forget its middle.[110] We must consider who, after the deaths of the entire royal family, will "the gored state sustain" (5.3: 313; 296). That Edgar is going to rule is just as clear in the Quarto, where Albany speaks the final lines, as it is in the Folio, where Edgar does, though the Folio speech assignment is helpful in making the situation more perspicuous.[111] The optimistic premise is that the experience of having been Poor Tom will lead the future King Edgar to take more than a little "care of this," to do everything he can to eliminate from his realm or kingdom the existence of naked, houseless, and unfed wretches. F. T. Flahiff points out that in much Elizabethan political discourse, the rule of the historical King Edgar was seen as having a utopian quality.[112] The elimination of gross superfluity would allow for each person to be "superfluous" in more than the poorest things.

This is the reconciliation of the attack and the defense of superfluity. The play's final lines are, as they should be, a homage to the sufferers and victims—to Cordelia, Lear, and perhaps Gloucester.[113] The stress on feeling in the final speech has to do with the importance of sincerity, but it should also serve to remind us of the role that feeling has been seen as playing in the imagination of social reform.[114] What must be "borne" remains a question, but the play does not merely brood intensely on the matter of inequality.[115] If we have been attending fully, we too have been at least vicariously exposed "to feel what wretches feel," and perhaps we too will be led by this to act in such a way that we can be seen to "show the heavens more just." It may be that one of the greatest works of art in our tradition does indeed have a palpable design upon us.

CHAPTER 6

The Tempest (1)

Power

Je suis la Puissance.
         —Prospero, in Aimé Césaire, *Une Tempête*

Service interested Shakespeare throughout his career.[1] An aspect of this topic that deeply concerned him was the issue of how a servant or subordinate is to respond to an obviously immoral command. I have argued that Shakespeare grew more and more insistent on the need for servants to resist such, that *King Lear* represents the culmination of this development, and that in the three romances prior to *The Tempest* it is taken as axiomatic that "Every good servant does not all commands / No bond but to do just ones" (*Cymbeline*, 5.1.6–7).[2] *The Tempest*, however, does not seem to fit into this picture. The "virtuous disobedience" theme does not, as we will see, entirely disappear from the play, but the focus of the play with regard to masters and servants seems to be elsewhere. Its focus, as my epigraph from Aimé Césaire suggests, is on the extent and possibilities of human power, of power conceived of as pure coercion, as the capacity to control the bodies and—as far as it turns out to be possible—the minds of rational beings. *The Tempest*, in other words, is about the practical or existential rather than the moral limits of authority, and about the psychology of its exercise. To this exploration, as my epigraph is also meant to indicate, the colonial context of the play is deeply relevant.

This essay falls into two parts. The first examines what can be called (by analogy with Thomas Kuhn's "normal science") "normal politics" in the play.[3] This is the politics in which Shakespeare's "axioms" about proper and improper obedience do apply, in which conspiracy and usurpation are familiar, and in which various other *topoi* and practices internal to European politics, Machiavellian and otherwise, operate. The second and larger part of this essay focuses on features that are distinctive to *The Tempest*: Prospero's "art" and, correlated with it, his two remarkable (and non-European) servants. The dynamics that operate in this context constitute what I will call "magical politics"—which is defined by being colonial.

As my references to Césaire signal, my exploration of the latter draws on the remarkable post–World War II phenomenon of commentators and writers using *The Tempest* to explicate actual colonial situations and struggles, an analytical and literary practice that began in earnest with Dominique-Octave Mannoni's *Psychologie de la colonisation* in 1950, and that culminated in Césaire's *Une Tempête* in 1969.[4] This essay goes in the other direction, using material from the analyses of colonialism derived from *The Tempest* as ways of reading *The Tempest*. The postcolonial appropriations are now relatively well-known, but have more often been used for political critique of the play than for detailed literary criticism of it.[5] The procolonialist afterlife of *The Tempest* has been taken more seriously by literary critics than has the anticolonialist afterlife of it.[6] Mannoni and Césaire help explicate the play's "magical" politics. In conclusion, the essay will return to the "normal" politics of the play and attempt to assess the relation between its two frameworks. I should state at the outset that I do not see myself as joining Paul Brown, Jonathan Goldberg, and others in exploring the "political unconscious" of the play, nor as joining Lori Leininger and others in finding meanings in it that the play does not want us to notice.[7] I understand the meanings that I ascribe to the play as fully intended.[8] In a way, what follows is a homage not only to Mannoni and Césaire but also to George Lamming's great meditation, "A Monster, a Child, a Slave" in *The Pleasures of Exile* (1960), which goes even further into the details of the play in a colonial context than Mannoni does, and in which Lamming claims that what he finds in his analysis is "part of the conscious stuff of his [Shakespeare's] thinking."[9]

Normal Politics

The most obvious of the moments in which the "proper disobedience" theme does get into *The Tempest* is Ariel's reported noncompliance with Sycorax, even though Ariel "was then her servant" (1.2.271).[10] This noncompliance, "refusing her grand hests" (1.2.74), is presented as having been more an ontological matter, a matter of sensibility or fastidiousness, than a moral one—"thou wast a spirit too delicate / To act her earthy and abhorr'd commands" (1.2.72–73)—but the refusal is clearly seen as praiseworthy. It is hard not to think of the "earthy and abhorr'd commands" as sexual—the "abhorr'd" / "ab-whored" pun was readily available—and the context is smarmily salacious ("for one thing she did / They would not take her life" [1.2.266–67]). Ariel's refusal of this "hest" would therefore function to differentiate Ariel, in the dialectic established in *King Lear*, from the type of servant that Edgar (as "Poor Tom") pretends to have been, and that Oswald would presumably have been willing to be, one who "serv'd the lust of [his] Mistris heart, and did the acte of darknesse with her."[11] Ariel will not "serve" in this way, but the question remains as to whether there are any other sorts of commands that he would not obey.[12] I have already suggested that the moral dimension of his refusal of Sycorax's grand hests is unclear. Prospero appreciates Ariel's fastidiousness—"delicate" is one of Prospero's favorite words for Ariel—and Prospero has obtained Ariel's services by freeing him from the punishment to which Sycorax's "unmitigable rage" at Ariel's disobedience condemned him (1.2.76). But are there circumstances in which Ariel would disobey Prospero? Are there commands he would disobey that were not physically degrading? We will return to this.

A more straightforward, if less spectacular, example of what we might call the "Lear-Pericles-Cymbeline" dialectic in the matter of service occurs in Prospero's narrative of the loss of his dukedom, a key instance of normal European politics. In describing how his wicked brother ousted him, Prospero stresses his brother's skill, as regent or deputy, at personnel management, or, in less anachronistic terms, at working the courtly mechanisms of reward and punishment.[13] Antonio soon got the hang of

> how to grant suits,
> How to deny them, who t' advance, and who
> To trash for over-topping. (1.2.79–81)

Antonio truly "perfected" these techniques, and through these familiar and strictly political skills, these management skills (I want to keep the edge of ordinariness), Antonio was able to do something that Prospero finds quite amazing. The language of Prospero's account becomes extremely interesting here. Shakespeare gives him three different phrases to describe the phenomenon, even though the first phrase seems more than sufficient, and the second and third merely synonyms.

Using the idea of subordinates as "creatures" of their social superiors, Prospero sees Antonio as having "new created / The creatures that were mine" (1.2.81b–82a). The line break is significant (and can be performed). Prospero sees Antonio as having been like the Christian God, creating out of nothing, rather than the Platonic demiurge, creating out of matter. Prospero reaffirms this description with "I say" ("new created / The creatures that were mine, I say") before seeming to back off from "new created" with the diminuendo that ends the line, "or chang'd 'em" (82b). But he reasserts a strong view at the beginning of the next line with "Or else new form'd 'em" (83a). This is an image of political power as truly transformative and godlike. The next line seems to retreat again, and to present Antonio's power as merely situational ("having both the key / Of officer and office"), but this "key" turns out to be musical and mystical rather than merely practical, for with (or in) this "key" Antonio "set all hearts i' th' state / To what tune pleased his ear" (83b–85a). Antonio established concord; he captured "hearts," not just bodies.

The result of all this was that the entire political class of Milan seems to have obeyed Antonio. He was able, with the active support of Alonso, the king of Naples, to levy a "treacherous army" in Milan (128), and to find a number of "ministers for th' purpose" of disposing of Prospero and Miranda (131).[14] The unexplained love that the Milanese "people," presumably plebeian (not, now, "the creatures," presumably courtly), bore Prospero prevented Antonio from having Prospero and Miranda straightforwardly murdered, but no one prevented Antonio from having them placed aboard an unrigged, rotten boat and put to sea. The deposed duke and his daughter were aided by a single courtly figure, who, like the virtuously disobedient Camillo in *The Winter's Tale*, "being then appointed / Master of this design," exceeded and countermanded his charge ("Out of his charity") and provided Prospero and his infant with luxurious as well as necessary items including the books that Prospero prized "above his dukedom" (1.2.162–68).[15] It is typical of *The Tempest* that it is not Gonzalo's moral heroism but his "charity" that is stressed, and that the disobedient nature of his action is never made explicit (contrast the "charity" of Gloucester in *King Lear* [3.3.14], which is explicitly recognized as "forbid" [3.3.19]). Gonzalo's act of forbidden charity seems to have been completely surreptitious; it was apparently never discovered and therefore was never identified as disobedience.

Yet *The Tempest* has a hard time acknowledging even this mild and obviously laudable intervention. At the end of the play, Prospero praises Gonzalo for being "a loyal sir / To him thou follow'st" (5.1.69–70). In context, this has to mean loyal to King Alonso. The implied contrast is with the king's brother,

Sebastian, the would-be usurper and (with Antonio) co-murderer of Alonso. In the moment of upper-class planned regicide and usurpation in the play—normal politics—Antonio, using his own successful usurpation as a model ("look how well my garments sit upon me" [2.1.267]), assures Sebastian that after Antonio kills Alonso "with this obedient steel" (2.1.278), the relevant human material will be equally "obedient." In a brilliant image, Antonio says of Alonso's followers, "they'll take suggestion as a cat laps milk" (2.1.283). Again the image is of gaining willing compliance. Shakespeare substitutes the complaisant cat for the normal dog who knows "naught ... but following," but the picture (and the contempt) is the same.[16] Gonzalo is marked for death, since he alone is not thus open to "suggestion." He would remain "a loyal sir" to his king. But this entirely omits Gonzalo's role in Prospero's story. It can only have been Alonso, the king of Naples, attracted by the promise of "homage" and "annual tribute" from Milan (1.2.113), who "appointed" Gonzalo, specifically identified as "a noble Neapolitan," to be "master of [the] design" to oust Prospero from the dukedom of Milan and install Antonio (1.2.162–63). The plan was clearly for Prospero (and his daughter) to die at sea. So, Gonzalo, in providing materials for Prospero's survival and anticipated further existence, was not, in the most literal sense, being "a loyal sir" to Alonso.[17] It seems to be the case that Prospero finds it difficult to praise disobedience even when it was virtuous and he himself the beneficiary of it. But that is Prospero's perspective—not necessarily that of the play as a whole, or of its author.[18] That Gonzalo might have been truly acting as a "loyal sir" to Alonso in undermining his plan is certainly not what Prospero has in mind.[19]

In the dramatized (as opposed to narrated) action of the play, there are a few moments in which the "virtuous disobedience" trope is at work. We are perhaps intended to feel a flicker of admiration for Ferdinand's abortive attempt to "resist" Prospero's accusatory power (1.2.468), and for Miranda's limited disobedience of Prospero (in telling Ferdinand her name [3.1.36–37]).[20] The most interesting of such moments occur in the Boatswain's dialogue with the aristocrats in the opening tempest, and in Ariel's dialogue with Prospero in act 5. In the latter moment, Ariel functions as a good counselor in the full moral sense.[21] Prospero is certainly in a state of high excitement; he has just been (and is perhaps still) in a towering rage. He has set his dogs on Caliban and company (stage direction, 4.1.253), and is exulting that "At this hour / Lies at my mercy all mine enemies" (4.1.261–62). Yet despite Ariel's fear of Prospero's anger—which on an earlier occasion had prevented Ariel from speaking out ("I thought to have told thee of it; but I fear'd / Lest I might anger thee" [4.1.168–69])—Ariel now suggests to Prospero that Prospero ought to "become tender" to his European enemies (5.1.19a).[22] Ariel should be seen as following Kent's advice in *King Lear* (borrowed from radical resistance theorist George Buchanan) about not being one of those servants who encourages "every passion / That in the natures of their Lords rebells" (2.2: Q 69–71; F 71–73).[23] Ariel's intervention against the passion that "rebels" in Prospero leads Prospero to side "'gainst [his] fury" (5.1.26). Ariel's intervention is truly an act of virtuous opposition. The fact that it succeeds should not blur its moral and political outlines. He is, at this moment, the virtuously outspoken courtier delineated in the fourth book of Castiglione's *The Courtier* and exemplified in the behavior of Kent in the first scene of *Lear*.

The Boatswain of the opening scene can hardly be described in courtly terms, yet he too can be seen as enacting a version of "virtuous disobedience." The political meaning of his action is quite complex. The Boatswain is peremptory and rude to his social superiors, grandly commanding them "trouble me not" (1.1.17–18). Yet his rudeness is entirely in the service of attempting to do his job. "You mar our labour" is his complaint (13). His behavior, for all its rudeness, is within a framework of social hierarchy. But the Boatswain is keenly aware of the limits of social and political authority. Nature defines these limits. He challenges the aristocrats thus: "if you can command these elements to silence, and work the peace of the present, we will not hand a rope more; use your authority" (1.1.21–23).[24]

Magical Politics

The Boatswain's comments on the limits of "normal" authority bring us to the central feature of *The Tempest*, the presence of non-normal authority in the play. As soon as we meet Prospero, we find out that he can apparently "command these elements to silence, and work the peace of the present." The name of this non-normal authority in the play is, as I have already suggested, "art," which here means magic.[25] Prospero's magic, his special power, is what makes the treatment of "authority" in this play special. It is also, I will argue (following Mannoni), what makes the focus of the play colonial. What Shakespeare seems to have intuited and embodied in the figure of Prospero is that, at their cores, the Renaissance idea of magic and the idea of colonial administration have the same fantasy content: namely, the idea of omnipotence. Both figures, the magus and the colonial administrator, are defined by having special kinds of servants—"spirits" or daemons on the one hand; "natives" on the other.[26] As Stephen Orgel notes, "What Prospero's magic chiefly enables him to do is control his servants."[27]

Christopher Marlowe seems to have first given voice to the crucial association between the colonialist and the magian fantasies.[28] When Marlowe's Dr. Faustus is first "glutted with [the] conceit" of magical power, and is asserting his resolve "To practice magic and concealed arts" to the friends (Valdes and Cornelius) who have urged him in this direction, thoughts of "the new-found world" are strongly present to all of them. Valdes expresses the core fantasy by coordinating the two kinds of servants.

> As Indian Moors obey their Spanish lords,
> So shall the spirits of every element
> Be always serviceable to us three.[29]

The rule of the Spanish in the New World is the closest analogue Marlowe can think of to the vision of magical omnipotence.[30] Shakespeare remembered this analogy.

The equation between magic and colonial administration helps explain many things in Shakespeare's magician play. Most importantly, it explains a central fact about which the critics have been remarkably incurious: why Prospero's "art" (unlike Faustus's) can only work in a particular locale. He can apparently do nothing to bring his enemies to his island ("bountiful Fortune... hath mine enemies / Brought to this shore" [1.2.178–80]), and he cannot, apparently, use his powers directly to get himself home and reseize his dukedom. What this means, interpretively, is that any attempt to read Prospero "straight" as a magus cannot be right.[31] A magus could use his powers anywhere. Seeing magic as equivalent to colonial administration explains a related point as well. It explains why, in contemplating his life off the island, Prospero imagines himself not as "this famous Duke of Milan" (5.1.192), but as a weak and vulnerable penitent looking toward death. Although there is some confusion about this in the scholarship (to which we shall return), Prospero does not see his homecoming as a regaining of his life and work but as an escape from them—he will "retire me to my Milan, where / Every third thought shall be my grave" (5.1.310–11). Life on the island, in other words, is not Prospero's nightmare but his wish-fulfillment dream. This is Mannoni's great insight—the centrality of a certain set of (infantile) psychological satisfactions to the experience of colonial administration.[32] Prospero's life and his work are on the island. Both Frantz Fanon and Césaire criticized Mannoni's views on the mentality of the colonized (or at least, how he presented his views), but they both accepted Mannoni's view of the psychology of the colonial administrator.[33] Fanon admiringly notes "the intensity with which M. Mannoni makes us feel the ill-resolved conflicts that seem to be at the root of the colonial vocation."[34] It is one of the most brilliant features of *Une Tempête* that at the end of the play Césaire's Prospero chooses to remain on the island.[35]

Mannoni distinguished sharply between the conquistador / explorer, on the one hand, and "the colonial," meaning the colonial administrator, on the other.[36] Shakespeare could have studied the psychology of the colonial administrator in the many accounts of his countrymen in Ireland and, especially, of the Spanish in the New World.[37] Seeing Prospero as embodying this psychology gets the focus of the colonial dimension of the play on the only place where it can plausibly be: on Prospero's relation to his non-European servants. For, apart from these relations, Prospero is a very odd colonizer. He is not, in fact, by the dominant English definition, a colonizer at all. The *True Declaration of the State of Virginia* (1610) explained that "a Colony is therefore denominated, because they [the settlers there] should be *Coloni,* the tillers of the earth, and stewards of fertilitie."[38] Colonies were often called "plantations," as in Bacon's "Of Plantations" (1625) or Francis Higginson's *New-England's Plantation* (1630).[39] A "plantation" was a militarily guarded and maintained agricultural settlement.[40] Cultivation, farming, and building were central to the English conception of colonization; they were what made colonization a (supposedly) "civilizing" endeavor.[41] The (attempted) conquest and resettlement of Ireland was the model.[42] Sir John Davies pours scorn on the Irish gentry because (except when they occasionally imitated the English) the Irish never "did build any stone or brick house" and "neither did any of them in all this time plant any gardens or orchards, enclose or improve their lands"; William Crashaw explains that the American natives need (and desire) "civility" for their bodies almost as much as they need (and desire) Christianity for their souls, since "a savage cannot plow, till, plant, nor set."[43] Prospero looks very odd indeed in this context.[44] He seems to have neither built, planted, nor "set" anything on the island. His "cell" seems to be a cave.[45] There is no indication that he grows anything, raises anything, or even has a garden on the island.[46]

We meet Prospero not at the moment of discovery or conquest but at a moment when he has already had a significant history on the island. The essence of Prospero's situation on the island is not cultivation, except in the mental sense.[47] He is a "governor" rather than a "planter," and "governors" could be thought of as especially (and sometimes only) appropriate for the uncivil and, especially, the non-European (see *OED*, s.v. "governor," definition 6a). A leader of the defiant local gentry on the Isle of Wight in the 1580s told the queen's newly commissioned governor of the island that "if he would needs be a governor," he "should go into the West Indies among the base people."⁴⁸ As Prospero experiences his situation, he is "among the base people." He has, as he experiences it, no peers, only inferiors: a boyishly androgynous "spirit," a fifteen-year-old daughter, and "a salvage and deformed slave."⁴⁹ Paradise! Not another adult European male (or female) for thousands of miles. When George Ogilvie established a plantation on the Santee River in South Carolina, he experienced himself as "like the Tyrant of some Asiatick Isle, the only free Man in an Island of Slaves."⁵⁰

This is the ideal situation for someone who has, as Mannoni wonderfully puts it, "a grave lack of sociability combined with a pathological urge to dominate."⁵¹ What Prospero learns about himself on the island that he did not and could not know about himself in Milan is that he had a capacity for exercising power over those distinctly not like himself (though his desire to be a magus perhaps suggests this).⁵² His gift is for being a "governor." The model that Shakespeare employs for Prospero's proceedings on the island can be seen as a Spanish rather than an English one (recall "As Indian Moors obey their Spanish lords"). Anthony Pagden states that while the British were concerned with rights over things and land, "the Spaniards were overwhelmingly concerned with rights over people."⁵³ Prospero is not at all concerned with things and land. Mannoni was right to speak of domination.⁵⁴ This is what concerns Prospero as a ruler—dominating his servants, the island's two named indigenes.

The first of the two that we encounter is initially addressed merely as "servant" (1.2.187). But something special already seems to be involved when, in the next line, the figure is addressed, in something like a formal invocation, by name, and with a possessive: "Approach, my Ariel." There seems to be an element of some sort of affection or intimacy here. Ariel's response recognizes both a social and a functional superior. "All hail, great master," he says, and we know from the witches in *Macbeth* that "All hail" is an especially obsequious mode of address.⁵⁵ The address then changes to "grave sir, hail"—which would seem to connote genuine, nonhierarchical respect, respect for a person rather than a position (as in Jonson's "Inviting a Friend to Supper," which begins, "Tonight, grave sir, both my poor house and I / Do equally desire thy company"). But what follows is a speech that is surprising both for the physical capacities it asserts—"be't to fly, / To swim, to dive into the fire, to ride / On the curl'd clouds"—and for the attitude of complete, willing, and uncritical subservience (or call it dedication) that it enunciates. Ariel comes to answer Prospero's "best pleasure" (1.2.190). The master is invited to exercise his authority: "to thy strong bidding task / Ariel and all his quality" (1.2.192–93).

Prospero gets right down to business. He makes it clear what sort of creature Ariel is, takes his special capacities for granted, and wants to know whether Ariel has acted punctiliously: "Hast thou, spirit, / Perform'd to point the tempest that I bade thee?" (1.2.193–94). Ariel's response is a rhetorical and descriptive tour de force. His narrative describes spectacular effects in both senses—the visual and auditory phenomena he produced and the impact that these had on those who experienced them. His first period ends with a statement that combines both effect and affect: "I flam'd amazement" (198a). He emphasizes his projective and (so to speak) gymnastic skills: "sometimes I'd divide . . . Then meet and join" (198b–201a). The effect was synesthetic, involving sight, sound, and smell simultaneously: "the fire and cracks / Of sulphurous roaring" (203b–204a). As Harry Berger notes, the narrative shifts into "high-toned epic personification" with the claim that all this made "most mighty Neptune . . . his dread trident shake" (204–6).[56] Prospero is pleased, using his wonted possessive ("My brave Ariel"), but he is not interested in the effects, only in the affect, the psychological effect that he intended for the spectacle to produce. "Who," he asks, "was so firm so constant, that this coil / Would not infect his reason?" (207–8a).

The idea was to drive the sufferers of the spectacle mad. Ariel assures Prospero that occurred ("Not a soul / But felt a fever of the mad" (208b–209a), but Ariel does not stop there; he gives further detail, specifying who stayed on the ship (the sailors) and who "Plung'd in the foaming brine," adding a special vignette about "the King's son, Ferdinand," who (like a good Elizabethan madman) seemed to think that he was possessed (210–215b). Ariel answers the question about the location of the apparent wreck straightforwardly, but as to the safety of the men, he again uses a grand style phrase, this time biblical rather than classical ("Not a hair perished" [217]), before straightforwardly reporting that he followed Prospero's instructions as to the disposition of the members of the royal party and the rest of the royal fleet but used his own discretion as to where he stowed the King's ship (referring, in the process, to a previous remarkable feat that he had done—fetching dew from "the still-vex'd Bermoothes" [224–237]).

Prospero commends Ariel for performing his charge "exactly." But it is impossible that Prospero had actually specified all the details that Ariel so volubly provides. Some of it was clearly improvised. Lamming was right to speak of the "pure and diabolical delight" that Ariel takes in narrating and performing all the harms and terrors he inflicts (aesthetic appreciation in the play is not morally coded).[57] Derek Cohen notes that Ariel, "like Hegel's bondsman, seems to discover in his labour a form of self-expression."[58] It is no wonder that, after all this inspired activity, Ariel is surprised when Prospero states that "there's more work" (1.2.238). That word, which suddenly suggests that doing the master's "pleasure" is not entirely a pleasure for the servant, brings a change of tone into the dialogue. The servant speaks up. Suddenly he is no longer presenting himself as a pure and willing instrument. "Is there more toil," he asks, and suddenly changes the framework, asserting a claim: "Since thou dost give me pains, / Let me remember thee what thou hast promis'd, / Which is not yet perform'd me" (242b–244). Something like a contract is implied here, and Ariel expects to be an object as well as an agent of "performance."

Prospero responds to the change in tone, not to the substance. He seems surprised that his servant should manifest any trace of self-concern. He trivializes it, treating it, as we would say, as if it were just a matter of "hormones"— "Why how now? moody?"[59] Prospero then plays dumb, as if the whole scenario were inconceivable—"What is't thou canst demand?" Ariel answers in clear and striking words: "My liberty" (243–45). He claims something like the legal status of an apprentice, an indentured servant, or a Roman slave who has been promised manumission.[60] The words have an effect on Prospero. He answers from within the contract idea, but insists that it includes no flexibility, no room for bargaining—"Before the time be out? No more!" But apparently this contravenes another agreement. Ariel points out that in return for perfect service and perfect obsequiousness—"no lies . . . no mistakings . . . Without grudge or grumblings"—Prospero has promised to reduce the term of service by a year.

Here, for a second time, Ariel has ventured to urge Prospero to remember something (243, 246). This idea—that Prospero should be reminded of something, that someone else's historical consciousness should be brought to bear on the present moment—outrages Prospero. He is so incensed at being quite gently reminded ("let me remember thee") that he turns the tables on Ariel and accuses him of being the one who is forgetting something. Prospero is in charge of the memory game, a game, as Lamming notes, that Prospero is an expert at.[61] Prospero claims that Ariel, in making his demand for "performance," has forgotten a fact—the key fact—about their relationship: it is based not in a contract between them but in Prospero's power. Prospero has used his power to benefit Ariel. He freed him from "a torment," and Ariel has "forgotten" to be properly grateful. Ariel flatly denies this (252), and Prospero accuses him of having exactly the mental attitude ("grudge") that Ariel has denied having: "Thou think'st it much to tread the ooze." Ariel also denies this—very reverently this time ("I do not, sir" [256])—and Prospero responds with an astonishing accusation and epithet: "Thou liest, malignant thing!" (257).

Suddenly there is no affection or comradeship, only a battle of wills. Again, and again, Prospero accuses Ariel of having "forgotten" a key fact—"Hast thou forgot / The foul witch Sycorax ... hast thou forgot her?" (257, 259). "No, sir," says Ariel, but this means nothing to Prospero. He insists that Ariel has forgotten the facts—"Where was she born?" Ariel answers, but Prospero is not content with his answer. Many critics assume that when Prospero says, "O, was she so?" he intends to correct or contradict Ariel, but, as Orgel points out, that cannot be so.[62] It is important to see the oddness of the situation here. Prospero is accusing Ariel of having "forgotten" something that Prospero could only know through Ariel having told it to him (the history of Sycorax). Prospero insists that he is in charge of "reminding" Ariel, regularly, of Ariel's own story—"I must / Once in a month recount what thou hast been" (261–62). Ariel is reduced to merely assenting to the truth of his own story: "Is not this true?" asks Prospero; "Ay, sir," says Ariel (267–68). The point of all this is for Prospero to evoke and Ariel to recall, as vividly as possible, the torment that Ariel had endured for his disobedience to Sycorax (painful confinement for twelve years in a cloven pine [274–281a; again at 285b–290a]). Prospero's role as savior must be in the foreground, with his unique art, more powerful than that of Sycorax (who could not undo the curse on Ariel [291]). Ariel must be properly—that is, supinely—grateful. "I thank thee, master" (293) is the expected and demanded response. Prospero is to be in charge not only of Ariel's behavior but also of his state of mind (as "without ... grudge" suggested). What Prospero means by "remembering" is seeing things, including Ariel's own past, exactly as he (Prospero) does.

One would think that the profession of gratitude would be enough, but Prospero is not finished. He recharacterizes Ariel's offense, and adds a major threat:

> If thou more murmur'st, I will rend an oak,
> And peg thee in his knotty entrails, till
> Thou hast howl'd away twelve winters. (1.2.294–96)

So, as a number of critics have noted, despite Prospero's contempt for Sycorax, he threatens, in effect, to become her.[63] He will reproduce the terms of Ariel's torment, and outgo them, imprisoning Ariel in a specially created space of hard wood rather than in Sycorax's "[pre-?] cloven pine" (277). He will also go Sycorax one better in the reason for the torture. Where she in her "unmitigable rage" (276) punished Ariel for actively disobeying, Prospero will punish him merely for expressing discontent, for, as Prospero puts it, murmuring.

"Murmuring" was the standard term in the English Renaissance Bible and in English Renaissance poetry for expressed or suppressed verbal reluctance to accept God's commands; biblically alert auditors would have noted this.[64] Prospero is assuming God's role here, relying not just on gratitude (for freedom from captivity) but on fear. No wonder Ariel ends by asking to be forgiven for the offense he has committed—such as it is—and promising to be the perfectly responsive servant: "Pardon, master: / I will be correspondent to command, / And do my spiriting gently" (296–98).[65] "Do so," says Prospero, who is finally willing to acknowledge that he remembers the contract—all that Ariel asked in the first place: "after two days / I will discharge thee." This puts Ariel into a proper framework of gratitude and reverence—"That's my noble master!"—and into a frenzy of obeisance: "What shall I do? Say what; what shall I do?" (300). Prospero finds this completely acceptable; he gives another command; and he ends this stretch of dialogue by admonishing Ariel to execute this new command "With diligence" (306)—hardly, one would think, an admonition that is necessary at this point.[66]

How to characterize the relation between Ariel and Prospero is a tricky matter. Ariel is initially, as we have seen, addressed as "servant," and seems to have a contract of sorts. But Prospero later states that Ariel characterizes himself as Prospero's "slave" (at 1.2.270).[67] A slave, after all, can be manumitted. So is there a difference in the play between being a slave and being a servant? Roberto Fernandez Retamar suggests that there is not.[68] In this context, the affection between Prospero and Ariel needs to be looked at carefully. It is largely part of the service relation, and not necessarily (as David Schalkwyk would like to posit) a benign part of it.[69] As with the opening tempest, Prospero's expressions of affection and appreciation for Ariel occur entirely in contexts of instrumentality. Ariel is the agent and embodiment of Prospero's "magic." It is through Ariel that Prospero can experience something like the infantile belief in "the omnipotence of thought" that Freud saw as the essence of magic and Mannoni saw as one of the great colonialist fantasies.[70] Prospero commands Ariel, "Come with a thought," to which Ariel replies, "Thy thoughts I cleave to" (4.1.164–65). Significantly, this formulation disturbs Frank Kermode, for whom it is part of the evidence that Shakespeare's characterization of Prospero's relation to Ariel is not "theurgically pure."[71]

Ariel sometimes seems virtually internal to Prospero. When, at the end of the second scene, Ferdinand seems (to Prospero) properly smitten with Miranda, Prospero notes that "It goes on ... As my soul prompts it," and then calls Ariel a "fine spirit" (423–24) where "spirit" follows very quickly upon "soul."[72]

The appreciation of Ariel for exact enactment of Prospero's wishes continues. After Ariel has delivered the great prepared speech through which Prospero attempts to take over the consciousness of his European enemies—again through producing madness (3.3.58)—Prospero commends him for performing "bravely," and notes, happily, that "Of my instructions hast thou nothing bated" (3.3.85). In the next scene, Prospero calls for his "industrious servant," to which Ariel responds, "What would my potent master?" (4.1.33–34). Prospero commands Ariel to bring the "rabble / O'er whom I give thee power" to where he and Ferdinand and Miranda are, to perform "some vanity of mine art," the masque. Ariel, on understanding that he is to do this posthaste, reassures Prospero that he will. But Ariel ends this particular assertion of willing obeisance with a question, one that suggests a different picture of the Ariel-Prospero relationship: "Do you love me, master? no?" (4.1.48).

This is a haunting and troubling moment. Schalkwyk worries that Prospero's response, "Dearly, my delicate Ariel," might seem "perfunctory."[73] But it is perfunctory, and immediately followed by a command (4.1.49–50). Jeffrey S. Doty observes of Prospero's use of the possessive here and at other places in relation to Ariel that it "is less a term of affection than an assertion of possession."[74] What the love between them seems to consist of is, on the one hand, the pleasure of seeing one's will fully instantiated, and, on the other, the pleasure of being the perfect instrument. Both are troubling pleasures. In Ariel's desire to be "loved" by his master, it looks as if what we have is an illustration of what Mannoni called "the dependence complex in its pure state."[75] It is the attitude in which Aristotle's "natural slave" permanently exists, a human (or, in Ariel's case, humanlike) figure that finds its purpose entirely in being an instrument.[76] Lamming calls it "degradation."[77] There is no question of being loved as an independent entity or consciousness.[78]

The possibility that there is a theological or mystical and, as Mannoni would point out, psychological realm in which service could be experienced as "freedom" cannot be denied.[79] But this is certainly not what Ariel had in mind when he spoke of his "liberty." Prospero has a vision of liberty for Ariel, telling him, "Thou shalt be as free / As mountain winds" (1.2.502), and again, "Thou shalt have the air at freedom" (4.1.265).[80] Yet Ariel's own vision of life after service is rather different. As revealed in his song in act 5 (5.1.88–94), it is a vision of happy oneness with nature, which seems to be conceived of in terms of infantile satisfactions: sucking ("Where the bee sucks, there suck I"); passively lying in an enclosed space ("In a cowslips' bell I lie"); being carried about by another ("On the bat's back I do fly"); and being protected ("Under the blossom that hangs on the bough"). Ariel is formally manumitted "to the elements" in the final line of the play (before the epilogue). But it looks (sounds) as if he wishes to lose his will to "the elements" and to be "loved" by them as he formerly was by Prospero.[81] On Mannoni's model, "service" has corrupted Ariel's consciousness as thoroughly as domination has Prospero's.

This brings us, inevitably, to Caliban. He is first mentioned in Prospero's admonitory "reminding" Ariel of Ariel's story. Prospero's acknowledgment of Caliban having "a human shape" is parenthetical and contorted, but he is perfectly clear on the social function of "that Caliban, / Whom now I keep in service" (285–86).[82] Caliban seems strictly parallel to Ariel. Shakespeare appears to be introducing us to Prospero's household, and doing so in order of rank: child, upper servant, lower servant. As we have already seen, no clear distinction from Ariel is implied when Prospero refers to Caliban as "my slave" (310). What is distinctive is the nature of Caliban's "service." It has to do with biological sustenance.[83] Prospero's situation strikingly duplicates that of the Virginia settlers, who, in Ralph Lane's report on the first colony in 1584, were utterly dependent on help from "the savages" for survival.[84]

Yet Prospero's initial summoning of Caliban has no practical point. Caliban assumes that when Prospero calls for him, what is wanted is for Caliban to perform what is apparently his most normal and characteristic task, that of log-fetching, and Caliban asserts (from offstage) that "there's wood enough within" (1.2.316). Prospero must accept the truth of this, since he asserts that wood-carrying is not what he desires; rather, he tells Caliban, "there's other business for thee" (317). Yet Prospero ends this initial interaction by commanding, "Fetch us in fuel" (368a). So apparently there was no "other business," though this rather mysterious phrase is repeated after the command for fuel—"be quick, thou 'rt best, / To answer other business" (368b–369a)—and is followed by a threat of torture for hypothetical future disobedience (370–73). The initial summons was a mere exercise in authority. Prospero's command was not, in fact, that Caliban do anything but that he appear and "speak" (316). Interaction, apparently, was what Prospero wanted. In response to Prospero's formal invocation of him as a "poisonous" bastard begotten "by the devil himself" on his "wicked dam," Caliban produces an elaborate and multifaceted curse that picks up the reference to his mother (321–26). Prospero assures Caliban that he will be tortured for such later (327–32).[85] Their relationship seems to be one of straightforward enmity. The economic arrangement would seem to explain this, to explain why Caliban, as Miranda says, "never / Yields us kind answer" (310–11). A servant or slave could well be imagined to resent having to do continuous physical labor, and a master could well respond to this resentment with equal and opposite hatred. But it turns out that the situation is much more complex. Instead of responding to Prospero's list of tortures (cramps, side-stitches, etc.), Caliban provides a historical narrative. This is the third of these that we have heard. The first two were by Prospero, who has given his own story (as he sees it) and Ariel's (as Prospero sees it). But Caliban gives his own. What he narrates (334b–346a) is not a story of straightforward enslavement but of a mutually beneficial and affectionate relationship that somehow ended in the current hostility.[86] Prospero responds by calling Caliban a "most lying slave" (346b).

This immediately echoes Prospero's response to Ariel's "reminder"—"Thou liest, malignant thing!" (1.2.257). We recall that what Prospero means by calling one of his subordinates a liar is not that the servant or slave in question has said something untrue—Prospero never claims this—but that this figure failed to mention a fact that Prospero considers to be crucial. Ariel had not made reference to his torture and imprisonment by Sycorax, and Caliban has not made reference to what Prospero calls Caliban's attempt "to violate / The honour of my child" (349–50). So, for Prospero, not to understand and tell one's own story as Prospero understands it is to lie.[87]

Interestingly, Caliban does not deny the rape charge. He is unrepentant—again, he does not lie—and this episode is taken as revealing the irredeemable, evil essence of Caliban's "vile race."[88] Yet Prospero's account of Caliban's sexual transgression is, as Mannoni first argued, and a number of commentators since have agreed, a justification for, rather than a rational explanation of, hatred and coercion.[89] Responses other than sadistic enslavement were surely possible.[90] But not for Prospero. What made Caliban's attempt on Miranda unpardonable? One answer to this question may have to do with problems of sexuality and of incest fantasies (a major topic of *Pericles*).[91] But the answer that I want to pursue has to do with Prospero's overwhelming self-concern. The attempt on Miranda—assuming its reality—was not, in Prospero's mind, an attack on her person but on her "honour," a marker and prerogative of class status.[92] It was not so much an attack on her as on him—on "the honour of my child." Prospero is the injured party.[93] He treated Caliban beautifully (1.2.348)—and Caliban betrayed him. Like Ariel, who has murmured and dared to remind Prospero, Caliban has been ungrateful. He has betrayed Prospero's trust. Prospero, as he sees it, bears no responsibility for his harsh treatment of Caliban; it is forced on him by Caliban's betrayal of him. In that amazing early colonialist document the *Requerimiento*, the Spanish carefully explain that if their (proper) demands for obedience and reverence are not met, "we shall take away your goods, and shall do you all the mischief and damage that we can, as to vassals who do not obey," and it goes on to explain that all these ills that will be inflicted "are your fault."[94] So, according to this "logic," Caliban is responsible for Prospero's treatment of him.[95]

But the play takes us further into this matter. This is Prospero's second tale of betrayal. We must read the story of Caliban's "betrayal" of Prospero through the story of Antonio's betrayal of Prospero. Prospero imagines what he calls his "trust" to be an absolute that places an absolute obligation on its object. His trust in Antonio was, as Prospero says, "sans bound" (1.2.97). He put Antonio in a situation of impossible temptation—"casting" the government entirely upon him (1.2.75)—and then was utterly startled, shocked, and horrified when Antonio did not play by Prospero's rules and succumbed to the obvious temptation. And Prospero did exactly the same with Caliban. Caliban was fourteen or fifteen when Prospero appeared on the island, since Sycorax gave birth to Caliban there and sometime—presumably early on after her arrival—confined Ariel in the pine where Ariel did "painfully remain" for twelve years, during which time Sycorax died, and Caliban, who must have been weaned by then, survived on his own. This time span—twelve years—could not be more insisted on in the play. It is how long Prospero and Miranda have been on the island, as Prospero tells her (twice in one line): "Twelve years since, Miranda, twelve years since" (1.2.53). We also know how old Miranda was when they arrived—"not / Out three years old" (1.2.40–41). The precision and insistence on these numbers are striking, given how cavalier Shakespeare is about such matters elsewhere.[96] The numbers matter. Shakespeare wants it to be easy for us to calculate that at the time of the action of the play, Miranda is going on fifteen and Caliban on twenty-six or twenty-seven.[97]

So we must consider the domestic arrangements over which Prospero presided. He "lodg'd" an adolescent boy together in his "cell" with his daughter. When she was a young child, one could imagine—giving Prospero the benefit of the doubt—that this did not matter. But Prospero seems to have been sublimely indifferent to the fact that children grow up.[98] He was startled, shocked, and horrified when Caliban became sexually interested in Miranda once she reached or approached puberty—twelve years from the age of three being plenty of time for this to happen. So, consider the parallel "betrayals."[99] In the cases of both Antonio and Caliban (brother and surrogate or foster son), Prospero sees his boundless trust as having "awak'd" a preexistent "evil nature" in the recipient of it—this is said, it should be noted, of Antonio (1.2.93).[100] Prospero's "trust" no more acknowledged the independent personhood of its objects than his impositions of power and narrative do.

The sociopsychological fantasy embodied in *The Tempest* is of narcissistic withdrawal producing—in proper circumstances—magical power. Perhaps more clearly than Marlowe, Shakespeare recognized that magic, especially "white" (theurgic) magic, was the Renaissance name for what we would now think of as the Foucauldian conception of "power-knowledge," of knowledge functioning as a form of power.[101] But Shakespeare is explicit, as Foucault is not, that the ultimate meaning of power is physical coercion (Césaire seems to me to show his typical perspicacity in having his Prospero characterize himself as "la Puissance" rather than the more abstract "le Pouvoir," Foucault's term).[102] After Prospero's "Fetch us in fuel"—the practical pointlessness of which we have already noted—Caliban comments:

> I must obey: his art is of such pow'r,
> It would control my dam's god, Setebos,
> And make a vassal of him. (1.2.374–76)

Power is the capacity to coerce and enslave, to "control" in the very strong Renaissance sense of that term.[103]

Yet *The Tempest* is also strongly aware of the limits of coercive human power, even in a colonial situation. Through a combination of threats and bribes, Prospero can keep Ariel from "murmuring," but nothing Prospero can do can keep Caliban from cursing. Prospero threatens Caliban with a version of the most famous of early modern torture devices—"if thou neglect'st, or dost unwillingly / What I command, I'll rack thee with old cramps" (370–71). But while Prospero can make Caliban work, he cannot keep him from doing so "unwillingly." Neither surveillance nor punishment makes a difference. "His spirits hear me, / And yet I needs must curse," says Caliban (2.2.3–4). Caliban claims that all Prospero's conscripted workers do unwillingly what he commands, and that in fact they all "do hate him / As rootedly as I" (2.92–93). "Thought is free," says Stephano (2.2.121).[104] So, as Caliban's case makes clear, is the tongue—if one is willing, like Caliban in the play and the rebellious Henry Paine in the narrative on which scene 1 is partly based, to suffer for the use of it (Paine specialized in "settled and bitter" antiauthoritarian speech; in the 1611 "Articles, Lawes, and Orders, Divine, Politique, and Martiall for the Colony in Virginea," the second through fifth items concern speech-crimes—impiety, blasphemy, derision, etc.).[105]

The limits of Prospero's power are crucial to the political meaning of the play, both generally and in its colonial context. Yet the best political critics of the play have either refused to note or refused to give interpretive weight to these limits. This may be because these critics have assumed that if the play is critical of colonialism, it must be criticizing a presentation of colonial *success*. Paul Brown sees the action of the play as producing a "new solidarity" in the aristocratic class.[106] Peter Hulme is insistent that "in its own terms Prospero's play is undoubtedly a success; it achieves what it wants to achieve."[107] Stephen Orgel takes full note of Prospero's failure with Antonio, yet concludes from this that since Antonio remains impenitent, it must be the case that "penitence *is not what Prospero's magic is designed to elicit* from his brother."[108] What Prospero really wants, says Orgel, is his dukedom back—and this he gets. Stephen Greenblatt follows Orgel here. After noting that "the truculence of the villains at the end of the play marks the limit of Prospero's power," Greenblatt withdraws from the point by adding that "at the very moment that the limit is marked, the play suggests that *it is relatively inconsequential*"—since Prospero gets his dukedom back.[109] Curt Breight takes the "success view" even further and denies that Prospero intends to renounce his power when he returns to Milan.[110]

But just as the play is explicit that Prospero intend to "retire" to Milan (5.1.310), it is explicit that he desires to transform his enemies. He wants to affect their minds, their hearts, their consciences. This (as Greenblatt knows and emphasizes elsewhere in his essay) is one of the great fantasies of power in the period, in and out of the colonial context.[111] Prospero's aim, repeatedly highlighted, is not only to get his dukedom back; he could do that merely by revealing himself. His "business," Ariel says in Prospero's words, is to get Prospero's enemies to remember—"for that's my business to you" (3.3.69). Getting figures to remember in the way he wishes them to has, as we have seen, been Prospero's "business" all along, but his aim in relation to his aristocratic European enemies is not, as with Miranda, to produce awe ("are not you my father?" [1.2.55]), or, as with his island subordinates, to produce or to justify "service." His aim, with regard to those who "did supplant" him from Milan (2.2.70), is twofold. It is to produce, first, contrition—"heart-sorrow" (3.3.81)—and then, reform, "a clear life ensuing" (82). This is the exact Protestant definition of penitence.[112] Prospero's whole "project" with regard to his European enemies consists, he says, in their "being penitent"; it is "the sole drift" of his purpose (5.1.28–29).[113]

At the end of act 3, Gonzalo believes that Prospero has succeeded in this endeavor with all his European enemies. Watching the behavior of Alonso, Sebastian, and Antonio after they hear what the thunder says, Gonzalo concludes:

> their great guilt,
> (Like poison given to work a great time after)
> Now 'gins to bite the spirits. (3.3.104–6)

But it turns out that Gonzalo is wrong. Prospero can produce the physical and even the physicopsychological effects of guilt—he can produce hysteria and hallucinations and obscure the group's rational powers (5.1.67–68)—but he cannot affect their "spirits" in the nonphysiological sense. He cannot change their moral characters, their hearts in the nonphysiological sense. A similar moment occurred earlier when Prospero paralyzed Ferdinand with sword in hand and told him that he (Ferdinand) could not strike because "thy conscience / Is so possess'd with guilt" (1.2.473–74). Breight argues that Shakespeare is here demystifying the way that power seeks to impose false interpretations on its subjects.[114] Yet Shakespeare may here be pointing not to the emptiness of the fictions of power but to the fullness of their fantasy content, to the capacities that those in power wish that they had.[115]

Like torturers and tyrannical administrators of all sorts, Prospero can "play God," but Reformation Protestants knew that only the figure who does not have to play God can actually transform the will. Only God can produce "heart-sorrow / And a clear life ensuing." This was the central premise of Luther's "Ninety-Five Theses" and of the whole Protestant attack on the penitential system.[116] Fear of punishment may have been "attrition," but it was not contrition (Gonzalo in Césaire's play points this out).[117] Alonso, who does feel genuine remorse and does change his life ("Thy dukedom I resign" [5.1.118]), is Prospero's one clear success, and it seems to be grief over the (apparent) loss of his son that enables the process to work in Alonso. Sebastian, in act 5, seems to have developed a capacity for wonder (he sees the revelation of Ferdinand and Miranda playing chess as "a most high miracle" [5.1.177]), but relapses into cynicism at seeing Ariel and Caliban (at 5.1.263–65—"Will money buy 'em?"). Antonio, the major villain of the play—the deposer of Prospero, suborner of Sebastian, and would-be assassin of Alonso—remains, as Orgel noted, entirely untransformed. Just as Prospero cannot stop Caliban from cursing, he cannot make Antonio speak. Prospero can "forgive" Antonio, but he cannot change him, even though Antonio is repeatedly characterized as "unnatural" (5.1.74–79).[118] The entire speaking part assigned to Antonio in act 5 is a cynical line and a half responding affirmatively to "Will money buy 'em?" (he is sure that at least Caliban is "marketable" [5.1.265–66]). Shakespeare's point is not that Prospero does not really want to transform Antonio, but that he does really want to, and cannot.[119] This strikes me as very far from "inconsequential."

But perhaps Caliban is transformed. The humanist fantasy of morally uplifting the "uncivil" (whether "natives" or not) is a deep one.[120] In his final speech, Caliban says that he will "be wise hereafter, / And seek for grace" (5.1.295). The question is what to make of this. I do not believe that there is truly a theological dimension here, though Shakespeare obviously wants us to consider this possibility. We might share Joseph Warton's disappointment that "our author has not preserved [the] fierce and implacable spirit in Calyban to the end of the play"—something that Césaire did—but we may not need to worry that Shakespeare has "injudiciously put into [Caliban's] mouth words that imply repentance" in the full religious sense.[121] Shakespeare is using the language of "grace" in its lowest (sociopolitical) rather than its highest (theological) register. The "grace" that Caliban seeks is human, not divine pardon. Shakespeare wants us, I would argue, to feel the gap between these senses (Leininger would argue that he is trying to cover over this gap).[122] Where the Reformation deontologized grace in order to exalt it ("grace is not medicine, but favor"), Shakespeare here reduces the functional to the political.[123] The context is entirely sociopolitical. Seeing Prospero in full aristocratic garb, with "hat and rapier," in act 5 (84), Caliban notes, "How fine my master is," and immediately fears punishment (5.262–63). He dedicates himself to Ariel-like punctiliousness. When Prospero makes his "pardon" conditional on Caliban trimming Prospero's cell "handsomely" (5.292–93), Caliban says, "Ay, that I will."[124] The "wisdom" that Caliban dedicates himself to is merely the ability to recognize true earthly power and, therefore, the proper object of "worship." Reflecting on his former relationship to Stephano and Trinculo, Caliban says, "What a thrice-double ass / Was I, to take this drunkard for a god, / And worship this dull fool" (2.94–96).

These are the last words spoken by Caliban, and they point us to what is truly the most disturbing feature in Shakespeare's portrayal of this character. The hatred that Caliban feels for Prospero seems, in the circumstances of the play's diegesis, perfectly rational; the conspiracy that Caliban instigates is shocking in its imagined physicality—"batter his skull, or paunch him with a stake" (2.2.88)—but Caliban presents it as a tyrannicide (2.2.162; 3.2.40), which can always claim legitimacy. The sexual rapaciousness alleged by Prospero and implied by Miranda is never dramatized. We hear Prospero's account, but what we witness is Caliban's desire not for sex but for offspring (with, as Lamming was the first to suggest, "a political intent").[125] Caliban's hunger for servility, on the other hand, is fully staged. It is a datum. This is perhaps the deepest link between Ariel and Caliban—their hunger for dependence, not for liberty. Both of them want to be loved by a master. I referred earlier to "the dependence complex in its purest state" with regard to Ariel, but Mannoni made this claim in regard to Caliban.[126] Césaire entirely eliminated this element from his Caliban (and in Ariel's case, presents it as strategic).[127] Shakespeare's devotes a surprising amount of time and space to the scenes between Stephano, Trinculo, and Caliban (any stage production will confirm this). Here we see Caliban at his most degraded. Caliban's favorite promise to Stephano is to be his foot or boot licker or kisser. This occurs four times (2.2.149, 152; 3.2.22; 4.1.219), and is part of Caliban's equally explicit tendency toward idolatry. "I prithee," he says to Stephano, "be my god" (2.2.149). This all appalls us as degradation. It would have horrified Shakespeare's largely Protestant audience as much as it does us, for both related and different reasons—foot-kissing was associated with Roman Catholicism.[128]

Yet Mannoni seems to be right that Caliban feels abandoned by Prospero, and that servility (to Stephano and Trinculo) is, for Caliban, a mode of relationship.[129] Where Mannoni is wrong, however, is in asserting that Caliban does not also feel exploited by Prospero, and that Caliban lacks a conception of freedom. Caliban sees himself as having been usurped and forced into a subject position "Which first was mine own King" (1.2.344). What exactly this vision of self-rule means is never developed, but it certainly implies an absence of any coercive power.[130] He can certainly imagine freedom from forced physical and menial labor. Prospero can starve—or do his own "dirty work":

No more dams I'll make for fish;
Nor fetch in firing
At requiring;
Nor scrape trenchering, nor wash dish. (2.2.180–84)

Yet in the very next line, Caliban equates freedom with getting "a new master" (2.2.185). As we have already suggested, Mannoni argues (or ought to argue—he is not fully consistent), the encounter between native slave or servant and European "master" degrades the consciousness of both.[131]

What then do we want to conclude about Shakespeare's attitude in *The Tempest* toward colonial and toward "normal" politics? Certainly the play could have been experienced, in 1611 and throughout James's reign, as reinforcing the emphasis of the Virginia Company and its partisans (many of whom were friends or patrons of Shakespeare) on the need for strong government, for the use of force against native peoples, and for disciplined laborers without Caliban-like "dreames of mountaines of gold, and happy robberies."[132]

Yet the deepest fear of *The Tempest* seems to be not that England's struggling colonial ventures would fail, but that they would succeed. Pierre Bourdieu notes that in situations of direct, unmediated, or, as he happily calls it, "enchanted" domination, before "a system of mechanisms has been constituted capable of objectively ensuring the reproduction of the established order by its own motion," the dominator must work "directly, daily, personally" to produce the conditions of domination, which, Bourdieu adds, "are even then never entirely trustworthy."[133] This perfectly captures the difficulties of Prospero's relations to his island servants. As Meredith Skura points out, the question about Virginia at the time of the production of *The Tempest* was clearly "Is it worth it?"[134] Shakespeare can be seen as giving something close to a negative answer—not as an "aporia" but as a position.

But what of the fantasy of transforming souls? As David Kastan has shown, King James did not approve of princes who delighted in magicians and occult studies.[135] On the other hand, James reveled in the biblical language of kings "as Gods," who could "make and unmake their subjects."[136] It is surely no accident that the one image of thorough transformation by human means (not a "sea-change") in the play occurs within the realm of normal rather than of magical politics. The ability to "new create" and new form "creatures" is said to be attained not by magic but by knowing "how to grant suits, / How to deny them"—that is, by the skillful exercise of normal princely prudence. Prospero's one truly successful political venture is in this realm: he arranges a dynastically advantageous marriage for his daughter.

To sum up the "local" meanings, then, the partisans of the Virginia Company could have seen *The Tempest* as supporting them in the dark days of 1611, whereas King James could have seen the play as suggesting that colonial endeavors, for all their glamour, leave one weary and, in Shakespeare's wonderful word, "vex'd" (4.1.158). James could have seen the play as advocating a focus on normal politics, a policy of concentrating on his own court and on arranging advantageous marriages for his children, especially for his daughter, Elizabeth, who was fifteen in 1611.[137] On the other hand, when we recognize that the play's critique of "magical" politics is profound enough to undermine normal politics as well, we are perhaps reaching toward its deepest and nonlocal meaning.

CHAPTER 7

The Tempest (2)

Labor

Ever since the eighteenth century, it has been known that Gonzalo's primitivist fantasy in *The Tempest* (2.1.142–60) is a close adaptation of a passage in Montaigne's *Des cannibales*.[1] Yet the significance of this borrowing remains in question. Why did Shakespeare want this vision to be part of his play? An obvious answer is that he intended to critique it. The addressee of the speech (the King of Naples, Alonso) says to Gonzalo about this speech, "Thou dost talk nothing to me," and Gonzalo seems to accept this characterization (2.1.166–70). The younger members of Alonso's court party point out an obvious contradiction—"The latter end of his commonwealth forgets the beginning"—in that Gonzalo both asserts that the "commonwealth" that he is imagining knows "No sovereignty," and presents himself as "King on't" (2.1.152). This may be too easy a critique. The most famous imagined commonwealth of the period, More's Utopia, is a republic established by a king (Utopus).[2] But the undercutting remarks do seem to invite us to consider the vulnerabilities of either the vision itself or the attempt at imagining a "natural" society. Caliban would seem—at least as he is in the present moment of the play—to be a (new world?) "native" very unlike Gonzalo's "innocent people," so the play as a whole becomes, in Stephen Greenblatt's words, "an act not of homage but of aggression" toward Montaigne's apparent belief in the beauty of a "natural" society.[3] But that might not be the whole story either—especially when one takes into account the other essay of Montaigne's that Shakespeare cites. The presence of Montaigne turns out to have a deeply unsettling effect on the apparent value structure of Shakespeare's play.

In Praise of Idleness

If one follows David Quint, the "latter end" of *Des cannibales*—which concentrates on native warfare and its rituals—also "forgets the beginning" (or critiques it), and this means that the essay as a whole is much more critical of the native culture described than it might seem.[4] But in neither case—Greenblatt's or Quint's—does the undercutting reading respond adequately to the lyricism of the passages in question. Montaigne does seem to admire the "natural" society that he depicts before he gets into the discussion of the wars the natives wage, and we are almost certainly not intended to think of Gonzalo as merely an old fool.[5] It has got to be to his credit that he is capable of imagining a society without treason, and so forth, just as it is part of the sweetness of Montaigne's nature that he can imagine it.[6]

Certainly the passage raises the question of what "natural man" is like and equally certainly—if the borrowing is recognized—it brings the new world context into the play. But these considerations do not respond to the internal emphases of the two passages of description that Gonzalo provides. The first passage ends—after it lists all the things that the imagined society does not have (government, writing, social distinctions, agriculture, legal systems and conventions, "metal, corn, wine, or oil")—with the assertion that this society would have "all men idle." Gonzalo emphasizes this by adding an emphatic second "all" after this assertion ("all men idle, all" [2.1.150b]). He anticipates the charge that this is a sexist labor fantasy by adding "And women too," and he tries to preclude a hot sexual fantasy by adding that these "idle" women are "innocent and pure" (he had already dropped the mention of lack of clothing—*nuls vestemens*—from Montaigne's list of negatives).[7] Gonzalo could be seen as also forestalling a Quint-type critique by dropping Montaigne's mention of "pardon" (*le pardon*) being lacking, and by specifying in the next passage that there are no weapons in this society—no "Sword, pike, knife, gun, or need of any engine [of war]"—so that the "idleness" of Gonzalo's citizens is much more total than that of Montaigne's.[8] Unlike the society that Montaigne evokes, in Gonzalo's there are no cooking-grills as well as no swords.[9] The culminating thought is that "Nature should bring forth, / Of its own kind, all foison, all abundance, / To feed my innocent people" (2.1.158–60). The key idea is abundance ("foison") without labor—"without sweat or endeavour" (156).[10]

"Foison" is a rich word here, and though a French one, it is Shakespeare's alone. It does not appear in Montaigne or in Florio's 1603 translation, though Florio transliterates Montaigne's equivalent word, *uberté* (Florio's "ubertie"), and all three texts mention "abundance" (*abondance*).[11] "Foison" is rare for Shakespeare. He uses it once in the sonnets (in sonnet 53); once in *Antony and Cleopatra* (2.7.20); once in *Measure for Measure* (1.4.43); and once in *The Two Noble Kinsmen* (5.1.53).[12] The word always signifies benign natural fertility: "the spring and foison of the year"; the result of the Nile at its height; the "plenteous womb" of the year or of a happily pregnant young woman. In *Macbeth*, MacDuff assures Malcolm that Scotland has "foisons" enough to satisfy anybody (4.3.88). *The Tempest* is unique in that it contains two appearances of the word. The second is in the masque of Ceres (*The Two Noble Kinsmen* has "Ceres' foison"). Like Gonzalo's fantasy, the masque is another highly lyrical moment, but in the masque "foison" occurs in the evocation of a world extremely different from that of Gonzalo's Arcadian or golden age fantasy.[13] The contrast between the two appearances of this word can, I suggest, lead us to the deepest reason why Shakespeare inserted the passage from *De cannibales* into the play.

The masque of Ceres is precisely—as John Gillies says, "comprehensively"—opposed to Gonzalo's commonwealth.[14] It follows immediately upon and is meant to elaborate on Prospero's extraordinary warning to the young man of the affianced couple for whom the masque is being performed:

> If thou dost break her virgin-knot before
> All sanctimonious ceremonies may
> With full and holy rite be minister'd,
> No sweet aspersion shall the heavens let fall
> To make this contract grow; but barren hate,
> Sour-ey'd disdain and discord shall bestrew
> The union of your bed with weeds so loathly
> That you shall hate it both; therefore take heed,
> As Hymen's lamps shall light you. (4.1.14–23)

This is a world where the Latinate ponderousness and near pleonasm of "sanctimonious ceremony" is entirely positive; where the "rite" has to be not only "holy" but "full"; where a metaphorical "aspersion"—a religious term in a legalist context—is "sweet"; and where, most interestingly and significantly, a legal convention, a "contract," is seen as having the essential property of nature and being able to "grow." The contract here is with nature, so to speak. Unless the sanctimonious procedures governing sexuality are followed, the marriage will (Prospero says) become a source of pain and disgust—both in itself and in the presumably hateful offspring that it will produce (the "it" here in line 22 seems to be both the bed itself and the offspring). The young lords were quick to point out that it is unclear how Gonzalo's commonwealth, with no institutional structures, can be one of "innocent and pure" sexuality rather than being a world of "whores and knaves," but, in the world that Prospero demands, sexual "purity" is guaranteed by institutions and rules.

The masque of Ceres continues the emphasis on sexual constraint. Only "temperate nymphs" are invited, and they are invited to celebrate (again) "a contract" (4.1.133). Venus, who has no regard for the rules of marriage is excluded, so that no "wanton charm" can be done to the young couple "Whose vows are, that no bed-right shall be paid / Till Hymen's torch be lighted" (96–97). "Bed-right" is a wonderful pun, including both the legal right and the ceremonial rite. It might also in some sense include the natural right, but only within the other senses of the term. The masque is, most of all, a celebration of cultivation. It is not a "disorderly juxtaposition of pastoral and georgic elements" but an artful blending of these.[15] In the masque, nature brings forth nothing "Of its own kind." The opening invocation to the "bounteous" Ceres evokes her "rich leas / Of wheat, barley, vetches, oats, and pease" (4.1.60–61). This gives us both a sense of variety and a celebration of the most fundamental, ordinary, necessary, and long-standing cultivars, both grains and legumes. None of these can be counted on to grow wild.[16] As "vetches," which are mostly used for forage, suggests, there is a whole ecology here. Mountains and lowlands harmoniously and productively interact, throughout the seasons.

This is all planned. The next lines tell us that the "nibbling sheep" (living lawn mowers) of the mountains live adjacent to "flat meads" that are "thatch'd" (like dwellings) "with stover," which is specifically designed to support the sheep ("them to keep") through winter. The rivers of Ceres have "banks with pioned and twilled brims," which means, as Frank Kermode explains, that "the 'pioneers' have built embankments" that "are fortified by layers of branches crisscross."[17] These are then seen as serving, at Ceres's command in early spring, to adorn cool rivulets imagined as "cold nymphs" ("spongy April at thy [Ceres's] hest betrims" them). There is further evidence of cultivation, since the next landscape invoked is of "poll-clippt vineyards"—grapevines pruned in the spring (to produce better and more abundant fruit at harvest time). Finally, Ceres is seen as cooling herself off ("thyself dost air") at her "sea-marge, sterile and rocky hard." Gillies plausibly explains this rather surprising note of sterility as a celebration of boundaries, specifically of keeping the sea in its place.[18]

Within the diegesis of the masque, Ceres is being summoned by Iris to "entertain" Juno and, with Juno, to bless the contract, and, as expressed in grand language that includes but transcends the legal, "some donation freely to estate" on the well-behaved young lovers (the next passage is the one where the exclusion of Venus is asserted). Juno offers social and biological gifts that constitute human happiness (something like *eudaimonia*)—"Honour, riches, marriage-blessing, / Long continuance" (4.1.106–7).[19] Ceres, on the other hand, stays within her realm, the realm of cultivated nonhuman nature.[20] It is in Ceres's speech that the key word from Gonzalo's vision recurs. She offers "Earth's increase, foison plenty" (4.1.110). This seems at one with Gonzalo, but the next line specifies "Barns and garners never empty." The "foison" here is contained within and made available by human constructs. This is abundance within civilization. In further contrast with Gonzalo's vision, where the "foison" is, so to speak, automatically produced, so that there is no anxiety whatever attending it, Ceres here asserts that, through the means, human and natural, that she has specified, "Scarcity and want" will be avoided. So, in this vision, which includes winter, these exist as possibilities, though discounted.[21]

One other factor enters the "most majestic vision" at this point. After the "temperate nymphs" are called in to help celebrate the "contract" (again [4.1.133]), a set of male figures is called in to enter into a country dance (dancing being essential to masques). The male figures are "sun-burned sicklemen of August weary" (4.1.134). So, it turns out that the "foison" here envisaged requires not only human constructs ("barns and garners," "pioned" banks) but also serious human labor. This is real labor; it is not presented as pleasant or "redeeming." Those who do it are "weary" from it. As "pioned" implied—recall Othello's special contempt for "pioneers"—the humans involved are defined by their labor; they are "sicklemen" or "reapers" (4.1.139).[22] They can dance here, but, as in Robert Herrick's great poem about harvest celebrations, everyone knows that the pleasure of such an occasion is not meant to "drown" the pain of the workers, but, in Herrick's wonderful pun, "to make it spring again."[23] Vin Nardizzi correctly notes that sawyers are not included, but I am not sure that they (along with grape-pickers, etc.) could not be part of this "vision."[24]

One critic claims that the "sicklemen" here constitute "the only image of laborers" in a Jacobean masque.[25] This may or may not be true (I leave it to the masque scholars to sort this out), but it does point to a very striking feature of *The Tempest*: the issue of physical labor and who is to do it is regularly raised. The play is emphatic that (1) physical labor is necessary; and (2) only certain people (or classes of people) should do it.[26] It might well be that the most amazing feature of Gonzalo's vision is not "all foison" but, as I have already suggested (and Antonio has sneered), "all idle."

The issue of physical labor is present from the outset of the play. In the opening scene, the Boatswain instructs his aristocratic passengers to "keep below," saying, "You mar our labor: keep your cabins; you do assist the storm" (1.1.14–15). The Boatswain's concern, following the commands of his Ship-master, is to get "th' mariners" to work effectively. The aristocrats are making a lot of noise ("they are louder than the weather") and continue to get in the way. When the Boatswain's (presumed) blasphemy is answered with a curse ("A pox on your throat," shouts Sebastian), the Boatswain turns to him (and the whole aristocratic group) and says, "Work you then" (1.1.42).[27] This is an exasperated endgame retort, not a serious proposal. Antonio insists that the aristocrats are not afraid of drowning (1.1.44); they are apparently less averse to this outcome than they are to doing labor to prevent it. This may not seem surprising in a hierarchical predemocratic society, but it turns out that it actually is so. In William Strachey's narrative of the storm in Bermuda that was encountered by an English ship headed for Virginia in 1609, Strachey comments, wonderingly, on a phenomenon exactly opposite to what Shakespeare presents. Strachey notes that, in the storm, "the better sort, even our governor and admiral themselves, not refusing their turn ... There was not a passenger, gentleman or other ... but was able to relieve his fellow." To hammer the point home, Strachey makes explicit that this included "such as in all their lifetimes had never done [an] hour's work before."[28]

In *The Tempest*, aristocrats do not labor—even when their lives depend on it. Physical labor is done by others. This is as true of Prospero as it is of Antonio, Sebastian, and company. Prospero is entirely dependent on his native slave, Caliban, for physical labor. We learn bits about this figure. His mother was "that foul witch Sycorax," and he is "freckled" (1.2.258, 269, 283).[29] There is an early hint that the relation between Prospero and Caliban was not always hierarchical—Caliban is "that Caliban / Whom now I keep in service" (285–86)—but the relationship definitely is so "now." As Prospero and Miranda prepare to interact with Caliban, we learn two more things about their (current) relation to him: he is consistently surly to them (he "never / Yields us kind answer"), and Miranda has an aversion to him (1.2.310b–312a). But neither of these matter to Prospero because

> We cannot miss him: he does make our fire
> Fetch in our wood, and serves in offices
> That profit us. (1.2.313–15)

This is very odd. Of Prospero's two slaves or servants, one would think that the other one, the one who can do things that humans cannot ("dive into the fire . . . ride / On the curl'd clouds," etc.), would be the one who is indispensable.[30] But we are never told that about him. Ariel seems to be drawn on only for special occasions. He is needed for the particular moment of the play when Prospero's European enemies and their entourages have, unexpectedly ("By accident most strange" [1.2.178]) sailed into the realm in which Prospero can exercise his special power. Ariel is needed to carry out Prospero's "project" in relation to the Europeans (see 5.1.1), and to do things like creating the masque. Caliban's tasks, on the other hand, are specified as things that any able-bodied person could do—make a fire and fetch wood for it. Yet Prospero and Miranda "cannot miss" Caliban.

The point is that it is inconceivable that Prospero or Miranda should fetch their own wood or make their own fire. When Prospero pretends to see what Ferdinand, a prince, is willing to endure for his love of Miranda, Prospero assigns him Caliban's characteristic job of log-bearing.[31] Both the young prince and (apparently) Miranda see this activity as "baseness" (3.1.2 and 12); Ferdinand calls it a "mean task" and associates it with "slavery" (3.1.4, 62).[32] The other tasks that Caliban performs for Prospero and Miranda are not here specified, but although they are granted the dignity of being termed "offices," they must be of the same order as the two that are mentioned (log-bearing and fire-making).[33] Caliban's services are strictly "economic"—in the etymological not the modern sense, despite the mention of "profit." They have to do with the physical maintenance of the *oikos,* the household; they involve the provision of necessaries. Without Caliban, Prospero and Miranda would have no fire (definitely for heat—for "fuel," says Prospero [1.2.368], and probably for cooking, though there is, significantly, no direct mention of this). It is not clear that without Caliban the Prospero family would have food of any kind, animal, aquatic, or vegetable.[34] As Stephen Orgel says, "There is a great deal of physical labor to be done on the island, and except for the brief hour of Ferdinand's servitude, only Caliban can be made to do it."[35]

When Caliban imagines laboring for another master (Stephano, the drunken butler), Caliban promises to replicate the hunting and gathering that he has presumably done for Prospero:

> Let me bring thee where crabs grow,
> I with my long nails will dig thee pig-nuts;
> Show thee a jay's nest, and instruct thee how
> To snare the nimble marmoset; I'll bring thee

To clustering filberts, and sometimes I'll get thee
Young scamels from the rock. (2.2.167–72)

This is another version of something like "foison," and here too it comes through physical labor and a certain amount of ingenuity—snaring the marmoset, and, in the continuation of the speech, making "dams ... for fish." It is hard to imagine Prospero performing any of these actions, let alone even "meaner" tasks. When Caliban imagines leaving Prospero, Caliban states that he will no longer "scrape trenchering, nor wash dish" for his old master (2.2.184).

But the question might be asked, Why is all this a problem for the ruler? Shouldn't the fact of not physically laboring provide the ruler or master with leisure, allowing him to do, using Hannah Arendt's distinction, work rather than labor?[36] One of the interesting things about *The Tempest* is that although it definitely does denigrate physical labor, it does not seem to idealize work (or art). Prospero's rule is never easy or serene. This is obvious in the state of his relation to Caliban, but is largely true of Prospero's relation to Ariel as well. With regard to the staged tempest, Prospero has to assure himself that the result was what he intended, asking, with apparent anxiety, "But are they, Ariel, safe?" (1.2.217). When, after commending Ariel for doing his tempest job "exactly," Prospero informs him that "there's more work" for him (1.2.238), Ariel, as we have seen, does not receive this announcement happily.[37] Ariel experiences his work as labor. His service involves a promise of manumission; Derek Cohen thinks that the desire for freedom "motivates Ariel almost entirely."[38] Ariel is not, like Caliban, regularly tortured, but Ariel too acts under threat of punishment. He sometimes seems to take pleasure in his activity (as in his narrative of the tempest), but as far as I can see, it is only Caliban in the play who evokes the experience of laboring freely. Caliban remembers having done so for Prospero (1.2.339–40) and imagines doing so for Stephano (happily using his long nails, fetching "scamels," etc.).

Prospero never has a moment of relaxation. His "art" requires a constant assertion of will. We have heard him lecturing Ferdinand and Miranda before the masque, and we know that the masque, though it is indeed, as Ferdinand says, "Harmonious charmingly" (4.1.119), is truly a labor as well as a "work" of art. It is the product of Ariel as Prospero's "industrious servant" (4.1.32).[39] Prospero cannot even enjoy the production. It breaks off when he remembers the "foul conspiracy" against him (4.1.139). This would hardly seem a matter of grave concern, given the agents involved, but the recollection of it puts Prospero into a state of rage that Miranda claims is unprecedented ("Never till this day / Saw I him touch'd with anger, so distemper'd" [4.1.156]). One is tempted to say that Miranda has not been paying attention (or is extenuating), but perhaps this moment does constitute a special case. It may be that Prospero actually allowed himself to relax for a few moments, to enjoy the show and forget his consuming "project," and it may be his awareness that he allowed himself such a moment that puts him into such a state.[40] He devises a menu of physical torments for the lower-class conspirators, but then turns his attention to his real enemies, the aristocrats who deprived him of his dukedom. For them he has devised more upper-class torments, mental rather than physical ones—"inward pinches" rather than outward ones (compare 5.1.77 and 4.1.260). At the beginning of act 5, Prospero is delighted (and, again, perhaps a little surprised) that he has succeeded in imposing his will: "My charms crack not; my spirits obey" (5.1.2). Ariel reminds him that they are still doing "work" (5.1.4). And Prospero is still very angry.

In what is clearly a great moment in the play, Prospero decides not to continue the punishments he has inflicted on his enemies. In a beautiful image related to the poetry of the masque with its "crisp channels," Prospero restores his aristocratic enemies to the clear pool of sanity, removing "the ignorant fumes that mantle / Their clearer reason" (his fen-clearing is entirely mental [5.1.67–68]). But there is no pleasure in this for Prospero, and no letting go of anger. With regard to Antonio, he refuses even to acknowledge their kinship, and offers to "forgive" but not to forget, saying, "most wicked sir, whom to call brother / Would even infect my mouth, I do forgive / Thy rankest fault,—all of them" (5.1.130–32). This is juridical pardon. It is beyond what Montaigne's warrior cannibals do—recall that they do not have *le pardon*—but it is not reconciliation. The final acknowledgment of Caliban—"this thing of darkness I / Acknowledge mine" (5.1.275b–76)—is exactly parallel to this; it manifests the same mixture of official reconciliation and continued anger. The aristocrats are sorting out their servants and relations. "Two of these fellows" (Stephano and Trinculo) "you," Prospero tells Alonso, "Must know and own" (5.1.274b–275a); the other one Prospero must. Antonio remains, for Prospero, a "most wicked sir" (not a brother) and Caliban a "thing of darkness" (not a person).

That Prospero cannot enter into Miranda's wonder at the human creatures she beholds is not surprising. He also, however, does not seem able to enter into Gonzalo's joy. When Gonzalo prays that a "blessed crown" descend on the young couple, the one who says "Amen" is Alonso (5.1.201–4). To the invitation to "rejoice / Beyond a common joy" at all the outcomes (207), Prospero says nothing at all. For Prospero, the only model of productive life is one that involves constant work, constant effort of the will. The one moment in which he revels in his potency—"my so potent art"—is the speech in which he abjures it (5.1.50–51).⁴¹ Prospero's plan for himself, after witnessing the marriage of Ferdinand and Miranda in Naples, is not to rule in Milan but to "retire" there—yet again (5.1.310; see 1.2.91). The one future activity he imagines for himself is to devote "every third thought" to his death (5.1.311), which he almost certainly views as a relief. The sense of weariness at effort explains why the most beautiful and memorable speech in the play is not about fertility or productiveness but about quietly fading into nothingness—"into air, into thin air" (4.1.150).⁴² It is the consummation for which Hamlet "devoutly" wishes, and eliminates Hamlet's anxiety by placing dreams *ante* rather than *post mortem*. Like Hamlet, Prospero generalizes his meditation. The "we" whose revels have ended may be Prospero and the young couple, but the "we" who are "such stuff as dreams are made on" is all mankind.

But what is the alternative to this vision of blissful release from all activity (which is itself phantasmagoric)? One could imagine the role of work in productive life differently. One possibility would be that described in the commonwealth of Utopia, where the amount of labor required of any (almost every) individual is minimal and the total amount produced maximal; labor is not eliminated but is not constitutive of anyone's life—except those who choose to have it so.⁴³ Another possibility is the Protestant solution that Weber identified: to see work and labor as positive, as divinely approved.⁴⁴ Milton, for instance, saw work—though interspersed with rest—as part of human dignity; "other Creatures all day long / Rove idle, unimploy'd."⁴⁵ The absolute alternative to both work and labor is Gonzalo's commonwealth, a vision of human life where sustained effort is not necessary at all, and "idleness" reigns. Montaigne certainly found this an attractive idea. He found a strong tendency to idleness to be a determining aspect of his own character. But instead of seeing this as a flaw, he associated it with "freedom" (*liberté*). In *De la vanité*, Montaigne asserts that *la liberté et l'oisiveté* are his two ruling qualities (*mes maistresses qualitez*), and also his two "favorite qualities" (*mes qualitez plus favories*).⁴⁶ The connection between them is a shared antipathy toward "care" (*soing, soucy, solicitude*).⁴⁷

One might think that this would mean not caring at all about worldly things, and perhaps retreating as far as possible from them. But this is neither Montaigne's recommendation nor, in actual life, his practice. As Felicity Green notes, Montaigne's point in praising *l'oisiveté* "is not to commend pure inactivity and lethargy but rather to free himself from mental disquiet."⁴⁸ It is a matter of "managing one's will." The essay by that title, *De mesnager sa volonté* (3:10), is about freedom. It has, in a way that might seem unusual for Montaigne, a definite moral: *il faut mesnager la liberté de nostre ame*—"we must husband the freedom of our soul."[49] This liberty is a matter of internal equilibrium. It is not a matter of retreat. In life, one has to take on various projects—private, and even, when necessary, public. Montaigne says, "I do not want a man to refuse to the charges he takes on, attention, steps, words, and sweat and blood if need be."[50] The point is to attend to such charges "with the mind [or spirit] holding itself ever in repose . . . not without action but without vexation, without passion" (*l'esprit se tenant tousjours en repos . . . non pas sans action, mais sans vexation, sans passion*).[51] One must not have a "violent and tyrannical intensity of purpose." In particular, in chastising injuries, it is important to keep anger out of it (*nous en distrayons la cholere*). The ideal is to maintain, even in great affairs, *une grande nonchalance*. And, he says, *liberté*.[52] These latter two terms are the same for Montaigne.

The contrast of this ideal with the dramatized inner state of Prospero for virtually the entire play could not be more stark. Ferdinand's comment that when the masque breaks off, Prospero is "in some passion / That works him strongly" (4.1.144) conveys exactly Montaigne's sense that passion operates as a form of compulsion, as if from outside the self. Prospero himself states at this moment that he is, in exactly the term Montaigne warns against, "vex'd" (4.1.158). But, as we have seen, Prospero has been so from the beginning—in the opening interactions with Miranda, with Ariel, and with Caliban.[53] He is constantly "touched with anger" (recall that in the opening sentence of *De mesnager sa volonté*, Montaigne states that "In comparison with most men, few things touch me" (*peu de choses me touchent*).[54] Moreover, it should also now be clear that in Prospero's retreat to his library as "dukedom large enough," Prospero was also not following Montaigne's model.[55] So, as Lars Engle puts it, Prospero fails on "both sides of the Montaigne prescription," public and private.[56] The *Essais* offer a critique of the way Prospero conducts his life and his "project." This critique might seem to go unvoiced in the play, but this is where we must recall that Gonzalo's vision stresses idleness even more strongly than Montaigne's does. This means that to someone who knows the *Essais*, the evocation of golden age "idleness" might bring with it the critique of Prospero's passionate involvement in his project, his violent and tyrannical intensity of purpose.[57]

Strenuous Virtue

There seems, however, to be a major obstacle to this conclusion. It arises from the second borrowing from the *Essais* in *The Tempest*, a borrowing much more recently noticed and less well-known than that from *Des cannibales*. This is a passage from *De la cruauté*, a passage that seems to praise strong passion as necessary to virtue.[58] In the great moment of Prospero's moral self-correction, Prospero claims that he is going to let his "affections" toward his aristocratic enemies "become tender" (5.1.19–20). His reason for claiming that he will do this is that Ariel has suggested it, and Prospero reflects that if a "spirit" who is "but air" can imagine a human doing this, then it makes sense for an actual human to do it—on the categorical grounds of biological identity: "shall not myself, / One of their kind, that relish all as sharply, / Passion as they, be kindlier mov'd than thou art?" (5.1.21–24). The biological and ethical emphasis here relies heavily on the semantic range of "kind."[59] But it is important to retain an awareness that this sentence is a question. Prospero is contemplating an issue about feeling, not having one.[60] He is not here weeping.[61] And the next part of the speech changes direction. The issue of "kindness" is dropped. Instead of contemplating an internal change, Prospero announces that he is now, in this very moment, having one:

> Though with their high wrongs I am struck to th' quick,
> Yet with my nobler reason 'gainst my fury
> Do I take part: the rarer action is
> In virtue than in vengeance. (5.1.25–29a)

This is a decision, not an effusion of feeling. It is a decision made on the basis of a maxim ("the rarer action is...").[62] The decision is to act with or in "virtue." What virtue means here is for the agent to establish an internal ethical hierarchy in which "reason" is "nobler" than passion (conceived of as excessive—"fury") and to choose to take "reason" as his basis for action rather than taking its competitor, passion, as such. The condition of the objects of the action has nothing to do with the decision. It is a decision made entirely on principle through an act of simultaneous intellection and will. For purposes of self-consistency, Prospero adds a reference to his previously stated "business" in tormenting the court party—contrition and change of life (3.3.69, 81–82): "they being penitent / The sole drift of my purpose doth extend / Not a frown further" (29b–30a).[63] The grammar of this ("they being penitent") is nicely poised between being conditional and being indicative. It allows Prospero to present (to himself and, I suppose, to Ariel) a conditional as if it were indicative, as if the condition has been fulfilled. In any case, the decision has been made; it does not depend on seeing whether his courtly victims have indeed become penitent. Ariel is told to "release them" (30b) without being commanded to make any prior effort to ascertain the matter. The issue is bypassed under the guise of assuming its success. The decision has been made entirely on the basis of a conception of "virtue."

That conception is what brings Montaigne's essay "Of Cruelty" into Shakespeare's text. The essay begins with a reflection on the relation of virtue to vengeance:

> It seems to me that virtue (*la vertu*) is something other and nobler than the inclinations toward goodness (*la bonté*) that are born in us. Souls naturally regulated and wellborn follow the same path, and show the same countenance in their actions, as virtuous ones. But virtue means something greater and more active than letting oneself, by a happy disposition, be led gently and peacefully in the footsteps of reason. He who through a natural mildness and easygoingness (*une douceur et facilité naturelle*) should despise injuries received would do a very fine and praiseworthy thing [Florio has: "should no doubt performe a rare action"]; but he who, outraged and stung to the quick (*jusques au vif*) by an injury, should arm himself with the arms of reason against this furious appetite for vengeance, and after a great conflict should finally master it, would without doubt do much more. The former would do well, and the other virtuously; one action might be called goodness, the other virtue. For it seems that the name of virtue presupposes difficulty and contrast, and cannot be exercised without opposition.[64]

In these terms, Prospero's great speech, despite its abstract recognition of the natural ("kindness"), seems to move entirely in the grander arena of "virtue." Prospero could not perform the "rarer action" unless he were in the grip of a strong passion (Shakespeare shifts the domain of "rare" from the realm of nature (*facilité naturelle*), where Florio, following Montaigne puts it, to the realm of reason). So, as the final sentence in the quotation notes, the passion is the necessary occasion for the virtue. On this account, if Prospero were less incensed, he would be less virtuous.[65]

Almost all the critics and scholars who have noted this borrowing have read the passage in this way, as praise of "virtue."[66] But to read the passage in that way is not to attend to Montaigne's essay as a whole, and not even to its full opening paragraph. The next sentence after that on virtue needing internal opposition reads: "Perhaps this is why we call God good, strong, liberal, and just, but we do not call Him virtuous: His operations are wholly natural and effortless."[67] Suddenly it looks as if we are in a situation where we have to choose between being virtuous and being God-like. Something tricky is going on here. Montaigne continues to praise the effortfulness of virtue—"the easy, gentle, and inclining path that guides the footsteps of a good natural disposition is not the path of true virtue" (308; 92).[68] But suddenly Montaigne brings himself up short. He reflects that in the terms that he has established, Socrates "would be little deserving of commendation," since Socrates did not have unruly passions to be countermanded. Yet Montaigne holds Socrates to be "the most perfect soul that has come into my knowledge" (308; 93). Socrates was completely "at ease" in his soul (*à son aise*). So now there is a new ethical hierarchy. The person who has developed a character such that he does not have temptations to do wrong—that is, the person who has Aristotelian temperance (*sophrosyne*)—is ethically superior to the person who successfully struggles with such temptations (who has Aristotelian continence, *enkrateia*).[69] But, Montaigne continues, although the temperate person is morally superior to the continent one, the continent person is still finer (*plus beau*) than the person "simply provided with a nature easy and affable (*une nature facile et debonnaire*) and having an inborn distaste (*dégoustée par soy mesme*) for vice" (310; 95).

This still seems to allow for serious (if somewhat diminished) admiration of the continent person, the one who, through reason, overcomes strong internal opposition and has "virtue" in the sense that the opening of the essay defined. It makes sense that the third type of person is "innocent, but not virtuous." Merely avoiding falling into a vice is not the same as being virtuous. This all seems perfectly coherent. But suddenly the line of thought gets trickier. Montaigne decides that he will "say a word" about himself (311; *un mot de moy-meme* [96]). Needless to say, this "word" becomes, as Arthur Kirsch recognizes, "the essay's core subject."[70] Montaigne notes that he himself is of the third type mentioned above: "My virtue is a virtue, or should I say an innocence, that is accidental and fortuitous" (311; 96). He does not owe his freedom from major vices to his reason. He owes it to his nature, either first or second (he was either born so or his upbringing created it). Without effort, he holds "most vices in horror" (311; 97). He then reflects that reason produces opinions, and that in many cases (Epicurus is a key one), men's behavior is better than their opinions. This leads him to a rather startling question, one that brings us back to the opening discussion of (mere) "goodness" as opposed to "virtue": "Could it be true that to be wholly good (*pour estre bon à faict*) we must be so by some occult, natural, and universal property, without law, without reason, without example (*sans loy, sans raison, sans exemple*)?" (312; 97).[71] Innocence and goodness—without, without, without. We are back to *Des cannibales*. In case we have missed the connection, when Montaigne goes on to discuss his own "softness" (*mollesse*) of disposition (313; 98) such that he cannot stand cruelty even to animals, Montaigne notes that "savages do not shock me as much by roasting and eating the bodies of the dead as do those who torment and persecute the bodies of the living" (314; 100).[72]

So, even the opening passage on the "nobility" of virtue does not actually idealize effort, will, and care. Yet these are what *The Tempest* offers as essential to civilized life and to projects of any sort (colonial or reforming). Agriculture and household maintenance require labor, and labor—even in the most perfect civilized society (as in the masque)—requires an underclass to perform it. Everything is work. Even, as we have seen, pardoning is work. As in Gonzalo's vision, "endeavour" and "sweat" are equated. Genuine freedom is imagined only in a nonhuman context (Ariel merging with "the elements").[73] Inner freedom is no more available to Prospero than is any positive version of "idleness"—golden age or Utopian or Montaignian. No wonder that, as I noted earlier, the most positive fantasy that Prospero can entertain is to dissolve peacefully into nothingness—"into air, into thin air." If we take the matter one step further, and accept the naive but almost irresistible (and possibly correct) parallel between Prospero's situation and Shakespeare's, it would seem that by the time he wrote *The Tempest*, Shakespeare may have come to see writing and staging plays as work, and as coercive, morally dubious work at that.[74] He may have felt that he needed a secular "indulgence" to be set free (Epilogue, 20).[75] Montaigne, on the other hand, in his work as in his life, could rely on the *liberté* provided by *une grande nonchalance*.

CHAPTER 8

The Tempest (3)

Humanism

As his education would lead one to expect, Shakespeare was deeply involved with the materials that constituted the humanist curriculum.[1] This is transparent in the early comedies, though it has been seen in the early histories as well.[2] *The Comedy of Errors* is based on two Plautine comedies in a way that Shakespeare clearly expected his audience to recognize.[3] *A Midsummer Night's Dream* is equally open about its engagement with Ovid.[4] *Love's Labor's Lost* and *The Taming of the Shrew* are suffused with the "sweet smoke of rhetoric" (*LLL*, 3.1.61) and feature actual or mock schoolmasters. But *The Tempest* engages with this tradition in a particularly intense way. Like *Hamlet*, it features a central character who at least seems to fulfill the humanist fantasy (and partial reality) of an educated prince who makes practical use of his education, and in *The Tempest*, this figure is also, explicitly, a pedagogue.[5]

Much has been written about the play's engagement with the humanist tradition through its classical allusions and its unusually tight dramaturgy. But the dominant current view of the play's overall relation to this tradition is that it gives up on or critiques it. Jonathan Bate sees the play as (in Quentin Skinner's phrase about *Utopia*) "a humanistic critique of humanism," and, more strongly, "a renunciation of humanism's secular wisdom."[6] Goran Stanivukovic sees the play as revealing "the discontents of humanism," though it is a bit unclear in his essay what "humanism" is and what its "discontents" are, since humanism, on Stanivukovic's account, includes the positions of both Machiavelli and Erasmus, and so is fundamentally unstable.[7] It either does or does not have an ethical core. In my view, the humanist program of education in the classics is defined by its ethical core. It always includes what James Hankins calls "virtue politics."[8] In this view, Machiavelli, despite the interest he developed in the politics and society of ancient Rome, is not among the humanists.[9] I take Erasmus as the defining figure for "humanism" and the relevant figure for northern humanism, and I take Shakespeare's play not as critiquing the Erasmian tradition but as critiquing its central character for failing, as both a prince and a pedagogue, to live up to it.[10] I will argue that Prospero is, in other words, as much of a failure as a humanist as he is as a spiritual reformer.[11]

The play opens in a way that does not seem at all promising for any sort of humanistic perspective. Human action seems of no avail, and the only "hope" that the opening scene seems to hold out is for a kind of comic moral predestination—Gonzalo takes "comfort" from the belief he professes that the Boatswain's "complexion" guarantees the fellow hanging rather than drowning (1.1.28–33).[12] Despite the crude skepticism of the aristocrats, the sailors do seem to be doing as well as can be done in managing the ship in the tempest. But it turns out that resignation is the only real option—"The wills above be done" (1.2.66). The comedy of the first scene provides some sort of reassurance, since a tragic-seeming event is presented as a kind of farce. But the actual comfort that the play provides is that this whole apparently uncontrollable, apparently natural disaster was itself the product of "art."[13] The opening words of the second scene are stunning: "If, by your art, my dearest father, you have / Put the wild waters in this roar, allay them." The idea of having power over nature is itself a major fantasy, but the focus of the second scene's opening is not on power as such but on "art," on a (nonmanual) human skill and attainment. After the practitioner of this art reassures his daughter that "The direful spectacle of the wrack" was indeed only a spectacle, he then, in the course of explaining how he and his daughter came to be on "an uninhabited island," gives an account of his background that also serves to explain the nature of his "art."[14]

Prospero claims that he was reputed among "all the signories . . . the prime duke" and, in this exalted company, "for the liberal arts / Without a parallel" (1.1.71–73). He was also "transported / And rapt in secret studies" (76–77).[15] This combination would have identified him to the learned in Shakespeare's audience as someone who aspired to be a magus in the sense defined in Pico della Mirandola's *Oration [on the Dignity of Man]*.[16] For this figure, the liberal arts are merely "expiatory sciences," the necessary first step toward "the utter perfection of natural philosophy."[17] For Pico, this was, clearly, a culmination. But Pico, like other Neoplatonists, flourished under the Medici—at the cost of giving up the civic commitments, whether republican or not, of the earlier humanist tradition.[18] Pico boasted that he had "relinquished all interest in affairs, private and public (*omni privatarum et publicarum rerum cura*), and given [himself] over entirely to leisure for contemplation."[19] So this might seem an odd ambition for a "prime duke"—as indeed it was.

The civic humanists derided the person who "dedicated himself completely to theory and the delights of literature," stating that such a person, "whether a prince or a private citizen," perhaps "becomes dear to himself" but "is surely of little use to his city" (*at parvum certe utilis urbi aut princeps est aut privatus*).[20] So wrote Pier Paolo Vergerio in a letter on liberal education in 1402. The northern humanists, especially in England, maintained this perspective. At the very beginning of Thomas Starkey's *Dialogue between Pole and Lupset* (1533?), Lupset (the mouthpiece for Starkey) argues forcefully that "whosoever he be," who "by his own quietness and pleasure moved," leaves "the care of the common weal and policy," such a person "doth manifest wrong to his country and friends."[21] Similarly, Richard Mulcaster, the headmaster of the important Merchant Taylor's school, wrote in 1582 that those who "live to themselves" for "pleasure in their studie" are guilty of "the private abuse of a publik good."[22] David Kastan has shown that King James, though very conscious and proud of his own learning, advised his son to "delight in reading" but also to make sure that such reading conduced to "the principall ende," that is, "the discharge of [his] office."[23]

We can therefore assume that Shakespeare's audience had a complex, perhaps mainly negative attitude toward a prince who described himself as "neglecting worldly ends, all dedicated / To closeness and the bettering of my mind" (1.2.89–90)—a negative attitude that was intensified by Protestant antimonasticism and upgrading of the "worldly."[24] But on the island, as an apparently successful Neoplatonic magus, Prospero seems to have become much more pragmatic.[25] He has learned to rule, and he has learned to teach. The great aim of the humanist movement, in all its varieties, was never merely self-perfection; the aim was always to teach, and to teach did not mean to convey information or even skills but rather, as I have already suggested, to nurture or to create ethical beings. This is why eloquence was the central humanist value.[26] There is no doubt that, from a civic humanist point of view, Prospero was a failure when Duke of Milan. On the island, the lack of equanimity that we have discussed would be problematic for Prospero's standing as an ideal humanist prince. Erasmus opened his treatise on the education of "a Christian Prince" by stating that such a one should have "a quiet and placid trend of spirit . . . a nature staid . . . not excitable."[27] But the question of how to judge Prospero as a humanist pedagogue remains. This means considering his pedagogical relation to the two young persons in his charge: to his daughter, Miranda, and to Caliban, his servant and / or adopted son.[28] His relation to Ariel is not pedagogical; his relation to his European enemies involves, as we have seen, more a ministerial or priestly fantasy than a pedagogical one.[29]

Tutee Number One: Miranda

Prospero describes himself as having been a "schoolmaster" and an especially "careful" tutor to Miranda (1.2.171–74). The first thing to say about this is that Prospero would not have been doing anything unusual or "unorthodox" in educating his princess daughter.[30] As Sarah Gwyneth Ross has shown, many aristocratic and elite fathers in the period were dedicated to the education of their daughters, and sometimes took a direct hand in it.[31] Following the classicist Judith Hallett, Ross even speaks of "filiafocality."[32] Learned upper-class women were not outside the cultural norm by the late sixteenth and early seventeenth centuries. The model of female virtue consisting of a woman being "chaste, silent, and obedient"—the model so prevalent in the prescriptive handbooks—was not the only available cultural model.[33] "Learned"—meaning educated—virtue was the competing ideal. We can see this in Shakespeare's presentation of the haut-bourgeois father in *The Taming of the Shrew* who goes out of his way to procure tutors for his daughters not just in music but also in Latin and (apparently) Greek.[34] Moreover, the handbooks of William Gouge and company are irrelevant to Miranda, who is a princess.[35] The analogue to Miranda would be, for instance, the future Elizabeth I, who had very grand tutors (hired, in her case, by a notably learned lady, her stepmother, Katherine Parr, whose own education, supervised by her mother, was modeled on the household of the filiafocused Sir Thomas More).[36]

One unmistakable result of Miranda's education is that she—like Katherina Minola—is capable of elegant speech.[37] The body of the play—the shipwreck scene seems like a prologue[38]—opens with the skillful and elegant speech by Miranda that seeks the major goal of eloquence: persuasion. She begins with a conditional ("If by your Art"), into which a direct address is inserted ("my dearest father") before continuing the *protasis* with an alliterative and lyrical formulation ("you have / Put the wild waters in this roar") and proceeding to the *apodosis* containing, in good Latinate fashion, the main verb, which is followed by a preposition that points back to the middle of the sentence ("allay them"). It's both a lovely sentence and a lovely period. She continues in equally high descriptive and metaphorical language ("th' welkin's cheek"), yet the center of the speech is not descriptive but, in the rhetorical sense, ethical—evoking, in exclamatory fashion, the *ethos* of the speaker, her compassion: "O, I have suffered / With those that I saw suffer."[39] This is another elegant formulation, but its content is what is important. After a bit more description, the idea is reiterated in another exclamation, this time in a less abstract and almost physiological mode: "O the cry did knock / Against my very heart" (1.2.8–9).

The speech gets what it wants—reassurance that, despite appearances to the contrary, "There's no harm done" (1.2.15). Miranda's appeal to *ethos* has its effect. Her father recognizes "The very virtue of compassion" in her (1.2.27), and responds to it. An interesting question is whether this ethical stance, which establishes the immediate characterization of Miranda, is to be seen as the result of Prospero's pedagogy. Hiewon Shin thinks that it was "inculcated by Prospero's paternal instruction," which is therefore to be seen as also semimaternal ("androgynous").[40] But there is no evidence of Prospero ever manifesting such a feeling. It is true that he does not want to injure the inhabitants of the ship. But he does want them to suffer. When Ariel tells Prospero that the spectacular "performance" of the tempest led everyone aboard the ship to feel "a fever of the mad," Prospero is delighted (1.2.194–215). Later, after Prospero has toyed with his aristocratic enemies' hunger, he wants them, again, to feel "a fever of the mad" of the sort that could drive them to suicide (3.3.59–60); and he feels no compassion for the sufferings he inflicts on the lower-class conspirators. When he finally is persuaded to cease the psychological tormenting of his aristocratic enemies, he again speaks of "virtue." But this is not "The very virtue of compassion." It is, rather, the virtue of "nobler reason."[41] Miranda's compassionate nature is purely her own.

We get a glimpse of Prospero actually teaching Miranda when he tells her the story of how they came to be on the island. As he develops the narrative, discussing his commitment to study over government, and his reliance on his brother, he breaks off to ask whether Miranda is paying attention (1.2.77); when he continues, he accuses her of failing to do so (87); and then, as he approaches the climax of the story (his dethronement and expulsion), he again accuses her of not listening (106). She assures him, with a humorous hyperbole, that she is indeed listening ("Your tale, sir, would cure deafness"), but he does not acknowledge this. What he wants is to tell the story, and to tell it the way he wants to. The one moment in which he offers positive reinforcement is to commend

Miranda for asking a question that leads him into the next thing that he wanted to narrate and explain (139). He is not teaching Miranda "to speak up."[42] He is manifesting how wrought up he is, and making sure—unnecessarily—that he has her total attention, that she has no thoughts other than the ones that he is giving her. N. Amos Rothschild is right that Prospero seems here to be the sort of "choleric and punctilious tutor" that Montaigne (following Erasmus) criticizes.[43] Octave Mannoni states that in this conversation, Prospero "tries to treat [Miranda] as an equal, but fails."[44] I am not sure that he ever really tried. When Miranda attempts—very carefully ("O dear father")—to intervene when Prospero is incapacitating Ferdinand, Prospero exclaims, "What! I say, / My foot my tutor?" When she persists, he threatens to "chide" and possibly hate her (471–72, 479–80). He is being hyperbolical here, pretending rage and, in the first instance, making a kind of joke, but, as with so many hyperboles and jokes, a true attitude slips out.[45]

As a number of scholars have noted, Miranda is not always silent and obedient.[46] She reveals her name to Ferdinand (supposedly against Prospero's wishes), directly asks Ferdinand whether he loves her, and does seem to take the lead in formally establishing their engagement (3.1.37, 67, 87). Despite the fact that she and Ferdinand are playing out exactly the script that Prospero intends for them, it does seem right to credit Miranda with some spunk and autonomy here. She does, after all, as I have noted, have the special status of being a princess (which her "tutor" has known all along, even if she has not).[47] But if she is not always silent and obedient, she does seem to have learned the cardinal importance of the first and primary member of the traditional trinity of female virtues. It would be a "sin," she says, even to consider infidelity in her mother (1.2.118–19). The two males with whom she has a positive relation are both obsessed with her virginity. Ferdinand, on first seeing her, inquires whether she is "maid or no" (430). He may be asking whether she is a mortal creature rather than "the goddess / On whom" the music that he has heard attends (424–25), but when, twenty lines later, he offers to make her "Queen of Naples," he prefaces the offer with, "If a virgin." For all her erotic forwardness, she considers her "modesty" (that is, virginity) "the jewel in [her] dower" (3.3.54). This is the one substantive lesson that we have evidence that she has learned (aside from how to play chess).[48] Patriarchy is firmly internalized here. When Prospero says that he has been a "careful" tutor to her, the word should be seen to carry some of its early sense of proceeding with anxiety as well as its modern sense of proceeding with attentiveness.[49] Prospero seems to have been as "careful" in the ideological inculcation of this matter as he was lax in the practical enforcement of it. He relied on interpellation, and "trust" (in Miranda's case, successfully).[50]

But the major feature of Miranda's character—the one that is highlighted even more than her chastity and her compassionate nature—is her naivete. This is where Prospero's role as "schoolmaster" stands out as most morally questionable. Shin says that Prospero has "instructed her in the ways of the wider world," but this seems to be exactly what he has not done.[51] Her lovely first speech includes the thought that the ship ("the brave vessel") had "no doubt some noble creature in her" (1.2.8). This is very odd. Even if we accept the emendation of "creatures" for "creature" (which I am inclined to do) the statement sounds remarkably naive.[52] Why does Miranda not understand what a ship is, and what it would be carrying? Surely one or more of the books that Prospero prizes "above his dukedom" would involve descriptions of ships and seafaring. Miranda is surprised at how Ferdinand looks, but why has Prospero not given her—either directly or, again, through his "volumes"—some sense that there are young human males (other than Caliban) in the world?[53] Miranda's Platonic-sounding belief that beauty must reflect virtue (1.2.460–62) reads as naivete rather than philosophy, especially since she explains it so badly (contrast this with, for instance, Viola's decision to accept the doctrine as a conscious leap of faith).[54]

Prospero seems to have kept Miranda ignorant precisely in order to assert her naivete. As preface to his autobiographical narrative, Prospero characterizes her as "Ignorant of what thou art" (1.2.17). But whose fault is that? She claims not to have had any sense that he or she had an existence prior to their life on the island (22–23). That may have been true as far as her self-initiated thoughts went, but she can be prompted (to Prospero's surprise) to remember something from a prior existence, and she notes that Prospero has at various times teased her with the promise of their story, leaving her, as she says, "to a bootless inquisition" (1.2.35). George Lamming has noted the weirdness of this; as he writes, "It has taken [Prospero] twelve years to tell the child one or two things which any decent parent of his intelligence would have passed on long ago."[55] It is only when his enemies are in his power that he is prepared to reveal himself to her. Stanley Cavell's thinking about fear of self-revelation is more apt here than in relation to Edgar in *King Lear*.[56] Prospero only wants to be recognized when he has power over Europeans. He does not want his daughter to recognize him as a pitiful exile, and he does not want to recognize his daughter as an equal. He has kept his daughter ignorant of the most basic features of the behavior and appearance of Europeans so that he can patronize her "innocence."[57] Her most famous line—"O brave new world"—provides the crowning occasion for this (5.1.183). Unlike Pietro Bembo and Thomas More (and other Renaissance fathers with educated daughters), Prospero does not celebrate his daughter's learning or sophistication—or make such possible.[58]

Tutee Number Two: Caliban

With regard to the other young person in Prospero's care, we have more direct information about the pedagogic relationship between them. In the present of the play, the relationship between Prospero and Caliban is a pure master-servant or master-slave relationship, with Caliban doing menial labor.[59] But we are given a history of the relationship that shows it to have been, initially, a very different one. Caliban gives a detailed account of this phase:

> When thou cam'st first,
> Thou strok'st me, and made much of me; wouldst give me
> Water with berries in 't; and teach me how
> To name the bigger light, and how the less,
> That burn by day and night: and then I lov'd thee. (1.2.333–38)

This is a picture of pedagogy within a framework of love. The student is literally and figuratively nurtured by the teacher; he not only learns but enjoys learning, and comes to love his teacher. The picture goes beyond pedagogy in its insistence on reciprocity—not only does affection circulate but learning does as well; Caliban showed Prospero "all the qualities o' th' isle" (1.2.339). The latter is part of the colonial context of the play, but what is described here is something like a picture of equality. David Norbrook points out the importance of Caliban switching into the intimate form of the second-person pronoun in this part of his speech.[60] These lines are the most convincing evocation of interpersonal intimacy in the play. What is depicted seems much more substantial than the instant "love" that springs up between Ferdinand and Miranda, despite the hyperbolization of the latter.[61] And, unlike the "love" between Prospero and Ariel, the initial Prospero-Caliban relationship does not exist solely in the context of service.[62]

With regard to pedagogical models, the significant point is the context of love and pleasure. This was the humanist ideal. Learning was to be a pleasure. This is why, said Erasmus, "the ancients fabled the Muses to be comely maidens, given to the song and the dance, companions to the Graces"; it was the doctrine of the ancients, he explained, that success in study depended on "a relationship of good will (*mutua animorum benevolentia*) between student and master." Especially in the early stages of education, "delight" (*voluptas*) should "go hand in hand" with utility.[63] (Erasmus even recommended taste treats—though more directly pedagogical ones than Prospero's potation.)[64] Roger Ascham (Elizabeth Tudor's tutor) thought that the place of learning should, following Plato, be a scene "of play and pleasure."[65] Children "should be taught rather by love than by fear," as was "well-known and diligently used among the Grecians and old Romans."[66] The schoolroom, said Ascham, should be "a sanctuary against fear."[67]

But, of course, the pedagogical idyll between Prospero and Caliban did not last. Prospero came to see Caliban as someone whose behavior and sensibility could only be affected by physical pain, someone "Whom stripes" (whippings) "can move, not kindness" (1.2.347). The relation between them turned into one of mutual hatred, with physical coercion and abuse, on one part, and resentment and thirst for revenge, on the other. It is important to put this into the context of humanist educational theory. The humanists were, in general, strongly against corporal punishment in the learning process. They knew that they were fighting an uphill battle here, but it was central to their vision of educational reform. Aeneas Silvius Piccolomini argued (in 1450) that students should be guided by advice, not blows. He notes that it is "customary for pupils to be flogged," and that many authorities can be cited for it, but he says that "Quintilian and Plutarch have more weight with me when they say that boys must be led to honorable practices not by wounds but by admonitions and explanations."[68] The passage in Quintilian to which Piccolomini points was constantly cited by the humanists. Quintilian expresses his disapproval of beating students, despite, as he notes (in the first century C.E.), the authorities who support it.[69]

But it might be said that this is irrelevant to the revised Caliban-Prospero relationship, since the relationship is no longer a pedagogical one. But the issue of beating students and the issue of beating slaves turn out to be historically and conceptually linked. Quintilian's objection to flogging is that "it is a disgraceful form of punishment, and fit only for slaves" (*deforme atque servile est*). Erasmus makes this connection but takes it in a different direction. He was passionately against flogging in the educational process. But it turns out that he was against flogging in general—as a means of reforming anyone. He states that "there are people you could not mend by flogging," yet "if you used kindness and persuasion, you might lead them in any direction you pleased."[70] In discussing a schoolmaster who beat his students constantly in order to "humble" them—an idea that Erasmus loathes—he asks, "would anyone dream of training a slave or even a donkey in such a manner?" He goes on to discuss animal training, claiming that "the most ferocious animal can be subdued by gentle treatment, while the tamest can be aroused to anger by excessive harshness." He then picks up the issue of servility, which Quintilian flagged, pointing out that it is the mark of a servile nature to be restrained from evil only by fear. But Erasmus then makes an astonishing move. Going way beyond Quintilian, Erasmus suggests that not only should teachers not flog students but masters should not flog slaves. Masters should "remember that their slaves are human beings and not animals" (whom he has already suggested should be treated gently). No slave will be improved by being beaten. Those with a "sound disposition" will be better moved to moral improvement by admonitions than by beatings, and those without such (*insanabilis*) will only be led by beatings to harden themselves in wickedness and seek to contrive their master's murder (sound familiar?). But Erasmus goes even further. He sees the whole concept of slavery as incompatible with Christianity, speaking of *hoc vile servitutis nomen*.[71] So the idea that there is a human (or any) creature more appropriately treated with "stripes" rather than kindness is deeply anti-Erasmian.[72]

But my discussion so far has avoided consideration of the particular episode that transformed the relation between Prospero and Caliban. Using one of the humanists' great words for the quality they were seeking to inculcate in both teachers and students, *humanitas*, Prospero claims that he had used Caliban "with humane care" (1.2.345)—which includes both kindliness and humanistic pedagogy—until Caliban sought to "violate" Miranda.[73] This event led Prospero (and Miranda) to conclude that Caliban was morally uneducable. Caliban is characterized as a human creature on whom "any print of goodness would not take" (1.2.354). He therefore would show the limits of the humanist ideal of "imprinting" the recipient of learning, whether schoolchild or prince, with "goodness."[74] Caliban would be among the humans who cannot be so "imprinted," on whose natures, as Prospero says of Caliban later (changing the image), "Nurture can never stick" (4.1.188–89).[75]

As some of Erasmus's comments have already suggested, this view of any human was problematic for him. We recall the slave with the "unsound" (*insanabile*) disposition. The question was whether there are functioning human beings who are uneducable—that is, morally uneducable.[76] The issue was the crucial one of what education, ultimately, can do. The humanists split on this point. Most of the Italian humanists thought that there were limits to what even the best education could do in the face of certain kinds of nature or inherent character. Vergerio held that "the disciplines of letters take away neither madness nor wickedness." His examples are two Roman emperors, Claudius, whom Vergerio sees as having been insane but learned, and, most troubling of all, Nero, who was wicked and yet well educated.[77] Piccolomini thought that "as nature is blind without instruction, so instruction is defective without nature."[78] Castiglione seems to have thought the same thing; many princes "would be good, if their minds were properly cultivated," but some "are like sterile ground, and are by nature so alien to good behavior that no training can avail to lead their minds in the straight path."[79] Sir Thomas Elyot likewise thought that the kind of education he was advocating could work only "if nature repugn not."[80]

Erasmus, on the other hand, adopted the view that he ascribed to Lycurgus, that "nature [is] strong," but "education is more powerful still" (*Efficax res est natura, sed hanc vincit efficacior institutio*).[81] Erasmus thought that parents and others blamed "nature" too readily, and unjustly.[82] Sound instruction can always prevail.[83] But he went beyond the "Lycurgus" view. For Erasmus, the human infant's mind is, at worst, a "natural void" (*naturam vacuam*).[84] But his actual definition of (human) nature is more positive: "By nature I mean man's innate capacity and inclination for the good" (*Naturam apello docilitatem ac propensionem penitus insitam ad res honestas*).[85] More's imagined commonwealth can be read as a demonstration of the malleability and even essential goodness of human nature.[86] Elizabeth Hanson calls Erasmus's *De Pueris* "a passionate revolutionary manifesto proclaiming the plasticity of human nature."[87] But, for Erasmus as for More, this left the problem of original sin. The pagan philosophers, Erasmus notes, were flummoxed by the fact that—perhaps (*fortassis*)—we are more inclined to evil than to good, and he sees that "the Christian philosophy" provides an explanation. But Erasmus is not comfortable with this. Trying not to sound too heterodox, he concedes that belief in human proneness to evil cannot be false (*falsam esse non potest*), but he insists that nevertheless it is most true (*verissimum*) that the greater part of human evil derives from corrupt relationships and bad education (*maximam hujus mali partem manare ex impuro convictu pravaque educatione*).[88] Nero is, again, the hard case, but here too Erasmus seems to think that his education did not begin early enough.[89] Tyrannical behavior is produced by a combination of educational failure and unfortunate opportunity.

With the notable exception of Hanson, scholars have generally failed to take account of the Erasmian optimism in humanist pedagogy, especially among the northern humanists (despite Elyot). Jonathan Goldberg sees the humanistic program as specifically intended to produce failures as well as successes, "to indicate those incapable of education."[90] Goldberg follows Richard Halpern in seeing the project as a sorting mechanism with a "demonstrative" as well as a "disciplinary" function.[91] But the "disciplinary"—that is, educational—function was the defining feature of the program, and Erasmus consistently attributed student failure to inadequate or improper teaching.[92] To ignore this is to misrepresent his position.[93] Ascham, despite his Protestantism, is as optimistic as Erasmus is. Ascham states that if "the wisdom of the teacher" is added to "the goodness of nature," children can "most easily" be brought to lives of virtue and public service. He adds that they also need to be "kept up in God's fear and governed by His grace," but this does not change the position.[94] "The goodness of nature" is its basis.

Halpern and Goldberg both cite Richard Mulcaster in support of their view. Mulcaster did indeed worry about the education system overproducing, turning out more intellectuals or educated persons than there were employment possibilities. "Want of preferment" was the problem.[95] But this was a matter of historical contingency, of what the existing structures could provide. It was not intrinsic to the program.[96] Ideally, everyone, in all states of life, would be educated, if employment for all were possible, and if necessary manual and other labor would still get done. *Utopia* imagines a version of this—almost everyone labors (though only six hours a day), and everyone has access to public lectures on various topics ("a great number of [persons of] all classes [*ex omni ordine*] ... both males and females, flock to hear the lectures").[97] Erasmus imagined the ploughboy singing psalms as he worked; "the lowliest women" reading the Gospels and the Pauline epistles (at least in translation); and cities replacing (or being the equivalents of) monasteries as places of education and spirituality.[98] He noted that "not a few in number" who were born into humble circumstances have risen to high office, "indeed," he says archly, "sometimes to the supreme dignity of the papacy." He knows that this cannot come true for everyone, but *"all should be educated towards that end"* (*omnes huc educandi sunt*).[99] Omnes.

Goldberg does not see the humanist project as ever even imagining success of this kind—that is, success in educating everyone, regardless of class status and even of gender.[100] Goldberg insists that "Ascham's innocent and pure mind is not some *tabula rasa* assumed as the condition of *any* pedagogic subject"; rather, says Goldberg, "the goodness that Ascham would inscribe is directed at a good subject—a gentleman in short."[101] But in a passage that Goldberg actually quotes, Ascham asserts the most positive possible version of the *tabula rasa* (or *naturam vacuam*) view: "the pure clean wit of a sweet young babe is like the newest wax, most able to receive the best and fairest printing."[102] Similarly, Goldberg says that, for Mulcaster, "the sequence from mere being to well being" is not "simply a natural telos."[103] But Mulcaster's view is that it exactly is such. He follows Erasmus in defining the aim of education as "to help natur unto hir perfection"; "to perfit all those abilities, which natur endoweth our kinde withall."[104] Mulcaster leaves no one out; he asserts that "ther maie be some good done" by education "even in the heaviest wits."[105]

Prospero and Miranda see Caliban as (so to speak) a Nero type, one who learned but who was not, because of his nature, morally transformed thereby: "thy vile race, / Though thou didst learn, had that in 't which good natures / Could not abide to be with" (1.2.360–62).[106] But did Prospero (and possibly Miranda, if she was pedagogically involved) give up too soon?[107] Erasmus's remarks, and even Mulcaster's, might well lead one to think so. And Caliban is not one of "the heaviest wits." There is no indication that he lacked any cognitive capacities. The speaker of the "vile race" speech has to admit—though it is tucked away in a concessive clause—that "thou didst learn" (361). Caliban claims that his major "profit" from the language lessons he was given was that he now knows "how to curse" (1.2.366), but the play makes it abundantly clear that cursing by no means exhausts Caliban's linguistic capacities. He is capable of persuasion ("That most deeply to consider is / The beauty of his daughter" [3.3.96–97]), argumentation ("This island's mine by Sycorax, my mother"), and lyrical evocation ("the isle is full of noises" [3.3.133–41]). Despite what Prospero says, there seems to be no doubt that "nurture" can stick on Caliban's nature. Prospero's "pains" were clearly not "all, all lost, quite lost" on Caliban (4.1.189–90). Even more important, it is not true that Caliban is someone "Whom stripes may move, not kindness" (1.2.347). Prospero's initial treatment of him thoroughly "moved" Caliban. When Prospero stroked Caliban, and praised ("made much of") him, the result was "And then I loved thee" (1.2.335, 338). Strokes produce something very different from what "stripes" produce. When Stefano teaches language to Caliban in his own positive way ("here is that which will give language to you" [2.2.84–85]), Caliban responds with the same sort of generosity that he had formerly shown to Prospero ("I'll show thee the best springs; I'll pluck thee berries" [2.2.160]).

So, Caliban is neither cognitively nor emotionally impaired and does not seem to be "capable" only of wickedness (which is what "capable of all ill" [1.2.355] seems to claim).[108] He cannot plausibly be seen as an Aristotelian "natural slave"—a category that has been misapplied as well as misunderstood.[109] Prospero did not only, as Jonathan Bate says, "misread" Caliban.[110] Prospero chose to do so. The rape attempt undoubtedly called for some kind of rebuke, and it certainly called for a change in the domestic arrangements—though not necessarily for confinement to a barren "rock" (1.2.363–64) or to the reduction of Caliban's status to that of an "abhorred slave."[111]

What would an "Erasmian" response to the situation have looked like? This is a fantasy, but it is one that is worthwhile to attempt to reconstruct, and one that the play can be seen to provide material for doing so. We must look at the justification for the post-rape-attempt treatment that Caliban receives. The fullest account of this justification specifies the problem as lying not in the action that Caliban attempted but rather in the fact that his "race" had "that in 't which good natures / Could not abide to be with" (1.2.361–62). But it is never specified what the utterly condemnable "that" is. The editors do not provide a gloss, but in context, the inference that it is strong sexuality is hard to avoid. What makes this interesting is that the play does not seem to see such a psychological or biological feature as unique to Caliban, or as not "capable of" external control and internal acceptance thereof. Almost every critic of the play has noted the parallel between Caliban and Ferdinand in the task that Ferdinand is assigned (log-carrying, which is Caliban's most clearly designated task). But normally this parallel is taken to establish the difference between the two young males—the handsome and wellborn European prince and the "deformed" and illegitimate indigene. One labors willingly, one grudgingly, and so forth.[112]

However, as a number of less idealizing critics have suggested, one can run the comparison in the other direction, and take it as an invitation to see likeness as well as difference.[113] Ferdinand's nature also has "that in 't." He speaks as if everyone—or at least every male—has such. In asserting that he will not break Miranda's "virgin-knot" until he is officially sanctioned to do so, Ferdinand asserts that "the murkiest den, / The most opportune place, the strong'st suggestion / Our lesser genius can, shall never melt / My honour into lust, to take away / The edge of that day's celebration" (4.1.24–29). He has within him a "lesser genius" (lower nature?) that would see a murky den as an "opportune place" for a sexual encounter. Instead, he has been taught to wait. In return for this, he is assured by an external authority that, in the long run, he can count on a happy union and healthy offspring.[114] In the short run, he anticipates an especially keen sexual experience on his wedding night (there is something connoisseur-like in the imagination of "the edge of that day's celebration"). The patient state is produced in him by these promises and also by threats of the consequences that will ensue were he to allow his "honour" to melt into lust—

which seems, at one moment, to be at least partially occurring, since Prospero has to command him to cease doing something with or to Miranda. "Be more abstemious," says the watchful father (4.1.53). Ferdinand is monitored with as much "care" as Caliban was not.[115] So, a question arises that seems obvious, but has only rarely been considered: Why could not the same combination of threats, promises, and surveillance have produced the same results in Caliban?[116] It is not clear that Caliban's nature had anything "in 't" that Ferdinand's did not. In fact, Ferdinand seems more focused on sex as such than Caliban ever was. As was the case with Prospero's brother, an "evil nature" seems available to be "awak'd" in anyone if the circumstances are truly "opportune," and proper education, training, and "care" have not intervened. Erasmus's ambivalence about a tendency toward evil in humans is replicated in the play.

Prospero seems somehow to have expected that "bountiful Fortune" (1.2.178) or "Providence divine" (1.2.159)—the same?—was eventually going to allow him the dynastic outcome that he enjoys at the end of the happy afternoon in which his enemies were brought to the shore of his island: "his issue / Should become Kings of Naples" (5.1.205–6) as well as rulers of Milan. But what if "Fortune" had not been so bountiful? Would it not have made sense to cultivate Caliban, teaching him the value of postponement, so that Miranda would not "abhor" Caliban, and the island would eventually be peopled? Lamming raises this possibility and is not sure whether or not Prospero could live with it.[117] It would have been a path both prudent and beneficent—even if (to European eyes) Caliban does not have the "beauty" of Ferdinand (see 1.2.417–19).

Caliban's nature could not (or merely did not) resist the temptation posed by a "most opportune" situation, just as Antonio could not. Nor could Prospero. The attempted rape provided an opportunity. It "awak'd" something in Prospero's nature that, given the justificatory occasion, preferred the role of torturer to that of loving instructor.[118] Erasmus pointed out that the situation of being a tutor supplied, in a certain kind of nature, such an occasion; he "fancies he has gained for himself a private little empire," which leads him to act, in his domain, like a tyrant and enjoy exercising power in a cruel way.[119] The situation of the tutor, in other words, offered, psychologically, the same sort of perverse pleasure that Mannoni saw was offered to the colonial administrator.[120] Prospero's condescension to Miranda flowed from the same source as did his domineering over Caliban and Ariel: the perverse pleasure of misusing both power and authority.

PART III

Beliefs

CHAPTER 9

Shakespeare and Skepticism (1)

Religion

This essay is not about skepticism in the philosophical sense, epistemological skepticism.[1] Rather, it is about something closer to Protestant and "lay" skepticism; namely, skepticism about supernatural intervention and causation—and specifically about traditional (Catholic) versions of these. Much of the essay is an attempt to take seriously the well-known facts that two of Shakespeare's major plays are linked to books that are skeptical in this second sense: *A Midsummer Night's Dream* (1595?) to Reginald Scot's *Discoverie of Witchcraft* (1584); and *King Lear* (1605) to Samuel Harsnett's *Declaration of Egregious Popish Impostures* (1603). I will begin, however, with discussion of a skeptical and anti-Catholic play that does not have a companion text of this sort—though it does have a decidedly pre-Christian one—and I will end by suggesting, as I have with regard to motives, the way in which Shakespeare could draw powerfully on theological conceptions in radically skeptical and humanistic contexts.[2]

Let me say at the outset that this essay is not going to argue that Shakespeare was an atheist in the full modern sense. It will certainly suggest that he may have been so in the much looser sense in which Renaissance writers and polemicists used the term.[3] To be skeptical about exorcism, fairies, and witches (relics could be added to this list, but are not treated in this essay) did not imply religious disbelief, though supporters of witch beliefs suggested this.[4] Samuel Harsnett was not an atheist. Reginald Scot was not such either, though the case might appear to be harder here.[5] Disbelief in witches and traditional exorcism did not normally imply disbelief in the devil (though again, Scot might possibly be a hard case). It was possible, for instance, to think that popular witchcraft beliefs were a diabolical distraction from the real source and nature of evil, so that witchcraft beliefs were one of the devil's ways of sowing dissension among neighbors.[6] My claim will be that, with regard to the matters in question, Shakespeare was a skeptical rationalist of a Protestant or Erasmian sort—it is not clear whether, by the end of the sixteenth century, there was a difference between the two.[7] He may have shared some of Scot's "Familist" orientation (also Erasmian), in which "spiritual" entities turn out to be psychological rather than ontological.[8]

"O for my Beads"

The Comedy of Errors, which everyone agrees is an early play of Shakespeare's, and one in which he is parading his use of classical sources, is startling in its skepticism about the supernatural.[9] The classicism and the skepticism might seem to go together, but they need not (*The Winter's Tale*, for instance, is consistently classical in its setting, and, in some sense, strongly religious).[10] As Stephen Greenblatt points out, in the early play there is a full-fledged mock-exorcism.[11] Greenblatt is inclined to dismiss this episode as trivial in comparison to the supposedly richer treatment in *Twelfth Night* (1601), but I would argue that in *The Comedy of Errors*, this episode is much more deeply woven into the fabric of the play than it is in the later comedy. In *Twelfth Night*, the mock-exorcism does not have any edge to it. The fictional "Sir Topas" is a gentle parody of a Church of England curate; his exorcism consists of nothing more than the command "Out, hyperbolical fiend."[12] Feste is merely having fun at Malvolio's expense. Both plays show that Shakespeare knew that a clergyman might well be called in to treat a "lunatic." Madness, in the Elizabethan world, existed in a culturally uncertain space between the spiritual and the physical. Thanks to the work of Michael MacDonald, we have a detailed account by one of the most successful physician-psychiatrist-spiritual healers of the period, Richard Napier, who was a cleric, a doctor, and a magus. Madness and belief in demonic possession went together. MacDonald calculates that "more than 500 of Napier's patients" thought they were bewitched.[13] In such cases, Napier described his procedures thus: he started physiologically—"First let them blood"—and then went on to say, "Lord I beseech thee, let the corruption of Satan come out of this man, or woman or child that doth so trouble or vex her or him." Moreover, MacDonald notes, in such cases, Napier often used astrological amulets, which were "good against all spirits, fairies, witcheries, sorceries ... against all evil spirits, fairies, witcheries, possessed, frantic, lunatic."[14]

The "lunatic" in *The Comedy of Errors* is no more insane than Malvolio is—the whole situation is equally absurd—but the exorcist who is brought in is much closer to Napier than he is to "Sir Topas." Dr. Pinch may or may not be a clergyman, but he is called a "conjurer," and utters a formal adjuration:

> I charge thee, Satan, housed within this man
> To yield possession to my holy prayers
> And to thy state of darkness hie thee straight. (4.4.48–50)

This could be a Protestant adjuration, relying, as Puritan exorcists did, on the power of prayer.[15] But the final line of Pinch's "charge" takes the passage in different direction: "I conjure thee by all the saints in heaven." No Protestant would appeal to "all the saints in heaven"—not even Richard Napier.[16] Moreover, there is something slightly off, to Protestant ears about the assertiveness of "my holy prayers." Shakespeare would have counted on his audience identifying this figure as specifically Catholic.[17]

Mockery of both Catholic ritual and popular beliefs is deeply built into the play. When, in response to the attempt by Adriana, the wife of Antipholus of Ephesus, to get the man (Antipholus of Syracuse) she takes to be her husband to behave himself properly toward her, the Syracusan falls into a condition of epistemological doubt, but his foolish servant, equally shaken, exclaims, "O for my beads; I cross me for a sinner. / This is the fairy land; O spite of spites, / We talk with goblins, elves and sprites" (2.2.179–80).[18] The servant calls for his rosary ("beads"). Fairyland, goblins, and rosaries are equally mocked. And this continues. Dromio of Syracuse remains the mouthpiece for such beliefs. In narrating the story of his encounter with a fat, erotically demanding kitchen-wench, he presents her as a human version of a demonic force: "this drudge, or diviner, laid claim to me; called me Dromio ... told me what privy marks I had about me ... that I, amazed, ran from her as a witch" (3.2.124–28). "Privy marks" were a crucial piece of "evidence" in witchcraft prosecutions, but this passage clearly makes fun of the whole idea.[19] Even more daringly, the passage goes on to make fun of the superstitious use of scripture: "if my breast had not been made of faith ... she had transformed me."

At one key moment, it looks as if the problem of epistemological failure or incapacity in the play genuinely calls for a religious solution. Antipholus of

Syracuse is given a declaration and a prayer that both sound quite serious; they are phrased in a generalized way that seems to transcend the local context:

> here we wander in illusions
> Some blessed power deliver us from hence. (4.3.36–37)

This sounds like a recognizable fideist strategy: reason is hopeless, so we must opt for faith.[20] However, in the Folio (our only text), the words that immediately follow this eloquent plea are a stage direction: "Enter a Courtesan."[21] Upon seeing this character, who addresses Antipholus of Syracuse in a way that he finds puzzling, Antipholus of Syracuse's response is "Satan, avoid, I charge thee tempt me not" (4.3.46). Dromio of Syracuse follows suit, and, speaking of a "light wench," again cites scripture (and does so in the way that scripture cites scripture): "It is written, they appear to men like angels of light" (4.3.47).[22] In preparation for Dr. Pinch's appearance later in the act, exorcism is mocked. Antipholus (S) says to this "fiend," "I conjure thee to leave me and be gone" (65). His last words to her are "Avaunt thou witch" (71).

It is impossible to read *The Comedy of Errors* as anything but totally skeptical about witchcraft, about demonic possession, and about exorcism. In the fifth act, Adriana, the wife of Antipholus of Ephesus, echoes the language of witchcraft in stating that her husband "is borne about invisible" (5.1.187). But we know that she is ludicrously mistaken. Everyone in the play would have done better if they had done without theories of miracles and supernatural causation.

In speaking of the fifth act something must be said about the figure of the Abbess. She is certainly a more dignified figure than Dr. Pinch. But she accepts the possession theory of Antipholus of Ephesus's supposed madness and has her own set of cures, which are as interestingly and typically miscellaneous and eclectic as those of Drs. Pinch and Napier: "wholesome syrups, drugs, and holy prayers" (5.1.104–5). It is not clear that Shakespeare views her, in this regard, any differently than he views Dr. Pinch. Moreover, it is also not clear that her effort to use her status as a "religious" over the wife in the play is viewed as valid. By the end of the play, the Abbess has herself been identified as a wife, and her abbey, the place that she has claimed as a "sanctuary" (5.1.94), is thoroughly and very happily laicized. Any hint or remnant of a sacred locus apart from the family and the state is removed. The former Abbess invites the whole cast into the former abbey for an inclusive feast. Her final speech, the last serious speech in the play, is larded with religious terms, but the "Nativity" that is there celebrated seems purely secular or humanist and involves her movement out of a Catholic sense of holiness.²³

Passing Scot's Test: *A Midsummer Night's Dream*

In *A Midsummer Night's Dream*, Shakespeare seems to take up directly the question of credulity and of popular (Catholic) beliefs. Fairies were notably out-of-date as objects of belief in contemporary Protestant England and Scotland. Even in the *Daemonologie* (1597), where James VI strongly affirms—against, especially, "one called SCOT, an Englishman"—the existence and powers of witches and necromancers, James mocks the idea that "there was a King and Queene of Phairie, of such a jolly court & traine [that] ... naturallie rode and went, eate and drank, and did all all other actions like naturall men and women." He denounces belief in spirits "called the Phairie ... or our good neighbours" (associated with the figure "the Gentiles" called Diana) as "one of the sorts of illusions that was rifest in the time of Papistrie."²⁴ *A Midsummer Night's Dream* (1594–96?) cannot have been a response to the *Daemonologie*, but Scot's *Discoverie of Witchcraft* was available since the mid-1580s, and Scot's attitude to "good neighbours" was identical to King James's (though without the explanation of such illusions as demonically induced).²⁵

Scot certainly saw belief in fairies as "one of the sorts of illusions that was rifest in the time of Papistrie." He notes that, had he been writing his book a hundred years earlier, he would have failed to convince his countrymen "that Robin goodfellowe, that great and ancient bulbegger, had beene but a cousening merchant, and no divell indeed." But now that "poperie" has been sufficiently "discovered," says Scot, Robin goodfellowe ceases "to be much feared."²⁶ But where James saw an ontological difference between fairies and witches, Scot sees a continuity. Scot sees them as having exactly the same footing, ontologically and culturally. Part of Scot's strategy in *The Discoverie* is to show belief in the power of witches to be as ridiculous as belief in Puck (Robin Goodfellow). For instance, in discussing the belief that witches can consort with incubi, Scot explains that an incubus is a spirit, and, therefore (in Scot's metaphysics), entirely separate from matter.²⁷ To believe that an incubus can copulate with women, Scot tells his contemporary (presumably upper-class, sophisticated, male) audience, is to be no better than "your grandam's maides [who] were wont to set a boll of milk before him [an incubus] and his cousine Robin good-fellow, for grinding of malt or mustard, and sweeping the house at midnight" (67).

Robin Goodfellow is Scot's key example of a belief that was formerly widely held but is now, after the Reformation, fully exploded. Scot seeks to provide needed philosophical and historical perspective by reminding his readers that "heretofore Robin Goodfellowe, and Hob gobblin were as terrible, and also as credible to the people, as hags and witches be now" (105).

One might think that Shakespeare wrote *A Midsummer Night's Dream* to confute Reginald Scot. One might think that the point of the play, in which Robin Goodfellow (also known as "Hobgoblin" as well as "sweet Puck") is a central character, is to defend belief in fairies and credulity in general—and perhaps even (covertly) to defend the Old Religion. Perhaps Shakespeare believed, as Bacon pretends to, that a lack of belief in the spiritual world is much worse than superstition. Bacon's "Of Atheism" begins with an apparently resounding vote for credulity: "I had rather believe all the fables in the Legend, and the Talmud, and the Alcoran, than that this universal frame is without a mind."[28] For Reginald Scot, Samuel Harsnett, and all their Reformation fellow skeptics (with regard to the supposed powers of witches), the most fundamental historical-theological principle in this context is the recognition that, as Scot puts it, "the working of miracles is ceased" (39). Yet in a key speech in *All's Well That Ends Well*, Shakespeare seems directly to reject this principle: "They say all miracles are past; and we have our philosophical persons to make modern and familiar, things supernatural and causeless. Hence it is that we make trifles of terrors, ensconcing ourselves into seeming knowledge, when we should submit ourselves to an unknown fear" (2.3.1–6). Surely Shakespeare speaks through Lafew in this eloquent speech; the disdain for "philosophical persons" might be directed at Reginald Scot, who is brilliantly and accurately described as seeking to make "trifles of terrors." Yet in the play itself one might ask whether the cure of the King is to be thought of as "supernatural and causeless" or as the result of specific and experimentally derived pharmacological knowledge. The "receipt" that Helena uses on the King was "the dearest issue" of her father's medical practice on the basis of "his old experience."[29] It was "chief in power" against "that malignant cause" from which the King was suffering (2.1.104–11).

With regard to *A Midsummer Night's Dream* perhaps the best way to put the question is not whether it can be read as a defense of credulity ("Clap your hands if you believe in fairies") but whether it must be. Clearly it can be so read. It seems to be giving its audience a sort of Blakean choice. In "A Vision of the Last Judgment," Blake rejects the materialism, in all senses, of his contemporaries, and he mimics their voices: "What, it will be questioned, when the sun rises do you not see a round disk of fire somewhat like a guinea?" To which

Blake responds, "O no, no, I see an innumerable company of the heavenly host crying, Holy, Holy, Holy is the Lord God Almighty."[30] You can see the guinea-like disk or you can see the heavenly host; you can see spots in cowslips or you can see "rubies, fairy favors" (2.1.10–12); you can see the work of "that shrewd and knavish sprite / Called Robin Goodfellow" when cream will not churn to butter or when old women spill their drinks (2.1.36–38, 47–54); and you can see a contemporary cold and sodden spring as caused by dissension between the fairy king and queen (2.1.88–117). But is there anything of this sort that one has to see—that is, believe? The key question is this: Do the fairies do anything in the play that could not be accounted for otherwise? Scot is especially shrewd on this issue. He understands that claims to causation are strong claims. He questions whether we can consider something the cause of a phenomenon when, that supposed cause "being taken away," the phenomenon "happeneth nevertheless" (11). Claims about influence over the weather are, in fact, ones that he directly addresses. He is emphatic that "if all the divels in hell were dead, and all the witches in England burnt or hanged, I warrant you we should not faile to have raine, haile and tempests, as now we have" (2).

So, let us apply what we might call "Scot's test" to *A Midsummer Night's Dream*. Are there events that happen in the play that would not or could not have happened without the intervention of the fairies? The obvious candidates for such events in the play are the shifts in the male lovers' affections and the transformation of Bottom. There are a number of problems with taking the former set of phenomena as instances of nonnatural causation. First of all, the name of the "magical" juice that produces the shifts should give us pause; it is called "love in idleness" (2.1.168)—an abundance of aristocratic leisure. Shakespeare is telling us how to read this "juice." Second, we know, from data that is explicitly given in the text, that an instance of the phenomenon that the "love-juice" produces—a shift in the (female) object of a young man's affection, one that involves him renouncing his previous beloved—happened already before the play started. This had to have happened in order to produce the opening situation in which Demetrius, formerly engaged to Helena, is now a competitor with Lysander, Hermia's longtime fiancé, for the hand of Hermia. In other words, from an original state (call this State I) in which there were two couples—Lysander and Hermia; Demetrius and Helena—there was a shift that produced the opening situation, both young men in love with Hermia (State II). State III—both young men in love with Helena—was produced by the "juice." But State II was not.

The diagetical reality of State I is crucial to the play. The previous existence of State I is what gives force to the idea—necessary to a nondeconstructive (or at least, nondark) reading of the play—that the final alignment of the couples can plausibly be thought of as a return to a "natural" condition. This is what Demetrius claims about his situation at the end of act 4 (in love with Helena); he says that "as in health, " he has "come to [his] natural taste" (4.1.173).[31] What is important, from the point of view that we are pursuing, is that 1) this is a return to State I, the harmonious state—plausibly seen as a "healthy" one—in which there was no rivalry between the young men (or the young women), and 2) that the shift from that state to State II apparently "just happened." Demetrius, blessed with youth, wealth, and an abundance of aristocratic leisure, somehow found that he was in love with his friend's fiancé rather than his own. Heavens! This is irrational, perhaps, but has been known to happen in world history.[32] No fairies or (external) love-juices are required to explain it. Nor are any offered. The play offers us the fairies and the juice as a supererogatory "explanation" of such a phenomenon—if we want it. And of course the bad weather is caused by a feud in the royal household of the fairies. And old women spill their ale because Puck intervenes. We are in the world of Mercutio's Queen Mab.[33]

But surely the transformation of Bottom cannot be made "modern and familiar." The question here is whom the joke is on. Lucian (second century C.E.), normally taken as the author of *Lucius, or The Ass*, was one of the favorite authors of humanistic skeptics; Bacon thought him that supposedly rare thing, a "contemplative atheist."[34] A passage in *The Comedy of Errors* is immediately relevant. In the passage where Dromio of Syracuse calls for his "beads" and thinks he is in "the fairy land," he goes on to ask: "I am transformed, master, am I not?" (2.2.195). One of the high characters, a plain-spoken woman (Adriana's sister, Luciana), then says to him, "If thou art changed to aught, 'tis to an ass" (199). The joke, needless to say, is that he has been one all along. So it is (as his name suggests) with Bottom. When Bottom says, "This is to make an ass of me" (3.1.108), he is referring to his colleagues' apparent fear of him. No fairy was necessary to "make an ass" of Bottom. The physical ass-head is only, as it would have been recognized as being, a prop, and one that is simply materializing an existing state. "Please read allegorically," Shakespeare is again saying, as with "love-in-idleness" or when one of the male lovers speaks of being "wood [mad] within this wood" (2.1.192). Allegorical reading was one of Scot's major strategies.[35]

Yet, with regard to Bottom, the play may be more equivocal than this—not in relation to his "transformation" but in relation to his "vision." "The eye of man hath not heard, the ear of man hath not seen"—the biblical language in Bottom's Dream (4.1.203–12) is a garbled but perhaps not parodied version of the high words of 1 Corinthians 2:9 ("The things which eye hathe not sene, nether ear hathe heard . . . which God hathe prepared for them that love him").[36] It is hard to know how to take this comedic version of "the deepe things of God" (I Corinthians 2:10). Shakespeare seems to be letting up on his rationalism here. Northrop Frye thinks so.[37] Or maybe we are to read it as comedy and "no more yielding but a dream" (5.1.420). Be that as it may, one would think that the play surely undercuts the skepticism and rationalism of Theseus in his major speech at the beginning of act 5. There is no doubt about the rationalism of this speech. Despite how often the lines on the poet are quoted as praise—they have been used for National Poetry Day in the UK—Theseus's account of the poet in a "fine frenzy" stipulating names and locations for nonexistent entities ("airy nothings") is calculatedly equivocal; it recapitulates the ironic lyricism of Plato's *Ion*, and anticipates that of Bacon on poetry.[38] On the other hand, Theseus's account of the animistic urge is straightforwardly shrewd and almost technical in its terminological precision—if imagination "but apprehend some joy, / It comprehends some bringer of that joy" (5.1.19–20). Benign forces—benign agents (like fairies)—must be at work. Poetry, says Bacon, "doth raise and erect the mind." It does so by "submitting the shows of things to the desires of the mind." But the desire to see the world as animated and benign does not make it so. Again, there is no guarantee of contact with reality. What does have contact with reality, for Shakespeare's Theseus, as for Plato, is reason, which, as Bacon says, "doth buckle and bow the mind unto the nature of things."[39]

Bacon ends his discussion of poetry by conceding it some expressive value, but then remarking that "it is not good to stay too long in the theatre."[40] Shakespeare, on the other hand, did stay long in the theater; he spent the better part of his adult life working there. But this does not mean that Shakespeare did not know that theater was theater. At the level of "plot," so to speak, the joke is on Theseus. He scoffs at "fairy toys" at the beginning of act 5, when the fairies have been on stage for most of the play, and he scoffingly refers to "fairy time" just before the fairies take the stage again—with Robin Goodfellow doing just what Scot scoffed at, "sweeping the house at midnight." But are we supposed to take this *coup de théâtre* as a real argument? The lines the fairies are given mingle high mythology ("Hecate's team") with popular superstition (that there is a time of night when "graves, all gaping wide, / Every one let's forth his sprite / In the church-way paths to glide" [5.1.365–68]).[41] Oberon and company bless the ducal household with freedom from birth defects ("never mole, harelip, or scar" [5.1.373, 400]). If at this point, you want to believe that fairies are necessary for this . . . well, you have not been paying attention. That the play has an epilogue is a bit of a surprise, since Theseus has just insisted that a play, even a bad one, "needs no excuse" (5.1.341). Yet Shakespeare seems to feel that his play does. The epilogue does not ask us to clap our hands if we believe in fairies. Spoken by Robin Goodfellow, it may manifest a real anxiety that the learned Protestant aristocrats (the "gentles") in the audience would truly be tempted to "reprehend" a play that at least might be (mistakenly) taken as harkening back to the bad old days when Robin Goodfellow and Hob Goblin were credible, and before popery was "sufficiently discovered."[42] But it is important to remember that the point of Scot's book was not to attack belief in fairies—which he took to be obviously absurd—but to attack the much more relevant contemporary issue of prosecuting (supposed) witches. Theseus, like many commonsensical English magistrates, might, like Scot, have been as skeptical about the latter as the former.[43] Being on the side of the fairies might not put one on the side of the angels.

But before I move on to the other play deeply in dialogue with another text skeptical about popular (and Catholic) beliefs, I must briefly answer an obvious objection to the claims made above, especially with regard to witches. How could one possibly say that the author of *Macbeth* was skeptical about witches? Three of them appear in the very first lines of the play, and reappear later. Luckily, I do not have to make the case, since it was brilliantly made decades ago by Henry N. Paul in a classic of "Old Historicism."[44] Paul shows that the play was written for a king who had been a strong believer in witchcraft, and had written the *Daemonologie*, but who was, by the time of the composition of *Macbeth* (1605–6), well on his way to total skepticism on the issue.[45] The play, according to Paul, is intentionally written in a way that allows for learned skepticism (which Paul considers to be Shakespeare's view) as well as for popular credulity, and Paul further argues that this "double appeal" was already present in one of Shakespeare's major sources for the play, George Buchanan's (Latin) *History of Scotland* (1582).[46] As to the "weyard" sisters, Paul sees them as three old women "practicing sorcery" in a distinctively Scottish mode.[47] Basically, Paul sees the play as working to bring the king (and others in the audience) down the road to full rationalism, though not forcing them there—which seems right to me.

Mock-Devils and Mock-Miracles: *King Lear*

Turning now to *King Lear* (1605), the connection of the play to Harsnett's *Declaration* (and through Harsnett to Scot) is well established. As early as 1733, the greatest of Shakespeare's early editors, Lewis Theobald (Pope's "Tibbald"), noted that Edgar's mock "frenzy" is a "Satire levell'd at a modern fact," namely, the Catholic exorcisms of 1585–86, the fame of which was newly revived in 1603 by Harsnett's pamphlet.[48] Greenblatt has suggested that Harsnett's text was especially attractive to Shakespeare because the *Declaration* uses theater as "an explanatory model, at once metaphor and analytical tool," to debunk the Catholic exorcisms while at the same time accounting for their power over audiences.[49] But Shakespeare did not need Harsnett to provide him with the notion that madness, with its assertion of demonic possession, could be mimed. Against the grain of Greenblatt's "circulation" model—the claim, in this case, that Harsnett was somehow influenced by, as well as an influence upon, Shakespearean theater—Greenblatt notes that Erasmus's 1524 colloquy on exorcism uses the theatrical metaphor to debunk the practice of exorcism.[50] Erasmus had no connection to any actual theater. Shakespeare could have (and probably did) read the Erasmus colloquy for himself—the *Colloquies* were school texts and immensely popular.[51] In *The Discoverie of Witchcraft* (300–306), Scot translated most of Erasmus's colloquy on alchemy, which was paired by Erasmus with that on exorcism. But, again, *The Comedy of Errors* anticipates the point. In act 4, after Dr. Pinch had Antipholus of Ephesus bound (since "the fiend is strong within him"), Dromio of Ephesus advises his master to throw himself into the situation—"Wilt thou be bound for nothing? Be mad, good master; cry, 'The devil!'" (4.4.125–26). Shakespeare turned to Harsnett's pamphlet not because he needed it for exposition or analysis but because it expressed a position—about demonic possession and about the world—with which he agreed.

The audience of *King Lear* would have known from the play itself that Edgar was making up his whole autobiography as "Tom," an autobiography in which the experience of being pursued by "the foul fiend" bulks large. But Shakespeare might have sought to lead those like himself, who had just read the recently published Harsnett volume, specifically to recall the text. The names of many of the devils mentioned by Edgar-as-Tom are taken from Harsnett: Flibbertigibbet, Smulkin, Modo, and Mahu (3.4: Q 102, 126, 128–29; F 106, 130, 132–33; *Declaration* 240, 242), Frateretto (Q and F 3.6: 6; *Declaration*, 242), Obbidicut, and Hobbididence (Q 4.1.57; *Declaration*, 242, 295).[52] The mention in the Quarto of possessed "chambermaids and waiting-women" (4.1.59–60) is a direct reference to some of the "examinates" in Harsnett.[53] Those who caught these allusions would have been familiar with a spectacular, feigned, and Catholic discourse of demonic possession. In Harsnett, they would have been familiar (no pun intended) with a text in which, as in Scot's *Discoverie of Witchcraft*, the world of the spirit is sharply distinct from the world of matter, and even the "divine energie, power, and vertue" of the Eucharist is entirely a spiritual phenomenon

(*Declaration*, 301). In *A Declaration of Egregious Popish Impostures*, all postbiblical claims to access such power materially are shams. "The Sceptick" is a positive figure (*Declaration*, 251–52, 278). The "five fiends" who (in the Quarto) have been "in Poor Tom at once, of lust . . . of stealing . . . of murder" (4.1.56–58) recall Scot's allegorizing. The "five fiends" seem very much like the "seven divels cast out of Marie Magdalen," which, Scot explains, signifies not a specific number of entities but rather "an uncerteine number of vices" (429). "Tom's" seeing them as named demons is part of his (as of the examinates) miming of madness.

The demons in *King Lear* do not share even in whatever ontological ambiguity the fairies may have in *A Midsummer Night's Dream*. Unlike *Hamlet*, which seems committed to leaving its questions at least partially open, *Lear* might be said to participate less in Pyrrhonian than in Academic skepticism—instead of leaving everything open, neither asserted nor denied, it might be said to move all the way to "negative dogmatism."[54] The supernatural seems simply to be absent. Supernatural benevolence fares no better in the play than supernatural malevolence does. Miracles fare no better than demons. Critics who want to resist an entirely secular or disenchanted reading of the play—Greenblatt notable among them—sometimes suggest that it is only the wicked characters in the play who are skeptics.[55] It is rarely noted that the first mention of miracles in the play is a skeptical comment by a virtuous character. The King of France refuses to believe that "in this trice of time," Cordelia could have done something to justify Lear's changed treatment of her—"which to believe of her / Must be a faith that reason without miracle / Could never plant in me" (1.1: Q 209–11; F 219–21). He sticks, completely admirably, to reason. It might be argued that he is leaving open the possibility of being convinced by a miracle, but the point of his speech is to discount, not to affirm, the possibility. Edmund makes fun of Gloucester's belief that "the late eclipses" were portents of a bevy of social and political disasters (1.2: Q 97–105; F 95–108), calling it "foppery" and asserting the power of the will. Pretending to take Gloucester's view seriously, he mockingly asserts, "O these eclipses do portend these divisions" (123–24; 125–26). But Edgar is just as skeptical about astrology as Edmund is. When Edmund pretends to be taking seriously a prediction that he read the other day concerning "what should follow these eclipses," Edgar is surprised and asks, "Do you busy yourself about [F: with] that?" (1.2: Q 129; F 132). Edmund asserts that he does, and, in the Quarto, regales Edgar with an account that echoes Gloucester's on the awful "sequent effects" that the eclipses supposedly portended (Q 131–36). Edgar responds (in the Quarto) by mockingly inquiring of Edmund, "How long hast thou been a sectary astronomical?" (137).

Edgar is consistent in this regard. When he first sees his blinded father, he speaks of the "strange mutations" of the world (history, earthly life), not of the heavens (4.1: Q 8; F 11). So it is no accident that the character who discourses upon comic and ridiculous devils should also be what Harsnett calls a "miracle-minter." Obviously, Edgar's motives in creating a "miracle" for his father—involving an escape from another ridiculous fiend (with "a thousand noses," etc. [Q 4.6; F 4.5: 69–72])—are different from, much more benign than, the motives of the sadistic and ambitious Jesuit exorcists in Harsnett.[56] But the ontology of the situations is the same. In this episode, Shakespeare does truly draw on Harsnett's intimate knowledge of theater—that is, of classical (Roman) theater. Harsnett does make a reference to "your wandring Players" (211), and he does seem familiar with "the old Church-playes" (291), but he shows no awareness of contemporary London theater, with its grand, established theatrical buildings. Harsnett presents one of the Catholic exorcists discoursing in a manner that provides an exact model for what Edgar does at the supposed cliff near Dover, a model based squarely on Plautus (from a play that Shakespeare drew on in *Errors*):[57]

> the Miracle-minter deals heere with those formes and faces of devils as Sosia in *Amphitryo* dealt with the battaile at Teliboiis, who ranges two Armies, devides them into squadrons, wings, and flanks, and makes them meete and encounter, and none but himselfe alone is upon the stage. (*Declaration*, 313)

"Thy life's a miracle," says Edgar to a man who has fallen flat on his face from a kneeling position before and after being given an impressive imaginary narrative about the physical and spiritual perils of his situation (Q 4.6; F 4.5: 55). And none but themselves are alone upon the stage. Tonally and generically, this is a complex moment. Harsnett has a difficult time assigning a genre to the "theatrical" events that he is describing; he uses the term "Tragico-comaedia" (319; and see 203 et alia). Shakespeare's Harnsettian "miracle" may be comic, tragic, pathetic, or all of the above. It has been said that in this scene at Dover "the grotesque merged into the ridiculous reaches a consummation in this bathos of tragedy."[58] What the moment cannot be is straightforwardly religious.[59] In Erasmus's colloquy on exorcism, a fraudulent miracle is also invoked. The dupe in the colloquy is obsessed with demons. He is recovered from this by a letter from a spirit that he supposedly successfully exorcised, telling the dupe that there is a special place awaiting him in heaven. The comment made on this is that the jokers have not freed the man from insanity but merely changed its brand.[60] In the *Lear* scene, despite the beauty of the poetry in the lines evoking "the clearest Gods, who made their [or, in F, make them] honours / Of men's impossibilities" (Q 4.6; F 4.5: 73–74), these clear gods are as much a fiction as the fiend with a thousand noses.[61] Gloucester has just prayed that "Fairies and Gods" help the "poor man" prosper with his jewel (4.6; 4.5: 29). "*Think that* the clearest Gods," says Edgar (emphasis mine). He is telling Gloucester what to believe while leaving the truth-content of this belief spectacularly unasserted.

But exorcisms and miracles are one sort of thing. They are, even if one believes in them, extraordinary manifestations of divine presence. The most fundamental belief about such presence is the doctrine of providence, the belief that God's hand can be seen, with whatever difficulty, as active in human events.[62] This is different from belief in "the stars" or the fairies. Not to believe in providence is to extend religious skepticism past the point where Harsnett or (probably) even Scot would go. It approaches what would certainly have been called atheism. But *King Lear* seems to go there. As with the matter of the witches in *Macbeth*, on the matter of providence in *Lear*, we can rely on another great work of "Old Historicism," William Elton's *King Lear and the Gods*. Elton fudges a bit on the "atheism" question, equivocates between the play being pagan and the play being religiously syncretic, and, despite herculean efforts, is not able to discount every one of the apparently Christian references in the play (a point to which I will return), yet much of his argument, especially about providence, is fully persuasive.[63]

Elton's final chapter is a short but effective one called "Irony as Structure." He points out that every time in the play that it looks as if divine justice is going to be (or has been) shown, or as if right is about to triumph, or as if the gods will (at least) preserve the virtuous, something terrible happens. That the characters speak of "the gods" need not in itself undercut a providentialist perspective—they could have a pagan apprehension of the truth—but the ironic pattern does. "The gods" respond neither to Lear's prayers nor to his curses; when Albany says of the mortal wounding of Cornwall by his servant that "this shows you are above, / You Justices [Q: justicers]," his interlocutor immediately makes it clear that the intervention did Gloucester absolutely no good. "But O, poor Gloucester, / Lost he his other eye?" Albany cries in disbelief; "Both, both, my lord," says the nameless servant-messenger, who cannot fathom Albany's distress (4.2: Q 76–79; F 45–47). When the battle is joined between Cordelia's forces and those of the older sisters, Edgar's "pray that the right may thrive" is followed, three lines later, by "King Lear hath lost, he and his daughter ta'en" (Q and F:

5.2: 2, 6). Immediately following Albany's prayer that "the Gods defend" Cordelia (5.3: Q 249; F 230) is the stage direction, identical in both Q and F, "Enter Lear with Cordelia in his arms." To maintain piety, one could say that all this merely shows that providence is not humanly apprehensible, and one could quote Luther and Calvin on the "hidden God" to support this.[64] But the effect of the pattern in the play is to make it seem as if the divine is truly not active in human affairs. This is exactly the opposite of the conclusion that Calvin would want us to draw. The "principal purpose" of the narrative portions of the Bible, says Calvin, is "to teach that the Lord watches over the ways of the saints with such great diligence that they do not even stumble over a stone."[65] At the end of act 2, scene 2, Kent claims that "misery" has a special relation to miracles—"Nothing almost sees miracles," he asserts, "But misery" (Q 156–57; F 153–54). But it is not clear that by the end of the play, Kent still believes this. When Edgar urges Lear to "look up," Kent strongly demurs: "he hates him [Lear] / That would upon the rack of this tough world / Stretch him out longer" (5.3: Q 305–7; F 289–91). This is not the perspective of a man who expects misery to see miracles.

Insofar as there is an argument for providentialism within the play, it would focus on the destruction of the wicked rather than on the preservation or triumph of the virtuous. A. C. Bradley has some fine remarks on this.[66] The Quarto version is especially insistent on this. In the Quarto (and only in the Quarto), one of Gloucester's servants, who has just witnessed the blinding of Gloucester by Cornwall, says, "I'll never care what wickedness I do, / If this man [meaning Cornwall] come to good" (Q 3.7: 96–97). We find out fairly quickly that Cornwall has not "come to good." In the Quarto, the major part of the scene (4.2) that ends with the revelation to Albany of Cornwall's death and Gloucester's blinding is devoted to Albany's denunciation of Goneril, and to his predictions—not present in the Folio—that she too will come to no good ("She that herself will sliver and disbranch / From her material sap, perforce must wither, / And come to deadly use" [Q 4.2.33–35]). By the end of the play, Goneril has "desperately" fordone or "foredoomed" herself (5.3: F 265; Q 283), and Regan and Edmund (along with Cornwall) are also dead. It is possible to think, as Albany apparently does, that some sort of moral and metaphysical process is at work in this outcome (he speaks of "this judgment" [F] or "this justice" [Q] of the heavens), but all these deaths are given entirely clear naturalistic explanations—"If not, I'll ne'er trust poison [F: medicine]," says Goneril.

The focus of the end of the play is on the utterly incomprehensible and almost ludicrously gratuitous death of the innocent. Edmund countermands his command that Cordelia be killed, but that the command is carried out nonetheless is not the result of the suborned captain's eagerness or efficiency; it occurs through a lack of focus on the part of the virtuous. More precisely and ironically, it comes about from Albany's admirable interest in Edgar's "brief tale," which lasts for almost twenty lines (5.3: Q 175–187; F 173–185), and to which, in the Quarto, Edgar adds "something more"—about Kent's extraordinary service to Lear—for another seventeen lines (Q 5.3.198–215). "Great thing of us forgot!" (5.3: Q 230; F 211) would be hilarious were it not so awful. It takes us out of the moral realm entirely. As Albany rightly says in both Q and F, Cordelia's death makes the apparent moral transparency of the demises of Edmund and company "but a trifle" (5:3: Q 287; F 269).

With regard to the material manifestations of the supernatural in the world, it would seem, then, completely accurate to see the relation of *King Lear* to Harsnett's book as "one of reiteration," and of a reiteration, moreover, that is "neither superficial nor unstable." Greenblatt comes to this conclusion through a good deal of lucid and straightforward analysis, but his next sentence begins "And yet," and the remaining quarter of his essay is devoted to elaborating this reservation.[67] The argument becomes strained and obscure, but Greenblatt's discomfort with what we might call the "Eltonian" reading is apparent. For the "circulation" model to work, there has to be a sense in which the Catholicism and ritual that Harsnett mocked are somehow reinstituted by Shakespeare (providing the needed cultural circle). The play must be seen as somehow recuperating what it seems to be rejecting. Greenblatt does not quite read the Gloucester subplot in which the legitimate elder brother persecuted by "his skeptical bastard brother" is an allegory of the state of Catholicism in England, and especially of "the situation of the Jesuits in England," but he is tempted to do so.[68] But, as we have seen, Edgar, the elder brother, is just as skeptical as Edmund is, and though the Jesuits in England were certainly hunted, they hid with aristocratic sympathizers and did not wander about naked and starving.[69] This rather fanciful "resemblance" is then supposedly given historical plausibility by reference to the performance of a *King Lear* in 1610 in the house of a wealthy Catholic (who did shelter Jesuits) by a Catholic theater company. We know very little about this performance.[70] It is not certain that the play in question was Shakespeare's version rather than the revived older version that is certainly less skeptical than Shakespeare's (we know that the old play was printed in 1605 "As it was latelie Acted").[71] Maybe the 1610 performance was Shakespeare's version, maybe not. Maybe in it Edgar was seen as truly possessed. But in any case, all we can say is that the play that was performed was not seen as inherently anti-Catholic *by this audience.*

But Greenblatt's major argument is specific to great theater and to Shakespeare's play. Theater, at its grandest, apparently cannot be a purely secular experience. The claim is that since *Lear* generates "the hope for an impossible redemption"—which is taken to be equivalent to "the dream of exorcism"— the play validates this hope even while literally rejecting it.[72] But why not see the play as truly rejecting the dream of magical or even providential exorcism of evil? Greenblatt is certainly right that *Lear* is not, as Harsnett's *Declaration* is, a work of propaganda for the state religion. I am not sure, however, that *Lear* does not share the goal of the *Declaration* to lead us to loathe "impostures" and return unto the truth (*Declaration*, 335). I see no reason not to take Shakespeare as more rather than less skeptical than Harsnett, more truly secular. The deepest longing of the play may not be for the efficacy of rituals but for the possibility of an earthly social justice that would "show the heavens more just."[73]

Heavenly Eyes

Yet there do seem to be religious and even Christian moments in Shakespeare's play. Positive religious language certainly accretes, nonironically and nonambiguously, around the figure of Cordelia. The question is whether this suggests a supernatural presence in the world. The most unequivocally Christian language in the play occurs in the elaborate description, unique to the Quarto, of Cordelia's reactions to Kent's letters to her detailing the older sisters' treatment of Lear: "There she shook / The holy water from her heavenly eyes / And clamour moistened" (Q 4.3.29–30). Putting aside the fact that the Folio text lacks this scene, the question remains, In what sense are we to take this mention of "holy water"? Is this intended in a transcendental sense? If these tears are indeed, as I think they are intended to be, "holy water," they are such through a purely human capacity, and they have nothing to do with priests, institutions, incantations, demons, and so forth—the beliefs and uses of "holy water" that Harsnett savagely critiques (see *Declaration*, 280–81). Maybe compassionate tears really are holy water for Shakespeare (contrasting sharply with the "court holy water" referred to by the Fool earlier as a metaphor for flattery [3.2.10, Q and F]). "Heavenly" here is not clearly more than a seriously intended stock-phrase. Shakespeare (or whoever) may have had many reasons for cutting this scene, but he need not have worried that it undermined the nontranscendentalism of the play.[74] If this is "holy water," one need not believe in any nonhuman locus of holiness to reverence it. Only a fool of a sort very different from the one in the play would take it as containing "infused divine vertue" (*Declaration*, 274).

The hidden power that Cordelia invokes is within nature; she calls on the "unpublished virtues [vertues] of the earth" (Q 4.4; F 4.3: 16) in a strictly medical context. In the Quarto version of this scene, she is in dialogue with a "Doctor" who is clearly a medical person, not a divine.[75] She is interested in what "man's wisdom" can do (Q 4.4; F 4.3: 8).[76] Yet, at the very end of this scene, Cordelia is given the most explicit and unmistakable Christian reference in the play, a reference that seems certainly to point us beyond the human. In relation to reports both of Lear's condition and of the ongoing military situation, she states: "O dear father, / It is thy business that I go about" (Q 4.4; F 4.3: 23–24). The biblical reference here is unmistakable; Shakespeare must be having Cordelia echo "Knewe ye not that I must go about my fathers business?" (Luke 2:49; Geneva). But the question is what to make of this. It is extremely implausible that Shakespeare means us to see Cordelia as quoting or alluding. The pagan setting of the play has been too consistent for that. The words are hers, not the allusion. She means the words literally, providing Shakespeare's audience with a momentary experience of something like typology or double vision (even in the Christian scheme, the Old Testament "types" do not know that they are such).

One could, if one were given to a certain kind of criticism—as I am not—claim that Cordelia is a Christ "symbol" here, but unless one sees the mode of the play turning into allegory, it would remain important, as it is with *A Midsummer Night's Dream*, to distinguish between symbolic and literal representation. But here, following Paul Alpers, I would stress the literal.[77] It would be truer to the mode of this play and to the actual experience of this moment to see it as a recognition of "Christ-likeness"—of what selfless devotion *is like*. Moreover, to anyone who recalls the actual context of the biblical quotation, the interpretive situation becomes quite complex. What leaps out is exactly the literalness of Cordelia's claim. At the moment in Luke when the assertion is made, the boy Jesus is forcefully rejecting his (earthly) parents. He is speaking sharply to them in the process of rejecting his earthly father for a transcendental one. Cordelia is not doing any such thing; the "business" that she is taking on is entirely that of her earthly father. One might certainly view her actions as a form of piety, but it is piety as *pietas*, and there is no transcendental dimension to it.[78]

But what of Lear's vision of Cordelia as "a soul in bliss" (Q 4.7.44; F 4.6.40)? Elton ignores it in his discussion of the scene, and later states blandly that it "may indicate the happy state of the virtuous soul"—with the suggestion that this is not necessarily Christian.[79] Elysium is certainly a possibility, though "bliss" is very strong.[80] Even, however, if—despite inconsistency, anachronism, and so forth—one takes this to be a Christian reference (which obviously one need not), the point would still not be that a Christian afterlife exists, but (a) that Lear has recognized the moral stature of Cordelia, and (b) that Lear's grip on reality is still extremely shaky. The importance of the moment, and of the whole scene, is not what it asserts about transcendental realities, but (again) what it implies about human ones. What makes Cordelia "heavenly" here is precisely what made her "heavenly" and "holy" in the Quarto scene omitted from the Folio—her positive human qualities, her humanity in a normative sense. It is important here that Lear is mistaken. She is no more in heaven (or Elysium) than he is in hell—or rather, she is in the one in the same way that he is in the other. The moment is one of pathetic, moving, and lunatic fantasy, not of visionary reality. The ontological status of Cordelia as a "soul in bliss" is the same as that of Edgar's fiend with a thousand noses. Lear's vision of singing and gossiping with Cordelia in prison as if they were divine "spies" is another moment of lyrical and moving delusion.[81]

"And yet." I have discussed Greenblatt's "And yet." Here is my own. And yet—there is a serious sense in which a theological conception enters deeply into *King Lear*, and does indeed come to focus on Cordelia. In the final segment of this essay, I will try to demonstrate how profoundly the play is shaped by the ethical and psychological content of the central theological doctrine of the Reformation, but not by its specifically religious content. I mean to agree with Greenblatt that the relation of *King Lear* (and a number of the other plays) to theology is different from the relation to theology of Scot's or Harsnett's texts, and I mean to agree as well that there is a paradoxical dimension to this, and that it is deeply connected to Shakespeare's aims as a dramatist. The first essay in this book demonstrated that theological conceptions help Shakespeare dramatize his conception of evil in the presentation of Iago and his plans in *Othello*.[82] Here I want to show that Shakespeare's conception of goodness is similarly situated. The instance that I want to discuss occurs in the "recognition scene" (Q 4.7; F 4.6) that contains the "soul in bliss" assertion. I will argue that the "theology" of the scene lies not in any pattern of allusions but rather in its pattern of emotions and personal interactions.[83]

When one perceives the striking analogies between the interaction of father and daughter in this poetic scene, which is purely secular, and the dramatized interaction between agents in a great lyric poem that looks secular but cannot, on closer inspection, actually be so, the theological structure of Shakespeare's scene becomes unmistakably apparent. George Herbert's third poem entitled "Love," the culminating lyric of *The Temple*, dramatizes the psychological and moral difficulties that the human subject has in encountering completely unearned grace.[84] The human speaker, encountering embodied *agape*, is afflicted with overwhelming shame—"I cannot look on thee"—and with penetrating, specific remorse: "I, the unkind," he says (lines 9–10).[85] He wants nothing more than to be punished—"let my shame go where it doth deserve"—that is, to hell (lines 13–14). At the very least, he wants to serve ("My dear, then I will serve" [line 16]). But he is not allowed to do any of these things. Instead, he is told what he "must" do—"You must sit down" (line 17).[86] He must simply go along with getting something that has absolutely no relation to any calculus of justice or desert. Herbert is dramatizing the doctrine of grace here in its most uncompromising—and most joyous—Reformation formulation.[87]

The analogies with the scene in *Lear* (in both versions) are haunting—and informative.[88] In the "holy water" scene, we are told that because of his profound sense of "his own unkindness" to Cordelia "a sovereign shame" so "elbows" Lear that he "by no means / Will yield to see his daughter" (Q 4.3.40–42). Compare "I, the unkind … I cannot look on thee." In his analysis of shame, Stanley Cavell has pointed out that, in such moments, the refusal to look is correlated with a refusal to be seen, to be looked at.[89] In the recognition dialogue, Cordelia implores Lear, who is apparently still unable to do so, to "look upon me, sir." She also tells him what he "must"—or in this case, must not—do: "you must not kneel" (Q 57; F 53). Lear's impulse or desire to kneel is exactly parallel to "My dear, then I will serve" in Herbert's poem. In both cases, the proffered action is rejected; Cordelia's negative command is exactly parallel to "you must sit down," which rejects the offer of service. Most of all, Lear, like Herbert's human speaker, wants to be punished. Lear wants either to be allowed to stay in the hell he imagines himself inhabiting, where he imagines himself literally enduring burning shame ("mine own tears / Do scald like molten lead" [Q 43–46; F 39–42]), or to be justly executed by Cordelia—"If you have poison for me, I will drink it" (69; 66). Compare "let my shame / Go where it doth deserve." Lear reviews the scorecard of injuries: "your sisters / Have, as I do remember, done me wrong. / You," he says to Cordelia, "have some cause" (Q 71–72; F 68–69). He "knows" that Cordelia does not love him (Q 70; F 67), could not possibly do so. It turns out, however, that in both texts, love for an individual is not granted on the basis of merit. It flies in the face of justice and appropriate punishment, and is granted, as Cordelia says, completely freely, for "no cause" (Q 72; F 69). This is precisely the mode of completely unmerited, "unmotivated" love that

Luther thought was characterized only by divine love, which "does not find but creates its object."[90]

The way that theology enters into *Lear*, therefore, is through the deep structure of the Reformation doctrine of grace: the contrast between merit, calculation, and prudence, on the one hand, and grace or love, on the other. Reformation theology saw these concepts as sharply opposed to one another, and *Lear* does the same. The play starts with a confusion in Lear's mind between giving and earning. Is he giving his daughters their parts of the kingdom, or are they earning them? To recognize Shakespeare as secularizing the great Reformation contrast helps explain why Goneril and Regan are such powerful spokespersons for "reason," and why the initial confusion about love and quantity is savagely parodied in the pathetic equations of love with numbers in the second act of the play ("thy fifty yet doth double five-and-twenty, / And thou art twice her love" [2.4: Q 229–30; F 248–49]).[91] This act culminates in the moment when Lear comes to realize the irrelevance, even inappropriateness, of calculation to the deepest human needs.[92]

What Shakespeare does in *Lear* and elsewhere, in other words, is to create a thoroughly secular world in which terms like grace and sin, which, in Reformation theology, require a transcendental guarantee, are seen to exist and function without such: "I look down toward his feet—but that's a fable."[93] As Reginald Scot said, "the devil is no horned beast" (427). Shakespeare, like Scot, did not want us to believe in fables. One can enjoy "antique fables" and maybe even "fairy toys" (*MND*, 5.1.2) without belief, or with only theatrical "faith."[94] The demonic and the angelic exist in the human realm—"O, the more angel she"—equally mysteriously (*Othello*, 5.2.131). Theological conceptions were used by Shakespeare to point not to theological mysteries but to human ones.

CHAPTER 10

Shakespeare and Skepticism (2)

Epistemology

Current Shakespeare scholarship seems reasonably sure of two somewhat incompatible things: (1) we cannot be sure where Shakespeare stands on any particular issue, including religion (but he is sympathetic to Catholicism); and (2) we can be sure where he stands in the general philosophical world—that is, he was some sort of epistemological skeptic.[1] So, we cannot be sure of anything except that he was sure that we cannot be sure of anything. Yet we can be sure of some things. Shakespeare had, or came to have, a definite and firm position on a major ethico-political issue—namely, whether social or political subordinates should follow commands that seem to them obviously wicked or misguided.[2] Moreover, the essay previous to this one attempted to confute claim 1 with regard to some popular (Catholic) religious practices and beliefs about the supernatural. This essay will focus on claim 2, which (as I have suggested) is extremely widespread in current scholarship and criticism. My argument will be that Shakespeare was an anti-skeptic in the realm of epistemology, an epistemological realist.

Errors

This argument must begin, as did the argument that Shakespeare was a skeptic in relation to aspects of popular religion, with *The Comedy of Errors*. This is unsurprising, given the importance of error to the skeptical tradition. The play would seem to anticipate Descartes in a remarkable way. Indeed, if it had appeared in the mid-seventeenth century rather than the end of the sixteenth, it would certainly be seen as drawing on *Meditations on First Philosophy* (first printed in 1641) and perhaps also the *Discourse on the Method* (first printed in 1637). Descartes's *Meditations* begin with the problem of error or false belief. Descartes (or his surrogate in the philosophical fiction—let's call him "Descartes") states that he has been struck for a number of years by the number of false or dubious things (about the physical world) that he has come to believe. Having, in the dramatized moment ("today" [*hodie*]), decided that he is now old enough and in an optimal practical and psychological situation (leisure, solitude, and lack of anxiety [*mentem curis omnibus exsolvi*]), he feels himself ready to embark on the great project of seeing whether he can rid himself of all false beliefs (about the physical world) and thereby arrive at a basis on which to build something stable and permanent in the sciences.[3] He notes that he has based his previous cognitive structure on beliefs derived from sensory experience, and that sensory experience has sometimes led him astray. So, he now decides to take the path of prudence and not to have full confidence (*plane confidere*) in something that has previously deceived him. To make a new start, he is going to treat all the beliefs derived from his senses as if they were not merely dubitable but false.

But he finds that some of his sense perceptions seem indubitable—"that I am here, seated by the fire, wearing a winter dressing-gown, holding this piece of paper in my hands," and such. "How could I deny that these hands and this body are mine?" To doubt such matters would seem insane, and Descartes (and "Descartes") knows that he is not insane (he does not have crazy ideas like thinking that he has "an earthenware head," or is a pumpkin, or is made of glass).[4] He discounts this possibility.[5] Yet, after putting insanity aside, the narrator then recalls that he regularly has the experience of dreaming, in which state he has experiences just like those of madmen, and which seem to him just as obvious as that he is sitting by the fire, and so forth. This leads him to a thought that "astonishes" or stupefies him (*obstupescam* [*Meditationes*, 20])—not that he might be mad after all but that "there are no certain indications (*certis indiciis*) by which we may clearly distinguish wakefulness from sleep." Through this stupefying thought, he is led, at this moment, "almost" (*fere*) to think that he is asleep in the present, and possibly dreaming.

But "Descartes" moves past this moment of stupefaction. He accepts the point (for the time being at least) that he might, in the dramatized present, be dreaming. This would still leave him with certain beliefs that seem indubitable—"whether I am awake or asleep, two and three added together are five." But God is said to be omnipotent. This means that He could make it that Descartes goes wrong every time he adds two plus three. But that would seem to contradict the idea of God's goodness. Yet God certainly allows Descartes sometimes to go wrong. Why not all the time? So, "Descartes" apparently has to doubt absolutely all of his former beliefs, including the ones about arithmetic and geometry. He finds, however, that as a matter of psychological fact, he cannot actually do this. And he recognizes that, from a philosophical point of view, it does not really make sense to do this. He is aware that some of his former beliefs are highly probable, and that it is "much more reasonable to believe than to deny" many of them.

To force himself to doubt even the highly probable, he decides to postulate (to "suppose" [*supponam*]), as a conscious fiction, "that not God, who is supremely good and the source of truth, but rather some malicious demon [genius?] (*genium aliquem malignum*) of the utmost power and cunning has employed all his energies in order to deceive me." He resolves to treat all his beliefs about the physical world and his own physical existence as "the delusions [absurd fictions?] of dreams" (*ludificationes somniorum*), which he falsely believes in. He resolves further to "stubbornly persist" (*manebo obstinate*) in this epistemological posture, so that he will assent to no beliefs whatever—and therefore cannot be in error about anything. The meditation ends with "Descartes" struck by the difficulty of this project, and wishing to remain in the dreamlike state of delusion rather than awake into the apparently "inextricable darkness" of the problems he has raised.

All that is in Meditation 1—merely, for Descartes, the beginning. Five more Meditations follow, at the end of which "Descartes" (by then, Descartes) feels he has succeeded in establishing a stable and enduring foundation for the sciences, a foundation, in other words, that is more than highly probable. But Shakespeare's play might seem never to get beyond Meditation 1. The central character, Antipholus of Syracuse—the upper-class twin (with the same name as his brother) who is a stranger in the town (Ephesus) in which the play is set—finds himself, quite early in the play, in a mental state similar to that in which "Descartes" found himself in the course of Meditation 1. Antipholus of Syracuse quickly comes to lose all trust in the reliability of his sense-perceptions, and therefore, as in Descartes, of his ability to make sense of his experience. But unlike Descartes (or his persona in *Meditations*), who purposely, systematically, and merely heuristically puts himself into a state of uncertainty, Antipholus of Syracuse enters the play as a character who is psychologically prone to this state. From the very first moment when we meet him, Shakespeare presents this character as someone with an oddly weak conception of his own existence.

When, in undertaking, before dinner and a nap, to "view the manners of the town, / Peruse the traders, gaze upon the buildings" (1.2.12–13), Antipholus of Syracuse says he will "go lose myself" in doing this (1.2.30), the phrase seems to be merely a casual figure of speech for behaving like a good humanist traveler.[6] Yet when one of the many benign merchants in the play leaves Antipholus S. for a while to, in a very ordinary phrase, his own "content," this produces a verbally alert, poetical, and melancholy soliloquy (long before *Hamlet*):

> He that commends me to my own content
> Commends me to the thing I cannot get.
> I to the world am like a drop of water
> That in the ocean seeks another drop,
> Who, falling there to find his fellow forth,
> (Unseen, inquisitive) confounds himself.
> So I, to find a mother and a brother,
> In quest of them, unhappy, lose myself. (1.2.33–40)

This is not someone who can be counted on to have a robust sense of reality or of his own cognitive capacities. When the first of the "errors" in the play occurs, and this Antipholus, who has sent his servant to carry funds to the inn where he will be staying, is confronted with the servant of the other (resident) Antipholus and told to come home to dine with the resident's wife, the traveler immediately worries about his money. But his worry goes way beyond the ordinary. His soliloquy begins there—"They say this town is full of cozenage"—but continues:

> As nimble jugglers that deceive the eye,
> Dark-working sorcerers that change the mind,
> Soul-killing witches that deform the body... (1.2.97–100)

These (imagined) "dark-working sorcerers that change the mind" are startlingly close to the "malign genius" that Descartes so memorably postulates in the First Meditation.

The "foreshadowing" of Descartes's Meditation 1 continues even more strongly in the next scene in which Antipholus of Syracuse appears. He is confronted there with an apparently unaccountable phenomenon: an unknown woman addresses him by name as her husband and makes a passionate and eloquent speech to him about the meaning of marital oneness in relation to fidelity and infidelity.[7] Instead of replying that he does not know why she is saying all this to him, this Antipholus falls into the (it is hard not to call it) "Cartesian" dilemma about waking and sleeping. He profoundly doubts his own "waking" understanding of the world: "What, was I married to her in my dream? / Or sleep I now, and think I hear all this?" (2.2.173–74). He is in a state of "Cartesian" astonishment; recall: "I see so manifestly that there are no certain indications by which we may clearly distinguish waking from sleeping, that I am lost in astonishment." The Syracusan Antipholus suspects, almost in philosophical terms, that something is wrong—"What error drives our eyes and ears amiss?" (2.2.175)—but in his state of suspended judgment (*epoché*), he adopts the normal pragmatic attitude of the skeptic, ancient and modern, with regard to existing mores: "Until I know this sure uncertainty / I'll entertain the offered fallacy" (2.2.176–77).[8]

In the *Outlines of Pyrrhonism*, Sextus Empiricus summarizes the position thus: "Adhering then to appearances, we live in accordance with the normal rules of life, undogmatically, seeing that we cannot remain wholly inactive."[9] In the third part of the *Discourse on the Method*, the historical Descartes (now not "Descartes") explains that while pursuing the philosophical experiment dramatized in his *Meditations*, he adopted a "provisional morality" (*une morale par provision*) of obeying "the laws and customs of my country."[10] Montaigne similarly explained that his skepticism about the rational basis of laws led him to obey rather than to disobey them.[11] In the final soliloquy of the scene from which we have been quoting, Antipholus of Syracuse recapitulates the whole movement from cognitive uncertainty to social conservatism. But it is notable that he considers the possibility that, as we have seen, Descartes rejected even when Descartes was trying his hardest to dislodge his ordinary opinions—namely, the possibility that he is insane. In the face of Adriana and her sister's certainty, Antipholus of Syracuse says (to himself):

> Am I in earth, in heaven, or in hell?
> Sleeping or waking, mad or well advis'd?
> Known unto these, and to myself disguis'd?
> I'll say as they say, and persever so,
> And in this mist at all adventures go. (2.2.203–7)

"In this mist" seems exactly right for this play; compare the "inextricable darkness" by which "Descartes" feels threatened at the end of Meditation 1. Despite the play's unusually solid and detailed bourgeois setting (which is fully consistent with the Pyrrhonist respect for "appearances" and practice)—"The capon burns, the pig falls from the spit"; "the desk / That's covered o'er with Turkish tapestry"—*The Comedy of Errors* appears to have an extraordinarily dark view of human intellectual capacity. The major speech in praise of this capacity in the play ("Man, more divine . . . indued with intellectual sense") seems as ironic in its context as is the assertion of female inferiority that, uneasily and creakily, it subserves (2.1.20–22).[12] In the slapstick realm, the heads of the servants are constantly being treated as mere physical objects rather than as loci of intelligence—"an you use these blows long, I must get a sconce for my head and ensconce it too; or else I shall seek my wit in my shoulders" (2.2.36–39). Semantics are repeatedly reduced to somatics: "he told his mind upon mine ear" (2.1.48).[13] In the realm of the "higher" characters, the weakness of the fallen, or perhaps merely embodied, intellect is directly asserted. When Antipholus of Syracuse speaks of his "earthy-gross conceit, / Smothered in errors, feeble, shallow, weak" (3.2.34–35), the account is phrased in such a way as to make the problem seem general. Bertrand Evans speaks of a striking feature of this play as "the universal depth of the participants' ignorance."[14] The only way out of this impossible epistemological dilemma seems to be the one Montaigne envisions at the end of *The Apology for Raymond Sebond*: "letting himself be raised and uplifted by purely celestial means."[15] As Antipholus of Syracuse says, "here we wander in illusions— / Some blessed power deliver us from hence!" (4.3.36–37).

But, as we have seen, this is all a joke.[16] It is not a picture of the human condition. It is a picture of a particular—indeed, peculiar—character. It is a picture of the inner life of a person with a very weak grip on his mind and personal identity. We can see very clearly, in this case, how the plot of the play mandated the psychology of this character. Antipholus of Syracuse is searching all over the Mediterranean for his missing twin brother. For the play to proceed, Shakespeare has to make this character the kind of person to whom the obvious would not occur. One would think that he would immediately realize that what is happening is that he is being mistaken for his twin. The relevant contrast is with Viola in *Twelfth Night*. When Viola finds herself in exactly the situation that Antipholus of Syracuse finds himself in—being addressed by a stranger who claims an intimate relationship—Viola immediately, on the spot, realizes what must (or at least, might) be happening: "I, dear brother, be now ta'en for you!" (3.4.361).[17] The situation is slightly more complicated for Antipholus of Syracuse, since he is addressed by the name that he shares with his brother, but, on the other hand, he is the one looking for his long-lost brother (or rather, confounding himself and blurring his identity in his search for his identity). What is needed in the play, for reliable contact with reality to be attained, is not a miracle or a revelation but merely common sense. There are no more intractable epistemological dilemmas in the play than there are miracles, fairies, sorcerers, or witches.

Antipholus of Syracuse finally gets it: "I see we still did meet each other's man [i.e., servant] / And I was ta'en for him [Antipholus of Ephesus] and he [Antipholus of Ephesus] for me, / And thereupon these errors are arose" (5.1.386–88). "Errors" are exactly the problem. Descartes points out that errors only seem to be an obstacle to epistemological success. It is wise not to trust the senses "fully" (*plane*), since they are sometimes deceptive. But this is different from not trusting them at all. The key point is that the same intellectual capacity (that for making judgments about reality) that can go wrong also has within it the capacity for self-correction. As Descartes put the point in his typically devotional way, "He [God] has not permitted any falsity to exist in my opinion which He has not likewise given me the faculty of correcting."[18] That comes from the Sixth Meditation, the final one, which, it should be noted, ends with an answer to the dreaming argument. As all the best readers of *Meditations on First Philosophy* have understood, the text is an anti-skeptical one, seeking—as the opening sentence of the First Meditation makes clear—to make the world safe for epistemological realism.[19] Errors, by definition, can be corrected (otherwise, there would be no such category, and simply a realm of undifferentiated assertions in relation to which Pyrrhonian *epoché* would be the only rational position).

Ocular Proof

So, *The Comedy of Errors* can be seen as "Cartesian" in the philosophical (not religious) sense.[20] But what of other plays? A major candidate for demonstrating or asserting epistemological skepticism in Shakespeare is *Othello*. Ellen Spolsky sees the play as insisting on "the danger of relying on visual evidence as if it could deliver complete and thus reliable truth."[21] I am not sure what "complete" means here. It seems odd that "reliable" should require this, but that is what the sentence seems to say. Why "reliable" should require "complete" is never made clear. "Complete" evidence, relying on the senses, seems to be impossible because of "the modularity or multiplicity of knowledge itself"; apparently our various "modular systems" inevitably produce "structures of information which do not entirely confirm each other" (80). Again a modifier, another word like "complete" ("entirely") is being asked to do a lot of work. The upshot is that because of this modularity and lack of entire confirmation "fully consistent knowledge" will "never be available" (with "fully" here doing the work). Aside from the hyperbolizing adjectives and adverbs, I am not sure where the argument for these views is to be found (perhaps it is hidden in "modular"). But procedurally, the point seems to be that Spolsky holds this version of skepticism herself, and thinks that the play confirms or instantiates it.

She is right that the physical sense on which the play focuses is sight, the sense that is almost always (and understandably) given epistemological privilege. Spolsky is quite firm that "it is Othello's demand for 'ocular proof' that produces the disaster" (68). She asserts that "the false evidence of the misplaced handkerchief most literally fulfills Othello's demand for 'ocular proof'" (74). But is this true? I would argue that if Othello had stuck to his demand for "the ocular proof," the tragedy would not have happened. The dramatic context for the demand must be examined. It occurs in the great central scene of the play (3.3). Othello is beginning to be affected, as Iago says, with the "poison" of suspicion (3.3.328).[22] Othello has made the speech stating that, with the loss of his "tranquil mind," he has also lost his "occupation" as a happy practitioner and connoisseur of warfare (350–60)—a speech that even Iago finds surprising ("Is't possible, my lord?" [361]). Apparently Iago has succeeded beyond his hopes at this point. But here is where Othello pulls back from conviction and ferociously demands that Iago "prove" what he has claimed, and specifically that he provide "the ocular proof" (362–63). Iago retreats into his devoted "plain man" mode ("To be direct and honest is not safe"), and then seizes on the ambiguities of Othello's demand to be emotionally and intellectually "satisfied" about the matter of Desdemona's faithfulness or unfaithfulness (393).[23]

Iago presents this "satisfaction" as a demand for crude and voyeuristic pleasure: "how satisfied, my lord? / Would you, the supervisor, grossly gape on? / Behold her topped?" (397–399a). Suddenly the "grossness" is in the onlooker, not the (imagined) adulterous agents, and "the supervisor" takes on the meaning (available then as now) of instructor or director rather than merely overlooker.[24] Othello, of course, does not want that. But Iago has to go further. Othello could, after all, get over his revulsion at the imagined sight and insist that, if it is there to be seen, he does indeed want to see it, if not exactly "supervise." Iago states that it would be practically difficult to arrange this—"It were a tedious difficulty... to bring them to that prospect" (400–401)—and relies again on stimulating sexual horror in Othello ("where's satisfaction?" [404]). But Iago knows that this is still not good enough. He has to eliminate the very possibility of ocular proof, and move it beyond the realm of the difficult. The key move is this: "*It is impossible* that you should see this" (405; emphasis mine).

Once Othello accepts this claim, he is lost—thrown, as Iago wishes him to be, into the realm of "imputation" and "circumstances." Iago goes on to narrate the story of his (supposed) bedroom experience with Cassio (3.3.416–28), and begins to establish the spotted handkerchief as the possible agent of "ocular proof" of Desdemona's adultery (436–38). The trick is the substitution. The "ocular proof" that Othello demanded was of the sexual liaison itself, as Iago perfectly well understood. Othello is not, *contra* Andrew Cutrofello, making a philosophical mistake, and demanding "knowledge by acquaintance," direct knowledge, of something—Desdemona's love for Cassio—of which such knowledge is impossible.[25] The issue is not Desdemona's feelings but her behavior: has she slept with Cassio? That is what Othello is demanding "ocular proof" of. There is no reason why, if the adultery were going on, catching them in the act would be "impossible." A "tedious difficulty," perhaps; certainly not impossible. It is not even so clear that it would be such a "tedious difficulty." In a play that may well be related to *Othello*, Thomas Heywood's *A Woman Killed with Kindness*, there is in fact adultery going on between the wife and the husband's best friend, and the husband, without a great deal of effort, does indeed succeed in seeing the couple in his bed "close in each other's arms, and fast asleep."[26] If Othello had insisted on this sort of "ocular proof," and had decided not to act until he had such proof, and, meanwhile, to believe the actual evidence of his senses (Desdemona's appearance and her general behavior), Iago might not have succeeded.[27] Iago has to say "Yet we see nothing done" (3.3.437) in order to prevent Othello from having exactly that thought—that with regard to the supposed adultery, he has, in fact, seen nothing. When Othello later says, "I have seen her do 't," he is right—he has seen her kneel and pray (4.2.23).

As in *Much Ado About Nothing*, the actual (as opposed to manipulated) evidence of the senses is reliable. "If she be false, O then heaven mocks itself," Othello says of Desdemona's appearance, and he concludes, "I'll not believe it" (that is, the suspicion [3.3.282–83]). Iago has to remind Othello regularly *not* to trust his sensory experience. "O, the world hath not a sweeter creature," says Othello. "Nay, that's not your way," says Iago (4.1.180–81, 183). Othello would have been fine if he had followed his nose as well as his eyes. The smell of Desdemona's breath almost prevents Othello from killing her (5.2.16–17).[28] Moreover, if it be thought that Othello is presented as fundamentally unable to maintain a positive attitude toward Desdemona once the issue of sexual betrayal has been raised, he does maintain his positive attitude in response to Iago's initial invitation to jealousy. In a magnificent moment of sanity, Othello declares, "'Tis not to make me jealous / To say my wife is fair, feeds well, loves company, / Is free of speech, sings, plays, and dances well" (3.3.186–88). This deprives Iago of a number of moves he might indeed have made. But Othello, in a moment like this, understands that aristocratic wives have this sort of "freedom," and that "Where virtue is, these are more virtuous" (3.3.189).[29] He says, "I'll see before I doubt" (193), meaning that he'll see the adultery. He would have been fine if he had stuck to this resolve—and to the attitude out of which it emerged.

As all Shakespeareans know, the most famous treatment of *Othello* in relation to skepticism is by Stanley Cavell.[30] But it is not so clear that Cavell's essay is about epistemological skepticism in the Pyrrhonian or Cartesian sense—that is, about the general problem of knowledge with a special emphasis on beliefs about the existence of the physical world. It is not even clear that Cavell's essay is about the more contemporary version of skepticism, skepticism with regard to knowledge of other minds (meaning other persons).[31] Descartes touches on the latter—there is a moment in the Second Meditation when he looks out the window at a town square and notes that all that he physically sees are "hats and coats which could conceal automatons" (Cottingham, 21; *automata, Meditationes*, 32)—but Descartes does not see this as a special problem. Cavell seems to see the two kinds of skepticism as related, though I find his account of this obscure.[32]

Cavell's title for the essay, "Othello and the Stake of the Other," suggests that his focus will be on "staking," on placing (betting) one's entire sense of the comprehensibility of the world on another person in a way parallel to that in which Descartes stakes his belief that he cannot *always* be wrong in his mental operations—that the malevolent genie does not exist—on the necessary existence of a benign God. This suggestion is tidily expressed in the idea of Othello placing "a finite woman in the place of God" (126). But Othello's "stake" in his relationship is not well captured in cognitive terms, so Cavell's favorite formulation for what the philosophical skeptic does wrong—interpreting "a metaphysical finitude *as an intellectual lack*" (138; emphasis mine)—does not apply well to Othello.[33] If the "truth of skepticism" (141) is that other minds are not knowable the way stones are—though Descartes puts pressure on the way stones are known (see the wax experiment in Meditation Two)—the play stresses this truth more in regard to Othello's attempt to know Iago's mind than Desdemona's.[34]

Iago insists on "the truth of skepticism"—or pretends to. At the beginning of 3.3, when, after Cassio's exit and then Desdemona's, Iago is just warming up, there is an extended passage on the issue of coming to know what is in another person's mind. Iago provokes this, suggesting that he may have an opinion on the question re Cassio, "Is he honest?" (3.3.103). Iago avers, pretending to be scrupulous or epistemically modest, that Cassio is so "For aught I know." Naturally, Othello then asks, "What dost thou think?" Othello infers that there is "some monster" in Iago's thought, and demands, "If thou dost love me / Show me thy thought" (118–19) Othello then "shrewdly" notes that the outward behavior that Iago is manifesting ("these stops of thine") are, "in a man that's just," clear signs of effortfully suppressed inner turmoil.[35] Iago insists on his right not to utter his thoughts (3.3.136b–139a), but then shifts to asserting that it would be both improper and imprudent for him to do so (3.3.155–57). All this works, as it is intended to do, to make Othello more determined in his inquiry. "By heaven, I'll know thy thoughts," Othello cries (164b). It is in response to this that Iago utters "the truth of skepticism"—"You cannot [know my thoughts, even] if my heart were in your hand" (3.3.165).[36] That thoughts (of others) are not knowable in the way that physical objects are may be true. But that is not necessarily *a*, let alone *the*, truth of skepticism. Thoughts might be knowable some other way or ways. Moreover, in context, the fact that this may or may not be a deep truth about the human condition is barely relevant. The emphasis is much more on "thoughts" being in the agent's control with regard to uttering them (though not with regard to experiencing them—see 3.3.140–44) than about anything ontological or epistemological. Iago is perfectly able to communicate his "thoughts" to Othello, and Othello is perfectly able to come to know them.

By contrast, when Othello confronts Desdemona, he shows remarkably little interest in trying to know her thoughts. His first piece of behavior toward her, after his vow to himself and pact with Iago for "revenge" (3.3.463), is to think about the meaning of Desdemona's physical being, the moistness of her hand (3.4.36–44).[37] He then works to plant some thoughts in her: the elaborate mythological fiction about the handkerchief (3.4.57–77). Othello seems to consider the inner or mental as quite available for interpretation and manipulation—which it seems to be. Yet in dealing with Desdemona, he barely listens to her words. His focus is on his own feelings and, with regard to her, on her physical appearance. He wants her, as he thinks, to forswear and especially damn herself because she is, in the physical world, "like one of heaven" (4.2.37). When she tries to engage him in rational dialogue, asking that he make clear exactly how he thinks she has been "false"—"To whom, my lord? with whom? How am I false?" (4.2.41)—he refuses to answer. When, on a plausible hypothesis, she attributes Othello's strange behavior to the political situation ("this your calling back" [4.2.46]), he responds with an aria about his emotional dependence on her and inability to maintain "patience" (48–65). When she tries to get the focus shifted to his thoughts ("I hope my noble lord esteems me honest" [66]), he once again focuses on how awful it is that she is "so lovely fair and smell'st so sweet" (4.2.69). When she makes a powerful speech in her own defense, invoking biblical language ("to preserve this vessel for my lord" [4.2.85]), Othello does not respond to its power. He is focused on her person, not on her as a person, and he will not let his correct perceptions of the one lead him to correct thoughts about the other.

The next time we see Othello with Desdemona, he is again focused on her physical existence—on the whiteness and smoothness of her skin, on her "balmy breath" (5.2.4–5, 16). His project is to kill her in a way that preserves her bodily intactness.[38] He has no skeptical doubts about her bodily existence or about the independent status of her soul, which he assumes, in good Catholic fashion, can be cleansed through confession of her (presumed) sins (5.2.53).[39] Skepticism is not an issue. Shakespeare is interested in the bizarre mental / emotional state that Othello is in, not on the limitations of knowledge. Othello is profoundly in error, but the play leaves no doubt what the truth is. This brings me back to Cavell's reading of the play. After some provocative stage-setting remarks about *The Winter's Tale* and turning a woman to stone, Cavell's essay provides an existentialized account of Descartes's *Meditations*—Descartes wants "to know beyond doubt that he is not alone in the world" (126)—and an assertion (without argument) that Descartes cannot imagine other individuals to have the same ontological composition as himself (which somehow turns into "the problem of recognizing another to be Christ for oneself" [127]). The argument for the existence of God as necessarily deriving from the idea of God (the ontological argument) is turned into an argument about human nature and its necessary dependence on another conceived of as perfect.

Bracketing the plausibility of this as a reading of *Meditations*, the connection to *Othello* can now be made: the play (through the peripety of its main character) shows "the logic, the emotion, and the scene of skepticism" (128). This goes as follows: Othello's sense of the all-importance to him of his relationship to Desdemona shows "the stake necessary to best cases" (that is, the logic of skepticism); the "precipitousness" of his fall into jealousy is "the rhythm of skepticism" (which I suppose is imagined as very fast); and the extent of Othello's mental suffering is "the most extraordinary representation ... of the 'astonishment' in skeptical doubt" (this is "the emotion" of skepticism). Again putting aside the question of whether the "astonishment" in the First Meditation is real or pretended[40]—that is, granting Cavell his reading of *Meditations*—the connections to *Othello* now seem straightforward enough.

But we are then told that when Othello loses consciousness (at 4.1.43), it "is not from conviction in a piece of knowledge" (Desdemona's adultery) but in an effort to "stave off" some knowledge (128). The point is repeated when we are told that Iago "offers Othello an opportunity to believe something, something to oppose to something else he knows" (129). The problem, to use Cavell's title phrase, is a "disowning" of knowledge. Now this is all very interesting, and is the core of Cavell's final reading of the play. But it has nothing to do with skepticism, which is defined by *doubt* of knowledge, not by *refusal* of it. What Cavell goes on to provide—and I think we are genuinely indebted to him for this—is a cogent Freudian reading of the play.[41] The question becomes why Othello wants to believe Iago, what work this belief does for Othello. However terrible this belief is, "it must be less terrible than some other" (130). After making it clear that the realm in which the play operates is that of married sexuality, Cavell can ask his question in more specific terms: "What could be more terrible to [Othello] than Desdemona's faithlessness?" The paradoxical answer is "Evidently her faithfulness" (133). The next few pages explain this, culminating in the wonderful assertion, in response to the notion that Othello might have been impotent on his wedding night, that the problem, sexually, is that of "a success rather than a failure" (136).[42] Othello is frightened by Desdemona's sexuality, and by his own; he is "horrified by human sexuality, in himself and in others" (137), and by what human sexuality implies about the condition of the self (as embodied, not fully self-sufficient, etc.).[43]

There is much to be said for this reading, even though it makes Iago almost irrelevant to the play (Cavell barely mentions him). But my question about this reading in the context of the issue of skepticism is raised by Cavell himself. In a moment of self-consciousness two-thirds of the way through his essay, Cavell objects to his own reading—not on the basis of its correctness but on the basis of its relevance. After an eloquent paragraph about the complexities of human sexuality and Othello's relation to it, Cavell stops and exclaims, "But Othello certainly knows that Desdemona exists!" Cavell then follows up on this with the obvious question: "So what has [Othello's] more or less interesting condition to do with skepticism?" (137).

I think that this is a very good question. Cavell warns against asking it in the wrong "spirit" (138). I am sure that I am doing so. I do not see that Cavell ever provides an answer. The point seems to be that skepticism in general is a refusal rather than a questioning of knowledge, that the skeptic would rather question the possibility of knowledge than accept the knowledge of finitude, mortality, and the separateness of individuals. The problem becomes an ethical rather than an epistemological one, since what is needed is the acceptance of the knowledge that the skeptic (on this account) would deny, and the consequent need for acknowledgment of this knowledge and of the full existence of other individuals.[44] Whatever one thinks of all this, skepticism as consisting of doubt about the possibility of knowledge falls away. Epistemology, as I said, gives way to ethics. I am not sure that Descartes would recognize this picture of skepticism, and it is significant, I think, that at this point in the essay, Montaigne—not as a skeptic but as a commentator on human sexuality—supplants Descartes (139–40).[45]

That Within

Important as *Othello* is in current discussions of skepticism in Shakespeare, I cannot end without some discussion of *Hamlet*. My focus will not be on the question of the status of the (supposed) ghost in the play, though the play certainly raises this question and perhaps means to answer it in a Protestant-skeptical way (that is, that "the thing" is a demon, and that truly no traveler returns from the dead).[46] Peter Marshall points out that while ghosts are common in Elizabethan and Jacobean plays, *Hamlet* is, as Marshall says, "highly unusual" in "explicitly addressing the question of whether the apparition is really the spirit of Hamlet's father or a demonic illusion, and making it [this question] central to the action of the play."[47] Skepticism about whether "the thing" is a collective fantasy is answered; eighteen lines after Horatio is quoted as saying, "'Tis but your fantasy" (1.1.28), the thing appears. But skepticism about whether the thing is actually a ghost (the soul or spirit of a deceased human being) is never fully allayed. Hamlet vacillates on this, but Horatio seems to stay with his view of the thing as a demon.[48] That is an ontological and religious issue, a matter of "things in heaven and earth" (and elsewhere), not a strictly epistemological one.

But *Hamlet* does seem to be a play in which "other minds" skepticism is at work and, indeed, is both dramatized and thematized. When, early on, Hamlet claims to have "that within which passes show" (1.2.85), he may be claiming that there is something special about interior (emotional) experience, a claim that is one of the major sources of the "other minds" problem.[49] But it may be that

Hamlet is claiming that there is something special about *his* interior (emotional) experience. Later, he claims to have a special "mystery" of which Rosencrantz and Guildenstern are attempting to pluck out the heart (3.2.355–56), and he claims to have a special internal place for his affection for his true friend, Horatio, a "heart's core" or "heart of heart" (3.2.73). There is no doubt that Hamlet is, and considers himself to be, a person of deep feeling. He seems to see this as special to himself, but unquestionably the play is interested in the issue of how one can come to know the thoughts and feelings of another. Hamlet asserts his "mystery" in response to the concerted efforts that Claudius and his instruments (willing, like Rosencrantz and Guildenstern, or recruited, like Ophelia) are constantly making to find out what Hamlet is thinking and feeling. But the question is whether the play imagines such knowledge to be possible.

Hamlet resists being known in this way by Claudius and company, though he seems quite willing and able to speak his thoughts to his beloved friend.[50] His attempt to penetrate to the heart of Claudius's mystery through the power of theater—a humanist's and dramatist's fantasy—seems to have succeeded.[51] Claudius's conscience does seem to have been caught. Although Hamlet has less warrant to be sure of this (or that the "thing" is his father's ghost) than he comes to believe, this does not affect the question in general, since we do know, unequivocally, that the experiment succeeded.[52] So, it looks as if art can do what even very clever and pointed interpersonal manipulation cannot. This is borne out in the clearest case of (let's call it, to be *méchant*) penetration in the play: Hamlet's success with Gertrude.

It must be acknowledged, however, that between "The Mousetrap" and the closet encounter, there is a scene that seems to dramatize "other minds" skepticism precisely: Hamlet is standing right behind or at least fairly near the kneeling Claudius and thinks that Claudius is in the process of "the purging of his soul" (3.3.85), which would mean successfully repenting (in this Protestant world, no priestly presence or apparatus is needed for successful confession and repentance).[53] Hamlet, the most intelligent character we are likely to encounter in life or literature, makes, on the basis of correctly observed behavior, a wrong inference about another's inner state. So obviously behavior is not always revelatory of what it seems to be enacting. The play is deeply aware of this, of "actions that a man might play" (1.2.84). So we, even the most intelligent among us, can be wrong about another person's inner life.

But does this mean that that life is epistemologically unavailable? We can be wrong about almost anything, and on the basis of inferences drawn from perception. In Claudius's soliloquy, as in those of Hamlet, the speaker seems to have knowledge of his inner life and seems to be able to express such knowledge verbally. What if Hamlet could have heard Claudius's words? That would seem to alter the epistemological situation significantly.[54] With regard to observation of behavior, a certain amount of caution may be called for—as Descartes says, we must not trust "fully" (*plane confidere*) in observation—but that does not mean that further observation would not yield a more accurate result.[55] Deception is clearly a special case, but not one that leaves us entirely helpless in the face of it.[56] And with regard to the supposedly special status of one's relation to one's own mental states, it is important to note that one can be wrong about these as well.[57] It is certainly possible to believe that Hamlet's motive for not killing Claudius at this juncture may not be what Hamlet says it is; his motive (or motives) might be obscure to himself.[58] As Shakespeare recognized, that simply puts him in the same situation in relation to his own motives as he is to that of others, which lessens the epistemological problem of "other minds" by eliminating some of the apparent special privilege that we have in relation to our own. We can, as Shakespeare clearly knew, be right or wrong about both, and might have—at least at times—an inferential or merely postulated relation to both.

But, as I said earlier, the play suggests that the inner life of a person can be known to someone else; it also suggests that such knowledge can be communicated from the second-person perspective in such a way that it can serve to produce material that would only seem to be available to the first-person perspective. Hamlet's goal, in the confrontation with Gertrude, is to set up "a glass" for her wherein she "may see the inmost part" of herself (3.4.19), where this "part" is psychological or spiritual, not physical. Obviously this implies that this "inmost part" of one person can be brought into (conceptual) visibility by another. In the play, the means for doing this seems to be passionate speech in combination with visual aids. Hamlet is acting in his role here as "scourge and minister" (3.4.177). Glenn Clark has shown parallels between Hamlet's project and emotions here and those of English Protestant ministers, who were supposed to both rebuke and love the sinners to whom they preached.[59] But Hamlet's use of "this picture ... and this" suggests, as did his use of theater with Claudius, his humanist as well as his Protestant orientation.[60] Hamlet leads Gertrude to feel, or, better, to acknowledge and access guilt about her sexual attraction to Claudius, specifically to the elements of "reason" and "will" in it.[61] Hamlet's impassioned and intellectually complex presentation serves to give her as well as him access to Gertrude's "inmost part." "Thou turn's my eyes into my very soul," she tells Hamlet (3.4.89). This is a remarkable success, and one not troubled by any of the ambiguities that surround the catching of Claudius's conscience. Again, the play is highly optimistic about the possibility, through art—especially mixed media presentations (like theater or pictures plus words)—of "getting to" another, which implies having and conveying knowledge of their "inmost part." Assuming his role as lay minister, Hamlet instructs Gertrude in the Protestant version of penitence—"Confess yourself to heaven"—directly, without a priest—and change your life (3.4.151), though Hamlet's very Aristotelian reliance on the instrumentality of habit in doing the latter may suggest an Arminian rather than a strictly Calvinist theology.[62] Whether or not Gertrude truly does change her life in response to this encounter may be unclear in the play, but that is irrelevant to the matter of "other minds" skepticism.[63]

Recently, it has been suggested that the play ends on a note of epistemological and "practical" skepticism. James Kuzner acknowledges that Horatio evinces "epistemological confidence on several issues," but asserts that by the end of the play, Horatio is "epistemologically weak, unsure of who he is or who Hamlet was, unsure what is to be done."[64] Since Kuzner's book is in praise of "epistemological humility" (6), he basically admires Horatio's existence in this state despite or because of Horatio's "skeptical commitment to Hamlet without a clear picture of him" and his "skeptical commitment to Danish politics without a clear solution to political difficulties" (19). But does any of this hold up? Kuzner sees Horatio, at the end of the play, as torn between his friendship for Hamlet and the truth of what he knows (i.e., that Hamlet killed Polonius and is responsible for the deaths of Rosencrantz and Guildenstern). That is not in itself an epistemological issue, but in response to Horatio promising that he will "truly deliver" the substance of what he has summarized in general ("carnal, bloody, and unnatural acts . . . accidental judgments, casual slaughters . . . deaths put on by cunning and [forc'd] cause"),[65] Kuzner states that it is "unclear if this is truth" (17).

But where is the evidence that Hamlet does not want the facts known or that Horatio does not know them? Hamlet has already publicly asserted his role in Polonius's death (though, as we have seen, in a complicated way),[66] and has stated that the deaths of his two childhood friends are "not near his conscience" (5.2.58). As Kuzner knows, what Hamlet is concerned about is that he not be remembered as a traitor. When Hamlet stabs Claudius, the onlookers "all" cry out "Treason, treason!" (5.2.328), since no one but Horatio knows that Hamlet believes (rightly, if on insufficient evidence) that Claudius murdered his brother, the former king, to gain the throne ("things standing thus unknown").[67] When Hamlet tells Horatio to "report me and my cause aright" (5.2.344), his "cause"—legal and moral—must be the justification for his regicide.[68] There is no doubt what the "wounded name" (349) would be ("traitor"). The public justification for his action is, naturally, Hamlet's primary concern. But it should also be noted that before he falls into silence, Hamlet instructs Horatio to tell "th' occurrents more and less / Which have solicited" (5.2.363–64).

This sounds like a call for a pretty full account ("more and less"). And there is no doubt that Horatio is in a position to tell all this, having been uniquely privy to Hamlet's motives, plans, and actions. Horatio's summary of what he will tell ("carnal, bloody . . .") is striking and rather masterful. It does not include anything about Hamlet's philosophical musings—James Shapiro criticizes Horatio for this—but why should it?[69] There are, as Fortinbras rightly notes, a lot of physically present dead bodies to be accounted for, and others as well. Horatio is trying to gain attention for the story that he is going to tell—his summary is just the prologue—and he succeeds in this. "Let us haste to hear it," says Fortinbras. For better or worse, Horatio does offer a "clear solution" to the political difficulties of Denmark, suggesting (accurately) that he can confer legitimacy on Fortinbras's claim to have "rights" in the kingdom. Horatio's "epistemological confidence" never deserts him, as it should not. As Lars Engle says, it "survives modern skepticism."[70]

Shakespeare was skeptical about some things: fairies, demonic possession, the need for auricular confession. But from an epistemological point of view, he was indeed a Cartesian skeptic (though without God): one who believed that the senses, corrected as necessary by reason and judgment, are reliable, and that our minds can know the world and—to at least the same extent that we can know ourselves—other people.

CHAPTER 11

Mind, Nature, Heterodoxy, and Iconoclasm in *The Winter's Tale*

Both epistemological skepticism and religion figure largely in *The Winter's Tale*. The play can be seen as Shakespeare's final statement, so to speak, on both.[1] It is no accident that for this purpose, he chose a story about jealousy. Jealousy (in the plays) always seemed to mean, for Shakespeare, male jealousy directed to or at a woman to whom the man was or was about to be married, and it always took what might be called the vengeful rather than the prophylactic form, the form of conviction that a sexual betrayal had actually happened rather than the form of fear that such a thing could happen. This meant that the jealous male believed that he was in possession of a fact, a particular truth about the world, rather than (or along with) merely the possession of a general belief (that women were vulnerable, unreliable, oversexed, etc.). By the time of the composition of *The Winter's Tale* (1610–11), Shakespeare had already written at least two and probably three plays treating this version of jealousy: a comedy (or tragicomedy) in the late 1590s (*Much Ado About Nothing*), a major tragedy a few years later (*Othello*), and (probably) another mixed-genre play (*Cymbeline*) just a year or so before *The Winter's Tale*.[2] What made *The Winter's Tale* special was that it allowed Shakespeare to focus directly on the mind's relation to the world and on the world to which the mind relates.

The source for the play gave Shakespeare this opportunity. As is well known, the source was a highly successful Elizabethan novella by Robert Greene, *Pandosto: The Triumph of Time* (1588, 1592, 1595, 1607, 1609, 1614).[3] One attraction of Greene's text for Shakespeare may have been formal—*Pandosto* has a self-confessed genre problem. In the novella, after Pandosto, the King of Bohemia, is reunited with the long-lost daughter for whom he has had a serious bout of lust, Greene decides (partly because of this bout of lust) to "close up the comedy with a tragical stratagem," and have his erring king commit suicide in the final sentence of the tale.[4] Shakespeare was certainly, at this point in his career, interested in mixed genres: in particular, how to close up a (potential) tragedy with a comical stratagem.[5] But the main attraction of the novella must have been its topic and its treatment thereof. Despite the fact that Greene calls his work a "toy" and classified it among "trifles," it begins with the rather grand and sober reflection that "Of all the passions wherewith human minds are perplexed," jealousy is the most tormenting (156).[6]

Shakespeare may or may not have agreed with this observation, but what is striking about the presentation of this "passion" in the novella is that there is no villain involved in the generation of it. Pandosto's jealousy is entirely self-generated. Greene sketches out (or rather, postulates) a temporal and psychological process. It begins, in Pandosto, with some "doubtful [meaning, doubt-inducing] thoughts" about his wife and his childhood friend, the King of Sicily, Egistus, who is visiting Bohemia. These "thoughts" are general considerations that might be seen as the baseline conditions for erotic suspicion: the beauty of his wife (Bellaria), the "comeliness and bravery" of his friend, and the "fact" that "Love was above all Lawes" (158). A pyrological-psychological progression is outlined. The thoughts were repressed for a while ("a long time smothering in his stomach").[7] They then seem to become a definite idea (they "kindle in his mind a secret mistrust"); and finally they "grew at last to a flaming jealousy" (158–59). This was an entirely internal process, though based on observation as well as on generalizations (Bellaria "oftentimes" came into Egistus's bedchamber, and they would often "in privat ... passe away the time" [158]). The result was conviction: "Pandostoes minde was so farre charged with Jealousy, that he did no longer doubt, but was assured" (159). This conviction led Pandosto to destroy all the significant relationships in his life: with his wife, his children, his closest counselor, and with the other King, "who in his youth had been brought up with Pandosto" (157).

Intense male jealousy—but no Don John, no Iago, no Iachimo. Here truly the "monster" exists and is generated only in the mind (as Emilia initially thinks that Othello's is).[8] So, in distinction from *Othello*, Shakespeare did not have to split his focus. He did not have to treat the problem of evil—the kind of dedicated evil that Iago represents—along with the problem of jealousy. The absence of a villain (other than the jealous person himself) means that evil, in the fullest sense, need not exist in the later play. What would seem like a happy situation— an established marriage that has already produced a healthy young son and in which the devoted wife is pregnant with another child; a prolonged visit from a boyhood friend who has been absent for decades—is entirely destroyed by a belief, one that a king's mind has generated entirely on its own. So the play can be seen to be exploring, in the fraught territory of male sexual awareness, the problem not of skepticism but of the condition that makes skepticism possible: the fact that the realm of belief is not necessarily and wholly determined by the realm of reality. So Stanley Cavell is right that the play is "a response to what skepticism is a response to" and also about "recovery" from the damage that the epistemological fact can produce.[9] But where Cavell sees the play as overcoming skepticism in the only way that this can be done—not by refuting it but by addressing the psychological problem that underlies it (by, in his terms, "acknowledgment" rather than knowledge), I would argue that the play sees skepticism in a more traditional way, and does think that it can be refuted.[10]

The play, in other words, is more optimistic than Cavell is about getting out of the skeptical dilemma directly. Where Cavell thinks that the world will never be adequate to the mind, the play, in my reading, does not agree.[11] The skeptic (or skeptic equivalent) may be seen as trying to withdraw from the world, but the play can be seen as showing the world's resistance to this effort. As Janet Adelman puts it, the play emphasizes "the world's refusal to stay unmade."[12] It can thus be seen as continuing the position of what might be called Davidsonian anti-skepticism that I have attributed to Shakespeare. It can be seen to show a character learning to "re-establish unmediated touch with the familiar objects whose antics make our sentences and opinions true or false."[13] But the play goes even further. Its anti-skepticism is not simply a matter of asserting the existence of the world and its epistemological availability to the mind but also of asserting the fundamental goodness of the world. This is what the absence of a true villain allows. A maxim articulated by the (second) benign sea-captain in *Twelfth Night* can be taken as the basic premise of *The Winter's Tale*: "In nature, there's no blemish but the mind."[14] The imagery, the genre, the religious content, and even the extraordinary ending of the play all flow from the addition of this premise to the epistemological one.

Rotten Opinion

The central philosophical issue—the mind's relation to the world—is introduced in a subtle way in the brief opening scene, a dialogue, in prose, between a courtier of the visiting king of Bohemia and one of the courtiers of the host king of Sicily (Shakespeare reverses the roles in Greene, where the Sicilian is the visitor).[15] The visitors are about to depart; the topic of the conversation is the "magnificence" with which the Bohemians have been treated (1.1.12).[16] The Sicilian courtier explains that this flows from the childhood friendship between the kings. Shakespeare emphasizes this more strongly than Greene does (and adds the context of departure). Greene states that the Sicilian king was visiting Bohemia because he "was desirous to shew that neither tracte of time, nor distance of place could diminish their former friendship" (157). Shakespeare has the host courtier present the relation between the childhood friendship and the adult one of the kings somewhat differently. Shakespeare adds detail and imagery to Greene's statement, and has the Sicilian courtier present the childhood relationship as *guaranteeing* the adult one. "They were trained together in their childhoods," says Camillo, "and there rooted betwixt them then such an affection which cannot choose but branch now" (1.1.21–23). This is a humanist vision in which art—that is, discipline, education ("training")—is seen as part of a natural process; the botanical language of roots and branches is entirely positive.[17] There seems to be no room for slippage in this vision. The course of human emotions has the reliability, predictability, and benignity of natural processes ("affection ... cannot choose but branch").[18]

Yet the language of this rejection of agency is slightly troubling. "Cannot choose but" introduces, albeit negatively, a factor that stands apart from nature. The Bohemian king's counselor agrees about the "affection" between the two boyhood and now adult friends, stating, "I think there is not in the world either malice or matter to alter it" (1.1.31–32). Camillo then goes on to present a vision of children as having an entirely positive effect on adults (making "old hearts fresh" [1.1.37]). But again, we must pause a moment over a seemingly casual formulation. "There is not *in the world* either malice or matter to alter it"—"matter" is clearly a word that refers to stuff, substance "in the world." But what about "malice"? Is the relation of "malice"—a mental state—to "the world" as predictable as that of matter? Is malice "in the world" in the same sense that matter is? Can they so easily be put on the same plane? Does that "there is not ... matter" mean that there is not malice? In what sense are—or are not—mental states "in the world"?

These questions are taken up and dramatized in scene 2, the first major scene of the play and the first in verse. The sense of high society that obtained in the elegant badinage between the courtiers continues. We meet the two kings, Leontes of Sicily and Polixenes of Bohemia, and we meet Hermione, Leontes's queen. Where the issue—such as it was—between the two courtiers was how to characterize the grand entertainment that the Sicilian king has provided (a free gift, says the host's representative; an incomparable expense says the guest's), the "issue" now is whether the Bohemian king will be allowed to depart, as he wishes, the next day (after nine months in Leontes's court). Shakespeare makes the jealousy of his host king even more precipitous and even more unmotivated than did Greene. In Greene, as we saw, the omniscient narrator stipulated a prolonged mental process in Pandosto, whereas Shakespeare presents the jealousy as coming, effectively, out of nowhere. Leontes appears to be participating in the courtesy game, trying to get Polixenes to postpone his departure. Leontes's initial speeches are short and plain, but they do seem to be within the game (if only just barely). Having not succeeded in getting Polixenes to change his mind about the departure date, Leontes turns to his queen to enter the fray, apparently surprised that she has not done so before. Obviously, she is someone who normally speaks up. Leontes's first words to her are "Tongue-tied, our queen? Speak you."[19] It is only when Hermione does speak that we become aware that there has been something amiss in Leontes's behavior, in the curtness of his lines. She offers a humorous rhetorical critique: "I had thought, sir, to have held my peace until / You had drawn oaths from him not to stay" (1.2.27–29).

With more humorous hyperbole—"Will you," she says to Polixenes, "Force me to keep you as a prisoner / Not like a guest"—Hermione succeeds in getting Polixenes to agree to stay for another week. Leontes says nothing at this point, and, after the dialogue has moved to a different topic and shifted mode, asks, long after the appropriate moment, "Is he won yet?" (85). This is how Shakespeare begins to signal that Leontes is, as our idiom usefully would have it, in his own world. When Hermione goes off to converse with Polixenes, perhaps giving him her hand, Leontes reveals what Greene calls "a flaming jealousy." Of the behavior of Hermione and Polixenes, Leontes bursts out, to himself: "Too hot, too hot!" (108). Yet we have seen exactly what Leontes has seen, and it is hard to detect anything untoward in it. Greene's jealous king had much more to build on (recall that the Hermione equivalent "oftentimes" went into the bedchamber of the Polixenes equivalent). But we have nothing of the sort here—only humor, courtesy, and, as Hermione says, friendship.[20]

After the departure issue is resolved (and while Leontes is silent and distracted), Hermione moves into what is clearly a favorite and long-standing game between the three of them when she resolves to urge Polixenes to speak "Of my lord's tricks, and yours, when you were boys" (1.2.60). This is a court where people enjoy (or used to enjoy) hearing each other speak. Hermione's request allows Shakespeare to fill in, as Greene never does, something of the phenomenology of the boyhood friendship between the men. Pyschologically, this is crucial material. The picture is presented by Polixenes, as it must be, since at this point Leontes is incapable of calm, reflective, and humorous speech, but there is no doubt that the perspective Polixenes provides is meant to be shared by both grown-up kings.[21] Polixenes presents Leontes and himself as having been

> Two lads that thought there was no more behind,
> But such a day tomorrow as today
> And to be boy eternal. (61–63)

This is certainly a picture of happy carefreeness, but it cannot help but raise in our minds the question of what it would mean, in the resonant but rather disturbing phrase that Polixenes uses, to be "boy eternal."[22] Would this, in fact, be a good thing, and is there an equally positive version of adulthood to be imagined or, even, attained?

In responding further to Hermione's playful inquisition, Polixenes employs pastoral imagery to evoke the behavior of these temporally unaware boys. "We were," he says, "as twinn'd lambs that did frisk i' th' sun, / And bleat the one at th' other" (66–67a). The boys were indistinguishable from one another, and the pastoral imagery serves to present them as basically prehuman—their "frisking" seems to be in response to their natural environment, as were their vocal interchanges, which were undifferentiated and (perhaps therefore) did not have the status of actual speech. Instead, however, of developing the pastoral imagery further, Polixenes gives a philosophical and theological characterization of the picture he has just presented: "what we chang'd / Was innocence for innocence" (67b–68a). One could hardly be more emphatic about this. But we are fully, here, in the world of heresy. A mistaken idea of "epistemes" might lead one to think that such an idea of childhood was normal in a pre-Freudian age, but that would be to forget about "the fault and corruption of the Nature of every man that naturally is ingendered of the offspring of *Adam*; whereby man is very far gone from original righteousness, and is of his own nature inclined toward evil ... [and] deserveth God's wrath and damnation." That is from Articles of the Church of England (#9, "Of Original or Birth-Sin").[23] The equivalent Gallican article clarifies the fact that this "hereditary evil" is "truly sin," and is "sufficient for the condemnation of the whole human race, even of little children in the mother's womb."[24] All orthodox Christians accepted some notion of original sin, but Augustine's devastating critique of the ideas of infant and childhood innocence was most strongly embraced by the Protestant Reformers.[25] Calvin called infants "seeds of sin"—only corruption can spring from them.[26] Despite all the important recent work on Catholicism and medieval survivals in Tudor England, it is nonetheless worth remembering that in the early seventeenth century England was, officially and in practice, one of the major Protestant powers of Europe, and its Articles (as #9 suggests) were staunchly Calvinist.[27] Polixenes's speech asserts absolute childhood innocence in a way that would have been deemed heretical on both sides of the Great Divide. But the question remains as to what the content of the notion of childhood innocence is here—or, to put it another way, exactly what kind of heresy is being articulated, Gnostic or Pelagian.

Polixenes explicates "innocence" in his next lines: "we knew not / The doctrine of ill-doing, nor dream'd / That any did" (68b–70a). "The doctrine of ill-doing" is a strange and striking phrase. It is only sporadically and perfunctorily glossed by editors (perhaps because it contains no "hard words"), but it is puzzling. It could be more or less recuperated for orthodoxy by being interpreted as "the doctrine that condemns ill-doing" (the moral or Old Testament Law), but a less forced reading would take the phrase as suggesting that wickedness is something learned, something fundamentally intellectual and cultural. We would think of such a position as "Rousseauian," but it was available in the Renaissance in various forms. Bad teaching created evil in souls naturally pure. A modified version of this was held by Erasmus, as it was by Dante.[28] But this view is not the "normal," so to speak, heretical position. The "doctrine of ill-doing" leaves the purely biological and instinctive "innocent." The next and longer account that Polixenes gives is another negation of a negative (like "knew not ... ill"), but now biology rather than "doctrine" is the problem:

> Had we pursued that life,
> And our weak spirits ne'er been higher rear'd
> With stronger blood, we should have answer'd heaven
> Boldly 'not guilty.' (68b–74a)

"Stronger blood" here clearly means sexual maturity; "spirits" is being used in its physiological sense, and we are probably to recall that sperm was thought to have been made by heat from one of the kinds of "spirits" in the blood.[29] The idea is that sexual maturity is itself the Fall.[30] We are here moving into the Gnostic realm, where, as George Herbert put it, "The growth of flesh is but a blister" and "Childhood is health."[31] Polixenes ends his paean to boyhood with an afterthought. Despite the pagan setting, Shakespeare does not want him to sound *too* heretical.[32] Polixenes suddenly realizes that answering heaven "Not guilty" is bold indeed; and so he retreats, adding: "the imposition clear'd / Hereditary ours" (74b–75a). This is an attempt to acknowledge original—that is, hereditary—sin, but it is, as I said, and as the syntax indicates, an afterthought.[33] The sentence clearly could have ended at "not guilty." The final phrase sounds dutiful, and is, in any case, brushed aside. Moreover, the idea itself is weakly stated, with "imposition" suggesting something noninherent and externally applied.

In the immediate context, the idea of sin as "doctrine," something learned, falls away—though we will return to its importance. Hermione, who is as quick as she is witty and playful, picks up on the dominant and more fully expressed idea in Polixenes's speech, the notion that "stronger blood" caused the boys to fall from innocence: "By this," she says, "we gather / You have tripp'd since" [74b–75a]). Polixenes affirms that she has understood him correctly. Sexual attraction, he explains—or at least heterosexual attraction—is the problem:[34]

> O my most sacred lady,
> Temptations have since then been born to 's: for
> In those unfledg'd days was my wife a girl;
> Your precious self had then not cross'd the eyes
> Of my young playfellow. (75b–79a)

This is phrased in a courtly manner ("sacred lady... your precious self"), but Hermione is right to assert that what Polixenes is basically saying is that "your queen and I are devils" (sources of temptation and of falling).[35] She does not take this seriously, and, in fact, mocks the whole idea. Speaking for both regal wives, she states, "the offences that we have made you do, we'll answer" (82)—which must be read with implied quotation marks around "offences," just as "if you first sinned with us" must be read with implied quotation marks around "sinned." Hermione does not accept the view that sexuality is fundamentally sinful. She accepts the Protestant view of chaste sexuality within marriage.[36] The men in the play, however, seem prone to the Gnostic or Manichean view—always a temptation for Christianity, and perhaps especially so for Catholicism (with its ideally celibate male clergy)—that sexuality is fundamentally corrupting, and that it would be better to remain "boy eternal," where "boyhood" is imagined as a- or presexual.

We are now in a position to return to the question of jealousy and how it is presented in the play. What seems to have happened, judging from the imagery of the play, is that Polixenes's presence revived for Leontes the thought of boyhood "innocence"—lyrically and humorously expressed by Polixenes but experienced intensely by Leontes. In the opening prose scene, the youthful charisma of Mamillius, Leontes's young son, is imagined to have the power to make "old hearts fresh" (1.1.37). This works on Leontes, but in an ironic way. Instead of the thought of childhood (and Mamillius in particular) serving to reinvigorate Leontes's adult heart, it has served instead to make all adult behavior that is in any way eroticized or playful look corrupt to him. This would include Leontes's own sexual behavior, including his fatherhood of his son, and his role, if he accepted that he had one, in Hermione's current and very apparent pregnancy (this makes it clear, why, in some sense, he would want not to be responsible for it, and would want to project it onto his evil "twin").[37]

Leontes's first words to his son are "Art thou my boy?" (118). Cavell takes this to be a question that Leontes is seriously asking, and one for which "of course" he gets no satisfactory answer.[38] But that is not what is going on here. In this case, Leontes is pondering, playing on his knowledge, not his doubt. He is playing at doubting. He says about the boy's nose, "They say it is a copy out of mine" (121), and he disparages those who "say so," especially women, who "will say anything" (130). But his point is that he does in fact recognize his son as his. Though testimony is generally unreliable, "yet were it true / To say this boy were like me" (134). We are not in a Cartesian situation; Leontes finds his senses veridical.[39] What Leontes sees in his son is not a bastard but himself, himself as he wants to be, back in childhood:

> Looking on the lines
> Of my boy's face, methought I did recoil
> Twenty-three years, and saw myself unbreeched,
> In my green velvet coat, my dagger muzzled
> Lest it should bite its master. (152–56)

This is Leontes's equivalent of Polixenes's pastoral of presexual boyhood, but here the renunciation of adult male sexuality is more explicit. Leontes fantasizes about being "unbreeched"—back in a state of gender undifferentiation—and imagines himself free of the phallic dagger, which is a potential danger not to others but to himself.[40] Like the speaker of Marvell's "The Garden," Leontes wants to escape from aggressive sexuality, but Leontes's fantasy is of virtually becoming a plant ("in my green velvet coat"), and as in "The Garden," the fantasy is to be in the pastoral world not with another (even, as in Polixenes's vision, an identical twin) but to be there "alone."[41] Leontes does not want to kill his presexual, pre-male son; he wants to *be* him; to be, by himself, "boy eternal."[42] When the dagger is unmuzzled in adulthood, its penetrative power is frighteningly unstoppable. Misogyny and a general fear of sexuality mingle. Giving voice to a childish and appalled view of heterosexual intercourse, Leontes says that a woman's belly will "let in and out the enemy / With bag and baggage" (203–4).

Leontes loses not only any sense of sexuality as benign but also his grip on the innocence and ethical purity of aristocratic social intercourse, a mode of being that includes an element of flirtatiousness in its carefreeness, high spirits, and good humor. We might call this way of inhabiting and understanding social life "the code." Shakespeare consistently presents it as a model for sanity and *eudaimonia*.[43] But Leontes, like Othello in the moments when Iago's "poison" works in him, cannot inhabit the code, even though he is aware of it.[44] Just as Othello knows that it should not make him jealous "To say my wife is fair, feeds well, loves company / Is free of speech, sings plays, and dances well" (3.3.187–88), Leontes knows that "This entertainment [of Polixenes by Hermione] / May a free face put on, derive a liberty / From heartiness, from bounty, fertile bosom, / And well become the agent" (1.2.110-13). What is under suspicion, in both cases, is "free" behavior.[45] At her "trial," Hermione attempts to remind Leontes of the code (3.2.64–68); Leontes had showed both his awareness of the code and his alienation from it in using "How thou lov'st us show in our brother's welcome" as a provocation rather than a piece of genuine encouragement (1.2.73). Polixenes is right in saying that what has changed in Leontes is, in a deep sense, "his manners" (1.2.371)—or rather, his understanding of what "manners" are. Leontes cannot (now) see a difference between courtesy and lechery. And he cannot see adult playfulness as having anything in common with that of children—"Go play, boy, play; thy mother plays," says Leontes with disgust (1.2.187).[46] He has come to see playfulness and the whole realm of courtesy just as Iago does (or professes to). When Iago's minor dupe, Roderigo, ventures to say that Cassio's behavior toward Desdemona when she has disembarked before Othello is "but courtesy," Iago substitutes "Lechery," and assures Roderigo that "when these mutualities so marshal the way, hard at hand comes the master and main exercise" (2.1.259–60)—even though Iago himself knows that they really are mere "courtesies" (2.1.168–70).

But we recall that there is no Iago in *The Winter's Tale*. This helps us see the importance of the word "nothing" in the play. Psychoanalytic critics have alerted us to the importance in Shakespeare of "nothing" as a reference to female genitalia, and this certainly seems relevant.[47] But the reading I wish to pursue is, as I have already suggested, a more epistemological and metaphysical one, though one that can include the psychoanalytic. The point that this play makes, again and again, is that Leontes's state of mind does not correspond to any "thing" in reality, genital or otherwise. He gives to an airy nothing a local habitation (Polixenes, Hermione) and a name.[48] Compare Macbeth's recognition regarding the "dagger of the mind" that he thinks he sees: "There's no such thing" (2.1.48). Shakespeare uses the "thing / nothing" distinction just as carefully in *The Winter's Tale* as he does in *Macbeth* and *A Midsummer Night's Dream*. The jealous Leontes, in a speech of metaphysical self-reflection (however clogged and obscure)—the "Affection" speech—correctly observes that his mind "fellow'st nothing" (1.2.137–141a).[49] The view that Leontes is here attempting "to diagnose his own psychological condition" may be true, but that he is doing so "in a very positive spirit" cannot be sustained.[50] The appeal to reason or self-evidence that he goes on to make ("Then 'tis very credent" [141b]) is transparently self-undermining. The claim is that since "affection" can imagine the impossible and "fellow" with nothing, with "what's unreal," this makes it probable that it will "co-join with something," which Leontes then asserts that it has ("and I find it" [142–145a]). Northrop Frye brilliantly characterizes this speech as "a parody of creation out of nothing."[51] The problem is not that Leontes wishes the world to be "nothing"—Cavell's view—but that Leontes takes his thoughts to have the ontological status of "things."[52]

Later in this scene, Leontes tries to explain to Camillo that what Leontes is speaking of is (again) not "nothing." "Is this nothing?" Leontes asks (289) of the supposed behavioral evidence for his delusion before going into an aria on the term ("Why then the world and all that's in it is nothing, / The covering sky is nothing, Bohemia nothing, / My wife is nothing, nor nothing have these nothings, / If this be nothing" (290–293a). Camillo responds to this with a line that gives an extremely precise account of Leontes's condition as the play presents it. "Good my lord," says Camillo, "be cur'd / Of this diseas'd opinion" (293b–294). "Opinion" was a strong word in the period.[53] In the play, Shakespeare uses the term with philosophical precision. He uses it exactly the way Plato uses the term (*doxa* in Greek).[54] It is possible that Shakespeare read Plato in Ficino's Latin translation, but the important point is the structure of the usage, which Shakespeare, with his extraordinary absorptive capacity, could have picked up from many sources.[55] The key to this usage is that opinion contrasts with knowledge. The basis of the contrast is that opinion does not become knowledge until, to use Plato's image in the *Meno*, it is "tethered" to reality by correct explanatory reasoning.[56] There is a vast difference between an opinion, existing unstably in the mind, and a piece of knowledge, tethered to reality by a firm causal chain. Leontes thinks of himself as especially shrewd and perceptive, but it is not only in the "Affection" speech that he gets his philosophy wrong; he consistently does so.[57] In his speech about the spider in the cup, Leontes equates knowledge with opinion ("How blest am I / In my just censure! in my true opinion! / Alack, for lesser knowledge" [2.1.36–38]). Everyone else in the play understands the difference between knowledge and opinion. They understand that Leontes is living entirely in the world of belief, opinion (perhaps even "doctrine," as in misogyny or Iago's set of beliefs).[58] What Leontes needs, desperately, is knowledge, a state of mind that is tethered to reality. "How this will grieve you," Hermione says to him, "when you shall come to clearer knowledge" (2.1.96–97). Shakespeare does not see the passion of jealousy as (in Greene's words) "perplexing" the mind but rather as the product of the perverse creativity of the mind.[59]

Antigonus, one of Leontes's courtiers, is sure that the whole situation will be shown to be laughable when "the good truth" is known (2.1.199). Paulina, Antigonus's wife, enters the play to assert the "pure innocence" (2.2.40) not only of the newborn baby but also of the baby's adult mother. Paulina gives exactly the same account of Leontes's condition that Camillo does, and she expresses the account in a way that is even more central to the play. Speaking of Leontes's jealousy, Paulina refers to "the root of his opinion," which, she says, "is rotten / As ever oak or stone was sound" (2.3.89–90). It is central to this play that truth is, as Antigonus says, "good," that reality, the world of *things* (as opposed to nothing), the world called "nature," is entirely "sound"—that is, healthy, unflawed, innocent. The problem is that "opinion" does not have to be governed by "the law and process of great nature" (2.2.59).[60] In attempting to confute Leontes's "diseased opinion," Paulina points to the reliability and benignity of nature's "process"; the supposedly illegitimate infant looks just like its father, Leontes: "Although the print be little, the whole matter / And copy of the father" (2.3.98–99). Paulina lingers on the precision of biological reproduction—"The very mould and frame of hand, nail, finger"—which was much more accurate than mechanical reproduction in the period.[61] Leontes, as we have seen, had shared this view earlier, in relation to Mamillius, holding it to be true "To say this boy were like me" (1.2.134–35). But here he refuses to accept the evidence of his senses. Paulina is right to worry that the "good goddess

Nature, which has made" reliable bodies may not have "The ordering of the mind too" (2.3.103–5).

Redeeming the Words

We are now in a position to see what the task of the second half of the play must be. Shakespeare will have to redeem the terms and realms that have been slandered, the whole realm that stands apart from knowledge.[62] To see this happening, we must recognize that this realm is described not only by the philosophical term that we have examined but also by a number of related terms ("opinion" does not seem to be redeemable because, in this play, it seems to mean only—*contra* Plato—false belief). In speaking of Leontes's "diseased opinion," Camillo had spoken of "The fabric of his folly, whose foundation / Is pil'd upon his faith" (1.2.426–30). These terms—"folly" and especially "faith"—must be redeemed, shown to have a potentially or basically positive valence as well as a "diseased" one.[63] The vocabulary of playfulness and of sociality must be redeemed.[64] But the major realm to be redeemed is that of sexuality. An innocent version of (adult hetero-) sexuality must be convincingly presented. Such a thing must be part of what the play means by the goodness of nature. Shakespeare seems to want to assert—in dramatic form, so he cannot be prosecuted—a decidedly nonascetic version of the Pelagian heresy. We come back to the question of innocence. Childhood or infant innocence was asserted by both of the major groups that Augustine attacked, the Pelagians and the Gnostics. But where, as we have seen, the Gnostics saw the growth of flesh as "but a blister" and the divine spark in humans almost overwhelmed by "flesh," the Pelagians saw innocence as potentially continuing through adulthood and only ruined by actual moral failure.[65]

With this in mind, we can track the movement of the play beyond tragedy—indeed, all the way through to its astonishing but nonetheless extremely well-prepared-for conclusion.[66] The third act of the play opens with one of the few overtly mystical moments in Shakespeare, a description of the oracle at Delphos—that is, Delos—to which Leontes has been persuaded to submit his theories.[67] The oracle is associated with benign and productive nature ("The climate's delicate . . . / Fertile the isle"); with forgetting of the self (the noise of the oracle, says one of the messengers sent to it, "so surpris'd my sense / That I was nothing"—a positive use of this term); and with the realm of "knowledge" (we are assured that once the oracle's message is opened, "something rare . . .

will rush to knowledge" [3.1.21]).⁶⁸ Unlike Greene's, Shakespeare's jealous king ignores the oracle and is only brought to repentance by the death of his son, but Leontes does finally acknowledge that he was "transported" by his jealousy (3.2.156).⁶⁹ His "fancies" are condemned (3.2.179), and he is left contemplating his impotence in the face of the announcement that Hermione has died from grief over the death of their son. Paulina challenges the politically powerful king to bring "tincture or lustre" to the dead Hermione's lips, "or breath within" (3.2.203-4). Leontes leaves the stage (for the next act and a half) with a dedication of himself to a very chastened sense of "recreation"—"recreation" as mournful and self-lacerating spiritual "exercise" (3.2.239).⁷⁰ "Tears shall be my recreation," he says (3.2.238).

But Shakespeare wants "recreation" in the play to recover its joyful meaning, and he wants "creation," as in "re-creation" to do the same. The shift in genre away from tragedy occurs in the moment of the play's (and Shakespeare's) most famous stage direction (3.3.57).⁷¹ The bear that pursues Antigonus—the one person in the play other than Leontes who does believe that Perdita is a bastard—is a signal that we are in the world of romance rather than tragedy.⁷² The bear and the roaring sea that Lear imagines in the storm are, as G. Wilson Knight recognized, emblems of tragedy, but here they are literal, and seen through the eyes of low characters and through the medium of comic prose (in an incongruously elegant formulation, the bear "dined on" the gentleman [3.3.105]).⁷³ The class and medium shift signals the genre shift. Christopher Pye is right to speak of "calculated tonal instabilities" here.⁷⁴ Shakespeare seems to want to make sure that we recognize the move away from the thematic and representational world of tragedy by next bringing on a stage device at least as crude as that of the bear (or of the seacoast of Bohemia).⁷⁵ Act 4 begins, "Enter Time" (stage direction 4.1.0). We are being put in the position of naive viewers. And Shakespeare insists that there are worse places to be ("Of this allow, / If ever you have spent time worse ere now" [4.1.29-30]).

When the rogue Autolycus enters, singing "When daffodils begin to peer" (4.3.1), we are clearly in a different world, a world at once of happy celebration of nature's indomitability—"the red blood reigns in the winter's pale"—and of happy a- or immorality ("tumbling in the hay" and petty thievery). This is certainly a relief from the realm of tyranny and disaster. But it is not enough. Shakespeare wants to give us a vision even more positive than that of a spring-loving petty thief with a merry heart. The sheep-shearing festival scene (4.4) is by far the longest scene in the play. Shakespeare fills the stage with traditional village entertainments—ballads and Morris dances—in the representation of a familiar but threatened Elizabethan-Jacobean rural holiday.[76] The implicit celebration of nature and growth (and the human use of it) is obvious. But the most important figure in this scene is the grown-up (sixteen-year-old) Perdita. The figure who, as an infant, was the symbol, for Leontes, of sexual and social corruption becomes, as a nubile and socially apt young woman, the representative and spokesperson for happy and innocent sociality and sexuality.[77] Perdita as Queen of the Feast is, as Hermione was as actual queen, a well-spoken and gracious hostess. And Perdita is overtly and unabashedly sexual. She is also, as is her equally desirous princely boyfriend, chaste.[78]

In the famous dialogue on grafting in which Perdita rejects human art that "shares / With great creating nature," Polixenes rather condescendingly explains (I was tempted to say "mansplains") to her that "The art itself is nature" (4.4.86–97). He speaks of "mending" nature—as if there were something wrong with it—but then, using a *metanoia* or *correctio*, revises his statement, and shifts from "does *mend* nature" to "*change* it rather." Many critics think that Polixenes "wins" the discussion here—a point to which I will return—but Perdita remains unmoved. She says, "So it is," to Polixenes's grand summary (97), perhaps thinking it impolite to prolong the discussion. But when he tells her that she must act on her apparent agreement, she refuses. In a brilliant analogy, she likens interventionist gardening to the use of cosmetics; of biologically engineered plants, she asserts:

> I'll not put
> The dibble in the earth to set one slip of them;
> No more than were I painted, I would wish
> This youth should say 'twere well, and only therefore
> Desire to breed by me. (4.4.99–103)

She is completely at ease and unembarrassed at the idea of Florizel desiring "to breed" by her; and she insists that she wants this attraction to arise purely from nature without art—the "only" is important here.[79] In responding to Ferdinand's rather odd joke that in wanting to strew him with flowers she will make him "like a corpse," Perdita says: "No, like a bank, for love to lie and play on!" (4.4.130).[80] Chaste—meaning married—(hetero-) sexuality as happy and innocent adult "play" is accepted. We are a long way from "Go play, boy, play; thy mother plays" (1.1.185).

The festival scene continues this redemption of terms. "Affection," "fancy," and "madness"—words initially associated with Leontes's deluded state—are all presented positively, in relation to Florizel's love for Perdita (482–85). But a good deal of this long scene is taken up with Autolycus's activities, especially the sale and performance of printed ballads. The gullibility of the yokels is dramatized; they are prepared (it seems) to believe the absurd ballads (a usurer's wife giving birth to moneybags, etc.).[81] Autolycus's account emphasizes the raptness of the yokels' attention: "all their other senses stuck in their ears," says Autolycus, "no hearing, no feeling, but my sir's song, and admiring the nothing of it" (610–15). Autolycus takes practical advantage of the situation, but the interesting question is whether Shakespeare wants us to share in scorn for the yokels. As David Kaula has shown, Autolycus assumes the voice of a skeptical and educated Protestant, seeing the yokels as if they were superstitious and ignorant Catholics.[82] The yokels buy his wares as if his ribbons were relics and he were what Chaucer calls a "pardoner," a seller of indulgences—"as if my trinkets had been hallowed and brought a benediction to the buyer" (597–98).

But is there any element of respect for awe here, even in a primitive form? I am not sure. We may or may not be approaching the world of Bottom's Dream, which Bottom thought called for a ballad.[83] Are we to connect the response of the yokels to the ballads—"all their other senses stuck in their ears ... admiring the nothing of it"—with the noise of the oracle at Delphos, which "so surpris'd my sense, / That I was nothing"? Or are these profoundly different? Moreover, if we are experiencing the play in the theater, we are watching, presumably with rapt attention, a play with a stage bear and Father Time. The crude dramaturgy might have a point; it might, indeed, be part of the point of the play.[84]

The final act ties up all the themes the play has been developing, and returns to the questions of naiveté, faith, and superstition. I have already suggested that the play seems to accept a Catholic sense of penitence. In the first scene of act 5, Leontes reappears, and is described as having "perform'd / A saint-like sorrow" (5.1.1–2). This is Catholic in both theology and attitude.[85] I do not think there is any derogation implied in "perform'd" here; the stress is on having actually done something. But more internally to the play—since we do not see any of Leontes's penitential behavior—Leontes has been restored to a sense of the benignity of (hetero-) sexuality.[86] He describes his lost wife as "the sweet'st companion that e'er man / Bred his hopes out of" (5.1.11–12), a line in which the companionate and the procreative "co-join," as in Perdita's happy acknowledgment of Florizel's desire to "breed by" her.[87]

The second scene of act 5 ties up some tag ends of the plot and provides a buildup to the finale. The second scene consists (like the first of the play) entirely of prose, and it consists entirely of narration—nothing is shown.[88] The focus is on the royal and aristocratic reception of the story of Perdita's preservation and identity: "a notable passion of wonder appeared in them" (15–16). The aristocrats are here like the yokels at the ballad-singing; they are rapt, dumb in admiration. The connection is explicitly made. Ballads are mentioned, and suddenly seen as, if anything, too limited in their capacity to express extraordinary things: "such a deal of wonder is broken out within this hour, that ballad-makers cannot be able to express it" (23–25).[89] We are repeatedly told that the truth of the matter is "like an old tale" (28, 60). Shakespeare is toying with us. He has one of the narrators, just before Paulina's statue is mentioned, say of the spectators moved by the story of Hermione's death, "Who was most marble there changed colour" (88). Julio (Giulio) Romano—the only Renaissance artist mentioned by Shakespeare (who had apparently been reading Vasari)—has newly "performed," that is, finished by painting, his statue of Hermione, and we are told that if Romano could "put breath into his work," he would be better than Nature (97–99).[90] And so we are prepared for the final scene.

No first-time viewer, and probably not even any first-time reader, however shrewd and learned, could have seen this finale coming. In retrospect, the clues are obvious, but only so—in retrospect. It is extremely unusual in Shakespeare for him to withhold a key fact from the audience. There is only one other play in the entire corpus in which he does so.[91] In *The Winter's Tale,* with its Ovidian title and direct allusion to the Demeter (Ceres) / Persephone story, Shakespeare turns again, for his ending, to Ovid and gives us a version of the most famous story in our tradition about the powers and limits of art, the story of Pygmalion from book 10 of the *Metamorphoses*.

But Shakespeare had already—by the middle of act 3—adduced another context for this story. When Paulina unveils the statue and says, "behold, and say 'tis well'" (5.3.20), Shakespeare is giving a quite subtle hint of this other, nonclassical context. He is appealing to the biblically informed in his audience. They had already heard, and no doubt noted, a spectacularly overt reference earlier in the play to the book of Kings. When Antigonus agreed, because he was, as he said, "by oath enjoined," to take up Hermione's newborn baby and abandon her in some "remote and desert place," Antigonus prayed for the infant that "Some powerful spirit instruct the kites and ravens / To be thy nurses" (2.3.185–86). This is a "direct and directing" reference to the experience of the prophet Elijah, who was fed by ravens when "the word of the Lord" commanded them to do so (1 Kings 17:4–6).[92] No serious Bible reader could have missed the allusion. But the interesting question is whether such a reader or viewer would also recall what happens later in that same chapter. To do so allows us to see

Shakespeare's mind at work. He associated the Pygmalion story, the great classical story of animation, with an Old Testament analogue to it.[93] In the chapter that begins with Elijah fed by ravens, the prophet resurrects the son of a woman who has helped him (1 Kings 17:19–24). An audience member who recalled that might possibly—this is more of a stretch—have also heard the biblical resonance in Paulina's "behold, and say 'tis well" (5.3.20). When, in 2 Kings (after a tonally ambiguous episode involving bears [2 Kings 2:23–24]), Elisha redoes Elijah's animation of a child, the question of "being well" arises (2 Kings 4:23).[94]

Shakespeare wanted the biblical context of the final scene to become as present to the educated audience as the Ovidian one (he is perhaps coordinating chronologies). When Leontes finally does speak in the scene, he says to the statue: "Chide me dear stone" (24). This is a direct reference to a passage in Habakkuk: "For the stone shall crye out of the wall" (Habbakuk 2:11). In case someone missed the allusion, Shakespeare makes it again. In his next speech, Leontes says, "I am ashamed: does not the stone rebuke me" (37).[95] But again, the interesting issue is not only the direct allusion but the immediate context of the phrase quoted. The context in Habakkuk is a chapter strongly condemning idolatry, especially with regard to images: "What profiteth the image?" the prophet asks, "though he that made it trust therein." And the prophet particularly proclaims, "Wo unto him that saith to the wood, Awake, to the dumme stone, Rise up" (Habakkuk 2:18–19).

Shakespeare seems to be complicating his scene excessively by raising the issue of idolatry, but this seems to be exactly what he wishes to do.[96] The play certainly evokes some of the stances of traditional (late medieval) religion, but it does so, as Julia Reinhard Lupton notes, from a consistently Reformed perspective.[97] After the unveiling of the statue, the next great dramatic moment in the scene is Perdita's response (it was Perdita, after all, who was the instigator of the visit to Paulina's gallery on "hearing of her mother's statue" [5.2.92; and see 5.3.13]). The entire group is dumb with wonder—like the King and Camillo at the shepherd's recitation (5.2.10–16) or the yokels at the ballad-singing—until Paulina demands speech from Leontes ("first you, my liege" [22]), and Leontes "awakens" Perdita by calling attention to the girl's muteness and immobility (41–42). When Perdita responds by speaking, her first thought is of the problem of idolatry. She asks (presumably of Leontes):

> give me leave
> And do not say 'tis superstition, that
> I kneel, and then implore her blessing. (42b–44)

Any serious Protestant in Shakespeare's audience would have been very nervous about someone kneeling to a statue and "imploring" it for a blessing. It would indeed, as Perdita worries, have been seen as "superstition."[98] It was the fundamental image of Catholic idolatry—which many English Protestants experienced exactly the way the Hebrew prophets did idolatry. In the Book of Homilies, which represented the official position of the Church of England, the homily "Against Peril of Idolatry" is the longest, most elaborate, and one of the most passionate.[99] It sees the Old Testament prohibitions as completely reaffirmed by Christianity ("What a fond thing it is for man, who hath life and reason, to bow himself to a dead and insensible image, the work of his own hand?").[100] Michael O'Connell is right that what Perdita is proposing raises "the worst fears" of those concerned with the "peril" of idolatry.[101] Even an anti-Puritan like John Harrington, who defended the crucifix, was nervous about anyone kneeling before it.[102] Kneeling was a truly hot-button religious and political topic in early seventeenth-century England.[103]

Paulina perhaps prevents Perdita from kneeling, and certainly prevents her from kissing the hand of the statue. Paulina offers (or threatens) to remove the "image," as she calls it. But she also begins to suggest that something further is going to happen. With regard to the statue, the focus continues to be (as in the Giulio passage) on the limits of art—"Would you not deem it breath'd?" (64). "We are mock'd with art," says Leontes (68a), using a term bitterly that Paulina had used neutrally ("life as lively mock'd" [19]). Leontes is profoundly aware of the limits of art—"What fine chisel / Could ever yet cut breath?" (78a–79b). But, like Perdita earlier, he is prepared to act bizarrely: "let no man mock me, / For I will kiss her" (79b–80a)—presumably now on the mouth rather than (as Perdita wished) on the hand. In Ovid, the moment in which the statue comes alive is that in which Pygmalion, as Golding's translation says, "Did kiss her."[104] But in Shakespeare, this moment is not allowed to happen. Again Paulina intervenes:

> Good my lord, forbear:
> The ruddiness upon her lip is wet;
> You'll mar it if you kiss it, stain your own
> With oily painting. (80b–83a)

Shakespeare succeeds in making art an object of disgust here, and the erotic context intensifies it. We see now why we were told in the previous scene that the statue was "newly performed." The experience of what it would be like to kiss a newly painted statue is sensorily evoked: "stain your own [lips] / With oily painting." The descriptive phrase "oil painting" is brought vividly and unpleasantly to life here.[105] The statue is the ultimate "painted lady." Eroticism based on a woman being "painted" has already been rejected. Kissing a painted statue would have the same "marring" and "staining" effect as kissing a "painted woman." The danger here is not of poisoning but of impurity, ugliness, and disgust.[106] As is so often the case in the Hebrew Bible, the discourses of idolatry and of impure sexuality are brought together.[107]

At this point religious dread begins to take over the scene. Paulina and Shakespeare become very careful. The worry is that, if she makes the statue move, "you'll think ... I am assisted / By wicked powers" (88–90). This was a real worry, especially in the theater. A number of earlier plays (including one by the author of *Pandosto*) had, with great success, dramatized demonic magic on the public stage.[108] Shakespeare wants to make it clear that this is not what he is doing. He has Paulina make a strongly Protestant-sounding appeal, or perhaps just a strongly Pauline one: "It is required / You do awake your faith" (94–95). Not magic, but "faith" is what is demanded here—"faith alone," one might say. Where, before, Leontes had been "transported by [his] jealousies" (3.2.156) into a state of dangerous insanity, here he is equally "transported" (68) into "madness" (73), but these are now terms of responsiveness and wonder. Unlike the negative "faith" with which Leontes was afflicted ("his folly ... pil'd upon his faith"), this kind of faith does not involve any particular "opinion" but rather a generalized belief in the benignity of the cosmos: the belief that things might be better—rather than that they are worse—than they seem. So, this kind of faith directly opposes cynicism and pessimism.[109] It also involves passivity, rather than the manic activism of Leontes's previous state; he is now "content to look on ... content to hear" (92–93).[110] Something rare might rush to knowledge. And, as the Pauline injunction suggests, the religious framework suddenly widens here. Until this moment, the play has maintained a strongly Old Testament framework in its biblical references, but here, in notable contrast to the presentation of animation in both Ovid and the two books of Kings, the process is dramatized as happening without the intervention of bodily touch. As in the resurrection of Lazarus, the medium is going to be purely verbal. Jesus "cryed with a loude voyce, Lazarus, come forthe" (John 11:43).[111]

Leontes, at this point, seems not to share Paulina's worry that some who are there might think that "wicked powers" are involved. He commands, "No foot shall stir" (98). Nonetheless, the moment when the statue moves and steps down from its pedestal remains a terrifying one: "Start not," Paulina says, and she insists, once again, that her "spell is lawful" (104–5). Finally, we get what might be called the Pygmalion moment: "O, she's warm!" (109).[112] Leontes, in his joy, dismisses the question of the demonic, or rather, he tries to finesse it. "If this be magic," he says, "Let it be an art / Lawful as eating" (110–11). He tries, in other words, to remove the whole process from the realm of art into the realm of ordinary natural behavior, and he taps into the Pauline (and Protestant) theme of the liberation of eating from restrictive laws.[113] At this point, when it is virtually certain that the thing in question is or has become a living person and not a statue, Perdita is finally allowed by Paulina, indeed commanded by her, to kneel (119). Both the avoidance of idolatry and the human meaning of the moment entirely rest on the figure in question being a living person and not a dumb and lifeless image. As Jennifer Waldron notes, it is Hermione's ordinary human "actions" that are to be seen as "holy" (104), not her immobile presence.[114] Huston Diehl points out that wonder at the animate—and at the power that actually can install breath and warmth in a creation—is at the center of Protestant iconoclasm.[115] All dread of "superstition" disappears. Certainly a daughter can kneel to her mother.

Now, if we have been moved by this scene, if we have been caught up in it as it unfolded, if we have experienced the anxiety, the dread, and the joy, we have had to give up some of our sophistication and aesthetic distance; we have had to allow ourselves to be as enraptured by an improbable fiction as the yokels were in their ridiculous ballads—Hermione has either been hidden for sixteen years or "stolen from the dead."[116] In awakening our faith, we may have had to lose some of our contempt for credulity. To celebrate what Paulina calls "dear life"—"great creating nature"—we have had to adopt the attitude that Shakespeare calls "wonder," an attitude that Shakespeare might regard as fundamentally religious even in its most naive forms.[117] To sum up the play's religious content, it seems to reject a number of Protestant positions and attitudes: the insistence on original sin; the suspicion of purification through suffering; and, possibly, the critique of credulity. The play denies original sin, accepts purification through suffering, and may well be indulgent to credulity. On the other hand, it seems to accept with great enthusiasm two other Protestant positions: the idea of married sexuality as chaste; and the strong critique of idolatry.[118]

This brings me to a final question. In the famous dialogue on art and nature between Polixenes and Perdita, who does the play think is right? Perdita presents art and nature as sharply different, while Polixenes presents them as complementary. The ideology of the play seems to support Perdita: the person, Hermione, is infinitely more valuable than a statue of the person could ever be;

biological is more important than artistic reproduction.[119] But does the fact of the play support its stated ideology? After all, this whole celebration of nature is taking place within a work of art, and it is only the power of the work of art, its maker's excellence, that gets us to feel the power of its themes. So is the play ultimately a celebration of the power of art? Is Polixenes right, after all? Most critics seem to think this, and in general, Leonard Barkan's counsel that in the final scene, and the play as a whole, "we would be wise to perceive the mutual triumph of art and nature" has prevailed.[120]

This is genial, and almost irresistible.[121] But I wish to resist it. Along with a very small number of other critics, I think that Shakespeare actually did want his play to celebrate nature rather than itself, and I think that he did think that nature was greater than any human creation, and that to think otherwise was precisely the sin of idolatry.[122] It is hard for literary critics to believe that great writers could have thought that there was something more important than art, and could have embodied this belief in works of art, even great ones. George Herbert was capable of this, and so, I think, was Shakespeare. I think that, in general, artists are less idolatrous toward art (and artists) than critics are.[123]

NOTES

INTRODUCTION

Notes to epigraphs: Samuel Taylor Coleridge, *Coleridge on the Seventeenth Century*, ed. Roberta Florence Brinkley (Durham, N.C.: Duke University Press, 1955), 523. William Empson, "Still the Strange Necessity," *Argufying: Essays on Literature and Culture*, ed. John Haffenden (Iowa City: University of Iowa Press, 1987), 124–25.

    1. By "close reading," I mean reading that takes every detail in a stretch of text as potentially significant. Every commentator on the practice has emphasized the importance of slowness, of not simply "getting the point" and moving on, and the importance of noticing details. The founding and most eloquent exponent of the practice took it as defining what is or should be meant by "philology." In the preface to *Daybreak* (1887), Nietzsche asserted that a philologist is "a teacher of slow reading," and philology is "that venerable art which demands of its votaries one thing above all: to go aside, to take time, to become still, to become slow—it is a goldsmith's art and connoisseurship of the *word* which has nothing but delicate, cautious work to do and achieves nothing if it does not achieve it *lento*" (Friedrich Nietzsche, *Daybreak: Thoughts on the Prejudices of Morality*, ed. Maudemarie Clark and Brian Leiter, trans. R. J. Hollingdale [Cambridge: Cambridge University Press, 1997], 5). For twentieth-century exponents, see Viktor Shlovsky, "Art as Technique," in *Russian Formalist Criticism*, trans. Lee T. Lemon and Marion J. Reis (Lincoln: University of Nebraska Press, 1965), 3–24 (esp. 22); and Reuben A. Brower, "Reading in Slow Motion," in *In Defense of Reading: A Reader's Approach to Literary Criticism*, ed. Reuben A. Brower and Richard Poirier (New York: Dutton, 1963), 3–21. Recent commentators agree. See, in *ADE Bulletin* 149 (2010): John Guillory, "Close Reading: Prologue and Epilogue" (8–14); Jane Gallop, "Close Reading in 2009" (15–19); and Jonathan Culler, "The Closeness of Close Reading" (20–25). See also Emily Apter and Elaine Freedgood, "Afterword," in "Surface Reading," ed. Stephen Best and Sharon Marcus, special issue, *Representations* 108 (2009): 139–46. Jonathan Kramnick denies that close reading is "a particularly intense kind of attention" to texts. He insists that it is "a form of writing." This confuses the idea that close reading is a skill or a group of skills—certainly a valid point—with the necessity of these skills being manifested in writing (Jonathan Kramnick, "Criticism and Truth," *Critical Inquiry* 47 [Winter 2021]: 218–40, 222–23). Close reading *is* a particularly intense kind of attention to texts.

    2. Close reading need not be of this sort. Deconstruction is close reading committed to going against the grain of inferred authorial intention. See Paul de Man, "The Dead-End of Formalist Criticism," *Blindness and Insight: Essays in the Rhetoric of Contemporary Criticism*, 2nd ed., rev. (Minneapolis: University of Minnesota Press, 1983), 229–45, and "The Return to Philology," *The Resistance to Theory* (Minneapolis: University of Minnesota Press, 1986), 21–26.

3. I accept the view both that literary works "come out of a head, not out of a hat" and that "the poem belongs to the public" (W. K. Wimsatt Jr. and Monroe Beardsley, "The Intentional Fallacy," in *The Verbal Icon: Studies in the Meaning of Poetry* [1954; New York: Farrar Straus, 1964], 4–5). In "Against Theory" Steven Knapp and Walter Benn Michaels can be seen as putting the Wimsatt and Beardsley position on a firmer philosophical footing (as Bill Dowling argues); see *Against Theory: Literary Studies and the New Pragmatism*, ed. W. J. T. Mitchell (Chicago: University of Chicago Press, 1982), 11–30 and 89–94. However, I would see the relation between the implied author and the historical one as not necessarily to be severed—or as necessarily to be privileged. Anonymous works are certainly interpretable as are those, like the works of Shakespeare, for which we have no external authorial commentary. This is not to say that having such would not be interesting and potentially relevant; merely that it would not necessarily be so—its relevance would be a matter of judgment—and, in any case, such material would not be automatically regulative.

4. Elaine Auyoung in "What We Mean by Reading," *New Literary History* 51 (2020): 93–114, stresses the importance of the goal of showing or arguing how a text coheres.

5. See Donald Davidson, "On the Very Idea of a Conceptual Scheme," in *Inquiries into Truth and Interpretation* (Oxford: Clarendon Press, 1986), 183–98 (197); and, in the same volume, "Thought and Talk," 155–70. Compare J. L. Austin, "Other Minds," in *Philosophical Papers*, ed. J. O. Urmson and G. J. Warnock, 3rd ed. (Oxford: Clarendon Press, 1979), 76–116 (esp. 82). (For Augustine, reading according to charity meant finding the lesson of charity everywhere in the Bible; See Augustine, *On Christian Doctrine*, trans. D. W. Robertson [Indianapolis: Bobbs-Merrill, 1958], esp. 93).

6. That Shakespeare's plays were written to be read as well as staged is now, I think, established. The crucial work on this is Lukas Erne, *Shakespeare as Literary Dramatist* (Cambridge: Cambridge University Press, 2003), followed by Erne, *Shakespeare and the Book Trade* (Cambridge: Cambridge University Press, 2013). In 1623, the editors of the Folio (members of Shakespeare's acting company) were urging "the great Variety of Readers" to "Reade him . . . and againe, and againe." *The Norton Facsimile of the First Folio of Shakespeare*, prepared by Charlton Hinman (New York: W. W. Norton, 1968), 7 (A3r).

7. I would define a literary critical "reading" as an interpretive claim about a work or passage of a work that takes as its primary evidence material cited from the work itself. See also the essay cited in note 4 above.

8. *Measure for Measure*, 1.1.35–36. I realize that in this passage and elsewhere, Shakespeare does not use the term in the same sense in which I am using it (he means outcomes rather than matters for contemplation). But I cannot resist momentarily appropriating the lines for my purposes. Unless otherwise stated, citations of Shakespeare's works throughout this book will be to *The Complete Pelican Shakespeare*, ed. Stephen Orgel and A. R. Braunmuller (New York: Penguin, 2002).

9. See, inter alia, Arnold Hunt, *The Art of Hearing: English Preachers and Their Audiences, 1590–1640* (Cambridge: Cambridge University Press, 2010).

10. I have argued elsewhere that Shakespeare came to take a strong position on the matter of the necessity for subordinates of all kinds to resist plainly immoral commands. See Richard Strier, *Resistant Structures: Particularity, Radicalism, and Renaissance Texts* (Chicago: University of Chicago Press, 1995), ch. 7. The current book can be seen as extending the argument for Shakespeare having "positions."

11. I agree with Jonathan Kramnick that literary criticism "attempts to make true statements about literary texts" ("Criticism and Truth," 218). But Kramnick undercuts this by saying

that what truth means in literary studies is different from what it means in the sciences (237–39). He mocks the idea that iterability has any place in literary studies: "Do a reading the same way again to make sure that it yields the same results and you will appear to be losing your mind" (239). But I think that this is exactly what we do in testing the validity—that is, the truth—of an interpretation. Auyoung has a similar view that truth, in the normal sense, is not a major issue in evaluating literary interpretations, so that "critics are rarely under pressure to choose between competing interpretations of a text" ("What We Mean by Reading," 106). But critics routinely choose between such. These are adjudicated in the same way or ways that competing explanations in general are. See Peter Lipton, *Inference to the Best Explanation*, 2nd ed. (London: Routledge, 2004). As Empson says, reasons for interpretive claims are "like the reasons for anything else; one can reason about them" (William Empson, *Seven Types of Ambiguity*, 3rd ed. [New York: New Directions, 1947], 9).

12. I accept the distinction that Heather Love makes between description and interpretation, but think that she understates the role that the former plays in the latter. Moreover, I follow Empson (see the second epigraph to this introduction) in failing to see that it is an advantage to literary criticism to avoid the categories of "experience, consciousness, and motivation" (Heather Love, "Close but Not Deep: Literary Ethics and the Descriptive Turn," *New Literary History* 41 [2010]: 375). When Stephen Best and Sharon Marcus claim in their introduction to "Surface Reading" (see note 1 above) that such reading manifests "a true openness to *all the potentials* made available by texts" (16; emphasis mine), I think they fall into a contradiction. Charles Altieri makes a similar point when he notes that surface reading's "capacity for sponsorship" of different kinds of reading "is hampered by the oppositions produced by its basic metaphoric structure"—that is, the language of "surface" and "depth" (*Reckoning with the Imagination: Wittgenstein and the Aesthetics of Literary Experience* [Ithaca, N.Y.: Cornell University Press, 2015], 20).

13. See the introduction by Kenneth Dauber and Walter Jost to *Ordinary Language Criticism: Literary Thinking after Cavell and Wittgenstein* (Evanston, IL: Northwestern University Press, 2003). I basically agree with their desiderata for literary criticism (xvi–xx) except for the view that truth in literary criticism is a "rhetorical" matter (xx). See note 11 above.

14. See Austin, "Other Minds," 110–15. In chapter 9 of *Revolution of the Ordinary: Literary Studies after Wittgenstein, Austin, and Cavell* [Chicago: University of Chicago Press, 2017], Toril Moi suggests something like this. Altieri states the position clearly: "The skills we need to engage art objects are basically the same skills that we need to negotiate the many interpretive situations that we encounter in our daily lives" (*Reckoning with the Imagination*, 6). His notion of "attunement" (22, 199, and passim) gets at this, though he is more nervous about the cognitive dimension of this and more interested in the phenomenological dimension of it than I am.

15. See Rita Felski, *The Limits of Critique* (Chicago: University of Chicago Press, 2015), ch. 1.

16. I should add that what I am calling "deep" reading need not be "suspicious." The latter is defined by a particular relation between the surface meaning and the posited one, a relation of undermining. A deep meaning need not stand in this relation to the surface.

17. "A Plea for Excuses," in *Philosophical Papers*, 175–204.

18. Cavell provided a brief afterword to *Ordinary Language Criticism* (347–49).

19. For "ten leaves off" and "constellations of the storie," and for the Bible as a book that "lights to eternall blisse," see "The H. Scriptures" (2). *The Works of George Herbert*, ed. F. E. Hutchinson (Oxford: Clarendon Press, 1945), 58.

20. See note 1 above.

CHAPTER 1

1. All quotations from the *Nicomachean Ethics* (*NE*) are from the translation by Martin Ostwald (1962; Englewood, N.J.: Prentice Hall, 1999). Hereafter, citations of this work (Bekker page, column, and line numbers) will appear parenthetically in the text.

2. Quotations are from the Q2 text edited by Ann Thompson and Neil Taylor (Arden 3; London: Thomson Learning, 2006). I have also consulted the companion volume of Thompson and Taylor, *Hamlet: The Texts of 1603 and 1623* (Q1 and F, respectively).

3. The Folio (1623) text adds a half line, "Sir, in this audience," after "poor Hamlet's enemy," and has "mother" rather than "brother" in the final line of the speech.

4. In the notes to his Arden 2 edition (London: Methuen, 1982), Harold Jenkins argues for taking the madness seriously (566–67). This seems to me special pleading.

5. See J. L. Austin, "A Plea for Excuses," in *Philosophical Papers*, ed. J. O. Urmson and G. J. Warnock, 3rd ed. (Oxford: Clarendon Press, 1979), 175–204, esp. 184–85. The *Hamlet* case exactly corresponds to the case that Austin hypothesizes, though with a person rather than a donkey in question.

6. For character in Aristotle's ethics, see, inter alia, Nancy Sherman, "The Habituation of Character," in *Aristotle's Ethics*, ed. Nancy Sherman (Lanham, Md.: Rowman and Littlefield, 1999), 231–60; and Jonathan Jacobs, *Choosing Character: Responsibility for Virtue and Vice* (Ithaca, N.Y.: Cornell University Press, 2001), ch. 1.

7. For more on this speech and its implications, see "Shakespeare and Skepticism (2): Epistemology." The Q2-only speech in act 1 on the custom (of "wassail") that Hamlet deplores (1.4.18–38) is Aristotelian in its presentation of "habit" as of equivalent power with "Nature," but seems more Augustinian in its presentation of "custom" as negative, the *consuetudo* with which Augustine struggles in the *Confessions* (see VI: xi, xv; VIII: v, vii, ix, xi in *St. Augustine's Confessions*, trans. W. Watts, corr. W. H. D. Rouse [LCL: Cambridge, Mass.: Harvard University Press, 1977]). For commentary, see John G. Prendiville, "The Development of the Idea of Habit in the Thought of Saint Augustine," *Traditio* 28 (1972): 29–99. However, Hamlet's wassail speech does seem to imagine the possibility of change through moral effort, the possibility that the demeaning custom could, as Hamlet wittily puts it, be "honoured in the breach" (1.4.16–38). Paul Cefalu in "Damnéd Custom . . . Habit's Devil: Hamlet's Part-Whole Fallacy and the Early Modern Philosophy of Mind," in *Revisionist Shakespeare: Transitional Ideologies in Texts and Context* (New York: Palgrave, 2004), 145–72, recognizes the importance of the conception of habit to Hamlet's thinking, but (as his title suggests) basically sees Hamlet as only having the Augustinian view.

8. For the public dimension in the Folio version, see note 3 above.

9. For the social and affective dimensions of this interaction as occurring between aristocrats, and for analysis of Laertes's response, see "Happy Hamlet."

10. Christopher Crosbie, "Shakespeare, Intention, and the Ethical Force of the Involuntary," in *The Routledge Companion to Shakespeare and Philosophy* (New York: Routledge, 2019), 213. Crosbie uses some of the same passages from the *Nicomachean Ethics* that I do here and that I used in an earlier version of the essay in *Shakespeare and Moral Agency*, ed. Michael D. Bristol (London: Continuum, 2010), 55–68.

11. See "Combination, dissociation and complication" in Austin, "A Plea for Excuses," 195.

12. Quotations from *Othello* are from the edition by E. A. J. Honigmann (Arden 3; Walton-on-Thames: Thomas Nelson and Sons, 1996). The Revised Edition, with a new introduction by Ayanna Thompson (London: Bloomsbury, 2016) retains Honigmann's text and notes.

13. This description is from the first Stationer's Register entry for the play in 1598 (there is a second entry in 1600). See the Arden 3 edition of *The Merchant of Venice* by John Drakakis (London: Methuen, 2010), 417. The play is cited from this edition (hereafter referred to as "Drakakis"). I have also made use of the Arden 2 edition by John Russell Brown (London: Methuen, 1955; corr. 1961), hereafter "Brown." On the two Stationer's Register entries, see David Kastan, "Plays into Print: Shakespeare to His Earliest Readers," in *Books and Readers in Early Modern England*, ed. Jennifer Andersen and Elizabeth Sauer (Philadelphia: University of Pennsylvania Press, 2002), 31.

14. On how maritime commerce is presented in the play, see C. L. Barber, *Shakespeare's Festive Comedy: A Study of Dramatic Form and Its Relation to Social Custom* (Princeton, N.J.: Princeton University Press, 1959), ch. 7; and Theodore B. Leinwand, *Theatre, Finance, and Society in Early Modern England* (Cambridge: Cambridge University Press, 1999).

15. Lars Engle in *Shakespearean Pragmatism: Market of His Time* (Chicago: University of Chicago Press, 1993), 83, offers a lovely and, as he says, Empsonian paraphrase of Antonio's lines here, though the paraphrase may credit Antonio with more self-knowledge than he might actually be seen to have.

16. On this matter, see Lawrence Stone, *The Crisis of the Aristocracy, 1558–1641*, abridged ed. (London: Oxford University Press, 1967), chs. 9–10; Leinwand, *Theatre, Finance, and Society*, chs. 1–2; Craig Muldrew, *The Economy of Obligation: The Culture of Credit and Social Relations in Early Modern England* (London: Palgrave Macmillan, 1999); and Laura Kolb, *Fictions of Credit in the Age of Shakespeare* (Oxford: Oxford University Press, 2021).

17. This stage direction occurs in both Q1 and the Folio.

18. The starkness of the formulation "Where money is" leads to the thought that there is an unstated but highly significant distinction at work in the play between money and wealth. Belmont, where the "lady" lives, stands for "wealth"—it is inherited, unearned, and unselfconscious ("happy" in Mark Van Doren's formulation). Money is something else. See Mark Van Doren, *Shakespeare* (1939; Garden City, N.Y.: Doubleday, 1953), 80; and also W. H. Auden, "Brothers and Others," in *The Dyer's Hand* (New York: Random House, 1962), 233–34. Mark Netzloff in "The Lead Casket: Capital, Mercantilism, and *The Merchant of Venice*," notes that in the play "Portia's economic resources remain notably absent from representation" (*Money and the Age of Shakespeare: Essays in the New Economic Criticism*, ed. Linda Woodbridge [New York: Palgrave, 2003], 167).

19. On the scarcity of cash (in Elizabethan England), see, inter alia, Muldrew, *The Economy of Obligation*, 98ff.

20. On Renaissance and Reformation warnings against standing surety in the context of friendship (as opposed to medieval idealizations of this), see the appendices to Benjamin Nelson, *The Idea of Usury: From Tribal Brotherhood to Universal Otherhood*, 2nd ed. (Chicago: University of Chicago Press, 1969), 141–64. Auden borrows from Nelson quotations against standing surety from Ralegh, Lord Burleigh, and Luther in "Brothers and Others," 231–32. To get a sense of the complexity of the issue in the period, see stanzas 46–48 of Herbert's "The Church-porch" (lines 271–88), in *The Works of George Herbert*, ed. F. E. Hutchinson (Oxford: Clarendon Press, 1945).

21. As Harry Berger puts it, "The mere sight of Antonio drives Shylock into verse" (*Fury in the Words: Love and Embarrassment in Shakespeare's Venice* [New York: Fordham University Press, 2013], 47).

22. I am not sure whether Shakespeare intends for Shylock to know this reference here. Shakespeare could have Shylock falling into it with no awareness of the allusion, so the reader or

auditor can make the connection; or Shakespeare could have Shylock consciously assuming the role that Jesus condemns; or Shakespeare could intend for Shylock to reference the passage without recognizing that he is condemning himself. Any one of these seems possible to me, though the first seems least and the second most likely—that of Shylock consciously assuming the role. He seems to know the New Testament well, as his almost immediately prior reference to Jesus as "the Nazarite" who conjured devils into swine (1.3.30–32) demonstrates. For how that reference works, see M. Lindsay Kaplan, "*The Merchant of Venice*, Jews, and Christians," in *The Cambridge Companion to Shakespeare and Religion*, ed. Hannibal Hamlin (Cambridge: Cambridge University Press, 2019), 175–76.

23. Laura Kolb has suggested to me, on the basis of various texts in the period, that this is a ploy, "that Shylock is being strategic: hiding how much he has, while signaling a cautious willingness to extend himself for this customer" (pers. comm.). The speech seems to me to be improvised to cover up Shylock's absorption in his thoughts about Antonio, but Kolb may be right. Her point might be supported by Shylock, at the end of the scene, saying that he will "purse the ducats straight" (immediately)—apparently from his home (1.3.170).

24. This is an unusual way of referring to interest. The *OED* cites only this instance. Drakakis's note cites Philip Caesar's *A General Discourse Against the Damnable Sect of Usurers* (1578), which cites Jerome's commentary on Ezekiel as stating that "the word of God" calls usury "excesse." I have not been able to locate an English Bible that uses the term for usury. The relevant English Bibles seem to use the word "increase" in Ezekiel 18. Shakespeare may have wanted Antonio to use "excess" because of its general moral meaning as well as its specific financial one.

25. "Methought" or "Methoughts," in Shakespeare, generally introduces or refers to something the speaker finds strange, often a dream, a vision, or a fantasy. See, for instance, Bottom's speech about his "dream," where the word appears four times (*A Midsummer Night's Dream*, 4.1.203–13); Clarence's speech about his dream, where the word appears seven times (*Richard III*, 1.4.9–63); Posthumus on his vision of Jupiter (*Cymbeline*, 5.5.426–29); and Caliban on his dream of "riches" about to drop on him (*The Tempest*, 3.2.136–42).

26. As of 1571, interest up to 10 percent was legal in England. The Elizabethan Act of 1571 repealed the Edwardine Act of 1552, which had repealed the Henrician Act of 1545, which allowed the 10 percent rate. See Norman L. Jones, *God and the Moneylenders: Usury and the Law in Early Modern England* (New York: Oxford University Press, 1989).

27. Marc Shell, *Money, Language, and Thought: Literary and Philosophical Economies from the Medieval to the Modern Era* (Baltimore: Johns Hopkins University Press, 1993), 54.

28. Shell, *Money, Language, and Thought*, 54 n. 19, notes the oddness of Antonio not having insurance on his ships, and that this may be a matter of principle connected to the anti-interest zealotry.

29. Shell, *Money, Language, and Thought*, 49–50, suggests that Antonio's assertion that he does not "use" interest suggested the sheep ("ewes") to Shylock along with a connection to "Iewes." I am not sure. Shylock seems to tell the story as a favorite one.

30. No editor or critic, as far as I know, has found a direct precedent for the use of this story in this context.

31. See, inter alia, Barber, *Shakespeare's Festive Comedy*, 172.

32. For Aristotle, see *Politics* 1258b (book 1, ch. 10), where Aristotle explains that usury is called by the word *tokos*, which also means "breed" or "offspring," for "as the offspring resembles its parent, so the interest bred by money is like the principal which breeds it." Hence, Aristotle says, "we can understand why, of all modes of acquisition, usury is the most unnatural" (*The Poli-*

tics of Aristotle, trans. Ernest Barker [New York: Oxford University Press, 1958], 29). For Pound, see canto 45 in *The Cantos of Ezra Pound* (New York: New Directions, 1993), 230 (the theme, though not the phrase, is repeated in canto 51). For the medieval development of Aristotle's view, see John T. Noonan, *The Scholastic Analysis of Usury* (Cambridge, Mass: Harvard University Press, 1957).

33. I am not sure how to reconcile, in diegetical terms, Shylock's earlier lack of personal recognition of Antonio (see "This is Signior Antonio" at line 36) with the history presented here. Poetically, I am sure that Shakespeare wanted the difference between the speeches that I have tried to describe.

34. On the "blood libel," see R. Po-chia Hsia, *The Myth of Ritual Murder: Jews and Magic in Reformation Germany* (New Haven, Conn.: Yale University Press, 1988); E. M. Rose, *The Murder of William of Norwich: The Origins of the Blood Libel in Medieval Europe* (New York: Oxford University Press, 2015).

35. It is not entirely clear whether "spurned" is used literally or metaphorically in this passage, but "foot me as you spurn" seems to me to push toward the literal.

36. See J. H. Baker, *An Introduction to English Legal History*, 3rd ed. (London: Butterworths, 1990), ch. 14 ("Real Property: Feudalism and Uses") and the chapters that follow. The Statute of Uses (1536) was the major piece of Tudor legislation on real property. For more on Shylock's sense of property rights, and for further discussion of the legal meaning of "use," see "Shakespeare and Legal Systems: The Better the Worse (but Not Vice Versa)," 108–10.

37. Compare Eric Spenser, "Taking Excess, Exceeding Account: Aristotle Meets *The Merchant of Venice*," in *Money and the Age of Shakespeare: Essays in the New Economic Criticism*, ed. Linda Woodbridge (New York: Palgrave, 2003), 151.

38. This is the line with which Portia enters the trial scene (4.1.170). For an essay that questions the long-standing claim that on the Elizabethan stage there would have been a clear visual distinction between the two characters, see Emma Smith, "Was Shylock Jewish?," *Shakespeare Quarterly* 64 (2013): 188–219.

39. I give the King James version here because it articulates the point especially elegantly. Substantively, the verses in the Geneva version are the same: "Thou shalt not give to usurie to thy brother... Unto a stranger thou maiest lend upon usurie" (*The Geneva Bible: A Facsimile of the 1560 Edition*, intro. Lloyd E. Berry [Madison: University of Wisconsin Press, 1969]). In general, unless otherwise noted, I will give quotations from the Bible in the Geneva version, which was Shakespeare's Bible (see Richmond Noble, *Shakespeare's Biblical Knowledge* [New York: Macmillan, 1935]).

40. Nelson, *The Idea of Usury*, xix–xx, 4.

41. As Drakakis, following Brown, notes, this view appears in Thomas Wilson's *A discourse uppon usurye by waye of dialogue and oracions* (London: Tottell, 1572). It appears in "The Civilians or Doctours oration": "God ordeyned lending for maintenaunce of amitye, and declaration of loue, betwixt man and man" (Fo. 95^r). There is a modern reprint with an introduction by R. H. Tawney (London: G. Bell and Sons, 1925), where the quoted passage appears on pages 284–285.

42. Compare Auden, "Brothers and Others," 227.

43. Amanda Bailey, *Of Bondage: Debt, Property, and Personhood in Early Modern England* (Philadelphia: University of Pennsylvania Press, 2013), 53.

44. Brown, in his edition, has a useful note on what a "single bond" means here.

45. Antonio claims that "within two months," he expects "return / Of thrice three times the value of the bond" (1.3.153–55). This would mean that he is expecting to receive 27,000 ducats,

which would seem to be an immense amount, given that the 3,000 ducats of the loan is presented as a considerable sum.

46. See "It is no sin to deceive a Christian, / For they themselves do hold it a principle, / Faith is not to be held with heretics" (Christopher Marlowe, *The Jew of Malta*, ed. Stephen J. Lynch [Indianapolis: Hackett, 2009], 2.3.314–16).

47. It may be thought that in bringing up food (in "Fed with the same food") Shylock is undermining the picture of human solidarity, since the play is strongly aware of the kosher prohibition of pork. I do not think that this objection is valid. Mostly, even with kosher rules in place, Jews and other humans are "fed with the same food." Even those who keep kosher would not deny that they *could be* fed with the forbidden foods. A further thought along these lines has been raised with regard to "If you prick us do we not bleed." This has been seen to conjure the image of the bleeding male organ, and therefore connected to circumcision and to the bizarre myth of the menstruation of Jewish men (for the latter, see David Katz, "Shylock's Gender: Jewish Male Menstruation in Early Modern England," *RES* 50 [1999]: 440–62). I do not think the genital reference is at work in the speech either.

48. For a similar thought, see Terry Eagleton, *William Shakespeare* (New York: Blackwell, 1986), 42–43.

49. See Muldrew, *The Economy of Obligation*, on extensions, 174ff.

50. On the function and meaning of "my humour" here, see the Appendix to this chapter ("Say it is my humour").

51. This too is developed further in the Appendix.

52. Interestingly, George Granville's adaptation, *The Jew of Venice* (1701), which retains much of Shylock's part, omits the cat and the bagpipe, and keeps only the to-be-expensively-baned rat, moving directly from "To have it ban'd" to "What, are you answer'd yet?" (4.1.31–32). Granville also omits the whole narrative of Laban's sheep, merely having Shylock say, "You know the story" (3.1.72). Cited from *Five Restoration Adaptations of Shakespeare*, ed. Christopher Spencer (Urbana: University of Illinois Press, 1955).

53. Brown, 105, points out that there is a similar passage in Ben Jonson's *Every Man in his Humour*, where a character is said to be unable to "hold his water at reading of a ballad . . . a rime to him is worse then cheese, or a bagpipe." This suggests to Gail Kern Paster that "an inability to hear bagpipe music without an involuntary physical reaction may be conventional" (*Humoring the Body: Emotions and the Shakespearean Stage* [Chicago: University of Chicago Press, 2004], 206 n. 29). But Drakakis (355) points out that the lines appear only in the Folio edition of Jonson's play (1616) and not in the Quarto of 1598, which suggests that Jonson borrowed the image from this passage in Shakespeare.

54. Kenneth Gross has insisted on the importance of keeping to the Q1 and Folio version of line 57 ("As to offend himself being offended") and not, as many modern editors do, following Q2 in putting a comma after "offend." The Q1 / F version, as Gross notes, makes the element of self-offense more salient (*Shylock Is Shakespeare* [Chicago: University of Chicago Press, 2006], 69). Drakakis resists the comma.

55. Gross, *Shylock Is Shakespeare*, sees the speech as some kind of strategy, likening it to "the kind of parabolic acts of self-degradation characteristic of Old Testament prophets" (73). For discussion of another way of reading the speech as strategic (Gail Paster's), see the Appendix ("Say it is my humour").

56. For Iago's soliloquies as manifesting "the motive-hunting of motiveless malignity," see *Coleridge's Criticism of Shakespeare, A Selection*, ed. R. A. Foakes (Detroit: Wayne State University Press,1989), 113.

57. For Aristotle on proper pride ("high-mindedness," *megalopsychia*), see *NE* 1122a18–1123a33. The "high-minded" person "will show his stature in his relations with men of eminence and fortune, but will be unassuming toward those of moderate means" (1124b18–20).

58. On the social complexity and possible attractiveness of this position, see the chapter "Honest in *Othello*," in William Empson, *The Structure of Complex Words* (London: Chatto and Windus, 1964), 218–49.

59. See *Machiavelli's The Prince: A Bilingual Edition*, trans. and ed. Mark Musa (New York: St. Martin's Press, 1964), 82, 94.

60. For the Quarto, I have used *Shakespeare's Plays in Quarto: A Facsimile Edition of Copies Primarily from the Henry E. Huntington Library*, ed. Michael J. B. Allen and Kenneth Muir (Berkeley: University of California Press, 1981), *The Tragedy of Othello the Moore of Venice*, B2^r.

61. *The New Oxford Annotated Bible*, ed. Michael D. Coogan (Oxford: Oxford University Press, 2010) asserts that since the repeated word derives from a root meaning "to be," God's name "has a verbal rather than a noun form" (87). In *The English Bible, King James Version*, vol. 1, *The Old Testament*, ed. Herbert Marks (Norton Critical Edition; New York: Norton, 2012), Marks opines that a more accurate translation would be "I will be what I will be," but explains that "the KJV (via the Vulgate) reflects the early Greek translation, 'I am being'—an essentialist rather than a dynamic reading, which encouraged metaphysical definitions of God while abetting the efforts of early polemicists to demonstrate Plato's debt to the Bible" (117).

62. See *Paradise Lost*, 1.98 ("injur'd merit"), and 5.665 ("thought himself impair'd"). There may or may not be a slight difference between these two accounts, depending on whether there is a difference between "injur'd" and "impair'd." The latter may suggest a more existential condition. *Paradise Lost* is cited from *John Milton: Complete Poems and Major Prose*, ed. Merritt Y. Hughes (New York: Odyssey Press, 1957). Milton's knowledge of and admiration for Shakespeare are well known.

63. For the seriousness and consistency of Milton's commitment to classical ethics throughout his career, see Richard Strier, "Milton Against Humility," in *The Unrepentant Renaissance: From Petrarch to Shakespeare to Milton* (Chicago: University of Chicago Press, 2011), 248–83.

64. Saint Augustine, *The Enchiridion*, trans. J. F. Shaw, in St. Augustine, *On the Holy Trinity, Doctrinal Treatises, Moral Treatises*, Library of the Nicene and Post-Nicene Fathers, ed. Philip D. Schaff (Grand Rapids: Eerdmans, 1980), 240b.

65. A. O. Lovejoy, "Milton and the Paradox of the Fortunate Fall" (1937), rpt. in *Essays in the History of Ideas* (1948; New York: Capricorn Books, 1960), 277–95.

66. See A. O. Lovejoy, *The Great Chain of Being: A Study of the History of an Idea* (1936; New York: Harper, 1960), 61–80. Plotinus is the key formulator.

67. Plotinus repeatedly insists that the outflowingness of goodness is not a matter of deliberation. See *The Enneads*, trans. Stephen MacKenna, abr. John Dillon (London: Penguin, 1991), 138, 267, 354, 388–89. For the negative portrayal of deliberation as a model, see 295.

68. On the meaning of "free" in the description of Desdemona, see Richard Strier, "Freedom," in *Shakespeare and Virtue: A Handbook*, ed. Julia Reinhard Lupton and Donovan Sherman (forthcoming from Cambridge University Press, 2022).

69. See *Enneads*, 388. For the Platonic sources, see *Phaedrus* 247a, 253a-b, and especially *Timaeus* 29e (with "jealousy" as the translation), in *The Collected Dialogues of Plato*, ed. Edith Hamilton and Harrington Cairns (Princeton, N.J.: Bollingen, 1961), 494, 499, 1162.

70. Eliot distinguishes tough-mindedness from cynicism; see T. S. Eliot, "Andrew Marvell," in *Selected Essays of T. S. Eliot*, new ed. (New York: Harcourt Brace, 1950), 262.

71. See *The Ontological Argument: From St. Anselm to Contemporary Philosophers*, ed. Alvin Plantinga (New York: Doubleday Anchor, 1965).

72. On being a member of Christ's body, which is the church, in the Pauline epistles, see especially 1 Corinthians 12:12–27.

73. The overtly racist language in the play is given to Iago and his dupe-companion, Roderigo. Brabantio certainly considers Othello unfit for Desdemona, but his revulsion seems at least as much class- as race-bound.

74. Whether this fantasy has an erotic component—or, rather, what sort of erotic component it has—depends somewhat on what exactly "clyster-pipes" are. They are certainly lower-body connected, and the image of kissing them is meant to be disgusting, but the editors differ on whether the function of such "pipes" is anal or vaginal. Honigmann's note lists both possibilities. The *OED* lists only the anal, so that a "clyster-pipe" is a device for administering enemas.

75. On Iago as homilist, see Richard Mallette, "Blasphemous Preacher: Iago and the Reformation," in *Shakespeare and the Culture of Christianity in Early Modern England*, ed. Dennis Taylor and David N. Beauregard (New York: Fordham University Press, 2003), 382–414.

76. Catullus's lyrics 5 and 6 are probably the most famous "kiss poems" in what became a tradition; hiding from the eyes of others was crucial. See Alex Wong, *The Poetry of Kissing in Early Modern Europe: From the Catullan Revival to Secundus, Shakespeare and the English Cavaliers* (Cambridge: D. S. Brewer, 2017).

77. One might think that Richard III revels in his ugliness, but he revels in it insofar as it leads him to concentrate on what is truly important: power. When, in *All's Well That Ends Well*, Parolles is forced to give up his false self, he does not assert that he will go on as nothing but rather as the something ("the thing") that he is (4.3.323–24).

78. This is the suggestion that Honigmann (297) takes from Marvin Rosenberg, *The Masks of Othello* (Berkeley: University of California Press, 1961), 174–75.

79. The Third Decade, Story 7 from Giraldi Cinthio, *Gli Hecatommithi* (1567), trans. Geoffrey Bullough, in *Narrative and Dramatic Sources of Shakespeare*, ed. Geoffrey Bullough (New York: Columbia University Press, 1978), 7:252.

80. For more on this, see "Shakespeare and Skepticism (1): Religion."

81. On the relation between self-knowledge and knowledge of others, see "Shakespeare and Skepticism (2): Epistemology."

APPENDIX

1. I have commented on the overlap between "Old Historicism" (Tillyard's *The Elizabethan World Picture* and similar works) and what I call the new humoralism in *The Unrepentant Renaissance: From Petrarch to Shakespeare to Milton* (Chicago: University of Chicago Press, 2011), 18–19. Both types of scholarship present something like "the" Elizabethan world-picture. I have expressed some reservations about "humoralism," in particular in an e-conversation: "Shakespeare and Embodiment," *Literature Compass* 3 (2005): 15–17.

2. Gail Kern Paster, *Humoring the Body: Emotions and the Shakespearean Stage* (Chicago: University of Chicago Press, 2004), 203, 205, 207. Further citations of this work appear parenthetically in the text.

3. For critique along these lines, see Angus Gowland, "Melancholy, Passions and Identity in the Renaissance," in *Passions and Subjectivity in Early Modern Culture*, ed. Brian Cummings and Freya Sierhuis (London: Routledge, 2013), 75–93. For a different, nonhumoral take on Shylock's "stoniness," see Michal Zechariah, "Unmoved Emotions in Shakespeare and Milton" (Ph.D. diss., University of Chicago, 2021), ch. 1.

4. Lear's question is at 3.6: Q 71–72 ("makes this hardness"); F 34–35 ("makes these hard hearts"). Kent's puzzlement is at Q 4.3.34–35 (Q only). Kent's "solution"—"It is the stars, / The stars above govern our conditions"—is not an answer to this puzzle but a continuation of it. For the texts of *Lear*, I have used René Weis, *King Lear: A Parallel Text Edition* (London: Longman, 1993).

5. In 1579, "certain godly learned men" translated and published Martin Luther's *Commentary on Saint Paul's Epistle to the Galatians*. The "Argument of the Epistle" explains that "Like as the earth engendereth not rain, nor is able by her own strength, labour, and travail to procure the same, but receiveth it of the mere gift of God from above; so this heavenly righteousness is given us of God without our works or deservings" (Grand Rapids: Baker Book House, 1979), xxv. This text had a wide circulation in England. See Gordon Rupp, "Luther in England," in *The Righteousness of God: Luther Studies* (London: Hodder and Stoughton, 1953), 37–55. Carl Trueman and Carrie Euler note that the commentary on Galatians was "the most popular of all the Tudor translations of Luther" ("The Reception of Martin Luther in Sixteenth- and Seventeenth-Century England," in *The Reception of the Continental Reformation in Britain*, ed. Polly Ha and Patrick Collinson [Oxford: Oxford University Press, 2010], 63–82 [69]).

6. Richard A. Posner, *Law and Literature*, 3rd ed. (Cambridge, Mass., 2009), 236.

7. Paul Cefalu in *Revisionist Shakespeare: Transitional Ideologies in Texts and Context* (New York: Palgrave Macmillan, 2004) also sees Shylock as a "subjectivist on value" (96) but sees him as echoing Jean Buridan (1300–1358), who saw economic value as determined by desire and by willingness to pay (97).

8. Q1 has "Maisters of passion"; F and Q2 have "Masters of." Brown (Arden 2) prints "Master of" (106); Drakakis (Arden 3) has "Maistrice of." Drakakis's defense of this fanciful reading is that a gender ambiguity is intended (336).

9. For Aquinas, affections and passions are both movements of the soul, but passions are movements of the sensitive soul, whereas affections are movements of the intellective soul. As Nicholas Lombardo puts it, for Aquinas, "Unlike passion, affection does not necessarily imply either corporeality or passivity" (*The Logic of Desire: Aquinas on Emotion* [Washington, D.C.: Catholic University of America Press, 2011], 75). A clarifying essay is John Dryden, "Passions, Affections, and Emotions: Methodological Difficulties in Reconstructing Aquinas's Philosophical Psychology," *Literature Compass* 13:6 (2016): 343–50. See also Susan James, *Passion and Action: The Emotions in Seventeenth-Century Philosophy* (Oxford: Clarendon Press, 1997), 60–61. Russ Leo argues that Spinoza developed a precise distinction "between *affectus* and *passio*" ("Affective Physics: *Affectus* in Spinoza's *Ethics*," in Cummings and Sierhuis, *Passions and Subjectivity*, 33–49).

10. Shame is wonderfully treated in Paster's *The Body Embarrassed: Drama and the Disciplines of Shame in Early Modern England* (Ithaca, N.Y.: Cornell University Press, 1993).

11. See note 55 in "Excuses, Bepissing, and Non-Being."

CHAPTER 2

1. On Lear's "initial apportionment," see Richard Strier, *Resistant Structures: Particularity, Radicalism, and Renaissance Texts* (Berkeley: University of California Press, 1995), 178–80.

2. For Iago's assessment, see *Othello*, ed. E. A. J. Honigmann (Walton-on Thames: Nelson and Sons, 1997), 2.1.288–89. For the view that the marriage was internally doomed, see, inter alia, Edward A. Snow, "Sexual Anxiety and the Male Order of Things in *Othello*," *ELR* 10 (1980): 384–412.

3. "Hamlet and Lear are gay / Gaiety transfiguring all that dread." "Lapis Lazuli," lines 16–17, in *The Collected Poems of W. B. Yeats* (New York: Macmillan, 1956), 291.

4. I should say at the outset that my essay has little in common with Richard Chamberlain, "What's Happiness in *Hamlet*?," in *The Renaissance of Emotion: Understanding Affect in Shakespeare and His Contemporaries*, ed. Richard Meek and Erin Sullivan (Manchester: Manchester University Press, 2015), 153–74. Chamberlain's essay is an Adornian attempt at discerning the (possible) dialectical positivity of *unhappiness* in the play. For a general discussion of Shakespeare's conception(s) of happiness (without reference to Hamlet), see my essay on the topic in *Shakespeare and Emotion*, ed. Katharine A. Craik (Cambridge: Cambridge University Press, 2020), 275–87.

5. See *Hamlet*, ed. Harold Jenkins (London: Methuen, 1982), 2.2.5 for Hamlet's "transformation"; for Ophelia's characterization, 3.1.153. I will cite the play from this edition (hereafter "Jenkins"), though since the Jenkins edition is a conflated one, I will note when a passage appears only in the second Quarto (Q2) or the Folio (F). For Q2, I have used *Hamlet*, ed. Ann Thompson and Neil Taylor (London: Thomson Learning, 2006). For F (and the first Quarto [Q1]), I have used the companion volume of Thompson and Taylor, *Hamlet: The Texts of 1603 and 1623*.

6. See Rhodri Lewis, *Hamlet and the Vision of Darkness* (Princeton, N.J.: Princeton University Press, 2017).

7. Ellen MacKay has suggested to me that to see *Hamlet* in this way links it to one of Shakespeare's earlier tragedies, *Romeo and Juliet* (1595?). For "Golden lads and girls all must . . . come to dust," see *Cymbeline* 4.2.262–63.

8. Julia Lupton, *Thinking with Shakespeare: Essays on Politics and Life* (Chicago: University of Chicago Press, 2011), 69–96 (81).

9. Lupton, *Thinking with Shakespeare*, 86.

10. On the Elsinore setting, see András Kiséry, *Hamlet's Moment: Drama and Political Knowledge in Early Modern England* (Oxford: Oxford University Press, 2016), 90.

11. Gunnar Sjögren, "The Danish Background in *Hamlet*," *Shakespeare Studies* 4 (1968): 221–30 (223). See also Kiséry, *Hamlet's Moment*, 96–106. Belleforest set the story in Denmark, but not in Elsinore.

12. Sjögren, "The Danish Background in *Hamlet*," 224; and see Jenkins, 422–23.

13. Seth Lerer ignores the king and queen's comments about the early companionship of Rosencrantz and Guildenstern with Hamlet and mistakenly thinks that because they were at Wittenberg with him, they were "university friends" ("Hamlet's Boyhood," in *Childhood, Education and the Stage in Early Modern England*, ed. Richard Preiss and Deanne Williams [Cambridge: Cambridge University Press, 2017], 25). Horatio is Hamlet's university friend. For historical contextualization of Horatio's status as poor (see 3.2.59), as a university scholar, and as a friend of a high aristocrat, see Elizabeth Hanson, "Fellow Students: Hamlet, Horatio, and the Early Modern University," *Shakespeare Quarterly* 62 (2011): 205–29.

14. Hanson observes that Rosencrantz and Guldernstern are "tagged with the term 'gentle' or its equivalents five times in the thirty-five lines of their initial interview with Claudius and Gertrude" ("Fellow Students," 222).

15. Michael Neill, "'He that thou knowest thine': Friendship and Service in *Hamlet*," in *A Companion to Shakespeare's Works: The Tragedies*, ed. Richard Dutton and Jean E. Howard (Malden, Mass.: Blackwell, 2003), 319–38 (321–22); Christopher Warley, *Reading Class Through Shakespeare, Donne, and Milton* (Cambridge: Cambridge University Press, 2014), 47–72 (55–60).

16. I do not have a theory about why this passage (in Jenkins, 2.2.239–69a) does not appear in Q2. Jenkins mentions the possibility that the lines about Denmark being "a prison" might

have been thought to be offensive to Queen Anne (of Denmark), but he then rejects this theory (45, 467). Joshua Held has suggested to me that this passage of (relatively) lighthearted repartee shows Hamlet being even friendlier to Rosencrantz and Guildenstern in the Folio than he is in Q2. That may well be true, though I do not think that the absence of the passage in Q2 seriously affects the quality of the interaction.

17. I do not understand Hamlet's comment about being "dreadfully attended," and have not found a satisfactory gloss on it. Jenkins too seems puzzled (251).

18. With regard to Hamlet seeing Ophelia as a "willing pawn," I accept the "stage tradition," rejected by Jenkins (496–97), that Hamlet glimpses Polonius's presence when he suddenly asks Ophelia, "Where's your father?" (3.3.130–31). With regard to Hamlet's belief, at this point, in Gertrude's complicity, see his statement to her, early in the "closet" scene, that his killing of Polonius is "Almost as bad . . . As kill a king" (3.4.28–29).

19. Kent announces that he will be "unmannerly" when "Lear is mad" (1.1: Q 135–36; F 143–44). *King Lear, A Parallel Text Edition*, ed. René Weis (New York: Longman, 1993).

20. For Sir Andrew Aguecheek's claim, see *Twelfth Night*, 2.3.169. Part of the tragedy of Hamlet is that he did in fact love many of the people around him. Harold Bloom seems to me exactly wrong in asserting of Hamlet that "we have every reason to doubt his capacity to love anyone" (*"Hamlet": Poem Unlimited* [New York: Riverhead Books, 2003], 43).

21. I am afraid that I fell into this analogy myself in an earlier treatment of the two. See "Faithful Servants: Shakespeare's Praise of Disobedience," in *The Historical Renaissance: New Essays on Tudor and Stuart Literature and Culture*, ed. Heather Dubrow and Richard Strier (Chicago: University of Chicago Press, 1988), 104–33.

22. Frank Whigham, *Ambition and Privilege: The Social Tropes of Elizabethan Courtesy Theory* (Berkeley: University of California Press, 1984), 21. Empson was eloquent on the dangers of critical "high-mindedness"; see, for instance, his review ("'Mine eyes dazzle'") of Clifford Leech's 1963 book on *The Duchess of Malfi*, rpt. in William Empson, *Essays on Renaissance Literature*, ed. John Haffenden (Cambridge: Cambridge University Press, 1994), 2:110–14. It should be noted that "Neo-Christianity" is not the only form that such "high-mindedness" can take.

23. Joshua Scodel presents a fierce critique of the "sycophantic rhetoric" of Rosencrantz and Guildenstern, but has to note that "despite their sycophancy," they "do not seem especially ambitious or avaricious" ("Finding Freedom in Hamlet," *MLQ* 72 [2011]: 163–200 [177–78]).

24. Class status is very marked in this episode. Hamlet had "his father's signet in [his] purse" with which to reseal the letter (5.2.49), and he notes, at some length, the irony of having saved his life by a practice—"to write fair" (i.e., in a secretary hand)—that he had previously held to be below him ("a baseness" [5.2.32–36]). The difference between the socially high and the socially "base" is very present to Hamlet's mind here, so the line about "baser natures" is well prepared for.

25. The text (Q2 and F agree here) makes it clear that the document in question was formally sealed with the Danish royal seal and, as such things would have been, very carefully folded (5.2.50–52) to prevent inspection (see Jana Dambrogio and Daniel Starza Smith, *Dictionary of Letterlocking* [online: http://letterlocking.org]). Moreover, we know from the occasion when we have seen Claudius send a formal communication to a monarch that when he does so, he very carefully delimits the role of the bearers of the documents (1.2.33–38). Jenkins somewhat unhappily acknowledges (397) that there is no evidence in the text—despite what Hamlet seems to believe—that they knew what the commission they were carrying contained.

26. I believe that this view of the relationship is upheld by Alan Stewart, who sees the couple as essentially (though clandestinely) engaged before Polonius insists that Ophelia return Hamlet's

letters. See ch. 6, "Lovers' Lines: Letters to Ophelia," in *Shakespeare's Letters* (Oxford: Oxford University Press, 2008), 231–60.

27. On Ophelia's madness, see, inter alia, Elaine Showalter, "Representing Ophelia: Women, Madness, and the Responsibilities of Feminist Criticism," in *Shakespeare and the Question of Theory*, ed. Patricia Parker and Geoffrey Hartman (New York: Methuen, 1985), 77–94; Leslie C. Dunn, "Ophelia's Songs in *Hamlet*: Music, Madness, and the Feminine," in *Embodied Voices: Representing Female Vocality in Western Culture*, ed. Leslie C. Dunn and Nancy A. Jones (Cambridge: Cambridge University Press, 1994), 50–64; and Carol Thomas Neely, *Distracted Subjects: Madness and Gender in Shakespeare and Early Modern Culture* (Ithaca, N.Y.: Cornell University Press, 2004), 50–56.

28. James J. Marino brushes aside historical Elizabethan assumptions in favor of what he sees as theatrical ones; he argues that Ophelia's obedience to her father would have been seen (and should be seen) as a breach of theatrical conventions ("Ophelia's Desire," *ELH* 84 [2017]: 817–39 [esp. 822–24]). I am not sure.

29. Lupton, *Thinking with Shakespeare*, 87, takes some note of this.

30. Lewis, *Hamlet and the Vision of Darkness*, notes that Ophelia "has wit and learning enough to adapt a story about Hercules' decision-making," but goes on to criticize her for lack of "spirit" (123).

31. Almost every editor now asserts (with John Dover Wilson, *What Happens in "Hamlet"* [1935], 3rd ed. [Cambridge: Cambridge University Press, 1951], 134) that "nunnery" also means brothel here. If this meaning is present, it is a very Protestant joke, appropriate to a Wittenberg student, but it cannot be the primary meaning of the word in the context, where going to a nunnery is an alternative to being a "breeder" and getting married (3.1.122, 136–38). Jenkins (493–96) struggles with the issue, and warns that we must not "depose" the literal meaning (of nunnery as nunnery). Hamlet does seem to treat Ophelia as erotically corrupt insofar as she is included in his general condemnation of female erotic arts, but the "your" in "your paintings . . . your wantonness" (3.1.144–48) is generic, not particular (compare "your philosophy" at 1.5.175), and Hamlet ends the episode with another reference to a nunnery as a refuge from marriage.

32. *The Text of 1603*, ed. Thompson and Taylor, scene 6, ll. 40–41.

33. See, among many others, A. C. Bradley, *Shakespearean Tragedy*, foreword by John Bayley (London: Penguin, 1991), 138; and Jenkins's note on 4.7.125 (on Hamlet's "scruple").

34. See Jenkins's notes on 1.5.10–13 (453–54) and on 2.2.595–96 (483) on the possibility of the "thing" or "apparition" being a demon. Mark Matheson, "*Hamlet* and 'A Matter Tender and Dangerous,'" *Shakespeare Quarterly* 46 (1995): 383–39, sees the (supposed) change in Hamlet's character after his "return from the sea" as strongly and ideologically Protestant, and suggests that this "may develop out of the ideological preoccupations of the text as a whole" (391), but does not read the whole in terms of these Protestant "ideological preoccupations."

35. Quoted from Bullinger's *Decades* by Eleanor Prosser, *Hamlet and Revenge* (Stanford, Calif.: Stanford University Press, 1971), 102.

36. Stephen Greenblatt devotes a good part of a chapter to "St. Patrick's Purgatory" (*Hamlet in Purgatory* [Princeton, N.J.: Princeton University Press, 2001], 73–101), which he sees as relevant to Hamlet (233–34). Greenblatt mocks the idea that the play could be theologically coherent—that is, Protestant (239–40). Greenblatt sees Shakespeare as outwardly conforming to the Church of England while being "haunted by the spirit of his Catholic father" (249).

37. Oddly, the moment of popular rebellion in the play is treated neither in Andrew Fitzmaurice, "The Corruption of *Hamlet*," in *Shakespeare and Early Modern Political Thought*,

ed. David Armitage, Conal Condren, and Andrew Fitzmaurice (Cambridge: Cambridge University Press, 2009), 139–56, nor in Andrew Hadfield, *Shakespeare and Republicanism* (Cambridge: Cambridge University Press, 2005), ch. 6.

38. Margreta de Grazia, *"Hamlet" Without Hamlet* (Cambridge: Cambridge University Press, 2007), 159–65.

39. William Richardson (1783), quoted in de Grazia, *"Hamlet" Without Hamlet*, 161.

40. Jenkins is quite clear about this in his note on Hamlet wanting a "more horrid hent" for killing Claudius than when Claudius is (apparently) praying (513–15). Jenkins terms the tradition of refusing to take Hamlet's lines at face value "one of the most remarkable aberrations in the history of criticism" (513).

41. For classical and Renaissance sources and analogues to Polonius's precepts, see Jenkins's note (441–43), together with his warning that "it is a mistake to suppose they are meant to make him [Polonius] seem ridiculous" (443). In *Fictions of Credit in the Age of Shakespeare* (Oxford: Oxford University Press, 2021), Laura Kolb sees Polonius's speech as deeply representative of attitudes in the actual Elizabethan socioeconomic context (1–8).

42. Hamlet's lines here help make sense of Polonius's famous and famously opaque final precept concerning the relationship of "truth" to oneself and to others.

43. On aristocratic funerals, see, inter alia, David Cressy, *Birth, Marriage and Death: Ritual, Religion, and the Life-Cycle in Tudor and Stuart England* (Oxford: Oxford University Press, 2007), ch. 19, and Mervyn James, *Society, Politics and Culture: Studies in Early Modern England* (Cambridge: Cambridge University Press, 1986), ch. 5.

44. On the suicide issue, see Roland Mushat Frye, *The Renaissance "Hamlet": Issues and Responses in 1600* (Princeton, N.J.: Princeton University Press, 1984), 297–309, and Michael MacDonald, "Ophelia's Maimèd Rites," *Shakespeare Quarterly* 37 (1986): 309–17. MacDonald makes it clear that court records suggest, as the play itself does, that we should perhaps not be as confident as Frye is in asserting that an Elizabethan audience would have seen Ophelia's abbreviated rites as improper. The designation of the officiating figure differs in the early texts. He is "Priest" in F and Q1, but "Doct." (Doctor) in Q2. This may or may not be significant ("Doct." would perhaps make the figure more strongly Protestant). In any case, Laertes addresses him as a "churlish priest" (5.1.233). For that reason, Jenkins, who mainly follows Q2 (75), follows F here, and uses "Priest." For a defense of the Q2 reading, and the argument that this means the figure is Protestant, see Dover Wilson, *What Happens in "Hamlet,"* 69.

45. Frye, *The Renaissance "Hamlet,"* 309.

46. Frye, *The Renaissance "Hamlet,"* 245–49.

47. In the equivalent scene in Q1, Corambis also adds to Montano, "And bid him ply his learning" (scene 6, line 3).

48. Frye, *The Renaissance "Hamlet,"* 82–87; and see note 43 above.

49. De Grazia's attempt to use this passage to date the setting of the play to the eleventh century (*"Hamlet" Without Hamlet*, 64) is unconvincing, especially when it is recognized that what she sees as the major proof of this dating, the mention of the tribute that England owes the Danes (3.1.172), has a late Elizabethan relevance, which is made clear by Jenkins in his note on this line, and in the text to which Jenkins refers. See *Russia at the Close of the 16th Century. Comprising the treatise of "Of the Russe Commonwealth," by Dr. Giles Fletcher; and the travels of Sir Jerome Horsey, Knt, now for the first time printed entire from his own ms*, by Edward Bond (Hakluyt Society no. 20; London: Hakluyt Society, 1856), 239–42. This document also contains reference to Normandy.

50. Jenkins's note on the line makes the somewhat ambiguous status of fencing clear (460). Claudius claims, perhaps sincerely, to consider Laertes's skill at fencing one of the "unworthiest" of his fine "parts" (4.7.75).

51. On the fashionableness and complexity of the rapier in the period of *Hamlet*, see Sheldon Zitner, "Hamlet, Duellist," *University of Toronto Quarterly* 39 (1969): 1–18.

52. The praise of Laertes for aristocratic excellence is especially emphasized in Q2. The passage in which Claudius tells Laertes how Laertes has been praised (and how Hamlet reacted to this) and "the card or calendar of gentry" line are unique to Q2 (4.7.67–80; 5.2.106–34), as is Hamlet's meditation on Fortinbras and his military venture (4.4.32–66).

53. The only explanation that I can see for "envenom" is that it represents Claudius's inability to see aristocratic emulation as something positive.

54. Hamlet's deep interest in dueling, and apparent skill at it, can be seen as some justification for Ophelia thinking of him, in the past, as a "soldier" as well as a courtier and scholar. It also suggests, to get ahead of myself, that Fortinbras might be right about how Hamlet would have done "had he been put on." In this context, Paul A. Cantor speaks of Hamlet's "spiritedness" (*Shakespeare: Hamlet* [Cambridge: Cambridge University Press, 1989], 38–39).

55. On the functioning of the word "wrong" in this speech, see "Excuses, Bepissing, and Non-Being," where the speech is philosophically examined.

56. In "Ophelia's Maimèd Rites" MacDonald explains the difference between the verdicts of *felo de se* and *non compos mentis*.

57. The kinship of this image with Bassanio's story of his boyhood behavior with arrows confirms the aristocratic nature of the activity alluded to (on Bassanio's story, see "Excuses, Bepissing, and Non-Being," above, 22–23). The activity also seems to be connected to some notion of "innocence" (see *The Merchant of Venice*, 1.1.145).

58. Nicholas Bellinson has suggested to me that I have shown that Hamlet was always looking for "brothers." This leads me to take note of his status as an only child.

59. Many, perhaps most, editors do take Hamlet as disingenuous and Laertes as hypocritical (see the Thompson and Taylor Q2, for instance [450]). Jenkins (568) suggests a more complex view. Scodel sees Hamlet as "recalling the New Testament treatment of fellow Christians as 'brother,'" while seeing Laertes's response as mere "pretense" ("Finding Freedom," 196, 197).

60. Scene 17, line 100. The name is spelled Leartes throughout Q1. That text also, interestingly, has Hamlet dissuade Horatio from joining him in death not on the basis, as both Q2 and F have it, of generalized human feeling—"As th' art a man" (5.2.347)—but on the basis of love: "Upon my love, I charge thee let it go" (scene 17, line 105).

61. Bradley, *Shakespearean Tragedy*, 377.

62. In "Damnèd Custom . . . Habit's Devil: Hamlet's Part-Whole Fallacy and the Early Modern Philosophy of Mind," *Revisionist Shakespeare: Transitional Ideologies in Texts and Context* (New York: Palgrave Macmillan 2004], Paul Cefalu recognizes "the force of 'alone'" (149).

63. The word "trappings" might itself need further exploring. The *OED* only lists derogatory meanings, but I wonder whether a more neutral meaning was also available in the period. When Feste, in *Twelfth Night*, describes himself and Fabian and other members of the household as some of Olivia's "trappings," he is suggesting that despite their minor status, they are connected to her in a genuine way, not that they are unnecessary or worthless (5.1.8).

64. Frye, *The Renaissance "Hamlet,"* 97–100.

65. The speech here is quite opaque, but I believe that I have captured part of its meaning.

66. Frye, *The Renaissance "Hamlet,"* 94.

67. Baldesar Castiglione, *The Book of the Courtier*, trans. Charles S. Singleton (Garden City, N.Y.: Anchor, 1959), 122, 115.

68. *As You Like It*, 3.1.366–69.

69. Compare also the famous Lothian portrait of young John Donne. This portrait is widely reproduced, often on the cover of editions of Donne's poetry. For commentary, see John Donne, *The Elegies and the Songs and Sonnets*, ed. Helen Gardner (Oxford: Clarendon Press, 1965), 266–70 (the portrait is reproduced facing page 29), and Nick Davis, "Melancholic Individuality and the Lothian Portrait of Donne," *ANQ* 26 (2013): 5–12.

70. Frye, *The Renaissance "Hamlet,"* 214–20.

71. See the jacket of this book. Hals was almost certainly not aware of Shakespeare's play.

72. See Barbara Everett, *Young Hamlet: Essays on Shakespeare's Tragedies* (Oxford: Clarendon Press, 1989), 18.

73. Q1 scene 7, line 239. As I have already suggested (see note 13 above), the fact that the two were at Wittenberg with Hamlet does not imply that they only met him there.

74. On English actors performing at Elsinore in the 1580s and 1590s, see Sjögren, "The Danish Background in *Hamlet*," 227–28.

75. Lerer connects this to Hamlet's rhetorical and humanist education, and makes an interesting comparison with the young Saint Augustine ("Hamlet's Boyhood," 18–19).

76. For the consistency of Hamlet's aesthetic views, see Bradley's "Note" on the Player's Speech (*Shakespearean Tragedy*, 380–86). On the sources of and allusions in the speech begun by Hamlet and continued by the First Player, see Erica Sheen, "'These are the only men': Seneca and Monopoly in *Hamlet* 2.2," in *Shakespeare and the Classics*, ed. Charles Martindale and A. B. Taylor (Cambridge: Cambridge U Press, 2004), and Jonathan Bate, *How the Classics Made Shakespeare* (Princeton, N.Y.: Princeton University Press, 2019), ch. 8 ("Pyrrhus's Pause").

77. Sir Philip Sidney, *An Apology for Poetry or The Defence of Poetry*, ed. Geoffrey Shepherd (London: Thomas Nelson, 1965), 118. John Leonard has pointed out to me that Sidney's tyrant weeps but does not proclaim his malefactions. The proclaiming is Hamlet's addition, putting the element of public acknowledgment into the fantasy. Shakespeare probably knew that, as Jenkins points out (481), Plutarch specifies that it was a performance of Euripides's *The Trojan Women* that Alexander Pheraeus was watching, so the lines on Hecuba's grief in the Player's Speech would provide an immediate basis for having the story arise in Hamlet's mind at this point.

78. Right after telling the story of the tyrant being moved to tears by a well-made tragedy ("the very cunning of the scene"), Sidney immediately notes that it had no further effect on the tyrant's behavior. Sidney professes to believe that this is because Alexander did not sit through the whole play, but the claim is very lightly made.

79. I say "apparent success" because, as many critics have noted, when Hamlet substitutes "nephew" for "brother" in introducing the murderer of "Gonzago" (3.2.239), Claudius may well have taken this as his nephew (Hamlet) threatening him (see Dover Wilson, *What Happens in "Hamlet,"* 168–73). It turns out, however, that, in an important sense, "The Mousetrap" did work. Although Claudius neither wept nor (publicly) proclaimed his malefactions, the king's conscience was indeed "caught" by the play. The problem is that Hamlet could not know this. For a recent meditation on this problem, see Amir Khan, *Shakespeare in Hindsight: Counterfactual Thinking and Shakespearean Tragedy* (Edinburgh: Edinburgh University Press, 2016), ch. 2. Hamlet leaps to a conclusion that happens to be true. In philosophical terms, one would say that he only has a true belief where he thinks he has knowledge. The status of "the thing" remains unclear. While I agree with Ellen MacKay that there is a problem with Hamlet's reasoning here,

I do not agree that the whole episode is a deconstruction of the idea of theater affecting the conscience of a murderer (or that Hamlet himself was the one who shed tears for Hecuba) (*Persecution, Plague and Fire: Fugitive Histories of the Stage in Early Modern England* [Chicago: University of Chicago Press, 2011], 53–61).

80. Kiséry, *Hamlet's Moment*, 93.

81. I cannot explain the contradiction between the dramatization of Hamlet getting the idea here and the fact that he already had the idea and explained it to the players before the soliloquy began (2.2.531–36).

82. Bernard McElroy, *Shakespeare's Mature Tragedies* (Princeton, N.J.: Princeton University Press, 1973), 42; Bradley, *Shakespearean Tragedy*, 146–47. See also Everett, *Young Hamlet*, 24–25, and Harold Bloom, *Shakespeare: The Invention of the Human* (New York: Riverhead Books, 1998), 409. Bloom's insistence on a significant relation between Hamlet and the Falstaff of *Henry IV, Part 1* seems to me worth pondering.

83. Lupton, *Thinking with Shakespeare*, 94.

84. See *OED* "stomach," n. 8a: "spirit, courage, valour"; this shades into 8b: "pride, haughtiness." For a use of the term in the positive sense (equivalent, I believe, to *thymos* in ancient Greek), see Elizabeth I's famous speech to the troops at Tilbury in August 1588, where the queen said that though she had the body of "a weak and feeble woman," she had "the heart and stomach of a king." See *Elizabeth I: Collected Works*, ed. Leah S. Marcus, Janel Mueller, and Mary Beth Rose (Chicago: University of Chicago Press, 2000), 326.

85. For a recent essay that does see Hamlet's scholarly attributes as disqualifying him from a life of action and government, see Aysha Pollnitz, "Educating Hamlet and Prince Hal," in Armitage, Condren, and Fitzmaurice, *Shakespeare and Early Modern Political Thought*, 119–38. For the place of honor in the culture, see James, "English Politics and the Concept of Honour, 1485–1642," and the essay on the Essex revolt, chs. 8 and 9, in *Society, Politics and Culture*. For Hamlet's "spiritedness," see note 54 above.

CHAPTER 3

1. For Cavell on *Lear*, see "The Avoidance of Love: A Reading of *King Lear*," which first appeared in *Must We Mean What We Say? A Book of Essays* (New York: Scribner's, 1969), 269–353, and then in *Disowning Knowledge in Six Plays of Shakespeare* (New York: Cambridge University Press, 1987), 39–124, and then in *Disowning Knowledge in Seven Plays of Shakespeare* (New York: Cambridge University Press, 2003). I will cite this essay parenthetically by page number in *Disowning Knowledge* (hereafter *DK*; page numeration is identical in both editions of *DK*). For Berger on *Lear*, see Harry Berger Jr., *Making Trifles of Terrors: Redistributing Complicities in Shakespeare*, ed. and intro. Peter Erickson (Stanford, Calif.: Stanford University Press, 1997), chs. 3, 4, 13. I will cite this book parenthetically in the text.

2. See, for instance, Richard C. McCoy, "'Look upon me, Sir': Relationships in *King Lear*," *Representations* 81 (2003): 46–60. On a single page, "Stanley Cavell points out" and "Harry Berger points out" (49).

3. See, for instance, Colin McGinn, *Shakespeare's Philosophy: Discovering the Meaning Behind the Plays* (New York: HarperCollins, 2006).

4. Attempts like that of Reed Way Dasenbrock and a few others (Christopher Norris, Paisley Livingston, David Gorman) to interest literary scholars in what our colleagues in analytic

philosophy would consider disciplinarily normal or exemplary for them have not been notably successful. Despite *Literary Theory After Davidson*, ed. Reed Way Dasenbrock (University Park: University of Pennsylvania Press, 1993), Donald Davidson remains virtually unknown to literary scholars. In the world of Shakespeare studies, Lars Engle is unusual in making use of some analytic philosophy other than that of Cavell (and through him, Wittgenstein), especially Bernard Williams and Richard Rorty (see *Shakespearean Pragmatism: Market of His Time* [Chicago: University of Chicago Press, 1993]). Paul Cefalu makes use of the work of John Rawls and other analytic philosophers in *Revisionist Shakespeare: Transitional Ideologies in Texts and Contexts* (New York: Palgrave Macmillan, 2004). Speech-act theory has made some impact on Shakespeare criticism (see, for instance, Stanley Fish's essay on *Coriolanus* in *Is There a Text in This Class?* [Cambridge, Mass.: Harvard University Press, 1980], 197–245; Lynn Magnussen, *Shakespeare and Social Dialogue* [Cambridge: Cambridge University Press, 1999]; and David Schalkwyck, *Speech and Performance in Shakespeare's Sonnets and Plays* [Cambridge: Cambridge University Press, 2002]), but most of the work of twentieth-century Anglo-American philosophy has remained untapped by Shakespeareans and literary critics in general.

5. For Cavell doing philosophical writing that recognizably conforms (more or less) to the mode of American analytic philosophy, see the first three parts of *The Claim of Reason: Wittgenstein, Skepticism, Morality, and Tragedy* (Oxford: Clarendon Press, 1979).

6. The key philosophical essay is "Knowing and Acknowledging," in *Must We Mean What We Say?* 238–66, but all readers of Cavell would agree with Hilary Putnam that Cavell's notion of skepticism and how to overcome it is what "connects the many different parts" of his oeuvre ("Preface: Introducing Cavell," in *Pursuits of Reason: Essays in Honor of Stanley Cavell*, ed. Ted Cohen, Paul Guyer, and Hilary Putnam [Lubbock: Texas Tech University Press, 1993], vii). The titles of two of the three works cited in note 8 include "skepticism."

7. For Cavell's thoughts on the relation of psychoanalysis to philosophy, see "Psychoanalysis and Cinema: The Melodrama of the Unknown Woman," in *Images in Our Souls: Cavell, Psychoanalysis, and Cinema*, ed. Joseph H. Smith and William Kerrigan (Baltimore: Johns Hopkins University Press, 1987), 11–43 (esp. 26–29); rpt. in *Contesting Tears: The Hollywood Melodrama of the Unknown Woman* (Chicago: University of Chicago Press, 1996), 81–114.

8. For Cavell and literary study, see Michael Fischer, *Stanley Cavell and Literary Skepticism* (Chicago: University of Chicago Press, 1989); and two collections: *Ordinary Language Criticism: Literary Thinking After Cavell and Wittgenstein*, ed. Kenneth Dauber and Walter Jost (Evanston, Ill.: Northwestern University Press, 2003); and *Stanley Cavell and Literary Studies: Consequences of Skepticism*, ed. Richard Eldridge and Bernard Rhie (New York: Continuum, 2011).

9. For Berger's status in the humanities as a whole, see *A Touch More Rare: Harry Berger, Jr., and the Arts of Interpretation*, ed. Nina Levine and David Lee Miller (New York: Fordham University Press, 2009).

10. On Iago having this quality (or a hyperbolic version of it), and its relation to cynicism, see "Excuses, Bepissing, and Non-being." Rita Felski notes "the belief that the constitutionally suspicious are smarter and more sophisticated than the rest of us" (*The Limits of Critique* [Chicago: University of Chicago Press, 2015], 51).

11. In a remarkable essay, "Harry Berger and Self-Hatred" (in *A Touch More Rare*, 23–30), Kenneth Gross speaks of Berger's "skepticism of the self and its intentions" (25).

12. See "What Did the King Know and When Did He Know It? Shakespearean Discourses and Psychoanalysis," in *Making Trifles of Terrors*, 211ff. Berger's identification with Lacan has to do with Berger's eschewing of epigenetic claims with regard to characters (claims about infantile

experience), and with Lacan's insistence on the priority of language to ontology in analyzing mental processes.

13. This is different, I would argue, from my insistence on the opacity of motives in relation to some characters in Shakespeare (see "Excuses, Bepissing, and Non-Being: Shakespearean Puzzles About Agency").

14. See Sarah Beckwith, *Shakespeare and the Grammar of Forgiveness* (Ithaca, N.Y.: Cornell University Press, 2011), 186 n. 5. Cavell's influence is, as Beckwith says, "all-pervasive" in her book (x).

15. In his essay "Reading Harry Berger" (*Shakespeare Studies* 27 [1999]: 65–73), Cavell sees the "conjunction of interests" (65) between Berger's Shakespeare criticism and his own as consisting in their shared return to "a modified character-and-action" (Bradleyan) approach (Cavell, 67, quoting Berger, *Making Trifles of Terrors*, 25). Where they differ, for Cavell—aside from a dispute about shame vs. guilt (with Berger on the guilt side)—has to do with their attitudes toward the actual words said by characters (73).

16. This sentence echoes the title and to some extent the argument of "Must We Mean What We Say?," the essay that opens Cavell's first book and provides its title.

17. This points to where Cavell sees his own way of reading as different from that of Berger (see note 15).

18. Paul J. Alpers, "*King Lear* and the Theory of the 'Sight Pattern,'" in *In Defense of Reading: A Reader's Approach to Literary Criticism*, ed. Reuben A. Brower and Richard Poirier (New York: Dutton, 1963), 133–52. Citations of this work appear parenthetically in the text.

19. See Robert B. Heilman, *This Great Stage: Image and Structure in "King Lear"* (Baton Rouge: Louisiana State University Press, 1948), ch. 2 ("I Stumbled When I Saw").

20. Alpers himself falls into symbolizing (the storm, 140), into moralizing (re Lear, 149), into condescension (re Gloucester, 145), and into an occasional neat paradox (150). This shows the surprising difficulty of hewing to the literal in criticism and of avoiding moralism.

21. Nicholas Luke, in "Avoidance as Love: Evading Cavell on Dover Cliff," *Modern Philology* 117 (2020): 445–69, also criticizes Cavell's reading of the play, but his grounds for doing so are almost the opposite of mine. His essay responds to an earlier version of mine. In general, Luke finds Cavell too literal (458 n. 46). The reading Luke proposes is close to Heilman's: "We have to lose our sight, to become nothing, if we are truly to see" (457). Like Heilman, Luke is "reminded of Christianity's characteristic paradoxes" (463). Further, Luke seems to take "ordinary language" in the phrase "ordinary language philosophy" to mean something like language used to express the most ordinary (meaning "low") thoughts (463, 466). For Cavell's strictures against such an understanding of the phrase, see *DK*, 42–43.

22. All citations of the play are to *King Lear: A Parallel Text Edition*, ed. René Weis (London: Longman, 1993), which I prefer to the second edition (2010). When the line or lines in question appear in both versions of the play, but are numbered differently, I will give the Quarto (Q) first, and the Folio (F) line numbers from this edition (if no versions are indicated, the text and numeration are the same or vary by only a line). Significant differences between the Quarto and Folio texts will be noted.

23. This could be seen as a deeply Wittgensteinian point. That there need not be a common denominator to define a category is the argument of sections 64–91 of the *Investigations* (Ludwig Wittgenstein, *Philosophical Investigations*, trans. G. E. M. Anscombe [New York: Macmillan, 1953], 31e–43e). Cavell posits a common denominator in the references to eyes in the play.

24. See, inter alia, John Lascaratos and S. Marketos, "The Penalty of Blinding During Byzantine Times," *Documenta Ophthalmologica* 81 (1992): 133–44; Michael Evans, *Royal Deaths in Medieval England* (London: Palgrave, 2003), 36–37, 89–90. Edward Wheatley in *Stumbling*

Blocks Before the Blind (Ann Arbor: University of Michigan Press, 2010) points out that, in contrast with France, the punishment was rare in England after the thirteenth century, and regarded as particularly horrible and barbaric (ch. 2; esp. 42, 62).

25. This is somewhat more emphatic in the Folio. Early in the scene, Q has "villain Gloucester" where F has "traitor" (3.7.3), and at one point F has "treacherous villain" where Q has only "villain" (84). But in both texts, Gloucester is called "traitorous" in Cornwall's second speech (21), and both texts use the term throughout the scene (26, 30, 35).

26. For the importance to the play of all the ports being barred to Edgar, see *"King Lear* and Human Needs."

27. Cavell takes it as a premise that "recognizing a person depends upon allowing oneself to be recognized by him" (*DK*, 50). As far as I can see, he takes this to be either intuitively obvious or obvious upon reflection. I cannot see that an argument is given for it. That there is an ethical relationship between recognizing and being recognized does seem intuitively obvious; that there is a mutually constitutive relationship between them does not seem to me to be so. And I am not sure that Shakespeare believed this. To recognize others without allowing them to recognize you is a characteristic of one of Shakespeare's morally complex characters, Prince Hal (on Hal's "I know you all," see "Shakespeare and Legal Systems") and of his most developed villain, Iago. It is this that leads Stephen Greenblatt to give Iago's mode the chilling designation of "empathy" (see *Renaissance Self-Fashioning*, 224–29). Citing Iago, Martha C. Nussbaum notes the possibility that hatred "could generate knowledge of another" ("The Window: Knowledge of Other Minds in Virginia Woolf's *To the Lighthouse*," in Dauber and Jost, *Ordinary Language Criticism*, 76 n. 13).

28. Alan Macfarlane, "Illegitimacy and Illegitimates in English History," in *Bastardy and Its Comparative History*, ed. Peter Laslett, Karla Oosterveen, and Richard M. Smith (Cambridge, Mass.: Harvard University Press, 1980), 75.

29. See, inter alia, Lawrence Stone, *The Family, Sex, and Marriage in England, 1500–1800* (New York: Harper & Row, 1977), 107–13, and Ilana Krausman Ben-Amos, *Adolescence and Youth in Early Modern England* (New Haven, Conn.: Yale University Press, 1994).

30. "The Gloucester Family Romance," *Making Trifles of Terrors*, 57.

31. Edmund begins his great "Thou nature art my goddess" soliloquy with resentment at the legal significance of birth order (1.2.2b–6a). The "curiosity of nations" insists on this (compare the comment on "the courtesy of nations" by another younger son, Orlando in *As You Like It* [1.1.43–4]). But Edmund does come to focus on his status as a bastard (1.2.6b 15a). This is a choice, and it is one that he explains. He taps into an existing (semi-comic) mythology of the biological superiority of bastards due to their being begotten through better, livelier sex. One of Donne's early "Problems" is "Why have Bastards best Fortune?" Donne considers "the old naturall reason that these meetings in stolne love are most vehement, and so contribute more spirit than the easy and lawfull" (John Donne, *Paradoxes and Problems*, ed. Helen Peters [Oxford: Oxford University Press, 1980], 31). A "Paradox in Defense of Bastardy," in *The Treasury of Ancient and Modern Times* (London: W. Jaggard, 1613), 723–25, opens with the claim "that Bastards generally are begot in more heat and vigor of love . . . than most part of our legitimate children" (723).

32. Heilman, *This Great Stage*, 50.

33. Berger, *Making Trifles of Terrors*, 437 n. 16, gives a good list of the players.

34. Cavell asserts Austin's impact on him in "Notes After Austin," *Yale Review* 76 (1997): 313–22, and in many moments in *Little Did I Know: Excerpts from Memory* (Stanford, Calif.: Stanford University Press, 2010).

35. Luke in "Avoidance as Love" notes that I have raised this possibility (457 n. 44) but he is not interested in it. It is too literal a way of defusing the nonacknowledgment charge. Instead,

Luke (as his title suggests) accepts the refusal of acknowledgment picture but sees this as somehow positive, since "direct recognition can sometimes abort (true) recognition" and impede a mystical and theatrical "birth" (457).

36. In "Avoidance as Love," Luke seems to accept the suggestion that this is what Edgar is doing (460). I am not convinced by Ewan Fernie's reading of "burning shame" here as a "spiritual refining fire" (*Shame in Shakespeare* [London: Routledge, 2002], 201–2).

37. This is what Wittgenstein would call a "grammatical" point, a point about the conceptual structure of the way in which a word (in this case, "pretending") is actually used in a natural language (*Philosophical Investigations*, sections 90ff). For commentary, see, inter alia, Marie McGinn, "Grammar in the *Philosophical Investigations*," in *The Oxford Handbook of Wittgenstein*, ed. Oskari Kuusela and Marie McGinn (New York: Oxford University Press, 2011), 646–66.

38. Cavell's treatment of Cordelia includes an (as far as I know) unremarked-on and very odd moment of misogyny (or something), together with a refusal to credit the (Folio) text. Cavell is unhappy with the fact that (in F 1.1.81–82) Lear calls Cordelia "least" as well as last. Cavell states, very emphatically, that "the idea of a defiant *small* girl seems grotesque" (63; his emphasis). I have no idea why he thinks this. There is no reason to believe that Shakespeare did.

39. See Peter Erickson's introduction to Berger, *Making Trifles of Terrors*, xxvii–xxx.

40. In the prelude to his essay "Bodies and Texts" (*Representations* 17 [1987]: 144–66), Berger speaks of having to "protect" himself against his "own tendencies toward cynical reading" of, for instance, Cordelia in *King Lear* (145). I understand this need for "protection" against such, but think that the context of the remark (going to a performance of the play for such "protection") undermines it. Kenneth Gross in "Harry Berger and Self-Hatred" is aware of the issue, but claims that the work is "skeptical but never cynical" (23), and that its mode is "loving suspicion" (26). I think that the double way of reading this last phrase is not intended by Gross, but is apt. For a view of Berger's criticism similar to mine, see John D. Cox, *Seeming Knowledge: Shakespeare and Skeptical Faith* (Waco, Tex.: Baylor University Press, 2007), 26–28, 92–93.

41. There is a possible textual problem here, in "trial madam" (see the "Addenda" in *The Division of the Kingdoms: Shakespeare's Two Versions of "King Lear,"* ed. Gary Taylor and Michael Warren [Oxford: Clarendon Press, 1983], 486–88). It is odd that for all Berger's commitment to "text," he is largely uninterested in textual problems. As far as I am aware, there is only one moment (301) in *Making Trifles of Terrors* when Berger shows any awareness of the variant texts, despite a note characterizing Michael Warren's *The Complete King Lear, 1608–1623* (Berkeley: University of California Press, 1989) as "indispensable" (457 n. 23). Berger's first essay on the play in *Making Trifles* ("*King Lear*: The Lear Family Romance) came out in 1979 (*Centennial Review* 23: 348–76), before the "textual revolution" was fully visible, but after 1983, with *The Division of the Kingdoms*, the matter of the two versions was conspicuous.

42. For the Qb (corrected) as well as the Qa (uncorrected) readings and for F, see *The Parallel King Lear, 1608–1623* (part 1 of *The Complete King Lear*). For "Qa" and "Qb," see W. W. Greg, *The Variants in the First Quarto of "King Lear"* (London: Oxford University Press, 1940).

43. This is why attending a performance cannot "protect" Berger against his cynicism (see note 40). Two of the essays in *Making Trifles of Terrors* are entitled "Text Against Performance": the essay on the Gloucester family (ch. 3) and that on *Macbeth* (ch. 5).

44. For the "more assertive negations" and "darker sayings" that Berger's encounter with the "textual matrix" rather than performance allows him, see "Bodies and Texts," 145.

45. See *Narrative and Dramatic Sources of Shakespeare*, ed. Geoffrey Bullough (New York: Columbia University Press, 1978), 7:404.

46. One might think that this would make Berger a Kleinian, but his rejection of epigenetic accounts would rule this out, and he is uninterested in the other side of the Kleinian dialectic of "envy and gratitude" (see Melanie Klein, *Envy and Gratitude and Other Works, 1946–1963* [London: Hogarth Press, 1975]).

47. On salvage law and how it applies here, see the essay *"King Lear* and Human Needs," note 17.

48. When, for instance, George Herbert writes of condescension in "The Parson's Condescending," in *The Country Parson*, he is recommending the behavior, and seeing it motivated by love (*The Works of George Herbert*, ed. F. E. Hutchinson [Oxford: Clarendon Press, 1945], 283–84). A search in EEBO quickly reveals that the normal use of the word in the period is to describe either the "unexpressible condiscention of the Almighty" in the Incarnation ("Oh what condescention is here!") or good behavior reported or urged on the King or other powers. Joshua Scodel has reminded me that Adam is deeply grateful for Raphael's "friendly condescension" at the beginning and the end of book 8 of *Paradise Lost* (lines 8 and 649). See John Milton, *Complete Poems and Major Prose*, ed. Merritt Y. Hughes (New York: The Odyssey Press, 1957).

49. For an essay that focuses on this, see *"King Lear* and Human Needs."

50. As Gross beautifully puts it, making apt use of Wordsworth, "We need some kind of 'natural piety' toward such ways of speaking and the commitments they imply" ("Harry Berger and Self-Hatred," 30).

51. Putting aside the question of Edgar, neither Cavell nor Berger has anything to say about the heroism of Gloucester or the moral growth of Albany, who, in the Quarto, arrives at a magnificent denunciation of Goneril (Q 4.2.30b–35a; 36–48a) It is not surprising that "tough-minded" criticism like Berger's has no respect for these characters, but neither does high-minded criticism like Cavell's, who reserves his praise for Cordelia and France. High-minded criticism seems to generate scorn for "mixed" characters like Gloucester and Albany. Luke, in lamenting the death of Cordelia, follows Lear in asserting how much more Cordelia's life was worth than that of "rats and dogs," and then adds, "and Albanys" ("Avoidance as Love," 464). Compare the discussion of critical scorn for Rosencrantz and Guildenstern in "Happy Hamlet," and the citation there of Empson's comments on this phenomenon (note 22). In "Relation and Responsibility: A Levinasian Reading of *King Lear,*" *Modern Philology* 111 (2014): 485–509, Kent Lenhof commends the maximally exacting moral scheme of Levinas, and sees it as appropriate for *Lear*. This produces some fine (though perhaps hyperbolic) appreciation of Cordelia, but also odd moments like the discussion of Lear's "mistreatment" of Goneril and Regan (493). One knows what Lenhof means, but it seems oddly tone-deaf in the actual context of the play.

52. Samuel Johnson, "The Life of Gray," in *Lives of the English Poets*, ed. George Birkbeck Hill (Oxford: Clarendon Press, 1905), 3:441.

53. See *Philosophical Investigations*, section 109 for "bewitchment"; section 116 for "home."

54. Kenneth Dauber and Walter Jost see the work of Cavell as in some sense modeling "ordinary language criticism," though they are aware of the enormous difference between Cavell's "roundaboutness" and Wittgenstein's extreme straightforwardness (or, one might add, J. L. Austin's extreme lucidity). They see such criticism as standing against "the temptations of master formulations." See the introduction to *Ordinary Language Criticism: Literary Thinking after Cavell and Wittgenstein* (Evanston, Ill.: Northwestern University Press, 2003), xiii–xiv. Cavell seems to me to be often in the grip of a "master formulation." When Cavell's conceptual scheme and the thematic focus of a literary work (or a film) coincide, the results can be truly illuminating. This occurs, I think, when Cavell discusses the meaning of sex and marriage in *Antony and Cleopatra* [*DK*, 28–37] and in Hollywood films (see *The Pursuits of Happiness: The Hollywood*

Comedy of Remarriage [Cambridge, Mass: Harvard University Press, 1981]). The same can be said for Berger's suspicious mode. When it is textually justified, it is truly helpful, as I indicate in the discussion of *The Merchant of Venice* in "Excuses, Bepissing, and Non-Being," and in "*The Tempest* [1]: Power").

55. For further discussion, see the Introduction and "Excuses, Bepissing, and Non-Being" in this book.

CHAPTER 4

1. There is no mention of the play (hereafter *2H4*) in *The Law in Shakespeare*, ed. Constance Jordan and Karen Cunningham (New York: Palgrave MacMillan, 2007); it is mentioned in passing in the foreword to *Shakespeare and the Law*, ed. Paul Raffield and Gary Watt (Oxford: Hart Publishing, 2008), vi. Lorna Hutson comments on the play in "Not the King's Two Bodies: Reading the 'Body Politic' in Shakespeare's *Henry IV*, Parts 1 and 2," in *Rhetoric and Law in Early Modern Europe*, ed. Victoria Kahn and Lorna Hutson (New Haven, Conn.: Yale University Press, 2001), 166–98, but Hutson's essay, as its title suggests, is more concerned with countering the influence of Ernst Kantorowicz's *The King's Two Bodies* (Princeton, N.J.: Princeton University Press, 1957) than with reading *2H4*. Meredith Evans's "Rumor, the Breath of Kings, and the Body of Law in *2 Henry IV*," *Shakespeare Quarterly* 60 (2004): 1–24, is concerned with legitimation rather than law. Colin Burrow's essay (see note 11 below) comments in fine detail on parts of one set of scenes in the play. Virginia Lee Strain has argued for the centrality of legal reform in the play in "Legal Reform and *2 Henry IV*," in *The Oxford Handbook of English Law and Literature, 1500–1700*, ed. Lorna Hutson (Oxford: Oxford University Press, 2017), 277–97.

2. See Anon., *The Famous Victories of Henry the Fifth*, scene 4, in *Narrative and Dramatic Sources of Shakespeare: Later English History Plays*, ed. Geoffrey Bullough (London: Routledge and Kegan Paul, 1962), 4:309–10.

3. The play is cited from William Shakespeare, *King Henry IV Part 2*, ed. A. R. Humphreys (1966; Walton-on-Thames: Thomas Nelson and Sons, 1999).

4. There is some of this in the scene in *The Famous Victories* cited in note 2 above. In committing Hal to the Fleet in response to being given a "boxe on the eare" by Hal, the Chief Justice ("Judge") says: "in striking me in this place, you greatly abuse me, and not me onely, but also your father: whose lively person here in this place I doo represent" (310).

5. Thomas Hobbes, *Leviathan*, ed. C. B. Macpherson (New York: Penguin, 1968), ch. 16. See Henry S. Turner, "Corporate Persons, Between Law and Literature," in Hutson, *The Oxford Handbook of English Law and Literature, 1500–1700*, 467–84 (esp. 466–67) and the references there given.

6. Compare Strain, "Legal Reform and *2 Henry IV*": "The king's actual absence is essential to seeing the Chief Justice as upholding an office, as precisely not speaking for himself" (290–91).

7. See Hutson, "Not the King's Two Bodies."

8. On the title page of the sixteenth-century translation of *Utopia*, *De optimo reipulbicae statu* is translated as "the best state of a publyqye weal," but in the body of the text, "commonweal" is regularly used. On the term in England, see, inter alia, Whitney R. D. Jones, *The Tudor Commonwealth, 1529–1559* (London: Athlone, 1970), and Marku Peltonen, *Classical Humanism and Republicanism in English Political Thought, 1570–1640* (Cambridge: Cambridge University Press, 1995).

9. Compare "the judgement seat of Christ" in Romans 14:10 and 2 Corinthians 5:10.

10. This is the view of Strain in "Legal Reform and *2 Henry 4*."

11. For these scenes as providing real historical insight into the practices of late Elizabethan justices of the peace, especially in Gloucestershire, see Colin Burrow, "Reading Tudor Writing Politically: The Case of *2 Henry IV*," *Yearbook of English Studies* 38 (2008): 234–50, esp. 241ff.

12. Humphreys's note in *2H4* points to some of the scholarly attempts to identify the families and locales involved (159).

13. Aristotle, *Nicomachean Ethics*, trans. Martin Ostwald (Indianapolis: Bobbs-Merrill, 1962), 215 (1155a27).

14. See Christine M. Korsgaard, *Creating the Kingdom of Ends* (Cambridge: Cambridge University Press, 1996), 191–200; for the general orientation of Bernard Williams as relevant here, see Williams, *Moral Luck* (Cambridge: Cambridge University Press, 1996), essays 1 and 5. I am not aware that Williams ever commented directly on this passage. For further relevant philosophical work, and further references, see the introduction to the special issue on "Reasonable Partiality," *Ethical Theory and Moral Practice* 8 (2005): 1–10. See also the essays by Alan Thomas and by Theo Van Willgenburg in this issue (25–43, 45–62).

15. The term translated as "friendship" (*philia*) in the *Nicomachean Ethics*, books 8 and 9, covers the whole range of nonantagonistic relations between persons, from commercial to familial to affective relations. See John M. Cooper, "Aristotle on Friendship," in *Essays on Aristotle's Ethics*, ed. Amélie Oksenberg Rorty (Berkeley: University of California Press, 1980), 301–40.

16. E. M. Forster, *Two Cheers for Democracy* (London: Edward Arnold, 1951), 78.

17. Forster, 78.

18. See, inter alia, Shakespeare, *Henry IV Part I*, ed. A. R. Humphreys (1960; London: Routledge, 1988), xi–vviii (hereafter cited as *1H4*); and David Scott Kastan, "Killed with Hard Opinions: Oldcastle, Falstaff, and the Reformed Text of *1 Henry IV*," in *Textual Formations and Reformations*, ed. Laurie E. Maguire and Thomas L. Berger (Newark, Del.: University of Delaware Press, 1998), 211–27.

19. See, for instance, the discussion of capital punishment for robbery in the first book of *Utopia* and the notes thereon in *Utopia*, ed. Edward Surtz, S.J., and J. H. Hexter (New Haven, Conn.: Yale University Press, 1965). Anne Askew seems to have held that capital punishment was un-Christian. In *The lattre examinacyon*, she said: "Then the Byshopp said I shuld be brente. I answered, that I had searched all the scriptures yet coulde I never fynde there that eyther Christ or hys Apostles put anye creature to deathe" (*The Examinations of Anne Askew*, ed. Elaine V. Beilin [New York: Oxford University Press, 1996], 98).

20. On a major function of jokes as establishing (or solidifying) communities, see Ted Cohen, *Jokes: Philosophical Thoughts on Joking Matters* (Chicago: University of Chicago Press, 1999).

21. This is the fourth line of Shakespeare's sonnet 94, which begins, "They that have pow'r to hurt, and will do none." On the attitudinal and tonal complexities of this sonnet, see William Empson, *Some Versions of Pastoral* (1935; Norfolk, Conn.: New Directions, 1960), ch. 3; Edward Hubler, *The Sense of Shakespeare's Sonnets* (Princeton, N.J.: Princeton University Press, 1952), 95–109; Stephen Booth, *An Essay on Shakespere's Sonnets* (New Haven, Conn.: Yale University Press, 1969), 152–68; and Helen Vendler, *The Art of Shakespeare's Sonnets* (Cambridge, Mass.: Harvard University Press, 1997), 403–6.

22. Desiderius Erasmus, *The Praise of Folly*, trans. Clarence H. Miller (New Haven, Conn.: Yale University Press, 1979), 32.

23. Erasmus, *The Praise of Folly*, 39.

24. In *The Winter's Tale*, the newly gentled rustic (Clown) claims that gentles (aristocrats) have a special privilege with regard to lying on behalf of a friend, and not only of lying but specifically of swearing. Anyone can lie ("boors and franklins"—i.e., peasants and yeomen), but "If it be ne'er so false, a true gentleman may swear it in behalf of his friend" (5.2.155–58). This is obviously comic, but the Clown must be referring to something.

25. For the classic statement of this view, see E. M. W. Tillyard, *Shakespeare's History Plays* (London: Chatto and Windus, 1944), 265. It has been constantly reiterated. I have put the word *Aristotelian* in quotation marks in referring to this view, since it relies on a conception of the doctrine of the mean as an arithmetical and substantive doctrine, a doctrine of moderation, rather than as a rhetorical one, a doctrine of appropriateness. For a clear demonstration that "the doctrine of moderation is no part of the doctrine of the mean, nor is it a consequence of the mean," see J. O. Urmson, "Aristotle's Doctrine of the Mean," in Rorty, *Essays on Aristotle's Ethics*, 162. On the actual complexity of courage "as a mean," see the essay by that title by David Pears in the same volume, 171–87.

26. Strain, "Legal Reform and *2 Henry IV*," brings them together as "corruptive associations in the form of friendship and rebellion" (293).

27. For the romance provenance of this (imagined) feat, especially with regard to Lancelot, see the note in the Humphreys's edition of *1H4* (30).

28. For Hotspur as "one of the play's major selling points in its own time," and as one of the major reasons why *1H4* was the most reprinted of the Shakespeare quartos, see Roberta Barker, "Tragical-Comical-Historical Hotspur," *Shakespeare Quarterly* 54 (2003): 288–307.

29. See Paul A. Jorgenson, "The 'Dastardly Treachery' of Prince John of Lancaster," *PMLA* 76 (1961): 488–92.

30. That Prince John sticks "precisely to the terms of the oath" is noted by John Kerrigan in "Shakespeare, Oaths and Vows," *Proceedings of the British Academy* 167 (2010): 67.

31. Compare "I will also send wild beasts upon you, which shal spoile you, and destroy your cattel, and make you fewe in nomber: so your hye ways shalbe desolate" (Leviticus 26:22).

32. On this, see Humphreys's note in *2H4*, 26.

33. A virtually identical moment occurs in a later Shakespeare play, in the context of tension within another not so young couple. When Antony is berating Cleopatra after the disaster at Actium, the whole scene shifts when Cleopatra asks, "Not know me yet?" (3.13.162). On the connections between Falstaff and Antony (and Cleopatra), see Richard Strier, *The Unrepentant Renaissance: From Petrarch to Shakespeare to Milton* (Chicago: University of Chicago Press, 2011), ch. 3.

34. Erasmus, *Praise of Folly*, 31. Folly's position, it should be noted, is stronger than this. She goes on to claim that friendship also involves an ability with regard to one's friend "to be deceived, to be blind to his vices, to imagine them away, even to love and admire certain notorious vices as if they were virtues." I am certain that Mistress Quickly would agree with this as well, since, with regard to Falstaff, she seems to live it.

35. There is a nice note on the precision of Mistress Quickly's recollection in the Humphreys edition (88). In the two plays together, she is the third character whose relationship with Falstaff is given a precise duration. Bardolph, at thirty-two years, beats out Mistress Quickly by three (*1H4*, 3.3.45–47); and of Poins, Falstaff says, "I have forsworn his company hourly any time this two and twenty years" (*1H4*, 2.2.45–47). These relationships have remarkable—and very specifically marked—staying power.

36. Burrow, "Reading Tudor Writing Politically," does a remarkable analysis (244–49) of the economic and legal significance of what seems a throwaway line about "bullocks at Stamford fair" (*2H4*, 3.2.38).

37. I am not taking a position on the matter of whether the plays were initially conceived as a sequence, but I am suggesting that the end of the second play does seem to culminate the two. This is compatible with the view put forth by G. K. Hunter in *"Henry IV and the Elizabethan Two-Part Play," Review of English Studies*, n.s. 5 (1954): 236–48. Harold Jenkins, "The Structural Problem in Shakespeare's *Henry IV*," in *Structural Problems in Shakespeare: Lectures and Essays by Harold Jenkins*, ed. Ernst Honigmann (London: Thomson Learning, 2001), 3–22, sees the issue as rather more vexed.

38. For intelligent musing on this "brief, puzzling scene," see Hugh Grady, *Shakespeare, Machiavelli, and Montaigne: Power and Subjectivity from Richard II to Hamlet* (Oxford: Oxford University Press, 2002), 193.

39. Sir Philip Sidney, *An Apology for Poetry*, ed. Geoffrey Shepherd (London: Thomas Nelson & Sons, 1965), 100. Sidney saw poetry as providing an alternative to the brazen world of history, and potentially acting as a transforming agent. For a Middle English Land of Cockayne poem, see *Early Middle English Verse and Prose*, ed. J. A. W. Bennett and G. V. Smithers (Oxford: Clarendon Press, 1968), 138–44.

40. See David Bevington, "Equity in *Measure for Measure*," in *Shakespeare and the Law: A Conversation Among Disciplines and Professions*, ed. Bradin Cormack, Martha C. Nussbaum, and Richard Strier (Chicago: University of Chicago Press, 2013), 164–73.

41. Bevington, "Equity in *Measure for Measure*," 169; Virginia Lee Strain, *Legal Reform in English Renaissance Literature* (Edinburgh: Edinburgh University Press, 2018), 154–55.

42. *Measure for Measure* is cited from the edition by J. W. Lever (New York: Random House, 1967).

43. See Bullough, *Narrative and Dramatic Sources of Shakespeare: The Comedies, 1597–1603*, (London: Routledge and Kegan Paul, 1958), 2:399–530.

44. See Norman Jones, *God and the Moneylenders: Usury and Law in Early Modern England* (Oxford: Blackwell, 1989).

45. On the equation of usury and prostitution, see Lever's note on this passage (82).

46. Pompey's question seems to involve female as well as male youth, so that the issue moves from prostitution to "fornication" in general (brothels to service females does not seem to be imagined, but, in the play, the law against "fornication," premarital and noncommercial heterosexual sex, seems to be enforced only against the male partner).

47. On "sodomy," see, inter alia, Alan Bray, *Homosexuality in Renaissance England* (1982; New York: Columbia University Press, 1995); the essays by Janet E. Halley, Donald N. Mager, and Michael Warner in *Queering the Renaissance*, ed. Jonathan Goldberg (Durham, N.C.: Duke University Press, 1994); and Jonathan Goldberg, *Sodometries: Renaissance Texts, Modern Sensibilities* (Stanford, Calif.: Stanford University Press, 1992). On adultery, see Martin Ingram, *Church Courts, Sex and Marriage in England, 1570–1640* (Cambridge: Cambridge University Press, 1987), 150–54; and Laura Gowring, *Domestic Dangers: Women, Words, and Sex in Early Modern London* (Oxford: Clarendon Press, 1986), ch. 6.

48. On the complexities and ambiguities of Elizabethan marriage laws and practices, see Lever's introduction to *Measure for Measure*, liii–lv; Ernest Schanzer, *The Problem Plays of Shakespeare* (New York: Schocken, 1965), ch. 2; and Lawrence Stone, *The Family, Sex, and Marriage in England, 1580–1800* (New York: Harper & Row, 1977), 30–37.

49. In his defense of Escalus ("Equity in *Measure for Measure*"), Bevington mentions this second consideration (165), but does not discuss it. The Elizabethans and Jacobeans may have thought that it was appropriate for the legal system to take class status into account, and it may be that aristocrats were allowed special treatment in sexual as in other matters, but this is not clear

and, in any case, needs commentary. Escalus seems simply to mention Claudio's parentage, almost in passing, as something that he would take into account were he judging the case. He does not expand on the point or offer any sort of argument or explanation.

50. See Constance Jordan, "Interpreting Statute in *Measure for Measure*," in Cormack, Nussbaum, and Strier, *Shakespeare and the Law*, 101–20.

51. I believe that Strain is mistaken in calling this position "idiosyncratic," and I believe that she somewhat misunderstands what Angelo is saying here. She reprehends his position for ignoring the need for justices to "actively investigate" cases (see *Legal Reform in English Renaissance Literature*, 152). But the point here is that what a trial treats is the case before it. The claim is about what a trial does, not what a justice in general is to do.

52. For proof that this way of thinking was truly available in the period, there is a similar assertion of the irrelevance of individual moral purity to the functioning of a socially positive system in one of the treatises written to support James's project for the union of England and Scotland. See Paul J. McGinnis and Arthur H. Williamson, *The British Union: A Critical Edition and Translation of David Hume of Godscroft's "De Unione Insulae Britannicae"* (Burlington, Vt.: Ashgate, 2002), 70 (Latin), 71 (English): "As for the republic, motives don't matter. It's sufficient for the republic that we act for the public interest, even though we do it because it is expedient for our own private affairs." I owe my awareness of this text to work on the Union issue by Marie Theresa O'Connor.

53. As Debora Kuller Shuger notes, the play "leaves unanswered the objection Angelo raised earlier" (*Political Theologies in Shakespeare's England: The Sacred and the State in "Measure for Measure"* [New York: Palgrave, 2001], 64).

54. Shakespeare uses "Thought is free" in *Twelfth Night*, 1.3.65 and in *The Tempest*, 3.2.122. For the idea in *The Tempest*, see "*The Tempest* (1): Power" below. For the Roman juridical maxim ("No one is punished for thinking"), see *The Digest of Justinian*, 48.19.18, ed. Theodore Mommsen with Paul Krueger, trans. Alan Watson (Philadelphia: University of Pennsylvania Press, 1985), 4:850. For the importance of this idea in the English Revolution, see Richard Strier, "From Diagnosis to Operation: The 'Root and Branch' Petition and the Grand Remonstrance," in *The Theatrical City: Culture, Theatre and Politics in London, 1576–1649*, ed. David L. Smith, Richard Strier, and David Bevington (Cambridge: Cambridge University Press, 1995), 232.

55. G. Wilson Knight, "*Measure for Measure* and the Gospels," *The Wheel of Fire: Interpretations of Shakespearian Tragedy* (1930, 1949; New York: Meridian Books, 1957), 73–96.

56. Shakespeare had already given voice to such an argument in Portia's discourse on "the quality of mercy" (*The Merchant of Venice*, 4.1.194–97). In Isabella's speech, the argument might be less contextually compromised. On law in *The Merchant of Venice*, see the final section of the current chapter.

57. On the theocratic impulse in the play, see Shuger, *Political Theologies*, 36 and passim.

58. In one of the dramatic sources for Shakespeare's play (Giraldo Cinthio's *Epitia*), a character equivalent to Barnardine is mentioned ("the worst of criminals") but never appears (Bullough, *Narrative and Dramatic Sources*, 2:441). A person with a version of the name Falstaff is present in the historical record, but has nothing to do with Shakespeare's creation.

59. Bullough, *Narrative and Dramatic Sources*, 2:441.

60. Strain's celebration of "the reform of justice in *Measure for Measure*" occludes Barnardine, who is entirely unmentioned in her treatment (*Legal Reform in English Renaissance Literature*, ch. 4 [163]).

61. See James Q. Whitman, *The Origins of Reasonable Doubt: The Theological Roots of the Criminal Trial* (New Haven: Yale University Press, 2008).

62. On Hamlet's commitment to finding "a more horrid hent" than mere bodily death for Claudius (3.3.88), and the relation of Hamlet and Laertes as revengers, see "Happy Hamlet."

63. See Peter Lake, "Deeds Against Nature: Cheap Print, Protestantism and Murder in Early Seventeenth-Century England," in *Culture and Politics in Early Stuart England*, ed. Kevin Sharpe and Peter Lake (Stanford, Calif.: Stanford University Press, 1993), 257–84 (esp. 274); and see Shuger, *Political Theologies*, 128.

64. On Othello's legal thinking, see Richard Strier and Richard H. McAdams, "Cold-Blooded and High-Minded Murder: The 'Case' of Othello," *Fatal Fictions: Crime and Investigation in Law and Literature*, ed. Alison L. LaCroix, Richard H. McAdams, and Martha C. Nussbaum (Oxford University Press, 2017), 111–38.

65. This is parallel to what Bernard Williams and Thomas Nagel call "moral luck." See the essay by that title in the book by that title by Bernard Williams (see note 14), and the essay by that title in Thomas Nagel, *Mortal Questions* (Cambridge: Cambridge University Press, 1979).

66. Knight, "*Measure for Measure* and the Gospels," 95.

67. August Wilhelm Schlegel, *Lectures on Dramatic Art and Literature*, trans. John Black, 2nd ed. rev. A. J. W. Morrison (London: George Bell and Sons, 1904), 388.

68. Spring 2013 at the Goodman Theater in Chicago. At the very end of the play, in this production, Barnardine fatally stabbed Isabella.

69. One passage early after the "proclamation" concerning fornication is promulgated suggests that the brothels, as a business enterprise, have simply become an urban rather than a suburban franchise. The brothels in the suburbs are to be "plucked down"; those in the city "had gone down too, but that a wise burgher put in for them" (1.2.91–92).

70. Knight, "*Measure for Measure* and the Gospels," 96. Shuger's *Political Theologies* provides—with deep historical awareness—a reading of the play close to Knight's, but Shuger seems to waver between seeing the play's conception of Christian "justice" as radical or strange, and seeing it as perhaps practicable (133ff.).

71. This is Richard Posner's characterization of the (only) situation where the Sermon on the Mount does make sense ("Law and Commerce in *The Merchant of Venice*," in Cormack, Nussbaum, and Strier, *Shakespeare and the Law*, 305). The belief in the imminence of the end of the (historical) world in the Gospels and Pauline letters is a well-established topic in biblical studies. For one overview, see Ben Witherington III, *Jesus, Paul, and the End of the World* (Downer's Grove, Ill.: Intervarsity, 1992).

72. One clever way to respect both the Sermon (which penalizes thoughts) and an actual legal system (focused on acts) would be to see them as operating in separate realms, so that they could coexist. In one of the cases (number 15) presented in Alexander Sylvayn, *The Orator*, trans. L. P. (London: Adam Islip, 1596), "A Certain man bargained with a soldiour to kill his enemie, but afterwards repented him, and forbad him in any sort to touch him, to the end to hurt him: and this he did in the presence of two witnesses: the soldiour notwithstanding went on forward and killed him, and afterward was taken and condemned to die" (88). The question at issue is whether the man who initially suborned the soldier is also to be found guilty and executed. In his defense, the suborner who retracted says, "Trulie I confesse that *I have greatlie sinned against God, but as for the world, our thoughts and minds are free*, provided that they stretch not to the affecting of mischiefe," so that he is not to be punished by earthly justice (91–92; emphasis mine). *Measure for Measure* never articulates such a neat way of allowing both systems to operate. Shakespeare probably knew *The Orator*, and may have used its treatment of a case of the flesh bond with a Jew (number 95) in *The Merchant of Venice* (see Bullough, *Narrative and Dramatic Sources*, 1 [London: Routledge and Kegan Paul, 1966], 482–86), but

he does not seems to have used number 15. I owe my awareness of the suborner case to Christopher Crosbie, "Intention," Shakespeare Association seminar, "Boundaries of Violence," April 2021.

73. *The Merchant of Venice* is cited from the edition by John Drakakis (London: Methuen, 2010). I have also made use of the edition by John Russell Brown (1959; London: Methuen, 1964).

74. For the change in the contractual situation in the course of act 1, scene 3, see "Excuses, Bepissing, and Non-Being."

75. See Alberto Tenenti, "Gli schiavi di Venezia alla fine del Cinquecento," *Rivista Storica Italiana* 67 (1955): 52–69. The domestic focus of Shylock's speech is also accurate. Tenenti notes that "nell' Italia del secolo XVI lo schiavo è ormai sopratutto un oggetto di lusso, riservato ai nobili ed ai ricchi mercanti" [in Italy in the sixteenth century, the slave was above all a luxury item, reserved for aristocrats and rich merchants]—exactly the groups with which Shylock is concerned—and that "schiavitù nel Cinquecento si fa spiccatamente domestica" (54) [slavery in the sixteenth century was specifically domestic]. The view of slaves as primarily used in domestic contexts is supported by Dennis Romano, *Housecraft and Statecraft: Domestic Service in Renaissance Venice, 1400–1600* (Baltimore: Johns Hopkins University Press, 1996).

76. As William O. Scott puts it, what Shylock is doing here "effectively converts a loan transaction into a purchase." See Scott, "Conditional Bonds, Forfeitures, and Vows in *The Merchant of Venice*," *ELR* 34 (2004): 286–305 (301). The Constitution of the United States is ambiguous on whether slaves are persons or property (or both). See Paul Finkelman, "Slavery in the United States: Persons or Property," in *The Legal Understanding of Slavery: From the Historical to the Contemporary*, ed. Jean Allain (Oxford: Oxford University Press, 2012), 105–34, esp. 119.

77. See Amanda Bailey, *Of Bondage: Debt, Property, and Personhood in Early Modern England* (Philadelphia: University of Pennsylvania Press, 2013), 64–66.

78. For an explanation of why the Duke—on the basis of the actual legal system of Renaissance Venice—had to call in an outside judge, see Philip Goldfarb Styrt, *Shakespeare's Political Imagination: The Historicism of Setting* (London: Bloomsbury, 2021), chap. 6.

79. This point is made by Charles Fried in his "Opinion of Fried, J., Concurring in the Judgment [of Posner, J.]," in Cormack, Nussbaum, and Strier, *Shakespeare and the Law*, 156–58.

80. For the view that, confronted with the Shylock-Antonio contract, an actual Venetian court of the period "would have either severely punished lender and borrower alike or deemed them both insane and treated them accordingly," see Benjamin Ravid, "The Venetian Government and the Jews," in *The Jews of Early Modern Venice*, ed. Robert C. Davis and Benjamin Ravid (Baltimore: Johns Hopkins University Press, 2001), 26.

81. This is also explicit in Shakespeare's source. See *Il Pecorone* [*The Dunce*] by Ser Giovanni Fiorentino, in Bullough, *Narrative and Dramatic Sources of Shakespeare*, 1:472: "Since Venice had a reputation as a place of strict justice, and the Jew's case was legal and formally made out, nobody dared to deny him."

82. For a reading of the play in terms of the Old Law versus the New, see, inter alia, Barbara K. Lewalski, "Biblical Allusion and Allegory in *The Merchant of Venice*," *Shakespeare Quarterly* 13 (1962): 121–36.

83. This, I think, is what makes Stephen Greenblatt's marveling at Shylock not killing Antonio when he physically has the chance to do so beside the point ("Shakespeare and Shylock," *NYRB* 77 [September 30, 2010], 91). Shylock's reliance on the legal system is what leads both Posner and Fried to view Portia's second "hold" on Shylock as not legally valid. Working within the law cannot be a crime. See Posner, "Law and Commerce," 150; Fried, "Opinion," 160.

84. Lars Engle suggests something like this in *Shakespearean Pragmatism: Market of His Time* (Chicago: University of Chicago Press, 1993), 102, but his focus is philosophical (on "moral luck") rather than legal.

85. Fried, "Opinion," 161.

86. Janet Adelman puzzles over "why this specification" in *Blood Relations: Christian and Jew in "The Merchant of Venice"* (Chicago: University of Chicago Press, 2008), 125–27.

87. For an argument that the legal "resolution" of the trial scene in fact undermines the economic welfare of the city as it is presented in the play, see Thomas C. Bilello, "Law, Equity, and Portia's Con," in Jordan and Cunningham, *The Law in Shakespeare*, 123. This is similar to the position of Fried.

88. As Kenneth Gross points out, the word has never before in the play been applied to Shylock (*Shylock Is Shakespeare* [Chicago: University of Chicago Press, 2006], 103). On the rights of Jews as citizens or as *habitatores*, see Julius Kirshner and Osvaldo Cavallar, "Jews as Citizens in Late Medieval and Renaissance Italy: The Case of Isacco da Pisa," *Jewish History* 25 (2011): 269–318. See also Benjamin Ravid, "How 'Other' Really Was the Jewish Other? The Evidence from Venice," in *Acculturation and Its Discontents*, ed. David N. Myers, Massimo Ciavolella, Peter H. Reill, and Geoffrey Symcox (Toronto: University of Toronto Press, 2008), 19–55. Julia Reinhard Lupton stresses the importance of Shakespeare making Shylock "part of a world" (*Citizen-Saints: Shakespeare and Political Theology* [Chicago: University of Chicago Press, 2008], 79), but she takes for granted that Shylock lives in the ghetto (86–87, 98). Yet the play never mentions or hints at the existence of the ghetto (noted by Ravid, "The Venetian Government and the Jews," 26). Whether Shakespeare knew about the ghetto is unclear; he could have, though probably not by name (see Ravid, "Christian Travelers in the Ghetto of Venice: Some Preliminary Observations," in *Studies on the Jews of Venice, 1382–1797* [Aldershot: Ashgate, 2003], 111–24). No laws like those invoked by Portia actually existed.

89. See Harry Berger, "Marriage and Mercifixion in *The Merchant of Venice*: The Casket Scene Revisited," in Berger, *Making Trifles of Terrors: Redistributing Complicities in Shakespeare*, ed. and intro. Peter Erickson (Stanford, Calif.: Stanford University Press, 1997), 1–9. Oddly, Berger uses the term in relation to what Portia does to Antonio rather than to Shylock (9).

90. The exact financial terms of Shylock's punishment are unclear. The terms keep getting modified, and some of them are ambiguous. It is unclear what Antonio means by planning to have the half of Shylock's holdings initially designated for the state "in use" (376–79). Most critics and editors are quick to assert that this cannot refer to usury, and it is certainly true that the primary reference must be to holding land "in use" (for the meaning of which see B. J. Sokol and Mary Sokol, *Shakespeare's Legal Language: A Dictionary* [London: Continuum, 2010], 386). But in the context of the play it is impossible not to hear the excluded meaning. In any case, it is unclear how much of his estate, if any, Shylock will retain. Three things, however, are clear: (1) Shylock's life depends on his conversion; (2) he will lose control of at least half of his estate; and (3) he will not only lose the right to determine his heirs but must pass "all he dies possessed [of]" to someone who, it is explicitly noted, has acted criminally toward him—"the gentleman / That lately stole his daughter" (380–81).

91. It should be noted that the conversion under threat of execution is Shakespeare's addition to the story. It does not appear in *Il Pecorone*, where the last thing that is said about the legally defeated Jew is that he tears up the bond in frustration (Bullough, *Narrative and Dramatic Sources*, 1:474). Posner's attempt to present the conversion demand as nonobjectionable within the historical context is quite forced, and the extraordinary and almost consciously sophistical

ruling by Innocent III concerning stipulated "willingness" hardly helps the case, especially when the problem of the *conversos* is added (see Posner, "Law and Commerce," 148). For a useful historical overview, see *Forced Conversion in Christianity, Judaism, and Islam,* ed. Mercedes García-Arenal and Yonatan Glazer-Eytan (Leiden: Brill, 2020).

92. Richard H. McAdams claims to have located an instance in which Shakespeare portrays a legal process positively—and in Venice, no less. See his comments on act 1, scene 3 of *Othello* in "Vengeance, Complicity, and Criminal Law in *Othello*," in Cormack, Nussbaum, and Strier, *Shakespeare and the Law,* 123–25. I would reply that it is important, as McAdams notes in passing, that "the Duke is not a judge" and that the procedure in question is (as McAdams acknowledges) "informal" (124), not a set and formal legal process. My claim is that the more formal and official the legal situation—the more that what is presented is a legal system or is spoken of by a character as such—the more dubious Shakespeare became.

93. This is the butcher's proposal, seconded by Jack Cade in *Henry VI, Part 2,* 4.2.81.

CHAPTER 5

1. The medieval formulation is given in Chaucer's "The Monk's Tale": "Tragedie is to seyn a certeyn storie . . . Of hym that stood in greet prosperitee, / And is yfallen out of heigh degree / Into myserie"; the monk also adds that the central figure of such a story "endeth wrecchedly." (in *The Works of Geoffrey Chaucer,* ed. F. N. Robinson, 2nd ed. [Boston: Houghton Mifflin, 1961], ll. 1973–77). Enrica Zanin points out that this latter feature is a medieval one that early modern theorists often attributed to Aristotle, though it is not a view held in the *Poetics* ("Tragedy Ends Unhappily: The Concealed Influence of Medieval Poetics in Early Modern Theory of Tragedy," *Horizonte, Ausgabe* 2 [2017], online: http://hdl.handle.net/21.11108/0000-0007-C2D3-F).

2. Glenn Most has pointed out to me two ancient cases in which poverty is evoked: *Oedipus at Colonus* and Euripides's *Helen.*

3. The two unusual features (disfigurement onstage and poverty) are not unrelated. In *Resistant Structures: Particularity, Radicalism, and Renaissance Texts* (Berkeley: University of California Press, 1995), 192–93, I suggested a political reason for the extremely unusual onstage presentation of Gloucester's blinding, but this feature can also be seen as related to the play's treatment of poverty. Human vulnerability—physical vulnerability—is at issue in both cases. For a similar sense of the unusually sustained focus on poverty in *Lear,* see Chris Fitter, "'As Full of Grief as Age': Protesting Against the Poor Law in *King Lear*," in *Shakespeare and the Politics of Commoners: Digesting the New Social History,* ed. Chris Fitter (Oxford: Oxford University Press, 2017), 217–35.

4. Unless otherwise noted, for the text(s) of the play, I have used *King Lear: A Parallel Text Edition,* ed. René Weis (London: Longman, 1993), which I prefer to the second edition (2010). When the Quarto and Folio texts differ, I have given the line number first from the Quarto version in this edition, and then from the Folio. When the Quarto and the Folio texts are identical, I have given only the one citation. When quoting in sequence a number of passages from a particular scene, I have omitted the act and scene numbers unless the texts differ about these.

5. See Linda Woodbridge, *Vagrancy, Poverty, and English Renaissance Literature* (Urbana: University of Illinois Press, 2001), 219.

6. Critics sometimes write as if Cordelia simply refuses to participate in the "love-test." She attempts to do this, but when Lear, still in a kindly mode, tells her to "mend" her initial refusal "a little," she makes a highly significant speech, and one that is as long or longer than the speeches

her sisters have made (over eight lines in the Folio; at least nine in the Quarto). As Alex Schulman says, "She does not speak *like* Goneril and Regan, but she does speak" ("*King Lear* and the State of Nature," in *Rethinking Shakespeare's Political Philosophy: From "Lear" to "Leviathan"* [Edinburgh: Edinburgh University Press, 2014], 103). For a critic who writes as if Cordelia says nothing but "Nothing" (or "Nothing, my lord"), see Kent R. Lenhof, "Relation and Responsibility: A Levinasian Reading of *King Lear*," *Modern Philology* 111 (2014): 488–89. Lenhof wants her position to be more hyperbolic than it is (see "Resisting Complicity: Ethical Judgment and *King Lear*," note 51).

7. The conception of social life that Cordelia presents is clearly a classical one, one that Shakespeare's audience would have been familiar with from Cicero's *De Officiis* and Seneca's *De Beneficiis*. Both were widely available in Latin and in English translation. There is no doubt that Shakespeare knew the Cicero, since it was a school text (see, inter alia, T. W. Baldwin, *William Shakspere's Small Latine and Lesse Greeke* [Urbana: University of Illinois Press, 1944], 2:578–601). John M. Wallace has argued that Shakespeare knew and used Seneca's book (the longest of the moral essays) ("*Timon of Athens* and the Three Graces: Shakespeare's Senecan Study," *MP* 83 [1986]: 349–63; and "The Senecan Context of *Coriolanus*," *MP* 90 [1993]: 465–78). I do not agree with Schulman that Cordelia's perspective in this speech is a distinctively modern "rational-contractarian" one ("*King Lear* and the State of Nature," 104).

8. We have already met this meaning of "bred" in the play, when Gloucester tells Kent that Edmund's "breeding" has been at Gloucester's charge (1.1.8). And see Desdemona, who, in her equivalent speech about her bonds to her father and need, in marriage, to have "a divided duty," follows the order of "begot me, bred me." Desdemona acknowledges to her father, "To you I am bound for life and education" (1.3.182).

9. See François Hartog, *The Mirror of Herodotus: The Representation of the Other in the Writing of History*, trans. Janet Lloyd (Berkeley: University of California Press, 1988).

10. See Frank Lestringant, *Cannibals: The Discovery and Representation of the Cannibal from Columbus to Jules Verne*, trans. Rosemary Morris (Berkeley: University of California Press, 1997); Avramescu Catalin, *An Intellectual History of Cannibalism*, trans. Alistair Ian (Princeton, N.J.: Princeton University Press, 2009).

11. As Andreas Höfele points out, the distinction that Lear seems to draw here between the Scythian and the cannibal barely exists (*Stage, Stake, and Scaffold: Humans and Animals in Shakespeare's Theatre* [Oxford: Oxford University Press, 2011], 187 n. 57).

12. On Shylock's image, see "Excuses, Bepissing, and Non-Being." Höfele, *Stage, Stake, and Scaffold*, points out that Lear's image of himself as a dragon in his next speech has a similar density and opacity (183–87, 190).

13. On this belief in early modern English society, see Andy Wood, *Faith, Hope, and Charity: English Neighborhoods, 1500–1640* (Cambridge: Cambridge University Press, 2020).

14. For "neighbor" as a verb meaning "to associate in a neighborly way," the *OED* gives only one example from the early modern period, a very abstract occurrence in Bright's *Treatise on Melancholy* (1586). It lists the *Lear* passage under the definition "To bring or place near to some person or thing."

15. In a parallel to Lear's use of "neighbor" as a verb, he describes Cordelia as having been "strangered" by his oath (192; 202). I owe this observation to Kenneth Graham.

16. It is in response to this question that Jesus tells the parable of the Good Samaritan (Luke 10:30–35).

17. France is, or is pretending to be, concerned about the legal status of his claim to Cordelia when he says, "*Be it lawful*, I take up what's cast away" (1.1: Q 242; F 252; emphasis mine). The

normal realm of salvage law is maritime, and "cast away" might suggest this, as perhaps does "thrown to my chance" a few lines later. Bradin Cormack, in *A Power to Do Justice: Jurisdiction, English Literature, and the Rise of Common Law, 1509–1625* (Chicago: University of Chicago Press, 2007), 286, explains the distinctions between kinds of goods that can be salvaged from a wreck (flotsam, jetsam, and lagan). According to these categories, Cordelia would be jetsam (goods thrown overboard). Harry Berger Jr., in "*King Lear*: The Lear Family Romance," in *Making Trifles of Terrors: Redistributing Complicities in Shakespeare*, ed. and intro. Peter Erickson (Stanford, Calif.: Stanford University Press, 1997), notes that France is "no doubt invoking the law of salvage" (43), but Berger sees this as negative. See "Resisting Complicity: Ethical Judgment and *King Lear*," 82–83.

18. With regard to *Hamlet*, we cannot be absolutely certain that the addition of the other family story is Shakespeare's innovation, since we do not, as we do in the case of *King Lear*, have the earlier Elizabethan version.

19. *Narrative and Dramatic Sources of Shakespeare*, ed. Geoffrey Bullough (New York: Columbia University Press, 1973), 7:404–5.

20. R. H. Tawney, *The Agrarian Problem in the Sixteenth Century* (1912; rpt. New York: Harper and Row, 1967), 268.

21. See, inter alia, John Pound, *Poverty and Vagrancy in Tudor England*, 2nd ed. (London: Longman, 1986); A. L. Beier, *Masterless Men: The Vagrancy Problem in England, 1560–1640* (London: Methuen, 1985); Ian Archer, *The Pursuit of Stability: Social Relations in Elizabethan London* (Cambridge: Cambridge University Press, 1991).

22. "To My Esteem'd Friend, Thomas Boteler, Esq.," in Nahum Tate, *The History of King Lear* (1681), ed. James Black (Lincoln: University of Nebraska Press, 1975), 2. Shakespeare never explains Edgar's absence from the first scene. Tate, by rearranging the Lear and Gloucester plots, does.

23. See Jane Kingsley-Smith, *Shakespeare's Drama of Exile* (New York: Palgrave Macmillan, 2003), 127–28, on this and on what being "proclaimed" means.

24. William C. Carroll, *Fat King, Lean Beggar: Representations of Poverty in the Age of Shakespeare* (Ithaca, N.Y.: Cornell University Press, 1996), 194.

25. Simon Palfrey, *Poor Tom: Living "King Lear"* (Chicago: University of Chicago Press, 2014), 28.

26. The mention of "mills" is a bit of a puzzle here. Richard Knowles cites G. L. Kittredge's 1940 edition for noting that mills, like shepherd's cottages ("sheep-coates"), are "often distant from any village" (*A New Variorum Edition of Shakespeare: King Lear* [New York: MLA, 2020], 1:381. For Edgar's speech as revealing "the geography of the country of poverty," see Grigori Kozintsev, *"King Lear": The Space of Tragedy*, trans. Mary Mackintosh (Berkeley: University of California Press, 1977), 117.

27. Edgar's soliloquy is not a numbered scene in the Folio (there are no act or scene divisions in the Quarto). The soliloquy is part of act 2, scene 2 in the Folio. Alexander Pope's ten-volume edition (1728) was the first to treat the soliloquy as its own scene (Pope created many short scenes).

28. Henry Weinfield has raised the question of why Shakespeare uses "penury" rather than "poverty" here. I am not sure that I have a good answer. "Penury" is Latin in derivation rather than French—more elegant and perhaps even more emphatic.

29. For the "contempt of man" attributed to "the cosmos," see Laurie Shannon, *The Accommodated Animal: Cosmopolity in Shakespearean Locales* (Chicago: University of Chicago Press, 2013), 166.

30. On the original vs. the revised division plan, see Strier, *Resistant Structures*, 177–81.

31. Lars Engle would add a third, having to do with the refusal to use Lear's title. This is certainly present, but I am not sure that it is systematic, and in the scene of greatest cruelty, Lear is consistently referred to as "the King" (3.7.43, 48). See Engle, "Sovereign Cruelty in Montaigne and *King Lear*," in *The Shakespeare International Yearbook*, vol. 6, ed. Graham Bradshaw, Thomas Bishop, and Peter Holbrook (Aldershot: Ashgate, 2006), 119–39.

32. Thomas G. Olsen, "How Many Knights Had King Lear," *HLQ* 82 (2019): 193–219.

33. Virtually all modern productions, from Peter Brook's acclaimed 1971 film on, present the retinue acting in the way that Goneril claims they do.

34. On this, see Richard Strier, *The Unrepentant Renaissance from Petrarch to Shakespeare to Milton* (Chicago: University of Chicago Press, 2011), 108–110.

35. For the Folio stage direction, see *The Parallel King Lear, 1608–1623*, prepared by Michael Warren (Berkeley: University of California Press, 1989). The Weis edition substitutes "Knights" for "Attendants."

36. In the Quarto version of 1.3, Goneril is speaking to an unnamed Gentleman; in the Folio, it is Oswald ("Ste" for Steward). As with "Servant" vs. "Knight" in 1.4, the Weis edition does not record the differing speech-headings in 1.3. For these, see Warren, *The Parallel King Lear*.

37. Paul Cefalu seems to me to get the matter entirely backward in suggesting that there is a contrast between duty and affection in this speech and in the speeches to Lear of Cordelia and Kent in the opening scene (*Revisionist Shakespeare: Transitional Ideologies in Texts and Contexts* [New York: Palgrave Macmillan, 2004], 117, 120).

38. In the "recognition scene" between Lear and Cordelia, Cordelia asks for Lear's formal blessing ("hold your hand in benediction o'er me") and consistently addresses Lear in formal, indeed ceremonious, terms—not only as "Sir" but also as "my royal lord...your majesty...your highness" (4.7: 42, 80; 4.6: 38, 75).

39. For discussion of the manifold letters in the play, see Alan Stewart, *Shakespeare's Letters* (Oxford: Oxford University Press, 2008), ch. 5, though why letters are so prominent remains a mystery.

40. Aaron Tugendhaft has pointed out to me that this is parallel to God's instructions to the Hebrews (in the book of Kings) about the construction of the temple. The point is not the numbers and the materials in themselves but that they have been specified.

41. Compare Rosalie Colie, "Reason and Need: King Lear and the 'Crisis' of the Aristocracy," in *Some Facets of "King Lear": Essays in Prismatic Criticism*, ed. Rosalie Colie and F. T. Flahiff (Toronto: University of Toronto Press, 1974), 202.

42. On "antipathy," see Seth Lobis, "Sympathy and Antipathy in *King Lear*," in *Sympathy in Transformation: Dynamics Between Rhetorics, Poetics and Ethics*, ed. Roman Alexander Barton, Alexander Klaudies, and Thomas Miklich (Berlin: de Gruyter, 2018), 89–108. Lobis sees Kent as relying on the ontological meaning of "antipathy" ("physical determination" [96]), whereas I would see Kent as using an ontological reference to illustrate and rhetorically intensify an ethical point, one that he has explained at length in the speech about overly compliant servants (2.2: Q 66–74; F 68–76). I have treated this at length in *Resistant Structures*, 186–88. When Kent says that Oswald's "offense" is that "His countenance likes me not" [doesn't please me], Kent is not making the same point that he did in the antipathy lines. He is purposely being provocative.

43. On "personation" in this sense, see the discussion of the Lord Chief Justice's speech in act 5 of *2H4* in "Shakespeare and Legal Systems: The Better the Worse (but Not Vice Versa)."

44. These lines are unique to the Quarto (as 2.2.133–36).

45. All of the early uses of "comfortable" cited by the *OED* refer to emotional or spiritual experience.

46. As Stewart points out, "although a private Royal Post was in existence," letters in Shakespeare's plays always require an assigned personal messenger (*Shakespeare's Letters*, 12–13).

47. This is not to say that Peter Brook in his film was wrong to picture the transit but only to suggest that there was a reason why Shakespeare did not.

48. Presumably, Kent / Caius is on stage in the stocks during Edgar's soliloquy on becoming "Tom." This is easily staged, with the stocks toward the rear of the stage and Edgar stage front.

49. Compare Ewan Fernie, *Shame in Shakespeare* (London: Routledge, 2002), 192.

50. Compare Michael Ignatieff, "The Natural and the Social: *King Lear*," in *The Needs of Strangers: An Essay on Privacy, Solidarity, and the Politics of Being Human* (New York: Viking, 1985), 31. I am indebted to Ignatieff's remarkable chapter throughout. See also Emilia Jocelyn-Holt Correa, "Lear: De rey proprietario a súbdito y vagabundo. La relación entre propriedad, poder y dignidad en *El Rey Lear*," *Derechos y Humanidades* 24 (2014): 223–33.

51. The Folio is more insistent on this. Where the Quarto has Goneril entering saying, "Who struck my servant?" (2.4.158) the Folio has Lear saying, "Who stocked my servant?" (2.4.177).

52. Both Arendt and Agamben see themselves as relying on Aristotle's *Politics*. For Agamben, the key passage is *Politics* 1252b29–32: "When we come to the final and perfect association . . . we have already reached the *polis*—an association which may be said to have reached the height of full self-sufficiency; or rather we may say that while it grows *for the sake of mere life, it exists for the sake of the good life*" (*The Politics of Aristotle*, trans. Ernest Barker [New York: Oxford University Press, 1958]; trans. slightly emended and emphasis mine). At 1278b23–31, Aristotle distinguishes between the "chief end" of political association and persons coming together "merely for the sake of life."

53. Hannah Arendt, *The Human Condition* (Chicago: University of Chicago Press, 1958), 97. The distinction runs throughout the book, but is not always referred to in these terms. Giorgio Agamben uses the terms and builds on Arendt's distinction in *Homo Sacer: Sovereign Power and Bare Life*, trans. Daniel Heller-Roazen (Stanford, Calif.: Stanford University Press, 1998), 1–5. Agamben develops this in many other places; see *The Use of Bodies*, in *The Omnibus Homo Sacer* (Stanford, Calif.: Stanford University Press, 2017), 1206–13.

54. Margreta de Grazia, "The Ideology of Superfluous Things: *King Lear* as Period Piece," in *Subject and Object in Renaissance Culture*, ed. Margreta de Grazia, Maureen Quilligan, and Peter Stallybrass (Cambridge: Cambridge University Press, 1996), 23. Contrast Ignatieff, *The Needs of Strangers*, 51.

55. For destruction of one's clothing as, in the period, a particularly clear sign of madness, see Michael MacDonald, *Mystical Bedlam: Madness, Anxiety, and Healing in Seventeenth-Century England* (Cambridge: Cambridge University Press, 1981), 130–31.

56. Katherine Maus, *Being and Having in Shakespeare* (Oxford: Oxford University Press, 2013), 125. Maus recognizes that this attitude is marked as madness in the play, but somehow wants to see it as something more.

57. For the claim that the play "elevates an integrity in beasts that it asserts man lacks," see Shannon, *The Accommodated Animal*, 141. Shannon sees *Lear* as drawing on the "happy beast" tradition. But there are no happy beasts in the play.

58. Höfele, *Stage, Stake, and Scaffold*, 228.

59. The play takes no account of the ways that animals or birds or insects can build shelters. I owe this point to Martha Nussbaum. This makes a sharp contrast with Montaigne's "Apology

for Raymond Sebond," in *The Complete Essays of Montaigne*, trans. Donald M. Frame (Stanford, Calif.: Stanford University Press, 1943), 332–47.

60. In *Vagrancy, Poverty, and English Renaissance Literature*, Woodbridge notes the coincidence of the usages (220). Since Gloucester cannot have heard Lear's speech, the term is clearly on Shakespeare's mind.

61. John Gillies, "The Scene of Cartography in *King Lear*," in *Literature, Mapping, and the Politics of Space in Early Modern Britain*, ed. Andrew Gordon and Bernhard Klein (Cambridge: Cambridge University Press, 109–37 (125).

62. It is probably an accident that the unusual word "pelting" appears in both these passages, since the word is used in entirely different senses in each ("poor pelting villages" vs. "the pelting of this pitiless storm [Q: night]"). But I cannot help thinking that the recurrence signals some sort of connection between the passages in Shakespeare's mind (as does perhaps, to go out on the limb further, the alliteration of the "*p*'s").

63. Palfrey, *Poor Tom*, 53.

64. Ignatieff, *The Needs of Strangers*, 27.

65. Palfrey, *Poor Tom*, 54–55.

66. Stephen Greenblatt, *Shakespeare's Freedom* (Chicago: University of Chicago Press, 2010), 92. Marie Theresa O'Connor has shown that ideas of economic redistribution were truly "in the air" in 1605–06, when the play was written, in the context of the discussion of King James's proposal for the union of England and Scotland. But O'Connor shows that the play takes the idea much further than the pro-Union proponents of redistribution did ("Why Redistribute? The Jacobean Union Issue and *King Lear*," *Early Modern Literary Studies* [Sheffield] 16 [2016]: 1–27).

67. Walter Cohen, *Drama of a Nation: Public Theater in Renaissance England and Spain* (Ithaca, N.Y.: Cornell University Press, 1985), 334.

68. When Kent is expressing gratitude to Gloucester for providing Lear and company an accommodation better than the hovel, and intending to do even more than that, the Quarto has Kent say, "the gods deserve your kindness" (3.6.6). The Folio revises this to the more immediately intelligible "the gods requite your kindness," but I wonder whether the Quarto line may reflect the same idea of the gods or "heavens" getting credit for benevolent human action.

69. On Edgar's miracle, see "Shakespeare and Skepticism (1): Religion."

70. In the Quarto, the Fool has (by my count, using the Weis edition) sixteen lines after the appearance of "Tom." In the Folio, which does not include the mock-trial, the Fool has (by my count) twelve lines thereafter. He never reappears (the Folio gives him an exit line). In the two scenes in act 3 in which "Tom" appears (scenes 4 and 6), "Tom" has approximately ninety-three lines in the Quarto, and approximately eighty in the Folio (not counting the lines when Edgar speaks as himself).

71. See Carroll, *Fat King, Lean Beggar*, ch. 5.

72. The Quarto has "them of Bedlam."

73. Carroll, *Fat King, Lean Beggar*, 208. Among the Shakespearean exemplars, Carroll counts Christopher Sly from *The Taming of the Shrew* and Jack Cade (when impoverished) in *2H6*. But neither of them are vagrants of the sort that "Tom" purports to be, and their experience is not evoked at anything like comparable length.

74. Gillies, "The Scene of Cartography," notes that the evocation of poverty in the play "is uniquely authentic in the early modern theater" (126).

75. See MacDonald, *Mystical Bedlam*, 107.

76. See Richard Halpern, *The Poetics of Primitive Accumulation: English Renaissance Culture and the Genealogy of Capital* (Ithaca, N.Y.: Cornell University Press, 1991), 264.

77. On the late Elizabethan and early Jacobean periods as the great age of whipping and stocking vagrants, see Fitter, "'As Full of Grief as Age,'" 228.

78. Although the Folio does not include the "mock-trial" (Q 3.6.13–52), it does include the litany of types of dogs that "Tom" will supposedly scare off in response to Lear's imagination that three "little dogs" (his daughters?) are barking at him (3.6: Q 59–67; F 22–30).

79. Woodbridge, *Vagrancy, Poverty, and English Renaissance Literature*, 229.

80. For the emergence of Shakespeare's name on the quartos of the plays, see Lukas Erne, *Shakespeare as Literary Dramatist* (Cambridge: Cambridge University Press, 2003), ch. 2; for a useful chart, see Erne, *Shakespeare and the Book Trade* (Cambridge: Cambridge University Press, 2013), 14–15.

81. On the (possible) significance of *Lear* being played at court on St. Stephen's Night (December 26), see Leah S. Marcus, *Puzzling Shakespeare: Local Reading and Its Discontents* (Berkeley: University of California Press, 1998), 148–59.

82. *OED*, s.v. "sullen," A. adjective, 1.d. (designated "figurative" and obsolete"), with the first citation from Dryden in 1676.

83. See *The Two Gentleman of Verona*, 3.1.68–72; *The Taming of the Shrew*, 5.1.163–66.

84. Quoted from Thomas Dekker's *The Belman of London* (1608; based directly on Thomas Harman's *A Caveat or Warening for Commen Cursetors Vulgarely Called Vagabones* [1566, 1568, 1573]), in Knowles, *A New Variorum Edition*, 1:379 (cited originally in William Shakespeare, *King Lear, The New Variorum Edition*, ed. Howard Furness (Philadelphia: J. B. Lippincott, 1908), rpt. Mineola, N.Y.: Dover Publications, 2000), 136); emphasis mine. On Harman, see Carroll, *Fat King, Lean Beggar*, ch. 2; and Patricia Fumerton, *Unsettled: The Culture of Mobility and the Working Poor in Early Modern England* (Chicago: University of Chicago Press, 2006), ch. 3.

85. Compare Colie, "Reason and Need," 204.

86. On the striking lack of concern for the "worthiness" of the object of distribution here, and for those in Lear's "prayer," see Woodbridge, *Vagrancy, Poverty, and English Renaissance Literature*, 214. As Abel Athouguia Alves notes, all organized forms of poor relief in the period—across the religious spectrum—made a sharp distinction between the worthy and the unworthy poor ("The Christian Social Organism and Social Welfare: The Case of Vives, Calvin and Loyola," *Sixteenth Century Journal* 20 [Spring 1989]: 3–22).

87. Timothy Harrison alerted me to the shift in pronouns here.

88. Q's "stands" clearly means "withstands"; F's "slaves" is more difficult. "Enslaves" makes minimal sense. Some editors have suggested "makes it subservient to his superfluities and lust," which reads "slaves" in a normal sense, but might add too much to the passage. Johnson's gloss of "to slight or ridicule it" seems conceptually apt, if lexically unlikely. In any case, the "ordinance" in question has to be some sort of divine injunction to take care of the poor. See Knowles, *A New Variorum Edition*, 1:682–83.

89. In "'So Distribution Should Undo Excess': Recovering the Political Pressure of Distributive and Egalitarian Discourses in Shakespeare's *King Lear* and Early Modern England," *ELH* 86 (2019): 835–63, Chris Fitter argues that critics who equate the two speeches as both imagining a "more just" society are mistaken. He sees Lear's speech much as Greenblatt does, as merely recommending a "decorum of modest allocation" (841), whereas Fitter sees Gloucester's speech as genuinely radical. While it is certainly true that Gloucester's speech is more specific in its vision of social justice than Lear's, Fitter fails to respond to the extremity of Lear's speech and to the force of "physic" in it. The two speeches are indeed different, but I do not think that the difference runs along politico-economic lines. Where they truly differ is in their relation not to the economic realm but to "the heavens." Gloucester's speech is deeply religious, Lear's profoundly secular.

90. For the term as radical, see, inter alia, Terry Eagleton, *William Shakespeare* (Oxford: Blackwell, 1986), 82. Peter Holbrook points out that a late nineteenth-century British labor leader, Joseph Arch, began a speech at Stratford-on-Avon in 1878 using Gloucester's speech ("Shakespeare and Radicalism: The Uses and Abuses of Shakespeare in Nineteenth-Century Popular Politics," *Historical Journal* 45 [2002]: 369).

91. Judy Kronenfeld, *"King Lear" and the Naked Truth: Rethinking the Language of Religion and Resistance* (Durham, N.C.: Duke University Press, 1998), 175ff.

92. Fitter's argument that the word "did on occasion refer to large-scale reallocation" ("'So Distribution Should Undo Excess,'" 848) does not contradict Kronenfeld, who wavers between asserting that the term was not radical (*"King Lear" and the Naked Truth*, 173, 178) and asserting that it did not have to be so (201, 208) but could be (223). Compare Woodbridge, *Vagrancy, Poverty, and English Renaissance Literature*, 216–17.

93. Samuel Fleischacker, *A Short History of Distributive Justice* (Cambridge, Mass.: Harvard University Press, 2004), 2. Interestingly, as sources for the "positive community" view of the state of nature that might lead in such a direction, Fleischacker cites the literary tradition ("Virgil, Seneca, Ovid, and other poets" [146 n. 40]). But his claim is also disputable on historical grounds. I would question his treatment of the Franciscan tradition (36, somewhat modified on 42), and of the Diggers (148–49 n. 52, where he is troubled by the Diggers' appeal to "reason"). Kenneth Graham directed me to Fleischacker's book.

94. Cefalu's claim that Gloucester's empathetic response fails to "mediate an understanding of and respect for rights" seems to me quite mistaken (*Revisionist Shakespeare*, 129).

95. See Fernand Braudel, *The Structure of Everyday Life: Civilization and Capitalism, 15th–18th Century*, vol. 1 (Berkeley: University of California Press, 1992).

96. Compare Fitter, "'So Distribution Should Undo Excess,'" 845–46, 852–54.

97. I know of no direct evidence for Shakespeare's knowledge of *Utopia*. Gonzalo's imagined "commonwealth" in *The Tempest* has nothing at all to do with *Utopia* (see *"The Tempest* [2]: Labor"). More's *libellus* was, however, easily available in Latin (many editions) and in Ralph Robinson's English translation (1551; rpt. 1556, 1597).

98. See *The Complete Works of St. Thomas More*, vol. 4, *Utopia*, ed. Edward Surtz, S. J., and J. H. Hexter (New Haven, Conn.: Yale University Press, 1965), 128–31. Fleischacker's treatment of *Utopia* is extremely superficial, though he concedes that it constitutes "a partial exception" to his historical claim (*A Short History of Distributive Justice*, 44). He insists, however, that More's book is not meant to be taken seriously (48). I have contested this view in "Taking *Utopia* Seriously—and Positively," *Moreana* 54:2 (2017): 141–48.

99. Halpern similarly sees a deep connection between the play and *Utopia*, though I do not agree that they both "formulate a failed utopian response" (*The Poetics of Primitive Accumulation*, 265).

100. This does not contradict the view put forth in the previous chapter that literary works need not resolve the problems that they raise (see 89). To leave a problem unresolved is not the same as being contradictory in relation to it.

101. De Grazia, "The Ideology of Superfluous Things," 32.

102. See James H. Kavanagh, "Shakespeare in Ideology," in *Alternative Shakespeares*, ed. John Drakakis (London: Methuen, 1985), 159.

103. De Grazia, "The Ideology of Superfluous Things," 31.

104. De Grazia, 32.

105. Ignatieff, *The Needs of Strangers*, 35.

106. Kronenfeld, *"King Lear" and the Naked Truth*, 176.

107. Kronenfeld, 224. Kronenfeld cannot resist the scare quotes, and somewhat withdraws from this position on 228.

108. Henry James, *The Painter's Eye: Notes and Essays on the Pictorial Arts*, ed. John L. Sweeney (Madison: University of Wisconsin Press, 1989), 185. I owe this reference to William R. Veeder.

109. De Grazia sees the play and the period as equating property with identity. She may be right that, for the period, "what *one* is depends upon what one *owns*" (a homonym, she thinks, as well as an equation [34]). But *who* one is does not. Lear, Cordelia, Gloucester, and Edgar (as Edgar, not as "Tom") are all recognizably the same persons regardless of whether they have property or not. When, for instance, Lear says, "this is not Lear" (1.4: 219; 199), the hyperbolic nature of this response immediately shows that its speaker is indeed Lear. Personal identity—fundamental attitudes and ways of speaking—seems, in fact, remarkably stable in the play. To have nothing left of one's identity except one's style is to be *in extremis*, but the style and the values remain. Undowered Cordelia is "herself a dowry" (for the importance of this in relation to de Grazia's views, see Maus, *Being and Having in Shakespeare*, 119). De Grazia thinks she is following the historical analysis of J. G. A. Pocock in seeing (in the period) personality as a function of property (34), but Pocock is referring specifically to "*political* personality" ("Authority and Property: The Question of Liberal Origins," in *Virtue, Commerce, and History* [Cambridge: Cambridge University Press, 1985], 57, 70; emphasis mine).

110. Palfrey suggests that the dying Lear's request that a button be undone recalls Lear's unbuttoning in the storm (*Poor Tom*, 240). This is a nice connection, but relies on a Folio-only reading of Lear's speech at 3.4.97 / 101 ("come, unbutton heere"). This is a major textual crux. Qb has merely "come on"; Qa has "come on bee true." See Warren, *The Parallel King Lear*, 78–79. For "Qa" (the uncorrected Quarto) and "Qb" (corrected), see W. W. Greg, *The Variants in the First Quarto of "King Lear"* (London: Oxford University Press, 1940).

111. I am not sure where Marie Theresa O'Connor gets the idea that Kent's refusal might have invalidated Albany's offer ("Irrepressible Britain and *King Lear*," *Medieval and Renaissance Drama in England* 31 [2018]: 116). At this point Albany is, as Qa has him at the beginning of act 5 (5.1.4), "full of abdication." See Warren, *The Parallel King Lear*. Weis, *King Lear: A Parallel Text Edition*, fails to register this variant.

112. F. T. Flahiff, "Edgar: Once and Future King," in Colie and Flahiff, *Some Facets of "King Lear*,*"* 221–38, esp. 229–32.

113. In the Quarto, "The oldest have borne most," which requires a plural subject, and would include Gloucester; in the Folio, "The oldest hath borne most," which seems to refer only to Lear. The grammatical difference is noted in Knowles, *A New Variorum Edition*, 1:1014. In *The Structure of Complex Words* (London: Chatto and Windus, 1952), William Empson gives a wonderful account of the tone of the final couplet and its specific application to Lear (157).

114. Peter Holbrook defends "feeling" as a genuine force in historical reform in "The Left and *King Lear*," *Textual Practice* 14 (2000): 349–51. For a more general defense of this view in relation to the play, see Tom McAlindon, "Tragedy, *King Lear*, and the Politics of the Heart," *Shakespeare Survey* 44 (1992): 85–90. I should mention that I do not see "feeling" here and throughout the play as having the ontological entanglement that Amanda Bailey postulates (with "the magnetism that naturally conjoins all forms of matter"; "Speak What We Feel: Sympathy and Statecraft," in *Affect Theory and Early Modern Texts*, ed. Amanda Bailey and Mario DiGangi [New York: Palgrave Macmillan, 2017], 27–46 [36]).

115. Maus, *Being and Having in Shakespeare*, 130–31.

CHAPTER 6

1. For studies, see Mark Thornton Burnett, *Masters and Servants in English Renaissance Drama and Culture: Authority and Obedience* (New York: St. Martin's Press, 1997); David Evett, *Discourses of Service in Shakespeare's England* (New York: Palgrave Macmillan, 2005); Judith Weil, *Service and Dependency in Shakespeare's Plays* (Cambridge: Cambridge University Press, 2005); David Schalkwyk, *Shakespeare, Love and Service* (Cambridge: Cambridge University Press, 2008), and Elizabeth Rivlin, *The Aesthetics of Service in Early Modern England* (Evanston, Ill.: Northwestern University Press, 2012).

2. See Richard Strier, "Faithful Servants: Shakespeare's Praise of Disobedience," in *The Historical Renaissance: New Essays in Tudor and Stuart Literature and Culture,* ed. Heather Dubrow and Richard Strier (Chicago: University of Chicago Press, 1988), 104–33; expanded in Strier, *Resistant Structures: Particularity, Radicalism, and Renaissance Texts* (Berkeley: University of California Press, 1995), ch. 7.

3. See Thomas Kuhn, *The Structure of Scientific Revolutions,* 2nd ed. (Chicago: University of Chicago Press, 1970), chs. 2–5.

4. Rob Nixon, "Caribbean and African Appropriations of *The Tempest*," *Critical Inquiry* 13 (1987): 557–78; [Dominique] O. [Octave] Mannoni, *Psychologie de la colonisation* (Paris: Éditions du Seuil, 1950); Aimé Césaire, *Une Tempête* (Paris: Éditions du Seuil, 1969). For translations, see Mannoni, *Prospero and Caliban: The Psychology of Colonization,* trans. Pamela Powesland, 2nd ed. (New York: Praeger 1964), and Césaire, *A Tempest,* trans. Richard Miller (New York: Ubu Repertory Theater, 1992).

5. Joan Dayan, "Playing Caliban: Césaire's *Tempest*," *Arizona Quarterly* 48 (1992): 125–45, temptingly propounded the critical possibility ("Césaire teaches us how to return to the Shakespeare 'original'" [130]), and sees the works of Shakespeare and Césaire as deeply in dialogue, but her interest is more in what Césaire was doing than in what Shakespeare was.

6. For instance, Thomas Cartelli's "Prospero in Africa," in *Shakespeare Reproduced: The Text in History and Ideology,* ed. Jean E. Howard and Marion F. O'Connor (New York: Routledge, 1987), 99–115, sees the play's complicity in colonial discourse as part of its meaning, but does not see its usefulness to anticolonialist discourse as having this same status. Ania Loomba, *Gender, Race, Renaissance Drama* (Manchester: Manchester University Press, 1989), 145–46, also points out the dissymmetry in Cartelli's analysis. Lotfi Salhi, "*Une Tempête* Politicizing *The Tempest*: Césaire Rewrites Shakespeare," *International Journal of English Literature and Social Science* 2 (2017): 18–25, sees Césaire's play as simply corrective of the (supposed) proto-imperialism of Shakespeare's.

7. For the claim that the moments when it seems to problematize or contest colonialist discourse constitute or reveal the play's "political unconscious," see Paul Brown, "'This Thing of Darkness I acknowledge mine': *The Tempest* and the Discourse of Colonialism," in *Political Shakespeare: New Essays in Cultural Materialism*, ed. Jonathan Dollimore and Alan Sinfield (Manchester: Manchester University Press, 1985), 48–71, esp. 69. Jonathan Goldberg's view of the play is similar, though he uses "moments of textual trouble" to identify the play's unconscious (*Tempest in the Caribbean* [Minneapolis: University of Minnesota Press, 2004], 3–4). For the play as a triumph of systematic bad faith, see Lorie Jerrell Leininger, "Cracking the Code of *The Tempest*," in *Contemporary Critical Approaches to Shakespeare,* ed. Harry R. Garvin (Lewisburg, Pa.: Bucknell University Press, 1980), 121–31.

8. For a similar understanding of the antiauthoritarian elements in the play, see David Norbrook, "'What Cares These Roarers for the Name of King?': Language and Utopia in *The Tem-*

pest" (1992), rpt. in *Shakespeare: The Last Plays*, ed. Kiernan Ryan (London: Longman, 1999), 246–78. In speaking of the "cues and clues" that support his reading, Harry Berger Jr. also suggests that his anti-idealizing reading is intended by Shakespeare ("The Miraculous Harp: A Reading of Shakespeare's *Tempest*," in *Second World and Green World: Studies in Renaissance Fiction-Making* [Berkeley: University of California Press, 1988], 150).

9. George Lamming, *The Pleasures of Exile* (London: M. Joseph, 1960; rpt. with a foreword by Sandra Pouchet Paquet, Ann Arbor: University of Michigan Press, 1992), 13. My sense of what Lamming is doing corresponds to that of Peter Hulme in "Reading from Elsewhere: George Lamming and the Paradox of Exile," in *"The Tempest" and Its Travels*, ed. Peter Hulme and William H. Sherman (London: Reaktion Books, 2000), 220–35. But where Hulme is concerned to describe Lamming's insights into Shakespeare's play, my attempt is to develop and extend them (as with Mannoni and Césaire).

10. Unless otherwise noted, references are to *The Tempest*, ed. Frank Kermode (London: Methuen, 1958) ; hereafter "*The Tempest*, Kermode, ed." Where indicated, I have departed from Kermode's text for fidelity to the Folio (the sole text), for which I have used *The Norton Facsimile of the First Folio of Shakespeare*, ed. Charlton Hinman (New York: Norton, 1968), 19–37.

11. *King Lear: A Parallel Text Edition*, ed. René Weis (London: Longman, 1993), 3.4: Q 76–77; F 81–82. Citations from *King Lear* are to this edition.

12. I am using the male pronoun for Ariel, since it seems appropriate in this context, but I do not mean to deny the gender ambiguity or nonspecificity of the role. On this, see Bryan Reynolds and Ayanna Thompson, "Inspriteful Ariels: Transversal Tempests," in Bryan Reynolds, *Performing Transversally: Reimagining Shakespeare and the Critical Future* (New York: Palgrave Macmillan, 2003), 189–214.

13. Exactly what Antonio's designated position was before his usurpation of the dukedom is never made clear. In *Measure for Measure*, Angelo is referred to as "the Deputy," which would seem to be something like Antonio's position when he governed in Prospero's stead.

14. The army in question must have been composed of Milanese, otherwise it would not be "a treacherous army," merely an enemy one.

15. Prospero lists "rich garments, linens," and, perhaps in another category, "stuffs" as well as "necessaries" (1.2.164). Gonzalo was clearly imagining Prospero's survival, and did not want him to live a deprived life in his exile. We find out later that the "stuffs" must have included impressive household "utensils" (3.3.94) and, it turns out, a chess set.

16. For "Knowing naught, like dogs, but following," see *King Lear*, 2.2: Q 74; F 76.

17. For a view of Gonzalo's behavior that emphasizes his complicity rather than his resistance, see Evett, *Discourses of Service*, 197.

18. For a sharply contrasting reading, see Paul Yachnin, "Shakespeare and the Idea of Obedience: Gonzalo in *The Tempest*," *Mosaic* 24 (1991): 1–18. Yachnin reads the play as a whole as supporting only obedience. He sees Gonzalo's charity as a kind of sop to his conscience within the context of obedience.

19. For disobedience, in some circumstances, as true good service and loyalty, see Strier, "Faithful Servants."

20. For Miranda's action here as having political significance, see Melissa E. Sanchez, "Seduction and Service in *The Tempest*," *SP* 105 (2008): 50–82 (75).

21. For a recent treatment of counsel, see Ivan Lupić, *Subjects of Advice: Drama and Counsel from More to Shakespeare* (Philadelphia: University of Pennsylvania Press, 2019).

22. For further discussion of this moment, see "*The Tempest* (2): Labor."

23. For Buchanan, see *De Jure Regni apud Scotos, or, A Dialogue Concerning the Due Privilege of Government in the Kingdom of Scotland* (1689), 57–58. (The date of this English translation of Buchanan's treatise is worth noting.)

24. I have rejected the emendation of "present" to "presence" accepted by Kermode. See Stephen Orgel's comments on this in his edition of *The Tempest* (Oxford: Oxford University Press, 1987), 98; hereafter "*The Tempest*, Orgel, ed."

25. I have not followed Kermode in capitalizing this word, since the Folio, as is normal for early modern texts, capitalizes abstract nouns as a matter of course. But Kermode is right in suggesting that "art" is a term of art in the play.

26. On the theory of (high) Renaissance magic, and the importance in the theory of control over "daemons," see Kermode's introduction and appendix B (*The Tempest*, Kermode, ed.); and, inter alia, Robert H. West, *The Invisible World: A Study of Pneumatology in Elizabethan Drama* (Athens, Ga.: University of Georgia Press, 1939).

27. Orgel, introduction to *The Tempest*, Orgel, ed., 25; hereafter "Orgel, introduction".

28. I have borrowed the useful term "magian" from Harry Levin, "Two Magian Comedies: *The Tempest* and the *Alchemist*," *Shakespeare Studies* 22 (1969): 47–58.

29. *Doctor Faustus*, "B-Text" (1.1.115–17), in *Doctor Faustus, A- and B-Texts*, ed. David Bevington and Eric Rasmussen (Manchester: Manchester University Press, 1993). The "A-Text" version of these is slightly different, substituting "subjects" for spirits "of every element" (A: 1.1.124). The literal meaning is clearer in "B," but the political pun is richer in "A," and the connection to subjection is worth noting.

30. Jane Kingsley-Smith notes that "there was a connection between magic and colonialism in the magician plays of the 1580s and 1590s," but does not cite this key passage (*Shakespeare's Drama of Exile* [New York: Palgrave Macmillan, 2003], 166).

31. Compare Peter Hulme, *Colonial Encounters: Europe and the Native Caribbean, 1492–1797* (London: Methuen, 1986), 127–28.

32. Mannoni, *Prospero and Caliban*, 32, 203–4. It is important to note that Mannoni never denies the importance of economics to colonialism. His claim is that "the colonial is not looking for profit *only*," that he is also seeking and receiving a certain kind of pleasure, which it is essential to take into account "in any attempt to understand what is colonial about a colonial situation" (32 [emphasis mine], 204).

33. Elizabeth Fox-Genovese and Eugene D. Genovese note that whatever one wishes to say about Mannoni's views of the colonized, he "files a more blistering indictment of the colonizers" ("Illusions of Liberation: The Psychology of Colonialism and Revolution in the Work of Octave Mannoni and Frantz Fanon," in *Rethinking Marxism*, ed. W. Stephen Resnick and Richard Wolff [New York: Autonomedia, 1985], 129). In the *Discourse on Colonialism* (1955), trans. Joan Pinkham (New York: Monthly Review Press, 1972), 39–43, Césaire sees Mannoni as simply a racialist and a colonial apologist; Fanon, on the other hand, begins his discussion in "The So-Called Dependency Complex of Colonized Peoples," by stating that the "analytic thought" of Mannoni's work "is honest" (Frantz Fanon, *Black Skin, White Masks* [1952], trans. Charles Lamm Markmann [New York: Grove Press, 1967], 83–108). Césaire's play (as opposed to the *Discourse*) can be seen to embody his positive debt to Mannoni, who may have taught Césaire in the Lycée Schoelcher in Martinique in the 1920s (before Mannoni went to Madagascar). A Mannoni-like account by Césaire is quoted in S. Belhassen, "Aimé Césaire's *A Tempest*," in *Radical Perspectives in the Arts*, ed. Lee Baxandall (Baltimore: Penguin Books, 1972), 176. Césaire taught Fanon (also at the Lycée Schoelcher) in the early 1940s. In a reflection on *The Psychology of Colonization*, Mannoni said

that almost two decades later he "would essentially say the same things, but in a different way" ("The Decolonisation of Myself," *Race* 7 [1966]: 327–35 [328]).

34. Fanon, *Black Skin, White Masks*, 107. Goldberg notes that "the psychology Fanon describes is not all that far from Mannoni's" (*Tempest in the Caribbean*, 19).

35. Césaire, *A Tempest*, 65–66. Donald Pease states that in Césaire's play Caliban "persuades Prospero to remain and help in the process of decolonization" ("Toward a Sociology of Literary Knowledge: Greenblatt, Colonialism, and the New Historicism," in *Consequences of Theory*, ed. Jonathan Arac and Barbara Johnson [Baltimore: Johns Hopkins University Press, 1991], 115). This is wildly misleading. Césaire's Prospero makes the decision to stay for his own reasons, and, in his final speech before the epilogue, tells Caliban, "henceforth I will answer your violence with violence" (67).

36. Mannoni, *Prospero and Caliban*, 97.

37. Holinshed's *Chronicles* (1587), for instance, were "Of England, Scotland, and Ireland," and "news from the new world" was plentiful throughout Europe in the sixteenth century. For Shakespeare's reading in this material, see, inter alia, Kermode, introduction (*The Tempest*, Kermode, ed.), xxx–xxxiv. For the way the new and old world contexts interacted, see Barbara Fuchs, "Conquering Islands: Contextualizing *The Tempest*," *Shakespeare Quarterly* 48 (1997): 45–62. For the specifically Irish context, see Dympna Callaghan, "Irish Memories in *The Tempest*," in her *Shakespeare Without Women: Representing Gender and Race on the Renaissance Stage* (London: Routledge, 2000), 97–138.

38. *A True Declaration of the State of Virginia* (1610), in *New American World*, ed. David B. Quinn (New York: Arno Press, 1979), 5:255b. On the newness and conscious classicizing of this conception, see Quinn, "Renaissance Influences in English Colonization," *Transactions of the Royal Historical Society*, 5th series, 26 (1976): 73–93.

39. Prospero, it should be noted, never uses this word. The one use of it in the play (noted by Hulme, *Colonial Encounters*, 107) occurs, ironically, in the anticultivationist context of Gonzalo's golden age vision (2.1.138). Richard Halpern's reading of that speech misses the way in which Gonzalo's use of the term undermines its normal meaning rather than (as Halpern thinks) extending it ("'The Picture of Nobody': White Cannibalism in *The Tempest*," in *The Production of English Renaissance Culture*, ed. David Lee Miller, Sharon O'Dair, and Harold Weber [Ithaca, N.Y.: Cornell University Press, 1994], 262–92 [267]).

40. See Stephen Saunders Webb, *The Governors-General: The English Army and the Definition of the Empire, 1569–1681* (Chapel Hill: University of North Carolina Press, 1979), 39, 166, and 436–37.

41. See Anthony Pagden, *Lords of All the World: Ideologies of Empire in Spain, Britain, and France, c. 1500–c. 1800* (New Haven, Conn.: Yale University Press, 1995), 77–79. For the claim that the association of house-building, gardening, and farming with possession was particularly strong for the English, see Patricia Seed, *Ceremonies of Possession in Europe's Conquest of the New World, 1492–1640* (Cambridge: Cambridge University Press, 1995), ch. 1.

42. See Nicholas Canny, "The Ideology of English Colonization: From Ireland to America," *William and Mary Quarterly*, 3rd series, 30 (1973), 575–79, and *The Elizabethan Conquest of Ireland: A Pattern Established, 1565–76* (New York: Barnes & Noble Books, 1976); see also Webb, *The Governors-General*.

43. Sir John Davies, *A Discovery Of the True Causes Why Ireland was Never Entirely Subdued* (1612), ed. James P. Myers Jr. (Washington, D.C.: Catholic University of America, 1988), 165; W. Crashaw, *A Sermon Preached before . . . The Lord Lawarre, Lord Governour and Captaine Generall of Virginea . . . Febr. 21. 1609)* (London: William Welby, 1610), D4^r.

44. In *Shakespeare's Drama of Exile,* Kingsley-Smith recognizes that Prospero is "hardly a colonialist at all," but sees this as resulting from his status as an exile who longs, above all, to get back home (170). It is this longing that the Mannoni-Césaire reading would dispute.

45. Although Prospero speaks of his "house" at 4.1.18, it is never described or alluded to as a piece of architecture or as one of his own or Ariel's achievements. Caliban suggests that Prospero was somehow intending all along to build a "house" (2.2.95), but does not suggest that he had even begun the endeavor. I do not find plausible the suggestion that the supposedly intended "house" is a theater. See Vin Nardizzi, *Wooden O's: Shakespeare's Theatres and England's Trees* (Toronto: University of Toronto Press, 2013), 132–32.

46. Compare L. T. Fitz, "The Vocabulary of the Environment in *The Tempest*," *Shakespeare Quarterly* 26 (1975): 43.

47. Patricia Akhimie's discussion of *cultus animae* in *Shakespeare and the Cultivation of Difference: Race and Conduct in the Early Modern World* (New York: Routledge, 2018), 155–57, recognizes the normal English understanding of colonization as cultivation of land but blurs the picture by seeing intellectual "cultivation" as an equivalent ("Prospero uses the island in a less literal way to cultivate").

48. Quoted in Webb, *The Governors-General*, 14.

49. This is the description of Caliban in the cast list in the Folio (p. 37).

50. Quoted in Philip D. Morgan, *Slave Counterpoint: Black Culture in the Eighteenth-Century Chesapeake and Lowcountry* (Chapel Hill: University of North Carolina Press, 1998), 100.

51. Mannoni, *Prospero and Caliban,* 102.

52. Prospero apparently had no taste for and perhaps no aptitude for the kind of (ordinary) exercises of power of which, as we saw in Prospero's description of how he was usurped, Antonio was apparently a virtuoso. On "the colonial" as "very different from his former self," see Mannoni, *Prospero and Caliban,* 97.

53. Pagden, *Lords of All the World,* 78; see also 91 (on *encomiendas*).

54. Quentin Skinner and Philip Pettit have shown that there is an ancient and early modern political theory in which domination is the exact opposite of freedom. See Quentin Skinner in *Liberty Before Liberalism* (Cambridge: Cambridge University Press, 1997) and elsewhere, and Philp Pettit, in *Republicanism: A Theory of Freedom and Government* (Oxford: Oxford University Press, 1997) and elsewhere.

55. On hailing in *Macbeth*, see John Kerrigan, *Archipelagic English: Literature, History, and Politics, 1603–1707* (Oxford: Oxford University Press, 2008), 104–10.

56. Berger, "The Miraculous Harp," 152.

57. Lamming, "A Monster, a Child, a Slave," in *The Pleasures of Exile,* 97. The title of Lamming's essay does not include Ariel, since the "slave" in question is, presumably, Caliban, but some of Lamming's most telling points concern Ariel—as here. Berger also takes note of Ariel's pleasure in description ("The Miraculous Harp," 152).

58. Derek Cohen, "The Culture of Slavery: Caliban and Ariel," *Dalhousie Review* 76 (1996): 174.

59. We would say that this is a culturally "effeminizing" remark. I am not sure that this is anachronistic. See Rosalind's parodies of (supposed) female behavior, though boys also are "cattle of this color" (*As You Like It*, 3.2.98–99).

60. In "Industrious Ariel and Idle Caliban," in *Travel and Drama in Shakespeare's Time*, ed. Jean-Pierre Maquerlot and Michèle Williams (Cambridge: Cambridge University Press, 1996), 193–208, Andrew Gurr attempts to distinguish Ariel's relation to Prospero from Caliban's, but does not succeed in making the supposed distinction very apparent or convincing. After quoting Orgel's observation that Ariel is the "unwilling servant" of both magi in the play, Sycorax and

Prospero, Gurr then says, "Caliban by contrast has only become a servant or slave unwillingly" (197). So where is the contrast? Gurr also never makes it clear in what sense Caliban is "idle." This seems to rely on the same supposed contrast: Caliban, as opposed to Ariel, works unwillingly, and so, presumably—like a London apprentice in various tracts—wishes to be "idle." But, as Gurr points out, Ariel is the one whose situation is more like that of an apprentice (198).

61. Lamming, "A Monster, a Child, a Slave," 99, 115–16.

62. See *The Tempest*, Orgel, ed., 115–16.

63. See, inter alia, Orgel, ed., 22–23.

64. For "murmuring," see Exodus 16:7, Numbers 14:2, 27, 29, 36; in the New Testament, Luke 5:30, John 6:41. The Geneva Bible and the Authorized Version (1611) concur in this translation. English poets of the period used the term in this sense; see especially Herbert's "The Bunch of Grapes" and Milton's "When I consider how my light is spent."

65. Kermode (*The Tempest*, Kermode, ed., 28) points out the recurrence of forms of the word "gentle" in the play, and sees it as having a class as well as a behavioral meaning (xliii–iv). I am not sure that it has that connotation.

66. The command in question—"Go make thyself like a nymph o' th' sea" (301)—has generated a certain amount of critical puzzlement. It may, as Orgel suggests (*The Tempest*, Orgel, ed., 117), be appropriate for Ariel's next task—singing to Ferdinand about his supposedly drowned father (377–85), or it may simply be an arbitrary fancy.

67. Derek Cohen calls attention to the oddness of this attribution of self-characterization to Ariel—"my slave, / As thou report's thyself"—though I am not convinced that in this phrase Prospero is "acknowledging the moral ambiguity of his position" ("The Culture of Slavery," 162). I think Prospero is simply reminding Ariel of Ariel's position and of Ariel's normal acquiescence in it as opposed to his past lack of acquiescence in serving Sycorax ("Thou ... was then her servant").

68. Roberto Fernandez Retamar, "Caliban: Notes Toward a Discussion of Culture in Our America" (1971), in *Caliban and Other Essays,* trans. Edward Baker (Minneapolis: University of Minnesota Press, 1989), 16. Rivlin notes "the permeability between service and slavery" in the play (*The Aesthetics of Service*, 157), but seems to want to maintain the distinction. Similarly, Mary Nyquist first asserts an "obvious difference" between Ariel's servitude and Caliban's, but then speaks of "the brutal disciplinary regime" that Prospero had established for both ("Base Slavery and Roman Yoke," in *The Oxford Handbook of English Law and Literature, 1500–1700* [Oxford: Oxford University Press, 2017], 635–36).

69. See Schalkwyk, *Shakespeare, Love and Service*, 37–56 and passim.

70. Sigmund Freud, *Totem and Taboo,* trans. James Strachey, intro. by Peter Gay (New York: Norton, 1989), sec. iii, especially 97–107.

71. *The Tempest,* Kermode, ed., 143, Appendix B: "Ariel as Daemon and Fairy").

72. Elizabeth D. Harvey basically equates Ariel as a "spirit" with the physiological "spirits" in the blood ("Passionate Spirits: Animism and Embodiment in *Cymbeline* and *The Tempest*," in *The Oxford Handbook of Shakespeare and Embodiment*, ed. Valerie Traub [Oxford: Oxford University Press, 2016], 369–84). While this conflation may be culturally available, I think that it confuses rather than clarifies the relation between the characters in the play—who are, I believe, to be taken as separate characters, with specific and different psychological configurations.

73. Schalkwyk concedes that Prospero's response here is *"textually* perfunctory," but, as the italics indicate, Schalkwyk would like to see something richer here, something along the lines of Cavellian acknowledgment, but Schalkwyk can only phrase this possibility tentatively and hypo-

thetically ("To acknowledge love for the servant would signal the recognition" [*Shakespeare, Love and Service*, 111]).

74. Jeffrey S. Doty, "Experiences of Authority in *The Tempest*," *Shakespeare and the Politics of Commoners: Digesting the New Social History*, ed. Chris Fitter (Oxford: Oxford University Press, 2017), 241.

75. Mannoni, *Prospero and Caliban*, 107.

76. See *The Politics of Aristotle*, trans. Ernest Barker (New York: Oxford University Press, 1958), I.v.8 (13). For commentary on this postulated entity, see Mary P. Nichols, "The Good Life, Slavery, and Acquisition: Aristotle's Introduction to Politics," *Interpretation* 11 (1983): 171–83; Wayne Ambler, "Aristotle on Nature and Politics: The Case of Slavery," *Political Theory* 15 (1987): 390–410; and Martha Craven Nussbaum, "Shame, Separateness, and Political Unity: Aristotle's Criticism of Plato," in *Essays on Aristotle's Ethics*, ed. Amélie Oksenberg Rorty (Berkeley: University of California Press, 1980), 395–435 (esp. 415–22).

77. Lamming, "A Monster, a Child, a Slave," 99.

78. For a meditation on (and defense of) the idea that "a love relationship can be founded on inequality," see Aaron Kunin's remarkable *Love Three: A Study of a Poem by George Herbert* (Seattle: Wave Books, 2019), 106 (section 57).

79. For God's service as "perfect freedom," see the Collect for Peace in the 1559 text, in *The Book of Common Prayer: The Texts of 1549, 1559, and 1662*, ed. Brian Cummings (Oxford: Oxford University Press, 2011), 111, and see Kunin, *Love Three*. For claims that the prayerbook phrase is applicable to Ferdinand's love for Miranda, see "*The Tempest* (2): Labor," note 32.

80. For the connotations of mountain freedom that Prospero seems to be drawing on here, see Joshua Scodel, "'Sweet Liberty' and Literary Tradition in Milton's *L'Allegro*," a paper given to the Renaissance Workshop at the University of Chicago, and as a lecture at Yale University (available on YouTube).

81. I do not agree with Cohen that the primary feature of this vision is its "noncommunal" quality ("The Culture of Slavery," 173). It has been pointed out to me that while Prospero says that he "shall miss" Ariel (5.1.95), Ariel "never says the like to him" (from a reader for the Press).

82. The lines on Caliban's "human shape" (1.2.281–284a) are complex, but they do affirm Caliban's possession of such—"Save for" him (except for him) the island, prior to the arrival of Prospero and Miranda, was not "honour'd with" such a shape. That he may be, as the Folio cast list states, "deformed," suggests that he is, rather than that he is not, human (if he were not human, he would not be "deformed," merely shaped like something else—compare *Richard III*). Moreover, Caliban shares Prospero's ethico-biological pride in "a human shape," speaking contemptuously of "apes / With foreheads villainous low" (4.1.249).

83. See "*The Tempest* (2): Labor."

84. See "Ralph Lane's Discourse on the First Colony," in *the Roanoke Voyages, 1584–1590*, ed. David Beers Quinn (London: Hakluyt Society, 1955), 1:276–80.

85. On torture in the play, see Curt Breight, "'Treason doth never prosper': *The Tempest* and the Discourse of Treason," *Shakespeare Quarterly* 41 (1990): 25–27, and Akhimie, *Shakespeare and the Cultivation of Difference*, 169–76.

86. On the initial relationship of Prospero and Caliban, see "*The Tempest* (3): Humanism."

87. Compare Brown, "'This Thing of Darkness,'" 59.

88. Kermode discusses a premodern meaning of the term "race" in his introduction, xlii–xlvii; Orgel glosses the term as as "natural or inherited disposition" (*The Tempest*, Orgel, ed., 120). But the context here (spoken by a European of a non-European) seems to bring the usage eerily in

line with post-Renaissance racialist discourse. See Kim F. Hall, *Things of Darkness: Economies of Race and Gender in Early Modern England* (Ithaca, N.Y.: Cornell University Press, 1995), 6–8, 142–43, and Goldberg, *Tempest in the Caribbean*, 120–24. For the historical complexity of the term, see Ania Loomba, "Race and the Possibilities of Comparative Critique," *New Literary History* 40 (2009): 501–22; and *The Origins of Racism in the West*, ed. Miriam Eliav-Feldon, Benjamin Isaac, and Joseph Ziegler (Cambridge: Cambridge University Press, 2009).

89. Mannoni, *Prospero and Caliban*, 106 (and Part II, ch. 2). Mannoni has been followed in this view by many commentators, from Fanon (*Black Skins, White Masks*, 163–67) on. See Loomba, *Gender, Race, Renaissance Drama*, 150; Hall, *Things of Darkness*, 142–43; Seed, "'This island's mine': Caliban and Native Sovereignty," in Hulme and Sherman, *"The Tempest" and Its Travels*, 211.

90. For discussion, see "*The Tempest* (3): Humanism" below.

91. On incestuous fantasy in the play, see Mannoni, *Prospero and Caliban*, 106–7, and Jeffrey Stern, "The Cause of Thunder: A Psychoanalytic Reading of *King Lear, Pericles*, and *The Tempest*" (Ph.D. diss., University of Chicago, 1982). James Dougal Fleming argues that when Caliban says that Prospero "didst prevent" Caliban from a sexual relationship with Miranda, Caliban is accusing Prospero of having preempted him in this ("Prevent Is Not Prevent: Rape and Rhetoric in *The Tempest*," *Exemplaria* 15 [2003]: 451–72). Despite the philology that Fleming provides, I think this meaning contextually unlikely even if historically possible.

92. Tom MacFaul points out the prominence of "honour" here, but not its class significance (*Shakespeare and the Natural World* [Cambridge: Cambridge University Press, 2015], 185). James A. Brundage notes that in fourteenth- and fifteenth-century Venice "the higher the social status of the victim [of rape], the more severe the punishment [of the rapist]" (*Law, Sex, and Christian Society in Medieval Europe* [Chicago: University of Chicago Press, 1987], 530).

93. Apart from (or intertwined with) his own psychology, Prospero can be seen as relying on a legal view of rape as an assault on patriarchal authority and property rather than on the legal view that focuses on the victim's prior consent to the sexual act. The Elizabethan period has been seen as one in which official legal culture was making a transition from the former view to the latter. See Nazife Bashar, "Rape in England Between 1550 and 1700," in *The Sexual Dynamics of History: Men's Power, Women's History* (London: Pluto Press, 1983), 28–42, and Amy Greenstadt, *Rape and the Rise of the Author: Gendering Intention in Early Modern England* (Farnham: Ashgate, 2009), 31 and passim.

94. Translation in Sir Arthur Helps, *The Spanish Conquest of America and Its Relation to the History of Slavery and to the Government of Colonies* (1861), intro. M. Oppenheim (London: John Lane, 1900), 1:266 (for the whole document, 264–67). On the *Requirimiento*, see Stephen Greenblatt, "Learning to Curse: Aspects of Linguistic Colonialism in the Sixteenth Century," in *Learning to Curse: Essays in Early Modern Culture* (New York: Routledge, 1990), 28–30; and Seed, *Ceremonies of Possession*, ch. 3.

95. Seed notes that when Bartolomé de las Casas first heard about the *Requirimiento*, he "did not know whether to laugh or to cry" (*Ceremonies of Possession*, 71).

96. The problem of Hamlet's age is one notable example, as is the notoriously ambiguous time span of *Othello*.

97. For similar calculations, see *The Tempest*, Orgel, ed., 28 n.1. Bradin Cormack has raised the issue of why Shakespeare wanted this disparity of age between Caliban and Miranda, so they were not adolescents together. I think the answer is that Caliban has to be old enough, when Prospero and Miranda arrive on the island, to instruct Prospero on how to survive and to provide him the means for doing so.

98. Benjamin Jeffery has urged me, surely correctly, to see this "indifference" as either consciously or unconsciously wilfull, as a matter of being unwilling or unable to countenance loss or diminution of control.

99. In "Single Parenting, Homeschooling: Prospero, Caliban, Miranda," *SEL* 48 (2008): 373–93, Hiewon Shin opines that "arguably" Prospero is to blame for the attempted rape (376). She quotes a warning from Sir Thomas Elyot against mixed-sex education (starting from when a boy is seven). She does not see the parallel with Antonio.

100. In elaborating on this claim, Prospero seems to take some responsibility for this result, but the lines are very complicated: "my trust / Like a good parent, *did beget of him* / A falsehood in its contrary, as great / As my trust was" (1.2.93b–96a; emphasis mine). Whether there is a difference between Antonio's "evil nature" and Caliban's (supposed) "vile race" is an interesting question. The phrase used for Caliban is perhaps less abstract, since "vile" has a sociological meaning, and "race," while complex and ambiguous, seems to have a biological component (see note 88).

101. Michel Foucault, *Power-Knowledge: Selected Interviews and Other Writings,* ed. Colin Gordon (New York: Knopf Doubleday, 1980), ix, and chs. 5–6. Knowledge as power sounds Baconian, but Prospero's "project" does not seem to be the Baconian one of using power over nature to make nature more productive. Prospero's aims are entirely social, political, and (perhaps) moral. For an argument that Prospero's "art" is Baconian, see Elizabeth Spiller, "Shakespeare and the Making of Early Modern Science: Resituating Prospero's Art," *South Central Review* 26 (2009): 24–41. Césaire's Prospero is more Baconian than Shakespeare's.

102. For a useful collection of essays by Foucault and others on the topic, see *Power,* ed. Steven Lukes (New York: New York University Press, 1986). Judith Butler explores the Foucauldian view in *The Psychic Life of Power: Theories in Subjection* (Stanford, Calif.: Stanford University Press, 1997).

103. The *OED* "control, v." 5a cites Caliban's "controll my Dams god" in support of the definition "to overpower, overmaster." This sense is more normal in the period than the *OED* recognizes. Compare Donne's "For love, all love of other sights controls" in "The Good-morrow" (10).

104. For the legal genealogy of this phrase and its use early in the English Revolution, see "Shakespeare and Legal Systems," note 54. Annabel Patterson uses the phrase to point to what she believes to be the underappreciated antihierarchical strand in the play (*Shakespeare and the Popular Voice* [Cambridge, Mass.: Blackwell, 1989], 154–62 [esp. 160–61]).

105. It has long been known (see Kermode, ed, *The Tempest,* xxvii–xxviii) that Shakespeare took some of the details of the opening scene from William Strachey's *A True Repertory of the Wreck and Redemption of Sir Thomas Gates, Knight upon and from the Islands of the Bermudas: His Coming to Virginia and the Estate of that Colony then and After.* See *A Voyage to Virginia in 1609,* ed. Louis B. Wright (Charlottesville: University Press of Virginia, 1964). Strachey declined to quote Paine directly, but does give the gist of Paine's "unreverent" speech: "let the governor (said he) kiss, etc." (48). Paine is executed, but his speech, "with the omitted additions" after "kiss," echoes through the text. For the "Articles, Lawes, and Orders" of 1611, see Quinn, *New American World,* 1:222.

106. Brown, "'This Thing of Darkness,'" 63.

107. Hulme, *Colonial Encounters,* 120.

108. Stephen Orgel, "Prospero's Wife," in *Representing the English Renaissance,* ed. Stephen Greenblatt (Berkeley: University of California Press, 1988), 226; emphasis mine. See also Orgel, introduction, 51.

109. Stephen Greenblatt, "Martial Law in the Land of Cockagne," in *Shakespearean Negotiations* (Berkeley, CA, 1988), 146 (emphasis mine).

110. Breight, "'Treason doth never prosper,'" 20, 23.

111. Greenblatt, "Martial Law," 142–43, 150, 152.

112. See John Calvin, *Institutes of the Christian Religion,* ed. John T. McNeill, trans. Ford Lewis Battles (Philadelphia: Westminster Press, 1960), III.ii.1–3ff.

113. Sarah Beckwith in *Shakespeare and the Grammar of Forgiveness* (Ithaca, N.Y.: Cornell University Press, 2011) recognizes the relation between memory and repentance (151) but does not make clear that the conception of penitence at work here is the entirely nonceremonial and nonsacerdotal Protestant one. The Council of Trent explicitly anathematizes anyone who thinks "the best penance is merely a new life" (see *The Canons and Decrees of the Council of Trent,* 14th Session, chapters 3–8, trans. Rev. H. J. Schroeder [Rockford, Ill.: Tan Books, 1978], 104). Moreover, Beckwith's analysis treats the penitence imagined as that required to partake of communion in the Church of England. But there is no indication that the withdrawn feast in the play is Eucharistic; the play gives no hint of "sitting down and eating together" (Beckwith, 152) as the culmination of the penitential process. Moreover, the order of procedure is wrong: the feast is offered (insofar as it is) before penitence is demanded. And the play is notably lacking in a final feast or an invitation thereto.

114. Breight, "'Treason doth never prosper,'" 11–12.

115. The depth of this wish may explain the hyperbolical language with which, as we saw, Prospero described Antonio's success in the usurpation.

116. For a detailed exposition of the competing theologies of penance in the period, see Strier, "Herbert and Tears," *ELH* 46 (1979): 221–47.

117. Césaire, *A Tempest,* 33. Greenblatt alludes to this distinction (with regard to *Measure for Measure*) in "Martial Law," 140. Calvin distinguishes godly from "servile" fear (*Institutes,* III.ii.27, III.iii.4).

118. On the equivocal quality of Prospero's "forgiveness" of Antonio, see Orgel, introduction, 53, and the discussion in "*The Tempest* (2): Labor."

119. The consistency with which Antonio is portrayed as a villain, and his complete satisfaction with himself (see 2.1.267–71), make it clear that the idea of a transformed Antonio is entirely a fantasy of Prospero's. This point is developed in Benjamin Jeffery, "An Image on Water: A Reading of Shakespeare's *The Tempest*" (Ph.D. diss., University of Chicago, 2020)).

120. See "*The Tempest* (3): Humanism."

121. See Joseph Warton, *The Adventurer* (London: J. Payne, 1754), 2:160 (no. 97, October 9, 1753). I was alerted to this by Joshua R. Held, "Caliban and the Rhetoric of Sincerity: Postcolonialism, Performance, and the Self," *Christianity and Literature* 67 (2017): 71.

122. Leininger, "Cracking the Code," 127.

123. On grace as not medicine but favor, see Strier, *Love Known: Theology and Experience in George Herbert's Poetry* (Chicago: University of Chicago Press, 1983), 139 and 207.

124. Doty seems to me to underestimate the elements of coercion and fear that inflect Caliban's "willingness" here ("Experiences of Authority," 249).

125. Lamming, "A Monster, a Child, a Slave," 102. The dynastic reading is accepted by Orgel in "Shakespeare and the Cannibals," in *Cannibals, Witches, and Divorce: Estranging the Renaissance,* ed. Marjorie Garber (Baltimore: Johns Hopkins University Press, 1987), 54–55. Lamming's question as to why Caliban thinks the descendants with which he would "people the isle" (1.2.352–53) would be Calibans (102) is picked up by Jyotsna G. Singh, "Caliban Versus Miranda: Race and Gender Conflicts in Postcolonial Rewritings of *The Tempest,*" in *Feminist Readings of Early Modern Culture: Emerging Subjects,* ed. Valerie Traub, M. Lindsay Kaplan, and Dympna Callaghan (Cambridge: Cambridge University Press, 1996), 200. Seed adds that the aim to "people" a colonial possession was "a uniquely English" ambition in the Americas, so that Caliban is

presenting a frightening mirror-image of this project ("'This island's mine,'" 205). Julia Reinhard Lupton explains "peopling" as nation-founding (*Citizen-Saints: Shakespeare and Political Theology* [Chicago: University of Chicago Press, 2005], 176). Urvathi Chakravarty notes that not only is sex curiously absent from Caliban's fantasy, but Caliban seems to be imagining a procedure rather than an action. "Would't had been done!" (1.2.351) is, as Chakravarty says, "devoid of an agent or even an active voice"; she describes Caliban's fantasy as "almost parthenogenic" ("'I had Peopled Else': Shakespeare's Queer Natalities and the Reproduction of Race," in *Queering Childhood in Early Modern English Drama and Culture*, ed. Jennifer Higginbotham and Mark Albert Johnson [Cham, Switzerland: Palgrave Macmillan 2018], 59, 63). Both Seed (208) and Chakravarty (63) invoke cloning.

126. Mannoni, *Prospero and Caliban*, 107.

127. In a remarkable scene (2.1), Césaire presents Ariel and Caliban in dialogue—which makes us realize that there is no moment like this in Shakespeare. In *The Tempest*, the only moments when Ariel and Caliban appear on stage together are when Ariel helps Prospero hunt Caliban with "spirits in shape of dogs," and when Ariel is "driving in" Caliban, Stephano, and Trinculo (stage directions 4.1.254 and 5.1.254). In Césaire's scene, the two acknowledge each other as "brothers"—in suffering, in slavery, and in desire for freedom; they just "have different methods" (20). Ariel is clearly echoing Dr. King; Caliban, Malcolm X (he has said, "Call me X" [15]). Césaire presents the "brotherhood" as genuine, but seems to suggest that his Caliban is the more realistic of the two.

128. When Donne, in the elegy known as "Loves Progress," is arguing that the kiss grows more "refin'd" as it moves downward from the face, he notes that it "At the Papall foote delights to bee" (84). In *John Donne: The Elegies and the Songs and Sonnets*, ed. Helen Gardner (Oxford: Oxford University Press, 1965), Gardner comments on the recurrence of this image in anti-papal propaganda (135).

129. Compare Lupton, *Thinking with Shakespeare*, 216, though to see Caliban as entering into his "majority" here seems to me to simplify and idealize what Shakespeare presents.

130. On the complexities of Caliban's claim here, see Tom Lindsay, "'Which first was mine own king': Caliban and the Politics of Service and Education in *The Tempest*," *Studies in Philology* 113 (2016): 415.

131. On the inconsistencies in Mannoni, see Fanon, *Black Skin, White Masks*, esp. 85, and Fox-Genovese and Genovese, "Illusions of Liberation" (note 33 above). For balanced accounts, see Philip Chassler, "Reading Mannoni's *Prospero and Caliban* Before Reading *Black Skin, White Masks*," *Human Architecture* 5 (2007): 71–81; and Livio Boni, "The (Post)Colonial Condition, Between Marxism and Psychoanalysis: The Contribution of Octave Mannoni," *Actuel Marx* 61 (2017), trans. Robin Mackay [Cairn International], i–xvi, https://www.cairn-int.info/article-E_AMX_061_0153.

132. The need for strong government in Virginia is a major theme of Strachey's *True Repertory* and of the *True Declaration of the State* of *Virginia*; for the willingness to use force against the native peoples, see William Strachey, *A True Repertory of the Wreck and Redemption of Sir Thomas Gates, Knight upon and from the Islands of the Bermudas: His Coming to Virginia and the Estate of that Colony then and After*, in *A Voyage to Virginia in 1609*, ed. Louis B. Wright (Charlottesville: University Press of Virginia, 1964), 89; for the quoted phrase, see the *True Declaration*, 256 (and compare Caliban's dream "That the clouds . . . would open, and show riches / Ready to drop upon me" [3.2.139–40]).

133. Pierre Bourdieu, *Outline of a Theory of Practice*, trans. Richard Nice (Cambridge: Cambridge University Press, 1977), 190. Paul Brown ("'This Thing of Darkness,'" 60) uses Bourdieu's concept of "symbolic violence" with regard to Prospero's relation to Ariel.

134. Meredith Anne Skura, "Discourse and the Individual: The Case of Colonialism in *The Tempest*," *Shakespeare Quarterly* 40 (1989): 55

135. See David Scott Kastan, "'The Duke of Milan / And his Brave Son': Dynastic Politics in *The Tempest*," in *Critical Essays on Shakespeare's "The Tempest,"* ed. Alden Vaughan and Virginia Vaughan (New York: Twayne, 1997).

136. "A Speach to the Lords and Commons of the Parliament" (1609), in *The Political Works of James I*, intro. Charles H. McIlwain (Cambridge, Mass.: Harvard University Press, 1918), 307–8.

137. The play can also possibly be seen as arguing for a Protestant marriage—like the one, for instance, that Elizabeth eventually made in 1613 to the Elector Palatine. See Donna Hamilton, *Virgil and "The Tempest": The Politics of Imitation* (Columbus: Ohio State University Press, 1990), 41–42. In acknowledging the "dynastic" reading, I agree with Kastan, but I see this reading as following from the colonial one rather than as deflecting it.

CHAPTER 7

1. See Edward Capell, *Notes and Various Readings to Shakespeare*, vol. 2, pt. 4 (London, n.d. [1774?]), 63. For the text of *The Tempest*, I have used the edition by Frank Kermode (London: Methuen, 1958). Hereafter "*The Tempest*, Kermode, ed."

2. See *Utopia*, in *The Complete Works of Thomas More*, vol. 4, ed. Edward Surtz, S. J., and J. H. Hexter (New Haven, Conn.: Yale University Press, 1964), 113, 123 (English).

3. Stephen Greenblatt, "Introduction," in *Shakespeare's Montaigne: The Florio Translation of the Essays; A Selection*, ed. Stephen Greenblatt and Peter G. Platt (New York: New York Review Books Classics, 2014), xxviii.

4. David Quint, *Montaigne and the Quality of Mercy: Ethical and Political Themes in the "Essais"* (Princeton, N.J.: Princeton University Press, 1998), ch. 3.

5. There is a brief but cogent argument, against Quint, that the violence depicted in the essay is not "half-hidden," and is actually presented in a positive light, in Paul Yachnin, "Eating Montaigne," in *Reading Renaissance Ethics*, ed. Marshall Grossman (New York: Routledge, 2007), 164.

6. Will Hamlin notes that the passage from Montaigne "serves multiple purposes" in Shakespeare's play, but "above all that of establishing a perspective from which Prospero's plan of vengeance, dynastic marriage, and social unification may be understood as realistic and achievable, yet comparatively impoverished in its imaginative reach" (*Montaigne's English Journey: Reading the "Essays" in Shakespeare's Day* [Oxford: Oxford University Press, 2013], 88).

7. See Michel de Montaigne, *Essais*, 3 vols. (Paris: Garnier-Flammarion, 1969), 1:255 (hereafter *Essais*).

8. The presence of "pardon" (*le pardon*) in the list of words that are unknown to the natives is the launchpad for Quint's critique (*Montaigne and the Quality of Mercy*, 75–76). For *le pardon* being one of the things unknown to Montaigne's new world natives, see *Essais*, 1:255.

9. When citing and quoting from Montaigne in English translation, I have generally used *The Complete Essays of Montaigne*, trans. Donald M. Frame (Stanford, Calif.: Stanford University Press, 1958); hereafter "Frame" followed by a page number. However, when appropriate or necessary, I have used the early seventeenth-century translation by John Florio (see note 3 above and note 65 below). For the swords and grills, see Frame, 153; *Essais*, 1:256 (*leurs espées et des grils*).

10. William Rockett sees Gonzalo's "vision" as "a commentary on the way things would go to seed, from the Christian point of view, in the absence of discipline, toil, and vigilance" ("Labor and Virtue in *The Tempest*," *Shakespeare Quarterly* 24 [1973]: 77–84 [78]). I see no reason in the text for this assumption. Rockett's major premise is "the redeeming efficacy of work" in the play (78).

11. For *uberté*, see *Essais*, 1:259; for "ubertie," see Florio, ed. Greenblatt, 65.

12. The scene of *The Two Noble Kinsmen* in which the word appears (5.1) is generally accepted as written by Shakespeare. See *The Two Noble Kinsmen*, ed. Clifford Leech (New York: New American Library, 1966), xxiii–xxiv.

13. I am here relying on the typology of ideal societies in J. C. Davis, *Utopia and the Ideal Society: A Study of English Utopian Writing, 1500–1700* (Cambridge: Cambridge University Press, 1981), 20–40. Davis distinguishes sharply between Arcadian or golden age fantasies and utopias.

14. John Gillies, "Shakespeare's Virginian Masque," *ELH* 53 (1986): 673–707 (689). Where Gillies and I differ is on the weight he gives to Antonio and Sebastian's critiques of Gonzalo's golden age speech (see 685 and 689). James Kearney, in his otherwise excellent chapter on the play, "Book, Trinket, Fetish: Letters and Mastery in *The Tempest*," in *The Incarnate Text: Imagining the Book in Reformation England* (Philadelphia: University of Pennsylvania Press, 2009), makes the mistake of equating the two visions of "foison" (218).

15. Patricia Akhimie, *Shakespeare and the Cultivation of Difference: Race and Conduct in the Early Modern World* (New York: Routledge, 2018), 160.

16. These are also familiar European export products. In Robert Wilson's *The Three Ladies of London* (1584), Lady Lucre tells the European merchant, "Thou must carry over Wheate, Pease, Barly, Dates, and Fitches [vetches] and all kinde of graine" (sig B2^v). Shakespeare's list—without "Dates"—makes the items very English.

17. Note to 4.1.64 (*The Tempest*, Kermode, ed., 97).

18. Gillies, "Shakespeare's Virginian Masque," 690.

19. For *eudaimonia* in Shakespeare, see Richard Strier, "Happiness," in *Shakespeare and Emotion*, ed. Katharine A. Craik (Cambridge: Cambridge University Press, 2020), 275–87.

20. Gillies seems to me mistaken in conflating the two sets of blessings ("Shakespeare's Virginian Masque," 696).

21. I agree with Gillies that it is difficult to interpret Ceres's pledge that spring will arrive "at the very end of harvest" (4.1.115). This would seem to mean that winter would be eliminated, but "barns and garners" and stover would not be needed in a situation where there was no need for storage of agricultural products. The more difficult reading that Gillies proposes—"that spring and harvest will resist winter for as long as possible" ("Shakespeare's Virginian Masque," 697)—seems to make more sense in the context. Gonzalo's vision implies perpetual spring (Montaigne specifies "a very pleasant and temperate climate" [Frame, 153]; "*païs très-plaisante et bien temperée*" [*Essais*, 255]).

22. When Othello is imagining the most outrageous possible sexual behavior on Desdemona's part, he imagines her having slept with "the general camp, / Pioneers and all" (3.3.345–46).

23. Robert Herrick, "The Hock-Cart, or Harvest Home," in *The Complete Poetry of Robert Herrick*, ed. J. Max Patrick (New York: Norton, 1968), 140–42 (lines 54–55).

24. Vin Nardizzi, *Wooden O's: Shakespeare's Theatres and England's Trees* (Toronto: University of Toronto Press, 2013), 130.

25. Jeffrey Knapp, *An Empire Nowhere: England, America, and Literature from "Utopia" to "The Tempest"* (Berkeley: University of California Press, 1992), 235.

26. As James Kearney says, "Labor relations of the island are anything but mystified" (*The Incarnate Text*, 212).

27. As Kermode points out, the "blasphemous" words that the Boatswain must have uttered could not legally be present in the text staged in 1611 (note to 1.1.36 [p. 6]).

28. See William Strachey, *A True Repertory of the Wreck and Redemption of Sir Thomas Gates, Knight upon and from the Islands of the Bermudas: His Coming to Virginia and the Estate of that Colony then and After*, in *A Voyage to Virginia in 1609*, ed. Louis B. Wright (Charlottesville: University Press of Virginia, 1964), 10 and 12. For the relation of this text to Shakespeare's play, see "*The Tempest* (1): Power," note 105.

29. It is unclear what the significance of "freckled" is here. Presumably it suggests ugliness or imperfection, though neither the *OED* nor other Shakespearean usages suggest this. I have not found any editorial notes on the word. Probably it is used here as a synonym for "spotted," which is often negative, as in Edgar's description of Edmund as a "most toad-spotted traitor" (*King Lear*, 5.3: Q 134, F 130). "Freckled" would seem to imply that Caliban is fair-skinned, but in *Titus Andronicus*, Bassianus claims that Tamora's honor is as "Spotted, detested, and abominable" as Aaron's hue (2.3.73–74). So "freckled" shares some of the ethnological uncertainty that Leah Marcus has taught us to see in the description of Caliban's mother as "blue-ey'd" (1.2.269) (*Unediting the Renaissance: Shakespeare, Marlowe, Milton* [London: Routledge, 1996], 5–17). One intriguing possibility, if we take "freckled" literally and imagine Caliban as also literally "blue-ey'd," is that Caliban is imagined as Irish—certainly a savage race in English eyes (see the essay by Dympna Callaghan cited in "*The Tempest*" [1]: Power," note 37).

30. On the indistinguishability of the terms "servant" and "slave" in the play, see "*The Tempest* (1): Power," 145–46.

31. How these logs are produced is never addressed. Nardizzi (*Wooden O's*, 122) points to Prospero's claim to have "rifted" oak and "pluck'd up / The pine and cedar" (5.1.45–48). I say that Prospero "pretends" to test Ferdinand, since it is not clear that Ferdinand willingly takes on the "test" nor that Prospero takes it seriously. Prospero says that Ferdinand has "strangely stood the test" (4.1.7), but we never see Prospero directly assigning him a task or checking up on him. See the following note.

32. Ferdinand does not enjoy his task, and he is working "upon a sore injunction" (3.1.11). The play never suggests that "the odiousness of the work is redeemed by something inherent in it" (Rockett, "Labor and Virtue," 80). The "pleasures" that Ferdinand finds in his labors (3.1.7) are entirely extrinsic to them. David Evett's attempt to read Ferdinand's "with a heart as willing / As bondage e'er of freedom" (3.1.89–90) as echoing the freedom in service of the Church of England prayerbook seems to me unconvincing and grammatically unlikely (*Discourses of Service in Shakespeare's England* [New York: Palgrave Macmillan, 2005], 205). David Schalkwyk's view is similar (*Shakespeare, Love and Service* [Cambridge: Cambridge University Press, 2008], 105).

33. Kenneth Graham has raised the question of why these unnamed other tasks are designated as "offices." It may be that Prospero is trying to emphasize their importance, or it may be that he cannot bear even to mention such "mean" (menial) tasks.

34. On Prospero's lack of direct interest in food production (and on the colonial dimension of this), see "*The Tempest* (1): Power." As in the masque, Prospero seems to imagine actual production of food (rather than having it hunted and gathered for him) only in a European context.

35. "Introduction," *The Tempest*, ed. Stephen Orgel (Oxford: Oxford University Press, 1987), 25; hereafter "*The Tempest*, Orgel, ed."

36. Hannah Arendt, *The Human Condition* (Chicago: University of Chicago Press, 1958), secs. 3–4. On the general topic of Shakespeare and work, see the overview essay by that title by Michelle M. Dowd, *Literature Compass* 7 (2010): 185–94.

37. See "*The Tempest* (1): Power."

38. Derek Cohen, "The Culture of Slavery: Caliban and Ariel," *Dalhousie Review* 76 (1996): 161.

39. For an argument that *The Tempest* dramatizes the actual conditions of theatrical production in Shakespeare's theater, see Douglas Bruster, "Local Tempest: Shakespeare and the Work of the Early Modern Playhouse," *JMEMS* 25 (1995): 33–53.

40. For a similar reading of Prospero's "curiously overwrought state" here, see Christopher Pye, *The Storm at Sea: Political Aesthetics in the Time of Shakespeare* (New York: Fordham University Press, 2015), 149.

41. On the speech as recognizable bragging by a magician, see Barbara Mowat, "Prospero, Agrippa, Hocus Pocus," *ELR* 11 (1981): 288. That the speech is based on the self-praise of the most famous witch of antiquity, Medea, complicates the celebratory aspect of it. Shakespeare surely intended for much of his audience to recognize this source (book 7 of Ovid's *Metamorphoses*). Kearney notes that Prospero's vow to bury his book "deeper than did ever plummet sound" (5.1.56) echoes Alonso's speech about the "depth" of his grief (3.3.101), but discounts the idea that Prospero's abjuration is "a repetition of Alonso's despair" (*The Incarnate Text*, 220). I think it is.

42. James Kuzner asks the excellent question of how this speech can be intended to make Ferdinand "cheerful" (4.1.147), but I cannot see that Kuzner answers the question (*Shakespeare as a Way of Life: Skeptical Practice and the Politics of Weakness* [New York: Fordham University Press, 2016], 116). I would suggest that the vision of dissolution is the only thing that really does make Prospero "cheerful."

43. *Utopia*, 129, 131.

44. See Max Weber, *The Protestant Ethic and the Spirit of Capitalism*, trans. Talcott Parsons (New York: Scribner's, 1958).

45. *PL* 4.616–17, in John Milton, *The Complete Poems and Major Prose*, ed. Merritt Y. Hughes (New York: The Odyssey Press, 1957). Weber's evocation of the Protestant view of work is more rigorous than Milton's since Weber (in *The Protestant Ethic*, 87) reads the final lines of *Paradise Lost* as if Adam and Eve were to choose a place for work rather than, as the poem says, for "rest" (12.647).

46. *Essais*, 3:205, 183; Frame, 741, 759.

47. On "care" in the *Henry IV* plays, see "Shakespeare and Legal Systems" (93). It might be worth noting that Sir Toby's second line in *Twelfth Night* is to assert that he is sure "care's an enemy to life" (1.3.2).

48. Felicity Green, *Montaigne and the Life of Freedom* (Cambridge: Cambridge University Press, 2012), 142.

49. *Essais*, 3:216; Frame, 767.

50. *Essais*, 3:219; Frame, 770.

51. *Essais*, 3:219; Frame, 770.

52. *Essais*, 3:220; Frame, 771.

53. On the interaction with Miranda, see "*The Tempest* (3): Humanism"; on the interactions with Ariel and Caliban, see "*The Tempest* (1): Power."

54. *Essais*, 3:215; Frame, 766.

55. For a biography of Montaigne that stresses his involvements in the public life of his time, see Philippe Desan, *Montaigne: A Life*, trans. Stephen Rendall and Lisa Neil (Princeton, N.J.:

Princeton University Press, 2017 (the French title is Montaigne, *Une biographie politique* [Paris: Odele Jacob, 2014]).

56. Lars Engle, pers. comm.

57. For a contemporary defense of a position much like Montaigne's (though Montaigne is nowhere mentioned), see Brian O'Connor, *Idleness: A Philosophical Essay* (Princeton, N.J.: Princeton University Press, 2018), esp. ch. 5 ("Idleness as Freedom"). For "idleness" or nonchalance as a position of epistemological opportunity (with Montaigne as a model), see David Carroll Simon, *Light Without Heat: The Observational Mood from Bacon to Milton* (Ithaca, N.Y.: Cornell University Press, 2018), esp. ch. 1.

58. Credit for the discovery seems to go to Eleanor Prosser in "Shakespeare, Montaigne, and the Rarer Action," *Shakespeare Studies* 1 (1965): 261–64.

59. On this range, see Paul Yachnin, "Kindness: Animal Virtue in *The Tempest*," in *Shakespeare and Virtue: A Handbook*, ed. Julia Reinhard Lupton and Donovan Sherman (forthcoming from Cambridge University Press, 2022).

60. John S. Hunt seems to me mistaken in postulating affect here ("Prospero's Empty Grasp," *Shakespeare Studies* 22 [1994]: 277–313 [306]). Sarah Beckwith notes that Prospero's initial response to Ariel's comment on the distressed condition of the court party is a question ("Dost thou think so, spirit?" [5.1.19]), and she observes that this is unusual—"Prospero does not characteristically ask questions"—but she does not recognize that the continuation of Prospero's response is also in the questioning mode. She equates Prospero's embrace of "virtue" with his having "tender affections" (*Shakespeare and the Grammar of Forgiveness* [Ithaca, N.Y.: Cornell University Press, 2011], 148–49).

61. Prospero does claim to be weeping forty lines later when he restores the court party to their senses, but the explanation that he gives of this behavior does not, oddly, have to do with the situation of the sufferers but rather with the effect on him of Gonzalo's self-presentation as pitiful. Addressing Gonzalo, he says, "Mine eyes, even sociable to the show of thine, / Fall fellowly drops" (5.1.63–64). Leah Whittington notices this, and sees Prospero as barely holding onto his "empathy" when he turns back from Gonzalo to the court party ("Shakespeare's Virgil: Empathy and *The Tempest*," *Shakespeare and Renaissance Ethics*, ed. Patrick Gray and John D. Cox [Cambridge: Cambridge University Press, 2014], 98–120 [116]). Prospero's attitude toward the recovering sufferers strikes me as basically clinical, though beautifully expressed ("their rising senses / Begin to chase the ignorant fumes that mantle / Their clearer reason" [66–68]).

62. Compare Harry Berger Jr., "The Miraculous Harp: A Reading of Shakespeare's *Tempest*," in *Second World and Green World: Studies in Renaissance Fiction-Making* (Berkeley: University of California Press, 1988): "He [Prospero] is selecting rather than experiencing his response" (178). On the difference between Berger's reading of *The Tempest* (of which I highly approve) and his reading of *Lear* (which I criticize in "Resisting Complicity"), see the Introduction to this book.

63. For the relevant theology, see "*The Tempest* (1): Power."

64. *Essais*, 2:91; Frame, 306–7; for Florio, see *The Essays of Montaigne Done into English by John Florio*, with an introduction by George Saintsbury (London: David Nutt, 1893), 2:109 (this essay is not included in the collection cited in note 3). Hereafter, I will give page references to Frame and to *Essais*, vol. 2, in the text when citing this essay.

65. Jonathan Bate seems to me quite mistaken in asserting that what is being referred to here is "a strictly Christian version of virtue," and that "for Prospero, what finally matters is kindness" (*Soul of the Age: A Biography of the Mind of William Shakespeare* [New York: Random House, 2009], 128).

66. See Prosser, "Shakespeare, Montaigne, and the Rarer Action," 262; John Bender, "The Day of *The Tempest*," *ELH* 47 (1980): 235–58 (251); and Yachnin, "Eating Montaigne," 170, and "Kindness."

67. Unlike Frame, I have capitalized the pronouns referring to the deity here.

68. I have departed from Frame in translating *panchante* here as "inclining" rather than "sloping" because I think Frame's translation misses a wonderful pun in Montaigne's French.

69. See *Nicomachean Ethics*, book 7 (1146a10–12); trans. Martin Ostwald (Indianapolis: Bobbs-Merrill, 1962), 177.

70. Arthur Kirsch, "Virtue, Vice, and Compassion in Montaigne and *The Tempest*," *SEL* 37 (1997): 337–52. Kirsch and I have a similar view of the essay; we agree that where a figure like Gonzalo (or Montaigne) can "forgive instinctively," Prospero cannot (Kirsch, 345). Where Kirsch's view and mine differ is in what we see as motivating Prospero's "rarer action." Kirsch sees imagination as the motivating factor, which establishes (for him) a deep connection between Prospero and Montaigne (345–48). I take Prospero at his word, and see the "action" as entirely based on "reason." "Co-suffering" is, in my view, presented as a possibility that Prospero contemplates, not as something that he experiences. For an exploration of the connections in both character and behavior between Gonzalo and Montaigne, see Lars Engle, "Montaigne's Shakespeare: *The Tempest* as Test-Case," in *Shakespeare and Montaigne*, ed. Lars Engle, Patrick Gray, and William Hamlin (forthcoming from Edinburgh University Press, 2022).

71. The Garnier-Flamarion editor (Alexandre Micha) understands *à faict* here exactly as Frame does, glossing it *tout à fait* (*Essais*, 2:460).

72. For clarity here, I have slightly departed from the Frame translation. Quint notes that "Montaigne declares himself to be a softie" (*Montaigne and the Quality of Mercy*, 9).

73. For the confusions in Caliban's conception of freedom, and for Ariel's conception, see "*The Tempest* (1): Power." James Kuzner is unsure about whether Ariel's conception here counts as "freedom," but Kuzner correctly identifies it with "images of rest, of freedom from work and even from exertion altogether" (*Shakespeare as a Way of Life*, 111–12).

74. On Shakespeare's awareness of the "hard labor that drives theatrical illusion," see Elizabeth Rivlin, *The Aesthetics of Service in Early Modern England* (Evanston, Ill.: Northwestern University Press, 2012), 162; and Bruster, "Local Tempest."

75. It is probably worth saying that no one who took the idea of the granting of "indulgences" as a special papal privilege would use the term in this way, and imagine the persons in a theatrical audience having this privilege literally in their hands.

CHAPTER 8

1. The fundamental work on Shakespeare's education remains T. W. Baldwin, *William Shakspere's Small Latine and Lesse Greeke*, 2 vols. (Urbana: University of Illinois Press, 1944). For a more recent overview, see Colin Burrow, "Shakespeare and Humanistic Culture," in *Shakespeare and the Classics*, ed. Charles Martindale and A. B. Taylor (Cambridge: Cambridge University Press, 2004), 9–27. For a less cognitively oriented account of humanist education, in general and in relation to Shakespeare, see Lynn Enterline, *Shakespeare's Schoolroom: Rhetoric, Discipline, Emotion* (Philadelphia: University of Pennsylvania Press, 2012).

2. For the early comedies, see, inter alia, the essays by Vanda Zajko, A. B. Taylor, and Heather James in Martindale and Taylor, *Shakespeare and the Classics*; also Peter Holbrook, "Class X: Shakespeare, Class, and the Comedies," in *A Companion to Shakespeare's Works: The*

Comedies, ed. Richard Dutton and Jean E. Howard (Oxford: Blackwell, 2003), 67–89. For the early histories and humanist schooling, see Emrys Jones, *The Origins of Shakespeare* (Oxford: Oxford University Press, 1977).

3. See the essay by Wolfgang Riehle in Martindale and Taylor, *Shakespeare and the Classics*, and Riehle's *Shakespeare, Plautus and the Humanist Tradition* (Cambridge: D. S. Brewer, 1990).

4. See the essay by A. B. Taylor cited in note 2 above; Jonathan Bate, *Shakespeare and Ovid* (Oxford; Clarendon Press, 1994), ch. 4; Patricia Parker, *Shakespeare from the Margins: Language, Culture, Context* (Chicago: University of Chicago Press, 1996), ch. 3.

5. On a "set of rulers" who emerged in the early sixteenth century "devoted to the new learning," see Roland Bainton, *Erasmus of Christendom* (New York: Scribner's, 1969), 121. Bainton is paraphrasing a letter of Erasmus to Wolfgang Capito written early in 1517 (Letter 541 in *The Correspondence of Erasmus, Letters 446–593 (1516–17)*, trans. R. A. B. Mynors and D. F. S. Thomson [Toronto: University of Toronto Press, 1977], 263).

6. Jonathan Bate, "The Humanist *Tempest*," in *Shakespeare, "La Tempête": Études critiques* (Besançon: Université de Franche-Comté, 1993), 19 (Skinner), 5 (renunciation); Bate, *Soul of the Age: A Biography of the Mind of William Shakespeare* (New York: Random House, 2009), 130, 117; ch. 8, "The School of Prospero," includes most of Bate's earlier essay.

7. Goran Stanivukovic, "*The Tempest* and the Discontents of Humanism," *Philological Quarterly* 85 (2006): 91–119.

8. See James Hankins, *Virtue Politics: Soulcraft and Statecraft in Renaissance Italy* (Cambridge, Mass.: Harvard University Press, 2019).

9. Hankins, chs. 2 and 19.

10. For the centrality of Erasmus to northern humanism and to Shakespeare's education, see vol. 1, pt. 2, sec. A of Baldwin, *William Shakspere's Small Latine and Lesse Greeke*; see also Jones, *The Origins of Shakespeare*: "Without humanism, in short, there could have been no Elizabethan literature: without Erasmus, no Shakespeare" (13). In "The Humanist *Tempest*," Bate also takes Erasmus as his "main exemplar" (7). N. Amos Rothschild takes Montaigne as such, and sees Prospero failing as a humanist pedagogue in the light of Montaigne's essay on education ("Learning to Doubt: *The Tempest*, *imitatio*, and Montaigne's 'Of the Institution and Education of Children,'" *Yearbook of Research in English and American Literature* 29 [2013]: 17–34). It is not clear, however, that a critique where "dogmatism" is the problem and doubt the solution is relevant to *The Tempest*.

11. For Prospero's failure as a spiritual reformer, see "*The Tempest* (1): Power."

12. All citations of *The Tempest* are to the edition by Frank Kermode (London: Methuen, 1958 Hereafter "*The Tempest*, Kermode, ed." Other editions will be cited as needed.

13. As explained in "*The Tempest* (1): Power," note 25, I have not followed Kermode in capitalizing "art."

14. The list of the characters in the play that follows the text in the first Folio is headed by "The Scene, an un-inhabited Island." See *The Norton Facsimile of the First Folio of Shakespeare*, prepared by Charlton Hinman (New York: Norton, 1968), 37.

15. Stephen Orgel denies that there is "anything inherently mysterious" about Prospero's studies, since "they were, after all, the liberal arts" (*The Tempest*, ed. Stephen Orgel [Oxford: Oxford University Press, 1987], 106). But to assert this is to elide the mention of "secret studies."

16. For the publication history of the *Oration*, and when it developed the title by which we know it, see Michael Papio, "The *Oration*'s Printed Editions," in Pico della Mirandola, *Oration on the Dignity of Man: A New Translation and Commentary*, ed. Francesco Borghesi, Michael

Papio, and Massimo Riva (Cambridge: Cambridge University Press, 2012), 45–51; hereafter "*New Translation.*"

17. For reasons of availability and stylistic superiority, I have used the translation of the Oration in *The Renaissance Philosophy of Man*, ed. Ernst Cassirer, Paul Oskar Kristeller, and John Herman Randall Jr. (Chicago: University of Chicago Press, 1948), 230–54 (233, 247).

18. See Eugenio Garin, *Italian Humanism: Philosophy and Civic Life in the Renaissance*, trans. Peter Muntz (1947; New York: Harper & Row, 1965), ch. 3; Quentin Skinner, *The Foundations of Modern Political Thought* (Cambridge: Cambridge University Press, 1978), 1:113–18. On "civic humanism," a term initially coined and developed by Hans Baron, who associated it with republicanism, see Baron, *The Crisis of the Early Italian Renaissance*, rev. ed. (1955; Princeton, N.J.: Princeton University Press, 1966). For development and modification of Baron's view, see *Renaissance Civic Humanism: Reappraisals and Reflections*, ed. James Hankins (Cambridge: Cambridge University Press, 2000). For the view that Ficino had his own version of civic commitment, see Mark Jurdjevic, "Marsilio Ficino, Savonarola, and the Valori Family," *Past and Present* 183 (2004): 41–77.

19. Cassirer, Kristeller, and Randall, *The Renaissance Philosophy of Man*, 238; for the Latin, see *New Translation*, 188.

20. Pier Paolo Vergerio, *The Character and Studies Befitting a Free-Born Youth* (*De Ingenuis Moribus*), in *Humanist Educational Treatises*, ed. and trans. Craig W. Kallendorf (Cambridge, Mass.: Harvard University Press, 2002), 59 (English), 58 (Latin).

21. Thomas Starkey, *A Dialogue between Reginald Pole and Thomas Lupset*, ed. Kathleen M. Burton (London: Chatto and Windus, 1948), 22.

22. Richard Mulcaster, *The First Part of the Elementarie* (London, 1582), 12.

23. David Scott Kastan, "'The Duke of Milan / And his Brave Son': Dynastic Politics in *The Tempest*," in *Critical Essays on Shakespeare's "The Tempest,"* ed. Alden Vaughan and Virginia Vaughan (New York: Twayne, 1997), 236 (quoting from James's *Basilikon Doron*).

24. The classic study is Max Weber, *The Protestant Ethic and the Spirit of Capitalism*, trans. Talcott Parsons (New York: Scribner's, 1958).

25. On how to read Prospero's "magic," see "*The Tempest* (1): Power."

26. For a classic statement, see Hannah H. Gray, "Renaissance Humanism: The Pursuit of Eloquence," *JHI* 24 (1963): 497–514.

27. Desiderius Erasmus, *The Education of a Christian Prince*, trans. Lester K. Born (1936; New York: Norton, 1968), 139. On Prospero's lack of equanimity, see "*The Tempest* (2): Labor."

28. For Caliban as household servant, see Tom Lindsay, "'Which first was mine own king': Caliban and the Politics of Service and Education in *The Tempest*," *SP* 113 (2016): 397–423; for Caliban as adopted son, see Hiewon Shin, "Single Parenting, Homeschooling: Prospero, Caliban, Miranda," *SEL* 48 (2008): 373–93.

29. Rothschild in "Learning to Doubt" does treat the Prospero-Ariel relationship as pedagogical, and, following Bate ("The Humanist *Tempest*," 11; *Soul of the Age*, 121), faults Prospero for demanding "slavish imitation" from Ariel (24). But Ariel is a slave. What Prospero demands of him is not slavish imitation but slavish performance. When Prospero does "correct" Ariel (re Sycorax and Ariel's own history [1.2.261]), the point is not to get Ariel to repeat back what Prospero has said but to get Ariel to be properly grateful and properly fearful—to be "correspondent to command" (1.2.297). See "*The Tempest* (1): Power."

30. For the idea that this was unusual, see Shin, "Single Parenting," 382. For a supposedly "pervasive ambivalence about 'woman's place' in Renaissance life," see Lisa Jardine, "Cultural

Confusion and Shakespeare's Learned Heroines," in *Reading Shakespeare Historically* (London: Routledge, 1996), 48–64.

31. Sarah Gwyneth Ross, *The Birth of Feminism: Woman as Intellect in Renaissance Italy and England* (Cambridge, Mass.: Harvard University Press, 2009). It might be worth adding that Burckhardt had this same view; see Jacob Burckhardt, *The Civilization of the Renaissance in Italy*, trans. S. G. C. Middlemore (1929; New York: Harper and Row, 1958), 2:389–95 ("The Position of Women"). Interestingly, one of the editors of the German edition apparently felt moved to insert a dissenting footnote to this chapter (2:389 n. 4).

32. Ross, *The Birth of Feminism*, 12.

33. Ross, 5. For the handbooks, see, inter alia, Suzanne W. Hull, *Chaste, Silent, and Obedient: English Books for Women, 1475–1640* (San Marino, Calif.: Huntington Library, 1982).

34. For Greek, see *The Taming of the Shrew*, 2.1.81, 100.

35. Kathryn M. Moncrief, "'Obey and be attentive': Gender and Household Instruction in Shakespeare's *The Tempest*," in *Gender and Early Modern Constructions of Childhood*, ed. Naomi J. Miller and Naomi Yavneh (Farnham: Ashgate, 2011), 129–30, cites Mulcaster recommending that the highest educational provisions be made for "personages" including women, "as be borne to be princes," but Moncrief then goes on to see the handbooks as applicable to women's education in general. See Richard Mulcaster, *Positions Wherein Those Primitive Circumstances be Examined which are Necessarie for the Training up of Children* (London: Thomas Vautrollier, 1581), 180–81. Hereafter cited as "Mulcaster, *Positions*."

36. See *Katherine Parr: Complete Works and Correspondence*, ed. Janel Mueller (Chicago: University of Chicago Press, 2011), 5–6.

37. Katherina's linguistic skill is shown not only in her ability to praise the sun or the moon at will, as called for (4.5), but in her final speech, which, however its content is assessed (not an easy matter), is by far the longest and most eloquent speech in the play (5.1.142–85). See Elizabeth Hutcheon, "From Shrew to Subject: Petruchio's Humanist Education of Katherine in *The Taming of the Shrew*," *Comparative Drama* 45 (2011): 315–37; also Enterline, *Shakespeare's Schoolroom*, 114–19.

38. On the detachment of the opening scene from the rest of the play, see Benjamin Jeffery, "An Image on Water: A Reading of Shakespeare's *The Tempest*" (Ph.D. diss., University of Chicago, 2020).

39. On *ethos* as a means of persuasion, see Aristotle, *Art of Rhetoric*, trans. John Henry Freese (LCL; Cambridge, Mass.: Harvard University Press, 1975), 1.2.3–7. Rosalie Stoner has pointed out to me that in this moment, *ethos* and *pathos* come together.

40. Shin, "Single Parenting," 385.

41. For analysis, see "*The Tempest* (2): Labor."

42. Shin, "Single Parenting," 382.

43. Rothschild, "Learning to Doubt," 19. This characterization of Prospero seems right, but see the reservation expressed in note 10 above.

44. Octave Mannoni, *Prospero and Caliban: The Psychology of Colonization*, trans. Pamela Powesland, 2nd ed. (New York: Praeger 1964), 105.

45. Compare, in *Coriolanus*, Menenius's similar characterization of the First Citizen as "the great toe of this assembly" (1.1.154). For a reminder that in *The Tempest* as in *Coriolanus* this image is "open to tonal registers of irony, amusement, and teasing," I am indebted to a communication from Lois Kim. I am not sure, however, that this alters what Lorie Leininger calls the "crucial" status of the head-toe metaphor in the value structure of *The Tempest* ("The Miranda Trap: Sexism and Racism in Shakespeare's *Tempest*," in *The Woman's Part: Feminist Criticism of*

Shakespeare, ed. Carolyn Ruth Swift Lenz, Gayle Greene, and Carol Thomas Neely [Urbana: University of Illinois, 1980], 287). I would say the same of *Coriolanus.*

46. Shin, "Single Parenting," 386; Jessica Slights, "Rape and the Romanticization of Shakespeare's Miranda," *SEL* 41 (2001): 357–79 (esp. 369–70).

47. Lindsay, "'Which first was mine own king,'" might be right that Miranda manifests "the combination of submissiveness and assertiveness that early modern education sought to inculcate" (409), but this may not take full enough account of her special status as a princess.

48. Shin's claim ("Single Parenting," 387) that there is something shocking in Miranda knowing chess seems mistaken. Her citation of Kermode's note is misleading, since Kermode quotes a history of chess stating that "at chess, the sexes met on equal terms" (*The Tempest,* Kermode, ed., 123). Shin's quotation from the same history does not contradict this.

49. See *OED,* s.v. "careful," definition 2 ("Full of care, trouble, anxiety"), and see the opening of *1 Henry IV.*

50. On Prospero's laxity, and on the matter of "trust," see "*The Tempest* (1): Power."

51. Shin, "Single Parenting," 387.

52. In his edition of *The Tempest* (Cambridge: Cambridge University Press, 2002), David Lindley discusses this emendation sympathetically (228).

53. Miranda sometimes counts Caliban among human males and sometimes does not. At 1.2.448, she does (Ferdinand as the third such she has seen); at 3.1.51, she does not (Ferdinand as the second). I am not sure this revision signifies anything, since Miranda has already said that she does not "love to look on" Caliban (1.2.312), and presumably does not like to think about him either.

54. Kermode's note adds a phrase to try to make sense of Miranda's lines at 461–62; Orgel, in the note to the lines in his edition, adds a thought, and gives the Platonic explanation that Kermode provided (though noting that the speech expresses "more naiveté than Platonism"); Lindley, in his note, provides a whole dialectic. Viola, on the other hand, expresses very clearly her awareness that the Platonic view may be false, before deciding to accept the view nonetheless in her particular situation (*Twelfth Night,* 1.2.47–51).

55. George Lamming, *The Pleasures of Exile* (1960; Ann Arbor: University of Michigan Press, 1992), 115–16.

56. See Stanley Cavell, "The Avoidance of Love: A Reading of *King Lear,*" in *Must We Mean What We Say?* (New York: Scribner's, 1969), 269–353; *Disowning Knowledge in Six Plays of Shakespeare* (New York: Cambridge University Press, 1987), 39–124. For discussion of Cavell's view of Edgar, see "Resisting Complicity: Ethical Judgment and *King Lear.*"

57. Miranda's one moment of apparent sophistication—in the interchange with Ferdinand while they are playing chess (5.1.1714)—has never been satisfactorily elucidated. Her talk of "a score of kingdoms" is hardly part of realistic political discourse; it is perhaps better seen / heard as a naive person trying to sound sophisticated.

58. On Bembo and More (and others), see Ross, *The Birth of Feminism,* ch. 2.

59. On this, see "*The Tempest* (2): Labor."

60. David Norbrook, "'What Cares These Roarers for the Name of King?': Language and Utopia in *The Tempest*" (1992), rpt. in *Shakespeare: The Last Plays,* ed. Kiernan Ryan (London: Longman, 1999), 267.

61. I am certain that we are to take Ferdinand to be sincere when he avers that he loves Miranda "Beyond all limit of what else i' th' world" (3.1.72), but it is hard for a reader of Shakespeare not to hear an echo of Goneril's "Beyond all manner of so much" (*King Lear* [conflated text], 1.1.61). Hyperbole can sound empty even when it is meant to be full.

62. For this aspect of the Prospero-Ariel relationship, see "*The Tempest* (1): Power."

63. *De pueris statim ac liberaliter Instituendis declamatio* [*A Declamation on the Subject of Early Liberal Education for Children*], trans. Beert C. Verstraete, in *The Collected Works of Erasmus*, vol. 26, ed. J. K. Sowards (Toronto: University of Toronto Press, 1985), 291–346 (338); hereafter "*De Pueris* (Toronto)." For the Latin, I have used the text in Erasme, *Declamatio de Pueris Statim ac Liberaliter Instituendis*, trans. Jean-Claude Margolin [into French] (Geneva: Droz, 1966), 373–463 (449); hereafter "*De Pueris* (Latin)." It is worth noting that there was no distrust of this pleasure, as there was of the pleasure of solitary learning (see the works cited in notes 21 and 22 above).

64. *De Pueris* (Toronto), 339.

65. Roger Ascham, *The Schoolmaster*, ed. Lawrence V. Ryan (Charlottesville: University of Virginia Press, 1967), 6. The reference is to *Republic* 5.2 (537a): "Avoid compulsion, and let your children's lessons take the form of play" (*The Republic of Plato*, trans. Francis Macdonald Cornford [New York: Oxford University Press, 1945], 258).

66. Ascham, *The Schoolmaster*, 37.

67. Ascham, *The Schoolmaster*, 38.

68. Aeneas Silvius Piccolomini, *The Education of Boys* (*De Liberorum Educatione*), in Kallendorf, *Humanist Educational Treatises*, 137–39.

69. Quintilian, *Institutio oratoria*, trans. H. E. Butler (LCL; London: Heinemann, 1920), 1.3.13–18, beginning *Caedi vero discentes* (58–60).

70. Erasmus, *De Pueris* (Toronto), 326.

71. *De Pueris* (Toronto), 328; *De Pueris* (Latin), 431.

72. Montaigne's famous "cruel hatred" of cruelty is thoroughly Erasmian. See "Of Cruelty," in *The Complete Essays of Montaigne*, trans. Donald M. Frame (Stanford, Calif.: Stanford University Press, 1958), 313. On the other hand, Erasmus's good friend Sir Thomas More did not, on the evidence of *Utopia*, share Erasmus's utter detestation of slavery. See *The Complete Works of St. Thomas More*, vol. 4, ed. Edward Surtz, S. J., and J. H. Hexter (New Haven, Conn.: Yale University Press, 1965); hereafter "*Utopia*." The treatment of slavery in *Utopia* is a vexed issue; see 77–79 (among the Polyerites) and 191–92 (in Utopia). Whipping is used only in special cases; convicts (slaves) are forced to labor but are not confined or otherwise mistreated; manumission is possible. For a recent dark view, see Matthew Ritger, "Reading *Utopia* in the Reformation of Punishment," *RQ* 72 (2019): 1225–68.

73. I have departed from the Kermode edition and followed the Folio in printing "humane" rather than "human" as does Orgel in his edition of the play, and Lindley in his, and as do Virginia Mason Vaughan and Alden T. Vaughan in their Arden 3 edition of the play (London: Thomson Learning, 1999). For *humanitas*, see Bate, *Soul of the Age*, 118.

74. On this image in the play, see Jonathan Goldberg, "The Print of Goodness," in *The Culture of Capital: Properties, Cities, and Knowledge in Early Modern England*, ed. Henry S. Turner (New York: Routledge, 2002), 230–54.

75. One might think that in going from "imprinting" to "sticking," Prospero has already given up part of the claim, since "sticking" seems to be much less permanent. In *Framing Authority: Sayings, Self, and Society in Sixteenth-Century England* (Princeton, N.J.: Princeton University Press, 1993), ch. 3, Mary Thomas Crane considers various metaphors for humanist education, but this adhesive metaphor is not one.

76. Prospero might be seen as trying to finesse the question in 4.1.188–90 by referring to Caliban as "a devil," but this seems to be simply another way of saying that he resists "nurture."

77. Vergerio, *The Character and Studies Befitting a Free-Born Youth*, in Kallendorf, *Humanist Educational Treatises*, 39.

78. Piccolomini, *The Education of Boys*, in Kallendorf, *Humanist Educational Treatises*, 133.

79. Baldesar Castiglione, *The Book of the Courtier*, trans. Charles S. Singleton (Garden City, N.Y.: Doubleday, 1959), 329.

80. Sir Thomas Elyot, *The Book Named the Governor*, ed. S. E. Lehmberg (London: Dent, 1962), 14; and see 78, where Elyot restates the need for a "gentle nature" in the children to whom his educational project is addressed.

81. Erasmus, *De Pueris* (Toronto), 301; *De Pueris* (Latin), 385.

82. *De Pueris* (Toronto), 312.

83. *De Pueris* (Toronto), 317.

84. For *naturam vacuam*, see Erasmus, *De Pueris* (Toronto), 312; *De Pueris* (Latin), 405 (Margolin translates this as *une nature encore vierge* (Latin, 404).

85. See Erasmus, *De Pueris* (Toronto), 311; *De Pueris* (Latin), 401.

86. For an elaboration of this view, see Richard Strier, "Taking *Utopia* Seriously—and Positively," *Moreana* 54 (2017): 141–48.

87. Elizabeth Hanson, "No Boy Left Behind: Education and Distributive Justice in Early Modern England," in *Taking Exception to the Law: Materializing Injustice in Early Modern English Literature*, ed. Donald Beecher, Travis DeCook, Andrew Wallace, and Grant Williams (Toronto: University of Toronto Press, 2015), 185.

88. Erasmus, *De Pueris* (Latin), 419. The passage is translated in *De Pueris* (Toronto), 321, but I have translated the Latin more literally. In "Fallen Nature, Utopian Institutions, and (Radical) Medieval Christian-Aristotelianism," *Moreana* 54 (2017): 149–56, William Junker shows that there is a Christian tradition, going back at least to Aquinas, that supports this view. Junker shows that Dante held it. In the *Purgatorio*, an authoritative speaker (Marco Lombardo) states that it is "bad governance" that has made the world wicked, "and not nature" (*la mala condotta / è la cagion che 'l mondo ha fatto reo, / e non natura*" (16.103–5; Dante Alighieri, *The Divine Comedy: Purgatorio; Text and Commentary*, trans. Charles S. Singleton [Princeton, N.J.: Bollingen, 1973]). Singleton is shocked that original sin "is nowhere brought into the argument"; he calls it "a remarkable omission" (365). Junker's article is a response to articles by Strier (see note 86) and Walter Nicgorski in the same issue of *Moreana*.

89. Erasmus, *The Education of a Christian Prince*, 183.

90. Jonathan Goldberg, "The Print of Goodness," 237.

91. Richard Halpern, *The Poetics of Primitive Accumulation: English Renaissance Culture and the Genealogy of Capital* (Ithaca, N.Y.: Cornell University Press, 1991), 92–93.

92. See Erasmus, *De Pueris* (Toronto), 340 and passim.

93. Hanson sees Halpern's view as "a significant distortion" ("No Boy Left Behind," 183).

94. See Ascham, *The Schoolmaster*, 35.

95. See Mulcaster, *Positions*, 141. The entire chapter (37) is relevant. For the historical reality of this, see, inter alia, the appendix, "Seventeenth-Century Melancholy," in L. C. Knights, *Drama and Society in the Age of Jonson* (1937; Harmondsworth: Penguin, 1962), 261–74; and Mark H. Curtis, "The Alienated Intellectuals of Early Stuart England," *Past and Present* 23 (1962): 25–43. For a more recent piece on this issue, see P. B. Roberts, "Underemployed Elizabethans: Gabriel Harvey and Thomas Nashe in the Parnassus Plays," *Early Theatre* 21 (2018): 49–70.

96. Hanson sees a "fundamental contradiction" in Mulcaster's thinking between "his drive to think economically" and "the conviction, which he shares with Erasmus, that humanist learn-

ing not only is, but ought to be, universally desired" ("No Boy Left Behind," 196). In *A Culture of Teaching: Early Modern Humanism in Theory and Practice* (Ithaca, N.Y.: Cornell University Press, 1996), Rebecca W. Bushnell presents a concept of "decorum" as either resolving or eliding the contradictions in Mulcaster's thinking (114).

97. *Utopia*, 128–29.

98. For "the lowliest women" and the ploughboy, see *The Paraclesis* (1516), in *Christian Humanism and the Reformation: Desiderius Erasmus, Selected Writings*, ed. and trans. John C. Olin (New York: Harper and Row, 1965), 97; for cities replacing monasteries, see "Letter to Paul Volz" (1518), 130. It might be worth noting that in moments like these, humanist and Reformation ideals coincide.

99. See Erasmus, *De Pueris* (Toronto), 334 (emphasis mine); *De Pueris* (Latin), 441.

100. As Ross, *The Birth of Feminism*, makes clear, the program did not require schoolrooms for women, though it would seem that on a large scale, it would. Mulcaster insists that women should be educated, but notes that sending them to public grammar schools and to the universities is "not used in my countrie" (*Positions*, 168). It seems clear that he does not see any theoretical objection to such; there is merely "no president thereof." Moncrief has trouble acknowledging Mulcaster's "seemingly" progressive views on the education of women ("'Obey and be attentive,'" 129).

101. Goldberg, "The Print of Goodness," 237; Goldberg's emphasis.

102. Goldberg, "The Print of Goodness," 237; Ascham, *The Schoolmaster*, 34. Interestingly, Kermode misreads a passage on education in exactly the same way. Kermode says that Edward Phillips holds that "the want of nature can be partially supplied by education." But what Phillips says in the quoted passage is that if "that noble thing call'd Education" were "thoroughly and rightly prosecuted, [it] would be able to civilize the most savage natures, & root out barbarism and ignorance from the face of the earth" (*The Tempest*, Kermode, ed., xlvi).

103. Goldberg, "The Print of Goodness," 238. By "mere being," Mulcaster means those abilities "without the which theie [humans] could not once so much as live, or bear the name of men"; by "well being," he means those abilities "without the which tho theie live and continew men, yet ar theie extreme rude" (*The First Part of the Elementarie*, 31).

104. Mulcaster, *The First Part of the Elementarie*, 28.

105. Mulcaster, *The First Part of the Elementarie*, 37. Bushnell treats Mulcaster as "an advocate of corporal punishment" (*A Culture of Teaching*, 102; also 27 and 34). Unlike Erasmus, Mulcaster was an actual schoolmaster, but his pages on corporal punishment in *Positions* are nervous, and filled with reservations and qualifications (278–83).

106. On "race" here, see "*The Tempest* (1): Power," note 88.

107. The idea of Miranda as tutor to Caliban depends mainly on the "vile race" speech being assigned to her. There has been a long history of disagreement about this. William Davenant and John Dryden in their adaptation of the play (1667) gave the speech to Prospero (see *The Tempest, or the Enchanted Island* in *Five Restoration Adaptations of Shakespeare*, ed. Christopher Spencer [Urbana: University of Illinois Press, 1965], 1.ii.267), and some editors, from Lewis Theobald (1733) to G. L. Kittredge (1939), have agreed. More recent editors have retained the Folio speech heading, but have sometimes expressed doubt about it (see the introduction to the edition by Virginia Mason Vaughan and Alden T. Vaughan, 135; and David Lindley in his edition, 119). The Vaughans (following Kermode) state tentatively that Caliban's identification of Miranda as his teacher in the dialogue with Stephano about the man in the moon ("My mistress show'd me"; 2.2.138–41) "appears to corroborate" the claim that Miranda taught Caliban (215). The tentative-

ness is well founded. The passage does not establish Miranda as a serious educator. What Caliban ascribes to her teaching—to see the man in the moon with his dog and his bush—is (as the Vaughans, following Orgel [149], note) "folk legend" at best, and the stretch of dialogue in question serves, needless to say (as Trinculo does say [2.2.144–46]), to present Caliban at his least intellectually impressive. That the mechanicals in *A Midsummer Night's Dream* share the belief about the man in the moon [*MND*, 3.1.55–57] hardly alters its cultural status.

108. Kermode glosses "capable" in "capable of all ill" as "apt to receive the impression of." This is the literal meaning of the word, but does not, in context, seem strong enough, since it follows the denial of "any...goodness." Orgel seems more contextually accurate in glossing the word as "susceptible (only) to."

109. Matthew DeCoursey in "The Logic of Inequality: Caliban's Baseness in *The Tempest*," *Cahiers Élisabéthains* 64 (2003): 43–51, is mistaken in seeing Caliban as not having a human shape and (contradictorily) as a creature who can "legitimately" be enslaved along Aristotelian lines (48). The best readers of the *Politics* have recognized that Aristotle's conception of the "natural slave" is not intended as a justification for slavery in his society or elsewhere, and is not clearly presented as an actual possibility. For commentary, see "*The Tempest* (1): Power," note 76.

110. Bate, "The Humanist *Tempest*," 17; *Soul of the Age*, 127.

111. On the domestic arrangements, see "*The Tempest* (1): Power."

112. See "*The Tempest* (2): Labor," notes 31 and 32.

113. This was briefly suggested by Stephen Orgel in "Prospero's Wife," *Representations* 8 (1984): 5; it is taken for granted by Ian McAdam in *Magic and Masculinity in Early Modern English Drama* (Pittsburgh: Duquesne University Press, 2009), 341, and alluded to by John Kunat in "'Play Me False: Rape, Race, and Conquest in *The Tempest*," *Shakespeare Quarterly* 65 (2014): 310.

114. See "*The Tempest* (2): Labor," 158.

115. See "*The Tempest* (1): Power," 149.

116. Mannoni remarks in passing that Prospero "could have continued to civilize and correct" Caliban (*Prospero and Caliban*, 106). See also Julia Lupton, *Thinking with Shakespeare: Essays on Politics and Life* (Chicago: University of Chicago Press, 2011), 209.

117. Lamming, *The Pleasures of Exile*, 102.

118. Compare Leininger, "The Miranda Trap," 289: "Prospero needs Miranda as sexual bait, and then needs to protect her from the threat."

119. For the "little empire," see Erasmus, *De Pueris* (Toronto), 325; *De Pueris* (Latin), 425; for tyranny, see Toronto, 328; Latin, 433.

120. For Mannoni on this, see "*The Tempest* (1): Power."

CHAPTER 9

1. On epistemology, see "Shakespeare and Skepticism (2): Epistemology."

2. On the way Shakespeare draws on theological conceptions with regard to motives, see the discussion of *Othello* in chapter 1, "Excuses, Bepissing, and Non-Being."

3. Contemporary scholarly discussion of "atheism" in the Renaissance takes its orientation from Lucien Febvre's *Le problème de l'incroyance au XVIe siècle: La religion de Rabelais* (1942); *The Problem of Unbelief in the Sixteenth Century: The Religion of Rabelais*, trans. Beatrice Gottlieb (Cambridge, Mass.: Harvard University Press, 1982). William Elton's *King Lear and the*

Gods (San Marino, Calif.: Huntington Library, 1966) is in dialogue with Febvre. On skepticism in the period, see Richard H. Popkin, *The History of Skepticism from Erasmus to Spinoza* (1960; Berkeley: University of California Press, 1979).

    4. For relics, see the final essay in this book, "Mind, Nature, Heterodoxy, and Iconoclasm in *The Winter's Tale*." On charges of atheism, see the works by Febvre and Elton cited in the previous note; on possession-deniers as "atheists," see F. W. Brownlow, *Shakespeare, Harsnett, and the Devils of Denham* (Newark: University of Delaware Press, 1993), 65, 72; hereafter cited as "Brownlow."

    5. For Scot as on the edge of atheism, see Sidney Anglo, "Reginald Scot's *Discoverie of Witchcraft*: Scepticism and Sadduceeism," in *The Damned Art: Essays in the Literature of Witchcraft*, ed. Sidney Anglo (London: Routledge, 1977), 106–39, esp. 129; for Scot as an Erasmian (and Baconian), see Leland Estes, "Reginald Scot and His *Discoverie of Witchcraft*: Religion and Science in the Opposition to the European Witch Craze," *Church History* 52 (1983): 444–56. On the afterlife of Scot's book, see S. F. Davies, "The Reception of Scot's *Discovery of Witchcraft*: Witchcraft, Magic, and Radical Religion," *JHI* 74 (2013): 381–401.

    6. See George Gifford, *A Dialogue Concerning Witches and Witchcraftes. In which is laide open how craftily the Divell deceiveth not onely the Witches but many other and so leadeth them awrie into many great errours* (London, 1593).

    7. Almost all of Erasmus's works were on the Catholic Church's Index of Prohibited Books by the mid-sixteenth century or so. See Bruce Mansfield, *Phoenix of His Age: Interpretations of Erasmus c.1550–1750* (Toronto: University of Toronto Press, 1979), 26–27. On John Foxe's view of Erasmus as part of the Reformation, see Mansfield, 113.

    8. David Wootton argues that Scot's allegorizing of biblical narratives and episodes (such as the fall of Lucifer) links him significantly to the Familists ("Reginald Scot, Abraham Fleming, and the Impossibility of Witchcraft," in *Languages of Witchcraft: Narrative, Ideology, and Meaning in Early Modern Culture*, ed. Stuart Clark (New York: St. Martin's Press, 2001), 119–38. For Scot on the fall of Lucifer, which "onelie foreshewed the deposing and deprivation of king Nabuchadnez-zar," see *The Discoverie of Witchcraft . . . Whereunto is added An excellent Discourse of the Nature and Substance of Devils and Spirits*, ed. Brinsley Nicholson (Totowa, N.J.: Rowman & Littlefield, 1973), 421. Scot goes out of his way (perhaps disingenuously) to distance himself from "the familie of love and other such heretikes, as would reduce the whole Bible unto allegories," but in that very sentence he goes on to deny that in the story of the fall the devil actually entered into a snake (452). Scot is contemptuous of "grosse"—that is, literal—"conceivers of scripture" (427, 429, 433). For Erasmus's urging of Christians to disregard "the mere skin of scripture," and search into "its mystical spirit," see *The Enchiridion of Erasmus*, trans. Raymond Himelick (Bloomington: Indiana University Press, 1963), 106ff. For Erasmus and the spiritualists, see Richard Strier, "Martin Luther and the Real Presence in Nature," *Journal of Medieval and Early Modern Studies* 37 (Spring 2007): 271–303.

    9. For the dating of the play, see William Shakespeare, *The Comedy of Errors*, ed. R. A. Foakes (London: Methuen, 1962), xvi–xxiii; and the edition by T. S. Dorsch, rev. Ros King (Cambridge: Cambridge University Press, 2004), 38–40. All citations will be from the Dorsch-King edition.

    10. The three "romances" prior to *The Tempest* seem to relax their skepticism toward religion. For the peculiar theology of *The Winter's Tale*, see "Mind, Nature, Heterodoxy, and Iconoclasm in *The Winter's Tale*." *The Tempest*, on the other hand, does not develop its religious elements; the focus of the play is elsewhere (see "*The Tempest* [1]: Power").

11. Stephen Greenblatt, "Shakespeare and the Exorcists," in *Shakespearean Negotiations* (Berkeley: University of California Press, 1988), 114–15.

12. See *Twelfth Night*, 4.2.25.

13. Michael MacDonald, *Mystical Bedlam: Madness, Anxiety, and Healing in Seventeenth-Century England* (Cambridge: Cambridge University Press, 1981), 107.

14. MacDonald, *Mystical Bedlam*, 213.

15. On Puritan exorcists, see Keith Thomas, *Religion and the Decline of Magic* (New York: Scribner's, 1971), 483–87; and Brownlow, 62–74.

16. For confusion in the criticism about the doctrinal allegiance of Dr. Pinch, see Richard Strier, *The Unrepentant Renaissance: From Petrarch to Shakespeare to Milton* (Chicago: University of Chicago Press, 2011), 175–76. On the hesitance of even devoted adherents of the established church in the pre-Laudian period to call upon "the saints in heaven," see Strier, "'To all Angels and Saints': Herbert's Puritan Poem," *Modern Philology* 77 (1979): 132–45.

17. For the surprising social extent of theological awareness in the period, see Peter Marshall, "Choosing Sides and Talking Religion in Shakespeare's England," in *Shakespeare and Early Modern Religion*, ed. David Loewenstein and Michael Witmore (Cambridge: Cambridge University Press, 2015), 40–56; and Tessa Wright, *Cheap Print and Popular Piety, 1550–1640* (Cambridge: Cambridge University Press, 1991). Shakespeare almost certainly knew about the spectacular Catholic exorcisms of 1585–86 in Denham (Brownlow, 107–10). These are the topic of Harsnett's 1603 pamphlet, but Shakespeare did not need to learn about them there.

18. On Antipholus of Syracuse and epistemological doubt, see "Shakespeare and Skepticism (2): Epistemology."

19. On "privy marks," see Thomas, *Religion and the Decline of Magic*, 445–46; James Sharpe, *Instruments of Darkness: Witchcraft in Early Modern England* (Philadelphia: University of Pennsylvania Press, 1997), 178–84; Stuart Clark, *Thinking with Demons: The Idea of Witchcraft in Early Modern Europe* (Oxford: Oxford University Press, 1997), 84, 381–82, 424–25.

20. On the Reformation and fideist dialectic, see Popkin, *History of Skepticism*, ch. 11; and Richard H. Popkin and Arjo Vanderjagt, *Scepticism and Irreligion in the Seventeenth and Eighteenth Centuries* (Leiden: Brill, 1993).

21. See the text of the play in *The Norton Facsimile of the First Folio of Shakespeare*, ed. Charlton Hinman (New York: Norton, 1968), through line number, 1226.

22. On the passage not only citing scripture, but doing so in the way that scripture cites scripture, see Foakes's note on the line, which credits Richmond Noble, *Shakespeare's Biblical Knowledge* (London: SPCK, 1935) for the observation.

23. For a full-length argument that *The Comedy of Errors* endorses a Reformation rather than a Catholic conception of holiness, see Strier, *Unrepentant Renaissance*, ch. 4.

24. King James [VI of Scotland], *Daemonologie* (1597), in *Elizabethan and Jacobean Quartos*, ed. G. B. Harrison ([1922?]; rpt. New York: Barnes & Noble, 1966), 73–74. Anon., *News from Scotland* (1591) is also included in this volume.

25. On the dating of *A Midsummer Night's Dream*, see the edition by Harold F. Brooks (London: Methuen, 1983), xxxiv–lxvii, which I have used throughout.

26. Reginald Scot, *The Discoverie of Witchcraft*, xx ("To the Readers"). Further citations of this work appear parenthetically in the text.

27. For Scot's dualism, see *Discoverie*, 56; *An excellent Discourse*, 426–27. On the centrality of this to Scot's endeavor, see Anglo, "Reginald Scot's *Discoverie of Witchcraft*, 126–34; Clark, *Thinking with Demons*, 211–12; Robert H. West, *Reginald Scot and Renaissance Writings on*

Witchcraft (Boston: Twayne, 1984), 86–94; and Philip C. Almond, *England's First Demonologist: Reginald Scot and "The Discoverie of Witchcraft"* (London: Tauris, 2015), ch. 5.

28. Francis Bacon, *The Essays*, ed. John Pitcher (London: Penguin, 1955), 108. "Of Atheism" is paired with "Of Superstition," and must be read in that context. By the end of the second essay, it is quite clear that—if he had to choose, and despite the ringing affirmation quoted above—Bacon much prefers atheism to superstition. For the way in which Bacon's *Essays* sometimes affirm and sometimes undercut their initial assertions, see Richard Strier, *Resistant Structures: Particularity, Radicalism, and Renaissance Texts* (Chicago: University of Chicago Press, 1995), ch. 2.

29. On "experience" in medicine in the period, see Peter Dear, "The Meanings of Experience," in *The Cambridge History of Science*, ed. Katharine Park and Lorraine Daston, vol. 3 (Cambridge: Cambridge University Press, 2006), 106–31. On remedies, see Andrew Wear, *Knowledge and Practice in English Medicine, 1550–1680* (Cambridge: Cambridge University Press, 2000), ch. 2. For a wider perspective, see Elaine Leong, *Recipes and Everyday Knowledge: Medicine, Science, and the Household in Early Modern England* (Chicago: University of Chicago Press, 2018).

30. *The Poetry and Prose of William Blake*, ed. David V. Erdman (Garden City, N.Y.: Doubleday, 1965), 555 (punctuation and capitalization normalized).

31. Virtually all critics of the play take it to be significant, in a negative way, that the "love-juice" remains in Demetrius's eyes. Regina Buccola is typical: "Demetrius is blissfully married to Helena only because he is still suffering the effects of a fairy drug" (*Fairies, Fractious Women, and the Old Faith: Fairy Lore in Early Modern British Drama and Culture* [Selingsgrove, Pa.: Susquehanna University Press, 2006], 67).

32. Interestingly, the play presents this kind of erotic instability as characteristic only of young men—both Demetrius and Lysander manifest it in the play—but not of young women. Each of the young (human) women in the play is competely steady in her erotic commitment. Titania's passion for Bottom is the exception to the picture of complete female fidelity, and it is seen as an especially weird and uncharacteristic phenomenon ("O, how mine eyes do loathe his visage now," says Titania [4.1.78]).

33. *Romeo and Juliet*, 1.4.53–95. The plays are tightly linked; the play that the mechanicals put on for Theseus and company is a version of the Romeo and Juliet plot.

34. This text is included in the Loeb edition of Lucian, trans. M. D. McLeod (Cambridge, Mass.: Harvard University Press, 1967), 9:52–145 (on the authorship problem, see 9:47–51). Lucian is an important figure in the studies of both Febvre and Elton (see note 3 above). For Bacon's comment, see "Of Atheism," in *The Essays*, 109. For a general account of Lucian's influence, see Christopher Robinson, *Lucian and His Influence in Europe* (Chapel Hill: University of North Carolina Press, 1979).

35. See note 8 above.

36. The authorized version is very close to the Geneva version here, only altering the word order slightly.

37. Northrop Frye, *A Natural Perspective: The Development of Shakespearean Comedy and Romance* (New York: Columbia University Press, 1965), 108–9.

38. Whenever Socrates, in a Platonic dialogue, says that something comes from the gods (like "true beliefs" at the end of the *Meno*), one should be aware of having one's philosophical leg pulled (see *Ion* 533d–534e; *Meno* 99a–100b, in *The Collected Dialogues of Plato*, ed. Edith Hamilton and Huntington Cairns [Princeton, N.J.: Princeton University Press, 1961]). The point of the praise of poets in the *Ion* is to show them not to have knowledge (though, of course, what they do have is more "divine"). See Suzanne Stern-Gillet, "On (Mis)Interpreting Plato's *Ion*," *Phronesis*

49 (2004): 169–201. Alison Shell correctly notes that the orientation of Theseus's speech "is one of suspicion," but she backs away from this by asserting that the speech nevertheless presents "an attractive view of poetic creativity," and so Shakespeare is (as usual in her view) "having it both ways" (*Shakespeare and Religion* [London: Bloomsbury, 2010], 71).

39. Francis Bacon, *The Advancement of Learning*, ed. G. W. Kitchin (London: Dent, 1973), 83.

40. Bacon, *The Advancement of Learning*, 85.

41. On the status of this belief, sanctioned by neither Protestants nor Catholics, see Peter Marshall, *Beliefs and the Dead in Reformation England* (Oxford: Oxford University Press, 2002), 255–56. Hamlet seems to espouse this belief ("'Tis now the very witching time of night, / When churchyards yawn" [3.2.379–80]), but at the moment in which he does so, he believes that he has finally confirmed the account of the "ghost," and is in a state, as he himself recognizes, of hyperbolical overexcitement ("Now could I drink hot blood " [3.2.380]). With regard to the activities of "spirits" and of fairies and witches in *Hamlet*, these are reported as a report ("they say" it [1.5.161]). The folk-belief in question is presented as dubious, though beautiful ("so hallowed and so gracious"). A learned Protestant (Horatio) concedes, graciously, that he has heard such things and does "in part" believe them. On the "thing" (1.1.24) being the ghost of Hamlet's father rather than a demon, Horatio is continuously skeptical. See "Happy Hamlet," 55. All citations from *Hamlet* are from the edition by Harold Jenkins (London: Methuen, 1982).

42. Shell notes that while the consecration with "field dew" that the fairies promise to the ducal palace may "exploit Catholic nostalgia," the lines also "remind the audience that to link Catholics and fairies is to draw on the association of popery with superstition" (*Shakespeare's Religion*, 16).

43. On English magistrates refusing to prosecute, see Thomas, *Religion and the Decline of Magic*, 452, 459–60, 576. On the prevalence of witchcraft prosecutions in sixteenth-century Europe, see, inter alia, Brian Levack, *The Witch-Hunt in Early Modern Europe* (London: Longman, 1987). For the skeptical English magistrates, see Levack 182–84. For a study of a case in 1604 when the authorities—from Assize judges to King James himself—rejected accusations of witchcraft and possession, see James Sharpe, *The Bewitching of Anne Gunter* (New York: Routledge, 2000). On lay jurists at the height of the witchcraft persecutions in Europe (1480s–1530s) who argued against legal prosecution of supposed witches (and their supposed accomplices), see Matteo Duni, "Doubting Witchcraft: Theologians, Jurists, Inquisitors During the Fifteenth and Sixteenth Century," *Studies in Church History* 52 (2016): 203–31. Duni points out that the witchcraft accusations of this period were based on a newly developed theory of the devil's ability to operate physically in the world (205). The older (pre-Scholastic), canonical theory held that such claims were delusions. Scot can be seen as going back to the earlier view.

44. Henry N. Paul, *The Royal Play of "Macbeth": When, Why, and How It Was Written by Shakespeare* (New York: Macmillan, 1950).

45. On the change in James's views, see Paul, *The Royal Play*, 75–130. Paul is officially agnostic about whether James ever reached the point of total skepticism, but clearly tends toward the view that he did (87–89).

46. Paul, *The Royal Play*, 213–16.

47. Paul, *The Royal Play*, 61, 159.

48. Lewis Theobald, ed., *The Works of William Shakespeare* (London: A. Bettesworth & C. Hitch, 1733), 5:163–64. On the difficult (and as yet unsolved) question of why, in the context of a controversy with a Puritan exorcist, Harsnett produced a book on Catholic exorcisms of a decade and a half earlier, see Brownlow, chs. 4–5.

49. Greenblatt, "Shakespeare and the Exorcists," 106.

50. For the "circulation of social energy," see Greenblatt, *Shakespearean Negotiations*, 1–20. For Erasmus's "Exorcism, or The Spectre" (*Exorcismus, sive Spectrum*), see *The Colloquies of Erasmus*, trans. Craig R. Thompson (Chicago: University of Chicago Press, 1965), 230–37.

51. On the popularity of the *Colloquies*, see, inter alia, Thompson's introduction to his translation. For Shakespeare's connections to Erasmus, see "*The Tempest* (3): Humanism," and "Mind, Nature, Heterodoxy, and Iconoclasm in *The Winter's Tale*," notes 17 and 118.

52. Unless stated otherwise, all references to and citations of *King Lear* are taken from *King Lear: A Parallel Text Edition*, ed. René Weis (London: Longman,1993). References to and citations from Harsnett's *Declaration* are from the edition in Brownlow, 190–413 (page references in the text).

53. See the "Examinations" of Sara Williams, Friswood Williams, and Anne Smith in Brownlow, 339–387. The passage is unique to the Quarto. It may be the case that by the time the Folio version was composed, the Harsnett text was no longer current. For the possible date of the Folio version (and an argument that, apart from accidentals, many changes from the Quarto in the Folio are authorial), see Gary Taylor, "The Date and Authorship of the Folio Version," in *The Division of the Kingdoms: Shakespeare's Two Versions of "King Lear,"* ed. Gary Taylor and Michael Warren (Oxford: Clarendon Press, 1983), 351–468. For the record, I should say that I accept the main outlines of the authorial revision thesis. For a book-length attack on this view, see Sir Brian Vickers, *The One "King Lear"* (Cambridge, Mass.: Harvard University Press, 2016).

54. On negative dogmatism, see Popkin, *The History of Skepticism from Erasmus to Spinoza*, xvii. For *Hamlet* as purposely leaving its questions open, see Stephen Greenblatt, *Hamlet in Purgatory* (Princeton, N.J.: Princeton University Press, 2001), 239–40; Shell, *Shakespeare and Religion*, 113.

55. Greenblatt, "Shakespeare and the Exorcists," 121.

56. Even if one were to accept the denigration of Edgar's behavior to Gloucester that has become a staple in much *Lear* criticism today, it still would not make sense to equate Edgar with the figures of the fraudulent exorcists in Harsnett. In "Shakespeare and Harsnett: 'Pregnant to Good Pity'?," *SEL* 38 (1998): 251–64, Amy Wolf sees Shakespeare as critiquing Harsnett for sadism and lack of pity. I think that this responds correctly to Harsnett's tone and genre, but understates Harsnett's sympathy for (as Harsnett sees it) the victims. Harsnett was himself concerned about his tone, worrying that it might strike some as "too light and ironicall for one of my profession" (199). For a defense of Edgar's character against his critical denigrators, see "Resisting Complicity: Ethical Judgment and *King Lear*."

57. While the bulk of *Errors* derives from Plautus's *Manaechmi*, the episode of the husband locked out while his wife is inside his house with his look-alike is taken from Plautus's *Amphitryo*.

58. G. Wilson Knight, "*King Lear* and the Comedy of the Grotesque" (1930), in *The Wheel of Fire: Interpretations of Shakespearean Tragedy; with Three New Essays* (New York: Meridian Books, 1957), 171. Compare Jan Kott, "*King Lear* or *Endgame*," in *Shakespeare Our Contemporary*, trans. Boleslaw Taborski (Garden City, N.Y.: Doubleday, 1966), 142–49. As far as I can see, Kott does not acknowledge Knight's essay.

59. Compare Alex Schulman, "*King Lear* and the State of Nature," in *Rethinking Shakespeare's Political Philosophy: From "Lear" to "Leviathan"* (Edinburgh: Edinburgh University Press, 2014), 116.

60. *Colloquies*, ed. Thompson, 237.

61. There may be a significant difference between the ways that Q and F define the relation between the gods and "men's impossibilities." See Weis's note on the difference (past versus present). I am not sure which formulation, Q's past tense or F's present tense, is more skeptical.

62. For the breadth of belief in some version of this doctrine, see Alexandra Walsham, *Providence in Early Modern England* (Oxford: Oxford University Press, 1999): "Before 1640 the idea of an interventionist deity was very much part of the intellectual and cultural mainstream" (110).

63. For equivocations in Elton, *King Lear and the Gods*, see 48, 115, 238–39, 258. For a recent restatement of Elton's view of the critique of providentialism in the play, see David Loewenstein, "Agnostic Shakespeare? The Godless World of *King Lear*," in Loewenstein and Witmore, *Shakespeare and Early Modern Religion*, 155–71.

64. On Luther, see Phillip S. Watson, *Let God Be God* (Philadelphia: FortressPress, 1947); John Dillenberger, *God Hidden and Revealed* (Philadelphia: Muhlenberg Press, 1953). On Calvin, Edward A. Dowey, *The Knowledge of God in Calvin's Theology* (New York: Columbia University Press, 1952); Benjamin Warfield, "Calvin's Doctrine of God," and C. J. Kinlaw, "Determinism and the Hiddenness of God in Calvin's Theology," in *Articles on Calvinism*, ed. Richard C. Gamble (New York: Garland, 1992), 9:17–72, 161–73.

65. John Calvin, *Institutes of the Christian Religion*, ed. John T. McNeill, trans. Ford Lewis Battles (Philadelphia: Westminster Press, 1960), I.xvii.6.

66. A. C. Bradley, *Shakespearean Tragedy: Lectures on Hamlet, Othello, King Lear, Macbeth* (1904), foreword by John Bailey (London: Penguin, 1991), 280.

67. Greenblatt, "Shakespeare and the Exorcists," 120. Compare the flurry of three "but's" in two successive sentences at the bottom of 125.

68. "Shakespeare and the Exorcists," 121.

69. For a firsthand account, see John Gerard, *The Autobiography of a Hunted Priest*, trans. Philip Caraman (New York: Pellegrini and Cudahy, 1952); for the general picture, see Michael C. Questier, *Catholicism and Community in Early Modern England: Politics, Aristocratic Patronage, and Religion, 1550–1640* (Cambridge: Cambridge University Press, 2006).

70. For what is known, see John L. Murphy, *Darkness and Devils: Exorcism and King Lear* (Athens: Ohio University Press, 1984), ch. 3. Murphy's overall thesis is unclear.

71. The theatrical revival of the old play was probably what gave Shakespeare the impetus to turn to the story. The old *King Leir* was staged in 1594, and probably written sometime earlier (see *Narrative and Dramatic Sources of Shakespeare*, ed. Geoffrey Bullough [New York: Columbia University Press, 1973], 7:404–5.) For a useful comparison of *Leir* and Shakespeare's version(s), see James Shapiro, *The Year of "Lear": Shakespeare in 1606* (New York: Simon & Schuster, 2015), ch. 3.

72. Greenblatt, "Shakespeare and the Exorcists," 125.

73. See "*King Lear* and Human Needs."

74. I see the Folio as intensifying the darkness and the religious skepticism of the Quarto. But the argument of this chapter does not depend on this claim or on acceptance of the authorial revision thesis (see note 53 above).

75. In this scene, as in the final scene of act 4, the Quarto has a (medical) "Doctor" with Cordelia, while the Folio has a "Gentleman" instead.

76. In both the Quarto and the Folio, in the reconciliation scene, Cordelia tells the person who is attending on Lear, "Be governed by your knowledge" (Q 4.7; F 4.6: 17). Her hope that her kiss will act as "medicine" for Lear (24) does not contradict this.

77. See Paul J. Alpers, "*King Lear* and the Theory of the 'Sight Pattern,'" in *In Defense of Reading: A Reader's Approach to Literary Criticism*, ed. Reuben A. Brower and Richard Poirier (New York: Dutton, 1963), 133–52. For discussion of Alpers's essay and Stanley Cavell's divergence from it, see "Resisting Complicity: Ethical Judgment and *King Lear*."

78. On Cordelia's classical, especially Roman, values, see "*King Lear* and Human Needs," note 7. In the penultimate line of this scene, Cordelia speaks of "love, dear love" as the motive for her invasion of England, but that is not the whole story. She then adds, "and our aged father's right."

79. Elton, *King Lear and the Gods*, 238 and 258.

80. On Elysium, see, inter alia, Richmond Lattimore, *Themes in Greek and Latin Epitaphs* (Urbana: University of Illinois Press, 1942). For a survey of beliefs in the afterlife, see Bart D. Ehrman, *Heaven and Hell: A History of the Afterlife* (New York: Simon and Schuster, 2020).

81. Both Q and F have "Gods spies." Most editors print this as "God's," so that the play seems to make a sudden lurch into monotheism here, since all the other references to deities are not given the initial capital letter. But all mentions of deities in the early texts of the play are capitalized, starting with Kent's "Thou swearest thy Gods in vain" in 1.1 (Q 150; F 158). As far as I know, no modern edition indicates this. Elizabethan and Jacobean English did not have the convention of indicating possessives with apostrophes, and so the phrase "Gods spies" is radically ambiguous as to number. The Oxford version of the texts in *The Works of William Shakespeare*, ed. Stanley Wells and Gary Taylor, with John Jowett and William Montgomery (Oxford: Oxford University Press, 1986), is the only modern edition to capture this by not adding an apostrophe (leaving "Gods"). Kenneth Muir, in his Arden 2 edition (London: Methuen, 1964; 1972), notes the lack of the apostrophe in the early texts, and prints "Gods' spies." R. A. Foakes, in his Arden 3 edition (Walton-on-Thames: Thomas Nelson, 1997), also notes the lack of the apostrophe in Q and F, but inserts the singularizing apostrophe nevertheless. Modern conventions require an apostrophe *somewhere*. "Gods' spies" may be awkward but has the advantages of being consistent with the early texts and being a minimal rather than a maximal editorial intrusion. Elton provides a plausible pagan reading of "Gods' spies," with apt quotations from Plutarch and others (*King Lear and the Gods*, 252–53).

82. See "Excuses, Bepissing, and Non-Being," 36–39.

83. Here again, I am following Alpers ("*King Lear* and the Theory of the 'Sight Pattern,'" 149–52). Kent R. Lenhof's "Relation and Responsibility: A Levinasian Reading of *King Lear*," *Modern Philology* 111 (2014): 485–509, seems to be getting at a similar point, but the Levinasian formulations often seem hyperbolic and rather distant from the text (for specific problems with the Levinasian reading, see "Resisting Complicity: Ethical Judgment and *King Lear*," note 51, and "*King Lear* and Human Needs," note 6).

84. *The Works of George Herbert*, ed. F. E. Hutchinson (Oxford: Clarendon Press, 1945), 188–89. Through all the revisions and additions that Herbert made to his volume (see Hutchinson, liv-lv), Herbert kept this poem, unchanged from the first form in which we have it (in the "Williams manuscript"), as the final lyric—perhaps the final poem. "The Church Militant" is not a lyric and may not have been intended as the end of *The Temple*. The "Williams manuscript" places a "Finis" after "Love" (3), and there are five blank pages between that ending and "The Church Militant," which is given its own running title (see *The Williams Manuscript of George Herbert's Poems*, a facsimile reproduction with an introduction by Amy Charles [Delmar, N.Y.: Scholars' Facsimiles, 1977]).

85. For *agape* here, see Anders Nygren, *Agape and Eros*, trans. Philip S. Watson (New York: Harper and Row, 1969), 75–101.

86. Shakespeare's scene does not involve the host-guest framework that structures Herbert's poem or the Eucharistic resonance of its penultimate line, but the scene does capture what is clearly the central dynamic of the poem. Herbert called the poem "Love," not "The Holy Communion," "The Invitation," or "The Banquet" (titles of other poems in Herbert's volume). The

theology led both writers to think about love in the deepest sense, and courtesy in the deepest sense. On "ceremonious affection" and "courtesy" in *Lear*, see "*King Lear* and Human Needs," 118 and 122–23.

87. For a full reading of the poem in these terms, see Richard Strier, *Love Known: Theology and Experience in George Herbert's Poetry* (Chicago: University of Chicago Press, 1983), 74–83.

88. John D. Cox, *Seeming Knowledge: Shakespeare and Skeptical Faith* (Waco, Tex.: Baylor University Press, 2007), 89, accepts the analogy between this scene in *Lear* and Herbert's poem. The analogy was initially suggested in Richard Strier, "Shakespeare and the Skeptics," *Religion and Literature* 32 (2000): 171–89 (188–89), on which my discussion here draws.

89. See Stanley Cavell, "The Avoidance of Love: A Reading of *King Lear*," in *Must We Mean What We Say? A Book of Essays* (New York: Scribner's, 1969), 277–78; *Disowning Knowledge* (1987; Cambridge: Cambridge University Press, 2003), 49. For thoughts on the necessity of this correlation, see "Resisting Complicity: Ethical Judgment and *King Lear*," note 27.

90. Martin Luther, *Theses for the Heidelberg Disputation* (1518), in *Luther: Early Theological Works*, ed. James Atkinson (Philadelphia: Westminster Press, 1962), 278 (I have slightly emended the translation in consultation with the Latin text).

91. For Luther on "reason" in the context of grace as a "perverse leviathan," see "The Freedom of a Christian," in *Martin Luther: Selections from His Writings*, ed. John Dillenberger (Garden City, N.Y.: Doubleday Anchor, 1961), 71–72. For commentary, see Brian Gerrish, *Grace and Reason: A Study in the Theology Of Luther* (Oxford: Clarendon Press, 1962).

92. Compare Luther on the lack of considerations and distinctions in service to one's neighbor who is in need (the true Christian "does not distinguish between friends and enemies, or anticipate their thankfulness or unthankfulness"). This is part of the "freedom" of a Christian, and is expressed in the treatise by that title (75–76 [quotation from 76], 79–80). Reiterated in William Tyndale, *The Parable of the Wicked Mammon*, in Tyndale, *Doctrinal Treatises and Introductions to Different Portions of the Holy Scriptures*, ed. Rev. Henry Walter (Cambridge: Cambridge University Press, 1848), 95–98.

93. *Othello*, 5.2.286; see "Excuses, Bepissing, and Non-being." Sanford Budick, "Shakespeare's Secular Benediction: The Language of Tragic Community in *King Lear*," in *Religious Diversity and Early Modern English Texts*, ed. Arthur F. Marotti and Chanita Goldblatt (Detroit: Wayne State University Press, 2013), 330–51, seems to be getting at a similar point, but Budick's vocabulary of extreme humility and (Kantian) lack of consideration for the ordinary features of life seem to be quite far from the play. And Budick does not relate the play to any historical religious doctrine or position. Eric S. Mallin's *Godless Shakespeare* (London: Continuum, 2007) is quite different from my approach. Mallin sees Shakespeare as mocking religion, whereas I see him as drawing on it as a powerful and profound resource. Mallin comes closest to my view in his treatment of Cleopatra (114–18). D. Douglas Waters, in his admirable attempt to free the plays from unnecessary allegorizing and moralizing, argues that one should not dwell on the religious language in the plays, asserting (with regard to *Othello*) that "Shakespeare's language is not theological partially because his ideas are not theological" (*Christian Settings in Shakespeare's Tragedies* [Cranbury, N.J.: Associated University Presses, 1994], 200). This seems to me not to follow at all. That the language *is* often theological is beyond question. The issue is what to make of this. Simply dismissing it cannot be the right approach.

94. On theatrical "faith," see Richard C. McCoy, *Faith in Shakespeare* (New York: Oxford University Press, 2013), though Shakespeare may have been more skeptical about this than McCoy is; see "Mind, Nature, Heterodoxy, and Iconoclasm in *The Winter's Tale*."

CHAPTER 10

1. In *A Will to Believe: Shakespeare and Religion* (Oxford: Oxford University Press, 2014), David Kastan shows the weakness of the case for the Catholic Shakespeare (and the playwright's father), yet nonetheless backs away from the conclusion that Shakespeare was consistently Protestant into the claim that it is "impossible to know" what Shakespeare actually believed (30) and even into the highly skeptical but truly implausible claim that "it is impossible to *know* what anyone in the period 'actually' believed" (31; italics and quotation marks original). Can we not know what, for instance, Luther or Cardinal Bellarmine actually believed? For a recent book that sees living with "epistemological weakness" as the key to Shakespeare's works, see James Kuzner, *Shakespeare as a Way of Life: Skeptical Practice and the Politics of Weakness* (New York: Fordham University Press, 2016).

2. See "*The Tempest* (1): Power," note 2.

3. *The Philosophical Works of Descartes*, trans. Elizabeth S. Haldane and G. R. T. Ross (Cambridge: Cambridge University Press, 1931), 1:145; hereafter "Haldane and Ross." I have mostly used the Haldane and Ross translation, but sometimes have preferred the translation in vol. 2 of *The Philosophical Writings of Descartes*, trans. John Cottingham, Robert Stoothoff, and Dugald Murdoch (Cambridge: Cambridge University Press, 1984); hereafter "Cottingham." For the Latin, I have used *Meditationes de Prima Philosophia, texte latin et traduction du Duc de Lynes*, intro. Geneviève Rodis-Lewis (Paris: J. Vrin, 1978); hereafter "*Meditationes*."

4. Apparently thinking that one's body or one's head was made of earthenware or, especially, glass was a well-recognized rather comical version of insanity in the period. See Gill Speak, "An Odd Kind of Melancholy: Reflections on the Glass Delusion in Europe (1440–1680)," *History of Psychiatry* 1 (1990): 191–206. I owe my awareness of the glass delusion to Timothy Harrison (who credits his awareness of it to a lecture by Jean-Luc Marion).

5. In a key passage in his history of madness (first published in 1961), Foucault explains why, for Descartes in the *Meditations*, "madness is an altogether different affair" than sensory errors or dreaming (Michel Foucault, *History of Madness*, ed. Jean Khalfa, trans. Jonathan Murphy and Jean Khalfa [London: Routledge, 2006], 45). Derrida responded to this passage in "Cogito and the History of Madness" (originally published in 1964) by denying that Descartes really rejects this possibility, seeing him as only pretending to do so (see Jacques Derrida, *Writing and Difference*, trans. Alan Bass [Chicago: University of Chicago Press, 1978], 31–63, esp. 50–51). Foucault responded to Derrida's essay in an appendix to the second edition of the madness book (1972) with "My Body, This Paper, This Fire," in *History of Madness*, 550–74 (rpt. in Michel Foucault, *Aesthetics, Method, and Epistemology*, ed. James D. Faubion [New York: The New Press, 1998], 393–417), in which Foucault reasserted the legitimacy and importance for Descartes of the exclusion of madness. A view similar to Foucault's was developed independently in the Anglo-American analytic tradition by Harry G. Frankfurt, *Demons, Dreamers, and Madmen: The Defense of Reason in Descartes's "Meditations"* (Indianapolis: Bobbs-Merrill, 1970), 28, 36–40.

6. For the text of the play, I have used the edition by T. S. Dorsch, rev. Ros King (Cambridge: Cambridge University Press, 2004).

7. For the character of Adriana in the play, and for the play's attitude toward marriage, see Richard Strier, *The Unrepentant Renaissance: From Petrarch to Shakespeare to Milton* (Chicago: University of Chicago Press, 2011), 165–86.

8. On *epoché*, see Miles Burnyeat's introduction, and David Sedley, "The Motivation of Greek Skepticism," in *The Skeptical Tradition*, ed. Miles Burnyeat (Berkeley: University of California Press, 1983), 9–29.

9. Sextus Empiricus, *Outlines of Pyrrhonism*, ed. and trans. R. G. Bury (Cambridge, Mass.: Harvard University Press, 1933), 1: 8–10.

10. René Descartes, *Discourse de la méthode; Discourse on the Method: A Bilingual Edition*, ed. and trans. Georg Heffernan (Notre Dame, Ind.: Notre Dame University Press, 1994), 40, 41.

11. See "Of Custom, and Not Easily Changing an Accepted Law," in *The Complete Essays of Montaigne*, trans. Donald M. Frame (Stanford, Calif.: Stanford University Press, 1958), 77–90 (esp. 86).

12. On the illogic of the speech, see Strier, *The Unrepentant Renaissance*, 45–46.

13. On servants being beaten in the play, see Richard Strier, "Against the Rule of Reason," in *Reading the Early Modern Passions*, ed. Gail Kern Paster, Katherine Rowe, and Mary Floyd-Wilson (Philadelphia: University of Pennsylvania Press, 2004), 33–35; and Patricia Akhimie, *Shakespeare and the Cultivation of Difference* (New York: Routledge, 2018), ch. 2.

14. Bertrand Evans, *Shakespeare's Comedies* (Oxford: Oxford University Press, 1960), 4–5.

15. *The Complete Essays of Montaigne*, 457.

16. See "Shakespeare and Skepticism (1): Religion," 192.

17. David Simon has reminded me that Viola does not actually assert this here, but only hopes that it is so. But what is important for my argument is the fact that she has the thought.

18. Haldane and Ross, 191.

19. See, inter alia, Frankfurt, *Demons, Dreamers, and Madmen*; E. M. Curley, *Descartes Against the Skeptics* (Cambridge, Mass.: Harvard University Press, 1978).

20. My account of "Cartesian" skepticism—that is, anti-skepticism—sees the goal of the *Meditations* in strictly philosophical, not religious terms. Their aim, in the view I am adopting, is (as Harry Frankfurt puts it), the defense of reason, meaning of the reliability of properly applied reason, not the assertion of the necessity of God's existence for this. I do not mean to be taking a side on the long-vexed question of the nature or sincerity of Descartes's religious beliefs. I would, however, note that since the dreaming argument is answered philosophically, the role for which the postulation of God is needed is only to eliminate the "hyperbolical doubts" (*hyperbolicae . . . dubitationes* [*Meditationes*, 86])—of the highly probable (*valde probabiles* [*Meditationes*, 23])—that rely on the consciously adopted "suppose" of the evil demon that employs all its powers in deceiving Descartes. I thank Timothy Harrison for urging me to make this explicit.

21. Ellen Spolsky, *Satisfying Skepticism: Embodied Knowledge in the Early Modern World* (Aldershot: Ashgate, 2001), 68. Further citations of this work appear parenthetically in the text.

22. All quotations from and citations of *Othello* are from the edition by A. J. Honigmann (1996), intro. Ayanna Thompson (London: Bloomsbury, 2016).

23. On the importance of the "plain man" mode in the play, see Richard Strier, "Paleness vs. Eloquence: The Ideologies of Style in the English Renaissance," *Explorations in Renaissance Culture* 45 (2019): 91–120.

24. *OED*, n. supervisor, 1a.

25. See Andrew Cutrofello, "Is Othello Jealous? Coleridge and Russell contra Wittgenstein and Cavell," in *Shakespeare and Continental Philosophy*, ed. Jennifer Ann Bates and Richard Wilson (Edinburgh: Edinburgh University Press, 2014), 121–35.

26. Thomas Heywood, A *Woman Killed with Kindness*, scene 13, line 42, in *A Woman Killed with Kindness and Other Domestic Plays*, ed. Martin Wiggins (New York: Oxford University Press, 2008). The historical relation between the two plays (if any) is disputed. Peter Rudnytsky, "*A Woman Killed with Kindness* as Subtext for *Othello*," *Renaissance Drama*, n.s., 14 (1983): 103–24, sees *Othello* as responding to *A Woman Killed*. Honigmann, on the other hand, sees Heywood's play as a "reply" to Shakespeare's (355).

27. It might be objected that "ocular proof" is not necessarily in itself reliable. After all, in Shakespeare's first jealousy play, *Much Ado About Nothing* (1598?), a man is convinced of his fiancé's infidelity by a visual representation purporting to show the fiancé in a compromising position with another man. Claudio thinks he has ocular proof of Hero's infidelity. But this "proof" (the word is not used) relies on darkness, distance, and an elaborate charade. "Ocular proof," if the phrase is to have any meaning, requires optimal viewing conditions—such as the husband in *A Woman Killed with Kindness* has—and correct interpretation (thanks to Andrew Cutrofello for pressing me to make this explicit). A key scene in *Much Ado* in fact validates close and careful observation, the Friar's "noting of the lady" (4.1.158). This "experimental" knowledge (4.1.166) turns out to be veridical.

28. Colin McGinn, *Shakespeare's Philosophy: Recovering the Meaning Behind the Plays* (New York: HarperCollins, 2006) is certain that the marriage between Othello and Desdemona is unconsummated because "Desdemona's real love for him [Othello] would surely have shown through if they had enjoyed normal marital relations" (82). Apart from the bizarreness of this latter assumption (that successful sex "surely" indicates love), it is worth noting that something of the sort is, in fact, at work in the play, since *direct* sensory perception—"A fine woman, a fair woman, a sweet woman! (4.1.175–76)—is reliable therein.

29. For a similar moment, see "Mind, Nature, Heterodoxy, and Iconoclasm in *The Winter's Tale*," 237.

30. The essay on *Othello* was initially published as the final portion of Cavell's *The Claim of Reason: Wittgenstein, Skepticism, Morality, and Tragedy* (Oxford: Clarendon Press, 1979), 482–96. It is reprinted in *Disowning Knowledge in Six Plays of Shakespeare* (Cambridge: Cambridge University Press, 1987), 125–42, and in the "updated edition" (*Seven Plays*, 2003), with the same pagination. I will cite the essay from *Disowning Knowledge* (*DK*); page numbers from that volume will appear parenthetically in the text.

31. On the history and varieties of skepticism, see Burnyeat, *The Skeptical Tradition*, and *Skepticism: From Antiquity to the Present*, ed. Diego E. Machuca and Baron Reed (London: Bloomsbury, 2018). On skepticism about other minds, see the essay by Anil Gomes by that title in the Machuca and Reed collection, 700–713.

32. See *DK*, 6, quoting *The Claim of Reason*, 461–62. It is not clear which form of skepticism Cavell finds more basic. It might be fair to say that he thinks that object-skepticism provides the form, but mind-skepticism the content of skeptical doubt. In any case, he thinks general skeptical doubt unlivable, and something that philosophy inflicts on itself (as Wittgenstein would say), but that "other mind" skepticism is not only livable but part of the human condition. For the view that it is just as lunatic to hold "other mind" skepticism as world-skepticism, see Anita Avramides, "Perception, Reliability, and Other Minds," in *Knowing Other Minds*, ed. Anita Avramides and Matthew Parrott (Oxford: Oxford University Press, 2019), 107–26.

33. This formulation comes from Stanley Cavell, "Knowing and Acknowledging," in *Must We Mean What We Say? A Book of Essays* (New York: Scribner's, 1969), 238–66 (quotation on 263).

34. For doubts about whether other minds are known in any way different from the way that stones are, see Jerry Fodor as quoted in Gomes, "Skepticism About Other Minds," in Machuca and Reed, *Skepticism: From Antiquity to the Present*, 702; and Asa Wikforss, "Knowledge, Belief, and the Asymmetry Thesis," in Avramides and Parrott, *Knowing Other Minds*, 47 ("We should hesitate before giving up on the idea that such knowledge [knowledge of other minds] involves ordinary empirical justification").

35. There is a notable textual crux here, regarding how the voiced "stops" are designated. The Folio has "dilations" (emended by the eighteenth-century editor George Steevens to "delations,"

which is accepted by Honigmann). The Quarto has "denotements" (see *Shakespeare's Plays in Quarto*, ed. Michael J. B. Allen and Kenneth Muir [Berkeley: University of California Press, 1981], 811). Both readings make sense, but they are significantly different, and cannot be transforms of one another. On the Folio reading and the suggested emendation, see Patricia Parker, "Shakespeare and Rhetoric: 'Dilation' and 'Delation' in *Othello*," in *Shakespeare and the Question of Theory*, ed. Patricia Parker and Geoffrey Hartman (New York: Methuen, 1985), 54–74.

36. Compare McGinn, *Shakespeare's Philosophy*, 68: "This is an outright statement of the problem of other minds." Compare Cutrofello, "Is Othello Jealous?," 130.

37. On this moment, see Strier, *The Unrepentant Renaissance*, 14–16.

38. See Richard Strier and Richard H. McAdams, "Cold-Blooded and High-Minded Murder: The 'Case' of Othello," in *Fatal Fictions: Crime and Investigation in Law and Literature*, ed. Alison L. LaCroix, Richard H. McAdams, and Martha C. Nussbaum (Oxford: Oxford University Press, 2017), 111–38 (esp. 118).

39. While I do not believe, with Robert N. Watson, that the play is an anti-Catholic allegory (*"Othello* as Protestant Propaganda," in *Religion and Culture in Renaissance England*, ed. Claire McEachern and Debora Shuger [Cambridge: Cambridge University Press, 1997], 234–57), I do believe that it can be seen as embodying a critique of Catholic attitudes toward sexuality (see the discussion of Othello on Desdemona's hand cited in note 37 above).

40. As I have already suggested, in the *Meditations*, the clause after the claim about astonishment is a kind of joke: "And this astonishment *almost confirms me* in the opinion that I am asleep" (translation and emphasis mine). The Latin is equally careful (or arch): *fere . . . confirmet* [*Meditationes*, 20]).

41. If one believes, as Cavell came to do, that "philosophy is fulfilled in the form of psychoanalysis," the apparent shift in frameworks disappears. The argument for this, such as it is, appears in *Images in Our Souls: Cavell, Psychoanalysis, and Cinema*, ed. Joseph H. Smith and William Kerrigan (Baltimore: Johns Hopkins University Press, 1987), 11–43 (23).

42. This contradicts Cavell's earlier assertion that "there is reason to believe that the marriage has not been consummated," to which he added (even less plausibly) "anyway reason to believe that Othello does not know whether it has" (131). The "success" reading is much more powerful psychologically, as well as more interesting, than the failure one, and I think it is the reading that Cavell wants, so to speak, to go with, despite the contradiction of what he earlier said "there is reason to believe." Cavell tends, in general, to correct himself by addition rather than by revision.

43. For the possibility of historicizing this view more precisely than Cavell does, see note 39 above.

44. See Cavell, "Knowing and Acknowledging" (note 33 above). But the issue of sexuality, which emerges so powerfully in the *Othello* essay and is central to the introduction to *Disowning Knowledge* (which ends with a long discussion of Cleopatra's orgasms [31–37]), is not present in the early, more traditionally philosophical essay.

45. The essays cited are "On Some Verses of Virgil" and "Of Experience." *The Apology for Raymond Sebond* is no longer relevant.

46. See "Happy Hamlet," note 34.

47. Peter Marshall, *Beliefs and the Dead in Reformation England* (Oxford: Oxford University Press, 2002), 258.

48. Horatio's initial worry is that the apparition "In the same figure like the King that's dead" (1.1.44) will tempt Hamlet to suicide ("What if it tempt you to the flood, my lord . . . ?" [1.4.69]), which is certainly a demonic project. When Hamlet is convinced, on the basis of

Claudius's reaction to the performed play (or to Hamlet's commentary thereon) that the thing's "word" is reliable (regardless of its ontological status), Horatio simply affirms that he has seen the same reactions in Claudius that Hamlet has seen ("I did very well note him" [3.2.284]), affirming nothing further. *Hamlet* is cited from the edition by Harold Jenkins (London: Methuen, 1982), but I will indicate when a line or passage is unique to the Quarto or the Folio.

49. See Gomes, "Other Minds Skepticism," in Machuca and Reed, *Skepticism: From Antiquity to the Present*, 703–4.

50. McGinn's assertion of the necessity of "other minds" skepticism almost runs aground on his recognition that "language can seem like a solution to the problem" (*Shakespeare's Philosophy*, 63). But McGinn quickly moves to the much more comfortable topic (for a skeptic) of lying and deception. Cavell struggles with the problem of language and skepticism throughout *The Claim of Reason*, especially in pt. 1. In his essay on "Austin at Criticism," Cavell warns against adopting J. L. Austin's anti-skeptical position based on ordinary language and ordinary experience (*Must We Mean What We Say?* 110). For an argument that Wittgenstein's view of language is anti-skeptical, see Michael Williams, "Wittgenstein and Skepticism: Illusory Doubts," in Machuca and Reed, *Skepticism: From Antiquity to the Present*, 481–505. For the view that "successful communication proves the existence of a shared, and largely true, view of the world," see Donald Davidson, "The Method of Truth in Metaphysics," in *Inquiries into Truth and Interpretation* (Oxford: Clarendon Press, 1986), 201 and passim. See also the essays cited in note 54 below.

51. On "The Mousetrap" plan as a humanist fantasy, and on the problem of what Hamlet can legitimately conclude from the episode, see "Happy Hamlet."

52. On the crucial epistemological role for the reader or audience of Claudius's post-Mousetrap soliloquy, see Amir Khan, "My Kingdom for a Ghost: Counterfactual Thinking and Hamlet," *Shakespeare Quarterly* 66 (2015): 29–46, rpt. as ch. 2 of *Shakespeare in Hindsight: Counterfactual Thinking and Shakespearean Tragedy* (Edinburgh: Edinburgh University Press, 2016).

53. On the Reformation conception of repentance, see "*The Tempest* (1): Power," 151.

54. On the role of "testimony" with regard to knowledge of the inner lives of others, see J. L. Austin, "Other Minds," in *Philosophical Papers*, 3rd ed. (Oxford: Oxford University Press, 1973), 82, 112–15; Anil Gomes, "Testimony and Other Minds," *Erkenntnis* 80 (2015): 173–83.

55. Ramie Targoff suggests something of this sort in "The Performance of Prayer: Sincerity and Theatricality in Early Modern England," *Representations* 60 (1997): 49–69 (esp. 59).

56. See Austin, "Other Minds," 112; and Avramides, "Perception, Reliability, and Other Minds," 123. In a commentary on the book of Proverbs published in 1592, Peter Moffett notes that even when "a secret intent of the minde is cunningly hidden and closely concealed," it often happens that a person "indued with discretion, either by propounding of questions or by observing of gestures, soundeth and fisheth out the secret purpose of him who is so close." I owe this reference to Christopher Crosbie's paper, "Intention," for the Shakespeare Association seminar "Boundaries of Violence" (2021).

57. Compare Austin, "Other Minds," 110.

58. For Shakespeare's presentation of cases where a character's motives seem opaque to that character, see "Excuses, Bepissing, and Non-Being."

59. Glenn Clark, "Speaking Daggers: Shakespeare's Troubled Ministers," in *Shakespeare and Religious Change*, ed. Kenneth J. E. Graham and Philip D. Collington (New York: Palgrave Macmillan, 2009), 176–95. I see no reason to think that Hamlet is being satirized in this role here, as is proposed by R. Chris Hassel, "The Accent and Gait of Christians: Hamlet's Puritan Style," in *Shakespeare and the Culture of Christianity in Early Modern Europe*, ed. Dennis Taylor

and David N. Beauregard (New York: Fordham University Press, 2003), 285–310; and apparently accepted by Mareile Pfannebrecker, "Hamlet and Habit: The Renaissance Problem of Programmable Life," *Modern Philology* 118 (2020): 25–47 (37). That Hamlet's language is perhaps "over-the-top" here in its intensity, as Pfannebrecker suggests, does not mean that it is satirized.

60. Whatever form these "pictures" take (see Jenkins, ed., *Hamlet*, 517–19), they are physical objects.

61. Ellen MacKay, *Persecution, Plague, and Fire: Fugitive Histories of the Stage in Early Modern England* (Chicago: University of Chicago Press, 2011), denies this (66–69). Her point seems to be that the "grounds" for Gertrude's feelings of guilt are never made explicit (68). But it seems pretty clear that it is her present and past relationship with Claudius that is at issue.

62. As already suggested (see "Excuses, Bepissing, and Non-Being," note 7), I do not agree with Paul Cefalu that Hamlet "refuses to take seriously the possibility that virtuous habits might provide antidotes to vicious ones" ("Damnéd Custom . . . Habit's Devil: Hamlet's Part-Whole Fallacy and the Early Modern Philosophy of Mind," in *Revisionist Shakespeare: Transitional Ideologies in Texts and Contexts* [New York: Palgrave Macmillan, 2004], 158). I think that Pfannebecker is right that Hamlet's address to his mother "points to human plasticity outside and beyond childhood" ("*Hamlet* and Habit," 39).

63. Clark holds that Gertrude is not permanently changed ("Speaking Daggers," 183). I am not so sure. In the next scene, when Gertrude has to reveal the death of Polonius to Claudius, she tells Claudius that Hamlet was "Mad as the sea" at the time (4.1.7), thereby following Hamlet's instructions not to reveal that he is only "mad in craft" (3.4.190). See William Kerrigan, *Hamlet's Perfection* (Baltimore: Johns Hopkins University Press, 1994), 113–14.

64. *Shakespeare as a Way of Life*, 18. Further citations of this work appear parenthetically in the text.

65. "Forc'd cause" is the Folio reading; the Quarto has "for no cause."

66. On the complexities of Hamlet's apology to Laertes, see "Excuses, Bepissing, and Non-Being."

67. For the speech heading "All" in Q2 and F, see *The Three-Text "Hamlet,"* ed. Bernice W. Kliman and Paul Bertram, 2nd ed. (New York: AMS Press, 2003). I do not know why Ann Thompson and Neil Taylor, in their editions of both Q2 and F (London: Thomson Learning, 2006), substitute "Lords." They claim to be following the 1986 *Oxford Complete Shakespeare*, ed. Stanley Wells and Gary Taylor, in substituting "Lords" for "All," but that edition has "All the Courtiers." These emendations are not only textually unwarranted but also dramatically inferior to "All."

68. "Me and my cause a right" is the Q2 reading. The Folio has "me and my causes right" (see *The Three-Text "Hamlet"*). Given the lack of the convention of marking possessives, the Folio reading could also be "cause's right," though I have not seen any edition that adopts this.

69. James Shapiro, *A Year in the Life of William Shakespeare: 1599* (New York: HarperCollins, 2005), 299.

70. Lars Engle, "How Is Horatio Just? How Just Is Horatio?," *Shakespeare Quarterly* 62 (2011): 256–62 (quotation on 262). I share Engle's admiration for Horatio, which is much less guarded and tentative than Kuzner's. When I was asked (bizarrely) at a conference which Shakespeare character I identified with, I picked Horatio. Richard (then Judge) Posner rebuked me for aiming too low, but I maintained that this identification was aspirational. See the "Roundtable" in *Shakespeare and the Law: A Conversation Among Disciplines and Professions*, ed. Bradin Cormack, Martha Nussbaum, and Richard Strier (Chicago: University of Chicago Press, 2013), 318–20.

CHAPTER 11

1. These are not issues that are involved in *The Tempest* (or, for that matter, in *Henry VIII*, where religion is institutional and political, or in *The Two Noble Kinsmen*).

2. This is not certain, but seems to be the conclusion of John Pitcher's careful analysis of the dates of composition in the introduction to his Arden 3 edition of the play (London: Methuen, 2010), 84–90. I find Pitcher's analysis convincing.

3. I have listed only the editions published in Shakespeare's lifetime. For the place of *Pandosto* in Elizabethan and seventeenth-century print culture, see Lori Humphrey Newcomb, "'Social Things': The Production of Popular Culture in the Reception of Robert Greene's *Pandosto*," *ELH* 61 (1994): 753–81.

4. For ease of access, I will cite from the version of *Pandosto* in *Narrative and Dramatic Sources of Shakespeare*, ed. Geoffrey Bullough (London: Routledge & Kegan Paul, 1975), 8:156–99 (199). Further citations of this work appear parenthetically in the text.

5. On Shakespeare's interest in mixed genres, especially, tragicomedy, at this point in his career, see, inter alia, Pitcher's introduction, 7–13.

6. For Greene's comment on his work, see the dedication to "The Right Honorable George Clifford Earle of Cumberland," in *Pandosto. The Triumph of Time* (London, 1588), A2r ("trifles"), A2v ("this toy"). This prefatory matter is not included in Bullough.

7. "Smothering," as the *OED* and other instances in Shakespeare show, can be a conscious action of concealment, but the semantics and grammar here suggest something more like repression.

8. See *Othello*, 3.4.160–61: "It is a monster / Begot upon itself, born on itself."

9. See Stanley Cavell, "Recounting Gains, Showing Losses: Reading *The Winter's Tale*," in *Disowning Knowledge in Six Plays of Shakespeare* (Cambridge: Cambridge University Press, 1987), 198 (updated to *Seven Plays* [Cambridge: Cambridge University Press, 2003], same pagination); hereafter *DK*.

10. *DK*, 206. On acknowledgment, see Stanley Cavell, "Knowing and Acknowledging," in *Must We Mean What We Say? A Book of Essays* (New York: Scribner's, 1969), 238–66.

11. In technical (Wittgensteinian) terms, this means that criteria (for making assertions, especially about other minds) are not inherently disappointing, that it is not inherent to the human condition to find them so. Another way of putting it would be to hold that "that attunement with others in our criteria on which language depends" is not as fragile as Cavell thinks (*DK*, 206). See the position articulated by Donald Davidson quoted in "Shakespeare and Skepticism (2): Epistemology," note 50.

12. Janet Adelman, *Suffocating Mothers: Fantasies of Maternal Origin in Shakespeare's Plays, "Hamlet" to "The Tempest"* (New York: Routledge, 1992), 231.

13. Donald Davidson, "On the Very Idea of a Conceptual Framework," in *Inquiries into Truth and Interpretation* (Oxford: Clarendon Press, 1986), 198.

14. *Twelfth Night*, 3.4.352.

15. There is general agreement among critics that the geographic reversal was motivated by Shakespeare's desire to allude strongly in the play to Ovid's Proserpina-Dis-Ceres story in *Metamorphoses*, book 5, which is set in Sicily and which is "the winter's tale" (the story of how we got winter). See, inter alia, T. G. Bishop, *Shakespeare and the Theater of Wonder* (Cambridge: Cambridge University Press, 1996), 151ff. Perdita alludes directly to the story in her speech at the sheep-shearing festival about the flowers that she lacks (4.4.116–18). Cavell's claim (*DK*, 198) that we do not know what the tale is to which the play's title alludes is simply mistaken.

16. For the text of the play, I have used the edition by Stephen Orgel (Oxford: Oxford University Press, 1996), hereafter cited as "Orgel." Other editions will be cited as needed.

17. For this view of education in humanist theory (in Erasmus, Ascham, and Mulcaster), see "*The Tempest* (3): Humanism."

18. Derek Traversi has noted a possible ambiguity in "branch" here—as meaning either "flourish" or "separate"—and many critics (including Cavell, *DK*, 210) have endorsed this. But it seems to me that this ambiguity is certainly not intended by the dramatic speaker and probably not intended by Shakespeare, and that it is one that is, in any case, only available in retrospect (*An Approach to Shakespeare*, rev. ed. [Garden City, N.Y.: Doubleday, 1969], 2:298).

19. Charles Altieri is right that Leontes "is not blind to her [Hermione's] social abilities" ("Wonder in *The Winter's Tale*: A Cautionary Account of Epistemic Criticism," in *A Sense of the World: Essays on Fiction, Narrative, and Knowledge*, ed. John Gibson, Wolfgang Huemer, and Luca Pocci (New York: Routledge, 2007), 272.

20. For an appreciative reading of Hermione's role in the dialogue here, see Wilbur Sanders, *The Winter's Tale* (Brighton: The Harvester Press, 1987), 13–15ff.

21. As Peter Lindenbaum says, "there is every reason" to believe that Polixenes's feelings represent those of Leontes as well ("Time, Sexual Love, and the Uses of Pastoral," *MLQ* 33 [1972]: 11).

22. On the possible psychological implications of this phrase, see Coppélia Kahn, *Man's Estate: Masculine Identity in Shakespeare* (Berkeley: University of California Press, 1981), 215–16, and Adelman, *Suffocating Mothers*, 221–23. Gina Bloom usefully historicizes this nostalgia in "'Boy Eternal': Aging, Games, and Masculinity in *The Winter's Tale*," *ELR* 40 (2010): 329–56.

23. For the English *Articles of Religion* (1562), see B. A. Gerrish, ed., *The Faith of Christendom: A Sourcebook of Creeds and Confessions* (Cleveland: Meridian, 1963); quotation from 188. On Foucault's "Renaissance episteme," see, inter alia, Ian Maclean, "Foucault's Renaissance Episteme Reassessed: An Aristotelian Counterblast," *JHI* 59 (1998): 149–66.

24. *The Gallican Confession of Faith*, in Gerrish, *The Faith of Christendom*, 154.

25. For Augustine's picture of infantile psychology, see *Confessions*, 1.vi-vii. Saint Augustine, *Confessions*, trans. R. S. Pine-Coffin (Baltimore: Penguin, 1961), 24–28. Augustine's infant was not (like Freud's) sexualized but is full of desire to exercise power and of impotent and murderous rage at being unable to do so.

26. John Calvin, *Institutes of the Christian Religion*, ed. John T. McNeill, trans. Ford Lewis Battles (Philadelphia: Westminster Press, 1960), II.i.8.

27. There are many recent works on the place of Catholicism in Elizabethan England. Certainly the most important and influential of these is Eamon Duffy, *The Stripping of the Altars: Traditional Religion in England, 1400–1580* (New Haven, Conn.: Yale University Press, 1992). For the Calvinism of the Church of England Articles, see Gerrish's introduction to them, *The Faith of Christendom*, 164–85, esp. 173.

28. On Erasmus and Dante, see "*The Tempest* (3): Humanism," note 88.

29. On the "spirits" in the blood, see, inter alia, Robert Burton, *The Anatomy of Melancholy*, ed. Holbrook Jackson (New York: Random House, 1977), 148–49. For sperm as "'Blood, made White" by the body's heat, see Pitcher's note on 1.2.109. Pitcher cites Lawrence Babb, *The Elizabethan Malady* (East Lansing: Michigan State University Press, 1951), 129. Babb there cites Jacques Ferrand, *Erotomania* (Oxford, 1640), 261, and Thomas Cogan, *The Haven of Health* (London, 1589), 240, who explains how "some part of the profitable blood ... is woonderfullie conveighed and carried to the genitories, where by their proper nature that which before was plaine bloud is now transformed and changed into seede." When Polixenes later avers that if he has touched

Hermione "forbiddenly," his "best blood" should be turned to "an infected jelly," he is probably (given that the context is sexual) referring to his semen (1.2.412–13).

30. In speaking of "Edenic innocence destroyed by carnal knowledge," Orgel (25) wittily but misleadingly conflates the two differing accounts.

31. The quoted lines are the final two of Herbert's "H. Baptisme" (2). For Gnostic, or at least strongly dualist, tendencies in Herbert's poetry, see Richard Strier, "George Herbert and the World," *JMRS* 11 (Fall 1981): 211–36. On the Gnostic and Manichean "hostility to body and sex," see Hans Jonas, *The Gnostic Religion*, 2nd ed. (Boston: Beacon Press, 1963), 227 and passim. For the "Childhood is health" idea in seventeenth-century English poetry, see Leah Sinanoglou Marcus, *Childhood and Cultural Despair* (Pittsburgh: University of Pittsburgh Press, 1978); and Timothy Harrison, *Coming To: Consciousness and Natality in Early Modern England* (Chicago: University of Chicago Press, 2020), esp. chs. 3 and 4 (on Traherne).

32. Sanders states that the "austere Jansenist, James Smith, points out what a heterodox brand of Christianity this is" (12), but the reference given is mistaken (nothing of the sort appears on the pages cited), so it is impossible to know where or whether Smith made this (I think valid) point. My reading of "the imposition cleared" agrees with that of J. H. P. Pafford in his Arden 2 edition of *The Winter's Tale* (London: Methuen, 1963), 9 (hereafter "Pafford"), rather than that proposed by Lindenbaum in "Time, Sexual Love, and the Uses of Pastoral," 7–8. Lindenbaum himself recognizes that his reading "makes less theological sense" (8).

33. An exactly parallel moment occurs when one of the unnamed Lords in Leontes's court attempts to dissuade Leontes from sending Hermione to prison. The Lord will stake his life, he tells Leontes, on the fact that "the queen is spotless / I' th' eyes of heaven." But then he adds, "*I mean / In this* which you accuse her" (2.1.131–33, emphasis mine).

34. See Stephen Guy-Bray, *Homoerotic Space: The Poetics of Loss in Renaissance Literature* (Toronto: University of Toronto Press. 2002), 199–207. "Frisking" in the sun does not, apparently, count as erotic or sexual.

35. On "cross'd the eyes," see Adelman, *Suffocating Mothers*, 353 n. 50.

36. For Calvin's assertion of this view, see *Institutes*, IV.xii.26, 28. For Calvin on the weirdness of the Catholic Church at once insisting (falsely, in his view) that marriage is a sacrament, and calling it afterward "uncleanness, and pollution, and carnal filth," see IV.xix.35. For Luther, see the section on marriage in *The Pagan Servitude [Babylonian Captivity] of the Church*, in Martin Luther, *Selections*, ed. John Dillenberger (Garden City, N.Y.: Doubleday, 1961), esp. 332–34. For a full statement of the Protestant position that was influential in England, see Heinrich Bullinger, *The Christen State of Matrimony*, trans. Miles Coverdale (London, 1546); reprinted often. For scholarly overviews, see Charles H. George and Katherine George, *The Protestant Mind of the English Reformation, 1570–1640* (Princeton, N.J.: Princeton University Press, 1961), ch. 7; Roland M. Frye, "The Teachings of Classical Puritanism on Conjugal Love," *Studies in the Renaissance* 2 (1955): 148–59; and James Grantham Turner, *One Flesh: Paradisal Marriage and Sexual Relations in the Age of Milton* (Oxford: Clarendon Press, 1987).

37. Compare Cavell's observation that in the state of mind into which Leontes has gotten, Hermione's "faithfulness would be at least as bad as her faithlessness" (*DK*, 198). This, as Cavell points out, is parallel to his reading of Othello's psychology (for discussion, see "Shakespeare and Skepticism [2]: Epistemology").

38. *DK*, 203.

39. For Cartesian, see *DK*, 203. Orgel states that Leontes here treats truth as "independent of evidence" (21), but that is not accurate either. Here, Leontes does trust the evidence of his senses. What he rejects is the reliability of testimony. He trusts only himself.

40. On "breeching," Lawrence Stone writes that "it was a great moment for a [male] child." Stone explains that among the aristocracy, this took place at about six or seven and it was the moment when the male child was dressed in a distinctive way—in doublet (breeches) and hose—rather than in the long gown that both sexes wore (*The Family, Sex, and Marriage in England, 1500–1800* [New York: Harper and Row, 1977], 410).

41. In the fourth stanza of "The Garden," Marvell (or his "speaker") fantasizes that the classical deities who (notably in Ovid's *Metamorphoses*) pursued mortal women did so in order that the women could increase their erotic appeal by becoming plants ("Apollo hunted Daphne so / Only that she might into laurel grow"), and this speaker states that it would have doubled Adam's pleasure in Paradise if Adam could have been single there ("Two Paradises 'twere in one / To be in Paradise alone [lines 63–64]). On the fantasy of becoming a green plant as an escape from adult male sexuality, see Diane Purkiss, "Marvell, Boys, Girls, and Men: Should We Worry?" in *Gender and Early Modern Constructions of Childhood*, ed. Naomi J. Miller and Naomi Yavneh (New York: Ashgate, 2011), 181–92 (on breeching, see 188).

42. Cavell says that Leontes wants to "replace or remove" his son (*DK*, 199). But these are very different fantasies. Cavell opts for the latter; he sees Leontes as wanting to annihilate his son (and everything else). Wanting to replace him is a different matter, and seems to me closer to what Leontes actually fantasizes.

43. For *eudaimonia*, see the discussion of what constitutes it (translated as "happiness" or "flourishing") in book 1 of *The Nicomachean Ethics*. For commentary, see Thomas Nagel, "Aristotle on *Eudaimonia*," in *Essays on Aristotle's Ethics*, ed. Amélie Oksenberg Rorty (Berkeley: University of California Press, 1980), 7–14; John Cooper, *Reason and Human Good in Aristotle* (Indianapolis: Hackett, 1975), esp. sec. 2; Richard Kraut, *Aristotle: Political Philosophy* (Oxford: Oxford University Press, 2002), ch. 3. For a somewhat similar perspective on this play, see David Ruiter, "Shakespeare and Hospitality: Opening *The Winter's Tale*," *Mediterranean Studies* 16 (2007): 157–77. On *eudaimonia* in Shakespeare in general, see Richard Strier, "Happiness," in *Shakespeare and Emotion*, ed. Katharine A. Craik (Cambridge: Cambridge University Press, 2020), 275–87.

44. See "Shakespeare and Skepticism (2): Epistemology," 219.

45. See Richard Strier, "Freedom," in *Shakespeare and Virtue: A Handbook*, ed. Julia Reinhard Lupton and Donovan Sherman (forthcoming from Cambridge University Press, 2022).

46. Phebe Jensen connects this rejection of social "play" with anti-theatricalism and presents Leontes as adopting an "iconoclastic aesthetic" ("Singing Psalms to Horn-Pipes: Festivity, Iconoclasm, and Catholicism in *The Winter's Tale*," *SQ* 55 [2004]: 279–306 [282]). Jensen's position in *Religion and Revelry in Shakespeare's Festive World* (Cambridge: Cambridge University Press, 2008), ch. 5, is substantially the same. I find this connection unconvincing. I cannot see that the "playing" that Leontes here despises has anything to do with theater.

47. For this connection, see David Willbern, "Shakespeare's Nothing," in *Representing Shakespeare: New Psychoanalytic Essays*, ed. Murray M. Schwartz and Cóppelia Kahn (Baltimore: Johns Hopkins University Press, 1980), 244–63.

48. On Theseus's speech in *A Midsummer Night's Dream* (5.1.2–22), see "Shakespeare and Skepticism (1): Religion," note 38. In *Faith in Shakespeare* (Oxford: Oxford University Press, 2013), Richard C. McCoy makes the connection to Theseus's speech and reads that speech similarly (118).

49. On the complexity and obscurity of the term "affection" in Shakespeare, see the Appendix ("Say it is my humour") to the first chapter of this book.

50. See David Ward, "Affection, Intention, and Dreams in *The Winter's Tale*," *MHRA* 82 (1987): 545–554 (549).

51. Northrop Frye, "Recognition in *The Winter's Tale*," in *Fables of Identity: Studies in Poetic Mythology* (San Diego: Harcourt Brace, 1963), 115. For Christopher Pye, who alludes to Frye's comment, some version of creation ex nihilo is crucial to what Pye takes to be the play's engagement with political theology in the terms defined by Carl Schmitt ("Against Schmitt: Law, Aesthetics, and Absolutism in Shakespeare's *The Winter's Tale*," *South Atlantic Quarterly* 108 [2009]: 201).

52. For Cavell's view, see *DK*, 206 and 208 on "Leontes' wish for there to be nothing."

53. For the strength of the term, see Thomas Heywood's *The Four Prentices of London*, in which a whole family—four brothers, a sister, and a father—all fail to recognize each other because "strong opinion" blinded them. See the edition by William West in *The Routledge Anthology of Early Modern Drama*, ed. Jeremy Lopez (New York: Routledge, 2020), 4.5.130.

54. I would record that I have been anticipated in arguing this by Walter S. H. Lim in "Knowledge and Belief in *The Winter's Tale*," *SEL* 41 (2001): 317–34, but, as Lim graciously acknowledges in his headnote, his awareness of this motif in the play derives from my NEH seminar, "Renaissance and Reformation in Tudor-Stuart England." It turns out that Lim thinks that the play works to destabilize the distinction between knowledge and opinion, and to undermine the "privileged position" of faith (330–31)—views that I do not share. Lim purports to distance himself from Howard Felperin's deconstructive reading of the play, but ends up in a position more historicized but substantively indistinguishable from that in Felperin's "Tongue-Tied Our Queen? The Deconstruction of Presence in *The Winter's Tale*," in *Shakespeare and the Question of Theory*, ed. Patricia Parker and Geoffrey Hartman (New York: Methuen, 1985), 3–18. For a critique of Felperin's reading, see Richard Strier, *Resistant Structures: Particularity, Radicalism, and Renaissance Texts* (Berkeley: University of California Press, 1995), 43–45.

55. Ficino's translation (1484) was reprinted many times, and was available in England by the late sixteenth century. The 1578 edition and translation of Plato's works by Henri Estienne (Stephanus) and Jean de Serres was dedicated to Queen Elizabeth. But as Sears Jayne points out in *Plato in Renaissance England* (Dordrecht: Kluwer Academic Publishers, 1995), there is much less evidence of interest in Plato in England than elsewhere (France, for instance). On Shakespeare's extraordinary absorptive capacity, see T. S. Eliot's remark in "Tradition and the Individual Talent" that "Shakespeare acquired more essential history from Plutarch than most men could from the whole British Museum" (in *Selected Essays* [New York: Harcourt, Brace, 1950], 6).

56. Plato, *Meno* 98a; see *Plato's Meno*, trans. W. K. C. Guthrie, with essays edited by Malcolm Brown (Indianapolis: Bobbs-Merrill, 1971), 58. The word "opinion" is widespread in the Shakespearean corpus—according to the *Open Source Shakespeare Concordance*, it occurs in thirty-three of the plays—but it generally means either belief or reputation. The philosophically precise usage is unique to *The Winter's Tale*.

57. Frank Kermode, in the introduction to the Signet edition of *The Winter's Tale* (New York: New American Library, 1963), observes that Leontes is an intellectual (xxii–iii), "a powerful mind is disturbed by a passion it is unwilling to control" (xxix). Aaron Landau in "'No Settled Senses of the World can Match the Pleasure of that Madness': The Politics of Unreason in *The Winter's Tale*," *Cahiers Élisabéthains* 64 (2003): 29–42, uses Leontes's pride in his intellectual powers to cast him as a representative "rationalist." This requires Landau to downplay Leontes's madness—which the play insists upon. Moreover, to take "direct contact with transcendental truth" (34) as the normative Catholic ideal in the early modern period (or any other) is historically questionable.

58. Pitcher rightly calls it "solipsism" (38); Altieri, "Wonder," is right to insist on the "overriding resistance" of his court to Leontes's views and behavior (268).

59. Julia Reinhard Lupton, *Afterlives of the Saints: Hagiography, Typology, and Renaissance Literature* (Stanford, Calif.: Stanford University Press), 1996, sees this as resembling Protestant accounts of "inner idolatry" (188).

60. "Process" is a rich pun here, using its legal sense metaphorically (and, in the context, ironically) and its more general sense literally (see *OED*, s.v., 5a and 8a).

61. For the general inability of Elizabethan printers to produce identical copies, see D. M. McKenzie, "Printers of the Mind: Some Notes on Bibliographical Theories and Printing-House Practices," *Studies in Bibliography* 22 (1969): 1–75. For the observation that in the Renaissance "comparisons of mechanical and sexual reproduction, imprints, and children" are widespread, see Margreta de Grazia, "Imprints: Shakespeare, Gutenberg, and Descartes," in *Printing and Parenting in Early Modern England*, ed. Douglas A. Brooks (Basingstoke: Ashgate, 1988), 29–58 (34).

62. Lupton, *Afterlives*, speaks of "the redemptive transcription of key words and images" (209); James R. Siemon sees the continuity in terms but mistakenly assumes a continuity in meanings (*Shakespearean Iconoclasm* [Berkeley: University of California Press, 1985], 295).

63. Susannah Brietz Monta, "'It is requir'd you do awake your faith': Belief in Shakespeare's Theater," in *Religion and Drama in Early Modern England: The Performance of Religion on the Renaissance Stage*, ed. Jane Hwang Degenhart and Elizabeth Williamson (Burlington, Vt.: Ashgate, 2011), notes the transformation of the term "faith" in the play (131). "Folly" as benign is enacted in the play, but the term is not one of those that the play specifically redeems. The term does, however, come to be associated with harmless revelry ("our feasts / In every mess have folly" (4.4.10–11).

64. See Sanders, *The Winter's Tale*, 81, on "friend."

65. For the "blister," see note 31 above. For Augustine and the Pelagians, see, inter alia, Peter Brown, *Augustine of Hippo* (Berkeley: University of California Press, 1967), ch. 29.

66. Like most recent scholars, I do not believe that the final scene was added in revision (that is, after Simon Forman saw the play in May of 1611). That Forman does not mention the statue scene is the major reason for seeing it as a later addition (for Forman's account, see Orgel, 233; Snyder and Curren-Aquino, 262). For discussion (and rejection) of the revision theory, see Pafford's edition, xxiv-xxvi; Pitcher's edition, 90–93; and the edition by Susan Snyder and Deborah T. Curren-Aquino (Cambridge: Cambridge University Press, 2007), 63–66 (Curren-Aquino rejects the view but notes that Snyder accepted it).

67. On Delphos as Delos (and not a confusion between Delos and Delphi), see Pafford's note on the scene, in which he also points to a probable source for this passage in a mystical moment in the *Aeneid* (3:90–93).

68. On the positive use of "nothing" here in contrast to the way in which Leontes uses the term, see Peter Platt, *Reason Diminished: Shakespeare and the Marvelous* (Lincoln: University of Nebraska Press, 1997), 159.

69. Cavell sees this change from *Pandosto*—making the death of the son rather than the reading of the oracle the turning point—as central to the play. He argues that Leontes has to come to terms with his own repressed wish for this (*DK*, 195–96). Gina Bloom also sees this change as central; she argues (perhaps more plausibly) that Mamillius's death spoils Leontes's fantasy of escaping from age and death ("'Boy Eternal,'" 347). Altieri suggests that Cavell overstates the role of Mamillius in the play ("Wonder," 269).

70. I do not think that there is a reference to Ignatius Loyola's famous *Spiritual Exercises* here, but this vow definitely has a Catholic coloration in its insistence on repeated penitential behavior at the gravesite.

71. On the bear and tragicomedy, see Louise G. Clubb, "The Tragicomic Bear," *Comparative Literature Studies* 9 (1972): 17–30. See also Dennis Biggins, "'Exit pursued by a Beare': A Problem in *The Winter's Tale*," *Shakespeare Quarterly* 13 (1962): 3–13. In productions, the bear (an actor in some sort of "bear costume"—probably then as now) always elicits laughter. For discussion of the (unlikely) possibility that an actual bear was brought on stage in the original productions, see Orgel, 155–56.

72. Biggins's ethical criticism of Antigonus ("Exit Pursued," 11) is echoed in Alison Shell, *Shakespeare's Religion* (London: Methuen, 2010), 207–10, but could be mitigated, as was suggested to me by an actor who had played the part, by some (admittedly nontextual) stage business: Antigonus could die distracting the bear from the baby. For a critical essay that adopts this view, and provides a nuanced judgment on Antigonus, see Philip Goldfarb Styrt, "Resistance Theory, Antigonus, and the Bear in *The Winter's Tale*," *SEL* 57 (2017): 389–406.

73. G. Wilson Knight, *The Crown of Life: Essays in Interpretation of Shakespeare's Final Plays* (1947; New York: Barnes and Noble, 1966), 98.

74. Pye, "Against Schmitt," 205.

75. I agree with Orgel (38–39) that Bethell's suggestion that "the seacoast of Bohemia" was a well-known joke in the period is persuasive, and is another indication that the genre has shifted to romance (see S. L. Bethell, *The Winter's Tale: A Study* [London: Staples Press, 1947], 33–35).

76. See Pafford's note on sheep-shearing feasts (83). Lupton, *Afterlives*, observes that "the rustic contemporaneity infusing the scene's classical pastoralism already presses the evocation of paganism into a nostalgia for it" (206). For the contemporary status of such festivals, see Leah S. Marcus, *The Politics of Mirth: Jonson, Herrick, Milton, Marvell, and the Defense of Old Holiday Pastimes* (Chicago: University of Chicago Press, 1986).

77. Jensen's attempt to see Perdita as an anti-festive character because her manifestation of hospitality does not follow the raucous model of the shepherd's deceased wife (4.4.55–62) seems to me mistaken ("Singing Psalms," 296–97; *Religion and Revelry*, 217–18).

78. Florizel's disavowal of unauthorized sex (4.4.33–35) strikes me as less dubious than that of Ferdinand in *The Tempest* (see "*The Tempest* [3]: Humanism"). The comic-mythological context that Florizel invokes seems more playful than the tragic Virgilian one invoked by Ferdinand ("the murkiest den" seen as "the most opportune place" [*The Tempest*, 4.1.25–6]). For a contrary view, see Orgel, 45.

79. I have discussed this in "Finding Pygmalion in the Bible: Classical and Biblical Allusion in *The Winter's Tale*," in *The Bible on the Shakespearean Stage*, ed. Thomas Fulton and Kristen Poole (Cambridge: Cambridge University Press, 2018), 156–68.

80. For commentary on "like a corpse," see Adelman, *Suffocating Mothers*, 230. Perdita might even be implicitly redeeming the shopworn pun on "die" here.

81. This plays (lightly) on the supposed status of usury (taking interest) as *contra naturam* in making a lifeless substance "breed." See "Excuses, Bepissing, and Non-Being," note 32.

82. See David Kaula, "Autolycus' Trumpery," *SEL* 16 (1976): 287–303.

83. See the discussion of this moment in "Shakespeare and Skepticism (1): Religion."

84. Newcomb's article on the place of *Pandosto* in the literary and social culture of its day (see note 3 above) suggests that Shakespeare's choice of that text as the basis for a play may itself have signified cultural and status blending.

85. I have explored the contrasting Catholic and Protestant views of penitence in "Herbert and Tears," *ELH* 46 (1979): 221–47. Whether or not we accept that Leontes has "paid down / More penitence than done trespass" (5.1.3–4), his penitential "exercise" does seem to have been transformative. Curren-Aquino (41–47) argues strongly for this view.

86. Like Curren-Aquino (see pevious note), Carol Thomas Neely also sees a profoundly changed Leontes, emphasizing that he now honors Hermione's sexuality ("Women and Issue in *The Winter's Tale*," *Philological Quarterly* 57 [1978]: 190).

87. The companionate view of marriage was especially emphasized by Protestants; the procreative was central to the Catholic view (see note 36 above).

88. For a very positive reading of this scene (perhaps overly so), see Holger Schott Syme, *Theatre and Testimony in Shakespeare's England: A Culture of Mediation* (Cambridge: Cambridge University Press, 2012), ch. 5.

89. Monta ("'It is required,'" 133) rejects Paul Yachnin's argument for a distinction between aristocratic and peasant wonder in the play. The physical setting of 5.2 is distinctly aristocratic (Paulina has a "gallery" [5.3.10]), but the emotions described in it are not. For Yachnin's argument, see Anthony B. Dawson and Paul Yachnin, *The Culture of Playgoing in Shakespeare's England: A Collaborative Debate* (Cambridge: Cambridge University Press, 2001), 206.

90. On "perform'd," and for the relevant passage in Vasari, see Pafford's note on the passage and the discussion in Leonard Barkan, "'Living Sculptures': Ovid, Michelangelo, and *The Winter's Tale*," *ELH* 48 (1981): 655–58. But Romano was probably most widely known for supplying the images for one of the most famous works of pornography in the period, *I Modi* [*The Sexual Positions*] issued in book form with "sonnets" by Aretino. This may not be irrelevant, given the importance of a positive acceptance of sexuality in the play. On *I Modi*, see Bette Talvacchia, *Taking Positions: On the Erotic in Renaissance Culture* (Princeton, N.J.: Princeton University Press, 1999). Orgel refers to "the pornographic ideal" in discussing Shakespeare's reference to Giulio Romano, but does not relate this "ideal" to the play except to suggest that the "statue" should look like Romano's Ceres (*Imagining Shakespeare: A History of Texts and Visions* [Basingstoke: Palgrave Macmillan, 2003], 112–43).

91. The other case is the identity of the Abbess in *The Comedy of Errors* (see Bertrand Evans, *Shakespeare's Comedies* [Oxford: Clarendon Press, 1960], 9). *Errors*, it should be noted, has a romance frame.

92. I have borrowed "direct and directing" from Stanley Fish, *Self-Consuming Artifacts: The Experience of Seventeenth-Century Literature* (Berkeley: University of California Press, 1972), 211. The biblical reference is noted by Pafford (52).

93. For extended discussion of biblical materials in the play, see Strier, "Finding Pygmalion in the Bible" (see note 79).

94. The phrase occurs in only this verse in the Geneva Bible (2 Kings 4:23). Interestingly—though probably without relevance to *The Winter's Tale*—the phrase is more emphatically present in the Authorized Version (1611), where, after being introduced in verse 23, it is then reiterated four times in verse 26. I do not know whether Perdita's "This youth should say 'twere well" (4.4.102) is a foreshadowing of this moment in act 5.

95. The New Testament context of stones crying out—Jesus insisting, on his approach to Jerusalem, that, despite the objection of "some of the Pharises," his disciples were right in praising him loudly and "if these shulde hold their peace, the stones wolde crye" (Luke 24:37–40)—is not obviously relevant to the play. It might serve to suggest that what Leontes is imagining—the stone rebuking him—is appropriate. And since the humans are notably silent (5.3.21), it might be an occasion for the stone to "speak." It is not clear whether or not Jesus was recalling Habbakuk.

96. Lupton, *Afterlives*, sees the allusion to Habakkuk as introducing what she calls "the counter-rhythm" of iconoclasm into the play (215).

97. Lupton, *Afterlives*, 206, 216.

98. This is one of the rare uses of the term in Shakespeare. Aside from this moment, the word (as a noun) appears in exactly one other place—in *Pericles*, where the idea that it is bad luck to have a corpse on board a ship is denounced by Pericles (to the sailors) as "your superstition" (3.1.51). As an adverb, the word had already occurred in *The Winter's Tale* in a strongly Protestant usage when Antigonus decides "for once, yea superstitiously" to trust his dream-vision of Hermione (3.3.39–40). The adjectival form appears in *Julius Caesar* in a similar context (about trusting dreams and prodigies [2.1.195]); it is applied skeptically to "an old tale" in *Merry Wives* (4.4.26).

99. *Sermons or Homilies appointed to be read in Churches in the time of Queen Elizabeth* (London: The Prayer Book and Homily Society, 1825), 188–292.

100. *Sermons or Homilies*, 248.

101. Michael O'Connell, *The Idolatrous Eye: Iconoclasm and Theater in Early Modern England* (New York: Oxford University Press, 2000), 141. But O'Connell then goes on to argue that Shakespeare then supports "idolatry."

102. Harrington's epigram on "images" and the crucifix is *very* careful; he "allows" kneeling, but disallows adoration (see "To my dearest, a Rule for praying," in *The Epigrams of Sir John Harrington*, ed. Gerard Kilroy [Burlington, Vt.: Ashgate, 2009], 134).

103. See Lori Anne Ferrell, "Kneeling and the Body Politic," *Religion, Literature, and Politics in Post-Reformation England, 1540–1688*, ed. Donna Hamilton and Richard Strier (Cambridge: Cambridge University Press, 1996), 70–92.

104. *Shakespeare's Ovid, Being Arthur Golding's Translation of the "Metamorphoses,"* ed. W. H. D. Rouse (New York: Norton, 1966), 10.306.

105. Compare Peter Campbell's meditation on "oil paint's potential for unpleasantness," "At Tate Modern," *London Review of Books* [May 5, 2005]: 27.

106. On face-painting involving actual poison, and the cultural and theatrical resonances of that, see Tanya Pollard, "Beauty's Poisonous Properties," *Shakespeare Studies* 27 (1999): 187–210; developed further in Pollard, *Drugs and Theater in Early Modern England* (Oxford: Oxford University Press, 2005), chs. 3 and 4.

107. See Strier, "Finding Pygmalion in the Bible," esp. 163, 166.

108. See Robert Greene, *Friar Bacon and Friar Bungay* (Lincoln: University of Nebraska Press, 1963), scene 11, and also, of course, Marlowe's *Dr. Faustus*.

109. It is on this basis, I think, that the "faith" in question here can be connected to Christian faith. My position here is close to that which Northrop Frye articulates in *A Natural Perspective: The Development of Shakespearean Comedy and Romance* (New York: Columbia University Press, 1965), 122–23. McCoy's assertion that "we believe in [the] extraordinary outcome [of the play] because it never pretends to be an actual miracle" seems to me mistaken (*Faith in Shakespeare*, 143). Whatever else the scene does, it certainly at least "pretends to be an actual miracle." On the complexity of the response that the scene requires, see Bishop, *Shakespeare and the Theater of Wonder*, 162ff.

110. Working on *The Winter's Tale* has led me to recognize what might be called the aggressivity of opinions. I agree with James Kuzner that here, at a moment like this, something like "epistemological humility" is manifest, and I agree with him that the faith in question is not propositional belief, but I do not think it is as thoroughly devoid of content as Kuzner, following Agamben and Badiou, presents it as being, and I do not see it as a manifestation of skepticism. See James Kuzner, *Shakespeare as a Way of Life: Skeptical Practice and the Politics of Weakness* (New York: Fordham University Press, 2016), ch. 3 (esp. 101–2). For "opinion" being equated with something like aggression or dogmatism, see Nathaniel's praise of Holofernes for being (among other things) "learned without opinion" (*Love's Labor's Lost*, 5.1.5).

111. Sean Benson, *Shakespearean Resurrection: The Art of Almost Raising the Dead* (Pittsburgh: Duquesne University Press, 2009), sees the play as constantly referring to the Resurrection (Christ's), whereas the play refers only to biblical resurrections mediated by human agents, including Jesus. When Jesus is implicitly evoked, it is as an agent not an object of resurrection.

112. Golding continues: "In her body streyght a warmenesse seemd too spred" (10.306). In Ovid, the kiss has the same effect—*incumbensque toro dedit oscula: visa tepere est* (Ovid, *Metamorphoses*, trans. Frank Justus Miller, [LCL; Cambridge, Mass.: Harvard University Press, 1916], 10.281)—but here Golding's prolixity turns out to be a virtue. On "the discovery of warmth," see Sanders, 118.

113. Lupton, to the contrary, sees these lines as striving to move eating into the realm of art and ritual (*Afterlives*, 216). Huston Diehl's treatment of Paulina in relation to the biblical Saint Paul as understood in Protestant commentaries ("'Does not the stone rebuke me?': The Pauline Rebuke and Paulina's Lawful Magic in *The Winters' Tale*," in *Shakespeare and the Cultures of Performance*, ed. Paul Yachnin and Patricia Badir [Aldershot: Ashgate, 2008]: 69–82) does not actually deal with the matter of eating, though she mentions it (78). David Hillman describes this moment as part of the "rediscovery of the rightness and pleasure of eating" in the play (*Shakespeare's Entrails: Belief, Skepticism, and the Interior of the Body* [Basingstoke: Palgrave Macmillan, 2007], 168), though he then backs away from so purely affirmative a view (169–70). Cavell's claim (*DK*, 216) that this passage implies "that there is an unlawful as well as a lawful eating" seems to me exactly wrong. The passage takes "eating" as the model of lawful behavior.

114. Jennifer Waldron, *Reformations of the Body: Idolatry, Sacrifice, and Early Modern Theater* (New York: Palgrave Macmillan, 2013), 82. Compare "your holy looks" in the final speech of the play (5.3.148). On the Reformation sanctification (for the believer) of all the (lawful) ordinary activities and processes of life, see Strier, *The Unrepentant Renaissance: From Petrarch to Shakespeare to Milton* (Chicago: University of Chicago Press, 2011), 21, 38–39, 177–88ff., 228–29.

115. Huston Diehl, "Strike All that Look upon with Marvel: Theatrical and Theological Wonder in *The Winter's Tale*," in *Rematerializing Shakespeare: Authority and Representation on the Early Modern English Stage*, ed. Bryan Reynolds and William N. West (New York: Palgrave Macmillan, 2005), 19–34 (esp. 25–27). Platt is mistaken in asserting that "the reformers" were "seeking to push out" wonder (*Reason Diminished*, 20). They were seeking to redirect it, not to eliminate it.

116. On "empathetic wonder" in the final scene of *The Winter's Tale*, see Adam Max Cohen, *Wonder in Shakespeare* (New York: Palgrave Macmillan, 2012), 52. Cavell suggests that this scene asks that the audience of the play be "no longer spectators, but something else, more, say participants" (*DK*, 218).

117. Philip Fisher, *Wonder, the Rainbow, and the Aesthetics of Rare Experiences* (Cambridge, Mass.: Harvard University Press, 1998) sees religion as needing to put a "barrier across the path of wonder" (39), but this view is produced by Fisher's treating the Bible only through the issue of the rainbow.

118. I agree with Maurice Hunt about the "syncretism within Christianity" of the play ("Syncretistic Religion in Shakespeare's Late Romances," *South Central Review* 28 [2010]: 57–79), though Hunt does not specify exactly how this syncretism works. One might well ask, from a historical point of view, whether at the beginning of the seventeenth century it was possible to hold the sort of position that I have attributed to Shakespeare (in this play, at least). Erasmianism—though no longer in favor on either side of the great divide between the churches—may be the beginning of an answer (on Erasmus's posthumous standing, see Bruce Mansfield, *Phoenix of His Age: Interpretations of Erasmus c 1550–1750* [Toronto: University of Toronto Press, 1979]). Other

scholars have connected Shakespeare with Erasmus, though not in quite this detailed a way (see, notably, Jeffrey Knapp, *Shakespeare's Tribe: Church, Nation, and Theater in Renaissance England* [Chicago: University of Chicago Press, 2002]; and Robert B. Bennett, *Romance and Reformation: The Erasmian Spirit of Shakespeare's "Measure for Measure"* [Newark, Del.: University of Delaware Press, 2000]). But there is also a perhaps more surprising analogue. Some of the same collocation of positions can be found in Milton's poetry and prose: an exaltation of married sexuality; a vigorous iconoclasm; and a deep belief in "the faultles proprieties of nature" ("The Doctrine and Discipline of Divorce," in *Complete Prose Works of John Milton* [New Haven, Conn.: Yale University Press, 1959], 2:237). But neither Erasmus nor Milton shares Shakespeare's apparently benign view of credulity. My view of the religious content of the play approaches but does not fully accord with that of James Ellison, "*The Winter's Tale* and the Religious Politics of Europe," in *Shakespeare's Romances*, ed. Alison Thorne (Basingstoke: Palgrave Macmillan, 2003): 171–204. My view sees the religious content of the play as more eccentric than Ellison does, though equally irenic.

119. Compare the "Homily Against Peril of Idolatry": "Far better it were that the arts of painting, plastering, carving, graving, and founding had never been found nor used than one of them [i.e., the "weak and simple"] whose souls in the sight of God are so precious, should by occasion of image or picture perish and be lost" (263).

120. Leonard Barkan, "'Living Sculptures,'" 659.

121. Lupton, after arguing that the final scene enacts "the movement from the Church to its Reform" (*Afterlives*, 216), then backs away in her peroration and states that the "staging of iconoclasm is itself only apparent" (217). Even Diehl sees the play as finally achieving "a new, Protestant synthesis of art and nature" ("Strike All that Look upon," 28).

122. Pitcher, in the introduction to his edition, briefly defends Perdita's position over that of Polixenes (56); A. D. Nuttall defends the position at length in "*The Winter's Tale*: Ovid Transformed," in *Shakespeare's Ovid*, ed. A. B. Taylor (New York: Cambridge University Press, 2000), 135–39 (esp. 145–47). Maureen Quilligan also sees the play as praising life over art, biological over artistic reproduction ("Exit Pursued by a Bear: Staging Animal Bodies in *The Winter's Tale*," in *The Oxford Handbook of Shakespeare and Embodiment*, ed. Valerie Traub [Oxford: Oxford University Press, 2016], 506–25).

123. Barkan points out that "living sculptures" was Michelangelo's term "not for statues but for the real creations of nature" ("'Living Sculptures,'" 653). I am not so sure that in saying this Michelangelo meant to proclaim "the victory of sculpture" over nature as well as over painting. As for faith in Shakespeare-the-artist as the ultimate message of the play, the "Homily Against Peril of Idolatry" anticipates this, suggesting that if one were going to do any worshipping in relation to works of art, it would make more sense to worship the artists who made them rather than the works themselves (248). Needless to say, the homily is not recommending this.

INDEX

Adelman, Janet, 230, 281n86, 331n22, 332n35, 336n80
Agamben, Giorgio, 120, 286nn52–3, 338n110
agape, 208, 322n85
Akhimie, Patricia, 295n47, 297n85, 303n15, 325n13
Almond, Philip C., 318n27
Alpers, Paul, J., 68–9, 70, 71, 206, 270n20, 321n77, 322n83
Altieri, Charles, 253nn12, 14, 331n19, 334n58, 335n69
Alves, Abel Athouguia, 288n84
Ambler, Wayne, 297n76
Ambrose, Saint, 29
Anglo, Sidney, 316n5, 317n27
Apter, Emily, 251n1
Aquinas, St. Thomas, 45, 261n9, 313n88
Archer, Ian, 284n21
Arendt, Hannah, 120–21, 163, 286nn52–3
Aretino, Pietro, 337n90
Aristotle, on ethics, 15–9, 33, 35, 45, 169, 226, 254nn6–7, 313n88; on friendship (*philia*), 11, 92, 275n15; on happiness (*eudaimonia*), 160, 262n4, 303n19, 333n43; on the mean, 94, 276n25; on "natural" slaves, 146, 183, 297n76, 315n109; on persuasion, 310n39; on proper pride, 36–7, 259n57, 268n84; on tragedy, 125, 282n1; on usury, 27–8, 256n32, 257n37; *zoē* vs. *bios*, 120–121, 286n52
Ascham, Roger, 179, 182, 312n65, 331n17
Askew, Anne, 275n19 (quoted)
Auden, W. H., 29, 255nn18, 20
Augustine, Saint, 1, 37, 41, 233, 240, 252n5, 254n7, 259n64, 267n75, 331n25, 335n65
Austin, J. L.: on excuses, 4, 17, 254nn5, 11; impact on Cavell, 271n34; on instances, 69, 77; on other minds, 252n5, 253n14, 328nn50, 54, 56–7; prose style of, 273n54

Auyoung, Elaine, 252n4, 253n11
Avramides, Anita, 326n32, 328n56

Babb, Lawrence, 331n29
Bacon, Francis (Baconian), 140, 194, 196, 197, 299n101, 316n5, 318nn28, 34
Bailey, Amanda, 30, 108, 290n114
Bainton, Roland, 308n5
Baker, J. H., 257n36
Baldwin, T. W., 283n7, 307n1, 308n10
Barber, C. L., 79, 255n14, 256n31
Barkan, Leonard, 249, 337n90, 340nn120, 123
Barker, Roberta, 276n28
Baron, Hans, 309n18
Bashar, Nazife, 298n93
Bate, Jonathan, 171, 184, 267n76, 306n65, 308n10, 309n29, 312n73
Beardsley, Monroe, 252n3
Beckwith, Sarah, 68, 270n14, 300n113, 306n60
Beier, A. L., 284n21
Belhassen, S., 293n33
Bellinson, Nicholas, 266n58
Bembo, Pietro, 178
Ben-Amos, Ilana Krausman, 271n29
Bennett, Robert B., 340n118
Benson, Sean, 339n111
Berger, Jr., Harry: on *King Lear*, 75, 77, 80–4, 271n33, 272n41, 273n51, 284n17; and Lacan, 67, 81, 269n12; and Melanie Klein, 273n46; on *The Merchant of Venice*, 111, 142, 255n21, 281n89; as suspicious reader, 5, 6, 8, 66–7, 79, 269n11, 270nn15, 17, 272nn40, 43–4, 273n50; on *The Tempest*, 142, 292n8, 295n57, 306n62
Best, Stephen, 253n12
Bethell, S. L., 336n75
Bevington, David, 100, 277nn41, 49
Biggins, Dennis, 336nn71–2

Bilello, Thomas C., 281n87
Bishop, T. G., 330n15, 338n109
Blake, William (Blakean), 11, 194–5
Bloom, Gina, 331n22, 335n69
Bloom, Harold, 263n20, 268n82
Boni, Livio, 301n131
Booth, Stephen, 275n21
Bourdieu, Pierre, 155, 301n133
Bradley, A. C. (Bradleyan), 61, 64, 203, 264n33, 267n76, 268n82, 270n15
Braudel, Fernand, 289n95
Bray, Alan, 277n47
Breight, Curt, 151, 152, 297n85
Brook, Peter, 285n33, 286n47
Brooks, Harold F., 317n25
Brower, Reuben A., 251n1
Brown, John Russell, 257nn41, 44, 258n53, 261n8
Brown, Paul, 134, 151, 291n7, 297n87, 301n133
Brown, Peter, 335n65
Brownlow, F. W., 316n4, 317nn15, 17, 319n48
Brundage, James A., 298n92
Bruster, Douglas, 305n39, 307n74
Buccola, Regina, 318n31
Buchanan, George, 138, 198, 293n23
Budick, Sanford, 323n93
Bullinger, Heinrich, 264n35, 332n36
Burckhardt, Jacob, 310n31
Buridan, Jean, 261n9
Burnett, Mark Thornton, 291n1
Burnyeat, Miles, 324n8
Burrow, Colin, 98, 274n1, 275n11, 276n36, 307n1
Burton, Robert, 331n29
Bushnell, Rebecca W., 314nn96, 107
Butler, Judith 299n102

Caesar, Philip, 256n24
Callaghan, Dympna, 294n37, 304n29
Calvin, John (Calvinist, Calvinism), 80, 203, 226, 234, 300n117, 321n64, 331n26, 27, 332n36
Campbell, Peter, 338n105
Canny, Nicholas, 294n42
Cantor, Paul A., 266n54
Capell, Edward, 302n1
Carroll, William C., 126, 287n73, 288n84
Cartelli, Thomas, 291n6
Castiglione, Baldesar, 53, 138, 181
Catalin, Avramescu, 283n10
Catullus, 40, 260n75
Cavallar, Osvaldo, 281n88

Cavell, Stanley, on Descartes, 221–2; on *King Lear*: influence on criticism of, 270n14; on Cordelia's size, 272n38; on high-mindedness of, 273n51; on the symbolic meaning of blinding, 69–74, 76–7; on lack of acknowledgment: applied to Lear and Cordelia, 208–9; difference from Berger, 82–3, 270nn15, 17; Edgar's of Gloucester, 77–9, 177; Gloucester's of Edmund, 74–6; on *Othello*, 219, 221–3, 327nn42–3; on *The Winter's Tale*, 221, 238, 330n15, 331n18, 332n37, 333n42, 334n52, 335n69, 339nn113, 116; relation to philosophy, 5, 66–9, 85, 253n18, 269nn5–7, 270nn21, 23, 271nn27, 34, 273n54, 326n32, 327n44, 328n50, 330n11
Cefalu, Paul, 254n7, 261n7, 266n62, 269n4, 285n37, 289n94, 329n62
Césaire, Aimé, 133, 134, 139, 140, 150, 152, 153, 154, 291nn5–6, 292n9, 293n33, 294n35, 295n44, 299n101, 301n127
Chakravarty, Urvathi, 300n125
Chamberlain, Richard, 262n4
Chassler, Philip, 301n131
Chaucer, Geoffrey, 243, 282n1
Christian IV (of Denmark), 50
Cicero, 283n7
Cinthio, Giraldi, 42, 260n79, 278n58
Clark, Glenn, 225, 329n63
Clark, Stuart, 317nn19, 27
Claudius (Roman emperor), 181
Clubb, Louise G., 336n71
Cockayne, Land of, 99, 277n39
Cogan, Thomas, 331n29
Cohen, Adam Max, 339n116
Cohen, Derek, 142, 163, 296n67, 297n81
Cohen, Ted, 275n20
Cohen, Walter, 125
Coleridge, Samuel T., 1, 258n56, 325n25
Colie, Rosalie, 285n41, 288n85
Coogan, Michael D., 259n61
Cooper, John M., 275n15, 333n43
Cormack, Bradin, 284n17, 298n97
Correa, Emilia Jocelyn-Holt, 286n50
Cox, John D., 272n40, 323n88
Crane, Mary Thomas, 312n75
Crashaw, William, 140
Cressy, David, 265n43
Crosbie, Christopher, 18, 254n10, 280n72, 328n56
Culler, Jonathan, 251n1
Curren-Aquino, Deborah T., 335n66, 336n85

INDEX 343

Curtis, Mark H., 313n95
Cutrofello, Andrew, 218, 326n27, 327n36

Dambrogio, Jana, 263n25
Dante Alighieri, 93, 234, 313n88
Dasenbrock, Reed Way, 268n4
Dauber, Kenneth, 253n13, 273n54
Davenant, William, 314n107
Davidson, Donald, 1, 230, 252n5, 269n4, 328n50, 330nn11, 13
Davies, S. F., 316n5
Davies, Sir John, 140
Davis, J. C., 303n13
Davis, Nick, 267n69
Dayan, Joan, 291n5
Dear, Peter, 318n29
DeCoursey, Matthew, 315n109
de Grazia, Margreta, 56, 121, 130–31, 265n49, 290n109, 335n61
Dekker, Thomas, 288n84
de Man, Paul, 251n2
Derrida, Jacques, 324n5
Desan, Philippe, 305n55
Descartes, René (Cartesian), 227; and *The Comedy of Errors*, 10, 212, 213–4, 216; *Discourse on the Method*, 211, 214; and *Hamlet*, 225; *Meditations*, 210–12, 324n5, 325n20; and *Othello*, 219, 223; and *The Winter's Tale*, 236
Diehl, Huston, 248, 339nn113, 115, 340n121
Dillenberger, John, 321n64
Donne, John, 267n69, 271n31, 299n103, 301n128
Doty, Jeffrey S., 146, 300n124
Dowd, Michelle M., 305n36
Dowey, Edward A., 321n64
Dowling, Bill, 252n3
Drakakis, John, 256n24, 257n41, 258nn53–4, 261n8
Dryden, John, 261n9
Dryden, John (the poet), 314n107
Duffy, Eamon, 331n27
Duni, Matteo, 319n43
Dunn, Leslie C., 264n27

Eagleton, Terry, 258n48, 289n90
Ehrman, Bart D., 322n80
Eliot, T. S., 38, 259n70, 334n55
Elizabeth Stuart, 155, 302n137
Elizabeth Tudor (Elizabeth I), 174, 179, 268n84, 334n55
Ellison, James, 340n118

Elton, William, 202, 204, 206, 315n3, 316n4, 318n34, 321n63, 322n81
Elyot, Sir Thomas, 181, 299n99, 313n80
Empiricus, Sextus, 214
Empson, William, 1, 253nn11, 12, 255n15, 259n58, 263n22, 273n51, 275n21, 290n113
Engle, Lars, 166, 227, 255n15, 269n4, 281n84, 285n31, 306n56, 307n70, 329n70
Enterline, Lynn, 307n1
Erasmus, Desiderius (Erasmian), 190, 339n118; democratic view of education, 182, 314nn96, 98; on education and delight, 178–9, 312n63; on exorcism, 199, 201; on flogging, 179–180, 184, 185; and *Henry IV*, 94, 276n34; and Montaigne, 176, 312n72; and northern humanism, 171–2, 173, 308nn5, 10; on original sin, 181–3, 185, 234, 313n88; on the proper temperament of a ruler, 173; and Reginald Scot, 190, 316nn5, 8; and *The Tempest*, 9, 171–85
Erickson, Peter, 272n39
Erne, Lukas, 252n6, 288n80
Estes, Leland, 316n5
eudaimonia, 160, 237, 303n19, 333n43
Euler, Carrie, 261n5
Evans, Bertrand, 337n91
Evans, Meredith, 274n1
Evans, Michael, 270n24
Everett, Barbara, 267n72, 268n82
Evett, David, 291n1, 292n17, 304n32

Falls, Robert, 107
Famous Victories of Henry V, 274nn2, 4
Fanon, Frantz, 139, 293n33, 294n34, 298n89, 301n131
Febvre, Lucien, 315n3, 316n4, 318n34
Felperin, Howard, 334n54
Felski, Rita, 253n15, 269n10
Fernie, Ewan, 272n36, 286n49
Ferrand, Jacques, 331n29
Ferrell, Lori Anne, 338n103
Ficino, Marsilio, 238, 309n18
Finkelman, Paul, 280n76
Fischer, Michael, 269n8
Fish, Stanley, 269n4, 337n92
Fisher, Philip, 339n117
Fitter, Chris, 282n3, 288nn77, 89, 289nn92, 96
Fitz, L. T., 295n46
Fitzmaurice, Andrew, 264n37
Flahiff, F. T., 131
Fleischacker, Samuel, 129, 289nn93, 98

Fleming, James Dougal, 298n91
Florio, John, 157, 168
Foakes, R. A., 316n9, 317n22, 322n81
Fodor, Jerry, 326n34
Forman, Simon, 335n66
Forster, E. M., 93
Foucault, Michel (Foucauldian), 150, 299n102, 324n5, 331n23
Fox-Genovese, Elizabeth, 293n33, 301n131
Frame, Donald M., 307nn68, 71
Frankfurt, Harry G., 324n5, 325nn19–20
Freedgood, Elaine, 251n1
Freud, Sigmund (Freudian), 19, 35, 67, 145, 222, 233, 296n70, 331n25
Fried, Charles, 109–10, 280nn79, 83, 281n87
friend, friends (friendship), 7, 22; through aristocratic status, 58–65, 276n24; childhood friends (in *Hamlet*), 50–53, 262n13, 263n16; courtly, 232, 335n64; as danger to marriage, 218, 229–30; false promise of, 96, 97; indulgence of, 94, 97, 104, 276n34; legal treatment of, 92–3, 98, 323n92; material version of, 122–3; pre-sexual, 233–5; special depth of, 224; standing surety for, 24, 26, 255n20; and taking interest on loans, 28–30
Frye, Northrop, 197, 238, 338n109
Frye, Roland Mushat, 57–8, 61–2, 265n44, 332n36
Fuchs, Barbara, 294n37
Fumerton, Patricia, 288n84

Galenic physiology (humours; "spirits" in the blood), 4–5, 43, 152, 234, 296n72, 331n29
Gallop, Jane, 251n1
Gardner, Helen, 301n128
Garin, Eugenio, 309n18
Genovese, Eugene D., 293n33, 301n131
George, Charles H., 332n36
George, Katherine, 332n36
Gerard, John, 321n69
Gerrish, Brian, 323n91, 331n27
Gifford, George, 316n6
Gillies, John, 123, 158, 159, 287n74, 303nn14, 20–21
Giovanni Fiorentino, Ser (*Il Pecorino*), 280n81, 281n91
Gnostic heresy, 234, 235, 240, 332n31
Goldberg, Jonathan, 134, 181–3, 277n47, 291n7, 294n34, 298n88, 312n74
Golding, Arthur, 246, 339n112
Gomes, Anil, 326nn31, 34, 328nn49, 54

Gorman, David, 268n3
Gouge, William, 174
Gowland, Angus, 260n3
Gowring, Laura, 277n47
Grady, Hugh, 277n38
Graham, Kenneth, 283n15, 289n93, 304n33
Granville, George (*The Jew of Venice*), 258n52
Gray, Hanna H., 309n26
Green, Felicity, 305n48
Greenblatt, Stephen: on *The Comedy of Errors*, 190; on *Hamlet*, 55, 264n36, 320n54; on *King Lear*, 125, 199, 200, 204–5, 207; on *The Merchant of Venice* (Shylock), 280n83; on Montaigne and Shakespeare, 302n3; on *Othello* (Iago), 271n27; on *The Tempest*, 151, 156–7; on *Twelfth Night*, 190
Greene, Robert, *Pandosto*, 228–9, 231, 232–3, 239, 241, 330nn3, 6, 336n84; *Friar Bacon and Friar Bungay*, 338n108
Greenstadt, Amy, 298n93
Greg, W. W., 272n42
Gross, Kenneth, 47, 84, 258nn54–5, 269n11, 272n40, 273n50, 281n88
Guillory, John, 251n1
Gurr, Andrew, 295n60
Guy-Bray, Stephen, 332n34

Hadfield, Andrew, 265n37
Hall, Kim F., 298n88
Hallett, Judith, 174
Halley, Janet E., 277n47
Halpern, Richard, 126, 182, 289n99, 294n39, 313n93
Hals, Franz, 62
Hamilton, Donna, 302n137
Hamlin, Will, 302n6
Hankins, James, 172
Hanson, Elizabeth, 181, 262nn13–4, 313nn93, 96
Harman, Thomas, 288n84
Harrington, Sir John, 246, 338n102
Harrison, Timothy, 288n87, 324n4, 325n20, 332n31
Harsnett, Samuel, 189, 194, 198–9, 201, 202, 204, 205, 207, 317n17, 319n48, 320nn53, 56
Hartog, François, 283n9
Harvey, Elizabeth D., 296n72
Hassel, R. Chris, 328n59
Hegel, G. W. F, 142 (mentioned)
Heilman, Robert B., 68, 69, 76, 84, 270n21
Held, Joshua R., 263n16, 300n121
Helps, Sir Arthur, 298n94

Herbert, George, on condescension, 273n48; against "flesh," 234, 332n31; on grace, 300n123; against idolatry, 249; against invoking saints, 317n16; and *King Lear* ("Love" [3]), 208–9, 322nn84, 86, 323nn87–8; on love between unequals, 297n78; on murmuring, 296n64; providing a model for reading, 11; against standing surety, 255n20; on the theology of penance, 300n116
Herodotus, 113
Herrick, Robert, 160
Heywood, Thomas (*A Woman Killed with Kindness*), 218, 325n26, 326n27, 334n53 (*The Four Prentices of London*)
Higginson, Francis, 140
Hillman, David, 339n113
Hobbes, Thomas (Hobbesian), 90
Höfele, Andreas, 122, 283nn11–2
Holbrook, Peter, 289n90, 290n114, 307n2
Holinshed, Raphael (*Chronicles*), 294n37
Homilies, the Elizabethan Book of, 246, 338nn99–100, 340nn119, 123
Honigmann, E. A. J., 37, 254n12, 260nn74, 78, 325n26, 327n35
honor (honorable / dishonorable), 22, 54, 57, 60, 65, 95, 148, 179, 268n85, 304n29
Hsia, R. Po-chi, 257n34
Hubler, Edward, 275n21
Hull, Suzanne W., 310n33
Hulme, Peter, 151, 292n9, 293n31, 294n39
Hume, David (of Godscroft), 278n52
Humphreys, A. R., 275n12, 276nn27, 32, 35
Hunt, Arnold, 252n9
Hunt, John S., 306n60
Hunt, Maurice, 339n118
Hunter, G. K., 277n37
Hutcheon, Elizabeth, 310n37
Hutson, Lorna, 90, 274n1

Ignatieff, Michael, 124, 131, 286n50
Ingram, Martin, 277n47
Intention, authorial, 1–2, 198, 251n2, 252n3, 253nn11–2, 254n10, 292n8; as abstract term or concept, 45, 59–60, 81, 84, 102, 106, 269n9, 278n55, 280n72, 298n93, 326n27, 328nn50, 56, 333n50
Intentions, of characters, 18, 26, 35, 73, 269n11
Interpretation (as a "reading"), 1–4, 24, 27, 30, 36, 94, 102, 109, 131, 134, 152, 157, 196, 200, 204, 220–22, 230, 238, 252n5, 259n61, 270n21, 279n70, 323n87; misinterpretation, 10

Jacobs, Jonathan, 254n6
James, Heather, 307n2
James, Henry, 131
James, King, 154, 155, 173, 193, 287n66, 319nn43, 45
James, Mervyn, 265n43, 268n85
James, Susan, 261n9
Jardine, Lisa, 309n30
Jayne, Sears, 334n55
Jeffery, Benjamin, 299n98, 300n119, 310n38
Jenkins, Harold, on *Hamlet*, 254n4, 262nn5, 12, 16, 263nn17–8, 25, 264nn31, 33–4, 265n40–41, 44, 49, 266nn50, 59, 267n77, 329n60; on *Henry IV*, 277n37
Jensen, Phebe, 333n46, 336n77
Johnson, Mark Albert, 301n125
Johnson, Samuel, 4, 84, 288n88
Jonas, Hans, 332n31
Jones, Emrys, 308nn2, 10
Jones, Norman L., 256n26, 277n44
Jones, Whitney R. D., 274n8
Jonson, Ben (Jonsonian), 40, 141, 258n53
Jordan, Constance, 102
Jorgenson, Paul A., 276n30
Jost, Walter, 253n13, 273n54
Junker, William, 313n88
Jurdjevic, Mark, 309n18
Justinian (*The Digest*), 278n54

Kahn, Coppélia, 331n22
Kaplan, M. Lindsay, 256n22
Kastan, David Scott, 155, 173, 255n13, 275n18, 302n137, 324n1
Katz, David, 258n47
Kaula, David, 243
Kavanaugh, James H., 130
Kearney, James, 303n14, 304n26, 305n41
Kermode, Frank, 145, 159, 293nn24–6, 294n37, 296nn65, 71, 297n88, 304n27, 311nn48, 54, 312n73, 314nn102, 107, 315n108, 334n57
Kerrigan, John, 276n30, 295n55
Kerrigan, William, 329n63
Khan, Amir, 267n79, 328n52
Kim, Lois, 310n45
King, Martin Luther, 301n127
King Leir, 321n71
Kingsley-Smith, Jane, 284n23, 293n30, 295n44
Kinlaw, C. J., 321n64
Kirsch, Arthur, 169, 307n70
Kirshner, Julius, 281n88

Kiséry, András, 64, 262nn10–11
Kittredge, G. L., 284n26, 314n107
Klein, Melanie (Kleinian), 273n46
Knapp, Jeffrey, 304n25, 340n118
Knapp, Steven, 252n3
Knight, G. Wilson, 103, 106, 241, 320n58
Knights, L. C., 313n95
Knowles, Richard, 284n26, 288nn84, 88, 290n113
Kolb, Laura, 255n16, 256n23, 265n41
Korsgaard, Christine, 92
Kott, Jan, 320n58
Kozintsev, Grigori, 284n26
Kramnick, Jonathan, 251n1, 252n11
Kraut, Richard, 333n43
Kronenfeld, Judy, 129, 131, 289n92, 290n107
Kuhn, Thomas, 133
Kunat, John, 315n113
Kunin, Aaron, 297nn78–9
Kuzner, James, 226, 305n42, 307n73, 324n1, 329n70, 338n110

Lacan, Jacques (Lacanian), 67, 81, 269n12
Lake, Peter, 279n63
Lamming, George, 134, 142, 143, 146, 153, 177, 185, 292n9, 295n57, 300n125
Landau, Aaron, 334n57
Lane, Ralph, 147
Lascaratos, John, 270n24
Las Casas, Bartolomé de, 298n95
Lattimore, Richmond, 322n80
Leininger, Lori Jorrell, 134, 153, 291n7, 310n45, 315n118
Leinwand, Theodore B., 255nn14, 16
Lenhof, Kent R., 273n51, 283n6, 322n83
Leo, Russ, 261n9
Leonard, John, 267n77
Leong, Elaine, 318n29
Lerer, Seth, 262n13, 267n75
Lestringant, Frank, 283n10
Levack, Brian, 319n43
Lever, J. W., 277n48
Levin, Harry, 293n28
Lewalski, Barbara K., 280n82
Lewis, Rhodri, 262n6, 264n30
Lim, Walter S. H., 334n54
Lindenbaum, Peter, 331n21, 332n32
Lindley, David, 311nn52, 54, 312n73, 314n107
Lindsay, Tom, 301n130, 309n28, 311n47
Lipton, Peter, 253n11
Livingston, Paisley, 268n3

Lobis, Seth, 285n42
Loewenstein, David, 321n63
Lombardo, Nicholas, 261n9
Loomba, Ania, 291n6, 298nn88–9
Love, Heather, 253n12
Lovejoy, A. O., 38, 259n66
Loyola, Ignatius, 335n70
Lucian, 196, 318n34
Luke, Nicholas, 270n21, 271n35, 272n36, 273n51
Lupić, Ivan, 292n21
Lupton, Julia, 49, 50, 64, 245, 264n29, 281n88, 301nn125, 129, 315n116, 335nn59, 62, 336n76, 337nn96–7, 339n113, 340n121
Luther, Martin, 44, 80, 152, 203, 209, 255n20, 261n5, 323nn90–92, 324n1, 332n36
Lycurgus, 181

MacDonald, Michael, 190, 265n44, 266n56
Macfarlane, Alan, 75
MacFaul, Tom, 298n92
Machiavelli, Niccolò (Machiavellian), 36, 80, 134, 171–2
MacKay, Ellen, 262n7, 267n79, 329n61
Maclean, Ian, 331n23
Mager, Donald N., 277n47
Magnussen, Lynn, 269n4
Mallette, Richard, 260n75
Mallin, Eric S., 323n93
Mannoni, Dominique-Octave, 134, 138–41, 145, 146–7, 148, 154, 176, 185, 293nn32–3, 294n34, 295nn44, 51–2, 298nn89, 91, 301n131, 315n116
Mansfield, Bruce, 316n7, 339n118
Marcus, Leah Sinanoglou, 288n81, 304n29, 332n31, 336n76
Marcus, Sharon, 253n12
Marino, James J., 264n28
Marion, Jean-Luc, 324n4
Marketos, S., 270n24
Marks, Herbert, 259n61
Marlowe, Christopher, 24, 31, 139, 150, 258n46, 293n29, 338n108
Marshall, Peter, 223, 317n17, 319n41
Marvell, Andrew, 236, 333n41
Matheson, Mark, 264n34
Maus, Katherine, 286n56, 290nn109, 115
McAdam, Ian, 315n113
McAdams, Richard H., 279n64, 282n92, 327n38
McAlindon, Tom, 290n114

INDEX

McCoy, Richard C., 268n2, 323n94, 333n48, 338n109
McElroy, Bernard, 64
McGinn, Colin, 268n3, 326n28, 327n36, 328n50
McGinn, Marie, 272n37
McKenzie, D. M., 335n61
Micha, Alexandre, 307n71
Michaels, Walter Benn, 252n3
Michelangelo, 340n123
Milton, John, 37, 38 (quoted), 41, 117, 165, 259nn62–3, 65, 273n48, 296n64, 297n80, 305n45, 340n118
Moffett, Peter, 328n56
Moi, Toril, 253n14
Moncrief, Kathryn M., 310n35
Monta, Susannah Breitz, 335n63, 337n89
Montaigne, Michel de, 8, 156–7, 164–6, 168–70, 176, 214, 215, 223, 285n31, 286n59, 302nn3–9, 305n55, 306n57, 307nn70, 72, 308n10, 312n72, 325n11
More, Thomas, 174, 178; *Utopia*, 129, 156, 165, 171, 182, 274n8, 275n19, 289nn97–9, 303n13, 312n72
Morgan, Philp D., 295n50
Most, Glenn, 282n2
Mowat, Barbara, 305n41
Muir, Kenneth, 322n81
Mulcaster, Richard, 173, 182–3, 310n35, 313nn95–6, 314nn100, 103, 105, 331n17
Muldrew, Craig, 255nn16, 19, 258n49
Murphy, John L, 321n70

Nagel, Thomas, 279n65, 333n43
Napier, Richard, 190–91, 192
Nardizzi, Vin, 160, 295n45, 304n31
Neely, Carol Thomas, 264n27, 337n86
Neill, Michael, 50
Nelson, Benjamin, 29, 255n20
Neoplatonic (Neoplatonists), 38–9, 41, 172, 173
Nero, 181, 183
Netzloff, Mark, 255n18
Newcomb, Lori Humphrey, 330n3, 336n84
Nicgorski, Walter, 313n88
Nichols, Mary P., 297n76
Nietzsche, Friedrich, 11, 251n1
Nixon, Rob, 291n4
Noble, Richmond, 257n39, 317n22
Noonan, John T., 257n32
Norbrook, David, 178, 291n8
Norris, Christopher, 268n3
Nussbaum, Martha C., 271n27, 286n59, 297n76

Nuttall, A. D., 340n122
Nygren, Anders, 322n85
Nyquist, Mary, 296n68

O'Connell, Michael, 246, 338n101
O'Connor, Brian, 306n57
O'Connor, Marie Theresa, 278n50, 287n66, 290n111
Oedipus Tyrannos, 112
Ogilvie, George, 141
Olsen, Thomas G., 116
Orgel, Stephen, on *The Tempest*, 138, 144, 151, 152, 162, 293n24, 295n60, 296n66, 297n88, 298n97, 299n108, 300nn118, 125, 308n15, 311n54, 312n73; on *The Winter's Tale*, 332n30, 39, 336n71, 78, 337n90
Ovid (Ovidian), 171, 244–5, 246, 247, 289n93, 305n41, 330n15, 333n41, 339n112

Pafford, J. H. P., 332n32, 335nn66–7, 336n75, 337nn90, 92
Pagden, Anthony, 141, 295n53
Paine, Henry, 150
Palfrey, Simon, 115, 124, 290n110
Papio, Michael, 308n16
Parker, Patricia, 308n4, 327n35
Parr, Katherine, 174
Paster, Gail Kern, 43–7, 258nn53, 55, 261n10
Patterson, Annabel, 299n104
Paul, Henry N., 198, 319n45
Pears, David, 276n25
Pease, Donald, 294n35
Pelagian heresy, 234, 240, 335n65
Peltonen, Marku, 274n8
Penitence / Impenitence, 105, 151, 226, 243, 300n113, 336n85
Petit, Philip, 295n54
Pfannebrecker, Mareile, 329nn59, 62
Phillips, Edward, 314n102
Philoctetes, 112
Piccolomini, Aeneas Silvius, 179, 181
Pico della Mirandola, 172–3, 308n16
Pitcher, John, 330nn2, 5, 331n29, 334n58, 335n66, 340n122
Plato (Platonic), 38, 76, 136, 177, 179, 197, 238–9, 240, 259nn61, 69, 311n54, 312n65, 318n38, 334n55
Platt, Peter, 335n68, 339n115
Plautus (Plautine), 171, 201, 320n57
Plotinus (Plotinian), 38, 259nn66–7
Plutarch, 63, 179, 267n77, 322n81, 334n55

Pocock, J. G. A., 290n109
Pollard, Tanya, 338n106
Pollnitz, Aysha, 268n85
Pope, Alexander, 284n27
Popkin, Richard H., 316n3, 317n20, 320n54
Posner, Richard, 43, 45, 46, 47, 279n71, 280n83, 281n91, 329n70
Pound, Ezra, 27, 257n32
Pound, John, 284n21
Prendiville, John G., 254n7
Prosser, Eleanor, 264n35, 306n58, 307n66
Purkiss, Diane, 333n41
Putnam, Hilary, 269n6
Pye, Christopher, 241, 305n40, 334n51

Questier, Michael C., 321n69
Quilligan, Maureen, 340n122
Quinn, David B., 294n38
Quint, David, 157, 302nn5, 8, 307n72
Quintilian, 179–80

race, 148, 183, 184, 260n73, 297n88, 299n100, 304n29
Ravid, Benjamin, 280n80, 281n88
Reading, Shakespeare's, 2, 228–9, 238, 244, 294n37; allegorical, 196; as a critical genre, 2, 10, 252nn4, 7, 253n11; as democratizing, 182; as a kingly activity, 173
Readings, "close," 1, 4, 68, 251nn1–2; cynical, 79–84, 272n40; humouralist, 43–7; moralizing, 73–9, 273n51; "ordinary," 3, 5, 50 (face value), 68, 84–5, 253nn13–4; "promiscuously responsive," 3–4; "surface" vs. "deep," 3–6, 253n12; "suspicious," 4, 253n16; symbolic vs. literal, 6, 68–79
Requerimiento, 148–9, 298n94
Retamar, Roberto Fernandez, 145
Reynolds, Bryan, 292n12
Richardson, William, 265n39
Riehle, Wolfgang, 308n3
Ritger, Matthew, 312n72
Rivlin, Elizabeth, 291n1, 296n68, 307n74
Roberts, P. B., 313n95
Robinson, Christopher, 318n34
Rockett, William, 303n10, 304n32
Romano, Dennis, 280n75
Romano, Giulio, 244, 337n90
Rorty, Richard, 269n4
Rose, E. M., 257n34
Rosenberg, Marvin, 260n78
Ross, Sarah Gwyneth, 174, 311n58, 314n100

Rothschild, N. Amos, 176, 308n10, 309n29, 310n43
Rudnytsky, Peter, 325n26
Ruiter, David, 333n43
Rupp, Gordon, 261n5

Salhi, Lotfi, 291n6
Sanchez, Melissa E., 292n20
Sanders, Wilbur, 331n20, 332n32, 335n64, 339n112
Schalkwyk, David, 145, 146, 269n4, 291n1, 296n73, 304n32
Schanzer, Ernest, 277n48
Schlegel, August Wilhelm, 106
Schmitt, Carl, 334n52
Schulman, Alex, 283nn6–7, 320n59
Scodel, Joshua, 263n23, 266n59, 273n48, 297n80
Scot, Reginald, 189–90, 193–4, 195, 196, 197, 198, 199, 200, 202, 207, 209, 316nn5, 8, 317n27, 319n43
Scott, William O., 280n76
Sedley, David, 324n8
Seed, Patricia, 294n41, 298nn89, 94–5, 300n125
Seneca, 283n7
sexuality, 27, 35, 39, 100, 102–4, 148, 158–9, 184, 222–3, 235–7, 240, 242–3, 247, 248, 277n47 (sodomy), 327n39, 44, 333n41, 337nn86, 90, 340n118
Shakespeare, William, plays: *All's Well that Ends Well*, 194, 260n77; *Antony and Cleopatra*, 158, 273n54, 276n33; *As You Like It*, 62, 271n31, 295n59; *The Comedy of Errors*, 9–10, 11, 171, 190–193, 196, 199, 210, 213–6, 316n9, 317n23, 337n91; *Cymbeline*, 133, 135, 228, 256n25, 262n7; *Hamlet*, 4–5, 10, 15–8, 20, 22, 48–65, 171, 213, 223–7, 268n82, 284n18, 319n41, 320n54, 327n48, 328nn51, 59, 329nn62–3, 66; *Henry IV* (1 & 2), 6, 11, 81, 89–99, 268n82, 274nn1, 6, 275n10, 276n26, 277n37, 305n47; *Henry VI*, part 2, 282n92; *Henry VIII*, 330n1; *Julius Caesar*, 338n98; *King Lear*, 5, 7, 9, 11, 52, 66–85, 112–132, 133, 135, 136, 138, 177, 189, 198–209, 261n4, 263n19, 271n26, 272n41, 273nn47, 49, 283nn6–7, 284n18, 285n42, 287n66, 288n89, 289n92, 290nn111, 114, 292n16, 298n91, 304n29, 311n61, 320n53, 322nn78, 81, 83, 86, 323n93; *Love's Labor's Lost*, 171, 338n110; *Macbeth*, 35, 45, 48, 71, 112, 141, 158, 198, 202, 238, 272n43, 295n55; *Measure for Measure*, 7, 11, 100–107, 158, 252n8, 277n49, 278nn53, 60, 279nn70, 72,

292n13; *The Merchant of Venice*, 4–5, 7, 19–35, 42, 107–111, 113, 256n22, 266n57, 274n54, 278n56, 279n72, 281nn86, 89; *The Merry Wives of Windsor*, 338n98; *A Midsummer Night's Dream*, 6, 9, 11, 171, 189, 193–8, 200, 206, 238, 256n25, 315n107, 317n25, 333n48; *Much Ado About Nothing*, 218, 228, 326n27; *Othello*, 4, 9, 10, 11, 18–9, 20, 35–42, 48, 54–5, 105, 112, 160, 207, 209, 216–223, 228, 229, 237, 259n68, 260n73, 261n2, 279n64, 282n91, 283n8, 298n96, 303n22, 306n59, 315n2, 323n93, 325n26, 326n28, 35, 327nn36–7, 39, 42, 330n8, 332n37; *Pericles*, 135, 148, 338n98; *Richard III*, 35, 256n25, 260n77, 297n82; *Romeo and Juliet*, 196, 262n7, 318n33; *The Taming of the Shrew*, 91, 171, 174, 287n73, 288n83, 310nn34, 37; *The Tempest*, 6, 7–9, 133–185, 256n25, 274n54, 278n54, 289n97, 291nn6–7, 292n20, 294n37, 296nn65–8, 72–3, 297nn79, 81–2, 88, 298nn89, 91–3, 97, 301nn127, 129–30, 302n137, 303nn10, 14, 20–21, 304nn29, 31–4, 305n39, 306nn59–63, 65, 307nn70, 73, 309nn25, 28–9, 310n45, 311nn48, 53–4, 57, 61, 314n107, 315nn108–9, 113, 116, 118, 316n10, 330n1, 331nn18–9, 29, 336nn72, 75–8, 80, 85; *Twelfth Night*, 52, 190, 215, 230, 263n20, 266n63, 278n54, 305n47, 311n54; *The Two Gentleman of Verona*, 288n83, 299n105, 300nn118–9, 125; *The Two Noble Kinsmen*, 158, 303n12, 330n1; *The Winter's Tale*, 10–11, 126, 136, 190, 221, 228–249, 276n24; sonnets, 57, 158, 275n21
Shannon, Laurie, 284n29, 286n57
Shapiro, James, 227, 321n71
Sharpe, James, 317n19
Sheen, Erica, 267n76
Shell, Alison, 319nn38, 42, 320n54, 336n72
Shell, Marc, 26, 256nn28–9
Sherman, Nancy, 254n6
Shin, Hiewon, 175, 177, 299n99, 309nn28, 30, 311n48
Shlovsky, Viktor, 251n1
Showalter, Elaine, 264n27
Shuger, Debora Kuller, 278nn53, 57, 279nn63, 70
Sidney, Sir Philip, 53, 59, 63–4, 81, 99, 114, 267nn77–8, 277n39
Siemon, James R., 335n62
Simon, David Carroll, 306n57, 325n17
Singh, Jyotsna G., 300n125
Singleton, Charles S., 313n88
Sjögren, Gunnar, 49, 267n74

Skinner, Quentin, 171, 295n54, 309n18
Skura, Meredith, 155
slave, slavery, enslavement, 8, 108, 141, 143, 145, 146, 147, 148, 150, 154, 161–2, 178, 179–80, 183, 184, 280nn75–6, 295n57, 296nn60, 67–8, 297n76, 301n127, 304n30, 309n29, 312n72, 315n109
Slights, Jessica, 311n46
Smith, Daniel Starza, 263n25
Smith, Emma, 257n38
Smith, James, 332n32
Snow, Edward A., 261n2
Snyder, Susan, 335n66
Socrates, 169, 318n38
Sokol, B. J., 281n90
Sokol, Mary, 281n90
Speak, Gill, 324n4
Spenser, Eric, 257n37
Spiller, Elizabeth, 299n101
Spinoza, Baruch, 261n9
Spolsky, Ellen, 216–7
Stanivukovic, Goran, 171–2
Starkey, Thomas, 173
Steevens, George, 326n35
Stern, Jeffrey, 298n91
Stern-Gillet, Suzanne, 318n38
Stewart, Alan, 263n26, 285n39, 286n46
Stone, Lawrence, 255n16, 271n29, 277n48, 333n40
Stoner, Rosalie, 310n39
Strachey, William, 161, 299n105, 301n132
Strain, Virginia Lee, 100, 274nn1, 6, 275n10, 276n26, 278nn51, 60
Strier, Richard, on admiring Horatio, 329n70; on affective knowledge, 276n33; on biblical materials in *The Winter's Tale*, 337n93; on competing theologies of penance, 300n116; on a deconstructive reading of *The Winter's Tale*, 334n54; on Desdemona's hand, 327n37; on Dr. Pinch (*The Comedy of Errors*), 317n16; on Erasmus as "spiritualist," 316n8; on *eudaimonia*, 303n19; on grace, 300n123; on holiness in *The Comedy of Errors*, 317n23; on Iago's "plan" speech, 325n23; on Lear's initial division plan, 261n1, 285n30; on "Love" (3), 323n87; on marriage, the sexes, and hierarchy in *The Comedy of Errors*, 324n7, 325nn12–3; on Milton and classical ethics, 259n63; on prudence in *King Lear*, 117–8, 209; on the quality of being "free," 259n68, 333n45; on Reformation sanctification, 339n114; on the

Strier (continued)
   structure of Bacon's *Essays*, 318n28; on "Thought is free," 278n54; on virtuous disobedience, 252n10, 263n21, 291n2, 292n19
Styrt, Philip Goldfarb, 280n78, 336n72
Sylvan, Alexander (*The Orator*), 279n72
Syme, Holger Schott, 337n88

Talvacchia, Bette, 337n90
Targoff, Ramie, 328n55
Tate, Nahum, 115, 284n22
Tawney, R. H., 115, 257n41
Taylor, A. B., 307n2, 308n4
Taylor, Gary, 320n53
Tenenti, Alberto, 280n75
Theobald, Lewis, 198, 314n107
Thomas, Alan, 275n14
Thomas, Keith, 317nn15, 19, 319n43
Thompson, Ayanna, 254n12
Thompson, Craig R., 320n51
Tillyard, E. M. W., 260n1, 276n25
Traversi, Derek, 331n18
The Treasury of Ancient and Modern Times, 271n31
Trent, Council of, 300n113
Trueman, Carl, 261n5
Tugendhaft, Aaron, 285n40
Turner, Henry S., 274n5
Turner, James Grantham, 332n36
Tyndale, William, 323n92

Urmson, J. O., 276n25

Vanderjagt, Arjo, 317n20
Van Doren, Mark, 255n18
Vaughan, Alden T., 312n73, 314n107
Vaughan, Virginia Mason, 312n73, 314n107
Veeder, William R., 290n108
Vendler, Helen, 275n21
Vergerio, Pier Paolo, 173, 181, 318n29
Vickers, Sir Brian, 320n53
Virginia (colony), 140, 147, 150, 154–5 (company), 161, 301n132, 303n14

Waldron, Jennifer, 248
Wallace, John M., 283n7
Walsham, Alexandra, 321n62
Ward, David, 333n50
Warfield, Benjamin, 321n64
Warley, Christopher, 50, 51
Warner, Michael, 277n47
Warton, Joseph, 153
Waters, D. Douglas, 323n93
Watson, Philip, S., 321n64
Watson, Robert N., 327n39
Wear, Andrew, 318n29
Webb, Steven Saunders, 294n40, 295n48
Weber, Max, 165, 305n45
Weil, Judith, 291n1
Weinfield, Henry, 284n28
Weis, René, 285nn35–6, 320n61
West, Robert H., 293n26, 317n27
Wheatley, Edward, 270n24
Whigham, Frank, 53
Whitman, James Q., 278n61
Whittington, Leah, 306n61
Wikforss, Asa, 326n34
Wilbern, David, 333n47
Willgenburg, Theo Van, 275n14
Williams, Bernard, 92, 269n4, 275n14, 279n65
Williams, Michael, 328n50
Wilson, John Dover, 264n31, 265n44, 267n79
Wilson, Robert (*The Three Ladies of London*), 303n16
Wilson, Thomas, 257n41
Wimsatt, William K, Jr., 252n3
Witherington, Ben, III, 279n71
Wittgenstein, Ludwig, as anti-skeptical, 328n50, 330n11; on avoiding "schemes," 85, 273n53; 326n32; on categories not needing common denominators, 270n23; on "grammar," 272n37; on looking at instances, 69; prose style of, 273n54
Wolf, Amy, 320n56
Wong, Alex, 260n76
Wood, Andy, 283n13
Woodbridge, Linda, 126, 287n60, 288n86, 289n92
Wooton, David, 316n8
Wright, Tessa, 317n17

X, Malcolm, 301n127

Yachnin, Paul, 292n18, 302n5, 306n59, 307n66, 337n89
Yeats, William Butler, 48, 262n3

Zajko, Vanda, 307n2
Zanin, Enrica, 282n1
Zechariah, Michal, 260n3
Zitner, Sheldon, 266n51

ACKNOWLEDGMENTS

This book has had a long gestation. The essays in it were produced over a number of decades of thinking, reading, teaching, writing, paper-circulating, conference-attending, and public lecturing. Shakespeare has not always been my primary topic, but thinking about the plays has been a factor, implicit or explicit, in everything that I wrote or taught or lectured on from religious poetry to early modern philosophy. I turned, in graduate school, to Renaissance studies rather than nineteenth- and twentieth-century poetry through discovering the joy of teaching Shakespeare, and that joy has never left me. I have been fortunate to have been able to teach Shakespeare to wonderful graduate and undergraduate students at the University of Chicago for many years, and to have shared that responsibility and pleasure with the late David Bevington. This book has certainly profited from that experience.

The University of Chicago provided opportunities to present some of the materials that became this book in the faculty and graduate student Renaissance Workshop, which has been going strong since the mid-1980s. I am grateful to the students and the faculty members who have participated in those workshops over the years. They helped me hone and develop my thoughts. I am also grateful to the even more long-standing Chicago-area interdisciplinary faculty Renaissance Seminar at the University of Chicago for opportunities to present some of this material there. I know of no tougher, more learned, or more responsive group.

An organization that has been of enormous use to me and to so many is the Shakespeare Association of America. A good deal of this book was first presented in SAA seminars, and I am grateful to the organizers of and colleagues in the seminars in which I participated. Those seminars are a terrific venue in which to try out ideas and readings, having the amazing quality of being both relaxed and rigorous. I have been fortunate in being able to participate on a regular-irregular basis in the Columbia University Shakespeare Seminar, where I have been warmly welcomed and have benefited from the discussions of my own work and that of others. Venues in which material in this book was presented also include meetings of the Renaissance Society of America (including the memorable meeting in Florence), the Sixteenth-Century Conference, the Canadian Society for Renaissance Studies, the Midwest Conference on British Studies, and the Modern Language Association.

Versions of a number of the essays in this book were presented as lectures. I am deeply grateful to the scholars who invited me to give these and to the audiences who attended them. These opportunities have included lectures at universities in Australia (Sydney and Melbourne) and the Lloyd Davis Memorial Lecture at Queensland University in Brisbane, all through the courtesy of Peter Holbrook; and in Sweden at Uppsala University, thanks to Robert Applebaum. I was also honored to present material that has gone into this book as the Carol Brown lecture at Carnegie Mellon, as the Sharon O'Brian lecture at University of San Diego, as the Schick Lecture at Indiana State University, as the Strode Lecture at the University of Alabama at Tuscaloosa, as the Religion and Literature Annual Lecture at Notre Dame (thanks to Susannah Monta), and as the Nicholson Distinguished Faculty Lecture at the University of Chicago. I am grateful to audiences and colleagues at the other colleges and universities where I have had the opportunity to lecture or make workshop presentations: the University of California at Berkeley (English and History); the CUNY Graduate Center; Harvard University; University of Manitoba (thanks to Glenn Clark); University of Michigan; University of Nevada at Reno (thanks to Eric Rasmussen); New Mexico State University at Las Cruces; Occidental College; Princeton University; University of Texas at Austin; Wright College; and Yale University (twice). I wish I could record all the insight and encouragement I gleaned on those occasions.

Over the years, a handful of friends and scholars have read and commented on multiple pieces that have gone into this book. I am deeply grateful for the philosophically and textually sensitive comments of Lars Engle; for the helpfully unconvinced as well as the helpfully convinced responses of Theodore B. Leinwand and Henry Weinfield; for the always learned and often amiably contentious comments of Gail K. Paster; for the humane and psychoanalytically oriented comments of Jeffrey Stern; and, in a necessarily shorter time frame, for the copious and acute responses of my brilliant younger colleague, Timothy Harrison, who has tried to keep me *au courant*. Friends and colleagues have commented on individual essays: John Leonard, Ryan Netzley, Joshua Scodel, Philip Goldfarb Styrt, and Frank Whigham on "Happy Hamlet"; Jonathan Arac and Robert Pippin on "Resisting Complicity"; Kenneth Graham, Glenn W.

Most, Martha C. Nussbaum, and Quentin Skinner on "*King Lear* and Human Needs"; Bradin Cormack and the members of the Political Theory Workshop at the University of Chicago on "*The Tempest* (1): Power"; Kenneth Graham (orally) on "*The Tempest* (2): Labor"; Benjamin Jeffery (in his dissertation) on "*The Tempest* (1) and *The Tempest* (2)"; Kathy Eden and Rosalie Stoner on "*The Tempest* (3): Humanism"; Victoria Kahn on "Shakespeare and Skepticism (1): Religion"; Martha Devlin and V. Joshua Adams on "Shakespeare and Skepticism (2): Epistemology"; Leonard Barkan, Caryn O'Connell, and David Quint (orally) on the essay on *The Winter's Tale*. For responses to the Introduction, I am grateful to Jonathan Arac and to Loy D. Martin. The two readers for the University of Pennsylvania Press were extremely responsive and led me to see more exactly what I am doing in this book.

Together with those already mentioned, I am fortunate in friends who have provided intellectual as well as personal sustenance over the years: Akeel Bilgrami, Robert David Cohen, Roger Greenwald, Linda Gregerson, George Hoffmann, Steven Mullaney, Carol Rovane, Lisa Ruddick, Michael Schoenfeldt, Debora Shuger, Nigel Smith, William Veeder, and Robert von Hallberg. Stephen Greenblatt has been an actual and an imagined interlocutor in all my work on Shakespeare.

The dedicatee of the book, Camille Bennett, has been not only a co-conspirator in an almost absurdly happy marriage for over thirty years now but also a sharp-eyed proofreader and a brilliant commentator on both the substance and the procedures of the book. To say that I am grateful to her is a hopeless understatement.

www.ingramcontent.com/pod-product-compliance
Lightning Source LLC
Chambersburg PA
CBHW021848230426
43671CB00006B/307